Dictionary of Literary Biography

Dictionary of Literary Biography Documentary Series

Dictionary of Literary Biography Yearbooks

1980 edited by Karen L. Rood, Jean W. Ross, and Richard Ziegfeld (1981)

1981 edited by Karen L. Rood, Jean W. Ross, and Richard Ziegfeld (1982)

1982 edited by Richard Ziegfeld; associate editors: Jean W. Ross and Lynne C. Zeigler (1983)

1983 edited by Mary Bruccoli and Jean W. Ross; associate editor Richard Ziegfeld (1984)

1984 edited by Jean W. Ross (1985)

1985 edited by Jean W. Ross (1986)

1986 edited by J. M. Brook (1987)

1987 edited by J. M. Brook (1988)

1988 edited by J. M. Brook (1989)

1989 edited by J. M. Brook (1990)

1990 edited by James W. Hipp (1991)

1991 edited by James W. Hipp (1992)

1992 edited by James W. Hipp (1993)

1993 edited by James W. Hipp, contributing editor George Garrett (1994)

1994 edited by James W. Hipp, contributing editor George Garrett (1995)

1995 edited by James W. Hipp, contributing editor George Garrett (1996)

1996 edited by Samuel W. Bruce and L. Kay Webster, contributing editor George Garrett (1997)

1997 edited by Matthew J. Bruccoli and George Garrett, with the assistance of L. Kay Webster (1998)

1998 edited by Matthew J. Bruccoli, contributing editor George Garrett, with the assistance of D. W. Thomas (1999)

1999 edited by Matthew J. Bruccoli, contributing editor George Garrett, with the assistance of D. W. Thomas (2000)

2000 edited by Matthew J. Bruccoli, contributing editor George Garrett, with the assistance of George Parker Anderson (2001)

2001 edited by Matthew J. Bruccoli, contributing editor George Garrett, with the assistance of George Parker Anderson (2002)

2002 edited by Matthew J. Bruccoli and George Garrett; George Parker Anderson, Assistant Editor (2003)

Concise Series

Concise Dictionary of American Literary Biography, 7 volumes (1988–1999): *The New Consciousness, 1941–1968; Colonization to the American Renaissance, 1640–1865; Realism, Naturalism, and Local Color, 1865–1917; The Twenties, 1917–1929; The Age of Maturity, 1929–1941; Broadening Views, 1968–1988; Supplement: Modern Writers, 1900–1998.*

Concise Dictionary of British Literary Biography, 8 volumes (1991–1992): *Writers of the Middle Ages and Renaissance Before 1660; Writers of the Restoration and Eighteenth Century, 1660–1789; Writers of the Romantic Period, 1789–1832; Victorian Writers, 1832–1890; Late-Victorian and Edwardian Writers, 1890–1914; Modern Writers, 1914–1945; Writers After World War II, 1945–1960; Contemporary Writers, 1960 to Present.*

Concise Dictionary of World Literary Biography, 4 volumes (1999–2000): *Ancient Greek and Roman Writers; German Writers; African, Caribbean, and Latin American Writers; South Slavic and Eastern European Writers.*

Twenty-First-Century Canadian Writers

Dictionary of Literary Biography® • Volume Three Hundred Thirty-Four

Twenty-First-Century Canadian Writers

Edited by
Christian Riegel
University of Regina

A Bruccoli Clark Layman Book

THOMSON

GALE™

Detroit • New York • San Francisco • New Haven, Conn. • Waterville, Maine • London • Munich

Dictionary of Literary Biography
Volume 334: Twenty-First-Century Canadian Writers
Christian Riegel

Advisory Board
John Baker
William Cagle
Patrick O'Connor
George Garrett
Trudier Harris
Alvin Kernan

Editorial Directors
Matthew J. Bruccoli and Richard Layman

LIBRARY OF CONGRESS CATALOGING-IN-PUBLICATION DATA

Twenty-first-century Canadian writers / [edited by] Christian Riegel.
  p. cm. — (Dictionary of literary biography ; v. 334)
 "A Bruccoli Clark Layman Book."
 Includes bibliographical references and index.
 ISBN-13: 978–0–7876–8152–4
 ISBN-10: 0–7876–8152–0
 1. Authors, Canadian—21st century—Biography—Dictionaries. 2. Canadian literature—
21st century—Bio-bibliography—Dictionaries. I. Riegel, Christian.
 II. Series.

 PR9186.2.T94 2007
 810.9'97103—dc22
                                                              2007006151

Printed in the United States of America
10 9 8 7 6 5 4 3 2 1

Contents

Plan of the Series

. . . Almost the most prodigious asset of a country, and perhaps its most precious possession, is its native literary product—when that product is fine and noble and enduring.

Mark Twain*

The advisory board, the editors, and the publisher of the *Dictionary of Literary Biography* are joined in endorsing Mark Twain's declaration. The literature of a nation provides an inexhaustible resource of permanent worth. Our purpose is to make literature and its creators better understood and more accessible to students and the reading public, while satisfying the needs of teachers and researchers.

To meet these requirements, *literary biography* has been construed in terms of the author's achievement. The most important thing about a writer is his writing. Accordingly, the entries in *DLB* are career biographies, tracing the development of the author's canon and the evolution of his reputation.

The purpose of *DLB* is not only to provide reliable information in a usable format but also to place the figures in the larger perspective of literary history and to offer appraisals of their accomplishments by qualified scholars.

The publication plan for *DLB* resulted from two years of preparation. The project was proposed to Bruccoli Clark by Frederick G. Ruffner, president of the Gale Research Company, in November 1975. After specimen entries were prepared and typeset, an advisory board was formed to refine the entry format and develop the series rationale. In meetings held during 1976, the publisher, series editors, and advisory board approved the scheme for a comprehensive biographical dictionary of persons who contributed to literature. Editorial work on the first volume began in January 1977, and it was published in 1978. In order to make *DLB* more than a dictionary and to compile volumes that individually have claim to status as literary history, it was decided to organize volumes by topic, period, or

From an unpublished section of Mark Twain's autobiography, copyright by the Mark Twain Company

genre. Each of these freestanding volumes provides a biographical-bibliographical guide and overview for a particular area of literature. We are convinced that this organization—as opposed to a single alphabet method—constitutes a valuable innovation in the presentation of reference material. The volume plan necessarily requires many decisions for the placement and treatment of authors. Certain figures will be included in separate volumes, but with different entries emphasizing the aspect of his career appropriate to each volume. Ernest Hemingway, for example, is represented in *American Writers in Paris, 1920–1939* by an entry focusing on his expatriate apprenticeship; he is also in *American Novelists, 1910–1945* with an entry surveying his entire career, as well as in *American Short-Story Writers, 1910–1945, Second Series* with an entry concentrating on his short fiction. Each volume includes a cumulative index of the subject authors and articles.

Between 1981 and 2002 the series was augmented and updated by the *DLB Yearbooks*. There have also been nineteen *DLB Documentary Series* volumes, which provide illustrations, facsimiles, and biographical and critical source materials for figures, works, or groups judged to have particular interest for students. In 1999 the *Documentary Series* was incorporated into the *DLB* volume numbering system beginning with *DLB 210: Ernest Hemingway*.

We define literature as the *intellectual commerce of a nation:* not merely as belles lettres but as that ample and complex process by which ideas are generated, shaped, and transmitted. *DLB* entries are not limited to "creative writers" but extend to other figures who in their time and in their way influenced the mind of a people. Thus the series encompasses historians, journalists, publishers, book collectors, and screenwriters. By this means readers of *DLB* may be aided to perceive literature not as cult scripture in the keeping of intellectual high priests but firmly positioned at the center of a nation's life.

DLB includes the major writers appropriate to each volume and those standing in the ranks behind them. Scholarly and critical counsel has been sought in deciding which minor figures to include and how full their entries should be. Wherever possible, useful references are made to figures who do not warrant separate entries.

Each *DLB* volume has an expert volume editor responsible for planning the volume, selecting the figures for inclusion, and assigning the entries. Volume editors are also responsible for preparing, where appropriate, appendices surveying the major periodicals and literary and intellectual movements for their volumes, as well as lists of further readings. Work on the series as a whole is coordinated at the Bruccoli Clark Layman editorial center in Columbia, South Carolina, where the editorial staff is responsible for accuracy and utility of the published volumes.

One feature that distinguishes *DLB* is the illustration policy—its concern with the iconography of literature. Just as an author is influenced by his surroundings, so is the reader's understanding of the author enhanced by a knowledge of his environment. Therefore *DLB* volumes include not only drawings, paintings, and photographs of authors, often depicting them at various stages in their careers, but also illustrations of their families and places where they lived. Title pages are regularly reproduced in facsimile along with dust jackets for modern authors. The dust jackets are a special feature of *DLB* because they often document better than anything else the way in which an author's work was perceived in its own time. Specimens of the writers' manuscripts and letters are included when feasible.

Samuel Johnson rightly decreed that "The chief glory of every people arises from its authors." The purpose of the *Dictionary of Literary Biography* is to compile literary history in the surest way available to us—by accurate and comprehensive treatment of the lives and work of those who contributed to it.

The *DLB* Advisory Board

Introduction

Dictionary of Literary Biography Volume 334: Twenty-First-Century Canadian Writers covers the period from 1989, when the last volume in the *Dictionary of Literary Biography* on Canadian writing was published, to 2007. Writers from various age groups, styles, and ethnic backgrounds, as well as writers in all major genres, who have made a significant contribution to the literature of these years are included. Some of the subjects already had significant careers by 1989 and demonstrate a continuing vitality; others were only beginning to emerge at that time and made important places for themselves in the ensuing decade; and still others are relatively new to the Canadian cultural scene but have established themselves as important voices. The criteria used for including an author in the volume are critical and scholarly reception, commercial success, and whether his or her work reflects the larger Canadian historical, political, and cultural trends of the last decade and a half. Among those trends are the emergence into the literary mainstream of minorities, particularly of Asian and African Canadians; the increasing role of Aboriginal (North American Indian, First Nations, or Native Canadian) authors; and the formal and stylistic shifts as linguistic and literary theories of the 1960s and 1970s have become more firmly established.

Though well into its second century as an independent nation by the year 2000, Canada continued to be in a process of self-definition. The most dramatic shifts of the present era can be traced to the Constitution Act of 17 April 1982, which transferred formal control over the constitution from Britain to Canada. This event began a period of constitutional uncertainty that continues today. The central concerns are the status of the province of Quebec and the First Nations and the relationship of the provinces to the federation. Constitutional reform was attempted in 1987 with Prime Minister Brian Mulroney's Meech Lake Accord, which recognized Quebec as a society and culture distinct from the other provinces. The accord required ratification by all ten provinces by June 1990; it failed because of the objections of Manitoba and Newfoundland. During the summer of 1990; Mohawks in Oka, Quebec, barricaded a highway, and the resulting violence made the necessity of addressing Aboriginal concerns apparent. Another solution to constitutional problems was proposed in 1992 with the Charlottetown Accord; among its complex provisions were the establish-

ment of exclusive jurisdictions for the federal government and the provinces in various matters, a right of compensation if a province opted out of a constitutional amendment that transferred provincial powers to the federal government, and the elimination of barriers to the flow of goods, services, labor, and capital among the provinces. This time the ratification process involved a referendum for Quebec and a separate one for the remaining provinces and the two territories; the accord was resoundingly defeated. In 1995 the Quebec government held a referendum in an attempt to obtain a mandate to begin the process of separating from the nation. Opponents of independence won by a margin of 1 percent, underscoring the divisions in Quebec and reinforcing the sense that the nation's status was perilous.

The political scene during this period affirms the portrait of a divided country. Mulroney's Progressive Conservative Party government, ruling from 1984 to 1993, drew much of its support from Quebec. In 1991 the party's Quebec members of parliament formed their own party, the Bloc Québécois, under the leadership of former federal cabinet minister Lucien Bouchard, with the intention of aiding Quebec's independence movement. The Bloc Québécois was joined by the Alberta-based Reform Party of Canada, which had been founded in 1987. The Bloc Québécois became the official opposition after winning a significant number of seats in the 1993 federal election; that the opposition should be represented by a party whose goal was the altering of the fundamental structure of the nation was unprecedented in Canada's history. While the Liberal Party won the 1997 and 2000 federal elections by a large majority, the Bloc Québécois maintained its hold on Quebec's seats in Parliament; the Reform Party, renamed the Alliance Party in 2000, was entrenched in the western provinces from Manitoba to British Columbia; and the New Democratic Party and the Progressive Conservative Party elected members to Parliament in the Maritime Provinces (New Brunswick, Nova Scotia, and Prince Edward Island) and in the province of Newfoundland and Labrador. The Liberal Party drew its strength from Ontario and failed to dominate elsewhere. In Quebec the separatist party, the Parti Québécois, dominated the political scene. In order to become a truly national party, the Alliance Party merged with the Progressive Conservative Party in 2003 and formed a minority government in 2006. In the 2006 election, the Bloc Québécois elected many members of parliament from Quebec, even though the provincial government had changed from a separatist to a federalist one in the 2003 provincial election.

While Canadians were looking inward on the political stage, they were also building stronger ties to the outside world. Like many other nations, Canada was affected by globalization. During the late 1980s and early 1990s Canada negotiated with the United States and Mexico to form what became in 1993 the North American Free Trade Agreement. The agreement provided for the increased movement of goods and workers among the three nations and changed trade practices in fundamental ways. Further free-trade agreements were signed with Israel in 1994, with Chile in 1997, and with Costa Rica in 2001.

The political and economic patterns of the period are mirrored in Canadian writing: literary production occurs at a highly regional level as well as at the national level; well-established regional literatures contribute to the national literature, and writers from all provinces have Canada-wide profiles. Coinciding with the increase in international trade, Canadian writers such as Margaret Atwood, Timothy Findley, Alice Munro, and Michael Ondaatje achieved international success in the 1990s. Publishing reflects the regional and national nature of literary production: national publishers such as McClelland and Stewart and Canadian branches of U.S. firms such as HarperCollins, Alfred A. Knopf, and Random House are mostly based in Toronto, Ontario, though some, such as Douglas and McIntyre, are in Vancouver, British Columbia, and French-language houses are in Montreal, Quebec. Authors are subject to nationwide attention and have readerships from coast to coast. Much important writing is, however, published by regional concerns such as Killick Press in St. John's, Newfoundland; Goose Lane Editions in Fredericton, New Brunswick; NeWest Press in Edmonton, Alberta; Red Deer Press in Calgary, Alberta; and Ronsdale Press in Vancouver. Many writers who publish with regional presses have achieved significant profiles within their regions, and some have become nationally known.

In Canada, as in the United States, "little magazines" are important venues for writers; while regionally based and oriented, in Canada these magazines tend to be read from coast to coast as well as internationally. The work of most, if not all, emerging writers was first published in magazines such as *West Coast Line* and *Malahat Review* in British Columbia; *NeWest Review* and *Dandelion* in Alberta; *Grain* and *Wascana Review* in Saskatchewan; *Prairie Fire* in Manitoba; *New Quarterly, Descant, White Wall Review,* and *Arc* in Ontario; *Matrix* in Quebec; and *Fiddlehead, The Antigonish Review, Gaspereau Review,* and *TickleAce* in the Atlantic provinces. Furthermore, established writers tend to continue to publish in the little magazines. *West Coast Line* and the Toronto magazines *Open Letter* and *Brick* are important venues for experimental writing.

The development of regional and national literatures has been accompanied by increasing international exposure for Canadian writers. In 1990 Arnold E. Davidson noted that "For some time now Canadians have been certain that the country has produced a distinctive literature. More recently, much of the rest of the world has also begun to take notice." In Davidson's statement one can hear echoes of earlier critics, such as Desmond Pacey, who asserted in 1952: "It will no doubt come as a surprise to most of my readers to learn that there is someone who has the temerity to believe that the foundations of an essentially nationalist literature in Canada are, if not laid, at least in the process of being laid. For the average Englishman, and even a greater number of those who are well above the average in literary erudition, seems to be quite unaware that Canada is either able or anxious to produce anything other than wheat." Since Pacey's day, Canadian literature has become what Davidson calls "a major contemporary literary phenomenon." While the works of the leading writers are published by the largest Canadian houses and by foreign firms, many authors whose books are published by smaller regional presses have had them translated around the world. For example, Suzette Mayr's writing, which is published in Canada by NeWest Press, is also published in Germany, and Aritha van Herk, whose more-recent books have been published by Alberta firms, has significant followings in Germany and the Netherlands.

One sign of the emerging role of Canadian literature on the world stage is the increasing number of Canadian writers winning major international prizes. Ondaatje received Britain's Booker Prize in 1992; he was followed by Atwood in 2000 and Yann Martel in 2002. Anne Michaels won Britain's Orange Prize for fiction in 1997; the following year the prize went to Carol Shields, who had won the American Pulitzer Prize for fiction in 1995. Jane Urquhart received Le priz du meilleur livre étranger (The Best Foreign Book Award) in France in 1993, and Alistair MacLeod won the International IMPAC Dublin Literary Award in 2001.

While international recognition for Canadian writers is a sign of a vibrant literary scene, the establishment of several high-profile national awards since the 1990s signals the emergence of a uniquely Canadian literature. The Giller Prize, founded in 1994, is awarded to the best work of fiction published in a given year, and inclusion on the short list alone is guaranteed to bring a writer's work to national prominence. The Griffin Poetry Prize, launched in 2000, is awarded to a Canadian and a foreign poet; Canadian winners such as Christian Bök have achieved best-seller status. The Giller and Griffin Prizes join the Governor General's Literary Awards, which were first given in 1936, and the Writers' Trust of Canada Awards as key indicators of national success for writers. For poets in particular, the Governor General's Awards are one of the few paths to prominence across the country. Each region also has its own awards to bring local writers to public attention. Among these awards are the British Columbia Book Prizes, the Alberta Book Awards, the Manitoba Literary Awards, the Trillium Book Award (for Ontario), the Writers' Federation of Nova Scotia Awards, and the Writers' Alliance of Newfoundland and Labrador Provincial Book Awards. These awards often lead to national attention: writers such as Wayne Johnston of Newfoundland, Urquhart and Dionne Brand of Ontario, and Sandra Birdsell of Manitoba first came to prominence in their home provinces. (Lists of winners of the various awards can be found in an appendix to this volume.)

In her introduction to *The New Oxford Book of Canadian Short Stories in English* (1995) Atwood comments on the difficulty of defining "Canadianness": "In a country thousands of miles wide and almost as tall, which covers a terrain as diverse as the frozen Arctic, the Prairies, the West Coast rain forests, and the rocks of Newfoundland; in which fifty-two indigenous languages are spoken—none of which is English—and a hundred or so other also in use; and which contains the most cosmopolitan city in the world, the erstwhile true-blood Toronto the Good—it's kind of difficult to pin such a thing down." It is not surprising, of course, that a country that has not yet fully defined itself politically would be unable to do so in other domains. The work of the writers featured in this volume has no essential "Canadian" aspect; instead, the writing of the past eighteen years reflects a multicultural society composed of new migrants and descendants of earlier ones, as well as indigenous peoples who are only now—and slowly—being accorded respect as part of the nation. The diverse literary culture of the nation reflects the many perspectives that comprise the literal and imaginative terrain of the country. Furthermore, while in Canada, as elsewhere in the western world, the novel dominates public consumption of literature, poetry and drama continue to be important contributors to Canadian culture. The paucity of criticism of the latter forms should not be seen as reflective of their quality. It is only natural that in a nation whose literature is just coming into its own, the critical apparatus should also be in a state of development. Critical discussion of fiction has now reached a significant mass, and work on poetry and drama is slowly reaching a point at which an objective assessment of contemporary writing can be made.

Issues of race, ethnicity, and gender have become increasingly important aspects of public discourse in Canadian newspapers and magazines and on television, as well as in critical response to literary work. In 1998 Enoch Padolsky noted the "increasing racialization of the Canadian social and literary discourse over the last few years." Cultural production thus reflects the changes in Canadian society. As Padolsky remarks, "The reasons for this new racial awareness are complex and multi-origined. Contributing factors no doubt include changes to Canadian demography due to post-war non-European immigration; the discursive impact of the highly racialized society of the United States; the growing influence in Canadian intellectual circles of international post-colonial theory and 'Third World' perspectives; and increasing media attention in Canada to race relations."

This volume features the most important African Canadian and Native authors who have become established in the literary mainstream since the 1980s and 1990s. George Elliott Clarke remarks in the introduction to his anthology *Eyeing the North Star: Directions in African-Canadian Literature* (1997) that African Canadian communities and literatures have a long history that only began to be understood in all their complexity over the last decade or so. Certainly, the publication, readership, and awareness of African Canadian literature has grown significantly in recent years. Clarke also notes that the definition of African Canadian literature itself is fraught with difficulty: "How Canadian is it? The question is insidious, but it cannot be peremptorily dismissed, for the literature is awash in African-American and Caribbean influences." Black communities and the literature produced by African Canadians are as varied as any other communities and cultural production. African Canada is rooted in the migration of blacks from the United States following the American Revolution and the War of 1812 and the years leading up to the American Civil War. A significant immigration of blacks from the Caribbean began in the 1950s, peaked in the 1970s, and has continued through the 1990s and early 2000s; this population has been viewed as a separate group from the earlier African American immigrants. Furthermore, the Caribbean migration is not only Anglophone: while most English-speaking immigrants settled in Toronto, Montreal became the center of the French-speaking Haitian immigration, and significantly different cultural traditions have developed in the two cities. The African Canadian literature that emerged in the late 1980s and 1990s is identified by its varying cultural and historical heritages. The works of Clarke and Maxine Tynes, for example, reflect their Nova Scotian ancestry, while those of M. NourbeSe Philip and Dionne Brand demonstrate Caribbean influences; Dany Laferrière's writing shows his Haitian background, and Mayr's work combines Canadian, German, and Caribbean elements.

Native writing in Canada has a long history, originating in an oral tradition that predates European colonization of North America and still exists. Because of strong tribal identities and social organization, Aboriginal literature must be understood as a plurality of voices and contexts; furthermore, as colonial and postcolonial issues remain unresolved, Aboriginal literatures have a political and representational complexity that one should not try to simplify. In 1990 Thomas King noted, "when we talk about contemporary Native literature, we talk as though we already have a definition for this body of literature when, in fact, we do not." Aboriginal writing should be seen as a body of work that is in the process of definition. Writing in the 1980s, the 1990s, and the new millennium has contributed to that process, but the particular place of Native writing within the Canadian spectrum has yet to be fully determined. As King remarks, "What we have is a collection of literary works by individual authors who are Native by ancestry, and our hope [is that] . . . the sheer bulk of the collection, when it reaches some sort of critical mass, will present us with a matrix within which a variety of patterns can be discerned."

King is the most prominent Native Canadian writer of the first decade of the twenty-first century, and his career is exemplary of the changes that are occurring in Native literature. He is well known through his weekly national Canadian Broadcasting Corporation radio show and his many novels, short stories, and television scripts, and his work is a staple of courses in Canadian literature both at home and abroad. Among his frequent themes is the real and imagined boundaries of politics, race and ethnicity, nationality, or gender that separate humans from each other. His own life and career represent a challenging of such boundaries: King was born in California to a Cherokee father, raised by a German-Greek mother, and moved to Canada in 1979, when he was in his late forties; he is, nevertheless, considered a premier Canadian writer. The Métis writers Tomson Highway and Joan Crate reflect similar boundaries in their work. Highway and Native writers such as Jeanette Armstrong and Daniel David Moses address the racism, abuse in government- and church-run residential schools, and political activism that arose out of the colonial practices of the Canadian government in the twentieth century.

The themes of ethnicity, history, and origins evident in Aboriginal and African Canadian writing are also present in work by writers of other ancestries. M. G. Vassanji and Rohinton Mistry look at South Asian society and culture in Canada or elsewhere, while Ann-Marie MacDonald, Sheldon Currie, and Daniel MacIvor explore their Scottish descent, and Mayr and Marilyn Bowering examine their German roots. In her 1981 novel *Obasan* Joy Kogawa depicts the racist policies of the Canadian government during and after World War II that resulted in the internment and forced dispersal of thousands of Japanese Canadians, many of whom were citizens by birth. In her

1993 novel *Away* Urquhart explores the political turmoil that accompanied the shift from colonial status to nationhood, as well as the plight of the Irish underclass in the years leading up to Confederation in 1867.

Fiction, especially the novel, has been dominant in Canadian as in most Western national literatures in the twentieth century. Canada has produced a long list of internationally recognized fiction writers, and many new voices have emerged in the last fifteen years. Realism has traditionally predominated in Canadian fiction, and that trend continues in the work of new writers such as Brand, Johnston, Mistry, Urquhart, Vassanji, and Greg Hollingshead. Nonetheless, postmodernism and the linguistic theories of the 1970s and 1980s have influenced Canadian writing. Authors such as van Herk, Mayr, Birdsell, and Birk Sproxton are leaders in pushing the boundaries of realism and extending the possibilities of language. In their work self-conscious narration that challenges hegemonic and uncritical notions of history serve as counterpoint to the realist reconstructions of the past. In his novel *The Red-Headed Woman with the Black Black Heart* (1998), about an actual 1934 mining strike in Manitoba, Sproxton presents narrative as a slippery means of approach to history and history itself as at best tenuous and at worst elusive; he thereby places himself alongside prominent American novelists such as John Barth. The influence of postmodernism is evident in van Herk's rewriting of ancient myths and mythological figures in her *No Fixed Address* (1986).

Poetry has taken a backseat to fiction in popularity, but the poets of the last fifteen years have also made important contributions to Canadian culture. What is perhaps most striking about the Canadian poetry scene is its variety, as conventional poetry that looks back to nineteenth-century forms exists side by side with boundary-breaking postmodernist work. Poets who were able to innovate while working within conventional notions of lyrical poetry contributed most strongly to a sense of a developing tradition of Canadian poetry. Don McKay, for example, writes a primarily lyrical poetry that incorporates elements of pastoral and nature verse to present the personal interaction with the natural world in a fresh light. Similarly, Tim Bowling writes a conventionally formal poetry that employs Romantic and nineteenth-century notions of metaphor and the self in nature but shifts the context to the late twentieth century. Other poets, such as Crate and Brand, who also write fiction, as well as Tynes, employ lyrical modes to engage with contemporary theories of identity; the resulting poetry is highly personal, political, and social, and the lyrical mode avoids the common pitfalls of triteness and sentimentality. Clarke also writes about issues of identity, especially minority identity. For Bowering the lyrical mode is spiritual and meditative; her poetry engages with the complex relationship between self and world. Despite the predominance of more-conventional lyrical modes, writers such as Sproxton, Douglas Barbour, Dennis Cooley, and Steve McCaffery demonstrate the continuing vitality of linguistically oriented poetry. Influenced by the language poets, the Black Mountain Poets, and the *Tish* movement of the 1960s, named for a little magazine that published avant-garde poetry in Vancouver from 1961 to 1969, these writers have continued to refine their craft into the new millennium. McCaffery is the most purely linguistic poet writing in Canada at this time. Cooley and Sproxton employ the "vernacular muse"–a term coined by Cooley to explain the use of vernacular language and influences in literary writing–but also adapt genre as necessary to address the complexity of their material. The long poem, especially as developed by the American William Carlos Williams and the Canadian Robert Kroetsch, has been of particular interest to Cooley and Sproxton. Barbour has shown a remarkable range in theme, language, and form. Among emerging poets, Jonathan Hart and Jeanette Lynes work out of a tradition of lyric. Jon Whyte, who died at fifty in 1992, is included in this volume because his work is an important part of the avant-garde poetics that continue to influence early- twenty-first-century poetry. It pays attention to language, explores the long-poem form, and is highly visual in its use of typography and design.

Dramatic production in Canada continues to be strong, with lively theater communities in Vancouver, Edmonton, Calgary, Winnipeg, Toronto, Montreal, and Halifax, Nova Scotia. Like the fiction writers and poets, playwrights engage with conventional forms but also produce a great deal of experimental work. MacIvor, for example, writes surrealist monologues, and Guillermo Verdecchia has established himself as a highly metatheatrical dramatist. Issues of race, ethnicity, gender, and ancestry are of central concern to the dramatists, as they are to the fiction writers. MacDonald, for example, explores women's roles, as well as gay and lesbian themes, and Moses and Highway write complex plays that employ European and Native dramatic models to deal with Native, colonial, and postcolonial issues. All of these writers incorporate sometimes subtle and sometimes overt political themes in their plays, underscoring the role that drama has in challenging political responses to social problems in the country. Judith Thompson is exemplary in this regard, for her plays depict poor and marginalized people leading desperate lives that are fraught with violence.

The literary scene in Canada as the new millennium begins is vibrant and complex. Writers are faced with a country that is still in the process of defining itself politically, socially, and culturally. What has emerged from the tensions of this self-definition is a literary culture that investigates ancestry, ethnicity, and history, as well as contemporary society. Additionally, Canadian writers have engaged with the currents of international writing, both conventional and postmodern, to produce a strong and diverse literature.

–Christian Riegel

Acknowledgments

This book was produced by Bruccoli Clark Layman, Inc. Philip B. Dematteis was the in-house editor.

Production manager is Philip B. Dematteis.

Administrative support was provided by Carol A. Cheschi.

Accountant is Ann-Marie Holland.

Copyediting supervisor is Sally R. Evans. The copyediting staff includes Phyllis A. Avant, Caryl Brown, and Rebecca Mayo. Freelance copyeditors are Brenda Cabra, Jennifer Cooper, and Dave King.

Pipeline manager is James F. Tidd Jr.

Editorial associates are Elizabeth Leverton and Dickson Monk.

Permissions editor is Amber L. Coker.

Office manager is Kathy Lawler Merlette.

Photography editor is Crystal A. Leidy.

Digital photographic copy work was performed by Crystal A. Leidy.

Systems manager is James Sellers.

Typesetting supervisor is Kathleen M. Flanagan. The typesetting staff includes Patricia Marie Flanagan.

Library research was facilitated by the following librarians at the Thomas Cooper Library of the University of South Carolina: Elizabeth Suddeth and the rare-book department; Jo Cottingham, interlibrary loan department; circulation department head Tucker Taylor; reference department head Virginia W. Weathers; reference department staff Laurel Baker, Marilee Birchfield, Kate Boyd, Paul Cammarata, Joshua Garris, Gary Geer, Tom Marcil, Rose Marshall, and Sharon Verba; interlibrary loan department head Marna Hostetler; and interlibrary loan staff Bill Fetty and Nelson Rivera.

The editor's research assistants were Jerilyn Ninowski, Adam Dube, and Justin Dittrick.

Dictionary of Literary Biography® • Volume Three Hundred Thirty-Four

Twenty-First-Century Canadian Writers

Dictionary of Literary Biography

Jeannette Armstrong
(1948 –)

Rob Budde
University of Northern British Columbia

BOOKS: *Enwhisteetkwa: Walk on Water* (Penticton, B.C.: Okanagan Indian Curriculum Project, 1982);

Neekna and Chemai (Penticton, B.C.: Theytus, 1984);

Slash (Penticton, B.C.: Theytus, 1985; revised, 1988);

Seeking New Directions, Final Project Report: Phases One and Two (Penticton, B.C.: Okanagan Indian Learning Institute, 1986);

Aboriginal Perspectives of the Natural Environment, by Armstrong, James Dumont, and Donald R. Fiddler (Penticton, B.C.: Theytus, 1991);

Breath Tracks (Stratford, Ont.: Williams-Wallace, 1991);

The Native Creative Process: A Collaborative Discourse between Douglas Cardinal and Jeannette Armstrong (Penticton, B.C.: Theytus, 1991);

Whispering in Shadows (Penticton, B.C.: Theytus, 2000);

Dancing with the Cranes (Penticton, B.C.: Theytus, 2004).

OTHER: "Writing from a Native Woman's Perspective," in *In the Feminine: Women and Words: Conference Proceedings, 1983,* edited by Ann Dybikowski and others (Edmonton: Longspoon Press, 1985), pp. 55–57;

"Traditional Indigenous Education: A Natural Process," in *Tradition Change Survival: The Answers Are within Us* (Vancouver: UBC First Nations House, 1988), n. pag.;

"This Is a Story," in *All My Relations: An Anthology of Contemporary Canadian Native Fiction,* edited by Thomas King (Toronto: McClelland & Stewart, 1990), pp. 129–135;

"Words," in *Telling It: Women and Language across Cultures,* edited by the Telling It Book Collective (Vancouver: Press Gang, 1990), pp. 23–30;

"Racism: Racial Exclusivity and Cultural Supremacy," in *Give Back: First Nations Perspectives on Cultural*

Jeannette Armstrong (from the cover for Whispering in Shadows, *2000; Richland County Public Library)*

Practice, edited by Maria Campbell and others (North Vancouver: Gallerie, 1992), pp. 74–82;

"Trickster Time," in *Voices: Being Native in Canada,* edited by Linda Jaine and Drew Hayden Taylor (Saska-

toon: Extension Division, University of Saskatchewan, 1992), pp. 1–5;

*Looking at the Words of Our People: First Nations Analysis of
Literature,* edited by Armstrong (Penticton, B.C.:
Theytus, 1993);

We Get Our Living Like Milk from the Land, edited by Armstrong and others (Penticton, B.C.: Theytus, 1993);

*Metamorphosis: Manifesting and Respecting Diversity in Our
Transformation,* edited by Armstrong and others
(Penticton, B.C.: Theytus, 1995);

"Sharing One Skin: Okanagan Community," in *The
Case against the Global Economy and for a Turn toward
the Local,* edited by Jerry Mander and Edward
Goldsmith (San Francisco: Sierra Club Books,
1996), pp. 460–470;

"Invocation: The Real Power of Aboriginal Women,"
in *Women of the First Nations: Power, Wisdom and
Strength,* edited by Christine Miller, Patricia
Chuchryk, Marie Smailface Marule, Brenda
Manyfingers, and Cheryl Deering (Winnipeg:
University of Manitoba Press, 1996);

*Standing Ground: Strength and Solidarity amidst Dissolving
Boundaries,* edited by Armstrong and Kateri
Akiwenzie-Damm (Penticton, B.C.: Theytus, 1996);

"The Disempowerment of First North American Native
Peoples and Empowerment through Their Writ-
ing," in *An Anthology of Canadian Native Literature in
English,* edited by Daniel David Moses and Terry
Goldie, second edition (Toronto & New York:
Oxford University Press, 1998), pp. 239–242;

"Land Speaking," in *Speaking for the Generations: Native
Writers on Writing,* edited by Simon J. Ortiz (Tuc-
son: University of Arizona Press, 1998), pp. 175–
194;

Native Poetry in Canada: A Contemporary Anthology, edited
by Armstrong and Lally Grauer (Peterborough,
Ont. & Orchard Park, N.Y.: Broadview, 2001).

SELECTED PERIODICAL PUBLICATIONS–
UNCOLLECTED: "Discipline and Sharing: Educa-
tion in the Indian Way," *Fourth World Journal,* 1
(Winter 1985–1986): 73–88;

"Bridging Cultures," *Columbiana: Bioregional Journal for
the Intermountain Northwest,* 30, no. 14 (1989): 28–
30;

"Cultural Robbery: Imperialism–Voices of Native
Women," *Trivia,* 14 (1989): 21–23;

"C is for Culture," *Herizons,* 7 (Spring 1993): 40;

"I Stand With You against the Disorder," *Yes! Magazine*
(Winter 2006).

Jeannette Armstrong is one of the most prominent
First Nations authors in Canada and a groundbreaking
leader in First Nations publishing, creative-writing

instruction, and environmental awareness. She has published novels and poetry, edited anthologies, and developed educational programs. Through her novels,
poetry, essays, teaching, and social activism, Armstrong
has become a well-respected figure in both Canadian literature and First Nations politics. With her traditional
knowledge of natural medicines, she carries ideas of
healing into all that she does. She is a member of the
traditional council of the Penticton Indian Band and is
executive director of the En'owkin Centre, a postsecondary school teaching traditional Okanagan philosophy and practices. Her novel *Slash* (1985) was, like
Maria Campbell's *Halfbreed* (1973) and Beatrice Culleton's *In Search of April Raintree* (1983), a watershed book
in the development of First Nations and Métis literature.

Jeannette Christine Armstrong, an Okanagan
Indian, was born in 1948, the grandniece of Hum-Ishu-
Ma (Mourning Dove), the first Native American
woman novelist. Armstrong received a traditional education from Okanagan elders and her family on the
Penticton Indian Reserve, in south-central British
Columbia. From her family she learned the Okanagan
Indian language. She has studied traditional teachings
for many years under the direction of the Okanagan
elders, and this knowledge is central to her writing and
activism. Armstrong argues that these kinds of roots are
lacking in Western culture, which has become filled, she
says in her article "I Stand with You against the Disorder" (2006), with "people without hearts" because of
their lack of family bonds across generations, their dis-
harmony and alienation from the land, and their distance from a sense of community sharing. These
essential aspects of healthy living are lost, she says in
her essay "Sharing One Skin: Okanagan Community"
(1996), in the face of attention to an "individual sense
of well-being without regard to the well-being of others
in the collective." In "The Disempowerment of First
North American Native Peoples and Empowerment
through Their Writing" (1998) Armstrong says that she
feels the responsibility as a representative of her people
to convey the power of the "self-sustaining" indigenous
groups that are still on the land and are perhaps the
only remaining "protectors of Earth." Part of this effort
involves resisting "cultural imperialism" and coming to
terms with the effects of "totalitarian domination," but
underlying her message is a deep faith in humanity and
a call for proactive and cooperative action. Armstrong's
integrity revolves around these beliefs and a desire to
heal an ailing planet.

While her Okanagan education is central to her
intellectual position, Armstrong also graduated from
institutions of higher education. She received a diploma
of fine arts from Okanagan College in 1975 and a bach-

elor of fine arts from the University of Victoria in 1978. During her studies she received both the Mungo Martin Memorial Award (1974), a scholarship for students of First Nations ancestry, and the Helen Pitt Memorial Award (1978) for her writing. Armstrong later began working at the En'owkin Centre, which was created in 1981 as a training and gathering place on the Penticton Indian Reserve and includes an extensive library on Okanagan culture. The center features a school of writing and programs in teacher training, adult education, and community development. It has ties with Theytus Books, a First Nations publisher. The word *en'owkin* translates as a dynamic of communal decision making, voluntary cooperation, and gentle integrative processes. Armstrong's early writing displayed her desire to educate the youth of her people. Both *Enwhisteetkwa: Walk On Water* (1982) and *Neekna and Chemai* (1984) are books for children that include messages of reverence and respect for First Nations traditions. *Neekna and Chemai* describes Okanagan culture and traditional life patterns in the context of natural cycles. The story is about two girls living in the Okanagan Valley before European contact.

Published in 1985, Armstrong's first novel, *Slash,* quickly became a landmark literary phenomenon that initiated a new era in First Nations writing. Aimed at educating First Nations youth, the book offered alternative visions of cultural identity, conflict resolution, and community. The novel centers on a young Okanagan man, Tommy Kelasket, and the traditional Okanagan customs that are threatened by North American white culture. *Slash* presents an anatomy of assimilation and reasserts an autonomous, decolonized First Nations identity. Armstrong does not shy away from representing the sometimes brutal truths of real-life addiction, crime, and racism, but the novel harbors messages of hope and healing, as well. Connections to community and self-awareness are central to Tommy's struggle, especially as it concerns aboriginal identity and a sense of self-worth in conflict with a dominant and unforgiving white environment.

Armstrong did not initially intend *Slash* to be a novel. In a 1993 interview with Janice Williamson she discussed how the project was meant to be a re-creation of history for the Okanagan Indian Curriculum Project in 1982. As a researcher for the En'owkin Centre, Armstrong set out to revise the curriculum for eleventh-grade American Indians by conducting interviews with people in the community on their experience of recent history in the United States and Canada. In this way, as Dee Horne notes in *Contemporary American Indian Writing: Unsettling Literature* (1999), *Slash* is a product of "social memory" rather than written history. Armstrong finally

Paperback cover for the first edition, 2000
(Richland County Public Library)

chose to follow the story of one person in order to retell and replace the histories created by dominant society.

Slash is framed with a prologue and epilogue in which the narrator (presumably Tommy) reminisces about the past, remembering childhood innocence, a violent and chaotic adolescence, and finally an adult sense of peace and clarity. The novel is made up of four long chapters: "The Awakening," "Trying It On," "Mixing It Up," and "We Are a People." In "The Awakening," Armstrong draws out the opposing values and cultural markers that distinguish Indians from whites, those social elements that make up "contact," and the ensuing struggle over influence in young Indian lives. She draws a line between Eurocentric capitalist ideology and Okanagan tradition. Tommy learns from his father, his Uncle Joe, and an elder, Pra-cwa, and he returns to this spiritual instruction later in life. He feels most at ease and whole when engaged in some of the traditional rituals of his people.

Tommy is called "Slash" and an unrevealed Okanagan name; his European-influenced warrior nickname and unrealized First Nations identity suggest the various cultural tensions in his life. In the second and third chapters Tommy runs through a myriad of roles as a social activist, vagabond, criminal, protester, healer, and street brawler. He relearns some of his heritage in prison and experiences the 1972 Trail of Broken Treaties Caravan, in which he hears the testimony of many First Nations and American Indian experiences. These middle chapters especially are picaresque, depicting a thinly connected series of events involving many fleeting and flat characters. The episodes come across as individual stories and seem to carry the tones and rhythms of a distinctive oral tradition. This quality is further accentuated by Armstrong's use of idiom and vernacular in the writing; these markers of the storytelling tradition, of a speaking voice passing on an educational story, set *Slash* apart from the literary and historical discourses it seeks to unsettle.

Throughout the smaller incidents and anecdotes, Tommy keeps a central, if tenuous, connection to his home and family in the Okanagan region. Among the issues that emerge are the distinction between native traditionalists and assimilationists and the way the white systems of government, economics, and law all collude to ease First Nations people into an assimilated role. The concluding chapter of *Slash* solidifies the theme of native self-determination, as Tommy seems to discover balance and a solid foundation in traditional indigenous values. One of the criticisms of the novel is that it is too polemical, that it sacrifices artistic nuance in favor of political statements about native issues. The dialogue often appears as speeches on issues of cultural assimilation, disputed land claims, the American Indian Movement, treaty rights, and constitutional reform. Those who defend the novel argue that these issues are central to First Nations identity and that a young man of Tommy's nature would invariably encounter these arguments and tensions. In *Thresholds of Difference: Feminist Critique, Native Women's Writings, Postcolonial Theory* (1993), Julia V. Emberley argues that the novel deliberately intervenes in the easy separation of fact from fiction. At one point Tommy wonders "why they [colonizers] didn't show things that really happened." Historical events appear in the novel as remembered and revised: the Trail of Broken Treaties Caravan (which commemorated the Trail of Tears migration of 1838–1839), the Battle of Wounded Knee, and the alleged murder of activist Anna Mae Aquash in 1975. *Slash* can easily be read as a teaching aid for young native people who wish to see the "other" side of the story and who wish to transcend anger and achieve a firm sense of self-affirmation. The novel does not flinch from specific issues and the harsh reality of a racialized Canadian social environment and offers a counterhistory, both in terms of the representation of assimilation and colonization of North America Indians and the ways in which Tommy's story is personalized.

In 1989 Armstrong became the director of the En'owkin School of International Writing, affiliated with the University of Victoria. She still teaches creative-writing classes at the school, committing herself to training other young First Nations writers. The school is the first of its kind and has become a highly influential center for creative writing and ecological education. Around the time she became the director of the school, Armstrong began work on several nonfiction projects. *The Native Creative Process: A Collaborative Discourse between Douglas Cardinal and Jeannette Armstrong* (1991) explores in a direct and collaborative way the distinctive nature of the artistic process of First Nations people. Armstrong's environmental concerns and outlook are found in *Aboriginal Perspectives of the Natural Environment* (1991), created in collaboration with James Dumont and Donald R. Fiddler. She contributed the essay "Racism: Racial Exclusivity and Cultural Supremacy" to *Give Back: First Nations Perspectives on Cultural Practice* (1992), a volume of cultural and political discussion on race issues in Canadian culture that also features contributions by writers such as Lee Maracle and Campbell. Armstrong also served as an editor for *We Get Our Living Like Milk from the Land* (1993), an historical and political account of the Okanagan nation and its resistance to assimilation. In addition to these texts, "Words," Armstrong's contribution to *Telling It: Women and Language across Cultures* (1990), and her oft-quoted essay "The Disempowerment of First North American Native Peoples and Empowerment through Their Writing," first published in *Gatherings* in 1990 and included in *An Anthology of Canadian Native Literature in English* (1998), established her as a leading essayist on issues of First Nations culture and politics.

Armstrong's *Breath Tracks* (1991) is a collection of poems written in a variety of styles, from quietly reflective to politically insistent to abstractly imagist. What remains constant is her attention to the land, nature, and the centrality of maintaining a strong, autonomous First Nations identity. The book is divided into four sections: "From the Landscape of Grandmother," "History Lesson," "Fire Madness," and "Wind Woman." As a whole, *Breath Tracks* takes on an empathic but tender tone; it both teaches and soothes.

"From the Landscape of Grandmother" is largely made up of carefully arranged poems in which single words and phrases form loose columns. A reading of these poems becomes an undirected and fluid process of making reading connections, much as one might do in "reading" a natural setting or vista. This sequence concentrates largely on the natural world, with titles such as "Glaciers," "Winds," "Green," and "Butterflies." The loose structure of the poems indicates a relationship to landscape and nature based on release rather than control. One poem in this image-based series contrasts sharply with the others. "Words" begins with the line "words are memory" and is a contemplation of the power of memory, "the sharing / in what we select / to remember" and the importance of the "landscape of grandmother."

The poems in "History Lesson" are more topical. The title poem in the sequence is a retelling of the discovery and settlement of North America: "Out of the belly of Christopher's ship / a mob bursts." The poem recounts the terror and savagery of that "conquest" and mourns the loss of something sacred for both the colonizers and colonized. This political and politicizing voice is heard again in other poems, such as "Music the Tyrant Dances To" and "Grief Is Not the Activity That Heals."

The last two sections of *Breath Tracks* concentrate on healing through mourning and through celebration. "Indian Woman," a poem that encapsulates a movement of both history and individual identity, has received particular attention. The poem consists of a series of assertions beginning "I am. . . ." In the first half of the poem the assertions are derogatory and demeaning, but midway through the poem the speaker realizes that "some one is lying." The remaining lines are assertions of strength, purpose, and a "sacred trust." "Indian Woman " and "History Lesson" have both been anthologized.

Armstrong's novel *Whispering in Shadows* (2000) continues her legacy of making challenging political and social commentary but with the accompaniment of an engaging and emotionally charged story. Penny, a Native American of the Okanagan nation, is an artist, environmental activist, single mother, student, and cancer patient. In telling Penny's story, Armstrong uses poems, letters, diary entries, and a characteristic picaresque narrative. The novel explores Penny's various activities as the artistic, activist, and private aspects of her life mingle in her struggle for personal integrity. She encounters oppression and threats but always seems to find a firm grounding in her home, where she learns much from her *tupa* (grandmother). Penny travels the world battling for indigenous rights and ecological sustainability. Entwined in the personal politics of the people around her are the complex systems of power that inform the entire globe. As in *Slash*, activism and social awareness come across in strong political conversations.

Because of Penny's work and the obvious autobiographical connections to Armstrong herself, the novel does not come across as disingenuous. Through Penny, *Whispering in Shadows* becomes an analysis of the systems of "globalization and supremacy" in which "the colour of oppression and racism is money and blood."

With Penny's death from cancer, Armstrong conveys two final sentiments. First, Penny's dying raises a political issue as she becomes aware of the carcinogens she ingested throughout her life and the hypocrisy of much of the food industry. Second, she dies at home, dreaming of blueberries and the place where she grew up, listening to and learning from her *tupa*. The grounding provided by home and family is not shaken by her cancer and suggests that no oppressive power can take away such a foundation. The conclusion of the novel leaves room for hope and regeneration. *Whispering in Shadows* continues Armstrong's work in both creating positive images of First Nations identity and informing readers of a variety of pressing ecological and humanitarian issues. As a civil-rights activist she continues to fight for the rights of indigenous peoples in land claims and ecological issues. She has worked as a consultant for the Center for Ecoliteracy in Berkeley, California, contributed to the collection *The Case against the Global Economy and for a Turn toward the Local* (1996), and traveled as part of an international delegation of indigenous peoples to the Mexican state of Chiapas to report on the 1994 Zapatista uprising. She served as an indigenous judge for the First Nations International Court of Justice, held in Ottawa in 1996. In 2000 Armstrong was awarded an honorary doctorate from St. Thomas University in Fredericton, New Brunswick.

Armstrong received the 2003 Buffett Award for Indigenous Leadership for her community work, education initiatives, and indigenous-rights activism. The award recognizes her work as executive director of the En'owkin Centre. She has consulted for other organizations, including the Esalen Institute in Big Sur, California; the Omega Institute in Rhinebeck, New York; the Center for Creative Change at Antioch University in Seattle; and the Institute for the Humanities in Salado, Texas. Armstrong has also served on the Council of Listeners for the International Testimonials on Violations of Indigenous Sovereignty, sponsored by the United Nations.

Jeannette Armstrong continues her writing and activism, speaking and holding workshops across the globe. Her commitment to the development of Native American creativity and her insights into social and political issues are known and respected among First Nations people. Her contributions to a variety of educational and activist projects reflect a desire to create new ways of understanding and experiencing the world.

Interviews:

Victoria Freeman, "Rights on Paper," *Fuse Magazine,* 11 (March–April 1988): 36–38;

Hartmut Lutz, in his *Contemporary Challenges: Conversations with Canadian Native Authors* (Saskatoon: Fifth House, 1991), pp. 13–32;

Freeman, "The Body of Our People: An Interview with Jeannette Armstrong," *Paragraph,* 14, no. 3 (1992): 9–12; republished as "The Body of Our People: Jeannette Armstrong," in *The Power to Bend Spoons: Interviews with Canadian Novelists,* edited by Beverley Daurio (Toronto: Mercury, 1998), pp. 10–19;

Janice Williamson, "What I Intended Was to Connect . . . And It Happened," in her *Sounding Differences: Conversations with Seventeen Canadian Women Writers* (Toronto & Buffalo: University of Toronto Press, 1993), pp. 7–26;

Glenn Welker, "Chiapas Is Global," *Indians.org* (March 1994) <http://www.indians.org/welker/global.htm>;

Michael P. Kennedy, "An Interview with Jeannette Armstrong: The Writer as Image Maker and Breaker," *NeWest Review,* 20 (October–November 1994): 9–11;

Karin Beeler, "Image, Music, Text: An Interview with Jeannette Armstrong," *Studies in Canadian Literature/Etudes en Littérature Canadienne,* 21, no. 2 (1996): 143–154;

Kim Anderson, "Reclaiming Native Space in Literature/ Breaking New Ground: An Interview with Jeannette Armstrong," *West Coast Line,* 31 (Autumn 1997): 49–65.

References:

Noel Elizabeth Currie, "Jeannette Armstrong and the Colonial Legacy," *Canadian Literature,* nos. 124–125 (Spring–Summer 1990): 138–152;

Julia V. Emberley, *Thresholds of Difference: Feminist Critique, Native Women's Writings, Postcolonial Theory* (Toronto & Buffalo: University of Toronto Press, 1993);

Margery Fee, "Upsetting Fake Ideas: Jeannette Armstrong's *Slash* and Beatrice Culleton's *April Raintree*," *Canadian Literature,* nos. 124–125 (Spring–Summer 1990): 168–180;

Barbara Hodne and Helen Hoy, "Reading from the Inside Out: Jeannette Armstrong's *Slash*," *World Literature Written in English,* 32 (Spring 1992): 66–87;

Dee Horne, *Contemporary American Indian Writing: Unsettling Literature* (New York: Peter Lang, 1999);

Manina Jones, "Slash Marks the Spot: 'Critical Embarrassment' and Activist Aesthetics in Jeanette Armstrong's *Slash*," *West Coast Line,* 33 (Winter 2000): 48–62;

Angeline O'Neill and Josie Boyle, "Literary Space in the Works of Josie Boyle and Jeannette Armstrong," *CLCWeb: Comparative Literature and Culture: A WWWeb Journal,* 2 (March 2000) <http://clcweb-journal.lib.purdue.edu>;

Janice Williamson, "Biocritical Essay on Jeannette Armstrong," in her *Sounding Differences: Conversations with Seventeen Canadian Women Writers* (Toronto & Buffalo: University of Toronto Press, 1993), pp. 341–342;

Williamson, "Jeannette Armstrong: 'What I Intended Was to Connect . . . and It's Happened,'" *Tessera,* 12 (Summer 1992): 111–129.

Douglas Barbour

(21 March 1940 –   )

Christian Riegel
University of Regina

and

Neta Gordon
Brock University

BOOKS: *Land Fall* (Montreal: Delta Canada, 1971);
A Poem as Long as the Highway (Kingston, Ont.: Quarry Press, 1971);
White (Fredericton, N.B.: Fiddlehead, 1972);
songbook (Vancouver: Talonbooks, 1973);
He & She & (Ottawa: Golden Dog Press, 1974);
Visions of My Grandfather (Ottawa: Golden Dog Press, 1977);
Shore Lines (Winnipeg: Turnstone, 1979);
Worlds Out of Words: The SF Novels of Samuel R. Delaney (Frome, U.K.: Bran's Head, 1979);
In by One, Out by Four, by Barbour and others (Edmonton: Instant Poetry Press, 1980);
The Pirates of Pen's Chance: Homolinguistic Translations, by Barbour and Stephen Scobie (Toronto: Coach House, 1981);
The Harbingers (Kingston, Ont.: Quarry, 1984);
Visible Visions: The Selected Poems of Douglas Barbour, edited, with an introduction, by Smaro Kamboureli and Robert Kroetsch (Edmonton: NeWest Press, 1984);
Canadian Poetry Chronicle, 1984: A Comprehensive Review of Canadian Poetry Books, appendix by Allan Brown (Kingston, Ont.: Quarry Press, 1985);
Story for a Saskatchewan Night (Red Deer, Alta: Red Deer College Press, 1990);
bpNichol and His Works (Toronto: ECW Press, 1992);
Daphne Marlatt and Her Works (Toronto: ECW Press, 1992);
John Newlove and His Works (Toronto: ECW Press, 1992);
Michael Ondaatje (New York: Twayne / Toronto: Maxwell Macmillan Canada, 1993);
Fragmenting Body etc. (Edmonton: NeWest Press, 2000; Applecross, Australia & Cambridge: Salt, 2000);
Breath Takes (Toronto: Wolsak & Wynn, 2001);

Douglas Barbour (from the cover for Story for a Saskatchewan Night, *1990; Bruccoli Clark Layman Archives)*

Lyric/Anti-Lyric: Essays on Contemporary Poetry (Edmonton: NeWest Press, 2001);
A Flame on the Spanish Stairs: John Keats in Rome (Victoria: Greenboathouse, 2002);
Continuations, by Barbour and Sheila E. Murphy (Edmonton: University of Alberta Press, 2006).

OTHER: "Poet as Philosopher: Louis Dudek," in *Poets and Critics: Essays from Canadian Literature, 1966–1974,* edited by George Woodcock (Toronto: Oxford University Press, 1974), pp. 110–122;
"Down with History: Some Notes towards an Understanding of *Beautiful Losers,*" in *Leonard Cohen: The*

Artist and his Critics, edited by Michael Gnarowski (Toronto & New York: McGraw-Hill Ryerson, 1976), pp. 136–149;

"Frank Davey: Finding Your Voice to Say What Must Be Said: The Recent Poetry," in *Brave New Wave,* edited by Jack David (Windsor: Black Moss Press, 1978), pp. 65–82;

"The Phenomenological I: Daphne Marlatt's *Steveston,*" in *Figures in a Ground: Canadian Essays on Modern Literature Collected in Honor of Sheila Watson,* edited by Diane Bessai and David Jackel (Saskatoon: Western Producer Prairie, 1978), pp. 174–188;

The Story So Far 5, edited by Barbour (Toronto: Coach House, 1978);

"John Newlove: More than Just Honest Despair; Some Further Approaches," in *RePlacing,* edited by Dennis Cooley (Downsview, Ont.: ECW Press, 1980), pp. 256–280;

The Maple Laugh Forever: An Anthology of Comic Canadian Poetry, edited by Barbour and Stephen Scobie (Edmonton: Hurtig, 1981);

"Samuel R. Delany," in *Science Fiction Writers: Critical Studies of the Major Authors from the Early Nineteenth Century to the Present Day,* edited by E. F. Bleiler (New York: Scribners, 1982), pp. 329–336;

Writing Right: Poetry by Canadian Women, edited by Barbour and Marni L. Stanley (Edmonton: Longspoon Press, 1982);

Beverly Harris, Gloria Sawai, and Fred Stenson, *Three Times Five: Short Stories,* edited by Barbour (Edmonton: NeWest Press, 1983);

Richard Sommer, *Selected and New Poems,* edited, with an introduction, by Barbour (Montreal: Véhicule Press, 1983);

"J. R. R. Tolkien" and "Roger Zelazny," in *Supernatural Fiction Writers: Fantasy and Horror,* edited by Bleiler (New York: Scribners, 1985), pp. 675–682, 1113–1119;

"Notes towards an Identification of Regionalism in Canadian Poetry," in *Regionalism and National Identity: Multi-Disciplinary Essays on Canada, Australia, and New Zealand,* edited by Reginald Berry and James Acheson (Christchurch, N.Z.: Association for Canadian Studies in Australia and New Zealand, 1985), pp. 569–577;

"Day Thoughts on Anne Wilkinson's Poetry," in *A Mazing Space: Writing Canadian Women Writing,* edited by Shirley Neuman and Smaro Kamboureli (Edmonton: Longspoon Press/NeWest Press, 1986), pp. 179–190;

Tesseracts²: Canadian Science Fiction, edited by Barbour and Phyllis Gotlieb (Victoria: Porcépic Press, 1987);

"The Heavenly Rhetoric of Thine I: Some Versions of the Subject in Book I," in *Tracing the Paths: Reading*

& Writing The Martyrology, edited by Roy Miki (Vancouver: Talonbooks, 1988), pp. 172–188;

"Re: Viewing: Giving and Receiving in Canadian Poetry, or the Role of Reviewing in the Reception of Poetry in English Canada in the 20th Century," in *Problems of Literary Reception,* edited by E. D. Blodgett and A. G. Purdy (Edmonton: Research Institute for Comparative Literature, University of Alberta, 1988), pp. 49–60;

"Canadian Travelers on an Orient Express(ion): John Thompson's *Stilt Jack* and Phyllis Webb's *Water and Light,*" in *Essays in Canadian Literature: Proceedings from the Second International Conference of the Nordic Association for Canadian Studies, University of Lund, 1987,* edited by Jørn Carlsen and Bengt Streijffert (Lund, Sweden: Nordic Association for Canadian Studies, 1989), pp. 1–18;

Beyond Tish, edited by Barbour (Edmonton: NeWest Press / Vancouver: Westcoast, 1991);

"The Rhetorical Strategies of Eli Mandel: Some Notes," in *The Politics of Art: Eli Mandel's Poetry and Criticism,* edited by Ed Jewinski and Andrew Stubbs (Amsterdam & Atlanta: Rodopi, 1992), pp. 193–200;

"Poetry Anthologies of the Future/The Future of Poetry Anthologies," in *Precarious Present/Promising Future? Ethnicity and Identities in Canadian Literature,* edited by Danielle Schaub, Janice Kulyk Keefer, and Richard E. Sherwin (Jerusalem: Magnus Press/Hebrew University, 1996), pp. 160–182;

"William Gibson," in *Science Fiction Writers: Critical Studies of the Major Authors from the Early Nineteenth Century to the Present Day,* second edition, edited by Bleiler (New York: Scribners, 1998), pp. 309–322;

"Writing Both Ends of the Spectrum: Some Notes on John Kinsella's Poetry," in *Fairly Obsessive: Essays on the Works of John Kinsella,* edited by Rod Mengham and Glen Phillips (Nedlands, Australia: Centre for Studies in Australian Literature / North Fremantle, Australia: Fremantle Arts Centre Press, 2000), pp. 30–44;

Dennis Cooley, *Bloody Jack,* revised edition, introduction by Barbour (Edmonton: University of Alberta Press, 2002).

SELECTED PERIODICAL PUBLICATIONS– UNCOLLECTED: "Poet as Philosopher," *Canadian Literature,* 53 (1972): 18–29;

"Phyllis Gotlieb's Children of the Future: *Sunburst* and *Ordinary, Moving,*" *Journal of Canadian Fiction,* 3, no. 2 (1974): 72–76;

"Wholeness and Balance in the Hainish Novels of Ursula K. Le Guin," *Science-Fiction Studies,* 1, no. 3 (1974): 164–173;

"David Canaan: The Failing Heart," *Studies in Canadian Literature*, 1, no. 1 (1976): 64–75;

"bpNichol: The Life of Letters and the Letters of Life," *Essays on Canadian Writing*, nos. 7–8 (Winter 1977–1978): 97–108;

"Extended Forms: One Book & Then Another: The Canadian Long Poem," *Australian-Canadian Studies*, 5, no. 2 (1987): 81–89;

"Transformations of (the Language of) the Ordinary: Innovation in Recent Canadian Poetry," *Essays on Canadian Writing*, 37 (Spring 1989): 30–64;

"Late Word at the Kitchen Table: Phyllis Webb's *Water and Light*," in *West Coast Line*, 35 (Winter 1991–1992): 103–117;

"'The Man with Seven Toes': Michael Ondaatje's Expressionist Version of an Australian Legend," *Australian-Canadian Studies*, 10, no. 1 (1992): 19–43;

"Some Things I Think about When I Think about 90s Poetry & Poetics," *Open Letter*, 9 (Spring 1995): 37–44;

"Some New Zealand Poets in Europe/Europe in Some New Zealand Poems," *Poet's Voice*, 2 (June 1995): 80–99;

"'De tour ces mots en suspens mon souffle, aucun ne m'appartient': La Poesie de E. D. Blodgett"="'Not One of Any Word That Floats upon My Breath Is Mine': The Poetry of E. D. Blodgett," *Ellipse*, 57 (Spring 1997): pp. 55–68;

"Contemporary Canadian Poetry circa 1998: Some Notes," *Kunapipi: Journal of Postcolonial Writing*, 20, no. 3 (1998): 105–114;

"The Violent Logic of Late Capitalism: Jack Womack's SF," *Foundation: The International Review of Science Fiction*, 72 (Spring 1998): 20–33;

"George Bowering and the Extended Form of Poetics," *West Coast Line*, 36 (Winter 2001–2002): 25–36.

Douglas Barbour is a poet, publisher, professor of English, and literary critic whose prolific output has spanned several decades. Barbour is noted for his close attention to the effects of language; he is described by George Melnyk in *The Literary History of Alberta* (1999) as a writer who "uses language as a mirror that reflects upon itself and its linguistic structures." Barbour has a significant reputation in his home province of Alberta and is well known throughout Canada, but he also has a strong following in Australia and England. In 1984 he was awarded the prestigious Stephan G. Stephansson Award for Poetry. He is an innovative poet who has consistently questioned conventional approaches to lyric writing and to poetic form over the course of his writing career.

Douglas Fleming Barbour, the younger of two sons, was born in Winnipeg on 21 March 1940 to E. Phyllis Wilson Barbour and Harold Douglas Barbour, a professional fund-raiser. Barbour grew up in Winnipeg and, as much of his writing attests, has a strong attachment to the prairie landscape that surrounds the city. He did not read or write poetry growing up, but he read science fiction widely, as well as best-selling novels, most of them British and American. His high-school counselor suggested that he study engineering, and he enrolled at McGill University in Montreal in 1958, at first taking engineering courses and then general science classes. By chance Barbour enrolled in a modernist poetry course taught by the influential poet and critic Louis Dudek. Exposure to the works of modernist poets, especially those of Ezra Pound and T. S. Eliot, provided a spark for Barbour to explore the reading and writing of poetry. After several semesters, he left McGill to study English literature at Acadia University in Wolfville, Nova Scotia. Graduating in 1962 with a B.A. in English, he stayed in Nova Scotia to begin work on an M.A. at Dalhousie University in Halifax. He earned the degree in 1964, with a thesis on the works of Ben Jonson. During his time in Nova Scotia, Barbour began to explore more seriously the world of contemporary poetry. He read the works of experimental American poets such as Robert Duncan and Charles Olson, and he began to write poetry more seriously, from the beginning working only with open forms. In the early 1960s Barbour read issues of Dudek's little magazine, *Delta*, which kept him informed of developing poetics in Canada. He also read Dudek's long poems *Europe* (1954), *En México* (1958), and *Atlantis* (1967), which influenced his later penchant for extended forms.

As Barbour completed his first two academic degrees, he established a pattern of writing poetry and scholarly work side by side. He decided to carry on with his scholarly work by earning a doctorate in English at Queen's University in Kingston, Ontario, where he focused on science fiction. While at Queen's, Barbour was on the staff of *Quarry*, a literary magazine, where he worked with writers such as Michael Ondaatje, Gail Fox, David Helwig, and Tom Marshall. In his early years at Queen's, he was introduced to the poet and artist Barrie Phillip Nichol (whose name appears in his published works as bp Nichol or bpNichol), who became a good friend and an important influence. In 1966 Barbour married Sharon Nicoll. As his doctoral studies progressed, he began his teaching career, first at Alderwood Collegiate Institute in Etobicoke, Ontario, for the 1968–1969 academic career. In the fall of 1969 he became a professor in the English department at the University of Alberta, which was at that time in a period of expansion. That same year Barbour met Stephen Scobie, who was also beginning a teaching career at the university and with whom he began collaborating on poetry, including sound poetry: verse, usually intended for recitation, in which the primary consideration is the sound of words rather than meaning and syntax.

During his first years of teaching English and creative writing at the University of Alberta, Barbour served on the editorial boards for two literary journals, *The Merry Devil of Edmonton* from 1969 to 1971 and *White Pelican* from 1971 to 1975. In particular, his work on *The Merry Devil of Edmonton* and *White Pelican* represents his earliest collaboration with Scobie and reveals his broad concerns with the relationship between poets and critics; the work of younger, little-known Edmonton poets; the poetics of space and locality; and literary experimentation in genres such as concrete poetry.

Early in his career at the University of Alberta, Barbour published several books of poetry, beginning with *Land Fall* and *A Poem as Long as the Highway,* both published in 1971. *Land Fall* is an unusual volume in his early corpus in that most of the poems are short and spare. In "The Demoiselle Cranes," he compares the phenomena of nature to an artist's work of shifting description into fundamental image:

> These are the grey lines on white
> as on a precious parchment, the
> artist old and skillful, his brush
> insistent in single decisive lines.

Much of the imagery in *Land Fall* reveals Barbour's interest in the collapsing of sensory perception, chiefly of sight and sound. In "Sibelius' Autumn," the poetic persona ratifies his rapport with the Finnish composer Jan Sibelius both by "seeing" Canadian images in his music—"your / harmonies rise / with that rising wind / sweeping across the prairie"—and by describing the local scene in terms of sound: "a harsh rising resonance / of brown and yellow rushing / to corpses on ground." Several other poems in the volume, including "Poem: The Distances," "A Poem of Harsh Outlines," and "Out of the Auncient Historye," call attention to a specificity of vision, emphasizing the particularity of the prairie landscape as well as the specific moment of poetic apprehension, as in "Edmonton October Poem": "this grey parades, pervades / thought." Barbour's interest in "vision" is signaled in his repeated exploration of what the "eye" sees, as in "Moonlit Poem," and in what the eye "suspects," as in "Fog." The poems in *Land Fall* are primarily short lyrics, but "Out of the Auncient Historye" initiates a short sequence of landscape poems.

Barbour's interest in poetic sequences is more fully explored in *A Poem as Long as the Highway;* indeed, several of the themes in the *Land Fall* series are also present in the longer sequence. A prevalent theme in both sequences, though more explicitly in *A Poem as Long as the Highway,* is that the poetic apprehension of natural landscape reveals the desire for a return to a less technological, more primitive, and more innocent world.

A Poem as Long as the Highway, much of which was originally broadcast on the Canadian Broadcasting Corporation (CBC) radio program *Anthology,* takes up the route connecting Ontario to the West Coast and explores the effects of the human destruction of the landscape. Barbour is explicitly critical of "the machines brawl / earth movers / destroyers / of forest for / thin grey lines on a map." Barbour writes of a westward road trip taken by the speaker and his lover. The poems reflecting the early parts of the trip present a pessimistic view of the creation of the highway and its effects on the natural world, but once the travelers reach the prairies, this negativity relents. In both the prairie and the mountain poems, Barbour returns to the issues of vision and perspective as well as to the problem of describing landscape—how the artistic rendering of the natural is somehow as false as, although perhaps less destructive than, technological transformation. In "this poem is about the mountains" he writes, "Language is not so massive / nor memory clear / to combine to fulfill / the whole of it." Although the middle section of *A Poem as Long as the Highway* is almost entirely focused on descriptions of landscape and how to express them, the final poems of the volume allow a human element to penetrate the trip; the final two poems, "friends/visits" and "'Geoffrey: a babe at arms,'" widen the investigation of the journey.

During the early 1970s Barbour taught in the fall and winter in Edmonton but spent considerable time on the coast in Vancouver during the spring and summer, where he was in contact with the poets and other writers from the vibrant arts scene in that city. In *White* (1972) Barbour continued to explore the conventions and implications of the serial poem. The note that closes the volume states, "these poems are part of a continuum from which they came. in a continuum there are many orders. i have given then *[sic]* an order. any order would do. any order would be a correct order. read them as you will." The "order" provided by Barbour is primarily time-oriented, marking the varied features of winter in terms of seasonal change. Although often explicitly marked in terms of time, the poems are not presented in strictly chronological order. Following "the melancholy spirit of the North," which describes "April showers of / light white flakes," are two poems that return to the apex of winter. In "an appendix" the speaker

> stand[s] in
> a mass of white
> illumination cold
> glare of sun white in
> bright sky.

The second section of the poem "hoar frost" includes a speaker who is blinded by the combination of sun on snow and who muses on the human inability to capture the truth of "winter's frigid clarity." The speaker of the third section, however, articulates a different frame of mind, despite the fact that the "white" (the glare) persists; here the white shows "every step, each / footprint," which are "like thin lines of ink."

Barbour's *songbook* (1973) is concerned with exploring the sense that the language of poetry, the expression of the emotions of a single speaker, might be set to music. Barbour employs lyric conventions, highlighting the subjectivity of the speaker and the relationship between words and music, and conveys a sense of exuberance and celebration. As with *A Poem as Long as a Highway* and *White,* a sense of temporal, almost seasonal, chronology is maintained in *songbook,* as is indicated in "song 51":

> a continuous story
>   in song from
> day to day
>   these poems display
> the bones / articulate
>   narration

Within this loose continuum of articulating the "day to day," Barbour explores such themes as the power of song and poetry, the difficulties of self-knowledge and ignorance, and the energy of the seasons.

In "song 61" the speaker gives an account of his dialogue with a man:

> What does poetry do
> *then?* he asked me
> not having liked my poems,
> not thinking them "poems" at all he said.

The speaker's response is *"If possible, poetry sings. / Sings poetry, if possible,"* and the ways that poetry may sing or celebrate song are fully explored throughout *songbook.* Many of the poems in the collection take up not only how poetry sings but also how it sings to and of others— for example, a lover or another writer. The volume includes several poems for Barbour's wife, as well as for authors such as Earle Birney, Gwendolyn MacEwen, and Ursula K. Le Guin.

In the prefatory poem of Barbour's *He & She &* (1974) the speaker declares that "Someday im going to write a poem / about our fights," and, indeed, the bulk of the volume explores various conflicts between the two titular lovers. The opening poem asserts, by way of a comparison to a scar left from a dog bite, that such fights leave marks that are both painful and hidden; the core poems in the collection try to get underneath the surface of conflict, focusing on mood, rhythm, and emotional patterns rather than actual events. There are three core poems: "she complaind of a headache / cried for 12 seconds," "the sprung poem," and "when guests arrive." The first is the shortest; its main function is to make explicit Barbour's goal of rethinking the tradition of the love lyric by juxtaposing formal poetic idiom with colloquial speech and the contemporary moment: it is the "radio" that sends a "compleynt upon the air." In the next two core poems, which consist of several sections, this juxtaposition continues, as in the first section of "the sprung poem," which contrasts colloquial, almost conversational, stanzas with ones that are full of dense poetic rhythms and images:

>   Now you bend
> in the garden/ your thighs smooth
> ly slyly solicit mine
> while our faces frown lines we
> think harsh thoughts refuse
> such invitations.
>   O Lady
> i hate to bitch but
> how did it start this time?

Barbour reimagines the lyric persona of the poet-lover who must respond to his lady's contradictory demeanor—her tendency to "solicit" and at the same time "refuse such invitations."

The incongruities in idiom that run throughout *He & She &* reinforce the central theme, first articulated in the fourth section of "the sprung poem," the sense of imbalance felt between the lovers:

> here there
> is no
>   balance:
>   the sheet
> falls
>   away

This section of the poem explores the tension between the passion of anger and the passion of sex. In a further section of "the sprung poem," the speaker admits that "always / the tension / is there is / alive," whereby the idea of balance (or imbalance) is replaced by "tension." The ever-present tension ultimately results in the tenderness of an early morning described in the final section of this poem.

Between *He & She &* and his next book, *Visions of My Grandfather* (1977), Barbour completed work on his dissertation, which he defended in 1976. He also wrote extensively on new Canadian poetry, with more than one hundred book reviews appearing in a roughly ten-year period. In 1977 he began his long association with NeWest Press, a literary publishing house that was founded in Edmonton by Melnyk. Barbour was active on the editorial board, along with other writers such as Rudy Wiebe, Robert Kroetsch, Henry Kreisel, and Aritha van Herk. *Visions of My Grandfather* was written from 1971 to 1972. Much of the experimentation with rhythm, sound, and space found in Barbour's poetry collections of the 1970s is absent from this work. The opening section picks up on the title of the collection, with its emphasis on seeing. A major thematic focus of the volume is the question of how the vision of one man, as evidenced in his visual art, might be conveyed to his grandson and how the speaker-grandson's poetry might capture both a vision of what his grandfather saw and who his grandfather had been. The first section plays on the phrase "drawn in," referring at once to how "the country" is represented visually in the grandfather's paintings and drawings; how both the grandfather and the speaker are lured, almost spellbound, by landscape; and how the speaker is compelled by his grandfather's vision. The subject of the second section shifts from vision to voice, or how each may be substituted for the other. The last stanza describes the landscape "as texture," revealing that, for the artist, the country is somehow always art.

Barbour draws connections between visual and poetic art in several poems from *Visions of My Grandfather* that variously explore the processing of the visual into language, the differences between the grandfather's and the speaker's visions, and the way perception changes. Moments in the cultural history of Canada are mingled with biographical details from the grandfather's life:

> (from the fields you had known, from the flat harsh land
> scape your folk had settled, & his kind too, Grove came to read his
> visions. . . .   but you
> listend & Lorne Pierce listend. recognized the raw talent of the
> West.

A theme that emerges from the work is the celebration of Western and prairie art, with Barbour's own love for that particular landscape becoming part of a personal and public heritage. Only in the final section does the speaker acknowledge that such a love, although possi-

bly inherited from a family member, somehow excludes the human; he admits that, like his grandfather, he has a tendency to "ignor[e] the possible vertical figure / moving / on a white ground."

Shore Lines (1979) is framed by two poems that represent Barbour's overt exploration of sound poetry. Both "Summer's Sea Son" and "Our Lady of the slowly freezing lakeshore—november" work to establish the connection between the sounds of water and language:

> shal om shal lom sh sh shal lom
> shallow shal low shal om shalom osh
> shun osh shun osh shun oshun

The lapping of the waves suggests a quiet ("low") meditation ("om"), which is both a peaceful greeting and leave-taking ("shalom"). In "Our Lady" the changing of water into ice is both aurally and visually connected to the tension between "cycles" and "is," as well as to the myth of "Isis," Egyptian goddess of both fertility and death.

The poems in *Shore Lines* also take up the exploration of transitional spaces, such as the shore and the change of seasons. The first section, "dreaming," deals with the loss of control experienced during dreams and nightmares. The second section, "walking long beach," also takes up the subject of borders and the instability they project, this time in an exploration of the tension between the seeming infinity and exhaustiveness of the beach and the evidence of time's ravages to be seen in the production of "organic wrecks." Many of the ideas surveyed in "walking long beach" are reintroduced in the fourth and final section, "maligne canyon poems," in which the erosion of rock by water is compared with human pain.

In 1979 Barbour published a critical study, *Worlds Out of Words: The SF Novels of Samuel R. Delaney,* which grew out of his dissertation, "Patterns of Meaning in the SF Novels of Ursula K. Le Guin, Joanna Russ and Samuel R. Delany, 1962–1972." Barbour examines Delany's "craft-consciousness," his interest in metafiction, and his experiments with language that challenged "conventional estimates of what science fiction is." Barbour's critique also seeks out the tension between the ethical and the aesthetic that he sees as underlying Delany's fiction, whether he was writing according to traditional patterns of the quest story, experimenting with a complex series of cultural and literary allusions, or concentrating on matters of complex structure and language. Despite his increasing focus on poetry, Barbour has maintained an interest in science fiction and fantasy throughout his career, teaching various courses at the University of Alberta on the subject.

In 1980 Barbour formed the poetry-publishing firm Longspoon Press with Scobie and Shirley Neuman, but the press did not have a long life, and its activities were eventually taken over by NeWest Press. That same year Barbour traveled to the United States to perform sound poetry in the duo Re: Sounding with Scobie, by that time a noted Canadian poet. They continued the partnership with *The Pirates of Pen's Chance: Homolinguistic Translations* (1981). Barbour and Scobie acknowledged Nichol and Steve McCaffery as influences, underscoring the importance of the small community of language-oriented poets at work in Canada in the late 1970s and early 1980s. *The Pirates of Pen's Chance* was published by the respected Coach House Press, which specializes in experimental and avantgarde verse. In working with homolinguistic translation, Barbour signaled his developing interest in language as both subject and medium for poetic exploration. The process of writing the poems for *Pirates of Pen's Chance* was overtly and self-consciously experimental, as Barbour and Scobie note in the afterword. Homolinguistic translation is defined as "translation from English into English." The transfer from one text to another is varied: "some are closed, formal systems, which allow very little leeway to the translator, and some are wide-open, free-association processes which allow the translator unlimited freedom." A basic principle is that the poet works from an original text, a poem or other piece of writing, and then shifts or "translates" it into the context of a new creation: "The new texts may be comic, or surreal, or totally abstract. One of the things which fascinates us about this type of experimentation is the way in which it can push language to the outer edges of meaning: in these cases, the new texts hover on the borders of intelligibility, never wholly rejecting meaning, but never wholly embracing it either."

While the range of originating texts in *The Pirates of Pen's Chance* is broad, there is a dominating focus on literary work—criticism, theory, poetry, or fiction. Thus, works from canonical figures such as William Shakespeare, John Milton, William Wordsworth, and Robert Browning are used, as well as texts from significant Canadian writers, such as Leonard Cohen, Duncan Campbell Scott, Phyllis Webb, Ondaatje, and Sheila Watson. There are also works by writers who extended the uses of language in poetry, such as the modernists Eliot, Pound, and James Joyce and the Canadian poets Nichol, Kroetsch, and Dennis Lee. The end result is a process of writing that allowed Barbour and Scobie to extend the range of their work and their engagement with language and literature: "These translations take us, as writers, in directions we would never have gone without the stimulus of this process. The poems are unlikely to have been written in our own voices; they free us from the expressive demands of the lyric ego."

Barbour and Scobie identify three types of homolinguistic translation in *The Pirates of Pen's Chance*: metonymic, acrostic, and structural translations. All three pose challenges to readers and compel them to be active participants in the understanding of the texts. Metonymic translation is the replacement of words in the original text "by words which *we* associate with them, through synonyms, comparison, paraphrase, analysis, expansion, contraction, puns, allusions both literary and personal, and even all the devious methods of the composers of cryptic crossword-puzzle clues." Writing and reading metonymical translations involves a linguistic engagement that requires writer and reader to "play" with words and linguistic structures in order to comprehend the poems. Barbour and Scobie define acrostic translation as "(a) letter/word acrostics, in which the first *letter* of *every word* spells out the original text; (b) word/line acrostics, in which the first *word* of every *line* spells out the original text." Structural translation occurs when the poets draw "*all* the words" they use "from the original texts, without alteration." Thus, the resulting poem in a translation would include the words from the original, but the arrangement in the new text would be up to the poet: "our 'own' poetic activity here is confined to rhythmic annotation, and of course the decisions of where to start and where to stop."

The Pirate's of Pen's Chance is divided into two sections, "Minimal Lists" and "Steinways." An afterword provides a definition of terms and method and a list of notes for each poem that provides the source text, the author of the translation (either Scobie or Barbour), and the method of translation. The notes are essential to a full understanding of the book, as they provide information on how to read each of the poems. The first poem in "Minimal Lists," "Agricultural implement," is exemplary of the method of the book as a whole. A translation of William Carlos Williams's "The Red Wheelbarrow" (1923), it is a "new" piece with only minimal direct relation to the source text. The first section is identified as a metonymical translation, and the title of the poem itself indicates the relation of the new text to the original, for the wheelbarrow in Williams's poem is shifted to the larger category of agricultural implements. The original set of four couplets in Williams's poem is translated into two numbered sections: the first formally mirrors the original in its eight lines of couplets, but the second adds another eighteen lines, arranged in triplets. The second section is identified as a letter/word acrostic, so that the first letter of every word spells out the original poem. In the second section of *Pirates of Pen's Chance,* Barbour and Scobie

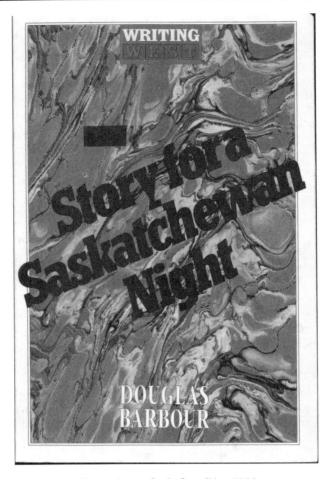

Paperback cover for the first edition, 1990
(Bruccoli Clark Layman Archives)

work from Gertrude Stein's "A Carafe That Is a Blind Glass," from *Tender Buttons* (1914). The first poem in the series, Scobie's "The Love Song of Alice B. Toklas," is a letter/word acrostic of the original text, and thus readers are provided with the source text that will help them to read the translations to follow. When the first letter of each word in a line is combined, as for example in the opening lines, Stein's text can be read:

> Alice knitted. I never did.
> I never grew lonely.
> Alice said something.
> Alice never died.
> Alice could outlast unruly servants.
> I needled . . .

Stein's text, then, is "A kind in glass and a cousin."

In 1984 Barbour and Scobie toured Germany, Denmark, and Sweden performing their sound poems. That same year Barbour published *The Harbingers*, a small volume of poetry first written in 1968–1970 and revised for publication at a writing retreat at Emma Lake, in northern Saskatchewan, in August 1981. Although composed and revised over a long span of time, *The Harbingers* reflects Barbour's development as a poet into the mid 1980s. He continued with his formalistic concerns, employing blank spaces, the arrangement of words on the page for visual effect, and varying stanza forms. He also made use of wordplay, sound patterns, and the melodic potential of language.

Thematically, *The Harbingers* reflects several of the concerns that Barbour explored in his earlier works, including nature, love, the relation of the self to the other (including the natural world), and the role of the perceiving self in relation to writing and language. The poem moves through a three-part cycle of the seasons, shifting from fall to winter to spring. Barbour establishes a strong connection between the speaker and the natural world around him. Not only is the speaker strongly aware of his perceptions, he is also aware of the natural world as it shifts from fall to winter and then to spring.

The Harbingers is an eighteen-page poem with two epigraphs, the first from a song by the early-twentieth-century Texas bluesman Blind Lemon Jefferson and the second from the seventeenth-century English poet George Herbert. The epigraphs are indicative of the wide range of literary and cultural texts that have influenced Barbour's works. The choice of a song lyric for the first epigraph reflects his continuing interest in the relationship between song and poetry and, by extension, lyric verse. He formally theorized this interest in his critical essay "Lyric/Anti-Lyric: Some Notes on a Concept," first published in 1984 and later collected in *Lyric/Anti-Lyric: Essays on Contemporary Poetry* (2001). Jefferson's song is the rumination of a man near death: "Now I'm looking funny in the eye / Pretty Momma I believe I'm fixin to die." He awaits the "two white horses in the night" who will take him to his deathbed. Barbour incorporates the imagery of the horses of death into the thematic content of his long poem: they come, "their sound precise / as steps to the block / clip / clop quick," to "draw the black hearse."

In 1984 Barbour traveled widely in Australia and New Zealand, where he read from his works. He returned to those countries for readings several times in the coming years. *Visible Visions: The Selected Poems of Douglas Barbour* (1984) presents key poems from his earlier works as well as seventeen new poems, many of which were republished in later volumes. The collection, which allows for a retrospective look at the development of Barbour's complex poetics, includes an introduction by the editors, Kroetsch and Canadian literary critic Smaro Kamboureli. They remark on Barbour's range as a poet as well as the major threads in his approach to poetry: "He can become at once the lyric poet and the author of a long poem because he is so deliberately a language poet. He foregrounds language, not only with his puns and his punctuation and his arrangements on the page, but also in his consciousness that language is not a 'tool' towards other ends but itself the substance of its own concern." In one of the new poems in the collection, "Earth song/body song," Barbour continues with his exploration of language, lyric, landscape, and desire. The title announces the connections that he wishes to emphasize—that the human is a perceiving body that struggles through language to encompass and articulate the nature of experience:

> knowledge is in sight   *in*
> *situ*   this place we stand
> at the end of the route
> rooted to the spot   &
> somehow   knowing

Barbour thus continues to explore seeing, knowing, and the particulars of the moment of perceiving in a specific place. "Earth song/body song," like many other of his earlier poems, works to find the language to make the immediate experience of perceiving a place and a landscape something that can be articulated. It also foreshadows the poems that he was to write over the course of the next fifteen years that ultimately became *Breath Takes* (2001). With *Visible Visions,* Barbour also achieved strong recognition for his work by winning the Stephan G. Stephansson Award for Poetry.

A collection of one hundred of Barbour's reviews was published in 1985 as *Canadian Poetry Chronicle, 1984: A Comprehensive Review of Canadian Poetry Books.* The book serves an historical purpose in that it chronicles a key period in Canadian poetry publishing, and it covers all of the major poets writing at that time, including writers such as Daphne Marlatt, Alden Nowlan, Nichol, Ralph Gustafson, and Frances Itani.

In 1986 Barbour traveled to Iraq to read at a poetry festival in Baghdad, where he was arrested and detained while innocently taking photographs. Although he was held for only a short time, this experience is incorporated into the sequence "A Baghdad Journal," from *Story for a Saskatchewan Night* (1990), a collection that brings together several poetic forms Barbour had employed earlier, including the serial poem, concrete poetry, homolinguistic translation, and experiments with formal constraints. In "A Baghdad Journal" Barbour confronts the chaos of a foreign culture and a convoluted war. The poem includes both prose and poetic sections:

> where in the midst of these bloody festivities loud voices ranting in their chanting for the victory to come is the quiet voice of the quiet memory the 20 flies buzzing on the ceiling the silence after love in a city without pictures or applause i couldnt hear any of this in the country so determinedly at war the poets are part of the troops with their own front lines

The themes in *Story for a Saskatchewan Night* include explorations of the language of landscape, the nature of the encounter with narrative, and literary versus political self-consciousness. The title work is a serial poem that identifies the prairie as the site of a collision between silence and story, as the place where silence or absence functions as a story. The sounds of the landscape, along with its hidden creatures, are explored, as is the complex aboriginal tradition of the trickster figure. The first section presents a speaker who claims repeatedly that he has "no story," that there "is no story," that "this isnt narrative hell / its not even complaint." In the subsequent sections the speaker's hesitancy ultimately becomes the impetus for a story.

In 1990 Barbour toured and read in England, where he was to return in 1996, giving his works further international exposure. In the years following *Story for a Saskatchewan Night,* he turned his attention to writing criticism on significant Canadian poets, publishing studies on John Newlove, Marlatt, and Nichol in 1992. The influence of these writers on his own work is clear. Barbour shares Marlatt's interest in phenomenology, perception, and complex rhythms and syntax, as well as her kinship with influential American poets such as Olson and Duncan and with the West Coast Canadian movement centered around *Tish* magazine. Nichol's innovations in the sound and visual aspects of poetry are also clear influences on Barbour's developing style. Another critical study by Barbour, *Michael Ondaatje* (1993), represents his interests in both poetic and fictional forms.

In the mid to late 1990s Barbour continued to travel widely and read his poetry wherever the opportunity arose. He went to South Korea in 1993, Austria in 1994, and Israel in 1995; that year he also completed an extensive tour of New Zealand and Australia, where he performed with Scobie. Barbour was the keynote speaker at a 1998 conference in Tenerife on Canadian poetry and read from his own works.

There was a significant gap between *Story for a Saskatchewan Night* and Barbour's next book of poetry, *Fragmenting Body etc.* (2000), which was published in Canada, England, and Australia. The international editions reflect the following he has garnered outside of his native country. The collection shows Barbour's ongoing interest in homolinguistic translation. The first three sections of *Fragmenting Body etc.* employ as source texts the forty-eight essays in the three-volume *Fragments for a History of the Human Body* (1989), edited by Michel Feher, Ramona Naddaff, and Nadia Tazi. The three sections comprise serial poems with the thematic focus suggested by the original texts; together they make up a multipart long poem.

The first section follows the editorial plan of the first volume of *Fragments for a History of the Human Body* by examining the relationship of the human body to the divine, to the bestial, and to the machines that imitate or simulate the human body. The poems work from excerpted passages from the original text: the first line of the translated text is taken from the original and given in bold, italicized type separated by a space from the ensuing poem. *"whole cadaver or of a part seems a virtual"* is exemplary of the formal and thematic interests of this section. The second line of the poem leads from the first but recasts or translates the context of the original and creates a new text:

reality

theres method when the dead cert finish
precedes the hearse

push a button watch a screen
slip on a glove
                    love
was never this carefully programmed
before

the only question left appears
in glowing letters

          what is the loss sustained
          on that body now
          "dead to the world"
          & why

The second section of *Fragmenting Body etc.* follows the pattern of the first in its thematic relation to the original text, in this case the second volume of *Fragments for a History of the Human Body,* which explores the duality of the inside and outside of a body and the disjuncture between the two. Taking its cue from the third volume of *Fragments for a History of the Human Body,* the third section of *Fragmenting Body etc.* examines the social role of the body and how individuals become organs of a larger unit, such as the social body. As elsewhere in Barbour's oeuvre, poetry is at once a linguistic game, a formal experiment, and serious intellectual inquiry.

The fourth section of *Fragmenting Body etc.,* "Paratactical manoeuvres," comprises a ten-page sequence of poems. It is followed by "For bpNichol: These re-memberings: an elegiac sequence," in which Barbour connects his poetry to a tradition of elegy reaching back to English writers such as Thomas Hardy, Matthew Arnold, Percy Bysshe Shelley, and Milton, and to classical poets such as Theocritus, Moschus, and Bion. A close friend of Barbour, Nichol was a significant force in experimental poetry in Canada, and his death in 1988 left a void that Barbour attempted to address with this poetic sequence. As elsewhere, he employs formal, visual, and aural elements, but he also reflects the conventions of the elegy in his thematic use of natural imagery, such as the growing, maturing, and burning of leaves, and the invocation of the Orpheus myth through references to song.

Some of the poems in *Breath Takes,* published in 2001, first appeared in various literary magazines and in *Visible Visions.* Seventy-five of the eighty-seven poems are titled "breath ghazal," and they appear in a numbered sequence in the order in which they were written. The *ghazal* is an ancient Persian verse form that requires the poet to write thematically unlinked couplets that often work against a coherent narrative. Barbour follows these conventions; however, by omitting punctuation at the end of each couplet, he revises the form. Key concerns in these poems include communication and celebration, as in "breath ghazal 48," in which the "heavy sweetsmellin' smell of new-mown grass" is "heady," and in "breath ghazal 68," in which "beer and wine in warm dusk" are central elements. The cycle of the seasons is also frequently considered.

In the second section of *Breath Takes,* "& the Returns," Barbour continues his homolinguistic translations and allusions to other writers. Some of the poems are translations from works by Cohen; others, such as "in the dream Daphne" and "for Fred," were inspired by Marlatt and Fred Wah, two influential language-oriented poets. In this section the poems show strong elements of narrative, in contrast with the disjunctive and fragmentary nature of the *ghazals.* In "History: Manhattan-Montréal-Berlin," a prose poem, Barbour overtly works with several lines from Cohen's songs. Thematically, the poem is an examination of the poet's relationship to Cohen's music and poetry, as well as a contemplation of the transitory nature of contemporary life.

Lyric/Anti-Lyric: Essays on Contemporary Poetry, also published in 2001, is a volume in the Writer as Critic series from NeWest Press, a series that includes books by Scobie, van Herk, Frank Davey, and George Bowering. The title essay, first published in 1984, speaks most closely to Barbour's engagement with the notion of lyric poetry throughout his career. In the other essays he considers experimental and language-oriented poetry in Canada, New Zealand, and the United States. He examines works by Canadian poets such as Eli Mandel, Sharon Thesen, Webb, and John Thompson; New Zealand poets such as Allen Curnow, C. K. Stead, and Jenny Bornholt; and the American Susan Howe.

Barbour's chapbook *A Flame on the Spanish Stairs* was published in 2002 by Greenboathouse Books, a small poetry press based in Victoria. In it he continues to work in the modes that he has been developing for more than thirty years, paying close attention to the effects of language, employing formal innovation, and using source texts that are incorporated and translated into the fabric of his poems. He works once again with a canonical literary figure, John Keats. In a prefatory note Barbour writes, "These poems are fourteen line, quasi-sonnets, word/line acrostics based on phrases found in Keats's letters." The sixteen poems in the chapbook are all constructed in the same manner, working from the original text to create something new.

The first poem sets out the mode of the rest, with a word/line acrostic. The first words of every line are the original text, a line from a letter by Keats: "I find

that I cannot exist without poetry without eternal poetry half the day." From these beginnings, Barbour translates Keats's words into his own speaker's context, and Keats's need for poetry becomes a starting point for the poet's rumination about his own need for writing and fashioning language: "I know now I always wanted to write, to / find a way to release the dreams / that spelled desire onto the page." Thematically, *A Flame on the Spanish Stairs* addresses many of the concerns that Barbour has explored elsewhere, including the relation of desire to language, self to other, and self to death. Inspired by Keats's reflections on death in his letters, Barbour returns to the contemplation of death that he also explored in *The Harbingers* and in the sequence about Nichol in *Fragmenting Body etc:*

> the death I know so intimately claims
> more of me each day
> I weep shamelessly & wish to
> have a good dying   but I have
> known too many bad ones.

In 2005 Barbour became professor emeritus at the University of Alberta. The following year he published *Continuations,* a long poem of twenty-five sections written in collaboration with Arizona poet Sheila E. Murphy, whom he had met in 2000 when performing with Scobie in Phoenix. The sections in *Continuations* are built out of six-line stanzas that were alternately written by each poet and exchanged via e-mail almost on a daily basis during a period of five years; the afterword to the collection asserts, "this format inherently possesses flexibility that facilitates fluid interchange, and allows a blending of resources associated with diverse backgrounds and experience." The collaborative process gives rise to stanzas that are often connected by associative wordplay, sonic experimentation, and thematic variation and accumulation. Frequently, a single word will crop up in several succeeding stanzas, accruing shifts in meaning as each poet riffs on the preceding stanza. In section xii, for example, a reference to smoke that "floats across the sound / of what's left" after an apocalyptic fiery disaster begets the image of "the lightest finger / ed note floated out from over" two stanzas later and, still later, the image of

> one wan
> and wandering / caught
> up in clouded floating
> over / lost now in
> the shifting city's streets.

Many of the sections deliberate about the medium of technology and how it affects and directs the writing process; section vii, for example, queries the process of collaborative writing by e-mail:

> mechanical?   or only thought
> s to be there found
> as cutting   edging   as there
> now   in the midst of
> chips strewn   the glare
> illuminates the hidden.

The thematic core of *Continuations,* however, is a celebration of a universal spirit, which is often figured in terms of triumphant sound or song, such as "counted / counter / tenored notes rising as / the sun."

In his career as a poet and critic, Douglas Barbour has had a prolific output and has built a significant reputation in Canada and internationally. As a strongly language-oriented poet, he has experimented with the possibilities of language, but his works remain largely accessible, as his readers across the world attest. Bar-

bour has emerged as one of the most important poets in contemporary Canadian literature.

References:

Charlene Diehl-Jones, "'Theres More Nothing to Say': Unspeaking Douglas Barbour's 'Story for a Saskatchewan Night,'" in *Negation, Critical Theory, and Postmodern Textuality,* edited by Daniel Fischlin (Dordrecht & Boston: Kluwer Academic, 1994), pp. 241–257;

George Melnyk, *The Literary History of Alberta,* volume 2: *From the End of the War to the End of the Century* (Edmonton: University of Alberta Press, 1999), pp. 71–72, 91, 173–174;

Wayne Tefs, "Douglas Barbour: The Land Was Ours before We Were the Land's," in *RePlacing,* edited by Dennis Cooley (Toronto: ECW Press, 1980), pp. 143–148.

Sandra Birdsell

(22 April 1942 –   )

Barbara Pell
Trinity Western University

BOOKS: *Night Travellers* (Winnipeg: Turnstone, 1982);

Ladies of the House (Winnipeg: Turnstone, 1984);

The Missing Child (Toronto: L. & O. Dennys, 1989; London: Vintage, 1990);

The Chrome Suite (Toronto: McClelland & Stewart, 1992; London: Virago, 1994);

The Town That Floated Away (Toronto: HarperCollins, 1997; New York: HarperCollins World, 1998);

The Two-Headed Calf (Toronto: McClelland & Stewart, 1997);

The Russländer (Toronto: McClelland & Stewart, 2001); republished as *Katya* (Minneapolis: Milkweed, 2004);

Children of the Day (Toronto: Random House Canada, 2005).

Collection: *Agassiz Stories: Night Travellers and Ladies of the House,* introduction by Robert Weaver (Winnipeg: Turnstone, 1987); republished as *Agassiz: A Novel in Stories* (Minneapolis: Milkweed, 1991).

PLAY PRODUCTIONS: William Kurelek, *A Prairie Boy's Winter,* adapted by Birdsell, Martha Brooks, and David Gillies, Winnipeg, Gas Station Theatre, 22 December 1984; revised, Winnipeg, Gas Station Theatre, 21 December 1985;

The Revival, Winnipeg, Gas Station Theatre, 13 November 1986.

PRODUCED SCRIPTS: "Places Not Our Own," television, *Daughters of the Country,* First Choice, 24 June 1987;

"Niagara Falls," television, *The Way We Are,* CBC Manitoba, 9 November 1987;

"Summer Storm," television, *Family Pictures,* CBC, Fall 1988;

Another View of the North, radio, CBC, June 1992;

The Town That Floated Away, radio, CBC, September 1992;

Sandra Birdsell (photograph by Robert Eidse; from the dust jacket for Katya, *2004; Richland County Public Library)*

The Waiting Time, radio, CBC, March 1993.

OTHER: "From the Bottom of the Lake," in *Trace: Prairie Writers on Writing,* edited by Birk Sproxton (Winnipeg: Turnstone, 1986), pp. 133–139;

Gabrielle Roy, *Where Nests the Water Hen,* translated by Harry L. Binsse, afterword by Birdsell (Toronto: McClelland & Stewart, 1989).

SELECTED PERIODICAL PUBLICATION–UNCOLLECTED: "'And Things That Go Bump in the Night,'" *Prairie Fire,* special issue on Canadian Mennonite writing, 11, no. 2 (1990): 184–190.

Although Sandra Birdsell came relatively late to a writing career, after fifteen years as a wife and mother, and her corpus is still relatively small, she is regarded as an important Canadian writer with a distinctive voice. In her novels and stories she unsentimentally portrays the sordid lives and inarticulate longings of working-class women not frequently found in Canadian fiction. Favoring subjective voice over objective plot and sympathy over judgment, Birdsell transcends ideological feminism in her fiction to express universal aspirations and, often, quiet desperation.

Sandra Louise Bartlette was born on 22 April 1942 in Hamiota, a small town in southern Manitoba, to Louise Schroeder Bartlette, of Russian Mennonite heritage, and Joseph Roger Bartlette (originally Berthelette), a Métis and a Roman Catholic. She was the fifth of eleven children to survive infancy. In 1943 the family moved to Morris, also in southern Manitoba, where Sandra's father became the town barber. The death of her next-older sister, Annette, of leukemia in 1948 isolated Sandra in the middle of the family. As a result, she became a rebellious loner and troublemaker to get attention.

Birdsell's family was a microcosm of the religious and cultural tensions in exceptionally multicultural Morris. Her mother and father were, as she told interviewer Andrew Garrod, "very strong-willed, very rebellious people" who married outside their religions and cultures. Consequently, family quarrels usually centered on religion, and Birdsell recalls the childhood trauma of hearing her mother tell her father that he was going to hell because he was Roman Catholic. She also inherited her parents' tales. As she recalls in the essay "From the Bottom of the Lake" (1986), "Both my parents told us stories. My mother's were stories of [Mennonite] suffering, life and death kinds of stories. My father's stories were often [aboriginal] tales of trickery, or Red River carts and Louis Riel. He told stories about magic and medicine." (Red River carts, large-wheeled carts used to transport goods in western Canada before the advent of railroads, were a symbol of Métis culture; Riel was a nineteenth-century Métis leader.)

Morris, on the banks of the Red River south of Winnipeg, represented the conformity, mediocrity, and hypocrisy Birdsell loathes. The town also was the source of her dominant fictional metaphor—the apocalyptic flood. She was terrified as a child to discover that her family lived on land that was once covered by the ancient Lake Agassiz; the Red River flooded in 1950, destroying much of Morris. As a rebellious teenager she first hitchhiked out of town in 1957. Forced to return, she finished tenth grade and then, already pregnant, married Stan Birdsell, a factory worker from nearby

Manitou, on 1 July 1959. With him she left Morris—but not its stories—for good.

The Birdsells moved around southern Manitoba for several years, finally settling in Winnipeg in 1964. They had three children, Roger, Angela, and Darcie, and for almost twenty years Birdsell worked as a homemaker, supplementing family earnings as an income-tax clerk, salesperson, and cocktail waitress. She had always written for pleasure. A poem about dying that she wrote at age eleven won a school contest, and she started a novel at twelve. Even as a busy wife and mother she kept journals and wrote pen-pal letters. In the mid 1970s, with all of her children finally in school, she began writing articles for local newspapers and considered a career in journalism.

When Birdsell's father died in June 1973 after a long illness, she turned to creative nonfiction. "I'll Come on Sunday" records her sense of loss and her attempt to capture life in stories. It won second prize in the *Winnipeg Free Press* Nonfiction Contest (1975) and first prize in the *Reader's Digest* Creative Writing Contest (1978). By that time Birdsell had already had several stories published in small newspapers and literary journals, but she was aware of her lack of educational and literary background. She read *Stories from Western Canada* (1972) and *Short Story Masterpieces* (1954) and was influenced by Sherwood Anderson, Katherine Mansfield, William Faulkner, Eudora Welty, and especially Flannery O'Connor. She also took two creative-writing courses, at the University of Winnipeg in 1978 with James Walker and at the University of Manitoba in 1979 with Robert Kroetsch.

Kroetsch in particular introduced Birdsell to the works of Manitoba authors such as Gabrielle Roy and Margaret Laurence, which gave her the courage to write as a woman and a Westerner. As she notes in "From the Bottom of the Lake," "it was a great liberation for me when I realized that it was possible for me to write out of the prairies about small-town people, and for that writing to have a universal appeal." Kroetsch challenged Birdsell to take her writing seriously. He wrote a recommendation that brought her a $2,000 Manitoba Arts Council grant to develop a series of stories that she had begun writing in his class; the grant also gave her legitimacy as a full-time writer in her family's eyes.

In 1982 these stories were collected as *Night Travellers,* which received excellent reviews and won the prestigious Gerald Lampert Memorial Award in 1984. William French, the influential reviewer from the Toronto *Globe and Mail,* compared his discovery of Birdsell with Alice Munro's debut fourteen years earlier and said that her "Manitoba reputation . . . deserves to become national" (24 March 1983). The thirteen stories in *Night Travellers* center on the Lafreniere family of Agassiz, a small town in southern Manitoba. The father, Maurice, tries to escape his Métis heritage and achieve respectability through his position as town barber, his marriage to a Mennonite girl from a strict family, and their six children. In the first story, "The Flood," Maurice gains the status of Old Man River because of his instinctive understanding of the waters that inundate the town, but in "Boundary Lines" he repudiates his native uncle. Only at his death near the end of the book, in "Journey to the Lake," does Maurice symbolically repossess his language and his people. His wife, Mika, embodies all the hard, frustrated, and oppressed women of Birdsell's fiction in "Stones" (a metaphor for her bitter laughter) and "The Rock Garden," a stony symbol of her imprisonment in the circles of wife and motherhood. In the title story of the collection, Mika finds fulfillment in a brief extramarital affair, but—denounced by her Mennonite father and pregnant again by her violent, drunken husband—she succumbs to her bondage.

The Lafrenieres' daughters, Truda, Betty, and Lureen, are the narrative foci for six other stories in *Night Travellers*. ("Judgement" is anomalous: the characters, Mika's parents, and the genre, fantasy humor, are at odds with the rest of the collection.) Truda is the timid artist in the family who discovers the wonder of her independent imagination in "Truda." Lureen is the rebel torn between her Métis heritage and her mother's Mennonite family in "The Day My Grandfather Died." Betty is the good girl who becomes the embodiment of Birdsell's themes of sexual temptation in "Flowers for Weddings and Funerals" and of sexual abuse in "Wednesday Circle," "The Wild Plum Tree," and "There Is No Shoreline," in which, as a middle-aged mother, she finally packs away her tragic memories and finds peace.

Birdsell's second short-story collection, *Ladies of the House* (1984), was seen as a sequel to *Night Travellers*. The ten stories are set mostly in Winnipeg, where the Lafreniere women are joined by other women friends. Some critics who had praised the earlier collection complained that this one had a less-unified structure and a darker tone. Alberto Manguel, however, enthusiastically praised *Ladies of the House* as confirmation of "Birdsell's position as one of the best short-story writers in the language" (*Books in Canada,* January–February 1985). The two collections were republished together as *Agassiz Stories: Night Travellers and Ladies of the House* (1987); the American edition was titled *Agassiz: A Novel in Stories* (1991), a questionable marketing ploy that confused and annoyed some critics.

The first story in *Ladies of the House,* "The Bride Doll," recounts Truda's childhood romanticization of a

"Birdsell is one of our best writers – no compromises, no hesitance, a full canvas." – Michael Ondaatje

Sandra Birdsell

THE CHROME SUITE

Cover for the 1995 reprint edition (Richland County Public Library)

pathetic Agassiz wedding between a retarded boy and a marginalized Paraguayan girl. It contrasts with another story, "Toronto Street," in which the adult Truda, alone in a dingy apartment without husband or children, imagines a tenuous connection with her neighbor. In "Moonlight Sonata," Betty waits for her delinquent son to come home, remembering her own youthful rebellion and her mother's anguish. Most of the narratives in the collection are filtered through Lureen, with echoes of Birdsell's own life and some foreshadowing of her second novel, *The Chrome Suite* (1992). In "Falling in Love" Lureen, abandoned by her lover, Larry, tries to hitchhike home and is given some advice on love and faith by an unlikely angel. In "Ladies of the House," Lureen (now married to Larry and with two children) remembers other women, seduced and abandoned by men, waiting at the windows of their houses. In "Spring Cleaning," Lureen and her fellow housewives substitute the cleaning ritual for faith and grace on Easter week-end. In "The Bird Dance," an epistolary story, Lureen's teenage daughters counsel her not to allow the faithless Larry to exploit her any further. Caught in a "bloody bird dance for the past twenty years" but terrified of loneliness and poverty, Lureen represents all of Bird-sell's admittedly autobiographical women–"the trapped wingless birds becoming women locked, caught inside tubes and uterus-shaped forms beneath the ground, but still dancing and balancing the moon in the palms of their hands." All the other women in *Ladies of the House* are similarly trapped. Lureen's friend Bobbie desper-ately fantasizes about a perfect life in "Dreaming of Jeannie." In "Niagara Falls" Mika's sister Elizabeth, who is finally liberated by the death of her husband, can choose to go to the falls alone. Mika herself, sur-rounded by her children and grandchildren in "Keep-sakes," retells a symbolic story from her childhood "in Russia [where] they once buried a woman who wasn't dead."

The characters in the two collections that make up *Agassiz Stories* are working-class people who lead gritty lives of poverty, abuse, and quiet desperation but nevertheless aspire to meaning and fulfillment. In "San-dra Birdsell's *Agassiz Stories:* Speaking the Gap" (1990), Charlene Diehl-Jones associates Birdsell with the Amer-ican writers of "dirty realism." At the time she was writing the stories in these collections, she was particu-larly influenced by New York writer Grace Paley's sto-ries about working-class people and by Maksim Gor'ky's *My Childhood* (1914) and *The Life of a Useless Man* (1908), with their depiction of the strength of the human spirit to survive in a cruel society without losing a sense of humor.

Birdsell has repeatedly denied that she has a femi-nist agenda since her female protagonists suffer the marginalization and exploitation not only of gender but also of class. Although her naturalistic vision seems bleak and pessimistic, she told interviewers Eric McCormack, Kim Jernigan, and Peter Hinchcliffe that she was merely being truthful to her experience in depicting the inevitability of some women's lives with "honest realism." In *Agassiz Stories* she was certainly expressing the anger and frustration that led her to end her marriage in 1984, despite her personal and eco-nomic fears of independence: "I wrote the stories out of a sense of anger, of what I felt had been done to me as a woman . . . by a man, and by the institution of marriage and by the church."

The collections in *Agassiz Stories* embody the genre, prevalent in Canadian literature, of the linked story sequence or cycle, although *Night Travellers* is united by setting, time, and characters much more than *Ladies of the House*. In "From the Bottom of the Lake"

Birdsell writes that she was unaware of this established genre, but her frustration with "the restrictiveness of the short-story form," which demands character compart-mentalization and plot resolution within a few pages, led her to return to the same characters and tell other aspects of their lives, connecting her stories like "beads on a string" or "pieces of a puzzle."

The repetitions of place, character, theme, and symbol must be understood for a full appreciation of Birdsell's "puzzles," but they make a considerable demand on the reader. In some stories the protagonist is not named and must be deduced from details identify-ing her in earlier stories; in others, important symbols–for example, the two "question marks" of the swing ropes in "The Rock Garden" and Betty's cutoff braids in "Keepsakes"–connect not only stories but even the two collections. As Birdsell pointed out to Garrod, she writes "short story collections like people write novels," but her primary commitment is to letting the characters' voices determine the narrative line, usually a first-person narrative for a flamboyant character and third person for a contemplative one. The structure of the individual stories is also circular, fragmented, and nonlinear because of the subjectivity of her protag-onists. Birdsell told interviewer Alan Twigg that she prizes her "ability to go in and out of the mind almost within the same sentence. That's the way memory works." Above all, she rejects moral judgments about her characters' inevitable failures, existential hopes, and hard-won epiphanies. Abby H. P. Werlock suggests that "Birdsell's technique involves multiple perspectives with minimal information, challenging her postmodern read-ers to fill in the gaps."

Birdsell was a founding member of the Manitoba Writers' Guild in 1981, served as writer-in-residence at the Winnipeg Public Library (1985–1986) and at the University of Waterloo (1987–1989), and taught cre-ative writing at Red River Community College. She also began writing plays and screenplays, adapting Wil-liam Kurelek's children's story *A Prairie Boy's Winter* (1973) for the stage with Martha Brooks and David Gil-lies in 1984 and writing the play *The Revival* in 1986. Birdsell wrote several scripts for the National Film Board of Canada and the CBC. During this period she also married her second husband, the moviemaker Jan Zarzycki.

Birdsell's first novel, *The Missing Child* (1989), won the W. H. Smith/*Books in Canada* First Novel Award, although only after a controversial four-way tie and the intervention of the editor of *Books in Canada*. In it she revisits her childhood fear of the return of the primor-dial Lake Agassiz, which now represents the great changes, danger, and violence (especially toward chil-dren) that seem to be rising to inundate society. Influenced by Gabriel García Márquez and Anne Tyler, Birdsell incorporated elements of magic realism into the story of Minnie Pullman, whose simplicity and amnesia stem from the childhood abduction, rape, and murder of her twin sister. The novel is also full of other missing children, exploited and destroyed by the self-serving adults in Agassiz, who despise and pollute the river and are finally destroyed in its apocalyptic judgment. Near the end another girl, the archetypally named Sandra Adam, is also found raped and murdered, a casualty of her father's neglect and the church people's hypocrisy. As the pastor lusts after a parishioner and the justice of the peace covers up the theft of First Nations lands and artifacts, the multicultural townspeople pursue their corruption and adultery, ignoring signs of impending doom. When the waters rise, Minnie floats away to rejoin Jeremy, her savior in an imagined heaven, from which she "will never, never again, choose to be born."

Birdsell told McCormack, Jernigan, and Hinchcliffe that *The Missing Child* is a "fantasy novel" with "real people," structured like a movie or a symphony. It begins with a biblical prologue, "In the Beginning" (which foreshadows the ending), citing Zech. 2, Dan. 9, and the Song of Solomon to introduce the themes of divine love and judgment. Within this fated circle, the book is divided into days over the period of one week, marked by several scriptural references from Genesis to Revelations and framed by two symbolic signs: "Drive Carefully, We Love Our Children" and "THE VALLEY ENDS TOMORROW."

Minnie and her friend Annie are the only sympathetic figures in *The Missing Child*; their marginalization is an indictment of the rest of the characters. Birdsell's narrative voice moves fluidly in and out of their minds and between past and present and fantasy and reality in a kaleidoscope of impressions. The novel lacks unity, however, because of the tenuous connections of plot and character. Birdsell admitted later that the unwieldy structure was a result of her attempt to write a novel like a movie. Even her most sympathetic and perceptive reviewer, Stephen Dunning, called this structure a "recipe for confusion," although he found unity in Minnie's "mysterious suffering" and the "Gnostic" hope for salvation in her escape from life to celestial realms (*Event*, 1990). Although Birdsell has repudiated the narrow-minded Mennonite fundamentalism of her family and her youth, she has repeatedly affirmed the mysticism, spirituality, and religion with which she leavens the naturalism of her novels.

The critics' reactions to *The Missing Child* were generally as polarized as the verdicts of the hung jury for the First Novel Award. Some found the multiplicity of story lines and fragmented structure confusing, the bizarre characters and fantasy elements unbelievable,

Dust jacket for the first U.S. edition, 1991 (Richland County Public Library)

and the misanthropic worldview even more pessimistic than the outlook in Birdsell's previous works. Others praised the postmodern and magic-realist inventions of the novel. Virtually every critic extolled Birdsell's beautiful prose, rhythmic dialogue, and memorable images. The most appreciative ones recognized the town of Agassiz as the real protagonist and the large cast, complex plot, and symbolic flood as elements of an apocalyptic revelation about contemporary society.

In 1992 Birdsell's second novel, *The Chrome Suite*, secured her growing reputation when it was nominated for a Governor General's Literary Award for Fiction and won the McNally Robinson Manitoba Book of the Year Award. Birdsell was also honored in 1993 with the most prestigious literary award for women in Canada, the Marian Engel Award, given to "a Canadian woman writer in mid-career, recognizing her collective works and the promise of her future contribution to Canadian literature."

The Chrome Suite continues Birdsell's autobiographical fascination with family life and evokes her sense of loss at the death of her sister Annette in 1948. As she told interviewer Stephen Smith in 1992, an "undercurrent of longing and desire" was triggered in her by Denys Arcand's movie *Jesus of Montreal* (1989) and her rereading of Rainer Maria Rilke's *Duino Elegies* (1923). The themes of the novel are found in the epigraph, a poem by Mark Strand, "Keeping Things Whole" (1964), in which the speaker announces: "Wherever I am / I am what is missing" and "I move / to keep things whole." Throughout the novel the protagonist, Amy Barber, keeps moving on to try to escape the loss and absence caused by the death of her thirteen-year-old sister, Jill, from cancer in the summer of 1959 and by her family's dysfunctional responses to it: her mother's fundamentalist religion, her father's obsession with the past and his ultimate desertion, and her older brother's surrender to alcohol and sex. In contrast, Amy's futile longing and attempts to fill "the presence of absence," which is "the human condition," as Birdsell told Smith, are allied with her desire for immortality and transcendence, symbolized by her childhood belief that she has miraculously survived a lightning strike and thereby can fly.

After being raped and losing her best friend in a car accident, Amy flees her hometown, miscarries her baby, desperately marries a failed country-and-western singer, and, nine years of misery later, leaves him and their five-year-old son, whom she had begun abusing in frustration. In 1992, at age forty-two, Amy recalls the death a year earlier of the only person she has ever loved, a Polish moviemaker who was ending their six-year affair when he was accidentally shot while filming a confrontation between First Nations and the Royal Canadian Mounted Police in northern Ontario. At the end of the novel, she is left alone again, with a possibly cancerous lump beside her breastbone that symbolizes "the absence of me." As Birdsell quotes Rilke, all these absences only make "'emptiness vibrate' in ways that do *not* comfort."

In response to the critics' confusion over *The Missing Child,* Birdsell dispensed with magic realism and presented the human existential condition bleakly and directly in *The Chrome Suite,* reinforcing her naturalism with her usual cyclical structures; as she explained to Garrod, "everything moves in a circle—there is no beginning and no ending." *The Chrome Suite* has a complex structure (although clearer than that in *The Missing Child*), with a double frame of 1991 within 1992 encompassing Amy's generally chronological retrospective beginning in 1959. The intricate combination of first- and third-person voices, present and past tenses, and an objective, italicized commentary that at times contradicts the subjective narrative suggests the self-reflexive, metafictional ambiguity of Amy's screenwriter

recollections: "Yes, she can remember. But can she be trusted? Can one trust a person who seizes every occurrence that passes by in the street and changes it instantly the second her eye rests on it?" At the end she burns her "sniveling, whiny" journals and, perhaps, her home movies in a gesture of courageous perseverance or lonely despair; as usual, Birdsell refuses clarity or closure. Ironic references to Margaret Atwood's *Surfacing* (1972), however, suggest that Birdsell's heroine will at least survive and that her text is a refutation of her Polish lover's Eurocentric contempt for Canadian culture and female experience.

In the 1990s Birdsell took her place as a prominent writer in the Canadian literary community. She served on fiction juries; mentored younger writers; taught creative writing at the University of Toronto (1993), the Banff School of Fine Arts (1993), and the University of British Columbia (1996); and was writer-in-residence at the universities of Lethbridge (1990), Alberta (1991), and Prince Edward Island (1991). Her next short-story collection, *The Two-Headed Calf* (1997), was nominated for the Governor General's Literary Award in fiction and won the 1997 Saskatchewan Book of the Year Award.

In *The Two-Headed Calf* Birdsell navigates her familiar territory of loss, conflict, and frustrated desires within typically fragmented and nonlinear plots. The title story portrays the naturalistic tragedy that all of her characters struggle against: "How was it possible not to be imprinted by other people's histories, their secret fears and desires? Whether we accommodated this inheritance or pushed against it . . . the result was the same." This conflicting determinism is even more schizophrenic for those from multiracial backgrounds, such as the protagonist, Sylvia, the illegitimate child of a Mennonite mother and Métis father, who feels like a "two-headed calf" in a fairground freak show: "which head . . . had determined when the calf slept, woke up, ate, what direction to go? . . . Perhaps . . . one message cancelled the other and the calf's heart stopped beating."

As in Birdsell's earlier collections, strained family relationships dominate these nine disparate stories of conformity and betrayal set in urban and rural Manitoba. The first two stories are paired by a mother-daughter relationship, although the time sequence is reversed to complicate the causality. In "I Used to Play Bass in a Band," Lorraine recalls how her adult daughter, symbolically named Christina, tries to save the lost souls of the world but capriciously abandons them to her mother's guilt. "The Midnight Hour" portrays the younger Christina, who "wants more" than her mother but "wants to know, most of all, what it is she wants" and gets nothing but grief from her divorced parents. In

"A Necessary Treason" the juxtaposed stories of an iconoclastic Mennonite mother and her rebellious, secular daughter parallel the treasonous dreams of the two strong women. In "The Man from Mars" a family that has escaped from a repressively primitive Mennonite colony suffers "a profound poverty of goods and knowledge" until the misfit father steps "into the path of an oncoming car" and frees them. "Phantom Limbs" is another story of betrayal—of marriages, friendships, and finally of faith itself.

The final three stories in *The Two-Headed Calf,* according to reviewer Nancy Wigston, "share a nightmarish, positively creepy quality" in which dysfunctional families have created a chaotic world (*Quill & Quire,* May 1997). In "Disappearances" elderly grandparents try to understand and support a granddaughter who has beaten another elderly couple to death. In "Rooms for Rent" a home invasion by welfare recipients leaves the elderly Lila feeling angry and guilty but mostly confused in a surrealistic contemporary world: "I don't know what anything means anymore." "The Ballad of the Sergeant Brothers" is a somewhat melodramatic story of lost love and literally drowned hopes, ending with a final, poignant image of a "garden of concrete sculptures," including "the figure of a sightless man looking skyward, his mouth open like a bird forever wanting to be fed."

Birdsell's only children's book, *The Town That Floated Away* (1997), is dedicated to Richard Birdsell, her grandson, "who said 'How about writing a little book just for me, please?'" With delightful illustrations by Helen Flook, the book won the 1997 Saskatchewan Children's Literature Award. It narrates the adventures of Virginia Potts, who is left behind when her town floats away on another of Birdsell's apocalyptic floods. A "morphan" because she has lost not only her "Preposterously Protective Parents" but also her whole community, she begins to shrink, despite the ineffectual ministrations of Madame Galosh, a representative of self-serving capitalism, and Mr. Edgar, an obtuse man of science. In the end, the strong, sensible children rectify the errors of the irresponsible, foolish adults, and family and community are restored.

Birdsell handles the conventions of children's literature well, with nonsense, wordplay, toilet jokes, heroes, villains, and faithful animals. There are probably too many plots, lessons, and themes. Some elements that have sent critics hunting for allegorical meanings seem like in-jokes for adults. *The Town That Floated Away* is, however, a humorous fantasy without the dark overtones of children's books by writers such as Roald Dahl.

In 2001 Birdsell served as writer-in-residence at McMaster University; that same year she published her

*Dust jacket for the first U.S. edition, 2004
(Richland County Public Library)*

third novel, *The Rußländer,* to great acclaim. It won the 2001 Saskatchewan Fiction and Book of the Year awards and was short-listed for the prestigious Giller Prize. The novel was published in the United States as *Katya* in 2004. In *The Rußländer* Birdsell returns to her Mennonite heritage with a more mature, sympathetic perspective than in her first books. In 1994 she told Joan Thomas, "I'm older now and I'm wiser, and I think I have a much kindlier, more generous view of the people that I wrote about in the beginning." She specifically revisits the history of her grandmother, whose family fled the aftermath of the Russian Revolution in 1923 to come to Canada, part of the Mennonite diaspora called the Rußländer.

In *The Rußländer* fifteen-year-old Katherine "Katya" Vogt escapes the massacre of her family and friends and the rape of her sister and others by hiding in a hole in the ground. This trauma and many other calamities of the Russian Civil War—including terror, disease, and starvation—reduce Katya and her compatriots from affluent, comfortable, and somewhat secularized but religiously legalistic collaborators with the czarist regime to desperate, persecuted aliens in a cruel, chaotic world. Katya, now almost one hundred and living in Winnipeg, tells her story to a young researcher who (like Birdsell herself) has taken a Mennonite heritage tour of Ukraine to preserve the stories of the past for future generations. He cites a Russian proverb, "Dwell on the past and you'll lose an eye, . . . ignore the past and you'll lose both of them." *The Russländer* has a happy ending, rare for a Birdsell novel: Katya has married her savior, Kornelius; learned that "love prevails" over all evils; and now has seventy-three descendants, as yet untouched by "accidents or heartbreak." To her usual themes of loss, betrayal, and discrimination, Birdsell adds love, hope, redemption, and the triumph of the human spirit. The graphic violence in the text is thus balanced with peace and grace.

The mainly chronological structure of *The Russländer* traces the fall of the Mennonite community, with archetypal imagery from Psalm 23 providing the section titles. The community moves from an idyllic Eden in part 1, "In Green Pastures," to the evils of paradise lost in part 2, "In the Presence of Enemies," to the hope of the Exodus in part 3, "Surely Goodness and Mercy." Birdsell sacrifices suspense for significance by giving a 15 November 1917 newspaper report of the massacre of Katya's family on the first page of the novel; the following pages of childhood delight and naiveté about the impending disaster, covering the period from 1910 to 1917, are contextualized by this report. The last pages of the novel are similarly framed by the metafictional device of Katya's delivering her story to the young archivist; the result is a somewhat belated reminder of the subjectivity of the story. As some critics have pointed out, the third-person narrative with limited point of view is rather weakly focused through Katya, who is a sympathetic but never strongly self-conscious voice.

In addition to her usual portrayal of strong, surviving women, Birdsell gives a complex, nuanced portrait in *The Russländer* of an entire culture, including churchmen whose legalism masks hypocrisy and landowners whose greed incites violence, as well as faithful, courageous, and sacrificial coreligionists. The sociological realism of this analysis is the result of her extensive research in Mennonite histories and archives, including the memoirs of her late great-uncle Gerhard P. Schroeder. Birdsell's religious skepticism may be the result of her own stance on faith, frequently compared to that of Rudy Wiebe, whose novel *Sweeter Than All the World* (2001), an epic history of five centuries of Mennonite sufferings (including those in Russia), was coinci-

dentally published at the same time as *The Russländer*. Brian Bergman contrasted Wiebe, a "devout Mennonite," with Birdsell, a "person of faith" who is incapable of belonging to a church and "doesn't feel any more like a Mennonite" after writing *The Russländer* but now understands and sympathizes more with her mother's family background (*Maclean's*, 22 October 2001).

Birdsell's novel *Children of the Day* (2005) deals with one day in June 1953 in the lives of the Vandals: Oliver, a Métis; Sara, a survivor of the 1917 Mennonite massacre narrated in *The Russländer*; and their ten children. Oliver and Sara are alienated from their respective families because of their union. Sara spends the day in bed, afraid that she is pregnant again and that her husband will desert her for his French childhood sweetheart, whose family would not let her marry a "half-breed," while Oliver wanders the countryside, struggling with the loss of his job as a hotel manager and with the loss of his people's land and heritage. He finally comes home, and Sara emerges from the bedroom. Oliver's brother, Romeo, accuses Sara's brother-in-law, Kornelius, of taking over the land—lost after the 1885 Battle of Batoche, which ended Friel's Métis rebellion—that rightfully belongs to the Vandals. In the end Kornelius buys land for a new home for Oliver's family, "because he understands from his old-country experience what it means to have land pulled out from under your feet and claimed by others."

Sandra Birdsell has lived in Regina since 1996. In early 2007 she was working on a new novel. She has earned her reputation as a writer who has amply fulfilled "the promise of her future contribution to Canadian literature" recognized in the 1990s. Her earlier misanthropic pessimism and postmodern plotlines have been moderated, but her trademark unsentimental realism and nonjudgmental voice guarantee her an appreciative audience for her future works.

Interviews:

Andrew Garrod, "Sandra Birdsell," in his *Speaking for Myself: Canadian Writers in Interview* (St. John's, Nfld.: Breakwater, 1986), pp. 12–33;

Eric McCormack, Kim Jernigan, and Peter Hinchcliffe, "A Conversation with Sandra Birdsell," *New Quarterly*, 8, no. 2 (1988): 9–22;

Alan Twigg, "Sandra Birdsell," in his *Strong Voices: Conversations with Fifty Canadian Authors* (Madeira Park, B.C.: Harbour, 1988), pp. 18–23;

Laurie Kruk, "Falling into the Page: An Interview with Sandra Birdsell," *Quarry*, 40, no. 3 (1991): 92–99;

Stephen Smith, "Suite Science: Sandra Birdsell's New Novel Goes Inside Out to Tell a Story of Loss & Remembrance," *Quill & Quire*, 58 (July 1992): 39;

Joan Thomas, "Taking Notice: An Interview with Sandra Birdsell," *Prairie Fire,* 15, no. 1 (1994): 80–85.

Bibliography:

Dallas Harrison, "Sandra Birdsell: An Annotated Bibliography," *Essays on Canadian Writing,* 48 (Winter 1992–1993): 170–217.

References:

Charlene Diehl-Jones, "Sandra Birdsell's *Agassiz Stories:* Speaking the Gap," in *Contemporary Manitoba Writers: New Critical Studies,* edited by Kenneth James Hughes (Winnipeg: Turnstone, 1990), pp. 93–109;

Isla Duncan, "'The Profound Poverty of Knowledge': Sandra Birdsell's Narrative of Concealment," *Canadian Literature,* no. 169 (Summer 2001): 85–101;

Dallas Harrison, "Sandra Birdsell (1942–)," in *Canadian Writers and Their Works: Fiction Series,* edited by Robert Lecker, Jack David, and Ellen Quigley, volume 12 (Downsview, Ont.: ECW Press, 1995), pp. 15–68;

Gabrielle Heinen-Dimmer, "The Whole Idea of Empathy: Prairie Realism and Female Narrative Structure in Sandra Birdsell's *Agassiz Stories,*" in *The Guises of Canadian Diversity: New European Perspectives,* edited by Serge Jaumain and Marc Maufort (Amsterdam & Atlanta: Rodopi, 1995), pp. 165–173;

New Quarterly, special Birdsell issue, 8, no. 2 (1988);

Andrew Stubbs, "The Rhetoric of Narration in Sandra Birdsell's Fiction," in *Acts of Concealment: Mennonite/s Writing in Canada,* edited by Hildi Froese Tiessen and Peter Hinchcliffe (Waterloo, Ont.: University of Waterloo Press, 1992), pp. 174–192;

Paul Tiessen, "Minnie Pullman and the Salvation of the Mennonite Church in Sandra Birdsell's *The Missing Child,*" in *On Being the Church: Essays in Honour of John W. Snyder,* edited by Peter C. Erb (Waterloo, Ont.: Conrad, 1992), pp. 123–149;

Abby H. P. Werlock, "Canadian Identity and Women's Voices," in *Canadian Women Writing Fiction,* edited by Mickey Pearlman (Jackson: University Press of Mississippi, 1993), pp. 126-41.

Papers:

Some of Sandra Birdsell's manuscripts and correspondence with the Turnstone Press are in the Turnstone Press Collection at the Elizabeth Dafoe Library, University of Manitoba, Winnipeg.

Marilyn Bowering

(13 April 1949 –   )

Jean Richardson
University of Alberta

BOOKS*: The Liberation of Newfoundland* (Fredericton, N.B.: Fiddlehead, 1973);

One Who Became Lost (Fredericton, N.B.: Fiddlehead, 1976);

The Killing Room (Victoria: Sono Nis Press, 1977);

The Book of Glass (Knotting, U.K.: Sceptre Press, 1978);

The Visitors Have All Returned (Erin, Ont.: Porcépic, 1979);

Sleeping with Lambs (Victoria & Toronto: Porcépic, 1980);

Giving Back Diamonds (Victoria: Porcépic, 1982);

The Sunday before Winter: The New and Selected Poetry of Marilyn Bowering (Toronto: General, 1984);

Anyone Can See I Love You (Erin, Ont.: Porcupine's Quill, 1987);

Grandfather Was a Soldier (Victoria: Porcépic, 1987);

Calling All the World: Laika and Folchakov, 1957 (Victoria: Porcépic, 1989);

To All Appearances a Lady (Toronto: Random House, 1989; New York: Viking, 1990; London: Hamilton, 1990);

Love As It Is (Vancouver: Beach Holme, 1993);

Autobiography (Vancouver: Beach Holme, 1996);

Visible Worlds (Toronto: HarperCollins, 1997; New York: HarperFlamingo/HarperCollins, 1998; London: Flamingo, 1998);

Human Bodies: New and Collected Poems, 1987–1999, introduction by Dave Godfrey (Vancouver: Beach Holme, 1999);

The Alchemy of Happiness (Vancouver: Beach Holme, 2003);

Cat's Pilgrimage (Toronto: HarperFlamingo Canada, 2004);

What It Takes to Be Human (Toronto: Penguin Canada, 2006).

PLAY PRODUCTIONS: *Hajimari-No-Hajimari,* Japan, Fall 1986;

Anyone Can See I Love You, Victoria, Bastion Theatre, January 1988;

Temple of the Stars, Victoria, Kaleidoscope Theatre, November 1996.

Marilyn Bowering (photograph © 1998 by Lincoln Clarkes Photography; from the dust jacket for Visible Worlds, *1998; Richland County Public Library)*

PRODUCED SCRIPTS: *Grandfather Was a Soldier,* radio, BBC Radio 3, November 1983;

Anyone Can See I Love You, radio, BBC Radio Scotland, March 1986;

Laika and Folchakov: A Journey in Time and Space, radio, CBC Radio, 1 November 1987;

A Cold Departure: The Liaison of George Sand and Frederic Chopin, radio, CBC Radio, 19 February 1989;

Divine Fate, motion picture, National Film Board of Canada, 1993.

OTHER: *Many Voices: An Anthology of Contemporary Canadian Indian Poetry,* edited by Bowering and David Day (Vancouver: J. J. Douglas, 1977);

Breaking the Surface, edited by Bowering and others (Victoria: Sono Nis Press, 2000).

Marilyn Bowering is a versatile and inventive writer of poetry, fiction, and drama whose works have been published, broadcast, and performed in North America, the United Kingdom, and Japan. She places her readers firmly in a well-constructed reality before moving them into the ephemeral world of dreams and visions. In a 1980 interview with Susan Yarrow, Bowering called this approach a combination of "romantic spirituality and something really pragmatic." Her preoccupation with the liminal space between the spiritual and the real makes her works unusual and an important addition to Canadian literature.

The daughter of Herbert James Bowering, a carpenter, and Elnora Grist Bowering, a purchasing agent, Marilyn Ruthe Bowering was born on 13 April 1949 in Winnipeg but grew up in Victoria. Raised in a Pentecostal home, she was exposed to a rigorous form of Christianity that played a major role in her early life. She was subject to a strict moral code in which any misstep led to damnation, and she accepted as normal a position outside of and separate from the wider community. This sense of separation led Bowering to shun mainstream images in her writing in favor of more-obscure personal references. Even her most ardent supporter, writer Dave Godfrey, notes in his introduction to *Human Bodies: New and Collected Poems, 1987–1999* (1999) that her "terrain can be difficult and her references are definitely not all available in her footnotes."

Other aspects of Bowering's early life were more conventional. She studied music "fairly seriously," she told Yarrow, as well as painting. She also wrote for others and for herself; for example, she recalls writing ghost stories for pajama parties at age eight. From a similarly early age, Bowering began composing poems in order to grapple with an idea or a feeling that she felt had to be put down on paper. At eighteen she announced that she was a poet, but her parents saw her writing as a form of rebellion and worried that she had chosen a hard life. While a student at the University of Victoria, Bowering took both psychology and political-science courses, but writing began to take up more of her interest. She received a B.A. in English in 1971 and then entered Robin Skelton's newly established creative-writing program at the same university. Skelton became her mentor, encouraging her and providing her with a sense of the worldwide community of poets. Bowering earned her M.A. in English, with a concentration in creative writing, in 1973. During her studies she worked as a script assistant and a radio control-room operator. She entered the doctoral program in Canadian literature at the University of New Brunswick in 1975 but dropped out after one year. In the following years she was employed as an instructor, editor, and writer-in-residence.

Bowering's literary career can be divided into two phases. The period from 1973 to 1987 was a time of apprenticeship in which her writing was characterized by the contemplation of personal issues. A more mature and accessible period dates from 1987 on. The poems from the early phase are not without merit, but they tend to be uneven and more than occasionally impenetrable to the reader. Bowering has said that each poem came from a story surrounding the poet. She did not write directly about this origin, so without the keys, her poems remained enigmatic. John Oughton wrote that Bowering tended to remove "a bit too much of the connective tissue between idea and image, making the poem difficult for the reader to explore" (*Books in Canada,* April 1983). Another difficulty for the reader, according to Chaviva Hosek in a review of *The Killing Room* (1977), was Bowering's choice of "a witchy female" persona. Hosek wrote that Bowering specialized in "mysterious narratives which are highly symbolic, full of secret, inaccessible knowledge about blood and bones" (*Fiddlehead,* Summer 1978).

Bowering's first book, *The Liberation of Newfoundland* (1973), is an experimental publication using a collage of photographs, poems, and prose to bring the particular setting of Newfoundland to life for the reader. Fluctuating between diary-like entries and more-distanced pieces, the text captures moments in the lives of those living in the harsh Newfoundland environment. The book received little critical attention. Bowering's next volume, *One Who Became Lost* (1976), is similar in approach to the first, but it is set in Greece, where Bowering was a writer-in-residence in 1973–1974, and the Queen Charlotte Islands, off the British Columbian coast, and it includes only poems. Interweaving anecdotes and dream visions from both the ancient Greeks and North American Indians, Bowering divides her book into three grouped sections, with an untitled first part followed by "One Who Became Lost" and "Slave Killer." According to M. Travis Lane, the first and third sections reflect each other with a focus on the different guises of the "Wild Woman Earth Goddess." Independent of the other two parts, the title poem is a "re-creation of ancient Indian belief and sensibility." Lane found Bowering's interest in violence and dream imagery intriguing. He also complimented her for her meticulous incorporation of dreams into her poetry without creating "surrealist messes" (*Fiddlehead,* Winter 1977).

*Dust jacket for the first U.S. edition, 1990
(Richland County Public Library)*

Douglas Barbour termed Bowering's 1977 book, *The Killing Room,* her first major collection, finding the poems powerful but ultimately "too bleak for most readers." He saw her as a talented writer fixated on "despair, acceding to death in all its forms without fighting back." Barbour found unsettling her representation of bitter violent lives in "so starkly absolute" terms, "so lacking in psychological exploration, that no hope at all remains" (*Dalhousie Review,* Autumn 1978). Indeed, the titles of the collection and of some of the poems–"His Flying Bones," "Raven I," "Raven II," "Foetus Bone," and "Vampires"–help to prove his point. In the interview with Yarrow, Bowering responded to this criticism by acknowledging that some of her readers viewed *The Killing Room* as "bleak." She felt that they often missed the satire.

Bowering's interest in menace and stressful environments continued in *The Visitors Have All Returned* (1979), her first book of prose. As in *The Liberation of Newfoundland,* evocative black-and-white photographs accompany and intensify the text. In the interview with Yarrow, Bowering explained that the creation of *The Visitors Have All Returned* began with a series of pieces that "all used the same characters and were related in tone and feeling and so on to each other." The book depicts the ongoing relationship between a woman who works in "leaps and jumps and associations" and a man who is an "A-to-B-to-C thinker." Bowering's "huge desire to do something really long and involved and complex" with these characters made short poems unworkable, so she chose prose. For her, the work is a "dialogue between two different kinds of logic" but with considerable movement, as each character begins to admit the other's ways into his or her own thinking. Bowering explained that she did not plan or expect this evolution in the fictional relationship but nevertheless felt satisfied with the end result. For her, *The Visitors Have All Returned* was the "most enjoyable thing" she had done up to that point. Despite Bowering's satisfaction with the convergence between the two main characters, reviewer Janet Giltrow thought the work emphasized not unity but disunity, with the speaker's theme being "her detachment from her husband, and eventually and ominously, from her daughter, and her resort to private images of ancient, childless figures traversing a mythic pastoral" (*Canadian Literature,* Winter 1980).

Bowering returned to poetry with *Sleeping with Lambs* (1980). In the time since the publication of *The Killing Room,* she had grown substantially as a poet. Her voice is more forceful, exploring an increasing range of themes. In sections such as "Wishing Africa" and "Sleeping with Lambs," her persona wanders through a variety of landscapes, while in "The Babe Within" and "The Origin of Doll" she is concerned with the body and childhood. David Macfarlane sensed her maturity and called the collection "poised . . . with a persistent devotion to craftsmanship." In his final judgment, Bowering's verse "is not particularly easy, and, at times, not very pretty, but it is always very good" (*Books in Canada,* May 1981).

Giving Back Diamonds (1982) is the last book of Bowering's apprenticeship period. As in her later poetry collections, the tone is more assured as she deftly clusters poems around themes of pain and unease. The title section deals with the end of a relationship, while "The Swan on the River of Death" concerns exploration. The most accessible poems are in "Mythical Stories," in which Bowering links mythological figures with the contemporary world. Her growing maturity as a writer was such that the volume caught the attention of poet and critic George Woodcock. Reviewing *Giving Back Diamonds* in *Canadian Literature* (Autumn 1983), he praised the book, claiming that the "diction is unerring; the tone is always appropriate; the poise is . . . assured."

The Sunday before Winter: The New and Selected Poetry of Marilyn Bowering (1984) marks the completion of the early period of Bowering's writing. Including poems from all of her previous collections, the volume is arranged chronologically. Reviewer Rita Donovan noted Bowering's depiction of "dark dreams and human isolation" (*Journal of Canadian Poetry,* 1984). The new poems in the section "The Sunday before Winter" dwell on fears, victimhood, dreams, and observations made in foreign locales.

In 1987 Bowering's publications began to attract more attention, in part because she was now producing poetry that reflected mainstream Canadian poetic interests. In a review of more than one hundred books of poetry published in 1987, Ronald Hatch noted a trend toward historical subjects (*University of Toronto Quarterly,* Fall 1988). Bowering joined the trend with *Anyone Can See I Love You* (1987), about Marilyn Monroe, and *Grandfather Was a Soldier* (1987), which deals with Bowering's grandfather's World War I experiences. Both mark an abrupt departure from her previous poetry. The cycle of poems in *Anyone Can See I Love You* chronicles the two parts of Monroe's life: her private life as Norma Jean Baker and her public projection as Monroe. No longer writing from a purely personal perspective, Bowering creates a vivid interior life for the movie star. *Grandfather Was a Soldier* is a more overtly researched work, drawing on testimony and archival documents. Bowering writes about her own experiences in researching her grandfather's military service. Traveling with the "ghost" of her relative, she visited the trenches of the Somme, the tunnels of Vimy, and the sloughs of Passchendaele. As Michael Mason noted in his review, Bowering was able to "take certain facts . . . and breathe life into the dead bones" (*Canadian Literature,* Autumn–Winter 1989). Moving between the present and the past, her photographic style brings an historical event close to the reader.

In 1989 Bowering published a book-length poem, *Calling All the World: Laika and Folchakov, 1957,* and her first novel, *To All Appearances a Lady.* The former concerns the dog carried aboard the Soviet satellite Sputnik 2 in 1957 and her trainer, Alexei Folchakov. Playing somewhat with the actual event by allowing the trainer to travel with Laika, Bowering re-creates a moment in space-exploration history that caught the world's imagination. In a short interpretative essay accompanying the text, Bowering describes Laika as an important figure in space exploration. The earliest living being to be launched into space, the dog represents "humanity's complex dream of discovery and adventure, . . . [and the] hope for something better." The narrator provides detailed descriptions of the passengers and their excitement about their space trip. The interweaving of details

from Folchakov's life and interstellar visits by a woman in blue and composer Sergey Prokofiev helps to lighten the foreboding that comes with knowledge of the certain death of both passengers.

In *To All Appearances a Lady,* Bowering combined her love of the coast of British Columbia with an interest in the past of the region to produce an historical novel. In a complex narrative that, according to Michael Thorpe, resembles a set of Chinese boxes, Bowering uses a West Coast pilot, Robert Lam, and his dead stepmother, Lam Fan, to tell the story. The protagonist is given a briefcase of family documents but finds them enigmatic. The key to these papers and his own life is supplied by Lam Fan's ghost during a voyage to a deserted whaling station along the coast. Bowering's use of two narrators in two different time periods brought sharp criticism from at least one reviewer. Susan Harvey felt that the almost constant time shift made the novel a case of "literary ping-pong. Just when you start to get involved in the story–wham!–you get bounced somewhere else" (*Globe and Mail,* 16 September 1989). The book received some enthusiastic reviews, however. Thorpe called *To All Appearances a Lady* "an extremely ambitious and substantial . . . novel" (*University of Toronto Quarterly,* Fall 1990), and Renee Hulan praised Bowering's eloquent prose (*Malahat Review,* June 1990).

After a four-year hiatus Bowering published *Love As It Is* (1993), a combination of one set of eleven poems and three sequences that show her continued interest in presenting travel anecdotes, exploring rural settings, and re-creating historical moments. The persona-driven approach first seen in *Anyone Can See I Love You* and *The Visitors Have All Returned* is also apparent. After a section in which the speaker wanders over the Newfoundland landscape, Bowering details the rural life of a family, the Mercers. "Eight Poems for Margaret, July–August, 1989" continues the rustic theme but in this case sensitively chronicles one woman, Bowering's friend Margaret Wilson, and her rapidly approaching death. "A Cold Departure," which reviewer Allan Brown called the "longest and most provocative part" of the book (*Antigonish Review,* Autumn 1994), is an imaginative reconstruction of the relationship of George Sand and Frédéric Chopin. Focusing on letters and considering each lover separately, Bowering captures the passion of this bittersweet liaison. Brown called *Love As It Is* Bowering's best book.

In *Autobiography* (1996) Bowering often employs an uncharacteristic unrhymed couplet form, writing fluently on a range of themes. Commenting on the section titled "The Mind's Road to Love" in his introduction to *Human Bodies,* Godfrey calls the exploration of love "Blakean in its mirrored simplicity and complexity."

Dust jacket for the first U.S. edition, 1998
(Richland County Public Library)

Bowering revisits the predatory natural world in "Nature's Children," but her vision does not remain bleak. *Autobiography* presents a playful world in which Susan Drodge sees a mixture of "technology and folklore, absurdity and pathos, angels and animals" at work. Bowering's continued interest in fantasy is seen in the depiction of an elderly married couple who lovingly create miniature human beings and then energize their bodies with a slight jab to the heart. The poem won the 1997 Pat Lowther Memorial Award, given by the League of Canadian Poets.

Bowering's love of complex narration, evident in *To All Appearances a Lady,* is also seen in her second novel, *Visible Worlds* (1997); reviewer Barbara Love found the "labyrinthine plot . . . almost impossible to summarize" (*Library Journal,* 15 June 1998). The novel tells the story of twin brothers born to German parents on the Canadian prairie in the 1930s and follows their lives over the course of three decades. Along with this family saga, Bowering also presents the story of a

young Russian woman's trek to the North Pole. Carol Berger wrote that *Visible Worlds* was not only the chronicle of a family but also a "fabulist invention filled with blazing comets, snowblindness and one-armed circus performers" (*Quill & Quire,* September 1997). Despite her enthusiasm, Berger believed the conclusion of the novel to be too hastily arranged. Love, with some reservations, found *Visible Worlds* "a novel of profound imagination and stylish writing." It received the 1998 Ethel Wilson Fiction Prize and has been published in the United States, England, Finland, Germany, and Greece.

Human Bodies: New and Collected Poems, 1987–1999, published in 1999, includes all of Bowering's poetry from the books *Anyone Can See I Love You* through *Autobiography.* Noting her interest in long poems with lengthy narrative arcs, reviewer David Jarraway called her an ambitious writer with a "painstaking as well as profound" mixture of observation and insight (*ARC,* Summer 2000). The new poems in the sections "When I Am Dead" and "My Heart Is Weighted" serve as reminders of Bowering's varied style. Inspired by an early-eighteenth-century text, the poems employ a variety of generic emblems. In "Letter to Janey" a narrator and an alter ego/double named Janey talk about dreams and incidents. "Gruta de las Maravillas" (Grotto of Wonders) is a prose meditation on Spanish life.

In the first part of *The Alchemy of Happiness* (2003) Bowering puts aside historical subjects and travel anecdotes to deal with her own childhood. "The Father and Mother Poems," "The Daughter Poems," and "The Alchemy of Happiness" move back into the territory of her earlier apprentice poems with a consideration of her parents and, to a certain extent, her religious upbringing. The focus shifts in "The Pink City," which concerns mental illness, with a vivid description of day-to-day life in a psychiatric ward. Written in the first person, this section includes boldly drawn portraits of fellow patients and medical staff. Bowering returns to travel descriptions in the final two sections, "Glen Lochay Diary" and "Calendar," in which the poems are ordered chronologically, with dates attached to each. This approach allows the reader to consider the possibility of narrative in the jumble of anecdotes.

In a 2004 article Andrea Colyn paraphrases what Bowering has said about her writing habits: "when she is focusing on writing poetry, inspiration for fiction seeps from it and the same happens for poetry when she is writing or researching fiction." This movement of themes and topics across genre lines is apparent in the novel *Cat's Pilgrimage* (2004), which draws on the adventures of a young woman from the "Glen Lochay Diary" section of *The Alchemy of Happiness.* The main character is fourteen-year-old Cathreen, who lives in a small Vancouver Island community but leaves on a quest to find her father in England. *Cat's Pilgrimage* is a vivid bildungsroman complete with murder, a Utopian community named Summerwood, and episodes of love. Despite the realistic quality of the narrative, Bowering also draws on her interest in magic to create a world where the everyday and fantasy intermingle with dramatic effect.

In her next novel, *What It Takes to Be Human* (2006), Bowering continues her interest in a youthful character's progress in an often hostile world. To prevent him from enlisting as a soldier during World War II, Sandy Grey's father commits him to a mental asylum. Sandy's experiences with sadistic doctors, brutal guards, and the other inmates form the core of the novel. Again, Bowering juxtaposes two worlds: the everyday world and the world of the mentally ill.

Marilyn Bowering is an important Canadian writer whose appeal extends far beyond her native country. In her writing about travel she captures the difficulties and rewards of adapting to new situations. Her works are intriguing because they do not dwell on a particular locale but shift as her concerns and experiences change. Another aspect of interest is her continuing exploration of the boundary between the everyday and the supernatural. Her mature works deal with fully formed characters in an intricately created world. Bowering's ability to carry the reader into unknown regions makes her writing of continuing interest.

Interviews:

Susan Yarrow, "A Marilyn Bowering Interview," *Waves,* 8 (Winter 1980): 43–50;

Chris Dafoe, "What Rhymes with Orange? Tale of Long, Strange Journey Could Lead to Literary Stardom; B.C.'s Marilyn Bowering Won't Allow Award to Guide Her Fortunes," *Globe and Mail,* 7 June 1999, p. C3.

References:

Andrea Colyn, "Canadian Poet Marilyn Bowering Stops in at Redeemer," *Crown,* 21 (7 April 2004) <http://thecrown.ca/issues/21-12/acolyn.html>;

Susan Drodge, "Trusting in Movement," *Canadian Literature,* nos. 164–165 (2000): 122–125.

Tim Bowling

(14 January 1964 –   )

Jan Olesen
University of Alberta

BOOKS: *Low Water Slack* (Gibsons, B.C.: Nightwood, 1995);

Dying Scarlet (Gibsons, B.C.: Nightwood, 1997);

The Thin Smoke of the Heart (Montreal & Ithaca, N.Y.: McGill-Queen's University Press, 2000);

Downriver Drift (Madeira Park, B.C.: Harbour, 2000);

Darkness and Silence (Roberts Creek, B.C.: Nightwood, 2001);

The Paperboy's Winter (Toronto: Penguin Canada, 2003);

The Witness Ghost (Roberts Creek, B.C.: Nightwood, 2003);

The Memory Orchard (London, Ont.: Brick Books, 2004);

Fathom (Kentville, N.S.: Gaspereau Press, 2006).

OTHER: "1958," in *Scaling the Face of Reason: An Anthology of Canadian Poetry,* edited by the Canadian Chamber of Contemporary Poetry (St. Catherines, Ont.: Canadian Chamber of Contemporary Poetry, 1994), p. 148;

"Young Eagle on a Piling," "The Last Sockeye," "Tides (A Poem to Myself)," and "Snowy Owl after Midnight," in *Breathing Fire: Canada's New Poets,* edited by Lorna Crozier and Patrick Lane (Madeira Park, B.C.: Harbour, 1995), pp. 25–30;

"The Rhododendron" and "Family Bible," in *Threshold: An Anthology of Contemporary Writing from Alberta,* edited by Srdja Pavlovlc (Edmonton: University of Alberta Press, 1999), pp. 259–262;

"Spectrum" and "A Small Essay in Honour of the Past," in *New Canadian Poetry,* edited by Evan Jones (Markham, Ont.: Fitzhenry & Whiteside, 2000), pp. 4, 6;

Where the Words Come From: Canadian Poets in Conversation, edited by Bowling (Roberts Creek, B.C.: Nightwood, 2002).

SELECTED PERIODICAL PUBLICATIONS–UNCOLLECTED: "Eastward Ho! A Saltwater Fisherman Finds There Is Life East of the Rockies," *NeWest Review,* 19 (June–July 1994): 67;

"Bad Haircuts and Bullies: A Few Thoughts on Poetry," *Event,* 27 (Spring 1998): 12–13;

"Al Purdy's 'Transient,'" *ARC,* no. 44 (Summer 2000): 42–43;

"Dark, and Rain in the Air," *Queen's Quarterly,* 109 (Fall 2002): 461–473.

The author of eight poetry collections and two novels, Tim Bowling sees the writer's role as that of a storyteller, no matter the genre. Uninterested in post-structuralist and deconstructionist techniques, he has striven to develop a more traditional naturalistic and narrative poetry. In an unpublished 2002 interview Bowling asserted that his "influences are too wide-ranging to start listing (poetry is only one part of that larger influence that includes everything else in the world)"; nevertheless, he acknowledged the American poets Robert Lowell and James Wright; the English poets Theodore Roethke, Philip Larkin, Dylan Thomas, Ted Hughes, Elizabeth Bishop, Adrienne Rich, and Seamus Heaney; and the Canadians Al Purdy, Irving Layton, Margaret Avison, Don Coles, Don McKay, and Don Domanski as primary influences. His poetry is mainly centered on the British Columbian coast, especially the Fraser River Delta, and he often uses the salmon as a metaphor: "All that symbolism, the cycle, the battling against odds, the dramatic reality of life and death intertwined. I have never been, nor will I ever be, annoyed to be labeled a nature poet," he said in an unpublished December 2002 interview. Bowling sees an intimate connection between civilization and wilderness. Asked about his sense of place, and the connection between the natural and the civilized, Bowling responded,

I've lived in Edmonton for eight years and I've learned one thing, as I put it in a recent poem: "all poems about the country are poems about the city." We can't escape being animals, being moon-directed, no matter how much we think we can. So, to answer your question briefly, wilderness and civilization intersect in the human spirit, plain and simple. Always have, always will. At least until we're all turned into computers.

Tim Bowling (from the cover for Dying Scarlet, *1997; Bruccoli Clark Layman Archives)*

Timothy Jon Bowling, the youngest of the four children of Harold "Heck" Bowling, a commercial fisherman, and Jean Stevens Bowling, was born on 14 January 1964 in Vancouver and grew up in the nearby town of Ladner with his sister, Nora, and two brothers, Rick and Bruce. He worked as a commercial fisherman with his father and brothers for several years. In the 2002 interview he noted that "the fishing was absolutely central to my apprenticeship as a writer. You can't do that kind of work and not brush against the awe at the heart of the natural world." He received a B.A. in English at the University of British Columbia in 1986. Beginning to write poetry seriously at the age of twenty-three, he won first place in the National Poetry Contest of the League of Canadian Poets for the poems in his first book, *Low Water Slack* (1995).

The title of the volume is taken from Fraser River fisherman parlance and refers to the moment when the tide slows down. Bowling uses the phenomenon as a metaphor to discuss the natural world, personal experience, and cultural diversity. The poems "Jack Spring," "Steelhead, Spawning," and "Dolly Varden" invoke images of the lush coast of British Columbia and marvel at the natural world while questioning the place of human beings within it. In "Hell's Gate 1913" Bowling contemplates the ecological costs of technological development:

> Millions perished at the gate. Major runs were wiped out, others
> devastated to the point of extinction. Bloody footprints filled
> the river and walked slowly back to the sea, pallbearing
> the last rich August of generations.

Unwilling to lay blame exclusively on technological progress, later in the poem Bowling measures the cost of traditional methods of fishing:

> At the mouth, the slaughter continued; cannery-crews worked day
> and night to pack the catch; groups of men on wharves, in skiffs
> and skows, raised their sharp gaffs against the sun, while
> weary voices called out the growing numbers of the dead.

"The Timsmith" is a tribute to John Sullivan Deas, a free mulatto from the United States who eventually owned and ran a British Columbia cannery in the 1870s. A tribute of a different sort, "West Coast Winter" gives a voice to Japanese Canadians interned during World War II.

Commenting on *Low Water Slack,* Michael Holmes notes that Bowling's "long-lined lyrics pulse with the rhythms of the West Coast, of community and meditation; often, he moves from the specific language and images of fishing and everyday life on the Fraser River to startling observations that set off universal reverberations." For Holmes, Bowling's first book is "a tight, mature, technical tour de force that suffers from none of the inconsistencies that usually plague a poet's early works."

In 1995 Bowling gave up commercial fishing and enrolled at the University of Alberta to pursue a master's degree in English. He was a National Magazine Awards finalist in 1996. In 1997 he completed his master's degree and published *Dying Scarlet,* his

Paperback cover for the first edition, 1997
(Bruccoli Clark Layman Archives)

second poetry collection. The title poem, for which Bowling won the Petra Kenney International Poetry prize, was inspired by an 1818 letter in which the Romantic poet John Keats referred to an expression of his friends: "They call drinking deep dying scarlet." Ignoring what scholars have called a misspelling of *dyeing,* Bowling uses "drinking deep" as a metaphor for living life to the fullest and writes of Keats that "the world loves him for drinking so deep." He acknowledges the influence of Keats's life and writing on him:

> in my wrists live the ghosts of all the words
> ever written in his, and his Queens English;
> they gather in my pulses, drinking life, dying scarlet.

In a review of *Dying Scarlet* for *The Fiddlehead* (Winter 1998) Brian Bartlett said that "if these poems are in some senses traditional, they're so in welcome senses of the word. While not characterized by structural fragmentation, mass-media citings, and unwavering irony and parody, they're clearly poems

written from the late twentieth century. They demonstrate that celebratory modes, moral questionings, and partial trust in language still have places in our poetry. Their acknowledgments of previous poets, rather than being tacked on for show, are engrained into the poems. Many passages in the book dig into palimpsests of memory and history—elegiacally, or whimsically, or both." Bartlett also noted that "Though Bowling's style and voice rarely resemble Purdy's, the poems sometimes evoke Purdy's in their generous curiosity about the past, especially in how it presses upon the present, how the dead and silent call forth responses from the living and speaking." Bowling takes the reader to a pre–World War II pool game played by his grandfather, writes a "Nocturne" on his mother's birth, and pays tribute to the deaths of his maternal grandparents. *Dying Scarlet* won Alberta's Stephan G. Stephansson Book Award for Poetry in 1998.

Bowling won the $5,000 grand prize at the International Poetry Festival in Orillia, Ontario, for "The

Rhododendron"; described as "technically daring," the poem beat out five thousand other entries from around the world. It is included in his third book of poems, *The Thin Smoke of the Heart* (2000). Many of the pieces are melancholic, but a lighter touch comes out in poems such as "NHL." Here Bowling reminisces about the simple, carefree time of youth, when the most important matters were "Blockbuster trades" and games of pickup hockey with his friends. The poem ends with a cheerful moment of revival:

The Past is Flawed except between friends—
Pete, we can go back whenever it rains
and Scrub those rink-boards white again.

Some reviewers asserted that the rigorous rhyme schemes in *The Thin Smoke of the Heart* draw attention from the thematic concerns of the poems.

Also in 2000 Bowling published his first novel, *Downriver Drift*. In the 2002 interview he insisted that he has not abandoned poetry for fiction: "Poetry remains my creative core; it lends itself better to quick leaps in image, which I love. And its intensity allows me to escape from the mundane necessity of prose, where the writer must lay the groundwork before he can spiral off into lyric heights (when novels contain only lyricism, they inevitably fail). In short, poetry can move quicker to the essential heart of things." He explained that "I started out with poetry for a simple reason: in my twenties, I lacked the maturity to sustain an interesting narrative over many pages that wouldn't simply be self-indulgent (I would add that almost no one can write a good novel under the age of 30). Lyric poetry allowed me to make a metaphorical or imagistic impression without boring or annoying the reader with my typical twenty-something angst. But I always planned to write novels. And once I was old enough to understand a few things about the world and living in it, I found that it became much easier to write 100,000 word narratives." He finds many similarities between the two forms of expression, he said: "I see fiction as a more social form, more involved in the mechanics of the world. As a result, there's usually a greater reliance on narrative as opposed to metaphorical logic. In my poetry, though, there's a strong narrative element, and in my novels, there's a definite attempt to achieve effects through image, metaphor, and symbol. So these definitions obviously blur." *Downriver Drift* is set in 1970s Chilukthan, a town at the mouth of the Fraser River. Vic Mawson is a fisherman facing the depletion of the salmon stocks and an unfriendly marketplace; his wife, Kathleen, is depressed because of a miscarriage eight years earlier; his daughter is obsessed by the death of the family dog; and his two sons dream, during evening drinking bouts,

of ways to escape their dead-end lives. Kathleen eventually pulls herself out of her depression, and the surprising arrival of a killer whale far up the river evokes the beauty and mystery of the British Columbia coast. At the end of the novel Ed Leary, the local union organizer, gives a speech in which he laments the capitulation of the unions to the big companies.

Bowling's next collection, *Darkness and Silence* (2001), reflects his move from the coast to the Alberta prairie. In the unpublished interview he asserted that "place is everything to me as a writer; everything is informed by the landscapes I've lived in. What I feel and what I think, what I imagine: these are all manifestations of where I've been." In *Darkness and Silence* Bowling puts the Alberta landscape to good use in poems such as "Alleys in Winter" and "Watching a Lone Rider Cross the Hills of the Red Deer River Valley." The book is divided into four sections. "To and Fro in the Earth" is a mix of nostalgia and history; "Five Elegies" includes tributes to people as diverse as former prime minister Pierre Trudeau and a fisherman lost at sea. The poem "Two Dogs" in the section "The God of Animal Patience" describes the speaker's passage between two neighboring dogs; their eyes staring at him make him feel "as though I'm at an intersection beyond which the road turns in a direction merely being human can never understand." As he pushes open the door to his house, all of history falls away; he is left alone on a "crack of earth," waiting to find his purpose in the world. In "The Sign of the Last Bed and Breakfast before Entering the Badlands," in the "Darkness and Silence" section, Bowling contemplates the slight moment of personal existence within the millions of years of geological history: "You are nothing but a hobby-craft / Shaped from the air."

The death of Purdy, an elder statesman of Canadian poetry, in 2000 prompted Bowling to embark on *Where the Words Come From: Canadian Poets in Conversation* (2002). The book comprises interviews of established Canadian poets such as Michael Ondaatje and Margaret Atwood by younger ones, including Christine Wiesenthal, Russell Thornton, and Anne Simpson. Bowling limits himself to some introductory remarks; he is neither a subject nor an interviewer.

Bowling's second novel, *The Paperboy's Winter,* was published in 2003. It is the coming-of-age story of Callum Taylor, who is returning to his hometown of Vancouver after his father's death. He finds traditional ways of life all but extinct, and old-timer Ezra Hemsworth's position in the community changed from tolerated eccentric to outcast. Callum had expected to "fish my own boat," get married, and "live in my own house"; instead, "fifteen years later, none of that happened, and my father was dead. Without his quiet,

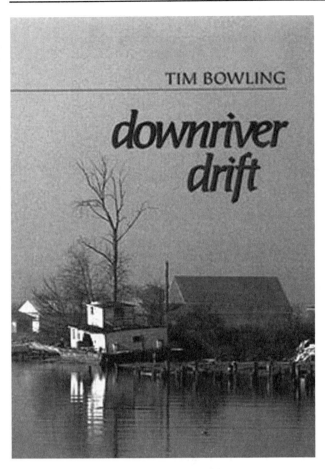

Paperback cover for the first edition, 2000
(<http://www.harbourpublishing.com>)

affectionate interest in my life, I had begun to drift, to find it difficult to rally to any serious engagement with the world." The loss of order and direction in his life is parallel to the path that the Canadian nation has taken: "And somehow the gentleness of my father seemed to have faded from my country as well; all was faster,

harsher, colder. As if shocked into sight, I woke to a place and a time from which I was, at heart, dislocated."

There is more than a passing similarity between *The Paperboy's Winter* and Bowling's collection *The Witness Ghost*, also published in 2003. Here the speaker expresses feelings of loss, anger, and frustration over the death of his father. *The Witness Ghost* is reminiscent of American poet Donald Hall's highly lauded collection, *Without*, published in 1998 after the death of his wife, Jane Kenyon. The difficulty of writing about the dead is indicated in the title poem:

> Yet I woke this morning,
> and will always wake,
> to your voice
> and the hopeless task of replication,
> to string along the verb
> without breaking
> the first, struck silver
> of dew, and listen for
> the dying-as-it's-born
> echoing afterclang of hush.

The Witness Ghost was nominated for the 2003 Governor General's Literary Award in poetry.

Tim Bowling is an active participant in the vibrant literary scene in Edmonton, where he is often featured at poetry readings, such as the Olive series, and fiction readings. He and his partner, Theresa Shea, have three children: Dashiell, Sadie, and Levi.

References:

Michael Holmes, "Why Poetry Still Matters: Canadian Poets Tim Bowling, Gregory Scofield, and Esta Spalding Offer Three Reasons," *Quill and Quire,* 63 (November 1997): 39–40;

Ross Leckie, "The Rhetoric of Romanticism," *Fiddlehead,* 206 (Winter 2001): 122–123;

Sheila Martindale, "Poet on Deck," *Canadian Author,* 71 (Spring 1996): 14–15.

Dionne Brand
(7 January 1953 –)

Debra Dudek
Deakin University

BOOKS: *'Fore Day Morning: Poems* (Toronto: Khoisan Artists, 1978);

Earth Magic (Toronto: Kids Can, 1979);

Primitive Offensive (Toronto: Williams-Wallace, 1982);

Winter Epigrams; & Epigrams to Ernesto Cardenal in Defense of Claudia (Toronto: Williams-Wallace, 1983);

Chronicles of the Hostile Sun (Toronto: Williams-Wallace, 1984);

Rivers Have Sources, Trees Have Roots: Speaking of Racism, by Brand and Krisanthana Sri Bhaggiyadatta (Toronto: Cross Cultural Communications Centre, 1986);

Sans Souci and Other Stories (Stratford, Ont.: Williams-Wallace, 1988; Ithaca, N.Y.: Firebrand, 1989);

No Language Is Neutral (Toronto: Coach House, 1990);

No Burden to Carry: Narratives of Black Working Women in Ontario, 1920s–1950s, by Brand and Lois De Shield (Toronto: Women's Press, 1991);

We're Rooted Here, They Can't Pull Us Up, by Brand, Peggy Bristow, Linda Carty, Afua Cooper, Sylvia Hamilton, and Adrienne Shadd (Toronto: McClelland & Stewart, 1994);

Bread out of Stone: Recollections, Sex, Recognitions, Race, Dreaming, Politics (Toronto: Coach House, 1994; enlarged edition, Toronto: Random House, 1998);

Grammar of Dissent: Poetry and Prose, by Brand, Claire M. Harris, and M. Nourbese Philip, edited by Carol Morrell (Fredericton, N.B.: Goose Land, 1994);

In Another Place, Not Here (Toronto: Knopf, 1996; New York: Grove, 1997; London: Women's Press, 1997);

Land to Light On (Toronto: McClelland & Stewart, 1997);

At the Full and Change of the Moon (Toronto: Knopf, 1999; New York: Grove, 1999; London: Granta, 1999;

A Map to the Door of No Return: Notes to Belonging (Toronto: Doubleday Canada, 2001);

thirsty (Toronto: McClelland & Stewart, 2002);

What We All Long For: A Novel (Toronto: Knopf Canada, 2005);

Inventory (Toronto: McClelland & Stewart, 2006).

Dionne Brand (photograph by Amy Gottlieb; from the cover for Sans Souci and Other Stories, *1989; Thomas Cooper Library, University of South Carolina)*

OTHER: "Dionne Brand," in *A Caribbean Dozen: Poems from Caribbean Poets,* edited by John Agard and Grace Nichols (Cambridge, Mass.: Candlewick Press, 1994).

SELECTED PERIODICAL PUBLICATIONS–UNCOLLECTED: "Abortion Justice and the Rise of the Right," *This Magazine,* 23 (September 1989): 31–32;

"Out There," *Malahat Review,* 100 (1992): 115–119;

"Who Can Speak For Whom?" *Brick: A Literary Journal,* 46 (Summer 1993): 256–281;

"What I Would Be if I Were Not a Writer: Dionne Brand," *Brick: A Literary Journal,* 50 (1994): 5–6;

"Harold Sonny Ladoo," *Brick: A Literary Journal,* 72 (Winter 2003): 158–163.

Dionne Brand is a poet, a novelist, a short-story writer, an essayist, an oral historian, and a documentarian. In Brand's writing, however, these categories are not separate: she writes poems that are oral histories, novels that are poetic, and histories that are cinematic; she personalizes her documentaries and tells stories in her essays. All of her work is political; she says, "I am a woman and Black and lesbian, the evidence of this is inescapable and interesting." Brand creates written and visual texts that challenge the reader or viewer to bear witness to the world through her words and images and to participate in making the world better for all peoples.

Brand has lived in the Caribbean and Canada, and much of her work focuses on the ways in which she occupies both of these places. Recurring words, phrases, and themes thread themselves between and within her texts. The words "here" and "hear" are frequently repeated as Brand examines the "here" that is Canada, which, she argues in *No Language Is Neutral* (1990), is a place in which one frequently cannot "hear," and the "here" that is the Caribbean, a place where language is "strict / description and teeth edging truth. Here was beauty / and here was nowhere." A quotation from *Toronto Life* on the back cover of her 2002 volume of poetry, *thirsty,* says, "You don't read Dionne Brand, you hear her." Brand is certainly being heard in Canada, as is evidenced by her national prizes and nominations. In 1990 her *No Language is Neutral* was short-listed for the Governor General's Literary Award for poetry; in 1996 her *In Another Place, Not Here* was short-listed for the Trillium Award and the Chapters/ *Books in Canada* First Novel Award; in 1997 she won the Governor General's Literary Award for poetry and the Trillium Award for *Land to Light On;* and in 2003 her *thirsty* (2002) was a finalist for the Trillium Book Award and the Griffin Poetry Prize and won the Pat Lowther Memorial Award for Poetry.

Brand was born on 7 January 1953. In *A Caribbean Dozen* (1994) she says,

> I was born in the south of Trinidad in a village called Guayguayare. Our house was so close to the ocean that when the tide came in the pillow tree logs on which the house stood were almost covered by surf. When I was four or so my grandmother, who brought me up, moved to San Fernando, but every holiday we would return to Guaya where my grandfather lived. It is the place I remember and love the most. . . . each time I go back to Trinidad I always go to Guayguayare just to see the ocean there, to breathe in the smell of copra drying and wood burning and fish frying.

Brand moved to Toronto in 1970. She worked as a counselor at the Immigrant Women's Centre, on the Black Youth Hotline, and as a community-relations worker for the Board of Education. In "Bread out of Stone" (1990) she writes: "I've worked in my community for eighteen years, licking envelopes, postering lamp-posts, carrying placards, teaching children, counselling women, organizing meetings though I never cooked food, chanting on the megaphone though I never made a speech, calling down racists, calling down the state, writing about our lives so we'd have something more to read than the bullshit in the mainstream press. I've even run off to join a revolution. But I haven't bent my back to a Black man, and I have loved Black women." In 1975 she graduated from the University of Toronto with a B.A. in English and philosophy.

In 1978 Brand published her first collection of poetry, *'Fore Day Morning.* The twenty-five poems move between warm and cold places, between fear and belonging, and between past and present; many of them flow in narrow columns down the page. In poems such as "Afro West Indian immigrant" she examines the divided sensibility of an immigrant to Canada:

> I feel like a palm tree
> at the corner of Bloor and Yonge
> in a wild snow storm.
> Scared, surprised, trying desperately to appear unper-
> plexed
> put out, sun brown naked and a little embarrassed.

In 1979 Brand published a collection of children's poems, *Earth Magic,* followed by *Primitive Offensive* (1982) and *Winter Epigrams; & Epigrams to Ernesto Cardenal in Defense of Claudia* (1983). Claire Harris, writing about the ways in which "black writers in Canada are searching for a language which instantly identifies their work as black. . . . and at the same time creating a channel to/ from an authentic black sensibility," calls *Primitive Offensive* "the most complete and elegant treatment of the authentication theme in Canadian poetry. . . . The poem turns the familiar curses on their heads, and makes them praise songs. Most important the 'I' is transformed into the subject of her own life, and in the end becomes the warrior 'naked woman.'"

In 1983 Brand participated in the revolution in Grenada as an information officer for the Caribbean People's Development Agencies and for the Agency for Rural Transformation. She was evacuated after the American invasion. In 1984 she published another poetry collection, *Chronicles of the Hostile Sun.* In 1986 she co-authored with Krisanthana Sri Bhaggiyadatta the nonfiction book *Rivers Have Sources, Trees Have Roots: Speaking of Racism* as part of a series of antiracist literature published by the Cross Cultural Communication Centre. The text moves between the voices of the authors and the voices of people they interviewed. Also in 1986 Brand helped found *Our Lives,* the first black women's newspaper in Canada, and worked as a facilitator for the Ontario Federation of Labour Women's Committee, the Ontario Federation of Labour Workers of Colour Conference, and the Metro Labour Council Anti-Racism Conference. In addition, she joined the board of a battered-women's shelter.

In 1988 Brand published *Sans Souci and Other Stories,* ceased working on her Ph.D., and began working with the National Film Board of Canada's Studio D. She served—at different times—as writer, director, and associate director for the documentary trilogy *Women at the Well,* comprising *Older, Stronger, Wiser* (1989), *Sisters in the Struggle* (1991), and *Long Time Comin'* (1993). She writes in *Bread out of Stone* (1994) about the process of creating *Older, Stronger, Wiser:*

> I've dreamt this film as a book, dreamt it as a face . . . a woman's face. . . . I write it, try to make everyone else dream it, too; if they dream it, they will know something more, love this woman's face, this woman I will become, this woman they will become. I will sacrifice something for this dream: safety. . . . As the cutting ends, I feel the full rain of lesbian hate. It hits the ground, its natural place. It mixes with the soil ready with the hate of women, the contempt for women that women, too, eat.

In 1990 the volume *No Language Is Neutral* established Brand as a major poet in Canada. The volume is divided into three sections: "Hard against the Soul," "No Language Is Neutral," and a continuation of "Hard against the Soul." The first section of "Hard against the Soul" consists of the single poem "I," the title of which might be read either as the Roman numeral one or as the first-person voice; not until the final section, comprising the poems "II" through "X," does the reader see that the first poem is part of a numbered series. The first poem opens, "this is you girl, this cut of road up / to Blanchicheuse . . ."; poem "II" continues, "I want to wrap myself around you here in this line so / that you will know something, not just that I am dying."

The central section of the volume, "No Language Is Neutral," comprises thirteen loosely narrative poems that fill the pages as rectangular blocks of text. These poems are rich in the imagery, sound, and unusual line breaks that distinguish Brand as a poet who continually surprises and shocks the reader:

Paperback cover for the first U.S. edition, 1989 (Thomas Cooper Library, University of South Carolina)

consonant curses into choking aspirate. No language is neutral seared in the spine's unravelling. Here is history too. A backbone bending and unbending without a word, heat bellowing these lungs spongy, exhaled in humming, the ocean, a way out and not anything of beauty, tipping turquoise and scandalous. The malicious horizon made us the essential thinkers of technology. How to fly gravity, how to balance basket and prose reaching for murder.

In 1991, after a year as writer-in-residence at the University of Toronto, Brand gave public readings in England, Scotland, and the Netherlands. She also went to South Africa to participate in the New Nation Writers' Conference, which celebrated the release from prison of Nelson Mandela. In addition, she published, with the assistance of Lois De Shield and the Immigrant Women's Job Placement Centre, *No Burden to Carry: Narratives of Black Working Women in Ontario, 1920s–1950s;* all royalties from the book go to the Immigrant Women's

Paperback cover for the first U.S. edition, 1997 (Thomas Cooper
Library, University of South Carolina)

Job Placement Centre. The fourteen narratives collected in *No Burden to Carry* demonstrate how different
the working lives of black women in Canada from the
1920s to the 1950s were from those of black men and
white women.

From 1992 to 1994 Brand taught in the English
department at the University of Guelph. In 1994 she
published two works of nonfiction: *We're Rooted Here,
They Can't Pull Us Up,* co-authored with Peggy Bristow,
Adrienne Shadd, Sylvia Hamilton, Afua Cooper, and
Linda Carty, and *Bread out of Stone: Recollections, Sex, Recognitions, Race, Dreaming, Politics.* In the title essay of the
latter work Brand recalls: "Exasperated after hours of
my crying for sweet water, opening her mouth wide,
my mama would say to me, 'Look inside! Aah! you see
anything in there? You want me to make bread out of
stone?' . . . In my mama's mouth, I saw the struggle for
small things." Many of the eleven pieces address the
complexities of calling a place "home"; others focus on
race, on her role as a revolutionary and an activist, and
on herself as a writer, a reader, and a poet for whom

poetry is "something wrestling with how we live, something dangerous, something honest." In 1998 *Bread out
of Stone* was republished with four additional essays.

In 1996 Brand published her first novel, *In Another
Place, Not Here.* The work is arranged around the interlock-
ing stories of Elizete and Verlia. The first section follows
Elizete as she falls in love with the revolutionary Verlia.
The second half of the book is Verlia's story of leaving the
Caribbean, moving briefly to Sudbury and then to
Toronto to join the Movement, and finally returning to the
Caribbean to participate in the revolution. This part of the
novel moves between Verlia's stories of leaving and return-
ing and Elizete's story of searching for Verlia's past. *In
Another Place, Not Here* ends with Verlia leaping away from
the sound of American guns over the edge of a cliff and
into "another place" that is "not here"–a place that is "less
tortuous, less fleshy."

The poems in Brand's Governor General's Award–
winning 1997 volume *Land to Light On,* are about giving up
safety and revolutions, land and language, children and
the past; they are also about not giving up on poetry,
which uses a "pencil for explosives." Brand taught at the
University of British Columbia in 1999 and at York University in 2000. In a 2000 interview with Rinaldo Walcott
and Leslie Sanders, Brand said that her second novel, *At
the Full and Change of the Moon* (1999), is "about how imagination is long, and open. And how, really, you are always
guided by your imagination. . . . the past is also something
that hovers in our imaginations. And it repeats, and sometimes we can see it and sometimes we can't see it, and
sometimes it's forgotten deliberately, or unconsciously. But
it is this crumbling thing, this crumbling estate, or this
crumbling plantation which shadows the times that we live
in now."

In the same interview Brand said that Canadian critics look at texts by black authors as sociological or anthropological documents that will somehow explain black
people to the reader. Instead, she said, reading should be
"an act of faith . . . and . . . an act of investigation . . . a
knowledge-making enterprise. . . . The novel doesn't only
have to come to me, I need to go to it too. I have to go to
the text and I have to say, I'm going to learn some things
here. . . . Black writers in this country have still to receive
an intelligent reading. The kind of reading that says, 'No, I
don't know. I've never lived in that body but in good faith,
I will go where the book is going because I am interested
in what human beings do.'"

From 1 September 2000 until 31 August 2002
Brand was the Ruth Wynn Professor in the women's
studies department at Simon Fraser University. In 2001
she published an autobiography, *A Map to the Door of No
Return: Notes to Belonging.* "The Door of No Return" is
the door on the west coast of Africa "out of which Africans were captured, loaded onto ships heading for the

New World." At the beginning of the text Brand states, "I am interested in exploring this creation place—the Door of No Return, a place of emptied beginnings—as a site of belonging or unbelonging." The book is a series of recollections that bring together and reshape many of the people, events, and moments that Brand has written about in her previous works. In 2002 she followed *A Map to the Door of No Return* with the poetry collection *thirsty*.

Between 2002 and 2006 Brand was a Distinguished Visiting Professor at St. Lawrence University in New York and wrote one novel and one book of poetry. The novel, *What We All Long For* (2005), which won the 2006 City of Toronto Book Award, is the story of four friends who were all "born in the city from people born elsewhere." It is as much a narrative about the crevices and expressways of Toronto as it is about the silent and spoken longings of the city's inhabitants. *Inventory* (2006), which was nominated for the 2006 Governor General's Literary Award for Poetry, recounts the devastations apparent in the opening years of the twenty-first century as death tolls rise globally. The seventh and final section of this inventory of bodies that live, love, work, and die briefly charts happiness before the final four lines of the book:

I have nothing soothing to tell you,
that's not my job,
my job is to revise and revise this bristling list,
hourly.

Also in 2006 Brand was made a fellow of the Royal Society of Canada. She is currently professor and University Research Chair in the School of English and Theatre Studies at the University of Guelph.

Dionne Brand is a poet and a revolutionary who believes in the power of language. As she said in a 1997 interview with Eva Tihanyi, "I'm a poet firstly, and that's what I absolutely love. Everything else comes from there. I have to have poetry going on to feel a certain sanity. The shape and order of poetry, its ability to contain universes of ideas which can lift you out of the immediate dread of living—and I don't mean lift you by deceit or fantasy but by clarity, a kind of sense-making which doesn't spare you the dread but offers you this clarity which is like being able to feel air or night, to feel the intangible. I like the way in which poetry makes you reach for perfect speech, the perfect expression of your breath, your singular breath, at the same moment as it joins you to all other breathing."

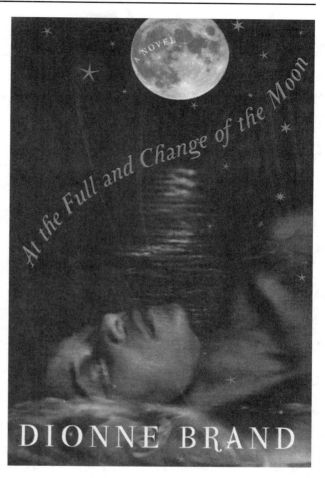

Dust jacket for the first U.S. edition, 1999
(Richland County Public Library)

mond (Toronto: Oxford University Press, 1990), pp. 271–277;

Charmaine Perkins, "Brandishing a Powerful Pen: Interview with Dionne Brand," *Kinesis* (June 1995): 16–17;

Lynnette D'anna, "In Conversation with Dionne Brand," *Prairie Fire,* 17 (Summer 1996): 9–19;

Eva Tihanyi, "Unredeemed Grace: Eva Tihanyi Speaks with Dionne Brand," *Books in Canada,* 26 (March 1997): 8–9;

Rinaldo Walcott and Leslie Sanders, "At the Full Change of CanLit: An Interview with Dionne Brand," *Canadian Woman Studies/Les Cahiers de la Femme,* 20 (Summer 2000): 22–26.

Interviews:

Dagmar Novak, *Other Solitudes: Canadian Multicultural Fictions,* edited by Linda Hutcheon and Marion Rich-

Reference:

Claire Harris, "Poets in Limbo," in *A Mazing Space: Writing Canadian Women Writing,* edited by Shirley Neuman and Smaro Kamboureli (Edmonton: Longspoon & NeWest Press, 1986), pp. 115–125.

Bonnie Burnard

(15 January 1945 –)

Jeanette Lynes
St. Francis Xavier University

BOOKS: *Women of Influence* (Regina: Coteau, 1988; London: Women's Press, 1993);
Casino and Other Stories (Toronto: HarperCollins, 1994; New York: HarperCollins, 1994);
A Good House (Toronto: HarperFlamingoCanada, 1999; New York: Holt, 2000; London: Doubleday, 2000).

OTHER: *Coming Attractions: Stories by Sharon Butala, Bonnie Burnard and Sharon Sparling* (Ottawa: Oberon Press, 1983);
"Moon Watcher," in *More Saskatchewan Gold,* edited by Geoffrey Ursell (Moose Jaw, Sask.: Coteau, 1984), pp. 243–259;
The Old Dance: Love Stories of One Kind or Another, edited by Burnard (Moose Jaw, Sask.: Coteau, 1986);
"Sister," in *Sky High: Stories from Saskatchewan,* edited by Ursell (Regina: Coteau, 1988), pp. 335–350;
"Patsy Flater's Brief Search for God," in *Lodestone: Stories by Regina Writers,* edited by Ven Begamudré (Saskatoon: Fifth House, 1993), pp. 1–18;
"Deer Heart," in *The New Oxford Book of Canadian Short Stories,* edited by Robert Weaver and Margaret Atwood (Toronto, Oxford & New York: Oxford University Press, 1995), pp. 318–325;
Stag Line: Stories by Men, edited by Burnard (Regina: Coteau, 1995);
"It Almost Always Starts This Way," in *Dominant Impressions: Essays on the Canadian Short Story,* edited by Gerald Lynch and Angela Arnold Robbeson (Ottawa: University of Ottawa Press, 1999), pp. 9–15;
"Ten Men Respond to an Air-Brushed Photograph of a Nude Woman Chained to a Bull," in *Great Stories from the Prairies,* edited by Birk Sproxton (Calgary: Red Deer Press, 2000), pp. 305–316.

The two landscapes that have shaped Bonnie Burnard's life thus far also inform much of her writing: small-town southwestern Ontario, where she was born and spent her childhood, and the prairies. Widely

Bonnie Burnard (photograph by Melanie Burnard; from the cover for A Good House, *1999; Bruccoli Clark Layman Archives)*

anthologized both in Canada and internationally and frequently broadcast on CBC Radio, Burnard's writing has been recognized by several literary awards.

Burnard was born on 15 January 1945 in Petrolia in southwestern Ontario. In 1974, after graduating from the University of Western Ontario in London with a B.A. in English, she moved to Regina, Saskatchewan. She was fiction editor of *Grain Magazine* from 1982 to 1986 and served on the board of the Saskatchewan publisher Coteau Books from 1983 to 1987. She won the W. O. Mitchell Bursary for writing in 1983 and the City of Regina Writing Award in 1984. In 1986 she edited an anthology of short fiction, *The Old Dance: Love Stories of One Kind or Another.*

Burnard's first collection of her own short stories, *Women of Influence,* was published in 1988. The fourteen stories average six pages in length; three are around a dozen pages. The first story, "Nice Girls Don't Tell," recounts the summer reunion of three middle-aged women; the almost casual "offstage" manner in which the narrator refers to the death of one woman's child makes the tragedy all the more horrific: "Ruby was thirty-six when Jason rode his new red ten-speed bike into the intersection. She's been a bad drunk ever since." The opening paragraph of "Music Lessons" deftly sketches the homogenizing force of socialization on a generation of females: "Most of us who grew up in that time, in that place, in that little subclass of well off girls in well off towns seem now to me interchangeable, like foundlings. We all grew up around the same rules, the same expectations. Among the many things we did in my town, with a strangely limited variation in skill, was play the piano. We were all taught to play by Mrs. Summers." The piano teacher, with her perfect chignon, "elegant sculptured legs," and "wonderful carriage" is one of Burnard's "women of influence." But the young narrator, Elizabeth, gains a deeper insight into the pianist that shatters the surface illusion of flawless femininity: "Before each lesson I would stretch up to those windows and watch her coming to the door. . . . And always, just before she put her hand to the knob, she prepared a smile." Mrs. Summers must construct a self before confronting an endlessly scrutinizing world. When Mrs. Summers's husband dies, the piano teacher's mask gradually falls away. She no longer makes herself up; she exposes long-sublimated anger when she strikes Elizabeth's hands "with her crossword puzzle book just before Christmas"; and she displays photographs of her lovers on the piano. "Word got out, of course. Lovers on the piano. It wasn't good. Soon music students were taking the longer walk across the tracks to the new high school teacher who, it was said, was just as qualified, if not quite so experienced."

In "The Replacement" a substitute teacher's trappings of perfection are similarly peeled away by a keen observer for whom watching intensifies into an almost obsessive voyeurism: "I moved into the big bedroom when my brother left home for university; I was thirteen. Miss Dickson moved in with our next-door neighbour, the widowed Mrs. Dunn, a few months later. Her bedroom window, a movie screen rectangle, faced mine above the blue snow-covered lawns. She had drapes, pink and black, flamingos in a dark swamp, and there was an orange blind as well, a second assurance of privacy, but she never pulled the drapes and I could watch her easily through the ancient blind, watch her silhouette, slightly enlarged, her angles, slightly distorted." The "dark swamp" is a metaphor for Miss Dickson's lonely, inner struggles as the young narrator watches the teacher sink into alcoholism over the course of a winter. Furthermore, Miss Dickson allows herself to be

Paperback cover for the first edition, 1988
(Bruccoli Clark Layman Archives)

watched: the teacher's complicity comes to light near the startling denouement of the story but is already present in its opening paragraph. The narrator herself becomes a teacher and, at the end of the story, returns home and is framed in her own "movie screen rectangle" window while a different teacher boards with Mrs. Dunn.

In "Grizzly Mountain" a couple take a last hike on the edge of a wilderness before their breakup. In "Joyride" two truckers trap a woman driving alone to a lake on an open stretch of prairie highway between their vehicles and threaten her with a knife. In "The Knife Sharpener" a six-year-old girl is nearly abducted by an old man with a face that is a "sickly, ashen colour." In Burnard's fictional world, hazard tends to lurk just under a seemingly innocuous surface. In "Landscape" a retired couple discover that their son is gay; when Edgar, the narrator's husband, cuts John out of his will, the narrator retaliates by chopping down all of the forty-year-old trees on the family property except

Paperback cover for the first edition, 1999
(Bruccoli Clark Layman Archives)

for two maples. One of the maples holds a rotting tree house, symbolic of domestic ruin. The narrator's ax-wielding attack on nature is foreshadowed by the opening scene of "Moon Watcher," in which Marg slams a hammer against the locked shutters of her cottage in retaliation for her husband's infidelity. The final story in *Women of Influence,* "Reflections," recounts an elderly couple's visit to the cemetery, at the wife's insistence, to locate their plots. The story is narrated first from the husband's point of view and then from the wife's, allowing Burnard to reveal how each remembers different aspects of their life together and to capture a central paradox of marriage: the togetherness, yet aloneness, of the partners.

The nine stories in Burnard's second collection, *Casino and Other Stories* (1994), range from twelve to twenty-six pages in length. Her sustained delineation of the lakeside dance hall and the beach occupies the first five pages of the title story and is so detailed that the texture of the "crisp sleeveless summer blouses" worn

by teenage girls who "carry trays of burgers and shakes to cars full of tired families or wide-awake young men" is palpable, as are the "white hot afternoon sand" and the "sticky blacktop" casino road. A single grain of sand is examined at close range: "THE BEACH is wide, composed of fine white sand. At least it looks white, especially at night. But the individual grains are really tan, interspersed with black. It's always a surprise to find black grains, but you can see them in the daytime when you take a handful of sand and let it sift through your fingers. Black like pepper." Burnard focuses on four men, revealing two phases in their lives: their halcyon days at the casino, narrated in the present tense, and their lives years later, told in the future tense. Jack is a skinny kid who, while dancing with American girls, "lies through his teeth, tells them he's rich and brilliant, a superachiever. . . . JACK will run into trouble at university. . . . Jack will remain extraordinarily thin all his life, as will his sons. When he is quite old, he will remember the Casino and the Saturday night dances. He will remember the words of songs and the way the lake smelled different after dark." Grady, "before he's too old to move," will pull his partner "from her brocade chair and waltz her round the room, humming a sad old love tune he remembers from the lake to lend some rhythm to their steps." Duncan's attendance at "an occasional dance at his golf club" and Norm's dance with his granddaughter at her wedding weave their lives back to their earlier dance-hall days.

In "Nipple Man" a history professor's conventional sexual fantasies are brought up short when he dates a woman whose body is a "war zone": she has lost a breast to cancer. In "Crush" a girl exposes her breasts to the married man whose children she babysits. Walking in after the man has left but while her daughter is still undressed, the girl's mother says: "I had a crush on your father. That's how it started with us, because I had a crush on him. . . . I think it's the same. You've made a fool of yourself. . . . Women have this feeling so they will marry, so they will have children. It's like a grand plan. . . . You've got to learn to control this thing, this feeling, until that man is there for you." After having had the "grand plan" explained to her, the girl runs to a grass-filled ditch beyond the cornfields, "leans back into the grass," "throws her arms up over her head," and "stares, for as long as she can, at the hot July sun."

Like "Casino," the final story in the collection, "Ten Men Respond to an Air-Brushed Photograph of a Nude Woman Chained to a Bull," focuses on male experience. Among the men who respond to the photograph are two who created it: the photographer and the publisher of the "magazine with very good distribution and surprisingly classy ads" in which it appears. The photographer "who captured the image" lives alone and "hangs out in malls a lot"; he "didn't know the blonde at the farm" and sees the photograph as only a technical exercise, a play of light. The publisher argues for the harmlessness of the images he sells: "The bruises are made up. We've never allowed ourselves to get pulled into the kind of stuff where people can get hurt." Richard, a reader of the magazine, says "I just like long legs." Don claims that "Nobody's forcing anything." John, echoing the publisher's argument, says, "Nobody's getting hurt here" and claims that the photograph is "almost an aesthetic thing with me." The only one who strongly objects to the photograph on moral grounds is Harvey, who finds the magazine in his seventeen-year-old son's dresser. Compared to Harvey's outrage, Father Michael's complaint on finding the photograph taped to the wall inside the confessional seems lukewarm. The responses are conveyed in the first person except for that of five-year-old Ryan, who, with a neighbor boy, Cody, finds the magazine in a bathroom drawer. Ryan is the last male to respond to the photograph, and even at his age he intuits the illicit nature of what he has found: "he knows he's discovered something, something no one would have told him about if he hadn't found it for himself." The boy's discovery is compared to "the dark round thing that grows under his mother's arm, a mole, she said, it's only an ordinary mole, which he saw by mistake the very last time he charged into her room without knocking."

After the publication of *Casino and Other Stories*, Burnard moved back to London. The book was shortlisted for the prestigious Giller Prize for fiction and almost received the Saskatchewan Book of the Year Award and the Periodical Publishers Award. In 1995 Burnard won the much-coveted Marian Engel Award, which recognizes female writers in midcareer for their body of work and carries a $10,000 cash prize.

Burnard's only novel to date, *A Good House* (2000), follows the working-class Chambers family of Stonebrook, Ontario, from 1949 to 1997, with a flashback to 1936–"the year King George died" and the year Bill Chambers married Sylvia Ferguson. During World War II, Bill watches "the three most useful fingers of his right hand leave his hand" to be "kicked . . . overboard" by "the guy beside him." More central to the novel than Bill's war injury is the disfiguring of his daughter, Daphne, when she falls during a trapeze act in 1952; her broken jaw distorts her face and marks her for life. Daphne is doubly "marked" because she has two children with a man she does not marry–a rebellious act in small-town Ontario in the 1960s. In Daphne's "experience kids with a physical oddness

were not mocked so much if they'd had an accident, as she had . . . from what she knew, you had to be born with something wrong to get the worst of it." This distinction is borne out when Daphne's brother, Paul, and his wife have a mentally handicapped daughter, Meg, who must be protected from "People who were stupid and cruel, all the time." In 1995 Bill, who is in failing health, begins calling his second wife, Margaret, by his first wife's name. In the final scene Margaret is sitting at the kitchen table with family photographs spread out before her: "she would decide that before too much time passed, someone with a fine hand should write all their names on the back of the pictures, in full, the placement of names replicating the placement of the bodies, like a key, or maybe it was more properly called a legend. Yes." The closing passage of the novel replicates the cinematic style of the opening as the Chamberses watch a videotape of the wedding of Daphne's daughter, Maggie:

> They would see themselves standing up from their chairs after it was done, after all the promises had been made. They would laugh watching the bridal party fool around down at Stonebrook Creek while the still photographer worked so hard to pose them. . . . They would see Josh reach back to help Maggie, their hands lifted and extended to each other like dancers from another century as she tried to get a foothold beside him on a large, flat rock. . . . Then, as Stephen's camera work was softly praised, they would move with him away from the bridal party, away from the bridge. They would follow for a few minutes along the bank of the creek, the water moving fast and churned to mud in the middle of the current but much cleaner, almost crystal clear, in the pools along the edge. . . . And from a perfectly focused, extreme close-up of a Scotch thistle, so sharply, delicately barbed, its small, spiny flowers so perfectly mauve in the sunlight, they would be quickly lifted back to a long view of Stonebrook Creek turning through town on its way to the lake, its movement like a muscle twisting and their perspectives briefly jolted, just as Stephen intended.

With *A Good House* Burnard achieved the pinnacle of recognition for a Canadian fiction writer: the Giller Prize for 1999.

Interview:

Linda Morra, "Inside a Good House: An Interview with Bonnie Burnard," *Books in Canada*, 30 (November–December 2001): 14.

Reference:

Margaret Laurence, *A Bird in the House* (Toronto: McClelland & Stewart, 1970).

George Elliott Clarke

(12 February 1960 –   )

Debra Dudek
Deakin University

BOOKS: *Saltwater Spirituals and Deeper Blues* (Halifax: Pottersfield, 1983);

Whylah Falls (Vancouver: Polestar, 1990; enlarged, 2000);

Provençal Songs (Ottawa: Magnum, 1993);

Lush Dreams, Blue Exile: Fugitive Poems, 1978–1993 (Halifax: Pottersfield, 1994);

Provencal Songs II (Ottawa: Above/ground, 1997);

Whylah Falls: The Play (Toronto: Playwrights Canada Press, 1999);

Beatrice Chancy (Victoria: Polestar, 1999);

Treason of the Black Intellectuals? (Montreal: McGill Institute for the Study of Canada, 1999);

Gold Indigoes (Durham, N.C.: Carolina Wren Press, 2000);

Execution Poems: The Black Acadian Tragedy of "George and Rue" (Wolfville, N.S.: Gaspereau, 2001);

Blue (Vancouver: Raincoast, 2001);

Africadian History (Kentville, N.S.: Gaspereau, 2001);

Odysseys Home: Mapping African-Canadian Literature (Toronto: University of Toronto Press, 2002);

Québécité: A Jazz Fantasia in Three Cantos, music by D. D. Jackson (Kentville, N.S.: Gaspereau, 2003);

George and Rue (London: Harvill Press, 2005; Toronto: HarperCollins Canada, 2005; New York: Carroll & Graff, 2006);

Illuminated Verses, photographs by Ricardo Scipio (Toronto: Canadian Scholars Press, 2005);

Black (Vancouver: Polestar, 2006);

Trudeau: Long March / Shining Path (Kentville, N.S.: Gaspereau, 2007).

PLAY PRODUCTIONS: *Beatrice Chancy,* dramatic reading, Toronto, Theatre Passe Muraille, 10 July 1997;

Beatrice Chancy, opera, libretto by Clarke, music by James Rolfe, Toronto, Music Gallery, 18 June 1998;

Québécité, jazz opera, libretto by Clarke, music by D. D. Jackson, Guelph, River Run Centre, 5 September 2003.

George Elliott Clarke (photograph by Thomas King; from the dust jacket for George and Rue, *2006; Richland County Public Library)*

PRODUCED SCRIPT: *One Heart Broken into Song,* motion picture, Canadian Broadcasting Corporation, 1999.

OTHER: *Fire on the Water: An Anthology of Black Nova Scotian Writing,* 2 volumes, edited by Clarke (Lawrencetown Beach, N.S.: Pottersfield, 1991, 1992);

Border Lines: Contemporary Poetry in English, edited by Clarke, Ruth Grogan, Victor Li, R. Ross, J. A. Wainwright, and A. Wallace (Toronto: Copp-Clark, 1995);

Eyeing the North Star: Directions in African-Canadian Literature, edited by Clarke (Toronto: McClelland & Stewart, 1997);

"Must We Burn Haliburton?" in *The Haliburton Bicentenary Chaplet: Papers Presented at the 1996 Thomas Randall Symposium,* edited by Richard Davies (Wolfville, N.S.: Gaspareau, 1997), pp. 1–40;

"Towards a Conservative Modernity: Cultural Nationalism in Contemporary Acadian and Africadian Poetry," in *Cultural Identities in Canadian Literature / Identités culturelles dans la literature canadienne,* edited by Benedicte Mauguiere (New York: Peter Lang, 1998), pp. 49–63;

"African-Canadian Literature," in *Companion to African Literatures,* edited by Douglas Killam, Ruth Rowe, Bernth Lindfors, Gerald M. Moser, and Alain Ricard (Oxford: James Currey / Bloomington: Indiana University Press, 2000);

"Race and Racism in Canadian Literature," in *Encyclopedia of Literature in Canada,* edited by W. H. New (Toronto: University of Toronto Press, 2002), pp. 922–926.

SELECTED PERIODICAL PUBLICATIONS–UNCOLLECTED: "Michael Ondaatje and the Production of Myth," *Studies in Canadian Literature/ Etudes en Litterature Canadienne,* 16, no. 1 (1991): 1–21;

"White Niggers, Black Slaves: Slavery, Race and Class in T. C. Haliburton's *The Clockmaker,*" *Nova Scotia Historical Review,* 14, no. 1 (1994): 13–40;

"The Road to North Hatley: Ralph Gustafson's Post-Colonial Odyssey," *Journal of Eastern Townships Studies / Revue d'Etudes des Cantons de l'Est,* 9 (Fall 1996): 21–42;

"White Like Canada," *Transition,* 73 (1997): 98–109;

"Letters to Young Poets," *Germination,* 11, no. 2 (1998): 14–15;

"Cool Politics: Styles of Honour in Malcolm X and Miles Davis," *Jouvert: A Journal of Post-Colonial Studies,* 2, no. 1 (1998) <http://social.chass.ncsu.edu/ jouvert>;

"*Beatrice Chancy:* A Libretto in Four Acts," *Canadian Theatre Review,* 96 (Fall 1998): 62–77;

"'Play Ebony Play Ivory' by Henry Lee Dumas,'" *Brick,* 62 (Spring 1999): 48–49;

"Racing Shelley, or Reading *The Cenci* as Gothic Slave Narrative," *European Romantic Review,* 11 (Spring 2000): 168–185;

"Reading Ward's 'Blind Man's Blues,'" *Arc,* 44 (Summer 2000): 50–52;

"Canadian Biraciality and Its 'Zebra' Poetics," *Intertexts,* 6 (Fall 2002): 203–231;

"Raising Raced and Erased Executions in African-Canadian Literature: Or, Unearthing Angélique," *Essays on Canadian Writing,* 75 (Winter 2002): 47–68;

"Still More Lost Careers," by Clarke, Eavan Boland, Dionne Brand, Robert Creeley, and Hugh Brody, *Brick,* 71 (Summer 2003): 109–114;

"The Critique of African-Canadian Literature," *Journal of Canadian Studies/Revue d'Etudes Canadiennes,* 38 (Spring 2004): 5–8;

"Afro-Gynocentric Darwinism in the Drama of George Elroy Boyd," *Canadian Theatre Review,* 118 (Spring 2004): 77–84;

"'This Is No Hearsay': Reading the Canadian Slave Narratives," *Papers of the Bibliographical Society of Canada/Cahiers de la Société Bibliographique du Canada,* 43 (Spring 2005): 7–32;

"Anna Minerva Henderson: An Afro–New Brunswick Response to Canadian (Modernist) Poetry," *Canadian Literature,* 189 (Summer 2006): 32–48.

Poet, lyricist, playwright, literary critic, and professor George Elliott Clarke is a seventh-generation Canadian of African American and Mi'kmaq descent. Nova Scotia, and specifically the history and culture of black Nova Scotians, have been central to Clarke's work. He has edited three anthologies dedicated to black writers in Canada, and his own writing revisits personal and collective histories and genres that embody the richness of black cultures. Clarke is, perhaps, best known for coining the term *Africadia,* which he defines in the introduction to *Fire on the Water: An Anthology of Black Nova Scotian Writing* (1991, 1992) as the merging of "*Africa* and *Acadia* (a word which derives–like *Acadie*–from the Mi'kmaq suffix, *cadie,* which means 'abounding in')" and which once meant both Nova Scotia and New Brunswick; "*Africadia* signifies Black Nova Scotia, an African-American-founded 'nation' which has flourished for more than two centuries." Africadians are people who live in Africadia, including the black Loyalists who settled in Nova Scotia after the American Revolution and their descendants. Clarke said in a 1998 interview with Anne Compton that in both his creative and his critical work he is "trying to establish an Africadian or African-Canadian vision, or perspective, on Canadian history and politics–and/or a personal vision attempting to rescue or assert certain aesthetic/political viewpoints combatting the hegemony of the standard aesthetic/political viewpoints."

Clarke's books are multimedia pieces of art, which are both aesthetically stunning and politically mobilizing. Black-and-white photographs from a variety of artists and archives, including the Public Archives of Nova Scotia and the National Archives of Canada, and from his own collection are placed beside the words in all of his major works. Clarke said in a 1996 interview with Maureen Moynagh that photographs and history are "means of contesting that constant erasure, which

*Paperback cover for the first edition, 1999
(<http://www.amazon.ca>)*

runner-up for the 1983 Bliss Carman Award for Poetry, Clarke was also writing lyrics for the a capella folk-gospel quartet Four the Moment.

Clarke's first collection of poems, *Saltwater Spirituals and Deeper Blues* (1983), was written and published while he was a student at the University of Waterloo, where he helped found the Creative Writing Collective. He told Compton: "*Saltwater Spirituals,* even though it was a reflection of, and a reaction to, my Nova Scotian history, was at the same time very much informed by what I had been studying in a way that hadn't yet been filtered out. The material hadn't yet been transmuted into my own voice. I was writing the poetry I thought I should be writing as opposed to stuff I had to write." *Saltwater Spirituals and Deeper Blues* is divided into three sections: "Soul Songs," "Blues Notes," and "The Book of Jubilee." More conventional in style than his later works, which are often written in what Clarke calls "Blackened English," speech, poems such as "Amherst African Methodist Episcopal Church" rely on devices such as alliteration:

brown-blown fall fields yield
to spring-sprung green garb
with blackthread train tracks
all along the tantramar marshes.

Clarke graduated with a B.A. Honors in English in 1984. In 1985 he protested against racism in the Annapolis Valley of Nova Scotia by organizing the Weymouth Falls Justice Committee. In 1985–1986 he was a social worker in the Annapolis Valley, and from 1987 to 1991 he was an aide to Member of Parliament Howard McCurdy in the House of Commons in Ottawa. He earned an M.A. in English from Dalhousie University in 1989.

Whylah Falls (1990), Clarke's second book, was written while he was working on his doctorate in English at Queen's University. It is based on the 8 June 1985 killing in Weymouth Falls of Graham Jarvis-Cromwell, a black man, and the acquittal of the accused killer, who was white. Like much of Clarke's later work, *Whylah Falls* represents an historical event that is revised through Clarke's imagination. As he writes in the poem "Absolution," "Every word, every word, / is a lie. But sometimes the lie / tells the truth." One of the recurring features of Clarke's writing, which is evident in the epic poetry of *Whylah Falls,* is his insistence on blending forms so that the song-like cadences and truths of everyday speech often balance violent events. This technique is evident in a passage from "The Passion of Pablo and Amarantha," the section that precedes the murder at the center of the poem:

has led ultimately I think to racism, to the idea that 'you folks do not count; you're not even a fit subject for history.' There's a whole side of Maritime/Canadian life that has been repressed, and it's the duty of us who are creating right now to address that fact."

Clarke was born in Windsor Plains, Nova Scotia, on 12 February 1960 to William Lloyd Clarke, a railway baggage handler, social worker, encyclopedia salesman, bartender, taxi driver, and self-taught intellectual, and Geraldine Elizabeth Johnson Clarke, a teacher and day-care center director. In 1979 he enrolled at the University of Waterloo. That same year he assisted in establishing the Black Youth Organization of Nova Scotia. In 1981 he won First Prize for Adult Poetry in the annual competition sponsored by the Writers' Federation of Nova Scotia. He worked as a legislative researcher in the Ontario provincial parliament in Toronto in 1982–1983. During this time, besides writing the poems for which he was

Come, my love, come, this lonely, passionate,
Nova Scotian night. Your voice trembles like wings,
Your bones whisper. Under the moon, I stroll
The shadowed road, awaiting your dark eyes
And sandalled feet. My love, if I have to,
I will pace this blue town of white shadows
And black water all night, if I have to.

Whylah Falls earned Clarke the 1991 Archibald Lampman Award for Poetry. It was reprinted four times before the tenth-anniversary second edition, which features a new introduction and an added section titled "The Apocrypha"; both have appeared in slightly different versions elsewhere. It was a runner-up in the 2002 Canada Reads competition, which made it a bestseller. The first volume of *Fire on the Water* was published in 1991; the second volume appeared the following year. Clarke received his Ph.D. in 1993 with a dissertation titled "The Similarity of Margins: A Comparative Study of the Development of English Canadian and African American Poetry and Poetics."

The year after Clarke received his doctorate, he published *Lush Dreams, Blue Exile: Fugitive Poems, 1978–1993*. The collection supplements the Canadian literary canon by reworking traditional English genres and by parodying iconic Canadian literature, such as Michael Ondaatje's "There's a Trick with a Knife I'm Learning to Do," to which Clarke pays homage—and, as he says in "Standing Your Ground"—to which he does damage in "Five Psalms for Paris":

There's a trick with a verb that I'm learning
To do, splintering French and hand language
With *deux Algériens,* whose history
Is frontiers, curried currencies, white sex,
And contraband cigs strong enough to swill.

From 1994 to 1999 Clarke was assistant professor of English at Duke University in Durham, North Carolina. Four scenes from his then-unpublished play, *Beatrice Chancy* (1999), were presented at the Vancouver Press Club on 19 November 1995. In 1997 Clarke edited *Eyeing the North Star: Directions in African-Canadian Literature*. In the introduction to the anthology he notes that African-Canadian literature comprises "The King James scriptures melded with East Coast spirituals, New Orleans jazz, Bajan calypso, and Nigerian jit-jive. Steel drums and steel guitars harmonized. A discourse diced with Motown slang, Caribbean Creole, approximated Queen's English, gilt Haitian French, Canuck neologisms, and African patois."

A dramatic reading of *Beatrice Chancy* was performed at Theatre Passe Muraille in Toronto on 10 and 11 July 1997. The play had begun as a libretto for an opera with music by the Canadian composer James

Paperback cover for the first edition, 2001
(<http://www.canadacouncil.ca>)

Rolfe; the opera premiered at the Music Gallery in Toronto on 18 June 1998 and ran through 20 June.

In 1998 Clarke received the Portia White Prize for Excellence in the Arts from the Nova Scotia Arts Council. That same year he was awarded a Bellagio Center Residency by the Rockefeller Foundation of New York, which allowed him to stay at the Villa Serbelloni in Bellagio, Italy, for one month. Also in 1998 Clarke accepted a one-year position as the third Seagram Visiting Chair of Canadian Studies at McGill University, where he delivered the paper *Treason of the Black Intellectuals?* as the Seagram Annual Lecture; it was published in 1999 by the McGill Institute for the Study of Canada. In the lecture he argues that being black and being Canadian should not be seen as static, binary oppositions: "It is necessary that we understand that we are creating . . . an African-Canadian literature, one that is a branch of Canadian literature, but which also maintains definable, Africanist oral/linguistic strategies, as well as a special relationship to song, rhythm, and a specific history." In 1999 Clarke was awarded an honorary doctorate of laws by Dalhousie University and became professor of English at the University of Toronto.

The play *Beatrice Chancy* was published in 1999. In his afterword Clarke states: "This work moves in sympathy with many visions of the true but often altered story of Beatrice Cènci, beheaded at the age of twenty for the crime of parricide, on September 11, 1599, in Rome, Italy." Clarke transfers the story of the Cenci family, which has been told by writers such as Percy Bysshe Shelley, Alexandre Dumas *père,* and Antonin Artaud, to the Africadian context in the years 1801–1802. In Clarke's version Beatrice is the daughter of a black slave and her white master, Francis Chancy. The play begins with Beatrice's return from the nunnery to which Chancy sent her three years previously to maintain her purity. Beatrice reunites with her beloved, Lead, but their love is doomed by Chancy's incestuous passion for her and his hatred of Lead and the other slaves. The play, however, is not all tragedy, for in the end the slaves, except Lead, free themselves literally and in song:

> I'm chasin the moon, chasin the moon,
> No more auction block for me.
> Moonlight's branchin through the trees,
> Many thousand gone.

Clarke's insistence on interweaving beauty and tragedy are apparent both in the reworking of the plot to include a love story between slaves and in how he uses poetry to represent both beauty and violence. For example, when Chancy strikes Lustra, *"Her mouth's a wet rose";* and when Beatrice is flayed, "Blood wept from his whip." Even more complicated are the ways in which Clarke gives Chancy some of the most poetic lines in the play, as when he says to Beatrice:

> Your lips halved to sing
> You pray, moaning–
> Chaste voluptuousness.
> Your perfume on my face
> Is like apples tumbled
> In an autumn grove,
> A place where *Poetry* comes to die.

Clarke wrote the screenplay for *One Heart Broken into Song* (1999), for which he was named Outstanding Writer of a Canadian Feature Film by the Black Film and Video Network in 2000. That same year he was awarded an honorary doctorate of letters by the University of New Brunswick and published the chapbook *Gold Indigoes.*

Also in 2000 Gaspereau Press released a hand-printed limited folio edition of Clarke's *Execution Poems: The Black Acadian Tragedy of "George and Rue."* All sixty-six copies were sold within a month, and a trade edition was published in 2001. The poems tell the story of his cousins

George and Rufus Hamilton, who killed a Fredericton taxi driver and were hanged in July 1949. Clarke provides context for the murder by allowing George and Rue to reveal the brutality that is commonplace both in their family lives and in the communal life of Fredericton. In the poem "Public Enemy" Rue says:

> Fredtown was put up by Cadians, Coloureds,
> and hammers. Laws and lumber get made here.
> Bliss Carman got made here. Why should I put up with
> this hard-drinking, hard-whoring, hardscrabble town?
> I want to muck up their little white paradise here.
> I want to swat their faces til I'm comfortable in my gut.
> I want to give em all headaches and nausea:
> I'll play *fortissimo* Ellington, blacken icy whiteness.
> I'll draw blood the way Picasso draws nudes–
> voluptuously.

In "The Killing" George and Rue discuss the murder:

> *Rue:* Here's how I justify my error:
> The blow that slew Silver came from two centuries back.
> It took that much time and agony to turn a white man's
> 　　whip
> into a black man's hammer.

> *Geo:* No, we needed money,
> so you hit the So-and-So,
> only much too hard.
> Now what?

Execution Blues won the 2001 Governor General's Literary Award for Poetry. That same year Clarke was awarded the National Magazine Gold Medal for Poetry for poems published in the journal *Prairie Fire.*

Also in 2001 Clarke published *Blue,* a collection of poems he had written while living in the United States. The pieces are dedicated to, or composed in the styles of, writers such as Ovid, the Marquis de Sade, Ezra Pound, Colette, Claire Harris, André Alexis, Suzette Mayr, and Dionne Brand. In his introduction to the collection, "Turning Blue," Clarke writes about seeing these poems as left over from *Beatrice Chancy,* as poems that give voice to the villain of that play, and as poems that may be a reversal of the character X in *Whylah Falls,* who is a kind of anonymous, unembodied persona. He says, "I craved to draft lyrics that would pour out–Pentecostal fire–pell mell, scorching, bright, loud: a poetics of arson." In the section "Blue Elegies," poem "III. iii" ends,

> Listen: An unflinching clarity will issue in the only legitimate
> response: scabrous, scatological, flamboyantly raw poems.
> Our Saviour–Shakespeare–shakes these devils with his icy,
> cutting, unappeased hatred. My revanchism is simpler. When
> a riposte arrives, I cite D'Annunzio: *Me ne frego.*

Clarke explores the language of violence and violation in poems such as "Colette, Translated," the fourth stanza of which reads:

Let her sweet, vicious face sparkle:
I'll plug her with wine, then hit her,
Then peg her cute, puckered circle—
Invigilating a litre.

In the later sections of the book the theme of the poems shifts from violation to lamentation. "Ashen Blues" opens with the tragic poem "Elegy for Mona States (1958–1999)," in which the speaker says to his cousin: "At nine, we tussled and frolicked, golden, in hayfields, / Your yellow hair aflame and nerve-wracking as sunlight"; her voice "was like a silk scarf holding gravel." In the end, she has "broken your face with a bullet, / Smithereened your own da Vincian portrait." In a review for the on-line bookstore Poetry Spoken Here, Diana Brydon writes: "The poems in *Blue* burst with erudition, with explicit and implicit reference to sources he names at the beginning, and some he doesn't. He invokes, quotes, and in some cases challenges these sources with a grandeur that is thrilling—so engaged is he with his subjects and their matter, so exacting in his expectations of words, and of poetry's capacity to express both artistic and moral vision."

Clarke's groundbreaking *Odysseys Home: Mapping African-Canadian Literature* (2002) comprises twelve essays on universalism, nationalism, liberalism, and conservatism and includes an exhaustive bibliography of African Canadian literature. Clarke received the Martin Luther King Jr. Achievement Award from the Black Theatre Workshop of Montreal in 2004. In 2005 he received an honorary doctorate from the University of Alberta and the Pierre Elliott Trudeau Fellowship Prize, worth up to $225,000 over three years. Also in 2005 he published his first novel, *George and Rue*, which is organized around the symbols of whip, hammer, and rope and elaborates on the story he published in poetic form in *Execution Poems*. The work was nominated for many literary prizes and won the 2006 Dartmouth Book Award in fiction. Another 2005 publication was *Illuminated Verses*, which celebrates black women in Clarke's poetry and Ricardo Scipio's nude color photographs. In "II–CALYPSO" Clarke writes, "She be ebon to the bone, / a velvet poem, composed / of silent, indelible ink."

Clarke's poetry collection *Black* was published in 2006. In the introductory section, "BLACK *Power*," he states: "These poems are *black*, deviant, defiant. Inked in the shadow of *Blue* (2001), they also echo The Great Republic's gregarious rages." That same year Clarke was the recipient of the Order of Nova Scotia, the highest honor awarded by the province; the Poesis Premiul from *Poesis* magazine of Romania; and an honorary doctorate from the University of Waterloo. In 2007 he was granted a twenty-five-day residency at the International Writers' and Translators' Center of Rhodes in Greece and published the opera *Trudeau: Long March / Shining Path*, with music composed by D. D. Jackson, treating the life and times of Canada's fifteenth prime minister.

Bringing together history and fiction, complicating notions of honesty and lies, and striving to make sure that black voices are not silenced, George Elliott Clarke insists on beauty in his writing, no matter how painful the subject matter might be. His character Beatrice Chancy says, "I was dreaming, dreaming too much, / As if love could extinguish history," but Clarke refuses to extinguish history and prefers to rewrite it to include voices that were previously excluded from mainstream white versions.

Interviews:

Maureen Moynagh, "Mapping Africadia's Imaginary Geography: An Interview with George Elliott Clarke," *ARIEL: A Review of International English Literature*, 27 (October 1996): 71–94;

Anne Compton, "Standing Your Ground: George Elliot Clarke in Conversation," *Studies in Canadian Literature*, 23, no. 2 (1998): 138–164;

Christl Verduyn, "Opera in Canada: A Conversation: G. E. Clarke and Linda Hutcheon," *Journal of Canadian Studies*, 35 (Fall 2000): 184–198.

Dennis Cooley

(27 August 1944 –   )

Karen Clavelle
University of Manitoba

BOOKS: *Leaving* (Winnipeg: Turnstone, 1980);

Fielding (Saskatoon: Thistledown, 1983);

Bloody Jack (Winnipeg: Turnstone, 1984; revised and enlarged edition, Edmonton: University of Alberta Press, 2002);

Soul Searching (Red Deer, Alta.: Red Deer College, 1987);

The Vernacular Muse: The Ear and Eye in Contemporary Literature (Winnipeg: Turnstone, 1987);

Dedications (Saskatoon: Thistledown, 1988);

Perishable Light (Regina, Sask.: Coteau, 1988);

Eli Mandel and His Works (Downsview, Ont: Essays on Canadian Writing, 1992);

this only home (Winnipeg: Turnstone, 1992);

Burglar of Blood (Winnipeg: Pachyderm, 1992);

Goldfinger (Winnipeg: Staccato, 1995);

Sunfall: New and Selected Poems 1980–1996 (Concord, Ont.: Anansi, 1996);

Passwords: Transmigrations between Canada and Europe (Kiel: I & F Verlag, 1996; revised, 2000);

Irene (Winnipeg: Turnstone, 2000);

The Bentley Poems (Winnipeg: Pachyderm, 2000);

Seeing Red (Winnipeg: Turnstone, 2003);

Country Music: New Poems (Vernon, B.C.: Kalamalka Press, 2004);

the bentleys (Edmonton: University of Alberta Press, 2006).

OTHER: *RePlacing,* edited, with a contribution, by Cooley (Toronto: Essays on Canadian Writing, 1980);

Draft: An Anthology of Prairie Poetry, edited, with contribution, by Cooley (Winnipeg: Turnstone, 1981);

"Prairie / Sun / Earth: Livesay's Changing Selves," in *A Public and Private Voice: Essays on the Life and Works of Dorothy Livesay,* edited by Lindsay Dorney, Gerald Noonan, and Paul Tiessen (Waterloo, Ont.: University of Waterloo Press, 1986), pp. 107–125;

"Some Principles of Line Breaks," in *Trace: Prairie Writers on Writing,* edited by Birk Sproxton (Winnipeg: Turnstone, 1986), pp. 141–156;

Dennis Cooley (courtesy of the author)

"Fielding," "shapes of frost," "corvus brachyrhnchos," "by the red," "dear valentine," "day hardens," and "Travelling Back," in *Section Lines: A Manitoba Anthology,* edited by Mark Duncan, contribution by Cooley (Winnipeg: Turnstone, 1988), pp. 53–64;

Gabrielle Roy, *Garden in the Wind,* introduction by Cooley (Toronto: McClelland & Stewart, 1989);

"Notes on Birk Sproxton's *Headframe,*" in *Contemporary Manitoba Writers: New Critical Studies,* edited by Ken Hughes (Winnipeg: Turnstone, 1990), pp. 146–162;

Inscriptions: A Prairie Poetry Anthology, edited, with contributions, by Cooley (Winnipeg: Turnstone, 1992); "small light from our window," "that's it then isn't it," "me holding your hand holding back," "a certain muskiness a numbness," "never planned it this way," "the morning after," "don't you see philip don't you see," "by the gosh i just waltzed him," "look he says look at this," and "& you do you look up," in *Beyond Borders: An Anthology of New Writing from Manitoba, Minnesota, Saskatchewan, and the Dakotas,* edited by David Williamson and Mark Vinz, contribution by Cooley (Winnipeg: Turnstone, 1992), pp. 63–74;

"An Awful Stumbling Towards Names: Ross and the (Un)Common Noun," in *From the Heart of the Heartland: The Fiction of Sinclair Ross,* edited by John Moss, contribution by Cooley (Ottawa: University of Ottawa, 1992), pp. 103–124;

"This Mute Intransigent Place: Eli Mandel *In/Out of Place,*" in *The Politics of Art: Eli Mandel's Poetry and Criticism,* edited by Ed Jewinski and Andrew Stubbs (Amsterdam & Atlanta: Rodopi, 1992), pp. 93–103;

"Nearer by Far: The Upset 'I' In Margaret Atwood's Poetry," in *Margaret Atwood: Writing and Subjectivity,* edited by Colin Nicolson (New York: St. Martin's Press, 1994; London: Macmillan, 1994), pp. 68-93;

"a curse on a critic," in *Uncommon Wealth: An Anthology of Poetry in English,* edited by Neil Besner, Deborah Schnitzer, and Alden Turner (Toronto: Oxford University Press, 1997), pp. 651–652;

"Portuguese Journal 1995," in *New Worlds: Discovering and Constructing the Unknown in Anglophone Literature. Presented to Walter Pache on the Occasion of His 60th Birthday,* edited by Martin Kuester, Gabriel Christ, and Rudolf Beck (Munich: Ernst Vögel, 2000), pp. 381–391.

SELECTED PERIODICAL PUBLICATIONS– UNCOLLECTED:

POETRY

"12 Poems from *Love in a Dry Land,*" *West Coast Line,* 12 (1993–1994): 7–14;

"7 Selections from 'Love in a Dry Land,'" *Prairie Fire,* 14 (Winter 1995–1996): 22–27;

"the hospital" and "From the Portuguese Journal," *Prairie Fire,* 19 (Spring 1998): 8–14, 77–96;

"29 Poems from 'Love in a Dry Land,'" *It's Still Winter: A Web Journal of Contemporary Canadian Poetry and Poetics,* no. 5 (July 2002) <http://quarles.unbc.ca/winter/number_5.2/index.html> [accessed 3 January 2006].

NONFICTION

"Davey's Locker," *CVII,* 2, no. 2 (1975): 42–44;

"Keeping the Green: Robert Duncan's Pastoral Vision," *Capilano Review,* 8–9 (1975–1976): 368–386;

"Of That Time, of This Place," *CVII,* 3, no. 3 (1977): 26–27;

"Fire and Ice," *Arts Manitoba,* 1, no. 2 (1977): 70–71;

"to be clean as broken stone," *CVII,* 3, no. 3 (1977): 26–27;

"Uncovering Our Dream World: An Interview with Robert Kroetsch," by Cooley, Robert Enright, and David Arnason, *Arts Manitoba,* 1, no. 1 (1977): 32–39;

"There's This and That Connection," by Cooley, Enright, and Arnason, *CVII,* 3, no. 4 (1977): 28–33;

"Antimacassared in the Wilderness: Art and Nature in *The Stone Angel,*" *Mosaic,* 11, no. 3 (1978): 20–46;

"Double or Nothing: Eli Mandel's *Out of Place* and *Another Time,*" *Essays on Canadian Writing,* 10 (1978): 73–81;

"CanLit: Surrender or Revolution," *Canadian Dimension,* 3, no. 4 (1978): 48–51;

"Three Recent Tish Items," *Canadian Poetry,* 3 (Fall–Winter 1978): 92–102;

"Dennis Lee: Latter-Day Matthew Arnold in the Critical Fields," *Sphinx,* 3, no. 2 (1979): 60–67;

"Loss and Confusion," *Canadian Forum,* 59 (1980): 34–35;

"Robert Duncan's Green Worl(d)s," *Credences,* 8–9 (1980): 152–160;

"Robert Duncan's Poetics," *boundary 2,* 8, no. 2 (1980): 45–73;

"David Arnason Interview," *Föstudagur,* 20 (1981): 2–3;

"'we will try to act like human beings': Celestial Navigation as Anti-Authoritarian," *Malahat Review,* 83 (1988): 127–137;

"Matching the Word to the World," *Border Crossings,* 8, no. 4 (1989): 25–30;

"Recursions, Excursions and Incursions: Daphne Marlatt Wrestles with the Angel Language," *Line,* 13 (1989): 66–79;

"Essaying the Tangible Medium: Notes in the Technology of Writing," *Border Crossings,* 10, no. 4 (1991): 7–8;

"Reading Writing and a Rhythm Tick: Land and Language in Canadian Poetry," *ZAA: Zeitschrift für Anglistik und Amerikanistik,* 39, nos. 3–4 (1991): 262–275;

"The First Four Books," *Essays on Canadian Writing,* 45–46 (1991–1992): 37–66;

"The Ampersand in the Garden: Kroetsch and Impeded Narrative," *Open Letter,* ninth series, nos. 5–6 (1996): 93–114;

"From the Portuguese Journal," *New Quarterly*, 18, no. 1 (1998): 114–125;

"One Hundred Years of Manitoba Poetry: A Sketch," *Prairie Fire*, 20 (Winter 2000): 109–121;

"David Arnason's *Marsh Burning* and Other Stories," *Prairie Fire*, 22 (Spring 2001): 100–111.

Dennis Cooley is a humanist, poet, writer, editor, critic, teacher, mentor, and literary evangelist. His influence extends well beyond his students and colleagues at the University of Manitoba and the writing community of Winnipeg to the larger domain of the Canadian prairies and the Canadian and international literary communities.

Cooley was born in Estevan, Saskatchewan, on 27 August 1944, the second youngest of four children and the only son of Orin and Irene June Wilson Cooley. His parents were third-generation farmers in the Estevan area; his paternal and maternal grandparents had migrated there from Minnesota and Ontario, respectively, around the turn of the twentieth century.

In his 1989 autobiographical essay, "Matching the Word to the World," in the journal *Border Crossings*, Cooley recalls hearing his father and his uncle Walter Allison (the husband of his father's sister) speak of the hardships of the Great Depression and of playing baseball in Saskatchewan leagues in the 1930s and 1940s, and he attributes his own love of the game to them; baseball terminology plays a large part in both his poetry and his critical writing. Listening to radio broadcasts of the Reverend Tommy Douglas with his Grandmother Cooley raised Cooley's awareness of public speaking and introduced him to prairie socialism. Other voices, historical and fictional, that fired his imagination included nineteenth-century Métis rebel leader Louis Riel, Canadian prime minister John Diefenbaker, Alberta premier William Aberhart, and Saint Sammy in W. O. Mitchell's novel *Who Has Seen the Wind* (1947)—"fervent, outlandish, indignant, eloquent voices full of our yearning" that espouse the social values and down-to-earth honesty and decency of ordinary people. Those values, reinforced by his United Church upbringing, inform Cooley's work, and similar voices appear throughout his texts.

Cooley began writing at about eleven. He received encouragement from Doug Third, the principal of Hillside Public School, who was legendary both for his strictness and for his teaching ability. Cooley says in "Matching the Word to the World" that he "took to writing like a cow to corn," delivering dozens of pieces to Third. The writing "died off" in adolescence, but Cooley maintained his interest in the poetry of William Wordsworth: "Why Wordsworth I don't know, so far in his upland hermitage from the cindered and chickened yard, the rusted machinery and forests of ragweed on our farm. He snuck into my mind, so insinuated himself there, not even girls and basketball could quite keep him down."

The family lived on their farm northeast of Estevan until 1958, when Cooley's father took a job as a caretaker at a school in town. While attending high school at Estevan Collegiate, Cooley worked at the first supermarket in Estevan and later at a men's clothing store. He earned his university tuition with a job at the Estevan power plant.

Cooley enrolled at the University of Saskatchewan in 1962. He married Diane Sanderson in 1965. Cooley received a B.Ed. with distinction in 1966 and a B.A. with high honors in 1967. The University of Saskatchewan was one of the first in Canada to teach American and Canadian literature, but Cooley recalls that the "curriculum on the whole implied that poetry was written by dead Englishmen and sometimes, it seemed, for them." At the university, however, Cooley first heard of the poet Eli Mandel, who was also born and raised in Estevan. After earning his M.A. in 1968 with a thesis on Stephen Crane, Cooley received a Canada Council grant and a tuition scholarship to the University of Rochester in New York, where he taught freshman English while studying for his doctorate. He completed the degree in 1971 with a dissertation on the Black Mountain poet Robert Duncan. On his return to Canada he taught adult education in Estevan for a year. In 1972–1973 he worked for the Saskatchewan government as an administrative assistant.

In 1973 Cooley took a teaching position at St. John's College of the University of Manitoba, and the Cooley family, which by then included daughters Dana and Megan, moved to Winnipeg. There David Arnason, a professor whose influence on him Cooley describes as "huge," directed him away from American literature and the Romantics and toward the work of the Canadian Tish poets and bpNichol (pseudonym of Barrie Phillip Nichol). Arnason also introduced Cooley to the works of Canadian prairie writers; Cooley describes the effect on him of Margaret Laurence and Sinclair Ross as "powerful," and Ross's character Mrs. Bentley in *As for Me and My House* (1941) continues to inspire his poems. Other influences include the early-twentieth-century Canadian poets Raymond Knister, W. W. E. Ross, and Lawren Harris and writers of the 1970s such as Andrew Suknaski, Al Purdy, George Bowering, Douglas Barbour, and Michael Ondaatje. In 1975, as a founding editor of Turnstone Press, Cooley became involved in editing and publishing other people's work. Around 1977 he took on the challenge of writing his own poetry. Robert Kroetsch's long poem

Seed Catalogue (1977), which marked an important entry of the postmodern into Canadian poetics; characters such as Johnny Backstrom in his novel *Words of My Roaring* (1977); and his critical examinations of Canadian and prairie writing continue to inform Cooley's work.

In 1980 Cooley edited *RePlacing,* a collection of essays on prairie writing. In the introduction he identifies one of the main characteristics of prairie poets as the "use of the vernacular to speak of what they know in voices that are their own." The volume includes "A Checklist of Prairie Poetry in English" comprising "all titles of reasonably well-known writers produced mainly within the last ten years."

Also in 1980 Cooley published *Leaving,* a collection of ten of his own poems. In one of the poems, "Phoning," the use of words becomes a sensual and sexual act:

> I want to re
> lease the spell
> > spill the mute
> > jelly vowels lying
> > numb . . . and
> > small
> in the thick
> muscle of my heav
> y tongue
>
> would have them flail
>
> spinning across
> > thin mineral seas
> · · · · · · · · · · · · ·
> > > consonant
> sound in
> > > your heart's rising drum

Leaving includes the elegy "Fielding," which later evolved into a book-length poem of the same title. The subject of the poem, "you," is the lost father, grandfather, miner, baseball player, and sunburned farmer who settled the Canadian prairies in the 1930s, 1940s, and 1950s. He is connected to time and place by cultural "markers" such as the 1955 Massey Fergeson tractor, Hank Snow, Gene Autry, and the Orpheum movie theater and Canada Café in Estevan.

In 1981 Cooley edited *Draft,* an anthology of prairie poetry, as a companion volume to *RePlacing.* The enlarged version of *Fielding* appeared two years later. The poem opens with a definition from the *Oxford English Dictionary:*

> silent (si/lent) adj. [L. *silens* <prp. Of silere, to be silent, still, prop. <IE. Base *sei-, *si-, to rest, to let the hand fall, whence
> SEED, SIDE, Goth. *(ana)silan,* to cease (of the wind)]

That quotation is followed by one from the German existentialist philosopher Martin Heidegger: *"What is spoken is never, and in no language, what is said."* In *Fielding* Cooley's speaker searches for a sense of place in a series of journeys back and forth across the prairies between Estevan, Winnipeg, and Regina and across time. *Fielding* includes references to pastoral elegy, elegiac Old English verse, and seventeenth- and nineteenth-century elegy; it is informed by the elegies of John Milton, Percy Bysshe Shelley, and Walt Whitman and, especially, by Ezra Pound's *Pisan Cantos* (1949). Cooley employs unmetered lines, consonance and assonance, alliteration, variable numbers of unstressed syllables in a line, and compound words evocative of Old English verse. He imports into the text documents such as news headlines, a death certificate, a weather report, a transcript of a Canadian Broadcasting Corporation radio clip, and a child's letter. The transitoriness of such documents contrasts with the high solemnity of elegies such as Milton's *Lycidas* (1637) and Shelley's *Adonais* (1821). Milton and Shelley, drawing on the pastoral elegies of ancient poets such as Virgil, open their poems with an invocation to the muse; Cooley also invokes a muse, but with a distinctly postmodern turn: in *Fielding* the primary muses are silence and language, and a secondary muse is the mythological Orpheus entering the underworld. In keeping with the tradition of pastoral elegy, the poem represents both the poet and the one he mourns: the speaker's father is the metaphorical Orpheus who leads the protagonist to experience but not to consolation.

In 1984 Cooley published *Bloody Jack,* a postmodernist mock epic about the Manitoba outlaw John Krafchenko, who was hanged for murder in 1914. Endeavoring to restore the oral tradition in print form, he makes the pages "noisy" or "quiet" by using several typefaces and allowing the words to occupy the page in varying densities. Written in the spirit of such postmodernist poems as Ondaatje's *The Collected Works of Billy the Kid* (1970), Nichol's *Captain Poetry Poems* (1972), Kroetsch's *Seed Catalogue,* and Arnason's *Marsh Burning* (1980), *Bloody Jack* includes letters, anecdotes, gossip, newspaper articles, police reports, country-and-western songs, critical reviews, an IOU, a parody of a dictionary, musical scores, and a court document. The four texts that make up the work are fragments rather than sustained narratives. The preface includes four epigraphs: quotations from the literary theorists Julia Kristeva and Roland Barthes and from Bloody Jack himself and Ondaatje's Billy the Kid. The Ondaatje quotation, "Not a story about me through their eyes then," indicates that Jack and Billy are fictional constructs rather than real-life individuals and that the real subject of both works is poetry itself, not Jack Krafchenko or William Bonney. Cooley draws his read-

Paperback cover for the first edition, 1983 (Bruccoli Clark Layman Archives)

ers into participating in the construction and deconstruction of the book as joint creators in complicity with the poet. For example, in the text "Description of Krafchenko," Jack is fluent in six languages, a machinist, and an engineer; but this account is incongruous with the description derived from local gossip reported in "the oral tradition," in which an anonymous witness claims that Krafchenko "Couldn't write a single word. Couldn't read neither." The text "that fateful day" invites overt participation by being cast in "fill-in-the-blanks" form. Finally, comparing the appendix of the book to the visceral organ of the human body, Cooley writes,

> Perhaps, dear reader, you would like to remove this appendix. Go ahead, just cut
> it out. . . . Perhaps, if you are lucky, you will nick Cooley's conscience, his mind
> there on the margins, in the gutter. Go ahead. Take it out on him.

He thus brings to the fore the reader's role in the creation of the work and raises the question of where the

book actually ends. *Bloody Jack* evoked a violently negative response from one reviewer, Kathy Kolybaba, in *Border Crossings* (Fall 1985). As the titles of several of the reviews indicate, *Bloody Jack* provoked bewildered and irritated reactions from other reviewers, among them John Donlan in "The Road of Excess" (*Contemporary Verse II,* Spring 1986), Terry Goldie in "Cooleying It in a Deconstructed World" (*NeWest Review,* February, 1986), and Peter Barker in "Wanting Magic" (*Prairie Fire,* Winter 1988–1989). Bill Brydon seems to have wanted nothing less than truth in the clearly fictionalized prairie long poem (*Canadian Book Review Annual,* 1985). On the other hand, the headline for Ken Adachi's review in *The Toronto Star* (18 March 1985) declared "Prairie Poet's *Bloody Jack* a major work," and the review announced the arrival of a major new poet. In *Prairie Fire* (Winter 1988–1989) Lesley Petersen wrote that Cooley was "rehabilitating the male love poem," whereas Karl Jirgens in *Canadian Literature* (Summer 1986) admired Cooley's "Sleight of Hand" in *Bloody Jack.* Don Kerr in *Journal of Canadian Poetry* (1986) recognized the energy, enthusiasm, and generosity of the book, in which he found "the sound of the prairie talking to itself." Kenneth James Hughes in *NeWest Review* (November 1986) understood Cooley's impulse to "remind the reader that texts are at once powerful political acts and human constructions" in which there is room for reader participation. The most sustained critical response to *Bloody Jack* to date is Douglas Barbour's introduction to the revised and enlarged edition, published in 2002. Barbour writes that Cooley "shares with Ondaatje an interest in using documents in order to subvert the apparently solid reality they represent, and does so in *Bloody Jack* with an almost terrifying energy and savage delight." Barbour argues that Cooley's text raises the fundamental question of what poetry is or should be. *Bloody Jack* has moved from critical rejection through acceptance to the cusp of canonization.

Influenced by Walter Ong, Cooley argues in the essays collected in *The Vernacular Muse: The Ear and Eye in Contemporary Literature* (1987) for a knowledgeable response to speech-influenced twentieth-century postmodern poetry. In the introduction he differentiates between "ear poetry," which draws on spoken language and "abides by whatever sorts of rhymes—alliteration, emphatic repetitions in morphology, and puns (homonyms)—situate themselves in spoken language," and "eye poetry," which is based in "imagist, metaphoric, or expressive precepts that situate themselves in written language." In Cooley's opinion, one type of poetry neither precludes nor is superior to the other. In the essay "Placing the Vernacular: The Eye and Ear in Saskatchewan Poetry" he champions vernacular writing for the vibrancy it infuses as it "enacts roles, presents selves (plural rather than singular in its loyalties), rhetorically appeals to some audience, real or imagined. Imploring, scolding, teasing, begging, cajoling, exhorting, praying—the vernacular addresses someone and seeks to act on an audience." Cooley opens the essay "Breaking and Entering (Thoughts on Line Breaks)" with a poem comprising broken lines of varying lengths and words and phrases split in the process of breaking the lines. The altering of the words frees them from their limiting, print-imposed meanings. He notes that writers such as Mandel, Margaret Atwood, e. e. cummings, and Charles Olson show in their innovative line breaks what can be done with wordplay and physical limits, breath units, tentativeness, speech models, syntactic ambiguity, and visual effects. The remaining essays in *The Vernacular Muse* comprise critical discussions of Laurence, Duncan, Sinclair Ross, Ondaatje, and Dorothy Livesay. In his concluding statement in *The Vernacular Muse* Cooley focuses on "the reader as raider" and challenges the reader to be aware of his or her position in the text:

> Think where this puts the reader. Puts you off? Where it puts the poem. The poet. We set in motion a new series of relations. Realizations. When the new poem comes on line.
>
> A radical de-centering. Away / a way from the poet as prophet. No more metaphor moses. We witness the migration of authority from author to reader. Unauthorized entries, entreaties. "Oh where are you going" said reader to writer, said reader to writing. No treaties—an agnostic relationship. Reader as hero, breaking and entering.

Cooley's poetry collection *Soul Searching* appeared in 1987. Evocative of Milton's fallen archangels and the souls in Dante's *Inferno,* Cooley's feisty and rebellious souls are rude, outraged, lustful, greedy, manipulative, grim little "buggers." The poems seek to unseat the age-old hierarchy in which the soul is superior to the body. "Pale Horse, Pale Rider" brings the Apocalypse to twentieth-century America. "Burnt Out" hints at laxness in the soul's stewardship of the earth and juxtaposes the temporal nature of the universe with the human tendency to take daily life as a constant:

> star stutter of sperm
>   squirms like new freckles
> a tickle in god's throat
> · · · · · · · · · · · · · · · ·
>
>   shouts
>   dying out
>
>   so we sit & listen
>   to the measly silence of god
> his laryngitis
>   just shining
>   & shining
>   all the night long

"Body Parts" depicts a graveyard of salvaged auto-body parts managed by Mike, Gabe, and Pete,

twentieth-century versions of Milton's rebel angels. The poem evokes Golgotha and parodies the practice of grave robbing in nineteenth-century Europe. The black humor turns poignant at the end of the poem:

>   Pete *hes working*
> *for the Man* crams all the stuff
> into a big bag of skin
> · · · · · · · · · · · · · · · ·
> something's left out weve left
> something behind back there
> where broken bodies are stripped
> down & where hearts leak
> all over the floor.

Another poem, "Where It All Got Started," is a parody of the opening of the Book of Genesis.

Dedicated to Mandel, *Dedications* (1988) is a collection of poems about Cooley's family, friends, and colleagues; poets; baseball; and Estevan. In "estevan fair" the speaker recalls "the diesels in smoke and smoke smoking," "the midway the rub of neon husky / on spatters of cotton / spotting onto jeans into pockets / the young farmstrong thighs the sweet whisper of blood," "& yes lights yes silver breathing brightness breathing / ether swaths of ether into the night air shaking." Other poems in *Dedications* similarly fuse personal history with place and demonstrate Cooley's skill with the vernacular. In almost every book Cooley includes one piece that pays homage to early English verse: "now that aprylle's here" is his dedication both to the prairie spring and the historic form.

Many of the poems in the collection *Perishable Light* (1988) focus on place; for example, "on the way to estevan (thanksgiving, 1985)":

> this is our country
> it is here we tap in
> put our eager ear
> to the ground
> · · · · · · · · · ·
>
> this is our country
> it is here we fall
>   into place.

The phrases "this is our country" and "it is here we fall / into place" suggest the fall from innocence into knowledge from the biblical Garden of Eden. Seeds fall into place not randomly but into the "lines" in the furrows for which they are destined; similarly, words fall into lines and into place. In the poem "on the way to estevan"

thistles in ditches
    wait with dirt of the thirties
 silent
as children   when they listen
    in winds
on water   from run off
        of sun   & sounds
    trapped
  as march is
  in pails of winter

and weed seeds auger
in furrows of brains.

In the poem "prairie romance" the prairie "dawn comes / on rubber tires / in bull low / a grain truck growling / up the sky." The "sun / galloping across the 1:30 news" surrenders to "night when / the light / drops out / a wrecked transmission / spilling oil."

During the 1980s Cooley participated in cross-border literary events, organized conferences, and edited manuscripts for students, colleagues, and members of the community, as well as for Turnstone Press and *Border Crossings.* He also gave talks and workshops in high schools; judged writing contests; served as vice president, president, and committee member of the Manitoba Writers' Guild and as a juror for the Canada Council; gave radio and television interviews; and served on various committees at his college and university. In addition to his books, he published dozens of essays and poems in literary magazines. A literary conference at the University of Trier in Germany in 1989 led in 1990 to his becoming the first visiting professor of Canadian studies at that university. In the 1990s he gave more than eighty talks and scores of readings in Canada, Germany, France, Spain, Portugal, Poland, Ukraine, Russia, Hungary, the United Kingdom, and the United States.

In 1992 Cooley published the monograph *Eli Mandel and His Works* and edited *Inscriptions: A Prairie Poetry Anthology.* That same year he also published *this only home,* a book of poems inspired by the "breathtaking" and "stunning" photographic images of Earth from space and the tender and yearning accounts of Russian cosmonauts of the "lives they looked back to across the blackness" of space. The poems in *this only home* expand the regional ecological concerns of *Perishable Light* to the entire planet. The speaker is struck with wonder at the fragility of "earth inside its thin bubble / breathing / so thin you gasp in terror." For the cosmonauts, home is poignantly out of reach, and their worries and anxieties touch on the most fundamental of human fears: becoming disconnected. In "Annie" the speaker laments, "I cannot read / or write / home to you"; the speaker of "east of Eden" declares, "we do not want to be homeless / adams whirling in space / exiles from the garden"; and the speaker of "impaled on a trajectory" is "sick of heart for home / our hearts full of it."

Also in 1992 Cooley published *Burglar of Blood,* a small collection of poems in which Dracula serves as a metaphor for poetry. Cooley's Burglar moves from burgling bodies and their banks of blood in London to burgling bodies of authoritative discourse and their banks of words on the Canadian prairies. In *Burglar of Blood* language is all-powerful; belief in words yields salvation from the barren prairie. The Burglar is grave robber, necrophile, and savior:

burglar of salvation the seventh seal busted
before the distant and distinct roar
the city, suspurration in its great heart
I come as doctor, would relieve the pressure
a little loyal bleeding, it's a good thing for the realm
you should spend some time on me
to redeem currency it's a holy thing I do.

In 1995 Cooley taught at the University of Augsburg. That same year he published *Goldfinger,* a collection of postmodern rewritings of such fairy tales as Rumpelstiltskin, Snow White, The Frog Prince, Hansel and Gretel, and Jack and the Beanstalk in which the male characters are depicted as caring, vulnerable, and longing for love. In "two thirds of the sun," based on Sleeping Beauty, the speaker's mission is to hack his way through overgrowths of thorn and free the "briar girl" with an awakening kiss. Cooley's hero faces the grim prospect of touching a body "frog-belly white" with "stains all over her face," but he fulfills his task. In "the lost children" Cooley deconstructs the tale of Hansel and Gretel.

In 1996 Cooley published *Sunfall: New and Selected Poems 1980–1996. Sunfall* includes "police informer" and "every year my dad drew lines," popular favorites from his public readings, and "a curse on a critic," a parody of Alexander Pope's *Dunciad* (1728) in which he appeals for more open-mindedness among literary critics. *Sunfall* also includes several poems from Cooley's mostly unpublished collection "Love in a Dry Land," a body of work inspired by the unnamed diarist of *As for Me and My House.* These lyric poems visit sites of love, loss, and longing on the Canadian prairies. Cooley's elegy to his mother, who died on 26 December 1990, describes a photograph:

there is a small boy five maybe four he is dressed in
darkness he is wearing brown rayon pants & shirt to
match his mother has just bought
. . . .

there is sun in his eyes
where you stand in front of the sun
you have disappeared into over
—exposed to time & the picture they never took of you

you went into the picture
before they fell out of your hands
& you were dissolving
turning to light, losing your shadow.

Metalinguistic pieces in *Sunfall* include "every spring my mother poked spring"; "every year my dad drew lines"; "thats an oh oh," a response to Lorna Crozier's "Onion" in *The Garden Going on without Us* (1985); and "a series of shocking pre-positions & afterwords."

Finally, in 1996 Cooley also published *Passwords: Transmigrations between Canada and Europe,* which evolved out of a journal he began at the University of Trier on 27 April 1990. At the beginning of the book the speaker, in transit himself, uses migrating geese as a metaphor for the instinctive human drive to write. Somewhat later the speaker mocks "the mad egomania of the journal":

I! I! I! I! I! I! I! I! I! It shouts, all it can think a-bout, I, I, I, I, all the way home, All it wants to say—I I I I I. I said, I thought, I saw, I went, I ate. All it wants to talk about is itself. Aie aie aie, my dad would have said.

In *Passwords* Cooley continues his metalinguistic interests by looking for words' potential for multiple meanings: he presses German for puns, which are rare in that language. He honors literary forebears from Homer through John Donne; George Gordon, Lord Byron; Wordsworth; and Mandel. The poems about Dracula and Mrs. Bentley that are threaded through *Passwords* are examples of Cooley's characteristic engagement in dialogue with other writers.

In 1998 Robert Budde and Deborah Keahey edited a special Cooley issue of *Prairie Fire.* In the introduction they refer to the "'Cooleyesque' kind of tone, an odd blend of tender play and mock outrage." Birk Sproxton's contribution, "Dennis Cooley and the Canadian Love Song," considers Cooley's "reputation as a poet and theorist of the vernacular" and notes that "critics and theorists continue to turn to, and argue with his major work of criticism to date, *The Vernacular Muse.*" Sproxton writes that Cooley has consistently made "forceful and effective arguments concerning the importance of place in writing and writing in place" and "consistently places work from the prairie west within national and international contexts and within current theoretical debates about reading and writing in general." In "That Cooley: Vernacular Poetics" Ray Wilton

Paperback cover for the first edition, 1984 (Bruccoli Clark Layman Archives)

draws attention to Cooley's adamant opposition to "the privileging of any one mode of discourse" and his championing of "those who are devalued by such privileging."

In 2000 Cooley published his second book-length elegy, *Irene.* The father in *Fielding* is Orpheus transported to the south Saskatchewan prairie; *Irene* uses the myth of Persephone, the lost woman taken from her garden to the underworld. Both works are informed by the elegies of Milton, Shelley, Whitman, and Pound; unlike those elegies, however, and like *Fielding, Irene* resists consolation. In *Irene,* as in the Persephone myth, the silence of winter and death might be considered broken with the reappearance of purple flowers; but the speaker in *Irene* understands the fundamental difference between the two narratives: in the myth there is consolation in Persephone's seasonal return; in *Irene* there is "a woman, passing / in this poem there is / a woman / passing."

Irene demonstrates Cooley's metalinguistic concerns more subtly than does *Fielding*. In *Fielding* words fail the speaker, but the silence in *Irene* is even more bleak:

```
        memory dropping off
    all the words worn away
          the letters too silent
    that mark your box of dust
                  the whole world itself burnt
    past recognition before it began

            there is nothing
            past where it began
        there is nothing
                to say
            when you are dead to say
                        you are dead
        you are dead.
```

Also in 2000 Cooley published *The Bentley Poems*, responses to Ross's unfulfilled preacher's wife in *As for Me and My House* selected from the "Love in a Dry Land" poems. In this collection loneliness and sustained longing are as much a part of the prairie existence as crows, grain elevators, and deserted towns. *The Bentley Poems* refers to prairie institutions of the 1930s such as "Rawleigh's Medicated Ointment" and the community dance and describes the prairie winter "cracking / the panes / open with ice / sun in branches." Near the end of the collection the speaker says:

```
    i leave my heart where its skipped
    a beat our bodies eat
    letters laid in the grass like ancient runes
    distant skirl of bagpipes their terrible
    grief & longing
    loving the feel of the words in my mouth.
```

In 2003 Cooley published *Seeing Red,* a collection of poems in which Dracula is the object of willing victims' affection; the greatest object of affection, however, is poetry itself. The following year he published *Country Music.* John Lent remarks in his introduction to the collection that "Cooley is inviting the reader to listen to a different kind of music, surrender to the rhythms and complexities of jazz, say, after only being exposed to the more formal rhythms and complexities of classical music." This new music, Lent notes, is "closer to the physical and psychological rhythms of our day to day lives." In one sequence Cooley combines the Garden-of-Eden motif and the Bentley material: "me ms. Bentley a bent rib." Later in the same sequence he addresses the biblical Adam: "Listen Mr. Adam I would say / I would have to / give the devil his dew." Formally, Cooley explores the visual effects of using various type-faces and placements of words on the page, and he emphasizes the oral qualities of the language he uses.

Country Music is a collection of poems from "Love in a Dry Land," to which *The Bentley Poems* has become a prelude. In his introduction Cooley describes the "semantically intense, sinuous and irregular" pieces as poems that "allow room for eye, and room for the reader's psyche to enter, engage, come up for breath, and re-enter them." In another introduction to the book Craig McLuckie likens Cooley to "a seasoned old jazz pianist refining his 'chops,'" in that, like a musician, Cooley shifts fields "from classical composition . . . to the more open fields of notation developed by jazz musicians." Many of the poems exploit the written word in the manner of musical improvisation, as when a description of the mundane household activity of washing dishes takes a sudden turn to the sensual image of freckles and fine hair on skin and an equally surprising turn to sounds connected with feeding the dog:

```
    dishes clink and rattle the soft sound
    soap makes when they move your arms
          warm to their freckles
        the fine hair on your neck
    scrape scrape scrape 'mere pal
    smell of fried potatoes 'mon boy
                whh whhw whh
    click click click his feet say
```

The poems in *the bentleys* (2006) also belong to "Love in a Dry Land," of which *Country Music* is the first substantial published segment. The poems in *the bentleys* are loosely derived from the characters in *As for Me and My House* and find in the prairies a sense of the sublime:

```
    what this must have been once a vast
    just a fox came through and forever
    huge world so impossibly large
    buffalo and mosquitoes stampeded into never
```

In his oeuvre Dennis Cooley forges an indigenous lyricism that is appropriate to his time and place. He has taken on the project of resuscitating, renewing, and invigorating poetry.

Interviews:

Daniel S. Lenoski, "Voicing Prairie Space: Dennis Cooley Interviewed on *Bloody Jack*," *Line,* 7–8 (1986): 166–183;

Michael Bonar, "In Many Ways . . . An Interview with Dennis Cooley," *Essays on Canadian Writing,* 41 (1990): 1–15;

Herbert Zirker, "Di Brandt & Dennis Cooley: Interview-Readings," in his *Selected Essays in English Literatures, British and Canadian: Jonathan*

Swift, John Fowles, Margaret Laurence, Margaret Atwood, Di Brandt & Dennis Cooley (Frankfurt am Main & New York: Peter Lang, 2002), pp. 131–161;

Robert Budde, "Dennis Cooley: Dreaming His Way into the World," in his *In Muddy Water: Conversations with 11 Poets* (Winnipeg: J. Gordon Shillingford, 2003), pp. 103–122.

References:

Debbie D'Aoust, "Decentering the Text: Transgression and Dialogue in Dennis Cooley's *Bloody Jack*," in *Contemporary Manitoba Writers,* edited by Kenneth J. Hughes (Winnipeg: Turnstone, 1990), pp. 131–145;

Frank Davey, "A Young Boy's Eden," in *Reading Canadian Reading* (Winnipeg: Turnstone, 1988), pp. 213–229;

Deborah Keahey, *Making It Home: Place in Canadian Prairie Literature* (Winnipeg: University of Manitoba Press, 1998), pp. 86–94;

Robert Kroetsch, *A Likely Story* (Red Deer, Alta.: Red Deer College Press, 1995), pp. 66–82;

Kroetsch, *The Lovely Treachery of Words* (Winnipeg: Turnstone, 1989), p. 191;

Robert James Merrett, "Violence, Ecology, and Political Sense in Recent Canadian Poetry," *Queen's Quarterly,* 92–93 (1985): 509–523;

W. H. New, *Land Sliding: Imagining Space, Presence, and Power in Canadian Writing* (Toronto: University of Toronto Press, 1997), pp. 177–178, 195–196, 203;

Prairie Fire, special Cooley issue, edited by Keahey and Robert Budde, 19 (Spring 1998);

Laurie Ricou, *Literary History of Canada,* second edition, volume 4, edited by New (Toronto: University of Toronto Press, 1990), pp. 6, 33–34;

Andrew Stubbs, "Dennis Cooley," in *Canadian Writers and Their Works: Poetry Series,* volume 12, edited by Robert Lecker and Margery Fee (Toronto: ECW Press, 1996), pp. 19–124.

Douglas Coupland

(30 December 1961 –)

Jordan Stouck
University of Lethbridge

BOOKS: *Generation X: Tales for an Accelerated Culture* (New York: St. Martin's Press, 1991; London: Abacus, 1996);

Shampoo Planet (New York: Simon & Schuster, 1992; London: Simon & Schuster, 1993);

Life after God (New York: Pocket Books, 1994; London: Simon & Schuster, 2004);

Microserfs (New York & Toronto: HarperCollins, 1995; London: Flamingo, 1995);

Polaroids from the Dead (New York & Toronto: HarperCollins, 1996; London: Flamingo, 1996);

Girlfriend in a Coma (New York & Toronto: HarperCollins, 1998; London: Flamingo, 1998);

Lara's Book: Lara Croft and the Tomb Raider Phenomenon, by Courtland, Kip Ward, and others (Rocklin, Cal.: Prima, 1998);

Miss Wyoming (Toronto: Random House Canada, 1999; New York: Pantheon, 1999; London: Flamingo, 2000);

City of Glass: Douglas Coupland's Vancouver (Vancouver: Douglas & MacIntyre, 2000);

All Families Are Psychotic (Toronto: Random House Canada, 2001; New York: Bloomsbury, 2001; London: Flamingo, 2001);

Kami wa Nihon o nikunderu / God Hates Japan (Tokyo: Kadokawa Shoten, 2001);

Souvenir of Canada (Vancouver: Douglas & MacIntyre, 2002);

Encounters: School Spirit, by Coupland and Pierre Huyghe (Paris: Dis voir, 2002);

Hey Nostradamus! A Novel (Toronto: Random House Canada, 2003; New York: Bloomsbury, 2003; London: Flamingo, 2003);

Souvenir of Canada 2 (Vancouver: Douglas & McIntyre, 2004);

Eleanor Rigby: A Novel (Toronto: Random House Canada, 2004; New York: Bloomsbury, 2004; London: Fourth Estate, 2004);

Terry: Terry Fox and His Marathon of Hope (Vancouver: Douglas & McIntyre, 2005);

Douglas Coupland (photograph by D. J. Weir; from Jpod, *2006; Richland County Public Library)*

Jpod: A Novel (Toronto: Random House Canada, 2006; New York: Bloomsbury, 2006; London: Flamingo, 2006);

A Douglas Coupland Reader (E-text)*, edited by Robert G. May (Kingston: Queen's University, 2006) <http://post.queensu.ca/~mayr/Comp%20Coupland.pdf> (accessed 13 February 2007).

PLAY PRODUCTION: *September 10, 2001,* Stratford-on-Avon, U.K., The Other Place, 10 October 2004.

PRODUCED SCRIPT: *Everything's Gone Green,* motion picture, First Independent Pictures, 2006.

OTHER: *The Vancouver Stories: West Coast Fiction from Canada's Best Writers,* introduction by Coupland (Vancouver: Raincoast Books, 2005);

Peter York, *Dictator Style: Lifestyles of the World's Most Colorful Despots,* foreword by Coupland (San Francisco: Chronicle Books, 2006).

SELECTED PERIODICAL PUBLICATIONS–UNCOLLECTED: "Reverse Time Capsule," *Wired,* 3 (April 1995): 17;

"Clone, Clone on the Range," *Time,* 149 (10 March 1997): 74–75;

"A Message from Doug," *Vancouver Magazine* (January–February 2000);

"Strong and Free," *Maclean's,* 115 (25 November 2002): 22–26.

"Either our lives become stories, or there's just no way to get through them," says a character in Douglas Coupland's highly acclaimed first novel, *Generation X: Tales for an Accelerated Culture* (1991). The search for meaning in a capitalist and often amoral society is the central theme of Coupland's fiction. Since the publication of *Generation X,* Coupland's writings have explored diverse scenarios for constructing personal meaning in late-twentieth- and early-twenty-first-century North America, where traditional belief systems no longer apply and where corporations market ideals and lifestyles rather than mere products. Coupland's first novel resulted in his being hailed as the voice of "generation X," people born in the early 1960s to the early 1970s, and earned him a reputation for astute cultural observation and formal experimentation. In his subsequent novels and short stories he uses irony and postmodernist pastiche to criticize the materialism of contemporary society while searching for meaningful alternatives. Most critics continue to praise his original descriptions of modern life and his brilliant one-liners, but some find his writing style facile and limited. John Burns argued in the 2 August 2003 *Globe and Mail* (Toronto), Coupland's work presents "a lifelong moral quest" for meaning in a globalized world that has moved beyond the once-defining narratives of history and religion.

Coupland was born on 30 December 1961 on a Canadian Air Force base in Baden-Söllingen, Germany, the third of four children—all sons—of Dr. Douglas Charles Thomas and C. Janet Campbell Coupland. In 1965 the family moved to Vancouver. Coupland studied sculpture at the Emily Carr College of Art and Design; after graduating in 1984, he completed a two-year course in Japanese business science in Hawaii and worked briefly in Tokyo. He held his first solo sculpture exhibition at the Vancouver Art Gallery in 1987, and he continues to show his work nationally and internationally. In 1990 he began writing articles on art and lifestyles for magazines and journals in Vancouver. The following year he published *Generation X,* which became a best-seller in Canada and the United States and, according to John Fraser in *Saturday Night* (March 1994), established Coupland as "the self-wrought oracle of our age."

In *Generation X,* Claire, Dag, and Andy, the narrator, three friends in their late twenties, abandon their lives as entry-level corporate drones and move to Palm Springs "to tell stories and to make our own lives worthwhile tales in the process." There they work at "McJobs," Coupland's term for low-paying, low-prestige, low-dignity, no-future jobs in the service sector that are "Frequently considered a satisfying career choice by people who have never held one." Haunted by visions of nuclear apocalypse and resentful of previous generations for polluting the earth, the three share "bedtime stories" as they attempt to make their "small lives on the periphery" of late-twentieth-century society meaningful. Andy, Claire, and Dag finally abandon all traces of corporate America for Mexico, where they plan to open a hotel on the beach for "friends and eccentrics only" and allow people who tell good stories to stay for free. The novel ends ambiguously: on their way to Mexico, Andy experiences a moment of true meaning when he is grazed by a white egret and embraced by a group of mentally retarded teenagers.

Generation X is credited with defining a generation in terms of what Coupland calls "lessness," a philosophy according to which "one reconciles oneself to diminishing expectations." Coupland has described the characters in the novel as marginal people who wish to be recognized as part of a larger whole, and the notion of marginalization is reinforced by illustrations and slogans in the margins of the book. Ryan Moore argues that the "aggressive indifference" of Coupland's characters conceals a longing for community and emotional fulfillment. These characters confront the fact that traditional religious narratives are no longer meaningful in North American culture, yet the need for meaning remains. Set in the desert of Palm Springs, the novel recalls the journey of the Israelites into the desert in search of the promised land, as well as the desert quests of Jesus and John the Baptist. Andy's epiphany at the end suggests a religious experience constructed out of personally meaningful symbols rather than orthodox ones.

The publication of *Generation X* coincided with the release of the movie *Slacker* and the rise of the grunge-music movement in Seattle. These three phenomena were seized on by marketing executives, and *Generation X,* a work that criticizes materialist culture, became identified with advertising campaigns that sold beer, clothes, and concerts by appealing to generation X's supposed trademark irony.

In 1992 Coupland began writing regularly for *The New Republic* and *The New York Times* and published his second novel, *Shampoo Planet,* which deals with the group of young adults who follow generation X: the "global teens" born in the early to mid 1970s who approach consumer culture with a more optimistic, if mercenary, attitude than their predecessors. The protagonist, Tyler Johnson, was born on a hippie commune in British Columbia and lives with his divorced mother, Jasmine, who still clings to the hippie lifestyle. Tyler rejects that ethos and desires nothing more than a job in the Northern California high-tech sector. His extensive collection of hair-care products reveals his participation in the consumer culture as well as his acceptance of marketing slogans such as "What's on top of your head says what's inside your head." Tyler's grandparents, once literally engineers of American capitalism but now broke, recoup their assets through a pyramid scheme, the KittyWhip Kat Food System. "Old people will always win," Tyler notes, "the system is absolutely rigged in their favour." But the federal authorities swoop in, and Tyler's grandparents wind up "with nothing to show for it except a heap of consumer durables," which now includes many boxes of cat food. Alongside the anticapitalist humor, *Shampoo Planet* offers a more serious lament for the land that is devastated by industrialization: Tyler and his girlfriend, Anna-Louise, drive to Canada to reconnect with nature, only to discover that the forest has been clear-cut. Instead of the ancient ecological system that they expected, they find only "generations of bleeding orange tree rings." They return home to Lancaster, California, the site of "the Plants," the world's largest producer of hazardous chemicals. Tyler recalls the "Most Misshapen Potato" contests of his youth and the vocabulary of "hip high-tech" words that the Plants gave the citizens of Lancaster. The Plants' environmental destruction becomes the subject of a government clean-up project, and Tyler's sister and brother-in-law must go to work to detoxify the soil surrounding their home. At the end of the novel Tyler wins his dream job with a scheme to market the past in a chain of HistoryWorld™ amusement parks where customers can find "instant history" while recycling consumer waste. Critics, and Coupland himself, have stressed the hopeful message in *Shampoo Planet.*

Life after God, a collection of short stories published in 1994, explores loss of faith. The narrator of the final story, "1,000 Years (Life after God)," summarizes the problem:

> Life was charmed but without politics or religion. It was the life of children of the children of the pioneers—life after God—a life of earthly salvation on the edge of heaven. Perhaps this is the finest thing to which we may aspire, the life of peace, the blurring between dream life and real life—and yet I find myself speaking these words with a sense of doubt. . . .

> I think the price we paid for our golden life was an inability to fully believe in love; instead we gained an irony that scorched everything it touched. And I wonder if this irony is the price we paid for the loss of God.

The story traces the lives of seven friends from their teenage years, spent floating in "pools the temperature of blood" and "pretending to be fetuses," through the inevitable disappointments and losses of life, to the narrator's final realization that he needs God. "1,000 Years (Life after God)" concludes with the narrator's baptism. Other stories explore defining moments of loss, including the loss of childish illusions, the loss of a first love, divorce, and the death of a family member. In "The Wrong Sun" the voices of the dead recount their memories of the nuclear apocalypse in which they died. The narrator of "In the Desert" becomes lost and is eventually guided in the right direction by a God-like enigmatic stranger. "Little Creatures" questions the process of creation. Bird imagery pervades the collection; as the narrator of "Things That Fly" states, "birds are a miracle because they prove to us there is a finer, simpler state of being which we may strive to attain."

Reviewers, expecting Coupland's typical witticisms and ironic observations on contemporary life, had mixed responses to the collection. In *Books in Canada* (April 1994) Rita Donovan criticized the initial stories as incomplete and undeveloped, but she, like Guy Mannes-Abbott in the *New Statesman and Society* (29 July 1994), praised the final three narratives as spiritual explorations of what Mannes-Abbott called "the big questions."

In 1994 Coupland began writing for the computer magazine *Wired.* In preparation for an article he lived with some Microsoft employees and found material for his third novel, *Microserfs* (1995). The novel takes the form of a series of diary entries made in an Apple PowerBook laptop computer by Daniel Underwood, a computer programmer who leaves Microsoft to join a Silicon Valley start-up firm established by some friends; including e-mail exchanges, lists, computer code, and "subconscious" word files, the book is, like *Generation X,* formally innovative. Over the course of the novel each character undergoes various physical, emotional, and

Paperback cover for the first edition, 1991 (Richland County Public Library)

relationship transformations while collectively working on Oop! (Object Oriented Programming), a digital Lego system that allows users to construct and reconstruct a virtual world. The theme of *Microserfs* is humanity's changing relationship to technology. Daniel and Michael, the guru-like founder of Oop!, discuss machines both as products of human innovation and as reflections of human evolution. Noting that externalized computer memory has begun to exceed collective biological memory, Michael declares that "We've peripheralized our essence." Making a witty reference to the media reception of his own first novel, Coupland has Michael rant about "all of this media-hype generation nonsense going on at the moment. Apparently we're all 'slackers.' Daniel, who thinks up these things?'" Coupland shows that the "nerd" is the new ideal of masculinity: in the new technology-based economy, computer programmers like Daniel, who have high IQs and technical knowledge, not those with physical prowess and aggressive drives, have the money and power. Technology also overturns traditional generational hierarchies: Daniel's father is fired from IBM,

where he is regarded as obsolete, and goes to work for Michael, who belongs to the same generation as his son. Critics praised *Microserfs* for its depiction of the new technical age and for returning to the generational angst of Coupland's early work.

In 1995 Coupland declared in the article "Generation X'd" in *Details* magazine that "X is over." Registering his disgust with the co-optation of his novel by corporate marketing campaigns, he explains that *Generation X* sought to define a way of looking at the world rather than a literal generation. He exhorts readers to defy labels and keep a few steps ahead of the media game by refusing to sell their ideals and individuality. Since 1995 the initial, hype-based critical acclaim for *Generation X* has been succeeded by more-thoughtful analyses that focus on the themes of faith and redemption in the novel.

Polaroids from the Dead (1996) is a collection of essays and short stories, many of which had previously appeared in *The New Republic* and other magazines and newspapers. In his introduction Coupland describes the book as an exploration of the early 1990s worldview, "as though I've opened a kitchen drawer and found a Kleenex box full of already nostalgic Polaroid snapshots and postcards." In the first section, "Polaroids from the Dead," New Age teens, aging Deadheads, and nostalgic yuppies describe a December 1991 Grateful Dead concert in Oakland, California; the narratives are illustrated with snapshots from the 1960s. Section 2, "Portraits of People and Places," describes Vancouver, East Berlin, the Bahamas, California, and Washington, D.C., in terms of twentieth-century iconography. East Berlin, for instance, is not a post-Communist wasteland but a vibrant, contradictory terrain of shopping malls, postmodernist architecture, and pop music. The final section, "Brentwood Notebook," presents the neighborhood that was the setting for the deaths of Marilyn Monroe and Nicole Brown Simpson as a symbol of the vacuity and false glamour of celebrity culture. Lan Nguyen in *People* (8 May 1996) asked whether the book was simply a reproduction of cultural icons, a criticism of early 1990s society, or a combination of the two.

In 1997 Coupland contributed a short story to *Time* magazine, "Clone, Clone on the Range," that satirizes the hubris surrounding advances in biotechnology by depicting a world in which blackmailers hold hairbrushes hostage for DNA and captains of industry will their assets to cloned versions of themselves. The protagonists' cloned embryos are implanted in "Hereford mommies," but the cows are rustled before the end of the gestation period. The clones are, however, eventually reunited with their genetic prototypes.

Coupland's next novel, *Girlfriend in a Coma* (1998), begins in 1979. Eighteen-year-old Karen Ann McNeil makes love to her boyfriend, Richard, for the first time; nine months later, she predicts the end of the world, falls into a coma, and gives birth to a daughter, Megan. When she wakes up nearly eighteen years later, the world does end: people everywhere lie down and fall asleep, succumbing to the mind-numbing aspects of contemporary life. The problem, according to Karen, is "A lack of convictions—of beliefs, of wisdom, or even of good old badness. No sorrow, no nothing. People . . . only, well *existed*." Finally, only Karen, Richard, Megan, and Karen and Richard's group of friends, all of whom work for the American film industry in Vancouver, are left alive. The friends are given the task of "clearing the land for a new culture" by the ghost of another friend, Jared, who died the year before Karen fell into the coma; he says, "If you're not spending every waking moment of your life radically rethinking the nature of the world—if you're not plotting every moment boiling the carcass of the old order—then you're wasting your day." Unlike most of Coupland's works, in which relations between generations are antagonistic, here two generations work together in quest of a better world:

Jared and Karen are psychologically seventeen and eighteen, respectively, frozen in time by death and coma; Megan, born just after her mother entered the coma, is also eighteen; but Richard and the rest of the group are thirty-six. Reviewing the novel in two issues of *Canadian Literature,* Kegan Doyle (Summer–Autumn 1999) and W. H. New (Winter 1999) found the shift from cultural critique in the first half of the novel to a vision of apocalypse and renewal in the second half confusing. For Laura Miller in *The New York Times* (12 April 1998) and Nadia Halim in *Canadian Forum* (May 1998) the combination of satire and sincerity in the novel made it difficult to tell how seriously Coupland's exhortation to question the world should be taken and made the final pages of *Girlfriend in a Coma* awkward.

After contributing a brief reflection and an original story to *Lara's Book: Lara Croft and the Tomb Raider Phenomenon* (1998), a text that provides background material on the video-game heroine Lara Croft, Coupland published his fifth novel, *Miss Wyoming* (1999). John Johnson, a "semisleazebag movie producer," and Susan Colgate, a child beauty queen turned television actress turned bride of a rock-and-roll musician, meet in a Beverly Hills restaurant and fall in love. Both have recently experienced life-changing events—John nearly died, and Susan is the only survivor of an airplane crash—and are searching for something real in a Hollywood environment that is relentlessly fake and plastic. Yet, Hollywood also allows them to reinvent themselves over and over again. The novel owes much of its style to Hollywood movies: John and Susan's love story is idealized, there is a car chase and a detective subplot, and, at the end, John and Susan drive off into the sunset. The work concludes with a vision of the future as constant transformation where, phoenix-like, people will cast themselves into new fires and rise from the ashes, "always newer and more wonderful." Andrew Clark in *Maclean's* (17 January 2000) likened *Miss Wyoming* to F. Scott Fitzgerald's *The Great Gatsby* (1925), and Stan Persky in *Quill and Quire* (January 2000) likened it to Nathanael West's *The Day of the Locust* (1939)—novels in which characters reinvent themselves in a flawed world. Clark declared the work Coupland's best novel to date, citing its blend of high romance and moral symbolism. On the other hand, Peter Behrens in *The Globe and Mail* (8 January 2000) and Tom Shone in *The New York Times* (16 January 2000) found the tone artificial and the characterizations shallow.

In 1999–2000 Coupland created a line of tables with a "sculptural dimension" for the Edmonton company Pure Design. In 2000 he published *City of Glass: Douglas Coupland's Vancouver,* which combines brief, often unorthodox observations on the city with color photographs taken by Una Knox and others, including Coupland himself. The book is, in part, a tourist guide: Coupland writes, "I get lots of visitors every year, and they always ask the same questions about Vancouver. . . . So this book arises from both love and laziness: love, because I spent my twenties scouring the globe thinking there had to be a better city out there, until it dawned on me that Vancouver is the best one going." Coupland's entries are far from the usual tourist fare, however, as they include "Grow-ops," "Japanese Slackers," "Monster Houses," and "Main and Hastings," an intersection in the poorest postal code in Canada. *City of Glass* upsets stereotypes such as the "beads and granola" label attached to Vancouver by people from eastern Canada and the popular perception of Canada in the United States as a scenic wilderness. His tribute to Lions Gate Bridge, "one last grand gesture of beauty" before civilization ends, is reprinted from *Life after God*. Coupland concludes that "Vancouver is one of the few cities . . . that are bucking the trend toward homogenization and pasteurized global taste."

According to James Hopkins in the 15 September 2001 *The Times* (London), Coupland's sixth novel, *All Families Are Psychotic* (2001), puts the "fun" back into "dysfunctional." Ted and Janet Drummond are the divorced parents of Wade, Sarah, and Bryan. Ted is dying of liver cancer. Wade was discovered to have AIDS after he was shot by his father for having unwittingly had casual sex with his new stepmother, Nickie; the bullet passed through Wade into his mother, so Janet and Nickie are also infected. Bryan, who is chronically depressed, has impregnated Shw (her name is an acronym for Sogetsu Hernando Watanabe, a martyred hero of the Peruvian Shining Path terrorist faction), who is plotting to sell their child to baby traffickers. Sarah, a thalidomide baby missing one hand, is the most successful member of the family: she has overcome all odds to become an astronaut and is about to go into space; there she plans to conceive her mission commander's child, while her husband and the commander's wife carry on an affair back on Earth. The family has gathered in Florida to witness the shuttle launch. Janet is taking thalidomide again, this time as a treatment for AIDS, while Wade and his new wife have conceived through an expensive and artificial process that removes the HIV from sperm. The novel ends with the appearance of a sinister deus ex machina: Florian, heir to a Swiss pharmaceutical fortune, scours hotels around the world for used hairbrushes, towels, clothing, condoms, and envelopes from which DNA can be taken to clone celebrities. Able to access the latest in biotechnology and pharmaceutical advances, Florian cures Ted, Janet, Wade, and Nickie, and the question then becomes what each will do with his or her second chance at life. Janet will search for meaning in places

Dust jacket for the first edition, 1992 (Richland County Public Library)

"once forbidden" to her because of her 1950s notions of propriety, while Wade will, through his born-again Christian wife and soon-to-be-born child, search for meaning in religion and love. In the end, the Drummonds deliver a surprisingly hopeful message about the possibility of redemption and recovery. As the epigraph by pop artist Jenny Holzer states, "In a dream you saw a way to survive and you were full of joy." In *Books in Canada* (August 2002) John Oughton declared, "There is considerable evidence here that Coupland is maturing as a writer, developing characters with enough depth to surprise and move us"; but Adair Brouwer in *Quill and Quire* (August 2001) questioned the relentlessly hip dialogue, claiming that Janet speaks "like a downtown latte-culture chick." Both reviewers, however, recognized that Coupland is addressing contemporary anxieties about technology and moral relativism.

In 2001 Coupland published *Kami wa Nihon o nicunderu / God Hates Japan,* a novel with graphic images written in Japanese. He also exhibited a sculpture installation, *Spike,* at the Totem Gallery in New York. In 2002 and 2004, respectively, he published *Souvenir of Canada* and *Souvenir of Canada 2,* collections of photographs and observations on what it means to be Canadian in which he seeks to update timeworn tourist images of the country. Hockey, for example, is no longer a purely Canadian sport but a microcosm of Canada's battle to resist the Americans. Beer bottles represent the shift from English to American colonialism. The maple-leaf flag, adopted in 1965, is a democratically constructed icon that Coupland remembers being embraced amid much debate and national fervor. Products and images that are only significant to Canadians include chimo, Ookpik, maple walnut ice cream, and poutine. Canada, he proposes, is a "staggeringly" young country that can be whatever it wants to be: "the future still belongs to you."

Coupland collaborated with French artist Pierre Huyghe on a volume of commentaries on art, *Encounters: School Spirit,* which was published in French and English in 2002. His novel *Hey Nostradamus!* appeared the following year. It begins with a massacre at a North Vancouver high school reminiscent of the one at Columbine High School in Colorado in 1999. The shooters act out of a "generic sort of alienation we've all become too familiar with during the 1990s." The first section is narrated posthumously by Cheryl Anway, who is killed in the cafeteria. Cheryl is secretly married to Jason, a fellow member of the Youth Alive! Christian youth group, and has just found out that she is pregnant. Moments before her death, Cheryl scribbles, "GOD IS NOWHERE / GOD IS NOW HERE" on a notebook binder. Jason narrates the second part of the novel, set eleven years later, in 1999, in a letter to his twin nephews. Since the shootings Jason has avoided life in a haze of drugs and alcohol; he works sporadically in construction and bitterly rejects the religious fanaticism of his father, Reg. Reg treats his family harshly, questions whether both of his identical-twin grandsons have souls (since the embryo split after the moment of conception, the point at which Reg believes the soul is joined with the body), and calls Jason a murderer for killing one of the shooters in an attempt to save Cheryl. As Cheryl notes, Reg "used religion as a foil to justify his undesirable character traits. His cheapness became *thrift;* his lack of curiosity about the world and his contempt for new ideas were called *being traditional.*" The narration is taken over in 2002 by Heather, Jason's long-suffering girlfriend, after Jason has disappeared. The brief final section is narrated by Reg, who confesses all of the personal weaknesses and failings that he disguised with the outward forms of religion and at last gains some humanity and some empathy for his son. Burns's review in *The Globe and Mail* commended Coupland's fictionalization of the Columbine

tragedy to frame important questions, but Megan Harlan in *The New York Times* (6 July 2003) criticized Coupland's writing style as too casual for his subject matter and his four narrators—Cheryl, Jason, Heather, and Reg—as sounding too similar to one another despite their external differences.

Coupland's next novel, *Eleanor Rigby* (2004), offers yet another perspective on the search for meaning in contemporary North American society. His middle-aged protagonist, Liz Dunn, describes herself as "drab, crabby and friendless." After explaining that she suffers from loneliness, "our species' curse" (and the pervading emotion of the Beatles song that provides the title of the novel), she says, "People look at me and forget I'm here." Liz's loneliness is dispersed by the arrival, heralded by the appearance of the Hale-Bopp comet, of Jeremy, the son she had put up for adoption following a teenage pregnancy. Jeremy brings a period of joy and mystical revelation to her life, but he is terminally ill. While his living prophetic influence is brief, his death propels Liz into a quest for her own guiding visions and a more meaningful life. Reviews of this novel, as for many of Coupland's more-spiritual works, were mixed. Ali Smith in *The Guardian* (9 October 2004) praised the mature and inspirational vision of the novel, but Emily Nussbaum in *The New York Times* (2 January 2005) found the characters stereotypical and said that the novel "dwindles . . . into a high-art twist on chick lit."

In the summer and fall of 2004 Coupland produced an art installation titled *Canada House* consisting of a space filled with objects designed, according to his website, to "reflect on the notion of Canada." His play *September 10, 2001* premiered in 2004 as part of the Stratford New Work Festival. A monologue performed by Coupland himself, it offers his perceptions of the 1990s. In 2005 Coupland published *Terry: Terry Fox and His Marathon of Hope,* a collection of images of and short reflections on Fox, who attempted to run across Canada on a prosthetic leg in 1980 to raise money for cancer research.

In 2006 Coupland published *JPod: A Novel,* his most acclaimed recent work, about six "JPodders"— their last names all begin with *J*—who work together at a video-game-design company. Forced to embed a friendly-turtle sidekick into a skateboarding game in the middle of production, the JPod members spend much of the novel exploring ways to subvert the corporate culture. Set in a Vancouver suburb, *JPod* satirizes twenty-first-century consumerism as both meaningless and absurd—in a series of comic subplots narrator Ethan Jarlewski's family members are involved in illegal marijuana grow-ops, immigrant smuggling, and competitive ballroom dancing. In a final postmodernist move Coupland inserts himself into the narrative as a sinister deus ex machina. Reviewers responded to Coupland's astute social commentary; in *The New York Times* (19 May 2006) Dave Itzkoff wrote that the novel "is a work in which his familiar misgivings about life on the technological cusp are again invoked, but also one in which the skills he's been developing as a novelist pay off, where his satirical streak and his social consciousness finally stop fooling around with each other and settle down together." The novel was long-listed for the 2006 Giller Prize, given annually to an outstanding work of Canadian fiction.

Despite his critique of contemporary culture, Douglas Coupland remains hopeful for the future. In a review of *Polaroids from the Dead* Paul McEwan wrote in the *Globe and Mail* (24 August 1996) that Coupland's "theme is constant: How does one reconcile a fast-food culture, where values and loyalties are fleeting, with the desire for a life based on something more meaningful?" The moments of apocalypse and crisis that pervade his later works suggest that society cannot continue on its current destructive course. Instead, people must move forward and develop their own moral and spiritual frameworks. Coupland's use of irony, spiritual quests, apocalyptic visions, explorations of love, and narrative innovation are ways to rediscover meaning in a world where corporations sell ideals and television sitcoms serve as moral compasses.

References:

J. Brent Bill, "Douglas Coupland's World: Loneliness Virus," *Christian Century,* 117, no. 31 (2000): 1150–1152;

Coupland.com <http://coupland.com/> (accessed 13 February 2007);

Jefferson Faye, "Review Essay: Canada in a Coma," *American Review of Canadian Studies,* 31 (Autumn 2001): 501–511;

Mark Forshaw, "Douglas Coupland: In and Out of 'Ironic Hell,'" *Critical Survey,* 12, no. 3 (2000): 39–58;

Lori Kendall, "Nerd Nation: Images of Nerds in U.S. Popular Culture," *International Journal of Cultural Studies,* 2, no. 2 (1999): 260–283;

Eva-Marie Kröller, "The City as Anthology," *Canadian Literature,* 169 (Summer 2001): 1–6;

G. P. Lainsbury, "*Generation X* and the End of History," *Essays on Canadian Writing,* 58 (Spring 1996): 229–240;

Robert McGill, "The Sublime Simulacrum: Vancouver in Douglas Coupland's Geography of Apocalypse," *Essays on Canadian Writing,* 70 (Spring 2000): 252–276;

Ryan Moore, ". . . And Tomorrow Is Just Another Crazy Scam: Postmodernity, Youth, and the Downward Mobility of the Middle Class," in *Generations of Youth: Youth Cultures and History in Twentieth-Century America,* edited by Joe Austin and Michael Nevin Willard (New York: New York University Press, 1988), pp. 253–271;

Andrew Tate, "'Now–Here is my Secret': Ritual and Epiphany in Douglas Coupland's Fiction," *Literature and Theology,* 16 (September 2002): 326–338.

Joan Crate
(14 June 1953 –)

Joanna Mansbridge
Simon Fraser University

BOOKS: *Pale as Real Ladies: Poems for Pauline Johnson* (London, Ont.: Brick Books, 1989);
Breathing Water (Edmonton: NeWest Press, 1989);
Foreign Homes (London, Ont.: Brick Books, 2001).

OTHER: "The Wedding of My Sister-in-law," in *The Road Home: New Stories from Alberta Writers,* edited by Fred Stenson (Edmonton: Reidmore Books, 1992), p. 229;
"Betwixt and Between," in *Boundless Alberta,* edited by Aritha van Herk (Edmonton: NeWest Press, 1993), pp. 477–485;
"Willow Women," in *Eating Apples: Knowing Women's Lives,* edited by Catarina Edwards and Kay Stewart (Edmonton: NeWest Press, 1994), p. 302;
"The Man in The Moon," in *Alberta Lifestyles,* edited by Phyllis Ashley (Red Deer: Writers' Ink, 1994), p. 6;
"Shawnandithit," in *A Passion for Identity: An Introduction to Canadian Studies,* edited by David Taras and Beverly Rasporich (Scarborough, Ont.: ITP Nelson, 1997), p. 8;
"The Invisible Landscape," in *Fresh Tracks: Writing the Western Landscape,* edited by Pamela Banting (Victoria: Polestar, 1998), p. 265;
"The Invisible Landscape II: The Influence of the Western Canadian Landscape on Four Alberta Poets: Christopher Wiseman, Marilyn Dumont, Robert Hilles, and Louise Halfe," in *Literature of Region and Nation: Proceedings of the 6th International Literature of Region and Nation Conference,* edited by Winnifred M. Bogaards (Saint John: University of New Brunswick, 1998), pp. 180–191;
"Gleichen," in *New Life in Dark Seas,* edited by Stan Dragland (London, Ont.: Brick Books, 2000), p. 44.

SELECTED PERIODICAL PUBLICATIONS–
UNCOLLECTED: "Letters in Colour to Father" and "Thoughts of Charles," *Quarry,* 37, no. 4 (1988): 19–21;

Joan Crate (courtesy of the author)

"Prairie Greyhound," *Canadian Author and Bookman,* 63, no. 3 (1988): 17;
"Negative of You" and "The blizzard moans my name," *Canadian Literature,* 124–125 (Spring–Summer 1990): 16, 18;
"Dreams of My Father," *Grain Magazine,* 20, no. 1 (1992): 36;
"The Mistress' Reply to the Poet," *Canadian Poetry: Studies, Documents, Reviews,* 33 (1993): 55–64;
"Their Honeymoon Trip" and "Flight," *Poetry Canada Review,* 14 (1994): 11;

"Me, Camille, and Joey Malarky," *Prairie Fire,* 19, no. 2 (1998): 118;

"Leaving Home," "Back Pages," and "Down the Road," *Grain Magazine,* 26, no. 2 (1998): 21, 73, 81;

"Home and Native Lands (Inspired by Tomson Highway's *Kiss of the Fur Queen*)," *Prairie Fire,* 20, no. 2 (1999): 224;

"Full (for N.H.)," *Grain Magazine,* 28, no. 2 (2000): 75.

Although Joan Crate's creative output to date is relatively small, she is an important voice in prairie, Métis, and women's writing in Canada. Her poetry is technically complex, employing lyrical conventions in a sophisticated manner. In both her poetry and her fiction she explores the shaping of identity in a postcolonial world and examines the forces of history, society, and culture that frame existence in late-twentieth- and early-twenty-first-century Canada. Deeply personal and emotional, yet also subtly political, Crate's poetry and short stories have been published in anthologies, textbooks, journals, and magazines. She won the Bliss Carman Poetry Award in 1988 and a national award in a poetry competition sponsored by the Hope Writers' Guild in 1997.

Crate was born on 14 June 1953 in Yellowknife, the capital of the Northwest Territories, the second of the two children of Charles Brandell Crate, a Cree and French-German miner, and Lilian Grace Crate, a welder of English descent. After being injured several times in mining accidents, her father decided that a university degree might allow him to find a safer career; thus, when Crate was six, the family moved to Alberta. The father eventually became a teacher. During the 1960s the family moved to various locations on the prairies. Crate left high school early to get married: in June 1969 she married Lindsay Taylor, a journalist. She had two children while completing a communications course in Kamloops, British Columbia. She worked at CFJC-TV in Kamloops from 1975 to 1977, then moved to CKCK in Regina, Saskatchewan; at both stations she wrote commercials. After her marriage dissolved in 1981, Crate enrolled in the honors English program at the University of Calgary. She supported herself with student loans and part-time summer jobs. She received her bachelor's degree in 1985 and, while working part-time in the university theater department—she began as an usher and ended up as the theater manager—completed her master's degree in English (with distinction) in 1988. Her undergraduate honors project became her first book of poetry, *Pale as Real Ladies: Poems for Pauline Johnson* (1989), while her master's thesis, "Bone in the Mouth," became her novel, *Breathing Water* (1989).

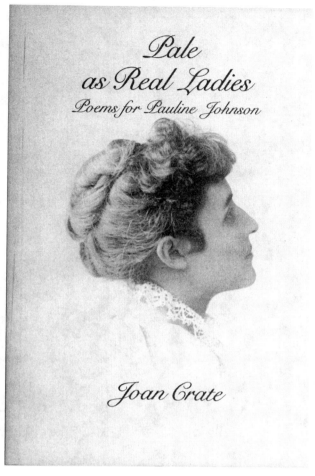

Paperback cover for the first edition, 1989
(Bruccoli Clark Layman Archives)

In *Pale as Real Ladies* Crate revives the voice of the half-white Mohawk princess E. Pauline Johnson (Tekahionwake), the first Native poet whose work was published in Canada. Johnson's writings achieved popularity at the beginning of the twentieth century amid the cultural tensions between Native people and European settlers. According to Veronica Strong-Boag and Carole Gerson, some of the poems draw on Betty Keller's *Pauline: A Biography of Pauline Johnson* (1981), "while others imaginatively fill the gaps between known events and link Johnson to Crate's own experience." Crate begins the volume by invoking Johnson's spirit: "I re-invent you. It is not your words I want. . . . It is the sound of your voice, your breath cool on my cheek, your insistent geniality, your travel, your toughness, your pretense. And your loneliness, your stretched thin days, desolation, illness, suffering." Crate maintains a balance of emotional, visceral, and intellectual elements throughout the collection. Some poems are spoken by Johnson, while others are dialogues

Paperback cover for the first edition, 1989 (Bruccoli Clark Layman Archives)

between Johnson and Crate. In "I am a Prophet" Johnson's voice is vivid and unsettling: "For ten bucks I will show you / every scar on my body / Another ten, you can make your own." A tone of desperation underlies some of the dialogue poems as the speakers search for connection.

The narrator of *Breathing Water,* Dione Harlumbus, is a Métis married to a Greek, Jorges ("Jo-Jo"), who is having an affair: "Jo-Jo, my husband, the father of my baby. That's why I married him, because he is Elijah's father, and because he wanted me too. . . . Jo-Jo said he loved me. People say that and, poof, things happen." The first third of the novel is lyrical and imagistic as Dione escapes her feelings of frustration and despair by retreating into a private imaginary world. The story of the shaman who "swam with the tide because it took him swiftly out into the open water, pushed his transformed sea otter body, neck stretched, tail taut, so that he was nothing but a swift line darting through the sea"

invades Dione's mind as she strokes Elijah's cheek. In times of despair the memory of her late father, for whom Elijah was named, provides a link to the past as he weaves tales of the "spirit people from the Underworld clambering over the earth." Yet, her father's voice is often obscured by the pervasive myths of the dominant European Judeo-Christian culture. She remembers asking as a child, "Yes, and what else Father? And then the people were hungry and the salmon people came to them with their bodies. . . ." But the memory is interrupted by a memory of the Christian ritual of Communion: "'This is my body,' the priest raised a gold chalice. 'Amen,' Mother sputtered." The Christian images of the blood and body of Christ threaten to overwhelm the corresponding Métis images of water and earth. The last section of the novel is a prosaic narrative of Dione's duties as a wife and mother that reveals that she is also having an affair. The conclusion of the work returns to the lyrical density of the beginning as Dione is finally able to let her father "go, so that I might find him where he is not—in myself, in my memory—and tell him to you, to me, to tell me, oh Elijah. . . . How I love you little one."

In 1990 Crate took a position as an English instructor at Red Deer College in Red Deer, Alberta. She and her common-law husband, Kamal Serhal, an engineer, with whom she has lived since 1982, have two children. In the late 1990s she helped develop a B.A. program in English that is offered through the University of Calgary with courses taught at Red Deer College.

Crate's second book of poetry, *Foreign Homes* (2001), is divided into three sections: "Dowries," "Loose Feathers on a Stone," and "Thieves." The second section comprises twelve elegiac verses about Shawnandithit, also known as Nancy April; the last known Beothuk to survive the genocide of her people in Newfoundland, Shawnandithit died of tuberculosis in 1829. Blending sympathy and anger, Crate reconstructs Shawnandithit's life in a series of vivid images. Shawnandithit is the symbolic wound, the embodiment of the sense of dispossession felt by many Native and Métis people. *Foreign Homes* explores the search for a sta-

ble identity amid alienation and dislocation: "Identity / is a hood ornament on the old clunker / I'm ready to sell if anyone's buying." True identity, Crate suggests, is established not individualistically but through belonging to a community that shares a common history. The final portion of the text features dialectical images of isolation and community, emptiness and abundance; for example, "The house is empty," but "We were full."

The work of Joan Crate explores the relationships between history and myth, between identity and alienation, and between individual and community. Incorporating her own experience of being Métis, Crate's poetry and fiction express the dislocation of body, mind, and spirit and examine the nature of myth, history, and identity. Her work also reveals possibilities for healing and awareness. Crate is part of the revival of a Métis mythology that investigates the past to find meaning and coherence in the present.

Reference:

Veronica Strong-Boag and Carole Gerson, *Paddling Her Own Canoe: The Times and Texts of E. Pauline Johnson (Tekahionwake)* (Toronto: University of Toronto Press, 2000), p. 6.

Lorna Crozier

(24 May 1948 –   )

Brenda Beckman-Long
University of Alberta

BOOKS: *Inside Is the Sky,* as Lorna Uher (Saskatoon: Thistledown, 1976);

Crow's Black Joy, as Uher (Edmonton: NeWest, 1978);

No Longer Two People, by Crozier, as Uher, and Patrick Lane (Winnipeg: Turnstone, 1979);

Humans and Other Beasts, as Uher (Winnipeg: Turnstone, 1980);

The Weather (Moose Jaw, Sask.: Coteau, 1983);

The Garden Going on without Us (Toronto: McClelland & Stewart, 1985);

Angels of Flesh, Angels of Silence (Toronto: McClelland & Stewart, 1988);

Martha Townsend: Island, by Crozier, Denise Desantels, and Louise Warren (Vancouver: Artspeak Gallery, 1991);

Inventing the Hawk (Toronto: McClelland & Stewart, 1992);

Eye Witness: Variations for the Spring Equinox (Victoria: Reference West, 1993);

Everything Arrives at the Light (Toronto: McClelland & Stewart, 1995);

A Saving Grace: The Collected Poems of Mrs. Bentley (Toronto: McClelland & Stewart, 1996);

The Transparency of Grief (Salt Spring Island, B.C.: [M]Other Tongue Press, 1996);

Language of Angels (Etobicoke, Ont.: Stewart House, 1998);

What the Living Won't Let Go (Toronto: McClelland & Stewart, 1999);

Apocrypha of Light (Toronto: McClelland & Stewart, 2002);

Bones in Their Wings: Ghazals (Regina, Sask.: Hagios, 2003);

Whetstone (Toronto: McClelland & Stewart, 2005).

Collections: *Before the First Word: The Poetry of Lorna Crozier,* edited by Catherine Hunter, afterword by Crozier (Waterloo, Ont.: Wilfrid Laurier University Press, 2005);

The Blue Hour of the Day: Selected Poems (Toronto: McClelland & Stewart, 2007).

Lorna Crozier (photograph by Don Hall; courtesy of Lorna Crozier)

PRODUCED SCRIPT: "Chile," by Crozier and Patrick Lane, radio, *State of the Arts,* Canadian Broadcasting Corporation, 4 October 1987.

OTHER: "The Edge of the Page: A Response to Barry McKinnon's *I Wanted to Say Something,*" as Lorna

Uher, in *RePlacing,* edited by Dennis Cooley (Downsview: ECW, 1980), pp. 106–111;

"Searching for the Poem," in *Trace: Prairie Writers on Writing,* edited by Birk Sproxton (Winnipeg: Turnstone, 1986), pp. 157–162;

A Sudden Radiance: Saskatchewan Poetry, edited by Crozier and Gary Hyland, introduction by Crozier (Regina, Sask.: Coteau, 1987);

"Speaking the Flesh," in *Language in Her Eye: Views on Writing and Gender by Canadian Women Writing in English,* edited by Libby Scheier, Sarah Sheard, and Eleanor Wachtel (Toronto: Coach House, 1990), pp. 91–94;

"Chile," by Crozier and Patrick Lane, in *Studio One: Stories Made for Radio,* edited by Wayne Schmalz (Regina, Sask.: Coteau, 1990), pp. 13–21;

Breathing Fire: Canada's New Poets, edited by Crozier and Lane (Madeira Park, B.C.: Harbour, 1995);

Alden Nowlan, *Selected Poems,* edited by Crozier and Lane (Don Mills, Ont.: Anansi, 1996);

"Piecing Together a Childhood: One Feminist's Beginnings," in *Click: Becoming Feminists,* edited by Lynn Crosbie (Toronto: Macfarlane Walter & Ross, 1997), pp. 30–36;

Desire in Seven Voices, edited, with contribution, by Crozier (Vancouver: Douglas & McIntyre, 1999);

Addicted: Notes from the Belly of the Beast, edited by Crozier and Lane, preface and contribution by Crozier (Vancouver: Greystone, 2001);

"What Stays in the Family," in *Dropped Threads: What We Aren't Told,* edited by Carol Shields and Marjorie Anderson (Toronto: Vintage, 2001), pp. 11–18;

Breathing Fire 2: Canada's New Poets, edited by Crozier and Lane (Roberts Creek, B.C.: Nightwood Editions, 2004).

SELECTED PERIODICAL PUBLICATIONS–
UNCOLLECTED: "A Western Poet's Journal from Montreal," *Prairie Fire: A Magazine of Canadian Writing,* 9, no. 1 (1988): 5–12;

"Foremothers / Fourmothers / For Mother . . .," *Contemporary Verse Two,* 12 (1989): 32–34;

"Who's Listening?" *NeWest Review,* 14, no. 3 (1989): 22–25;

"For the Sake of Insight," *Books in Canada,* 20, no. 7 (1991): 37;

"Writing My Father with Shame, with Terror," *Event,* 20, no. 1 (1991): 41–44;

"Leave My Soul Alone," *Medium,* 33, no. 2 (1993): 11–17;

"The Arduous Partnership: Memory and Invention," *West Word,* 13, no. 5 (1993): 1, 10–11; no. 6 (1993): 1, 10–11;

"Magic and Myth," *Books in Canada,* 23, no. 7 (1994): 38–39;

"The Shape of Human Sorrow: A Meditation on the Art of Poetry," *Border Crossings,* 13, no. 3 (1994): 34–39;

"A Secret Indulgence," *Matrix,* 45 (1995): 63–64;

"Talking Dirty," *Prism,* 33, no. 4 (1995): 7–10;

"So Much Sorrow, and Then Pancakes After," *Contemporary Verse Two,* 18, no. 4 (1996): 27–30;

"Sinclair's Secret," *Quill & Quire,* 63, no. 2 (1997): 44;

"Ghost House," *Western Living* (Vancouver Edition), 27, no. 6 (1997): 22b–24b;

"Comic Books, Dead Dogs, Cheer Leading: One Poet's Beginnings" and "Tips for Writers," *In 2 Print,* 13 (1998): 8–10, 12;

"In Memoriam, Pierre Elliott Trudeau," *Globe and Mail* (Toronto), 2 October 2000;

"My Older Brother," *Prairie Fire: A Magazine of Canadian Writing,* 21, no. 1 (2000): 62–63.

One of Canada's most widely read poets, Lorna Crozier tells stories and retells myths of Western culture from a female perspective. In her essay "Speaking the Flesh" (1990) she states that feminism has "stormed the bastille of our literature as well as other fortresses in our society" and has changed even "the oldest of stories, revised what many thought were untouchable texts." Among her literary "foremothers" Crozier acknowledges Virginia Woolf, Gabriela Mistral, Sylvia Plath, Eudora Welty, Margaret Atwood, P. K. Page, Anne Szumigalski, and Margaret Laurence, the last of whom has called Crozier "a poet to be grateful for." Drawing on the prairie landscape as a source of imagery, she combines a regional and a feminist poetics to represent the body, memory, desire, and grief and to address themes as diverse as politics, the environment, and metaphysics.

Crozier was born on 24 May 1948 in Swift Current, Saskatchewan, to Emerson and Peggy Ford Crozier. Her father, a displaced farmer, operated heavy machinery in the oil fields; her mother cleaned houses and sold tickets at the local swimming pool and at hockey games. Crozier grew up with stories of the farm and the Great Depression. In the first grade she wrote a poem that her teacher pinned on the bulletin board. "Maybe that early pat on the head explains why I thought I could be a poet even though I came from a bookless family," Crozier reflected in a 2002 interview with Elizabeth Philips.

After earning a B.A. in English from the University of Saskatchewan in 1969, Crozier married Lorne Uher, a high-school chemistry and physics teacher, and returned to Swift Current to teach high-school English. In 1974 she published a poem about her grandfather,

"Crozier locates her poems at the 'thresholds' of perception, where memory and the physical senses commune." – Mary di Michele, *Books in Canada*

INVENTING THE HAWK

Lorna Crozier

Paperback cover for the first edition, 1992 (Bruccoli Clark Layman Archives)

"Old Man with a Cane," in *Grain Magazine*. The editor, Ken Mitchell, suggested that she attend the Saskatchewan Summer School of the Arts at Fort San near Regina. There she took a creative-writing course from Mitchell, an experience that she compared in a 1993 with Barbara Carey to a "door opening in my head." She returned for several summers and met other Saskatchewan writers, with whom she formed a monthly workshop group named the Moose Jaw Movement in reaction to the Toronto-centered Canadian literary establishment.

Crozier's first book of poetry, *Inside Is the Sky* (1976), published under the name Lorna Uher, established her within the tradition of prairie literature that is characterized by landscape imagery. The poem "Vertical Man," for instance, alludes to Laurence Ricou's *Vertical Man, Horizontal World: Man and Landscape in Canadian Prairie Fiction* (1973). Crozier, however, uses the land as a trope for the female body, as in "Inner Space": "i look small / and earthbound / but inside / is the sky."

Crozier taught English at the University of Regina in 1976 and writing workshops at Fort San in the summers of 1977 and 1978. In her second volume, *Crow's Black Joy* (1978), also published under the name Uher, love lyrics such as "Commitment" and "I Want You" examine gender relations and split subjectivity. The collection won the 1978 Saskatchewan Poetry Prize.

In 1978 Crozier ended her marriage to Uher and joined Patrick Lane, a poet she had met at Fort San. In Winnipeg, where Lane was writer-in-residence at St. John's College of the University of Manitoba, Crozier and Lane co-authored *No Longer Two People* (1979). Crozier taught English at the University of Alberta in 1978–1979 and received a Canada Arts Council Grant for 1979–1980 to work on poems that became part of her M.A. thesis at the University of Alberta. She received the degree in 1980; the thesis was published that same year, under the name Uher, as *Humans and Other Beasts*. In tones that range from anger to humor, the female speaker explores themes of power, violence, and language. "This One's for You" is a parody of masculine bar talk; "Returning" considers the loss of innocence by alluding to the Eden myth; "The Taming of the Unicorn" draws on medieval mythology; "Mother Was a Lovely Beast" uses female archetypes; and "Morgain Le Fay" alludes to Sir Thomas Malory's *Morte d'Arthur* (1485).

In 1980 Crozier and Lane were in Ottawa, where Lane was writer-in-residence at the University of Ottawa. Crozier was writer-in-residence at the Cypress Hills Community College in Swift Current, Saskatchewan, in 1981 and director of communications for the Saskatchewan Department of Culture and Recreation in Regina from 1981 to 1983. She received a Saskatchewan Arts Board grant in 1982 and won a Saskatchewan Writers Guild poetry prize in 1983. she also won the Saskatchewan Senior Arts Award for 1983–1984. She reclaimed the name Crozier for *The Weather* (1983). The poems in the volume deal with landscape, politics, and gender from diverse perspectives. In a 1985 interview Crozier told Doris Hillis that the prairie is a "landscape of paradoxes": it is "beautiful and terrible," natural and altered. Many of the poems concern the vulnerability of wildlife, such as hawks, owls, bears, and buffalo. Crozier considers human vulnerability in "The Child Who Walks Backwards," about child abuse, and "Monologue: Prisoner without a Name," which bears witness to political prisoners in Chile. The long poem "The First Woman" retells stories of the "first white woman in the West," Marie Anne Lagimodière, while recalling losses of First Nations cultures after European contact. The narrative poems "Spring Storm, 1916," "The Women Who Survive," and

"Rooming House" tell stories of female members of Crozier's family.

Crozier was writer-in-residence at the Regina Public Library in 1984–1985. In her next collection, *The Garden Going on without Us* (1985), some of the poems reinterpret myths from a female perspective. "Forms of Innocence" retells the story of Leda and the swan as a woman might represent it. In "Myths" the speaker declares, "I was not made from a thin, dry rib," as Eve was created from Adam's rib in Genesis; instead, "We dreamed each other / at the same time and we dreamed a garden." In the sequence "The Sex Lives of Vegetables" the poem "Onions" speculates that if Eve had bitten an onion "instead of the apple, / how different / Paradise." Other poems in the sequence describe the phallic forms of carrots, the promiscuity of tomatoes, and the clitoral forms of peas in a pod. A provincial politician labeled the sequence pornography and asked the Manitoba government to stop funding school subscriptions to the Winnipeg arts journal *Border Crossings,* in which the poems were first published. The funding continued, and the journal was not banned from schools.

The Garden Going on without Us also exhibits a regional poetics. "Poem about Nothing" equates "nothing," paradoxically, with infinity—"Zero starts and ends / at the same place"—and goes on to show that the prairie landscape is not an empty space but a place of infinite possibilities. It also alludes to the erasure of the history that predates European settlement. The volume was nominated for a Governor General's Award in 1985.

While Lane was writer-in-residence at Concordia University in Montreal in 1985–1986, Crozier was supported by a Canada Council Grant. In 1986 they both became lecturers at the University of Saskatchewan in Saskatoon. In 1987 Crozier edited *A Sudden Radiance,* an anthology of Saskatchewan poetry, with Gary Hyland. In the introduction, which Allison Calder calls a "manifesto for prairie writing," Crozier challenges views of prairie literature that limit it to natural imagery and realist fiction and argues that paradox and multiple perspectives characterize the region's poetry.

In 1986 Crozier and Lane were part of a group of Canadian poets who were invited by the Catholic University, the Writers' Union, and Casa Canada to visit Chile, which was then under the military dictatorship of Augusto Pinochet. Afterward, they co-authored the radio script "Chile," which aired on the CBC's *State of the Arts* series on 4 October 1987 and won the Best Program Award at the National Radio Awards in 1988; it was published in 1990.

Poems from "Chile" are included in the "Angels of Silence" section of Crozier's *Angels of Flesh, Angels of Silence* (1988). "Fear of Snakes," the first poem in the volume, had won second prize in the Prism International Poetry Contest in 1986. Crozier associates a snake that a boy nails to a telephone pole with the bronze serpent that Moses lifted up on a pole (Num. 21:8–9) and to Christ on the cross. Instead of blaming Eve for the Fall and death of humankind, the poem presents her as a source of life and regeneration through her "seed," Christ, who redeems humanity. Another poem, "Mother Tongue," retells the Eden myth to redefine women's knowledge in terms of the female body and female desire. This knowledge is expressed in "womb-words," the "secret names that Eve knew" before Adam named the world.

Nowhere in the volume is female desire presented more clearly than in "The Penis Poems," which reverse poetic conventions by making the male body the object of a female gaze. The tone is erotic and satirical; Tanis MacDonald notes that Crozier's "demystification and eroticization of the penis propose ways of looking at the male body that acknowledge but do not support the fundamental structures of cultural masculinity." "Poem for Sigmund" and "What Women Talk About" contradicts Sigmund Freud's theory of penis envy. In the latter poem the speaker says:

Once on a TV talk show
I heard Germaine Greer, badgered by the host,
say, "Do you think a prick's the most interesting
thing we can put inside us?"
That got me thinking for a long time.

"Penis/Bird" retells a First Nations story about a young woman's pleasure in finding a penis that has grown wings. Crozier explains her writing strategy in the 1995 essay "Talking Dirty": "For me, writing about sexuality means finding the names, means moving out of a learned, imposed silence." "The Penis Poems" provoked some listeners to walk out of Crozier's readings.

Language is a central concern in the poem "Mother and I, Walking" and the section "Dreaming Domestic." A poem about sexual abuse, "Fathers, Uncles, Old Friends of the Family," records language that silences the female speaker. The section "Fisherman" and the long poem "Icarus" question the authority of language that is based on empirical knowledge. *Angels of Flesh, Angels of Silence* was short-listed for the Governor General's Award for poetry, and the "Angels of Silence" section won first prize in the CBC Radio Literary Competition for 1987–1988.

In 1989–1990 Crozier and Lane were writers-in-residence at the University of Toronto. They then returned to their lectureships at the University of Saskatchewan for a year. In 1991 Crozier took a position teaching creative writing at the University of Victoria.

In 1992 Crozier published *Inventing the Hawk.* "The Gardens within Us" is an elegy to Crozier's father, who died of throat cancer in 1990; he is also the subject of "Facts about My Father." "Repetitions for My Mother" and "Angel of Happiness" record Crozier's childhood memories of her mother, while "Time to Praise" relates family myths from multiple perspectives. "On the Seventh Day" retells the Genesis creation story from the perspective of God's wife. God is a "dreamy sort" who absentmindedly creates light for five days; his wife completes the creation for him but has insufficient time to make animals and humans immortal. The poem includes a creation myth to explain the prairie landscape's "thin line of soil / nudged against the sky." Crozier said in a 1993 interview with Barbara Carey, "One of the things I absolutely delight in is what Adrienne Rich calls 're-visioning': looking at the old stories, but looking at them in a new way; adding women to the story when women have been left out." in "Angel of Dragonflies" watching a dragonfly becomes a mystical experience: "It looks at you / as if it knows / exactly / who you are." In "The Language of Angels" the lines "Words, / thoughts, senses are all one body, / the body before you that burns" allude to Moses' burning bush, and the "silence" that "gathers . . . behind the rock they rolled from the tomb" refers to Christ's resurrection. According to E. F. Dyck in *NeWest Review* (June–July 1993), the scope of *Inventing the Hawk* makes Crozier not only "a model for all prairie writers" but also "heir" to a tradition of poetic invention that extends to the sixteenth-century English poet Sir Philip Sidney. The volume won the Governor General's Award, the Pat Lowther Poetry Award, and the Canadian Authors Association Award.

Everything Arrives at the Light (1995) includes the biblical epigraph "Be watchful, and strengthen the things that remain, that are ready to die," signaling familiar themes of perception, memory, and language. Paradoxes also recur: light and dark, life and death, pleasure and pain, and present and past. "The Sea at the End of the World" asks: "walk on water. / Is it not a miracle / to walk on earth?" In "Noah's Wife" the title figure loves the snail because "Like a woman the snail tucked itself / inside its shadow, slid on silence." Crozier experiments with the Persian form of the ghazal, five to twelve couplets, in the sequence "If I Call Stones Blue," which previously appeared in her chapbook *Eye Witness: Variations for the Spring Equinox* (1993). In "Photograph" the speaker is "obsessed / with the invisible." *Everything Arrives at the Light* won a Pat Lowther Award.

A Saving Grace: The Collected Poems of Mrs. Bentley (1996) explores the gaps and silences of the narrator of

Sinclair Ross's novel *As for Me and My House* (1941). Crozier's Mrs. Bentley admits that the art of her husband, Philip, lacks passion, as does their relationship; confesses her pleasure in making love with Paul, the local schoolteacher; reveals that she spied on Philip's affair with another woman, Judith; and acknowledges that she sent Philip a gift to add to his shame and Judith's pain after they discovered that Judith was pregnant.

Four of the poems in Crozier's *The Transparency of Grief,* winner of the 1996 (M)Other Tongue Press Poetry Chapbook Contest, are included in her volume *What the Living Won't Let Go* (1999). Crozier experiments with perspective, ranging from that of a fetus in the first section to the multiple viewpoints of sisters, brother, and parents on family politics in the second section. The third section approaches the past as both a burden and a gift: the speaker of "Wildflowers" acknowledges "the heart's strange fondness / for what is lost."

After living together for twenty-three years, Crozier and Lane were married in 2001. The following year Crozier continued her feminist revisionist project in *Apocrypha of Light*. Discussing the book at the 2003 Moose Jaw Festival of Words, Crozier said of Eve and the snake: "I wanted to give voice to a couple of creatures that didn't get to speak in Genesis." Other biblical characters also find a voice in the collection. In Genesis, to save his life Abraham deceives Pharaoh and King Abimelech into thinking that Sarah is his sister; in "The Barrenness of Sarah" Sarah, having been made a royal concubine, feels that she has been prostituted for her husband's gain. In "The Sacrifice of Isaac" Sarah claims that she rescued their son Isaac from being sacrificed by his father. In still other poems Lot's daughters and Jacob's daughter retell their stories of rape and incest as Crozier draws attention to what has been "erased from sermons or Sunday school teachings or the rants of TV evangelists." She sets her stories in the Canadian prairie. With characteristic humor, she writes of gophers in a religious context in "A Prophet in His Own Country." Crozier dedicates the poems "God the Father, "God the Mother," "God the Son," and "God the Daughter" to her family. "Book of Praise" is written in couplets inspired by Lane's *A Linen Crow, a Caftan Magpie* (1984). *Apocrypha of Light* was short-listed for the Pat Lowther Award. In 2003 she published *Bones in Their Wings: Ghazals.* Borrowing the form of Sufi mystics and Canadian poets such as Lane, Phyllis Webb, and John Thompson, Crozier writes couplets about love and wonder such as "Love is all flesh and then it's not / A fossil with the soft tissue gone" and "Saskatchewan / *Chew on that one,* said the wind."

Crozier returns in *Whetstone* (2005) to themes of language, silence, and loss. In "The Silence of Creation" she observes, "Far from the dream that is

Eden . . . when the blood of Adam's naming . . . fluttered, God said, 'Let there be silence.'"

In addition to her chapbooks and volumes of poetry, Crozier has written many essays. Seven writers discuss female desire in a collection that she edited, *Desire in Seven Voices* (1999); Crozier's essay is addressed to Lane. Her contribution to *Addicted: Notes from the Belly of the Beast* (2001) recalls the deception, loss, and betrayal she suffered, first as the child and then as the wife of alcoholics. She also addresses that subject in "What Stays in the Family" in *Dropped Threads: What We Aren't Told* (2001), a collection of women's writing edited by Carol Shields and Marjorie Anderson. Crozier and Lane have collaborated on three poetry anthologies: *Breathing Fire: Canada's New Poets* (1995), Alden Nowlan's *Selected Poems* (1996), and *Breathing Fire 2* (2004). Crozier received an honorary doctorate from the University of Regina in 2004 and a Distinguished Alumni Award from the University of Alberta in 2005.

Lorna Crozier has earned Canada's most prestigious literary awards and has made professional contributions as an editor, committee president of the Saskatchewan Artists' Colony, vice president of the Saskatchewan Writers' Guild, reviewer for CBC Radio, member of the League of Canadian Poets, and participant in Canadian schools' Writers in Electronic Residence program. She presents an intelligent, accessible, and often humorous voice among feminist writers of the late twentieth and early twenty-first centuries in work that consistently seeks female perspectives, whether the subject is memory, language, the female body, a bird, or a gopher. She continues to shape the future of Canadian literature as a poet and as a distinguished professor at the University of Victoria.

Interviews:

Doris Hillis, "The Real Truth, the *Poetic Truth:* An Interview with Lorna Crozier," *Prairie Fire: A Magazine of Canadian Writing,* 6, no. 3 (1985): 4–15;

Robert Enright, "Literary Landscaping: A Symposium on Prairie Landscape, Memory and Literary Tradition," *Border Crossings,* 6, no. 4 (1987): 32–38;

Bruce Meyer and Brian O'Riordan, "Nothing Better than Poetry? An Interview with Lorna Crozier," *Poetry Canada Review,* 10, no. 1 (1989): 1, 3, 28–29;

Barbara Carey, "Against the Grain: Lorna Crozier's Poetry Aims to Prick Holes in False Comforts," *Books in Canada,* 22, no. 3 (1993): 14–17;

Valerie Tamburri, "All Good Writing Is Risk: A Profile of Lorna Crozier," *Focus on Women,* 5, no. 12 (1993): 16–20;

Elizabeth Philips, "Seeing Distance: Lorna Crozier's Art of Paradox," in *Where the Words Come From: Cana-*

dian Poets in Conversation, edited by Tim Bowling (Roberts Creek, B.C.: Nightwood Editions, 2002), pp. 139–158;

Clarise Foster, "An Interview with Lorna Crozier," *Contemporary Verse Two,* 25, no. 3 (2003): 9–19.

References:

Gary Boire, "Transparencies: Of Sexual Abuse, Ambivalence, and Resistance," *Essays on Canadian Writing,* 51–52 (1993–1994): 211–232;

Deborah Bowen, "Phoenix from the Ashes: Lorna Crozier and Margaret Avison in Contemporary Mourning," *Canadian Poetry Studies, Documents, Reviews,* 40 (1997): 46–57;

Anne Burke, "Lorna Crozier: The Writing Is All," *Cross-Canada Writers' Magazine,* 10, no. 3 (1988): 5–6, 26;

Allison Calder, "Lorna Crozier," in *Encyclopedia of Literature in Canada,* edited by W. H. New (Toronto: University of Toronto Press, 2002), pp. 263–265;

Nathalie Cooke, "Lorna Crozier (1948–)," in *Canadian Writers and Their Works: Essays on Form, Context, and Development,* Poetry Series, volume 11, edited by Robert Lecker, Jack David, and Ellen Quigley (Toronto: ECW, 1995), pp. 77–155;

Dennis Cooley, "Correspondences: Two Saskatchewan Poets," *Border Crossings,* 12, no. 1 (1993): 4–5;

Susan Gingell, "Let Us Revise Mythologies: The Poetry of Lorna Crozier," *Essays on Canadian Writing,* 43 (1991): 67–82;

Gingell, "The Ways of Speech Made Plains: Saskatchewan Poetry Finds Its Voices," in *Writing Saskatchewan: Twenty Critical Essays,* edited by Kenneth G. Probert (Regina: Canadian Plains Research Centre, University of Regina, 1989), pp. 122–134;

Tanis MacDonald, "Regarding the Male Body: Rhapsodic Contradiction in Lorna Crozier's 'Penis Poems,'" *English Studies in Canada,* 28, no. 2 (2002): 247–267;

Fred Wah, "Saskatchewan Poetry," in *Essays on Saskatchewan Writing,* edited by E. F. Dyck (Regina: Saskatchewan Writers' Guild, 1986), pp. 197–219;

Lyle Weis, "Lorna Uher: 'A Poet to Be Grateful For'– Margaret Laurence," *Essays on Canadian Writing,* 18–19 (1980): 179–182.

Papers:

A collection of Lorna Crozier's manuscripts, correspondence, reviews, audio-visual tapes, and published versions of appearances on CBC Radio are in the University of Regina Archives.

Sheldon Currie

(25 February 1934 –   )

Jim Taylor
St. Francis Xavier University

BOOKS: *The Glace Bay Miners' Museum* (Ste. Anne de Bellevue, Que.: Deluge Press, 1979); title story enlarged as *The Glace Bay Miners' Museum: The Novel* (Sydney, N.S.: Breton Books, 1995);
The Company Store: A Novel (Ottawa: Oberon, 1988);
The Story So Far– (Sydney, N.S.: Breton Books, 1997);
Down the Coaltown Road: A Novel (Toronto: Key Porter, 2002);
Lauchie, Liza, and Rory (Winnipeg: Scirocco Drama, 2004).

PLAY PRODUCTIONS: *Lauchie, Liza, and Rory,* Festival Antigonish, Antigonish, N.S., Bauer Theatre, 13 August 1997;
Two More Solitudes, Festival Antigonish, Antigonish, N.S., Bauer Theatre, 13 August 1998;
By the Sea: Anna's Story, Festival Antigonish, Antigonish, N.S., Bauer Theatre, 19 August 2001.

PRODUCED SCRIPT: *Dies Irae,* by Currie and Mary Vingoe, television, CBC, 1993.

OTHER: "Comic Imagery in the Fiction of Flannery O'Connor," in *Realist of Distances: Flannery O'Connor Revisited,* edited by Jan Nordby Gretlund and Sally Fitzgerald (Aarhus, Denmark: Aarhus University Press, 1987), pp. 94–101;
"Tessie Gillis, Prophetic Storyteller," in *The Hand of a Woman: The Shaping of Cape Breton* (Sydney, N.S.: University College of Cape Breton, 2001), pp. 89–100.

SELECTED PERIODICAL PUBLICATIONS–UNCOLLECTED: "A Good Grandmother is Hard to Find: Story as Exemplum," *Antigonish Review,* 20, nos. 81–82 (1990): 143–156;
"David Adams Richards: The People on the Roadway," *Antigonish Review,* 25, no. 99 (1994): 67–75;
"David Adams Richards for the New Millenium," *Pottersfield Portfolio,* 19, no. 1 (1998): 41–42.

Sheldon Currie (from the cover for The Glace Bay Miner's Museum, *1979; Bruccoli Clark Layman Archives)*

Sheldon Currie's Cape Breton stories are greatly influenced by the doctrine of social justice preached by Moses Coady and the Rev. J. J. (Jimmy) Tompkins. Coady's *Masters of Their Own Destiny: The Story of the Antigonish Movement of Adult Education through Economic Cooperation* (1939), the manifesto of the struggle for social justice in eastern Nova Scotia, lays out the philosophy of economic freedom central to his and Tompkins's vision, which insists that the people take charge of their lives through cooperatives, trade unions, credit unions, and adult education. Since the founding fathers and the main spokesmen of the movement were Roman Catholic priests, and many of their parishioners were Catholic Highland Scots, the fundamental principles of the movement were grounded in Catholic social teachings. The protagonists of Currie's stories reflect Coady's

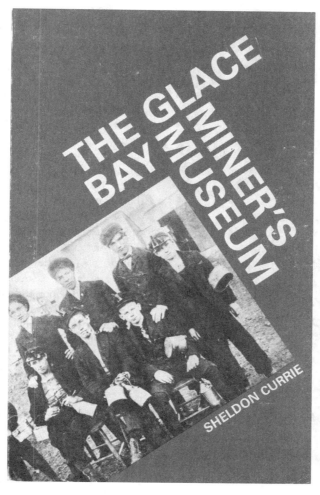

Paperback cover for the first edition, 1979
(Bruccoli Clark Layman Archives)

vision both in their insistence on self-determination and in their steadfast adherence to their Catholic faith.

Currie was born on 25 February 1934 to Charlie and Mary MacDonald Currie in Reserve Mines, Cape Breton, Nova Scotia. His father was a miner, an active union member, and an early supporter of the Co-operative Movement led by Tompkins and Frances Delores Donnelly, a Sister of Charity. Following graduation from St. Anne's High School in Glace Bay in 1951, Currie joined the Royal Canadian Air Force but left after less than a year of service. In 1953 he entered St. Francis Xavier University; he received his B.A. in English in 1957 and his B.Ed. in 1958. He taught English for a year at Digby Regional High School in southwestern Nova Scotia. In 1959 he married Dawn Wolstenholme of Moncton, New Brunswick, and began working on his M.A. in English literature at the University of New Brunswick. He received the degree in 1960 and was appointed assistant professor of English at St.

Thomas University in Chatham, New Brunswick. Two years later, he and his wife went to Alabama, where Currie pursued his doctorate in English while working as a graduate assistant. His lifelong fascination with the works of Flannery O'Connor began at that time.

In 1964 Currie was appointed assistant professor of English at St. Francis Xavier University. That same year his son Mark was born, followed by John in 1965, Mairi in 1967, and Rachel in 1970. He wrote a series of experimental short stories, the first of which, "He Said Parenthetically," was published in *The Antigonish Review* in 1970. His first collection of stories, *The Glace Bay Miners' Museum,* was published in 1979 by Deluge Press and marked him as an important writer in the Maritime Provinces. In these stories he chronicles, sometimes with trenchant humor and sometimes with touching pathos, the dominance of Celtic traditions and Roman Catholicism in the life of industrial Cape Breton.

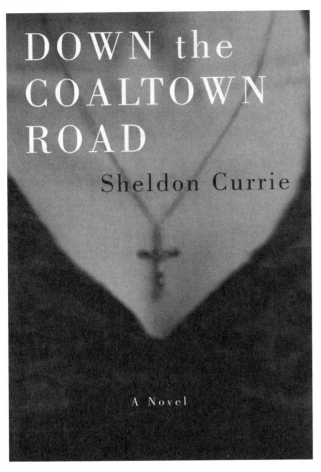

Dust jacket for the first edition, 2002
(<http://www.writers.ns.ca>)

The title story is a powerful satire depicting the exploitation of the Cape Breton people by the mining establishment, a moving elegy lamenting the loss of the Gaelic heritage, and a romantic tragicomedy. Neil Currie comes from St. Andrew's Channel, a pastoral part of Cape Breton, to the mining town of Glace Bay looking for work. Neil is the embodiment of the Celtic tradition that once nourished and gave meaning to the lives of the Cape Breton people: a kind of warrior-bard, he is witty, virile, and self-confident; speaks Gaelic; and plays the bagpipe. In the White Rose Café he meets Margaret MacNeil, who has no sense of her lost heritage or of her own identity. Like a clan chieftain of old, Neil strides into her life and rescues her from her stultifying and dreary existence in the mining town. After a swift courtship, they are married. Like Margaret, the rest of the MacNeils are ignorant of their Gaelic heritage, though her grandfather does know some old Scottish tunes. After a lifetime of working in the mines and breathing coal dust, he has developed silicosis; to be kept alive he must be thumped on the back every few hours to clear his lungs. Neil and Margaret's brother, Ian, are killed in a mine explosion; the grandfather dies as well, because Margaret, anxious for news about the disaster, is not at home to thump his chest. Margaret then creates a grotesque museum in which the body parts of her loved ones are stored in bottles of formaldehyde. The message is that the mutilation of these bodies is trivial compared to the way the miners are brutalized by the mine owners, and the body parts symbolize the various ways the Celtic heritage has been mutilated: Neil's severed tongue recalls the stifled tradition of Gaelic stories and songs; his fingers represent the loss of the skill to play the bagpipes; the grandfather's lungs, blackened with coal dust, proclaim the inhuman conditions that miners suffered; and finally, Ian's testicles attest to the extinction of the culture that had sustained the miners' Celtic ancestors when they first came to the New World. The organs are also associated with the crucified Christ; bodily mutilation and dissection are symbolically linked with the Crucifixion in many of Currie's early stories. The collection also includes "He Said Parenthetically," "Mary," "Sanabitur Anima Mea," "The Lovers," "Dic Mihi de Nostra," "Jesus Creep," "Her Wonders to Perform," and "Pomp and Circumstances." In these absurdist pieces, automaton-like characters who speak in a flat, unemotional manner attempt to do good but are thwarted by the blind forces of a nightmarishly mechanistic world.

Currie's novel *The Company Store* (1988) is told in flashback. Ian MacDonald, a miner's son whose ambition is to become a writer, is returning to Glace Bay from service in the air force in Ontario. On the train he recalls an earlier journey, when he left Cape Breton for the first time. The memory leads him to reflect on his ancestors, the Highland Scots, who "left behind sheep, dogs, shelter and every heavy thing, but they took as much of music, religion and literature as they could, and they hoped that whatever new they would acquire, they would keep what they landed with: each other and whatever was in their heads and hands." The two principal events in the novel are a mine disaster and the burning of the company store. The mine disaster is a realization of the fear of death or serious injury that is a constant in the lives of miners and their families: every day, as a miner's wife prepares her husband's lunch box, she is aware that it could be the last time she will ever see him alive. Yet, such possibilities are discussed with a gallows humor that is paradoxically lighthearted. Currie's instinct for outrageous Cape Breton characters and his keen sense of comic timing make the burning of the company store the set piece of the novel. Tired of being treated like chattel by the mine owners and being forever in debt to the company store, Ian's father, Angus, burned the store down. While the building was ablaze, a drunken miner emerged on the second-floor balcony carrying a pint of rum and dressed only in white long underwear; he was oblivious to, or unconcerned about, the flames that surrounded him. He played the orator in response to the crowd's collective yell for a speech; finally, he did a flip off the balcony with a chair on his back and landed in the street in a sitting position. From that day on, Ian observes, the miner was known to the nickname-loving Cape Bretoners as "Jack the Speaker." *The Company Store* was adapted by Mary Vingoe as a radio play for the CBC and later as a stage play for the Mulgrave Road Theatre in Guysborough County, Nova Scotia.

The Glace Bay Miners' Museum: The Novel (1995) includes new material depicting typical scenes from Cape Breton life such as card games, wakes, and mine mishaps. It won the CJCB Fiction Award in 1995 and was adapted by Wendy Lill, first as a radio play for the CBC and later as a stage play for the Mulgrave Road Theatre. The play has been in continual production since 1995 in Canada, the United States, and Britain. The novel was also adapted by Gerald Wexler and Mort Ransen for the 1995 movie *Margaret's Museum,* directed by Ransen and starring Helena Bonham Carter as Margaret. It received the award for Most Popular Canadian Film at the Vancouver International Film Festival and the Golden Seashell Award at the San Sebastián International Film Festival in Spain, both in 1995, and six Genie Awards at the Montreal Film Festival in 1996.

The story "Lauchie, Liza, and Rory," first published in *The Antigonish Review* in 1988, was adapted as a play by Currie and Vingoe for Festival Antigonish in August 1997. Liza is engaged to Lauchie but falls in love with his twin, Rory. She marries Lauchie but continues to yearn for Rory; after nearly twenty years of frustration, she finally achieves a kind of satisfaction when Rory shelters her from a storm. In a series of comical scenes the play explores themes of love, loyalty, and family solidarity in a typical Cape Breton community and the vagaries of the human heart as it chooses between individuals who are outwardly indistinguishable from each other.

In 1997 Breton Books published *The Story So Far—,* which includes stories from *The Glace Bay Miners' Museum,* excerpts from *The Company Store,* and three stories originally published in *The Antigonish Review.* In August 1998 Festival Antigonish produced Currie's play *Two More Solitudes,* which he adapted from his short stories "Dies Irae" and "On Parle par Coeur" (1979). It examines the French-English divide in Canada through the story of Ian, a young man from Cape Breton suffering from amnesia, who marries Yvette, a girl from Quebec. Eventually, Ian returns to Cape Breton, much changed but

still a Cape Bretoner. In 1999 Currie retired from St. Francis Xavier University and was awarded an honorary doctorate by St. Thomas University.

Currie's play *By the Sea: Anna's Story* (2001) is based on his novel *Down the Coaltown Road* (2002). It is a monologue in which Anna tells how she and Tomassio came from Italy to Cape Breton and were separated by Tomassio's death during World War II. The play was produced by Festival Antigonish in August 2001 and by Eastern Front Theatre in Dartmouth, Nova Scotia, in 2002.

Down the Coaltown Road deals with the internment of Cape Breton's Italian Canadians during World War II. It opens with a description of three buildings in Coaltown that "stand solid, the church in the middle, flanked on either side by the glebe house and the convent." The glebe, or priest's residence, is where Father Rod MacDonald lives; it is the temporary home of two nuns, Sister Helen and Sister Mary—who is Father Rod's own sister—who have come to Coaltown to assist in preparing the children for confirmation. The convent is the home of the nuns who teach in the adjacent school. The imposing church, "an immense mass of brown shingles, tall windows and doors, a medieval anomaly dominating the rows of company houses," proclaims the centrality of the Catholic faith to the community. The miners in their company-supplied houses "crouch in its neighborhood like legions of urban peasants." The narrator says that the Catholic Church "was the largest social institution in Coaltown and the only cultural institution where miners and their families were introduced to a foreign language and classical music. And like the majority of the Scots, Irish, and Acadians, the Italians were all Catholics. The parochial school was administered and taught by nuns, who by nature and profession tended toward charity, tolerance, and integration." The narration shifts from the omniscient narrator to Anna, whose words are set in italic type: she describes her life in Italy; her wedding to Tomassio, whom she inveigled into marrying her after she concluded that of all her suitors he was the one who could best meet her needs; and their immigration to Cape Breton. The omniscient narrator then tells of Father Rod's efforts to stop the mistreatment of the Italian population of Coaltown—especially Tomassio, whose hot temper and impetuous nature make him a target of the community's bigots. In his homily on the Gospel of St. Matthew at Tomassio's funeral, Father Rod says that the effort to rise above flawed human nature is a struggle against betrayal, the sin "that we despise most in others and forgive most easily in ourselves." The notion of betrayal provides the unifying thread in the novel: all of the characters struggle against betrayal, whether of others or of themselves. Father Rod states the theme of the novel when he declares that when Christ commanded, "Be reconciled with thy brother," he meant "that we be reconciled with those we betray and with those who betray us."

The theme of betrayal links the main plot—Tomassio and Anna's misfortunes and the Italian internment—with the subplot of the seduction of Helen Perenowsky. Just before graduating from high school, Helen became infatuated with a man who got her pregnant and deserted her. He was a German spy, and before leaving he acquired information about her brother's convoy and the strategic fortifications on the Cape Breton coast. Because of that information, her brother was killed in a German submarine attack. The novel concludes with Helen—now Sister Helen—preparing to meet her daughter for the first time since placing the child for adoption. The daughter has written to invite her mother to her wedding, and Sister Mary urges Sister Helen to reconcile herself with the child's father, the man who betrayed her. *Down the Coaltown Road,* like all of Currie's works, is filled with compassion and goodwill. Those who err do so out of misunderstanding or political compulsion or invincible ignorance. There are no villains—only well-intentioned but misguided human beings.

Though Sheldon Currie's writings are set in Cape Breton, they transcend the local to address the question of what it means to be human. His answers are always given with humor and reflect his Roman Catholic beliefs and his instinctive empathy for the poor and exploited. His works offer a vision of a world in which, while people's natural inclinations to goodness are distorted by pressures beyond their control, they manage to affirm their humanity.

References:

George Belliveau, "Glace Bay to Hollywood: A Political Journey," *Theatre Research in Canada,* 22 (Spring 2001): 46–57;

Dawn R. Dawnton, "Words, Words & Moving Pictures: The Mining of Sheldon Currie's Glace Bay," *Arts-Atlantic,* 14 (Winter 1996): 42;

Laura E. MacDonald, "Sheldon Currie: The Tricks of Adaptation," *In 2 Print* (Spring 1998): 38;

Peter Urquhart, "The Glace Bay Miners' Museum/ Margaret's Museum: Adaptation and Resistance," *Cineaction,* 49 (July 1999): 12–18.

Claire Harris

(13 June 1937 –   )

Leslie Sanders
York University

BOOKS: *Fables from the Women's Quarters* (Toronto: Williams-Wallace, 1984);

Translations into Fiction (Fredricton, N.B.: Goose Lane Editions, 1984);

Travelling to Find a Remedy (Fredricton, N.B.: Goose Lane Editions, 1986);

The Conception of Winter (Stratford, Ont.: Williams-Wallace, 1989);

Drawing down a Daughter (Fredricton, N.B.: Goose Lane Editions, 1992);

Grammar of Dissent: Poetry and Prose by Claire Harris, M. Nourbese Philip, Dionne Brand, edited by Carol Morrell (Fredericton, N.B.: Goose Lane Editions, 1994);

Dipped in Shadow (Fredricton, N.B.: Goose Lane Editions, 1996);

She (Fredricton, N.B.: Goose Lane Editions, 2000).

OTHER: "Poets in limbo," in *A Mazing Space,* edited by Shirley Neuman and Smaro Kamboureli (Edmonton, Alta.: Longspoon/NeWest, 1986), pp. 115–125;

"Mirror, Mirror, on the Wall," in *Caribbean Women Writers,* edited by Selwyn R. Cudjoe (Wellesley, Mass.: Calaloux, 1990), pp. 306–309;

"Ole Talk: A Sketch," in *Language in Her Eye,* edited by Libby Scheier, Sarah Sheard, and Eleanor Wachtel (Toronto: Coach House, 1990), pp. 131–141;

"Working with/out a Net," in *Crisis and Creativity in the New Literatures in English Canada,* edited by Geoffrey Davis (Amsterdam & Atlanta: Rodopi, 1990), pp. 71–75;

Kitchen Talk, edited by Harris and Edna Alford (Red Deer, Alta.: Red Deer College Press, 1992);

"Why I Write" and "Inside Passage," in *Into the Nineties,* edited by Anna Rutherford, Lars Jenson, and Shirley Chew (Armidale, New South Wales: Dangaroo, 1994), pp. 395–401.

SELECTED PERIODICAL PUBLICATIONS–
UNCOLLECTED: "Against the Poetry of Revenge," *Fireweed,* 23 (Summer 1986): 15–17;

Claire Harris (<http://www.athabascau.ca/dll/writers/harris.html>)

"Notes to the Great Canadian Novel," *Open Letter,* 9 (Spring 1995): 101–106;

"And the Heart Pauses for Breath," *Fireweed,* 56 (Winter 1996): 7–18.

Claire Harris is an elegant, precise, and challenging poet both in terms of her subjects and of her forms. Her concerns are many and include the complex impact of colonialism and racism, especially in the Caribbean Islands but also in Canada; the situation of women both as victims of oppression and as agents; and human brutality, which she examines both from the vantage point of its perpetrators and its victims. Harris's eye is far-ranging, but she always insists on her Canadian location. She does so not only to call into account the place she calls home but also to challenge the limits often placed on black poetic authority: the expectation that it will confine itself to racialized communities and their oppression. Widely respected, Harris has been invited to read in India and Brazil, as well as all over Europe and North America. As of 2007 her poems had been included in more than seventy anthologies and translated into Hindi and German, and her short stories had appeared in seven anthologies.

Harris's poetry is formally diverse, ranging from haiku to the long poem; two volumes, *Drawing down a Daughter* (1992) and *She* (2000), comprise single poems or poetic novels. She has said that it takes her three to four years to complete a volume, each of which is planned to be conceptually and thematically coherent. She publishes relatively few occasional poems, abandoning work that fails to further the evolution of a volume in progress. Her early choice of publishers was deliberate. She alternated between Williams-Wallace, a pioneering alternative Toronto press founded by Jamaican-born Ann Wallace that for more than a decade published the writing of immigrant women, particularly women of color, and Goose Lane Editions, a well-established Canadian firm formerly known as Fiddlehead. Since 1992 Goose Lane has published all her work and in 1995 republished her two Williams-Wallace collections, *Fables from the Women's Quarters* (1984) and *The Conception of Winter* (1989). By making these choices Harris insisted on her right to breadth of vision and range of audience.

Born in Trinidad on 13 June 1937, Harris was the second of six children and the older of two girls. Her father was a school headmaster and later inspector of schools; her mother retired from teaching to stay home and raise the children. Harris spent her early years in a succession of country towns near the capital, Port of Spain, and her summers at a country estate on the Lopinot River. In the country she was immersed in a world "far removed from the texts I read, or for that matter, the language and life of the towns," she recalled in a 2000 interview with Emily Allen Williams. "Finally, my earliest lessons were taught through story-telling." On both sides Harris's family had been relatively successful. "In Third World countries" to whom one is born "is the difference between life and death," Harris told Arun Mukherjee and Leslie Sanders in 1997, noting that her middle-class upbringing afforded her both education and the assurance that hard work and determination would be rewarded. Her education at St. Joseph's Convent in Port of Spain was classically British, "designed to produce a fully colonised subject"; yet, it provided her with "an indelible sense of great beauty, of possibility in language, even as it provided a theatre to observe human nature trapped in a struggle between worldly social and cultural attitudes and evils" and "a knowledge of duty to what was good."

In 1958 Harris entered University College Dublin to study English literature; she graduated in 1961 and returned to Trinidad to teach at St. Joseph's. She spent the following year studying at the University of the West Indies in Jamaica for a diploma in education, after which she returned to St. Joseph's. She planned to immigrate to New Zealand, where a job awaited her, but the death of her father in 1964 altered her plans. As the eldest daughter, she was expected to care for her mother, who was showing early signs of Alzheimer's disease. The mother's doctor advised a change of scene, and Harris's elder brother, who was living in Calgary, brought her there. Harris followed in 1966, having secured a position teaching English and drama in the middle grades of the Calgary Separate Schools. Her mother lived with her for the first three years. When Harris could no longer care for her, an aunt took her back to Port of Spain.

In 1974 Harris took a study leave and enrolled at the University of Lagos, where she earned a diploma in mass media and communications from a school the United Nations had established there. Her African trip was, "at the time, the great adventure of my life and jolted me into writing," she recorded in her first published collection of poetry, *Fables from the Women's Quarters*. She met the Nigerian poet and playwright John Pepper Clark, who encouraged her to write professionally and published her first work in *ODUMA,* a literary magazine produced by the English department at the University of Lagos. Harris also found inspiration, she told Williams, in the classroom, both teaching literature and drama, and from the teenagers she encountered daily, who gave her access "to raw experience and, occasionally, to a quality of desperation, I had only heard of or read about."

From 1981 to 1989 Harris served as poetry editor for the Alberta literary journal *Dandelion;* in 1983 she participated in the founding of *blue buffalo,* a journal of Alberta writing, and was its managing editor from 1984 to 1987. She has been an active member of the Writers Guild of Alberta from its inception in 1980.

In 1984 Harris published her first two collections, *Fables from the Women's Quarters* and *Translations into Fiction;* although the latter volume appeared after the former, it had been completed earlier. Both volumes evidence themes that have continued to preoccupy Harris in all of her work. The title *Translations into Fiction* indicates Harris's engagement with language and the effect of the bilingualism that marks the Caribbean's legacy of slavery and colonialism. Like Derek Walcott, Harris lays claim to both standard English and Caribbean vernacular; of particular concern to her is colonialism's invalidation of that vernacular, denying its precise and expressive capacity, and so also of the people who speak it. She sees English, whose literature she came to love, as inimical to her being and therefore in need of transformation. Translation, then, has particular resonance for this poet. The title poem suggests that displacement is a kind of translation: addressing an African mask "hauled from woods and worshippers to hang shackled to my wall," the speaker concludes, "You are left a fiction carved from a tree in Africa." When the mask is viewed out of its proper context, its original meaning is replaced by a fiction. In a related sense human experience does not easily translate, as when there is miscommunication, or racism. Stereotype, too, the poet would say, is a fiction. Actual translations are used as epigrams for many of the poems, including Gregor Sebba's of Rainer Maria Rilke, Guy Davenport's of Heraclitus, and W. S. Merwin's of Rūmī. Significantly left untranslated from the Spanish is the epigram of the poem "A Black Reading," in which the speaker says, "I dream of a new naming / new words new line / shaping a new world."

Other aspects of this first completed collection indicate preoccupations that have since come to characterize Harris's vision and form. Harris's investigations of human depravity in the volume are relentless and replete with images that are startling, horrific, and painful to contemplate. She scrutinizes both inhumanity committed by governments and brutal individual acts. The final section of *Translations into Fiction,* "Deformed Angels," includes "Who Would Suppose That He Could Forget Her," in which the romantic opening lines mask the compulsions of a serial killer. In the same section an untitled poem, introduced by the translation of a line by the Holocaust survivor Paul Celan, is divided into two columns. The left column relates the perspective of a young government soldier in Latin America using a baby as a football; in the right column, which is printed in italics, the speaker agonizes over whether the world always contained such horror. Finally, in this collection Harris uses typography, word placement, typeface, and poetic and prosaic line formations to render visual the energies and tensions that course through the poems, as well as to signal her intention of dislodging traditional English poetic

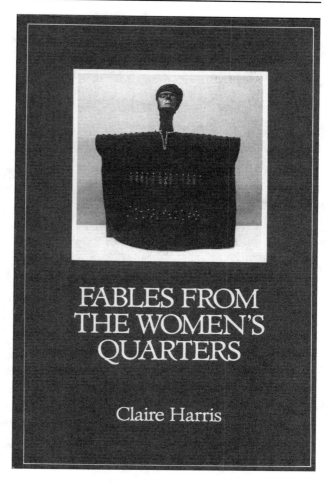

Paperback cover for the first edition, 1984 (Bruccoli Clark Layman Archives)

expectations. In a 2001 interview with Kwame Dawes, Harris spoke of the page as "where oral literature parts company with print" and acknowledged that she has a "very visual view of poetry. . . . Unlike other writers, poets have the gift of the page." While this early volume is modest in its formal experiments, formal freedom characterizes her later work. *Translations into Fiction* won the 1984 Writers of Alberta Poetry Award.

Fables from the Women's Quarters includes several long poems that speak from the marginal place to which the European relegates the "other." The collection opens with "Nude on a Pale Staircase," which depicts the deteriorating marriage of an Indian woman and an Italian man. Out of context in her husband's village, deprived of the extended family that would have sustained her in Assam, the woman is heartsick over news of massacres there that, to her husband, are only "a hell of a mess." The poem concludes:

She knows
he does not
see her
not as he used to
. . . .

Uprooted
dry pressed
between the pages of his
culture
the rough cut of her
foreignness
is faded to a nuance
he approves.

In "Where the Sky Is a Pitiful Tent" Harris counterposes passages from the testimony of Rigoberto Menchu, reproduced in italics beneath the stanzas, with the monologue of the wife of a Guatemalan indigenous freedom fighter:

I said *do not go*
you didn't answer. . . . You will not stop what you have
 begun
though I asked in the way a woman can
Since you have broken thus into life
soon someone will make a pattern
of your bones.

Setting is deftly sketched:

mist hides
sad mountain villages reluctant fields
still your son skips on the path laughing
he is a bird he is a hare
under skeletal trees.

Love, courage, anguish, and resolve infuse her speech, which is a testament to lives lost in freedom struggles the world over and to the families left behind.

Another long poem, "Policeman Cleared in Jaywalking Case," responds to a report in the *Edmonton Journal* that is cited as an epigram. The speaker addresses a fifteen-year-old black girl strip-searched and jailed for jaywalking: "Look you, child, I signify three hundred years in swarm around me this thing I must this uneasy thing myself the other stripped down to skin and sex. . . . . the child was black and female and therefore mine." Addressing the society that can so demean and destroy a child, the speaker recalls an incident in Trinidad when she was almost hit by a car while jaywalking. She contrasts the concern of the police, driver, and bystanders, which validated her life as precious, with the harsh violation of the child in Canada and con-

cludes: "but I fear most myself how easy to drown in your world dead believing myself living who stand 'other' and vulnerable to your soul's disease / Look you child, I signify." *Fables from the Women's Quarters* also includes Harris's first long poem, originally published by Clark in Lagos: "Seen in Stormlight," about her stay in Nigeria, depicts the country in political chaos. Prose commentary appears in italics at the bottom of the page, and footnotes explain terms and identify gods. Less typographically inventive than *Translations into Fiction, Fables from the Women's Quarters* is equally various in its forms, which range from free verse to dense paragraphs, both narrative and meditative; *Fables from the Women's Quarters* also includes haiku. The volume won the 1984 Commonwealth Award for Poetry for the Americas Region.

A theme that runs through many of the poems in Harris's next collection, *Travelling to Find a Remedy* (1986), is the question of possibility and volition; possibility is here understood on the level of atoms, as well as on the level of conscious choices made in what one poem calls the "accidental world." The long opening poem, "Every Moment: A Window," presents the thoughts of a man who has just murdered his wife; the poet intrudes:

now you stand here
thus
in this poem
an item
lifted from a newspaper
wondering.

The poem speculates on the chain of events that lead to the moment, postulating that "the window may crack / an opening through which we / may crawl bruised." The window also closes, however; at each moment, all is possible. A clue to the inspiration for the poem is that it ends with the man sitting in a chair, reading Paul Davis's *God and the New Physics* (1983). Other poems address more-benign moments of possibility: "Variations Two" meditates on choosing between an apple and an orange; "And So . . . Home" recalls resisting the speaker's mother's request to choose a particular color of hair ribbon. Yet, in a Harris poem one is often plunged into horror. In "Coming to Terms with the White Visibility of Death" a drowned child and a child killed by a car rise to the surface of the speaker's memory. "The Testimony of pPETER p pPETRUS" is a sober meditation on male consciousness, rendered playful through a sprinkling of unexpected *p*s. But the poem ends in a suicide that the title character of the next piece, the prose passage "Witness," is lured into witnessing. The title poem of the volume depicts a love affair in Africa and an offer of marriage that is refused because of insurmountable cultural differences. The early stanzas recount vivid moments of passion and spiritual and physical coupling; the later stanzas record the sober realization of custom and expectations. The speaker concludes: "There are advantages / to your ebon calm / your reason but I was not born to it." The most overtly philosophical of Harris's collections, *Travelling to Find a Remedy* suggests quests—physical, intellectual, and spiritual—none offering panacea, but all fruitful. The book won the Writers of Alberta Poetry Award in 1987.

Harris's 1989 volume, *The Conception of Winter,* begins with the section "Toward the Color of Summer," which follows three women friends on a trip to Barcelona. The poems are punctuated by "postcards," short poems in boxes sprinkled haphazardly across the page; for example:

SIGHTSEEING
my eyes
are
dead drunk
July 12, 1984.

Many of the poems in the section display a lyricism and gentleness that are rare in Harris's work. The speaker's companions' beauty, desires, and wistfulness are lovingly portrayed; sorrow also marks the trip, for another friend is dying back home in Calgary. For the speaker Barcelona's pleasures are also mitigated by a haunting history that is explored in "A Dream of Valor and Rebirth": it was the debarkation point for Christopher Columbus and the port for the "slave ship rising." The city thus invokes what Harris termed, in the interview with Dawes, "the worst catastrophe to have befallen the human race, and Earth . . . the movement of the West out of Europe." The middle section of the volume includes a series of meditations of the lives of women; "to every woman / a season / and a pattern / OF SURVIVAL," the speaker proclaims in the second poem in this section. The final section, "A Grammar of the Heart," is a long poem on the death of Harris's mother, whose life is rendered as "wild and full of grace."

Harris's best-known work, the 1992 volume *Drawing down a Daughter,* is a mixed-genre work relating the thoughts of a Trinidadian woman living in Calgary who is about to give birth to a daughter. The woman's African Canadian husband has gone to Trinidad to prepare to move the family there. For him, the move is a flight from racism to an environment where their daughter can grow up free of hatred; knowing the con-

straints of a small island society, the woman opposes the move. Over the course of a day the woman speaks to the unborn child, writes a journal for her, and recalls stories. She understands the challenges that will face her daughter:

Daughter to live is to dream the self
to make a fiction
this telling I begin
you stranded in a landscape of your time
will redefine shedding my tales
to grow your own
as I have lost our ancestors your
daughters will lose me.

She seeks to articulate a legacy for her child but confesses:

Daughter there is no language
i can offer you no corner that is
yours unsullied . . . all i have to give
is English which hates
fears your
black skin.

The narrative includes memories, advice, stories, sayings, even a recipe. The forms comprise prose and poetry; some of the poems are conventional free verse, while others are typographically adventuresome, with the words scattered across the page, lined up at both margins, or outlining a pregnant stomach and full breasts. The use of two fonts suggests different internal voices. The language varies from formal English to Caribbean vernacular, both in several registers. No language is adequate, a dilemma underscored by a theme that runs through the text: the question of "the matter of fact." Two linked prose narratives stress the difficulty of understanding what comprises reality and how language is implicated in this difficulty. The "matter of fact" brought under scrutiny is the intervention of a spirit from Trinidadian folklore into the affairs of humans. In this story La Diablesse takes vengeance on Burri, a city man who is prepared to abandon his pregnant country girlfriend, Jocelyn. The story seems incredible, except that the woman recalls hearing Burri tell her father, a respected man in the community, about his experience with a mysterious woman that led to the car wreck visible to all and confirmed in a police report. The story is told and retold by the principal speaker in standard English and by her aunt, as storyteller, in vernacular. An effect of this story is to insist that the reality defined by a Caribbean vernacular is as palpable, material, and ethical as that defined in any other fashion. The two languages define and articulate competing and

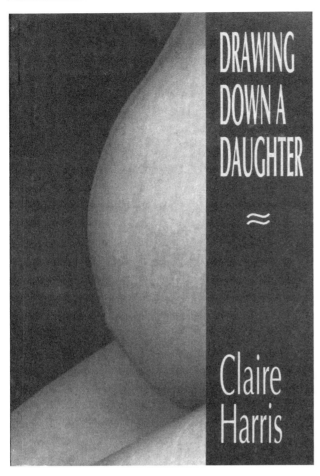

Paperback cover for the first edition, 1992 (Bruccoli Clark Layman Archives)

in some sense incommensurable realities. Despite the thematic concern with the lack of adequate language, in its eloquence and unconventionality *Drawing down a Daughter* probes those places where new language might evolve. A work of great intimacy and power, of all Harris's work *Drawing Down a Daughter* has garnered the most critical attention. It was short-listed for the prestigious Governor General's Prize for Poetry in 1993.

In her next work, *Dipped in Shadow* (1996), Harris confronts her readers with shocking Canadian realities. The opening poem, "O What Are You Thinking My Sisters," calls for attention to be paid to what follows; one stanza begins:

> what are you hatching my sister dear
> sister what are you
> hatching in your milk and cream
> skin.

"Nude in an Armchair" takes the perspective of a physically abused woman who did not stop her husband

from molesting their son and daughter at monthly gatherings of his friends: "on the first Saturday of every month . . . the girl is yOurs / the boy is yOurs." The poem, which includes transcripts from the mother's trial with marginal poetic commentary, is a portrayal of trauma, moral paralysis, and heartbreak. The typographical play "yOurs" links the father and the mother but also brings in the reader, enjoining the social responsibility that is a theme of the collection. "This Fierce Body" is a gentle and loving song of praise for a gay man dying of AIDS. "Sister (Y)our Manchild at the Close of the Twentieth Century," addressed to the mother of a marine, makes clear women's complicity in war and imperialism. Drawn from a newspaper account, the final poem in the collection, "Woeman Womb Prisoned," is a portrait of a fifteen-year-old girl giving birth to her father's child in the family bathroom; her brother assists her by taking the baby away. Its fate is not indicated.

In *She* (2000) Harris returns to the novelistic long poem she employed in *Drawing down a Daughter.* Depicting the mind of a woman afflicted with multiple-personality disorder, *She* takes the form of letters from Penelope-Marie Lancet, living in Calgary, to her sister, Jasmine-Marie Lancet-Maine, in Trinidad. At least six personalities appear; each writes in a different style, including elliptical yet vivid lyric flung across the page, terse questions ("i am not a shadow / or even a drift / from an other time / i am fiction / so who writes me? / love / penny"), long prose narratives, and even a script for a silent movie. Some personalities write in standard English, others in Caribbean vernacular. The letters are alternately anguished and hilarious. Multiple and fractured subjectivities are literalized and played out, becoming, finally, a cacophony of voices both historical and contemporary. Distraught over the termination of a false pregnancy, Penelope-Marie kidnaps a black baby adopted by white parents, telling her neighbors that he is her sister's child. Later, a childhood memory emerges of a sibling dropped down a well; the event is related calmly in prose by one personality, while another disintegrates in the telling. *She* extends the examination of language and its lack addressed by the woman in *Drawing down a Daughter.* What appears in the earlier work as lament is represented in *She* in all its torment. Penelope has many languages, but none is her own; thus, she is without language. She is ultimately reduced to babbling nursery rhymes, and the work resolves into a cry of anguish. "Ambitious and pulled off with heartbreaking flair, *She* is a virtuoso performance from a player who has earned her place in the spotlight," wrote Paul Vermeersch in *Quill and Quire* (May 2000).

In interviews and essays Harris confronts mainstream Canadian society's assumptions about black people and its expectations of black writers. As an outsider, she sees Canada in ways that it does not see itself. Coming from the West Indies, she told Sanders and Mukherjee, she recognizes the structures of colonialism in Canada. In her writing, she told Dawes, she claims "the full range of human interest and experience for my own," not restricting herself to topics such as racism that are deemed black writers' "only area of expertise, but ideas." In her essays Harris makes explicit her understanding of herself as a member of the African Diaspora, one who is in, but not entirely of, the West.

Considered one of Canada's most important black poets, Claire Harris writes deeply moral, courageous, and engaged poetry that is marked by searing images, memorable characters, precise language, and formal liberty. Making frequent use of newspaper accounts, her poems call attention to horrors to which most people have become inured and investigates human consciousness in moments of extremity. Her aim is to provoke her readers into seeing the world differently and into feeling the urgency of making it anew.

Interviews:

Monty Reid, "Choosing Control: An Interview with Claire Harris," *Waves*, 13 (Fall 1984): 37–41;

Janice Williamson, "Claire Harris: 'I dream of a new naming . . . '," in *Sounding Differences*, edited by Williamson (Toronto: University of Toronto Press, 1993), pp. 115–130;

Leslie Sanders and Arun Mukherjee, "A Sense of Responsibility: An Interview with Claire Harris," *West Coast Line*, 31 (Spring–Summer 1997): 26–37;

Emily Allen Williams, "An Interview with Claire Harris," *Wasafari*, 32 (Autumn 2000): 41–44;

Kwame Dawes, "Claire Harris," in *Talk Yuh Talk: Interviews with Anglophone Caribbean Poets*, edited by Dawes (Charlottesville: University of Virginia Press, 2001), pp. 61–72;

H. Nigel Thomas, "Claire Harris," in *Why We Write: Conversations with African Canadian Poets and Novelists*, edited by Thomas (Toronto: TSAR Publications, 2006), pp. 115–130.

References:

George Elliott Clarke, "Harris, Philip, Brand: Three Authors in Search of Literate Criticism," *Journal of Canadian Studies*, 35, no. 1 (2000): 161–189;

Lynette Hunter, "After Modernism: Alternative Voices in the Writings of Dionne Brand, Claire Harris and Marlene Philip," *University of Toronto Quarterly*, 62, no. 2 (1992–1993): 256–281;

Dannabang Kuwabong, "The Mother as the Archetype of Self: A Poetics of Matrilineage in the Poetry of Claire Harris and Lorna Goodison," *Ariel*, 30, no. 1 (1999): 105–129;

Kuwabong, "Reading the Gospel of Bakes: Daughters' Representations of Mothers in the Poetry of Claire Harris and Lorna Goodison," *Canadian Woman Studies*, 18, nos. 2–3 (1998): 132–138;

Sunanda Pal, "Celebration of the Black Being in Claire Harris's *The Conception of Winter* and *Drawing down a Daughter*," in *Intersextions: Issues of Race and Gender in Canadian Women's Writing*, edited by Coomi S. Vevaina and Barbara Godard (New Delhi: Creative Books, 1996), pp. 131–141;

Susan Rudy, "'What there is teasing beyond the edges': Claire Harris's Liminal Autobiography," *Essays on Canadian Writing*, 60 (Winter 1996): 78–99;

Ian Sowton, "An Autobiography. Of Sorts (Reading Claire Harris, *Drawing down a Daughter*)," *Open Letter*, 9 (Summer 1995): 25–34;

Teresa Zackodnik, "'Writing Home': Claire Harris's 'Drawing down a Daughter,'" *Ariel*, 30 (July 1999): 165–190.

Jonathan Locke Hart

(30 June 1956 –   )

Christian Riegel
University of Regina

BOOKS: *Theater and World: The Problematics of Shakespeare's History* (Boston: Northeastern University Press, 1992);

Northrop Frye: The Theoretical Imagination (London & New York: Routledge, 1994);

Breath and Dust, introduction by Robert Kroetsch (Edmonton: Mattoid/Grange, 2000);

Representing the New World: The English and French Uses of the Example of Spain (New York: Palgrave, 2001);

Dream China (Ottawa: BuschekBooks, 2002);

Dream Salvage (Ottawa: BuschekBooks, 2003);

Comparing Empires: European Colonialism from Portugese Expansion to the Spanish-American War (Houndmills, U.K. & New York: Palgrave Macmillan, 2003);

Columbus, Shakespeare and the Interpretation of the New World (New York: Palgrave Macmillan, 2003);

Contesting Empires: Opposition, Promotion, and Slavery (New York: Palgrave Macmillan, 2005);

Interpreting Cultures: Literature, Religion, and the Human Sciences (Basingstoke, U.K. & New York: Palgrave Macmillan, 2006).

OTHER: *Imagining Culture: Essays in Early Modern History and Literature,* edited by Hart (New York: Garland, 1996);

Explorations in Difference: Law, Culture, and Politics, edited by Hart and Richard W. Bauman (Toronto & Buffalo, N.Y.: University of Toronto Press, 1996);

Reading the Renaissance: Culture, Poetics, and Drama, edited, with contribution, by Hart (New York: Garland, 1996);

Making Contact: Maps, Identity, and Travel, edited by Hart and Glenn Burger (Edmonton: University of Alberta Press, 2003).

SELECTED PERIODICAL PUBLICATIONS— UNCOLLECTED: "When I stand with you," *Grain Magazine,* 14, no. 2 (1986): 28;

"Lost in Telling," *Grain Magazine,* 15, no. 4 (1987): 30;

"The Prodigal Father" and "Cries and Whispers," *Kirkland Review,* 1 (1997): 23, 26;

"From Turning," *Harvard Review,* 23 (2002): 31;

"#33 from Musing," *Cimarron Review,* 143 (2003): 26.

Jonathan Locke Hart is a scholar and editor who emerged in the late 1990s as an important voice in contemporary poetry. Hart's poems move from the present age to the ancient world to contemplate the relationship of the self to the grand sweep of history and literature.

Hart was born in Halifax, Nova Scotia, on 30 June 1956 to George Edward Hart, a public administrator in social policy and welfare, and Jean Maclean Jackman Hart, a librarian and painter. In Hart's early years the family lived in Ottawa; they then moved to Montreal, where he attended John Rennie High School from 1969 until they moved to Toronto in 1972. Hart graduated from Leaside High School in Toronto in 1974. As a teenager he played for championship hockey teams in Pointe Claire, Quebec, and Scarborough, Ontario; he was sent a letter of intent by Roger Nielson of the Peterborough Petes of the Ontario Major Junior Hockey League, but he declined the offer. In 1974 he entered Trinity College of the University of Toronto, where he studied under the literary scholar Northrop Frye. While still a student he was the runner-up for the prestigious E. J. Pratt Gold Medal in Poetry in 1978–1979. He received a B.A. with high distinction in 1978 and an M.A. in English literature in 1979. On 15 August 1981 he married Mary Alice Marshall, a lawyer. He completed his Ph.D. in English literature at the University of Toronto in 1983.

In the 1980s Hart published poems in the important Canadian literary magazines *Grain, Quarry,* and *The Antigonish Review.* He was a lecturer at the University of Alberta in 1984–1985, an assistant professor at Trent University in Peterborough in 1985–1986, a senior fellow at the Centre for Reformation and Renaissance Studies at Victoria College of the University of Toronto in 1986, and a visiting scholar at Harvard University in 1986–1987. In 1987 he became assistant professor of English at the University of Alberta. In 1989 he and his wife had twins, Julia Jackman and James Locke. Hart was promoted to associate professor in 1992 and full professor in 1995.

Hart established himself as one of Canada's most important literary scholars with a series of books, beginning with *Theater and World: The Problematics of Shakespeare's History* (1992) and continuing with *Northrop Frye: The Theoretical Imagination* (1994); he also edited or co-edited *Imagining Culture: Essays in Early Modern History and Literature; Explorations in Difference: Law, Culture, and Politics;* and *Reading the Renaissance: Culture, Poetics, and Drama,* all in 1996. In the late 1990s Hart developed with the University of Alberta Press the cuRRents series to publish new and reprinted titles featuring Canadian writers; the series, of which he is the editor, has included works by Sinclair Ross, Robert Kroetsch, and E. D. Blodgett. During these years Hart frequently spent his vacations, sabbaticals, and other leaves in London; Cambridge, Massachusetts; and Cassis, France. He traveled to China in 1993.

In 2000 Hart collected many of the poems he had written over the previous twenty-five years in *Breath and Dust.* The book is divided into four numbered parts and includes 123 mostly short poems linked by form and theme. The primary mode is the lyric; some of the poems show influences from Ezra Pound, Asian forms, and Roman models. The poems reflect the speaker's movements across geographical and psychic spaces. In his introduction to the volume Kroetsch says: "Here is the restlessness of the North American poet. Jonathan Locke Hart moves us through geographies of landscape, of history, of the psyche. But this poet is unique in his resolve to find a place, not to speak about, but to speak from." The poems move across a vast landscape that includes Newcastle; Australia; London and Hampstead Heath; Paris; Seoul; Beijing; Hong Kong; Toronto and Stratford, Ontario; and Lockeport, Nova Scotia. Kroetsch notes that in reading Hart's poems "we are reminded . . . of the constant motions that constitute our days," and the frequent shifts in place are signs of the "fluidity of our lives" in the modern period.

The poems in the second section–"Garden Zither," "Rain," "Chang'an Fall," "More Ruins," "Lost Farms," "To the Norther Border," and "Kept"–illustrate Hart's use of linked lyric. From two to four lines in length, each poem is a self-contained rumination on a singular moment of experience; for example, "Garden Zither" reads: "Life consumes us as death devours us: / At sunrise the poet thinks of impending night." These two lines are deceptively complex: out of the immediate moment–the poet's thoughts as he awakens in the morning–comes a philosophical understanding of the nature of living as mortal beings. As the series progresses, no overt mention is made of this theme;

Paperback cover for the first edition, 2000
(Bruccoli Clark Layman Archives)

rather, each poem subtly engages the theme by presenting a brief observed moment that connects to the larger idea of individual life as part of a broad historical sweep. "More Ruins," for example, reads:

It rains steadily along the Yangtze
The birds call above the dream
Of the six dynasties: the willows
Overgrow the great Taicheng.

Rooted in the perceptual moment of the rain along the river in the first line, the poem moves to the realm of dream and then to history and finally shifts back to the scene of the speaker's observation of the world around him.

Breath and Dust also includes more-extended poems such as the forty-two-line "Pointe Claire," which explores a childhood memory of a winter day:

A dawn so cold
The tongue rivets to steel and the youth
Trudges the snow-packed street towards the rink.

Paperback cover for the first edition, 2002
(<www.buschekbooks.com/>)

The focus shifts to the remembering speaker, who places himself within the poem in the line "I come to a field"; by the last stanza the speaker is fully conscious of the distance between past and present and about the role of writing poetry in the act of remembering:

In the season of my exile, here down the road
Removed I speak
To you who have never been
There.

Formally, Hart employs enjambment, half lines, and variable line lengths to create the effect of a dynamic movement through the currents of memory. In "Ancient Music" he uses line breaks to create effects of past and present and to heighten the sense of distance between the speaker and the female subject of the poem. In one passage he uses movement to develop the idea of the gap between the past and the present:

There are doorways to the yard
I may never enter: roses are like echoes.
My dreams move over the dead leaves
And hers skirt in the dark, whisper
Over the pond in a day too long
For the two of us.

After *Breath and Dust,* Hart published *Representing the New World: The English and French Uses of the Example of Spain* (2001). His second collection of poems, *Dream China,* appeared the following year. Like *Breath and Dust,* it is a series of linked lyrics; but while in the first volume the poems are titled and the links between sections and poems are subtle, in *Dream China* sequences are indicated by the numbering of the eleven sections and the numbering of the poems in a parallel series of Roman and Arabic numerals from the beginning of the volume to the end. The two sets of numbered poems do not progress evenly or correspondingly: for example, poems xxix and xxx immediately precede poems 34 and 35, which are followed by poem xxxi. The parallel tracks allow for a multiplicity of voices. *Dream China* is also more focused thematically than *Breath and Dust* and explores the self in the contemporary world in relation to the past, memory, family, and travel. In *Dream China* Hart examines the role of creativity in the perception of the world. "Paint and word," the speaker says in poem 39, "are small buttresses"; that is, creativity provides structures that enable one to endure the world. In poem xlv he notes that "this craft / itself a dream / decodes the signs of sleep." Contemplating the self in relation to history, the speaker in poem x notes that "my grandfather's / brother died slowly in the brigade / in Harrogate," and "other uncles . . . / fought in the Battle of Britain." Elsewhere he mentions figures such as Helen of Troy, Genghis Khan, and Marco Polo, affirming that he and his poetry are intertwined with thousands of years of history. He notes these connections in poem xxxiv:

This lone voice
mine
wavers amid

the words of the dead
spoken
as they wander

the earth from the east:
the strangeness

shaking my bones
the songs bread
from yeast.

Hart's third volume of poems, *Dream Salvage* (2003), comprises eleven sections of 105 linked numbered poems that once again deal with history, the relationship of the self to the world, and the role of creativity in perceiving the world. Here, however, he moves beyond the immediacy of perception that characterizes his earlier works and that is conventional in lyric poetry, so that the speaker is less likely to be identified with the poet. The opening sequences describe the Romans' violent conquest of Europe:

no prisoners, Germanicus said,
and the huge swift Germans fell

heaped and strewn
between the Rhine and Elbe.

Hart links the horror of ancient colonialism with the colonization of the Americas begun by Christopher Columbus and the conquering of Native Americans in New England: "the Natives massacred and massacring / playing heathen to the Elect." This passage questions his interest in history and his need to write about it:

why should anyone care
about people long past

ancestors or not?
the dead are forgotten

stray evidence
supports the myth

and theory. why
do I make a saga
of sleep?

Toward the end of the final section the speaker examines the relationship of his own family to world events in the past:

Europe tore itself and the world apart

our parents, grandparents, great-grandparents
were there for the bombs: I saw serial numbers

branded on forearms in my youth
and who is the savage now or ever was?

Also in 2003 Hart published *Comparing Empires: European Colonialism from Portugese Expansion to the Spanish-American War* and *Columbus, Shakespeare and the Interpretation of the New World* and co-edited *Making Contact: Maps, Identity and Travel*. In 2005 he visited Taiwan. That same year he published *Contesting Empires: Opposition, Promotion, and Slavery.* All of Jonathan Locke Hart's scholarly work deals with the connections between history and literature and with the effects of the past on the contemporary world. In his poetry he presents a sophisticated and complex voice that investigates poetic form, history, and the role of the self in the world.

Tomson Highway

(6 December 1951 –   )

Linda Morra
University of British Columbia

BOOKS: *The Rez Sisters: A Play in Two Acts* (Saskatoon, Sask.: Fifth House, 1988);

Dry Lips Oughta Move to Kapuskasing: a Play (Saskatoon, Sask.: Fifth House, 1989);

Kiss of the Fur Queen (Toronto: Doubleday Canada, 1998; Norman: University of Oklahoma Press, 1998);

Johnny National, Super Hero (Ottawa: Health Canada, 2001);

Caribou Song / atihko nikamom (Toronto: HarperCollins, 2001);

Dragonfly Kites / pimihakanisa (Toronto: HarperCollins, 2002);

Comparing Mythologies, Charles R. Bronfman Lecture in Canadian Studies Series (Ottawa: University of Ottawa, 2003)–includes "The Opposite of Prayer: An Introduction to Tomson Highway," by John Moss;

Fox on the Ice / Mahkesis Miskwamihk E-Cipatapit (Toronto: HarperCollins, 2003);

Rose (Vancouver: Talonbooks, 2003);

Ernestine Shuswap Gets Her Trout: A "String Quartet" for Four Female Actors (Vancouver: Talonbooks, 2005).

PLAY PRODUCTIONS: *A Ridiculous Spectacle in One Act,* Manitoulin Island, Ont., De-Ba-Jeh-Mu-Jig Theatre Company, 1985;

The Rez Sisters: A Play in Two Acts, Toronto, Native Canadian Centre, November 1986; New York, New York Theatre Workshop, December 1993;

Aria, Toronto, Annex Theatre, 1987;

New Song . . . New Dance, Toronto, Native Canadian Centre, 1988;

Dry Lips Oughta Move to Kapuskasing, Toronto, Theatre Passe Muraille, 1989;

The Sage, the Dancer, and the Fool, by Highway, Rene Highway, and Bill Merasty, Toronto, Native Canadian Centre, 1989;

Annie and the Old One, Montreal, Centaur Theatre, 1989;

Rose, Toronto, University College, 2000;

Incredible Adventures of Mary Jane Mosquito, Stratford, Ont., Stratford Summer Music Festival, 2001;

Tomson Highway (photograph by Michael Cooper; from the dust jacket for Kiss of the Fur Queen, *1998; Bruccoli Clark Layman Archives)*

Ernestine Shuswap Gets Her Trout, Kamloops, B.C., Western Canada Theatre, 2004.

OTHER: Geoffrey York, *The Dispossessed: Life and Death in Native Canada,* foreword by Highway (London: Vintage U.K., 1990);

"The Lover Snake," in *An Anthology of Canadian Native Literature in English,* edited by Daniel David Moses and Terry Goldie (Toronto: Oxford University Press, 1992), pp. 275–277.

Tomson Highway is widely acclaimed as a Native Canadian playwright, although he has also written a novel, children's short stories, and other forms of prose. In whatever genre he writes, Highway tends to infuse contemporary literary forms with elements of Native mythology, especially the Trickster figure Nanabush.

He frequently employs Cree or Ojibway phrases, reflecting his beliefs that certain aspects of culture defy translation and that he has been absorbed into a culture that makes few concessions to his own.

Highway was born on 6 December 1951 to Cree parents, Joe and Pelagie Philomena Highway, in a tent on an island in Maria Lake, north of the town of Lynn Lake on the Brocket Reserve in northwest Manitoba. His father was a fisherman, hunter, and champion sled-dog racer. The eleventh of twelve children—five boys and seven girls—Highway spoke only Cree until 1957, when he was removed from his parents' care and sent to the Guy Hill Indian Residential School, a Roman Catholic institution in The Pas. There he was required to speak English. He was also sexually abused by the priests who were his instructors. He attended Churchill High School in Winnipeg from 1966 to 1969. He studied piano at the University of Manitoba between 1970 and 1972 and in London, under William Aide, in 1972. He earned a bachelor of music with honors in 1975 and a bachelor of arts in English in 1976, both from the University of Western Ontario, where he worked with the playwright and poet James Reaney. Reaney introduced him to the work of Quebec playwright Michel Tremblay, which has influenced Highway's writing.

Giving up his plans to become a concert pianist, Highway was a program analyst for the Ontario Federation of Indian Friendship Centres and a cultural worker for the Native Peoples' Resource Centre from 1975 to 1978. For the next seven years he worked for such Native Canadian theatre companies as Northern Delights in Sioux Lookout, Ontario, and the De-Ba-Jeh-Mu-Jig Theatre Company on Manitoulin Island, Ontario. In 1985 he became artistic director of the De-ba-jeh-mu-jig Theatre Company; in 1986 he became artistic director of Native Earth Performing Arts, where he worked with such playwrights as Daniel David Moses and Monique Mojica.

Highway's career as playwright was launched by the success of *The Rez Sisters* (performed 1986, published 1988), about seven women who travel from the fictional Wasayshigan Hill Indian Reserve to Toronto to try to win the "Biggest Bingo in the World." On the bus they reveal to each other the most intimate details of their lives. The women attribute many of their problems to the reserve; in the opening scene Pelajia Rosella Patchnose declares that "Everyone here's crazy. No jobs. Nothing to do but drink and screw each other's wives and husbands and forget about our Nanabush." Pelajia's husband and sons have had to find "decent jobs" elsewhere; Annie Cook dreams of visiting her daughter, who lives with a French Canadian man in Sudbury; Marie-Adele Starblanket is dying of ovarian cancer and is preoccupied with ensuring the well-being

of her fourteen children after her death; Veronique St. Pierre remains childless in her second marriage, and her husband, Pierre, is an alcoholic who spends their money on his addiction; Zhaboonigan Peterson was sexually assaulted by two white boys who left her for dead; Emily Dictionary, beaten by her former husband, Henry Dadzinanare, left him to join a lesbian motorcycle gang and returned to the "rez" after her lover was killed by a semitrailer; and Philomena Moosetail regrets having given up her baby for adoption years ago when she was abandoned by her married white lover, for whom she had worked as a secretary. They all imagine the many ways that winning the "biggest bingo" might bring them freedom, happiness, respect, or relief. Philomena, who wins $600, uses it to install a "spirit white" toilet in her home. In *The Rez Sisters* the Trickster is a seagull, the bingo master, and the black bird of death who facilitates Marie-Adele's acceptance of her mortality and reappears when she is dying to embrace her in his "ever soft wings."

While revealing how detrimental the materialism of white culture, as reflected in their obsession with bingo, has been to the women's lives, Highway also depicts the mutually supportive environment and sense of community that they provide for each other. Their efforts to raise funds through bake sales, babysitting, and so forth to finance their trip to Toronto demonstrate their ability to work cooperatively to attain their goals, and Véronique cooks for Marie-Adele's fourteen children after the latter's death. Renate Usmiani notes that *The Rez Sisters* shows the influence of Tremblay's *Les belles-soeurs* (1968) but argues that the difference lies in how deeply the characters in each play have been affected by materialistic concerns. However mercenary the fantasies of the rez sisters may initially seem to be, they are balanced by the women's nurturing and caring relationships with each other. Many of their apparently self-interested desires have altruistic motivations, Usmiani points out; for example, if "Veronique dreams of a shiny new kitchen stove," she "also plans to use it to cook for all the motherless orphans on the reserve." *The Rez Sisters* shows, Usmiani suggests, "the essential humanism, life-affirming and hopeful world view of Native peoples," while *Les belles-soeurs* "reflects the negativism, nihilism and spiritual void of Western postmodern society." The play toured Canada and then went to the Edinburgh Festival. In 1987 it won the Dora Mavor Moore Award for Outstanding New Play and the Floyd S. Chalmers Canadian Play Award and was nominated for the Governor General's Award.

Highway's *Dry Lips Oughta Move to Kapuskasing* (1989) was developed at the Playwrights' Workshop Montréal. Here the seven main characters are male, while the Trickster is female—the opposite of *The Rez*

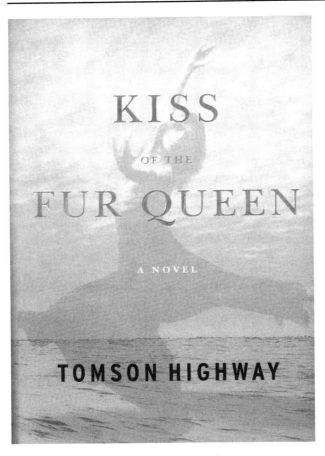

Dust jacket for the first edition, 1998 (Bruccoli Clark Layman Archives)

Sisters. The play centers on the hostility of the men when the women of the Wasaychigan Hill Indian Reserve decide to create a hockey team, the Wasy Wailerettes. While the rez sisters found the means to visit Toronto and win the "Biggest Bingo in the World," and the women in *Dry Lips Oughta Move to Kapuskasing* have the resources to form a hockey team, most of the male characters in both plays are irresponsible, powerless, or involved in self-destructive practices. Zachary Jeremiah Keechigeesik has been almost entirely assimilated into white culture and would like to open a bakery to produce—significantly—apple pies. Big Joey is still haunted by the violence he experienced at the Wounded Knee Reservation in South Dakota in 1973. Dickie Bird Halked has been abandoned by his real father, Big Joey, and is also mentally impaired by fetal alcohol syndrome, which affects his ability to communicate. Spooky Lacroix has overcome his alcoholism only to become a religious fanatic. Pierre St. Pierre is still an alcoholic. Creature Nataways's wife has left him for Big Joey, for whom he himself harbors homosexual desires. The Trickster appears as various female figures who

parallel the women characters: Patsy, Lady Black Halked, and Hera Keechigeesik. In a May 1998 interview with Susannah Schmidt, Highway said that this idea came to him when, during one of his visits to his dying father, he went to a tavern where the men stared at a stripper "like they were seeing God. . . . God as a woman, God as a stripper." He told Schmidt that much of his work examines how "misogyny has split the world": "why are women treated like this? God is a man, Jesus was a man. Until we conceive of God as female, women will not have that power to be treated with respect." From the image of the stripper in the tavern Highway conceived of a playful, irreverent figure who would undermine any attempt to be held accountable for humanity's problems. Thus, when Zachary calls on the "God of the Indian!" and demands to know "Why are you doing this to us?" his cry is both a parody of Christ's last words on the cross and an ironic appeal, since it is apparent that the characters are doing "this" to themselves. Roberta Imboden notes that in this play Nanabush is a comic figure who "allows the characters and the reader/audience to see the demonic, chaotic labyrinth in which the characters live in such a caricatured manner that a liberating process begins."

In the most shocking scene in the play, Dickie Bird rapes Patsy with a crucifix. Since all of the women characters are conflated with the Trickster figure, Patsy's rape represents the way in which Native culture and spirituality have been exploited by Western culture. According to Anne Nothof, the cross is a "literal weapon" and a symbol of how "Christian priests have tried to eradicate Native spirituality."

The one exception to the negative characterizations of male figures is Patsy's boyfriend, Simon Starblanket, who is trying to reintroduce Native cultural practices to the Wasaychigan Hill reserve. He plans to visit Wounded Knee, where Big Joey was injured, and he struggles to relearn the dances and chants of his ancestors. Patsy's stepmother is a medicine woman who, like Simon, makes an effort to revive Native practices and preserve Native values. Simon, however, dies when he loses control of his car on learning of Patsy's rape. This event seems to render the play bleaker than *The Rez Sisters,* but the bleakness is mitigated by Zachary's awakening at the end and realizing that everything that happened in the play was a dream. This ambiguous conclusion has elicited conflicting critical responses. Nothof believes that while the transformation from reality to dream holds "the possibility for a brighter future," the horrific events of the dream will linger in the minds of the audience: the "dramatization is more powerful than the comforting conclusion." Although feminists and religious activists were appalled by the violence in the play, it won the Dora Mavor

Moore Award for Outstanding New Play in 1989 and the Floyd S. Chalmers Canadian Play Award in 1990 and was nominated for the Governor General's Award.

The other plays Highway wrote in the late 1980s—*Aria* (1987), *New Song . . . New Dance* (1988), *The Sage, the Dancer, and the Fool* (1989), and *Annie and the Old One* (1989)—are considered less significant than *The Rez Sisters* and *Dry Lips Oughta Move to Kapuskasing* and have been left unpublished. All of these plays are concerned in various ways with Native culture and community and perseverance in the face of obstacles.

In 1994 Highway received the first Order of Canada bestowed on an Aboriginal writer. He was the Barker Fairley Distinguished Visitor in Canadian Culture at University College of the University of Toronto in 1997–1998. He has been writer-in-residence at the University of British Columbia, the University of Toronto, Simon Fraser University, and Concordia University and has received honorary doctorates from the University of Winnipeg, the University of Western Ontario, Laurentian University, the University of Windsor, and Brandon University.

Highway initially composed *Kiss of the Fur Queen* (1998) as a stage play, then transformed it into a screenplay and finally into a novel. Suzanne Methot notes that he wrote the work to purge his anger and bitterness over the abuse he and his brother, Rene, suffered at the residential schools: "this story needed desperately to be told" for the sake of his health and well-being. Rene, a dancer and choreographer, died of AIDS-related complications in 1990; the Cree dedication translates as "This one's for you, little brother." Highway has asserted that after he completed the novel, his rage and pain ebbed away. He wrote *Kiss of the Fur Queen* in Cree and translated for the sake of a larger audience, but some ideas could not be communicated in English; therefore, some Cree expressions are retained, and a glossary provides loose translations of them. Methot quotes Highway as saying that in "Cree, we don't have animate-inanimate comparisons between things. Animals have souls that are equal to ours. Rocks have souls, trees have souls."

The epigraph of the novel is a quotation from the poet and short-story writer Duncan Campbell Scott, who, as deputy superintendent-general of the Department of Indian Affairs from 1913 to 1932, implemented a brutal and repressive assimilation program and exhorted his agents to use their "utmost endeavours to dissuade the Indians from excessive indulgence in the practice of dancing." *Kiss of the Fur Queen* is divided into six parts, each of which is assigned a musical term that conveys the pace of the section. The novel opens with Abraham Okimasis winning the 1951 Millington Cup World Championship Dog Derby. As the champion,

Okimasis receives a kiss from the winner of the Fur Queen Beauty Pageant, which induces a vision sequence. The Fur Queen becomes a Trickster figure who reappears throughout the novel in various guises and acts as guardian of Okimasis's two children, the first of whom is seen descending "from the seven stars on her tiara." Since he was conceived on the evening of Okimasis's win, he is named Champion. The Fur Queen reappears on the birth of the next son, Ooneemeetoo, who becomes as talented a dancer as Champion is a musician. Champion and Ooneemeetoo are renamed Jeremiah and Gabriel, respectively, in the first of a series of acts of suppression of their Native cultural heritage. At age six they are placed in a Catholic residential school where they are forbidden to speak Cree or to engage in Native practices; they are also sexually abused by the priests.

At the school Jeremiah learns to play the piano, an instrument that further distances him from his cultural background. He is conditioned to see himself as white and to repel any suggestion that contradicts this belief. When he leaves the school, he represses his memories of the sexual abuse: "Some chamber in his mind slammed permanently shut. It had happened to nobody." The Fur Queen effects a transformation in Jeremiah that allows him to return to his Native roots. When Gabriel is dying toward the end of the novel, Jeremiah rejects the intervention of a Catholic priest and calls on a shaman, who burns sweet grass as part of a death ritual. The hospital fire alarms are set off by the smoke, but Jeremiah locks the door, exclaiming, "We have a right to conduct our own religious ceremonies, just like everyone else!" *Kiss of the Fur Queen* was shortlisted for the Chapters/Books in Canada First Novel Award and the Canadian Booksellers' Association Fiction Book of the Year Award.

Highway's play *Rose* was produced in 2000 but not published until 2003. In 2001 Highway received the National Aboriginal Achievement Award. That same year he published a children's book, *Caribou Song / atihko nikamom,* as the first in a trilogy titled Songs of the North Wind; it was followed by *Dragonfly Kites / pimihakanisa* (2002) and *Fox on the Ice / Mahkesis Miskwamihk E-Cipatapit* (2003). All three are written in both Cree and English. *Caribou Song* is a fictionalized account of an experience Highway shared with Rene when they were living with their parents in northern Manitoba; a similar episode occurs in *Kiss of the Fur Queen.* Joe plays the accordion, and his brother, Cody, dances to attract caribou; one day they are taken by surprise by a herd of about two thousand of the animals. Their grief-stricken parents assume that the boys have been trampled to death but find them playing, unharmed, on a large rock from which they watched the caribou pass by. That they are unscathed is evidence that the experience was a spiritual one. In *Dragonfly Kites* Joe and Cody make live "kites" out of dragonflies by tying their mother's sewing thread around the insects; they play with the dragonflies during the day and dream about them at night. They also give names to animals, sticks, and rocks, since in Cree no differentiation is made between human and nonhuman and animate and inanimate beings. In *Fox on the Ice* Joe and Cody are ice fishing with their parents. Their dog team runs after a fox, taking along a couple of unprepared family members who are sitting on the sled. Their dog Ootsie intervenes and saves the day. Brian Deines was a finalist for a 2002 Governor General's Literary Award for his illustrations for *Dragonfly Kites*.

Highway was invited to give the Charles R. Bronfman Lecture in Canadian Studies at the University of Ottawa in 2003. In his talk, which was published the same year, he compared the "mythologies" that have developed from Canadian and Native traditions.

Highway's play *Ernestine Shuswap Gets Her Trout: A "String Quartet" for Four Female Actors* was produced in 2004 and published in 2005. It focuses on four women who are preparing a banquet for the 1910 visit of the Canadian prime minister, Sir Wilfrid Laurier, at which the chiefs of the Shuswap, Okanagan, and Thompson people gave him a document that is known as the "Laurier Memorial." The play details the changes that transpire in the Native community as a result of the visit.

Tomson Highway has helped to establish mainstream Aboriginal theater in Canada. He is also important as an author of children's literature.

Interviews:

Nancy Wigston, "Nanabush in the City: A Profile of Tomson Highway," *Books in Canada*, 18 (March 1989): 8–9;

Hartmut Lutz, "Tomson Highway," in his *Contemporary Challenges: Conversations with Canadian Native Authors* (Saskatoon, Sask.: Fifth House, 1991), pp. 89–96;

Susannah Schmidt, "Interview with Tomson Highway" (May 1998) <http://www.playwrights.ca/portfolios/tomsonint.html> (accessed 31 January 2007);

Sandra Martin, "Finding Joy beyond the Rage," *Globe and Mail* (Toronto), 3 October 2001, p. R1.

References:

Alan Filewood, "Receiving Aboriginality: Tomson Highway and the Crisis of Cultural Authenticity," *Theatre Journal*, 46 (October 1994): 363–373;

Agnes Grant, "Canadian Native Literature: The Drama of George Ryga and Tomson Highway," *Australian Canadian Studies*, 10 (1992): 37–56;

Roberta Imboden, "On the Road with Tomson Highway's Blues Harmonica in *Dry Lips Oughta Move to Kapuskasing*," *Canadian Literature*, 144 (Spring 1995): 113–124;

Denis W. Johnston, "Lines and Circles: The Rez' Plays of Tomson Highway," *Canadian Literature*, 124–125 (Spring–Summer 1990): 254–264;

Suzanne Methot, "Universe of Tomson Highway: In Cree Cosmology, Everything's in Balance, Everything's Connected and Nothing's without Value," *Quill & Quire*, 64 (November 1998): 1, 12;

Daniel David Moses, "The Trickster Theatre of Tomson Highway," *Canadian Fiction Magazine*, 60 (1987): 83–88;

Anne Nothof, "Cultural Collision and Magical Transformation: The Plays of Tomson Highway," *Studies in Canadian Literature*, 20, no. 2 (1995): 34–43;

Robert Nunn, "Marginality and English-Canadian Theatre," *Theatre Research International*, 17 (August 1992): 217–225;

Jennifer Preston, "Weesageechak Begins to Dance: Native Earth Performing Arts Inc.," *Drama Review*, 9, nos. 1–2 (1987): 143–144;

Sheila Rabillard, "Absorption, Elimination, and the Hybrid: Some Impure Questions of Gender and Culture in the Trickster Drama of Tomson Highway," *Essays in Theatre*, 12 (1993): 3–27;

Renate Usmiani, "The Bingocentric Worlds of Michel Tremblay and Tomson Highway," *Canadian Literature*, 144 (Spring 1995): 126–142.

Papers:

Manuscripts for several of Tomson Highway's plays, including *The Rez Sisters*, *New Song . . . New Dance*, and *Dry Lips Oughta Move to Kapuskasing*, are in the Tomson Highway Collection, L. W. Conolly Theatre Archives, University of Guelph, Ontario.

Greg Hollingshead

(25 February 1947 –   )

Cliff Lobe
University of Lethbridge

BOOKS: *Famous Players* (Toronto: Coach House, 1982);
Spin Dry (Oakville, Ont.: Mosaic, 1992);
White Buick (Lantzville, B.C.: Oolichan Books, 1992);
The Roaring Girl (Toronto: Somerville House, 1995; New York: Putnam, 1997; London: Bloomsbury, 1997);
The Healer (Toronto: HarperFlamingo, 1998; London: HarperFlamingo, 1999; New York: HarperFlamingo, 1998);
Bedlam (Toronto: HarperCollins, 2004; New York: St. Martin's Press, 2006).

OTHER: Twelve poems in *T.O. Now: The Young Toronto Poets,* edited by Dennis Lee (Toronto: Anansi, 1968), pp. 1–7;
"The Sound," in *Aurora: New Canadian Writing 1978,* edited by Morris Wolfe (Toronto: Doubleday Canada / Garden City, N.Y.: Doubleday, 1978), pp. 110–120;
"The Story of Alton Finney," in *79: Best Canadian Stories,* edited by Clark Blaise and John Metcalf (Ottawa: Oberon, 1979), pp. 59–68;
"Defence of Floating," in *Writing Home: A PEN Canada Anthology,* edited by Constance Rooke (Toronto: McClelland & Stewart, 1997), pp. 152–158;
"Groff Conkin," in *Everybody's Favourites: Canadians Talk about Books That Changed Their Lives,* edited by Arlene Perly Rae (Toronto: Viking, 1997), pp. 139–140;
"Born Again," in *Turn of the Story: Canadian Short Fiction on the Eve of the Millennium,* edited by Joan Thomas and Heidi Harms (Toronto: Anansi, 1999), pp. 233–250;
"Life of Monsieur de Molière," in *Lost Classics,* edited by Michael Ondaatje, Michael Redhill, Esta Spalding, and Linda Spalding (Toronto: Knopf Canada, 2000; London: Bloomsbury, 2001);
"Lives of the Schmoes," in *Common Ground: A Celebration of Matt Cohen,* edited by Lee, Graeme Gibson, Wayne Grady, and Priscilla Uppal (Toronto: Knopf Canada, 2002), pp. 95–113;

Greg Hollingshead (photograph by Tara Nicholson; courtesy of the author)

"Fifty Cents a Copy," in *First Writes,* edited by Kelley Aitken, Sue Goyette, and Barbara Scott (Banff: Banff Centre Press, 2005), pp. 41–44;
"On Knowing Everything," in *What I Meant to Say,* edited by Ian Brown (Toronto: Thomas Allen, 2005), pp. 37–45.

SELECTED PERIODICAL PUBLICATIONS– UNCOLLECTED: "You Never Know" and "Mary Duncan," *Capilano Review,* 11, no. 1 (1977): 81–91;
"I Love Dragon Lady," *3-cent Pulp,* 4 (November 1978): 3–4;

"Seabright," *Capilano Review*, 14, no. 2 (1978): 5–10;

"Bedtime," *University of Windsor Review*, 14 (Spring–Summer 1979): 60–68;

"Story Story," *Quarry*, 30 (Autumn 1981): 94–101;

"Bishop Berkeley and the Gloomy Clerk: Pope's Final Satire on Deism," *Durham University Journal*, 75 (December 1982): 19–27;

"The Case for Berkeley's Authorship of *The Vanity of Philosophical Systems*," *Eighteenth Century Life*, 9 (January 1985): 51–64;

"The Search for Aldo Eagle (Part I)," *Malahat Review*, 72 (September 1985): 117–139;

"Fina Jim," *Fiddlehead*, 173 (Autumn 1992): 28–39;

"The Blue Chemical," *Canadian Fiction Magazine*, 77 (1992): 32–48;

"The Progress of Nature," *Canadian Fiction Magazine*, 85 (1994): 78–86;

"Writer in Residence," *Western Living*, 21 (June 1996): 20–22, 32;

"The Assistant," *Prairie Fire*, 17 (Summer 1996): 19–27;

"Short Story vs Novel," *University of Toronto Quarterly*, 68 (Fall 1999): 878–879;

"In Memoriam: Matt Cohen (1942–99)," *Writer's Union of Canada Newsletter* (February 2000): 6; revised, *Canadian Forum*, 78 (May 2000): 31;

"Writing *Bedlam*," *Brick: A Literary Journal*, 73 (Summer 2004): 109–113;

"The Fall Guy," *Alberta Views*, 7 (November–December 2004): 46–51;

"The Good News and the Bad News," *Canadian House and Home* (May 2005): 84, 86, 176.

Greg Hollingshead is a short-story writer, novelist, and scholar who has won the Governor General's Literary Award for Fiction and the Rogers Writer's Trust Fiction Prize and has been short-listed for the prestigious Giller Prize. He has also developed a strong international readership, particularly in England, the United States, China, and Germany. Writing primarily in a realist mode, Hollingshead is noted for his innovative use of narrative technique and for his portrayal of the banalities, absurdities, pains, and epiphanies of contemporary life.

Hollingshead was born in Toronto on 25 February 1947 to Albert and Joyce McGlashan Hollingshead and raised in Woodbridge, a suburb north of the city. His father worked at a cotton mill and was a clothier and municipal official; he was also, as Hollingshead told Christian Riegel in a 1997 interview, a "kind of uneducated philosopher" and storyteller. "I grew up in a rough neighbourhood," Hollingshead told Jon C. Stott in 1998, "and I didn't have a particularly happy home life. I spent a lot of time alone"; consequently, he "had time to fantasize" and to develop an "elaborate

interior world filled with secrets and stories." He then had the problem of "how to connect this inner world with the one outside." The relationship between subjective states and the external world is a theme in much of Hollingshead's fiction and is central to his scholarly work on the eighteenth-century idealist philosopher Bishop George Berkeley, whose interest "in how to talk about the connection between in here and out there," as Hollingshead put it in the Stott interview, was "a concern close to my heart."

Hollingshead first wrote poetry as a teenager; twelve of his poems were published in *T.O. Now: The Young Toronto Poets* (1968). He left home in his late teens and entered what he describes in "Writer in Residence" (1996) as "a long tunnel of rentals": "I lived in rooms with a desk and a bed, like cells. I rented other people's apartments and flats and houses." During this period he completed an Honors B.A. and an M.A. in English at the University of Toronto and traveled in Europe and North Africa. He studied in England for five years, receiving his Ph.D. from the University of London in 1974 with a dissertation on Berkeley. He told Mark Young in 1996, "I chose to do my PhD in the history of ideas and on a philosopher (George Berkeley) because I did not want to spend four years learning to think about literature like a critic. I ended up more a scholar than a critic." Returning to Canada with manuscripts for "three unpublishable novels," he took a position in 1975 as professor of eighteenth-century literature and creative writing at the University of Alberta.

In his fiction Hollingshead explores the central tension between physical and spiritual accounts of phenomena. This tension is often evident in the surreal elements that unsettle Hollingshead's fictional worlds, in which conscious and unconscious activity can seem equally uncontrollable and inexplicable. He is especially interested in transforming the details of everyday life into what he called in a 1996 interview with Kristjana Gunnars a "properly aesthetic object," a process he accomplishes, in part, by constant revision: as he explained to Gunnars, "for me, it's really just a matter of going over the material again and again and again, hundreds and hundreds of times, until all the things that have continued to bother me begin to really bother me and I'm able to do something about them."

In his essay "Defence of Floating" (1997) Hollingshead writes, "For as long as I can remember, it has been obvious to me that floating is the essence of life." He describes floating as a mode of being in which the things that seem most solid are revealed to be unsettled and indeterminate—for example, "the flowing upper mantle of the Earth." Floating through their lives, Hollingshead's characters find themselves in disjointed families and destructive relationships; it is difficult for them to ground themselves in the worlds they inhabit, much less to act. The characters seem to belong nowhere. Their problem is one of finding a home, which Hollingshead describes in "Writer in Residence" as "an order imposed upon the wilderness of the world that does more than afford shelter from the elements, that makes it your own." But, Hollingshead admits, "in my bones I know the world out there can never be mine, that this projection of familiarity is a vain illusion."

Dreams are a major theme in Hollingshead's fiction. He told Riegel:

> I think that dreams are traces of information that has come up in the course of a day that has been for whatever reason pushed aside because of distraction, because of repression, because of self-image or haste, and that pushing aside is essentially an emotional act that is a conflictual event on the verge of consciousness. Such events, I think, leave scars, if that is the word—traces anyway.

The traces, Hollingshead continued, reveal the disorder and disease beneath the "surface clarity" or "cleanliness" of daily life. "In my twenties," he explained to Riegel,

> I went through a process of being very attentive to my dreams, to the extent that I was more or less conscious all the time, because as the images came up, in my dreaming mind. It was making note or tracing and finding their origins. I had this idea that, given the Eastern saying, The wise man never dreams, all you have to do is figure out how to stop dreaming and you will become wise.

This process amounted to paying "attention during the day, so I was attempting to be alert enough so that I could process those little moments of impression as they occurred, so that the dreams would be quiet."

Hollingshead's first collection of short stories, *Famous Players* (1982), was edited by Matt Cohen. The two had met when Cohen was writer-in-residence at the University of Alberta. Hollingshead recalled in a 2000 tribute to Cohen, who died in 1999, that he was so impressed by Cohen's *Columbus and the Fat Lady, and Other Stories* (1972) that he began to write his own stories after a trip to Toronto with Cohen in the summer of 1976 on which "we talked for five days":

> As soon as I got out of the truck, I started writing short stories, and over the next six years Matt was often their first reader. At the end of a letter he'd scrawl, "Send more stories." Later, when I'd fumble out a contorted apology cum thank you for still another letter of reference, he'd say "Don't think about it" and change the subject. He was direct and generous and kind.

The short story suited Hollingshead's aesthetic vision. As he writes in his essay "Short Story vs Novel" (1999),

> The primary difference between the short story and the novel is not length but the larger, more conceptual weight of meaning that the longer narrative must carry on its back from page to page, scene to scene. It's not baggy wordage that causes the diffusiveness of the novel, it's this long-distance haul of meaning. . . . a scene in a novel spins off a good deal of its energy looking not only backward and forward in the text but also sideways, outside the text, towards the material world, to that set of common assumptions considered ordinary life. That energy is centrifugal, opening out, not constantly seeking to revolve upon its own still centre.

In contrast, in a "good short story"

> the meaning is not so abstractable, so portable, as it must be in a novel, but is more tightly and ineffably in the formal details of the text. . . . A scene in a short story—and there may be only one—operates with a centripetal force of concentration.

The protagonist of the title story of *Famous Players* is Charles "Bunny" Batten, an unsuccessful historian who wonders "what a profile of his life would look like if its peaks were the occasions on which he had met famous people." He moves from London to Los Angeles, a city filled with people who are "stripped of the pretences of life," "untroubled by history," and "eager to submit to the terrible morality of personal ambition," and resolves to become famous in ten years: "If he had not appeared on the *Tonight Show* by then he would either kill himself or go back to Canada." He writes a novel titled *Celebrity* that makes him rich and famous. He loves his own celebrity "for giving him a place, especially such a fun place, in history, but more than anything else he loved it for being so big and so sweet and so nothing at all." His fame reaches its apex on the *Tonight Show* when he collapses onto the actress Tuesday Weld, dead of a burst blood vessel in his brain. "Thanks to Bunny's demise on the *Tonight Show*," his last novel, *The Money-Seekers*, "sold six and a quarter million copies." In this satirical tale Hollingshead takes aim at the absurdity and emptiness of the desire to be a famous writer in a world in which—as Bunny's agent, Arthur Dankel, says—"Television makes books."

In "The Return of Harry the Dream," another story about a young writer, Hollingshead uses a realist frame to contain Arthur Burke's absurd and violent hallucinations. In this surreal tale it is difficult to say how much of the action takes place in Burke's imagination; Burke himself articulates the overlapping and ultimately inseparable domains of imagination and reality when he says to his neighbor, who is also a character in a

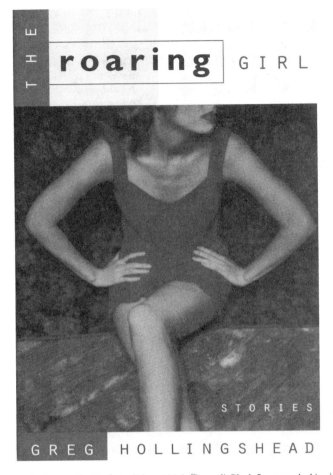

Paperback cover for the first edition, 1995 (Bruccoli Clark Layman Archives)

story he is writing: "I'm dreaming, Ike. You're . . . in my dreams."

Robert, the narrator of "My Father, with Both Hands," compiles a dream portfolio; his father, who wants to quit dreaming, says admiringly of the opus: "It's a bomb. It'll make Freud look like a featherweight. . . . You've got fifteen thousand odd words of truth here." Robert replies, "Dad . . . what I have said here . . . will bring the entire rotten edifice of this society crashing down!'" Robert's theory is that dreams are material traces of emotion, "a necessary aspect of the learning mechanism of the animal brain. They accompany the fixing of information, that is, certain patterns of response, useful for the brain to remember if it would ensure the survival of the organism." If not recorded and read, this material can settle in one's psyche like "globigerina," the "six to twelve thousand feet of ooze" that, according to Robert, covers "a third of the ocean floor." Robert points out that this substance is "composed mainly of broken homes." Robert's father, think-

ing of the dysfunctional and violent home he shares with his son and his wife, whom he calls "The Creature," objects to the metaphor: "Say bits of shells."

In 1983 Hollingshead married Rosa Spricer, a psychologist. They have a son, David. Hollingshead's next book was the novel *Spin Dry* (1992), in which the interpretation of dreams is the central problem. It opens with Rachel Boseman "driving in circles" in her subdivision, Village-on-the-Millpond, a sprawling development of houses and malls built on a garbage dump, like a "dreamer dreaming." When she hears a trumpet serenade played by the self-destructive and obsessive agoraphobic Cam Wilkes, it evokes in her mysterious feelings of loss. Wilkes's tune functions in the novel as an Orphic incantation that leads Rachel into the underworld of her subconscious. The dreams she narrates to her analyst at The Silver Dream Research Centre force her to address the increasing dissatisfaction, anxiety, and sense of meaninglessness she is experiencing in her suburban life. By writing down her dreams, Rachel tries to "write backwards in time, the last dream image evoking the one before, effects triggering causes, and so on back until memory flagged and sleep took over once more." Eventually, she begins to "see a familiar pattern emerging." The key to the pattern is the unidentified tune she heard Cam play; she believes that it is the same tune that her husband, Leon, tries to hum for her after he hears it when he dreams about the "dream guy." This hero figure for Leon and figure of authority and destruction for her—called Hal or Harry—haunts her imagination and refuses to be repressed, like the garbage bags on which Village-on-the-Millpond is built and that regularly "explode like land mines." She finally discovers by calling the Muzak Corporation that the name of the tune is *I Climbed the Rocky Mountains (But I Can't Get over You)*. It is the song that she and Leon heard through their bedroom window when they first moved to Village-on-the-Millpond and "used to leave the window open and make love all night. . . . It was our song." The novel ends three years after it began with the remarried Rachel driving home to the city and her new husband, John; she is singing to her daughter, Claire, "who slumped in her car seat and drooled on her hand." She has liberated herself from suburban life and the spectral figure of Harry, who "really had made the return trip to the dump, where the phantoms go," and she is confident that Claire will benefit from her insight and be prepared to live a different life: Claire "saw the light and colours and heard the wind and the engine and her mother's song and smelled and felt the warmth of her mother's love and had no thought, no thought at all, of Harry."

Hollingshead's second short-story collection, *White Buick,* also appeared in 1992. The title piece concerns an immigrant couple from an unspecified Middle Eastern country. It is narrated by the wife of the unemployed and abusive Kamal, whose white Buick compensates for his lack of status in a culture he reveres for its masculine and materialistic values. His attention to the car is inversely related to his affection for his wife. Explaining why she remains in the loveless and abusive marriage, the wife says: "When there are no children, it is necessary for one in the marriage to be the child"; she means Kamal. When the Buick's windshield is chipped by the metal ballast of a balsa-wood glider Kamal's solution is to evict their promiscuous tenant, Gabriella—the "whore" whose child's toy damaged the windshield—and "charge more rent and so build a garage." Before he can do so, his wife secretly repairs the windshield. "My husband, who is not a madman but a believer in the miracle of western technology, is convinced that in a wondrous emulation of the flesh of an animal, by means of some space-age fluid within the glass, the windshield of the Buick has *healed itself*." He believes the same about the car's door when it is scratched by a key: "The mark is not quite as deep as at first. It may take as long as a year, but it will heal. There seems to be a certain resiliency to the metal. The paint may need some touching up, but the metal, I have good expectation, will be recovered perfected." His wife similarly attempts to conceal the bruises on her face and body inflicted by her increasingly abusive husband, who eventually becomes involved with Gabriella.

"Your God Is Finished" is based on an unfinished fifteen-thousand-word autobiography that Hollingshead's father wrote about himself and his own father. Hollingshead told Riegel, "What struck me as I reread it was the recurrent theme that he never knew his father, just didn't know who the man was." In "Your God Is Finished" the narrator's grandfather was "a hard-working, no-nonsense man who towards his wife and children displayed no love and little compassion." The narrator's father shares the grandfather's "faith in certain features of the modern world. . . . He believed in asphalt and development and the commotion of progress. He believed in the adaptability of the human animal. If life could crawl out of the sea and grow lungs it could adapt to anything." The father has recorded his childhood experiences in a manuscript; when the narrator reads it, he realizes that both men feared emotional contact. The grandfather "would not have condoned my father's writing down his memories of childhood and he would not have understood my sifting through what my father has written for an understanding of a man I never knew." In the attic of the family home the narrator discovers a collection of gifts: the gifts the grandfather received were never opened, while those the father received were opened but never used. The gifts signified emotional attachments and responsibilities with which these silent men were uncomfortable.

McIntyre, the narrator of "When She Was Gone," is a retired police officer who apprehended a serial killer, Gordon Snider, twenty-five years earlier. Snider murdered several women, dismembered their bodies, and collected the parts as relics in his own hellish shrine: "It was like the lair of an animal," littered with "bones, big raw bones with strips of withered fat and muscle still attached. . . . Another head in a burlap sack in a cupboard. . . . There was a chair in the corner, made out of bones." McIntyre has not been able to let the case sink into oblivion: "I thought it did. It came back." He goes to visit Snider in the mental institution where the murderer is incarcerated. The head of the institution warns him that it is pointless to try to make sense of the nightmarish collection he discovered at the Snider home:

it's not that there aren't reasons for the way he turned out, a logic, his mother, and so forth. I'm not denying it's an interesting case. But I'd want to question very closely indeed anybody who'd try to generalize from it. This is a very disturbed individual, and that's the bottom line. We've got plenty of his type in here. . . . The point is, a man like Snider, you'd be better off rummaging through garbage cans.

In a commentary within the story, Snider explains his collecting of body parts:

Everybody has a place for salvage, whatever they might say or act like, and they watch over this place from day to day, protect it at any cost maybe. Different salvage might come and go, but it's always the same. A picture in a book or a magazine, a memory with a shine on it, or an actual souvenir of a person, it's a changing dream, that's all. Everywhere you look these days salvage is on display. It's like hair in a locket. Everybody knows this, everybody does it. . . . It would not be true to say I am not bothered by the things that were done. I have thought about them a good deal, not worried so much as tried to understand. I would say that blowing through the world is a wind of destruction. People huddle and say, You can know this, you can't know that. Others see the thing for what it is: a simple matter of salvage.

The explanation could provide McIntyre with a way to give some form to the horrors he has witnessed and the nightmares that have disturbed his imagination for twenty-five years.

In "Unacceptable People" the narration alternates among three characters: Jack Marquette, Brenda Popesque, and Cary Dean Griffith. On a superficial level, these characters are linked by alcohol, drugs, depression, desire, and deceit; on a deeper level they are connected by the "ineluctable mystery" of existence that each ponders. "You will be going along, things seem fine, everything's under control, and all of a sudden what happens?" Cary Dean says one night in the middle of an LSD trip. "What have you got? Phrases. A few scraps of advice, floating. It's pitiful. . . . is this what people mean when they say the human condition?" This bleak view is confirmed by Cary Dean's mother, who reminds him of how she took care of his dying father and then of her "last living friend," a woman "dying of throat cancer, from the cigarettes and the booze": "What a shame it was to go through the world with hardly a glance for the beauty of it, and what a waste they'd all made of their lives." After Brenda and Cary Dean commit suicide, Jack reflects:

These people come into your life and it is such chance and they are such a puzzle or such a drag that you almost think they are not really in your life at all. . . . Even though they are often boring or difficult, over the months or years you spend a lot of time with them because with them you do not have to worry about

yourself . . . you think you know these people better than you want to and you think you do not know them at all, but it is all the same. In the end it is a simple matter of lack of regard, and it cuts both ways. They were the stuff of your life, and now they are nothing but memories, and not loving them is suddenly no protection against their pain.

In "The Comfort of Things as They Are" Jeff, the father of a sick child, vows to be more vigilant about the myriad forces that threaten existence in a "terribly polluted world." Feeling confined and helpless in the hospital, Jeff wishes "that the window would open, so he could lean out and listen to the roar of the city in the ineluctable mystery of its operation."

Hollingshead finished *The Roaring Girl* (1995) while he was living in Paris in 1994–1995. In the title story Jim is eight when he learns that his mother's first pregnancy resulted in the miscarriage of a baby who was supposed to have been named Jim: "You made it, so you got the name," his father tells him. "It's not as if it wasn't like new." The information confirms Jim's feelings of alienation within his dysfunctional family. A mysterious stranger—a disheveled and brash adolescent girl—oversees his transition to adulthood and helps him to begin to speak about his ghostly double. Jim's brother Wayne is born shortly after the girl departs. Wayne is "a sickly baby, and his crying irritated the boy. Maybe if babies could measure up to the dead. Maybe if you could understand what they wanted. Maybe if they could talk." The narrator predicts: "All his adult life the boy will have a memory—and it will be imbued with that aura-vividness of life outside habit—of walking down the street with the girl." In this scene "he will not know who this was, will remember only his amazement at the time that they should be moving along at the same pace, that he should be contained in any form at all within that alien, unconscionable mind. And his heart will just roar."

In "The Naked Man" the eighteen-year-old narrator, Dennis Weatherall, buys a Studebaker and then leaves home for Australia. The Studebaker's presence in the garage has a strange effect on Dennis and his parents: it forces them—particularly Dennis, on his return—to come to terms with the past, to carry out the work of mourning, and, in a limited way, to say what cannot be said in this grieving family. Using the Studebaker to reveal the Weatheralls' family history, Hollingshead reveals Dennis's complex mixture of fear of being replaceable, his guilt for surviving, and his sense of inadequacy for not being able to "measure up to the dead."

Henry Stettmeyer, the narrator of "A Night at the Palace," is wondering, "Where did life go?" when he meets a friend, Bruce Harris, whom he has not seen for twenty-five years and who once saved his life. Harris has had a more adventurous life than Henry, and his arrival is timely: "You're drowning again," he says, and he promises to save Henry's life once more—this time with a night of debauchery with several of Harris's women friends at the rural home of Harris's in-laws, who are away. The outcome of the evening, however, is sober: spying on Harris making love to one of the women, Henry sees through Harris's persona when he hears her postcoital plaint—a cry that is "not animal and not human" that is followed by "another order of cry altogether . . . a prolonged and fluting whimper, febrile and kittenish." At this moment Henry realizes "that Harris was not the one I had imagined, and neither was he the one he now claimed to be, and I felt the force of him pass out of my heart, and the scales fall, and I looked about me and saw where I was, and this was squatting apelike and largely naked." *The Roaring Girl* received the Governor General's Literary Award for Fiction.

In Hollingshead's novel *The Healer* (1998) Tim Wakelin buys an isolated cabin near the town of Grant on the southern Canadian Shield, apparently in central Ontario. He has been commissioned to write a magazine article about a local girl, Carolyn Troyer, who possesses a miraculous ability to heal the sick. Wakelin, whose wife has recently committed suicide, is desperately in need of healing; Carolyn, who has been abused by her tyrannical father, Ross, can heal others but is incapable of healing herself. Wakelin decides not to write about Carolyn and her strange power, despite the cash advance he has received for the story:

> this was the real thing, the living fountainhead of that virtue. It was like being forgiven when you could not forgive yourself. Absolution from beyond. So strange. Such relief. Not to be another to submit her . . . to the scrutiny of a world that was always hungry for something new, this old. But would have needed to be there. If it wasn't to read it all wrong. If it wasn't to read it in the usual dreary ways, medical, psychoanalytical, or religious.

He wishes that "he could drop down before her and say, Okay, I'm ready. I wasn't before. Wrong auspices, phony pretext. All now given over, and I am wide open. Heal me. Or fail to, that's okay too. We can take it from here." After descending into the forest in a form of feral madness, Wakelin begins to keep a journal in which he writes: "With Carolyn Troyer I didn't know what I was getting into. I didn't understand that for some people there is no looking away." Wakelin has perfected a strategy of looking elsewhere to evade pain and sadness: "Either you look away and these things kill you slowly, or you face them and they blow you wide open." Medi-

tating on her own past and remembering her father's brutality and violent death, Carolyn thinks:

> There is no story. You do not, like a dreamer waking from a dream, insensibly provide the connections that will make sense of the pieces as if there were a series of events in the world. Thought is physical like the world, but it comes from the past, its connections are not here and now, they are vertical. You do not string them, you stack them. Memory is a story I tell myself. This is not memory. This is stacking. Like rock. Like earth and seeds. Like atomic fuel.

Set in the eighteenth century, Hollingshead's historical novel *Bedlam* (2004) considers the emergence of a new way to think about and speak of madness in the Age of Reason. It is a fictional account of the incarceration of James Tilly Matthews, the subject of the first book-length psychiatric case history in English, in London's infamous Bethlehem mental hospital, popularly known as Bedlam. The novel is narrated by Matthews himself; his wife, Margaret; and his physician, John Haslam. Matthews's madness is, ostensibly, the reason for his incarceration; but his narration is quite sane, in its metaphorical way, as are his well-reasoned petitions for release. He thinks that he is being confined because of his political activities; quoting the seventeenth-century playwright Nathaniel Lee, he says, *"They called me mad and I called them mad, and damn them, they outvoted me."* He is a republican sympathizer and a peaceful revolutionary and believes that he is being controlled at a distance by an "air loom gang" of French "magnetic agents" who want to implicate him in a treasonous plot. (This claim is not so outlandish when considered in the context of recent discoveries of forces such as Sir Isaac Newton's gravitation, Benjamin Franklin's electricity, Joseph Priestley's "phlogisticated" air, Antoine Lavoisier's chemistry, and Franz Anton Mesmer's "animal magnetism.") Matthews understands that "a man is not an island but a delicate play of connexion, and it takes very little to close down the game. But once that happens, he's a monster in disguise." Hollingshead leaves it for his readers to decide whether Matthews is a political prisoner or a lunatic. Brian Bethune said in his review in *Maclean's* (6 September 2004) that "*Bedlam* brings to mind that even paranoids have real enemies, as Henry Kissinger famously said about Richard Nixon."

In addition to teaching at the University of Alberta, Hollingshead has been director of the writing programs at the Banff Centre since 2000. He told Young that "the pervasive influence of deconstruction, which approaches literature more the way a writer does, turning readers into writers. . . . has opened the way for criticism to be more writerly, more admittedly subjective, more 'creative,' which in turn has helped generally to break down the old wall between critical and creative work in the universities. . . . In personal terms, I write two hours or so early in the morning then, about nine o'clock, I start my day. I wake up into my professorial role." He also does much of his writing at a cabin in Algonquin Park, Ontario.

In his fiction Greg Hollingshead documents the problems of alienation, isolation, loss, grief, ambivalence, indifference, paranoia, doubt, and disconnection that beset middle-class people in the modern age. He places readers in positions in which they must trace the forces that threaten to subsume identity and submerge the "floating" subject.

Interviews:

Chris Dafoe, "The Bemused Greg Hollingshead," *Globe and Mail* (Toronto), 1 January 1996, p. A8;

Mark Young, "Greg Hollingshead: *Blood and Aphorisms* Interview," *Blood and Aphorisms,* 22 (Spring 1996): 39–42;

John Ayre, "Hollingsview: John Ayre Speaks with Greg Hollingshead," *Books in Canada,* 25 (Summer 1996): 5–6;

Kristjana Gunnars, "Interview with Greg Hollingshead," *Prairie Fire,* 17 (Summer 1996): 6–18;

Christian Riegel, "Interview with Greg Hollingshead," *British Journal of Canadian Studies,* 12, nos. 1–2 (1997): 72–77;

Jon C. Stott, "Interview with Greg Hollingshead," in *The Harbrace Anthology of Literature,* edited by Stott, Raymond E. Jones, and Rick Bowers (Toronto: Harcourt Brace, 1998), pp. 1186–1189;

David Cameron, "The Language of the Lake," *Cottage Life* (March 2000): cover, 68–77, 94;

Chris Tenove, "Greg Hollingshead," *write,* 1 (Summer 2000): 28–32;

Jay Smith, "Hollingshead's Chronicles," *Vue Magazine,* no. 466 (23–29 September 2004): 13, 18;

Michael Bryson, "TDR Interview," *Danforth Review* (January 2005) <http://www.danforthreview.com/features/interviews/greg_hollingsh ead.htm>.

Wayne Johnston

(22 May 1958 –   )

Jim Taylor
St. Francis Xavier University

BOOKS: *The Story of Bobby O'Malley* (Ottawa: Oberon Press, 1985);

The Time of Their Lives (Ottawa: Oberon Press, 1987);

The Divine Ryans (Toronto: McClelland & Stewart, 1990; New York: Broadway, 1999; London: Anchor, 1999);

Human Amusements (Toronto: McClelland & Stewart, 1994);

The Colony of Unrequited Dreams (Toronto: Knopf Canada, 1998; New York: Doubleday, 1999; London: Anchor, 1999);

Baltimore's Mansion: A Memoir (Toronto: Knopf Canada, 1999; New York: Doubleday, 2000; London: Anchor, 2000);

The Navigator of New York (Toronto: Knopf Canada, 2002; New York: Doubleday, 2002; London: Cape, 2002);

The Custodian of Paradise (Toronto: Knopf Canada, 2006; New York: Norton, 2007).

PRODUCED SCRIPT: *The Divine Ryans,* motion picture, Imagex / TiMe Film und TV Produktion GmBh / Telefilm Canada / Nova Scotia Film Development Corporation / Labrador Film Development Corporation / Filmboard Berlin-Brandenberg, 1999.

SELECTED PERIODICAL PUBLICATIONS–UNCOLLECTED: "A Whale of a Time," *Saturday Night,* 110 (1995): 58–61;

"Rigged," *Saturday Night,* 114 (1999): 58–61.

Wayne Johnston (photograph by Jerry Bauer; from the dust jacket for The Colony of Unrequited Dreams, *1999; Bruccoli Clark Layman Archives)*

Newfoundland native Wayne Johnston achieved national recognition in Canada in 1985 with *The Story of Bobby O'Malley,* and his prestige has grown steadily as each new book was nominated for or received a coveted award. The historical novels *The Colony of Unrequited Dreams* (1998) and *The Navigator of New York* (2002) made his fame international. His work is marked by carefully crafted prose, a wry wit that mocks any form of pomposity or sanctimony, an appreciation of people's eccentricities and cultures, and carefully researched attention to historical detail. Because the decision to confederate with Canada convulsed Newfoundland for almost a decade before it occurred in 1949 and is still a sensitive issue, the Confederation debate casts its shadow on much of Johnston's work.

Johnston was born on 22 May 1958 in St. John's, Newfoundland, the first of five children of Arthur Reginald Johnston, a federal fisheries officer, and Genevieve Everard Johnston. The family was Roman Catholic in a province where religion largely determined one's education, social connections, and career opportunities. When Johnston was one year old, the family moved to his mother's childhood home, the Goulds, a farming community established in the wilderness in the late nineteenth century by his maternal ancestors and others who had abandoned fishing for a less precarious livelihood. Life there provided Johnston with material for his first three novels, all of which are notable for humor and odd characters.

Johnston completed an Honors B.A. in English at Memorial University in 1978. From 1979 to 1981 he was a reporter for the *St. John's Daily News*. He married Rosemarie Langhout in 1981 and completed his M.A. at the University of New Brunswick in 1984. From 1984 to 1986 he was poetry editor of *The Fiddlehead Magazine*.

In 1985 Johnston published *The Story of Bobby O'Malley,* which chronicles the coming of age of a boy in the fictional St. John's suburb of Kellies. Bobby's reminiscences of the rented houses where he spent his childhood supply the background for the antics of his parents, aunts and uncles, and schoolmates. Bobby's father, Ted, is a droll commentator on life's absurdities, the first of a type that appears in various guises in Johnston's later works. The Roman Catholic Church is everywhere—shaping personalities, determining responses, causing the O'Malleys' dysfunctional marriage, and serving as a target for Ted's satiric buffoonery. Bobby's struggle with adolescent torment, especially sexuality, is made humorously confusing by notions of sin absorbed from the Irish Christian Brothers and from his pious mother—at Bobby's conception, the only time the O'Malleys ever made love, Agnes fingered the bones on Ted's spine not, as he thought, out of passion but as beads to count off the Rosary. Much drama arises from Agnes O'Malley's ambition to have her son ordained a priest; and though he rejects this calling, at school he is treated with both ambiguous reverence and open scorn. Though fragmented at times, the novel establishes Johnston's keen ear for the Newfoundland idiom and his deft handling of comic situations. Yet, it is ultimately a dispiriting work: the O'Malleys' marriage is destroyed by Agnes's fear of sex; Bobby confuses goodness with celibacy and rejects his devout mother's values so that he can escape her smothering affection; and Ted's despair drives him to suicide. *The Story of Bobby O'Malley* won the Amazon.com/Books in Canada First Novel Award and the W. H. Smith Books in Canada First Novel Award.

The Time of Their Lives (1987) is even bleaker and more claustrophobic than Johnston's first novel, though it does have scenes of high comedy. The theme of the work is the dominion that parents, especially cruel ones, exercise over their children. The narrator is John Foley, grandson of Andrew and Irene Dunne—identified throughout as "Dad" and "Mom"—and son of Sheila and Tom Foley. Two communities outside St. John's supply the settings for a constant imbroglio: Harbour Deep is a fishing village; the Meadows is a farming community established by individuals who left Harbour Deep in the 1930s. Harbour Deep loyalists see Dad's rejection of the fishing life as a breach with tradition, and Dad's father disowns him for this treachery. Dad is even more tyrannical and mean-spirited with his family than was his own father; yet, his children recall life in the Meadows as "the time of their lives," and, forgetting that he was an unpleasant, envious, abusive man, they mythologize Dad into a beloved patriarch, tough and self-reliant. Throughout their lives the children compete with one another for Dad's approval. A typical incident involves Sheila's theft of money from her brother-in-law's business: a plan for repayment is reached, but Sheila's sister, Lew, carries the tale to Dad on the pretext that he might best accept the discovery of Sheila's shame from a family member. Dad never raises the issue with Sheila, and she is haunted by his silence for the rest of her life; Lew anxiously awaits his censure, fearful that he disdains her tattling. In such ways Dad keeps his children in bondage. The theme of parental tyranny reaches a climax in the relationship between Dad and his alcoholic son, Raymond, whose alienation from family members who try to deal with his addiction dominates the second half of the novel. Even as he breathes his last, Dad will not ask for Raymond, and Raymond refuses to visit his father until he is tricked into thinking that Dad has called for him. When Raymond himself is dying from alcohol poisoning, his totally self-centered life bestows on him a baffling heroic status as he holds court from his hospital bed—his throne, where no one else dares sit. Johnston won the Air Canada Award for Best Young Writer for the novel.

In 1988 Johnston was appointed writer-in-residence at the University of Regina. The following year he moved to Toronto, because he found that proximity to his material made writing impossible: he needed distance to be able distinguish the significant from the trivial in Newfoundland's culture and history.

The Divine Ryans (1990) recounts the snarled emotional development of Draper Doyle Ryan, whose family is called "the divine Ryans" because of the generations of nuns and priests it has produced. Draper Doyle's Aunt Phil, the sister of his dead father, Donald, is the adversary of all things Protestant and, together with her brother, Father Seymour, the scourge of anything having to do with sex. Funeral director Uncle Reg, another of Aunt Phil's brothers, is keenly sensitive to the suffering that Draper Doyle and his mother endure from the ignorance and bigotry of Aunt Phil and Father Seymour. The voice of life-affirming common sense, Uncle Reg enjoys puns and delights in whimsically adjusting famous quotations to fit random circumstances. After the Montreal Habs lose the Stanley Cup in 1966 to the Toronto Maple Leafs in a contest that to the Ryans represents the cosmic rivalry between Catholicism and Protestantism, Uncle Reg paraphrases John Donne: "Ask not for whom the phone rings. It rings for us." In a series of phantasmagoric nightmares confused with adolescent visions of sexuality, the ghost of Donald Ryan appears to Draper Doyle, tossing a hockey puck from hand to hand. For Draper Doyle and the Ryan clan, Donald, the former editor of St. John's Catholic newspaper, the *Daily Chronicle,* is a distant enigma. Only at the end of the novel does Draper Doyle recover the memory of the grotesque incident that revealed his father as a homosexual. The novel won the Atlantic Fiction Prize and the Thomas Raddall Atlantic Fiction Award.

Human Amusements (1994) is set in Toronto. Audrey Prendergast is the creator of *Rumpus Room,* one of the nation's most popular children's television shows; as Miss Mary, she is the host of the program, while her son, Henry, the narrator of the novel, plays the characters Bee Good and Bee Bad. Audrey produces a series on the life of Philo Farnsworth, the inventor of television, starring Henry as Farnsworth, that becomes a global cult hit. Henry regards the family's first television set, affectionately called the Gillingham for the repairman who installed the picture tube upside down, as a symbol of an innocent earlier time; he cannot bear to view the family's new color set, preferring to turn the Gillingham upside down and watch it in his room. The smell of the dust smoldering on the vacuum tubes and the gentle hum the set makes are a solace for him as he faces the trials of adolescence and celebrity status, and the upside-down television symbolizes Henry's adolescent rejection of the world as it appears. His father, Peter, a would-be novelist, is a witty, ironic commentator on the absurdities of life, especially life as portrayed on television; most of the humor in *Human Amusements* grows out of the playful exchanges between Henry's innocent speculations and his father's tongue-in-cheek responses. Peter abandons his life's work when he discovers that his wife has used her influence to arrange for it to be published by a New York firm in return for exclusive rights to a television biography of the Prendergasts—a genre that is the epitome of all that Peter considers superficial and vulgar. Humiliated and outraged because his manuscript has not been accepted on its own merits, he withdraws his consent for publication.

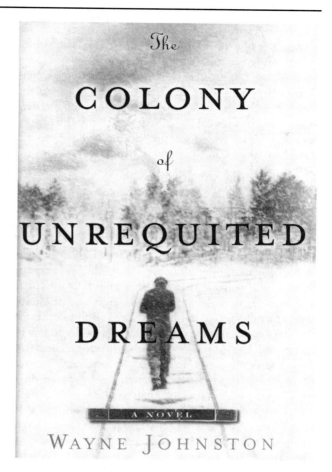

Dust jacket for the first U.S. edition, 1999
(Bruccoli Clark Layman Archives)

Johnston's 1998 novel, *The Colony of Unrequited Dreams,* is a fictionalized biography of Joey Smallwood, a key player in the 1948 referendum that joined Newfoundland with Canada and the first premier of the province after Confederation. The story begins with Smallwood's life in a chaotic home where his father's drunken rants are inspired by D. W. Prowse's eight-hundred-page *A History of Newfoundland* (1895); incensed by her husband's diatribes, Smallwood's mother throws the book out of the house and causes a small avalanche. Smallwood goes on to become an impoverished student at Bishop Feild, a private school in St. John's, where he suffers condescension from the sons of wealthy merchants and the contempt of his British teachers for everything colonial—they even despise themselves for their failure to find employment at home. After his expulsion from Bishop Feild for failing to achieve a grade of more than 45 out of 500 on "character," Smallwood becomes a reporter and gets a berth on the *S.S. Newfoundland* to investigate working conditions among Newfoundland sealers. Politically ambitious but recognizing that his poverty and lack of formal education preclude him from holding office, he calculates that his best chance of success lies in becoming a spokesman for the underprivileged. He adopts socialism and broadens his understanding of the doctrine by moving to New York, where he works for *The Call,* the voice of the socialist movement. The experience results in a lifelong distaste for theoretical socialism, whose proponents he perceives as individuals from the moneyed establishment "on sabbatical from lives of privilege."

He returns to Newfoundland and makes two treks into the wilderness to sign up railway workers and fishermen for unions. He then leads the movement for Confederation with Canada and becomes the province's first prime minister. Other notable figures depicted in the novel include Sir Richard Squires, head of the scandal-ridden Liberal Party and premier of Newfoundland from 1919 to 1923 and 1928 to 1932, who was responsible for the 1932 riots and the anti-government march on the Colonial Building; Peter Cashin, the charismatic unofficial leader of the Independents; and Dr. Alfred Valdmanis, director general of economic development in Smallwood's administration, who nearly bankrupted the province by persuading Smallwood to fund projects that were doomed to failure. After Smallwood fired him, it was discovered that he had been siphoning into his own pocket money from European companies that were receiving generous government grants. Johnston also introduces a fictional character, Sheilagh Fielding, an intelligent, beautiful cripple who becomes Smallwood's obsession from his schooldays to the end of his political career. Descriptions of the history and folkways of Newfoundland appear as entries in Fielding's private journal or as passages from her lifelong project, *Fielding's Condensed History of Newfoundland. The Colony of Unrequited Dreams* secured Johnston's reputation as one of Canada's important novelists. It was nominated for the Governor General's Literary Award for Fiction, short-listed for the Giller Prize, and won the Thomas Raddall Atlantic Fiction Award in 1998 and the Canadian Authors Association Award for Fiction in 1999.

Near the beginning of *Baltimore's Mansion: A Memoir* (1999), winner of the Charles Taylor Prize for Literary Non-Fiction, Johnston describes the arrival on 24 June 1904 of an enormous iceberg shaped like the Virgin Mary off the Newfoundland coast near his home in Ferryland. The date was considered portentous because it was not only the feast day of St. John the Baptist but also the day in 1497 when John Cabot first sighted Newfoundland. For Johnston's father, the Virgin Berg was the "first object he had seen both in real life and in a photograph"; thereafter, whenever he saw a photograph he recalled the photographer emerging from

under the blanket moments after the camera had exploded its charge of flash powder.

Johnston tells of learning in school that the colony founded in the 1620s by George Calvert, first Baron Baltimore, was first named Avalon; later, he read in his aunt Freda's copy of Thomas Malory's *Morte d'Arthur* (1485) that Avalon was the island where King Arthur sailed, accompanied by many fair ladies in black hoods weeping uncontrollably, after he had received his "grievous Wound." Johnston draws parallels between his world and Arthur's: aside from living on the Avalon Peninsula, which is shrouded in mist and fog like Arthur's Avalon, his father's name is Arthur Reginald, the middle name derived from *rex* (Latin for "king"). The images of the Virgin Berg and the barge carrying Arthur fused in his mind so that he pictured an iceberg made up of the Virgin and the "hooded Queens" of Arthurian legend. The most significant parallel is between Arthur's "grievous Wound" and Confederation, the "wound" inflicted on Newfoundland by its own inhabitants, seduced by the diabolical Smallwood. The connection between Confederation and Arthur's Wound is dramatically presented in the story of Brown's Document. Kenneth Brown, a committed anti-Confederate who reportedly had a document that would convince everyone at the National Convention of the folly of supporting Confederation, dropped dead on the convention floor just as he was about to reveal its contents; the document then disappeared. "Brown's Document," for Johnston, "was a phrase that invoked . . . the world of Malory's *Morte d'Arthur,* that the true king was always in exile while some pretender held the throne, that the honorable, by virtue of being honorable, must always lose. Brown lay on the floor, his long journey to the vale of Avalon begun, having suffered, like Arthur, a grievous head wound from which he could not recover."

In Prowse's *A History of Newfoundland* the young Johnston reads a letter to Lord Baltimore, dated 28 July 1622, reporting that a blacksmith's forge was completed on 24 June. For Johnston the uncanny coincidence on that date of Cabot's sighting of Newfoundland and the appearance of the Virgin Berg can only be interpreted as the hand of destiny in the unfolding of Newfoundland's history. Johnston's grandfather Charlie Johnston was a blacksmith; his forge becomes for Johnston a kind of sacred altar associated with the early history of Newfoundland, and the shattering of the anvil with one blow becomes an omen of the country's fragmentation. The last line of the memoir describes the images running through Johnston's grandfather's mind when he is dying at his forge of a heart attack brought on by the realization that Newfoundland will join Canada in seventy-six days: "All are fixed in a moment that for him will never pass."

Published in 2002, *The Navigator of New York* uses mysterious letters and documents to retell the story of the rivalry that embittered the Arctic quests of Dr. Frederick A. Cook and Lieutenant Robert E. Peary. The novel is narrated by the fictitious Devlin Stead, a lonely orphan living in St. John's with his aunt and uncle. Mysterious letters begin to arrive from Cook; from them Devlin learns that Cook, rather than Dr. Francis Stead, is his biological father. Amelia, Devlin's mother, was betrothed to Stead when she had an affair with Cook during a visit to New York. She had returned to Newfoundland, discovered that she was pregnant, and told Stead that she was violated at a party after having too much to drink. Stead had married her; but after Devlin was born, he had deserted the family and gone to New York, the center for Arctic expeditions. Shortly afterward, Amelia drowned. Peary employed both Cook and Stead as medical practitioners on his 1892 expedition to Greenland, where, after Stead told Cook the tale of his cuckolding, he was mysteriously lost. Devlin travels to New York to meet his father and becomes involved in the quest to reach the pole. Johnston presents Peary as petty, vindictive, self-deluded, arrogant, ruthless, and greedy for fame, while Cook is given the grace and acumen of a Renaissance courtier. The mantle of preeminent explorer is expected to pass to Cook, but Peary, whose Arctic Club of New York has authority over Northern exploration and decides who receives financial support, denies anyone else the opportunity to try for the pole. Forced to finance his own expedition, Cook falsely claims to have reached the North Pole five days before Peary. Devlin, who saves Peary's life at Etah when Cook rescues his stranded expedition, becomes the toast of New York society and is engaged to marry Kristine Summer, a cousin of his mother.

In 2004 Johnston became Distinguished Professor of Creative Writing at Hollins University in Virginia.

He commutes back and forth from Toronto. In 2006 he published *The Custodian of Paradise,* which brings back Sheilagh Fielding from *The Colony of Unrequited Dreams.*

Wayne Johnston's works teem with vibrantly drawn, intensely human characters who wrest high-spirited joy from their bleak Newfoundland surroundings and even from their deprivation. His literary voice is distinctive for its humor, satire, evocative description, and nuanced probing of psychological and interpersonal problems.

References:

Meira Cook, "On Haunting, Humour, and Hockey in Wayne Johnston's *The Divine Ryans,*" *Essays on Canadian Writing,* 82 (2004): 118–150;

Stan Dragland, "The Colony of Unrequited Dreams: Romancing History?" *Essays on Canadian Writing,* 82 (2004): 187–213;

Dragland, "My Cousin Ruby: When Wayne Johnston Published His Family Memoir, a Long-Lost Cousin in New York Called to Ask Why She Wasn't in It. So He Went to Visit," *National Post,* 21 December 2002, pp. B1–B3;

Danielle Fuller, "Strange Terrain: Reproducing and Resisting Place-Myths in Two Contemporary Fictions of Newfoundland," *Essays on Canadian Writing,* 82 (2004): 21–50;

Sophie Gironnay, "L'humour insulaire," *Actualitie,* 24, no. 2 (1999): 98–99;

Jeanette Lynes, "Strangely Strung Beads: Wayne Johnston's *Story of Bobby O'Malley,*" *Studies in Canadian Literature,* 15, no. 1 (1990): 140–153;

Cynthia Sugars, "Notes on a Mystic Hockey Puck: Death, Paternity, and National Identity in Wayne Johnston's *The Divine Ryans,*" *Essays on Canadian Writing,* 82 (2004): 151–172;

Herb Wyile, "From Roots to Routs: Cultivating Canadian Writing in an Electronic Age," *Essays on Canadian Writing,* 71 (2000): 215–223.

Thomas King

(24 April 1943 –   )

Jennifer Andrews
University of New Brunswick

See also the King entry in *DLB 175: Native American Writers of the United States.*

BOOKS: *Medicine River* (Markham, Ont.: Viking, 1990);

A Coyote Columbus Story (Toronto: Groundwood Books, 1992);

One Good Story, That One (Toronto: HarperCollins, 1993);

Green Grass, Running Water (Toronto: HarperCollins, 1993);

Coyote Sings to the Moon (Toronto: Key Porter, 1998);

Truth and Bright Water (Toronto: HarperCollins, 1999);

DreadfulWater Shows Up, as Hartley GoodWeather (Toronto: HarperCollins, 2002);

The Truth about Stories: A Native Narrative (Toronto: Anansi, 2003);

Coyote's New Suit (Toronto: Key Porter, 2004);

The Red Power Murders: A DreadfulWater Mystery, as Good-Weather (Toronto: HarperCollins, 2006).

PRODUCED SCRIPTS: *The One about Coyote Going West,* radio, Canadian Broadcasting Corporation, 1993;

Medicine River, radio, Canadian Broadcasting Corporation, 1993;

Borders, radio, Canadian Broadcasting Corporation, 1993;

Medicine River, motion picture, Canadian Broadcasting Corporation and Medicine River Productions, 1993;

Magpies, radio, Canadian Broadcasting Corporation, 1994;

Traplines, radio, Canadian Broadcasting Corporation, 1994;

Joe the Painter and the Bow River Massacre, radio, Canadian Broadcasting Corporation, 1996;

"Borders," television, *Four Directions,* Canadian Broadcasting Corporation, 1996;

Thomas King (photograph courtesy of James Ruppert)

Dead Dog Café Comedy Hour, radio, Canadian Broadcasting Corporation, 1996–2003.

OTHER: "My Friend's Father," in *Multi-Colored Maize,* edited by Ron Peat (Auburn, Cal.: Valley, 1981), p. 94;

The Native in Literature: Canadian and Comparative Perspectives, edited by King, Helen Hoy, and Cheryl Calver, introduction by King (Oakville, Ont.: ECW Press, 1987);

An Anthology of Short Fiction by Native Writers in Canada, edited by King (Toronto: Canadian Fiction Magazine, 1988); 125–132;

"Simple Suffering," in *Second Macmillan Anthology,* edited by John Metcalf and Leon Rooke (Toronto: Macmillan, 1989), pp. 56–61;

"Custer's Last Words," "Another Great Moment in Indian History," "The Truth about the Sioux and Puppies," "How to Entrench Native Rights," "How to Buy a Haida Bed," "How to Recognize Authentic Indian Jewelry," "How to Tell Regular Canadians from Real Indians," and "A Short History of the Hudson's Bay Company," in *Soundings,* edited by Yvonne Trainer (Calgary: Circle Five, 1989), pp. 15–19;

All My Relations: An Anthology of Contemporary Canadian Native Fiction, edited by King (Toronto: McClelland & Stewart, 1990);

"Native Literature of Canada," in *Dictionary of Native American Literature,* edited by Andrew Wiget (New York: Garland, 1994), pp. 12–18;

"The Open Car," in *Writing Away: The PEN Travel Anthology,* edited by Constance Rooke (Toronto: McClelland & Stewart, 1994): 147–155;

"The City on the Hill," in *Uncommon Wealth,* edited by Neil Besner and others (Toronto: Oxford University Press, 1997), p. 643;

"How I Spent My Summer Vacation: History, Literature, and the Cant of Authenticity," in *Landmarks: A Process Reader,* edited by Roberta Birks and others (Scarborough, Ont.: Prentice Hall, 1998), pp. 248–254;

"First Voices, First Words," special issue of *Prairie Fire,* edited by King, 22, no. 3 (2001);

"Where the Borg Are," in *Story of a Nation: Defining Moments in Our History* (Toronto: Doubleday Canada, 2001), pp. 279–291;

"Coyote and the Enemy Aliens," in *Our Story: Aboriginal Voices on Canada's Past* (Toronto: Doubleday Canada, 2004), pp. 155–174;

"Rocks and Trees and Water: A Boreal Dialogue," in *Rendezvous with the Wild: The Boreal Forest,* edited by James Raffan (Erin, Ont.: Boston Mills, 2004), p. 125.

SELECTED PERIODICAL PUBLICATIONS–
UNCOLLECTED: "The Star Thistles," *Toyon Review* (1976): 22;

"Note: Roadside Rock Art," *Journal of American Folklore,* 96 (1980): 60;

"Hanta Yo," *Utah Holiday,* 9, no. 9 (1980);

"N. Scott Momaday: Literature and the Native Writer. An Interview," *MELUS,* 10, no. 4 (1983): 66–72;

"Joe the Painter and the Deer Island Massacre," *Whetstone* (1987);

"Buffalo Poets," *Whetstone* (1987): 9–21;

"Not Counting the Indian, There Were Six," *Malahat Review,* 80 (1987): 76–81;

"How Corporal Colin Sterling Saved Blossom, Alberta, and Most of the Rest of the World as Well," *Whetstone* (1988): 29–33;

"Totem," *Whetstone* (1988): 29–33;

"The Closer You Get to Canada, the More Things Will Eat Your Horses," *Whetstone* (1989): 9–19;

"The Dog I Wish I Had, I Would Call It Helen," *Malahat Review,* 89 (1989): 79–87;

"Little Bombs," *West Magazine* (1990): 28–30;

"Prairie Time," *Western Living* (1990);

"A Seat in the Garden," *Books in Canada,* 19, no. 9 (1990): 13–16;

"Traplines," *Prism International,* 28, no. 4 (1990): 59-68;

"Other Stories, Other Voices," *Saturday Magazine* (31 March 1990): M13, M23;

"Godzilla vs. Post-Colonial," *World Literature Written in English,* 30, no. 2 (1990): 10–16;

"Coyote Learns to Whistle," "Coyote Sees the Prime Minister," and "Coyote Goes to Toronto," *Canadian Literature,* 124, no. 5 (1990): 250–253;

"It Is Dangerous to Read Newspapers," *Hungry Mind Review,* 19 (1991): 50–51;

"Domestic Furies," *Malahat Review,* 96 (1991): 26–33;

"Fire and Rain," *Border Crossings,* 11, no. 4 (1992): 94–97;

"Noah's Ark," *Descant,* 24, no. 3 (1993): 36–45;

"Native Writers of Canada: A Photographic Portrait of 12 Contemporary Authors," by King and Greg Staats, *Books in Canada,* 23, no. 5 (1994): 12–18;

"Shooting the Lone Ranger," *Hungry Mind Review,* 34 (1995): 36–37;

"Music," *Descant,* 92–93 (1996): 45–46;

"A Short History of Indians in Canada," *Toronto Life,* 31, no. 11 (1997): 68;

"Another Great Moment in Canadian Indian History," *Story* (1999): 62–70;

"Tidings of Comfort and Joy," *National Post,* 24 December 1999, pp. 10–11;

"The Garden Court Motor Motel," *Prairie Fire,* 22, no. 3 (2001): 207–211;

"Bad Men Who Love Jesus: The Lost Years," *New Quarterly,* 86 (2003): 210–212;

"Indians on Vacation," *Western American Literature,* 39, no. 2 (2004): cover, 144, 153, 168;

"Not Enough Horses," *Walrus,* 63 (2004): 63.

Thomas King is a versatile writer who explores the complexities of being Native and Canadian in novels, short stories, poetry, children's books, radio and television scripts, and photographs and, for six years, on a radio show broadcast by the Canadian Broadcasting Corporation. He is also an academic who has published essays about the state of Aboriginal literature in Canada, edited an anthology of contemporary First Nations fiction, and co-edited a collection of articles on the representation of Aboriginals from a Canadian and comparative perspective. Inspired as a young man by N. Scott Momaday's Pulitzer Prize–winning novel *House Made of Dawn* (1969), King recognized that there was a potential market for works by Aboriginal authors that did not replicate Native stereotypes. His narratives address some of the central concerns within contemporary First Nations populations, including self-definition, self-government, tribal alcohol abuse, and suicide rates. King's later works explore the complex historical relationships among Canada, the United States, and the tribes whose lands straddle the forty-ninth parallel.

Readers of King's work are struck by his skillful use of humor and his satiric commentary on the treatment of First Nations populations by national and local governments in Canada and the United States. He employs puns, layered allusions, and other forms of wordplay to examine from a Native perspective the impact of colonization and its legacy for Aboriginal communities. Influenced by the work of Harry Robinson, an Okanagan storyteller whose performance pieces record a disappearing tribal tradition, King's works also bring aspects of oral performance to the printed page.

King was born in Sacramento, California, on 24 April 1943 to a Cherokee father, Robert Hunt King, and a German-Greek mother, Kathryn Konsonlas King. His father, a soldier and an alcoholic, was absent much of the time and abandoned the family when King was five. Four years later he sent word that he wanted to return, but he never did and is presumed dead. King's mother raised King and his brother, Christopher, in a warehouse in Roseville that also housed her beauty shop. King's mother kept her sons aware of their Cherokee heritage and took them on trips to Oklahoma to visit their Aboriginal relatives. After attending a Catholic boarding school and completing high school in Roseville, King attended Sacramento State University for a year. He then took on a variety of jobs, becoming an actor, casino dealer, ambulance driver, and bank teller. After receiving a diploma in business administration from a junior college, he set off in 1964 on a steamer to New Zealand. While working as a photojournalist in New Zealand and Australia, he wrote his first novel, a story of American astronauts and Cold War Russians that remains unpublished. He returned to the United States in 1967. He took courses in drafting at Seattle Free University. In 1968 he enrolled at California State University at Chico. In 1970 he com-

pleted his bachelor's degree in English literature and married Kristine Adams. Their son, Christian, was born in 1971. That same year King became director of Native studies at the University of Utah. He completed his M.A. at Chico in 1972. He was associate dean for student services at California State University, Humboldt, from 1973 to 1977 and coordinator of the History of the Indians of the Americas Program at the University of Utah from 1977 to 1979. In 1979 he became assistant professor of Native studies at the University of Lethbridge in Alberta and began to write short fiction. He was divorced in 1981. He and his partner, Helen Hoy, had a son, Benjamin Hoy, in 1985. King defended his doctoral dissertation, "Inventing the Indian: White Images, Native Oral Literature, and Contemporary Native Writers," at the University of Utah in 1986. He wrote the introduction to *The Native in Literature: Canadian and Comparative Perspectives* (1987), a collection of scholarly essays on representations of Aboriginals, which he co-edited with Hoy and Cheryl Calver. He and Hoy had a daughter, Elizabeth, in 1988. In 1989 King joined the American Indian Studies program at the University of Minnesota at the rank of associate professor. The following year he published his first novel, *Medicine River*.

Medicine River traces the return of a Native photographer, Will, to the Alberta reserve of his childhood for the funeral of his mother, and his subsequent decision to stay there, aided by an old friend and trickster figure, Harlen Big Bear. Will's naiveté about his mixed roots—an Aboriginal mother and a white father who abandoned the family—is juxtaposed with Harlen's continued efforts to keep the photographer from returning to his urban life and his non-Native girlfriend. Will finds romance on the reserve with Louise Heavyman, a Native accountant who is pregnant with a child fathered by a former boyfriend. Will cultivates a strong bond with the baby, even though he is uncertain about his future with Louise. Will's position as an outsider coming back to the reserve is paralleled by that of David Plume, who participated in the standoff at Wounded Knee and feels alienated from those on the reserve who did not go there, and the handicapped Maydean Joe, who was taunted as a child by the other children, including Will. The novel explores the importance of the artist's relationship to a community as Will establishes a photography business on the reserve and compiles a calendar with pictures of the local people.

In this novel King employs repetition and movement between time periods to create a nonlinear narrative; for example, he incorporates into the first chapter fragments from his estranged father's letters to his now-dead mother. He also reorders syntax to convey the spoken word on the page.

In the essay "Godzilla vs. Post-Colonial," published the same year as *Medicine River,* King argues that Native literatures are not postcolonial because they did not depend on the arrival of Europeans in North America for their creation, nor are the literatures primarily products of colonial oppression. He proposes names for four vantage points from which to discuss Native writing. "Tribal" literature is work produced and disseminated exclusively within a Native community, usually in the language of the tribe. "Polemical" literature explores the conflict between Aboriginal and non-Aboriginal cultures, depicting modes of resistance used by Natives to maintain their communities. "Interfusional" literature combines oral and written narratives, relying on the structures and practices of the spoken word to shape the printed text; King offers the example of Robinson's *Write it on Your Heart: The Epic World of an Okanagan Storyteller* (1989). Extensive repetition of words and phrases and the use of an oral syntax characterize this kind of literature, which is best read aloud. Finally, "associational" literature focuses on a Native community, instead of individuals, depicting daily life in a flat narrative fashion that avoids conclusions or the imposition of judgments. Rejecting reductive stereotypes of Aboriginals, this type of literature reminds readers of the vitality of Native cultures and communities today. While providing only limited access to Native viewpoints, associational literature allows for realistic and complex representations of Native lives. King's own writing is typically interfusional and associational and, occasionally, polemical.

Also in 1990 King edited the groundbreaking *All My Relations: An Anthology of Contemporary Canadian Native Fiction.* In the introduction he provides a substantial discussion of several key debates in the field of Aboriginal literature, including questions of identity and authenticity. He begins with an examination of the title phrase, which, he argues, represents the extensive network of relationships that are integral to notions of Native identity and community. He points out that there is no real definition of the field of contemporary Aboriginal literature, because definitions of Native identity are still much contested. Rather than attempting to fix the concept, King contends that "our simple definition that Native literature is literature produced by Natives will suffice for the while." Moreover, he emphasizes the pervasiveness of oral traditions in contemporary texts and the significance of community and family to many of the authors included in the anthology. The vitality, creativity, and range of the narratives included in the collection, according to King, move beyond clichéd definitions of "Indian-ness" to consider the diversity of Aboriginal experiences, many of which do not fit non-Native expectations. King's story "The One about Coy-

ote Going West," which appears in the collection and was republished in his collection *One Good Story, That One* (1993), exemplifies the complexity of Native oral storytelling techniques and the contradictory nature of Coyote, who is both creative and destructive.

While serving as chairman of the Native Studies department at the University of Minnesota from 1991 to 1993 King published his first children's book, *A Coyote Columbus Story* (1992), in response to the quincentenary celebration of Christopher Columbus's "discovery" of America. While in the traditional narrative Columbus found virtually uninhabited lands, in King's text the voyage disrupts a well-established Native community. A female version of Coyote creates the world because she wants someone to play baseball with her. But the creatures have other tasks to perform, so she keeps producing animals in the hope of finding companions who will indulge her passion for the sport. Eventually, Coyote creates human beings, starting with Aboriginal people; they initially agree to play ball with her but soon turn to other activities. Finally, Coyote generates a group of European explorers; led by Columbus, they refuse to play ball and spend their time trying to put a value on everything and everyone they encounter. Chastised by the Natives for her mistake in bringing Columbus and his crew into the world, Coyote seeks to reestablish balance by creating another colonizing figure, Jacques Cartier. In response, the Aboriginal community and the animals hop on a train to Penticton, British Columbia, replicating the historical displacement of Native peoples who kept moving westward to escape European settlers. (King is also alluding to the location of Theytus Press, the only Aboriginal publishing house in Canada.) Coyote continues to hold out hope that she will be able to redirect Cartier's energies to the game of baseball. *A Coyote Columbus Story* is illustrated in psychedelic hues by the Métis artist Ken Monkman. It was nominated for a Governor General's Literary Award for children's literature.

A revised version of *A Coyote Columbus Story* aimed at adult readers appeared in 1993 in *One Good Story, That One,* along with nine other previously published stories that combine oral storytelling techniques with a comic twist. In "How Corporal Colin Sterling Saved Blossom, Alberta, and Most of the Rest of the World as Well" the mysteriously petrified bodies of Natives are claimed by a spaceship piloted by coyotes. Royal Canadian Mounted Police officer Colin Sterling tries to block the transfer of the bodies to the spaceship, insisting that he must protect the Natives, as Canadian citizens, from being kidnapped; but his efforts, which include the invocation of the name of Queen Elizabeth II, are futile. A local doctor suggests that perhaps the Aboriginals are happier with their "kidnappers," but Sterling continues

Dust jacket for the first edition, 1990 (Bruccoli Clark Layman Archives)

to believe that he should have saved them. Sterling's inability to hear the singing of the petrified bodies, which ask the coyotes why they did not arrive sooner, and his dismissive treatment of the Native community until the bodies are actually being removed parody the self-serving position of Canadian government agencies and small towns whose "concern" for the First Nations population masks a desire to control them. "Joe the Painter and the Deer Island Massacre" and "A Seat in the Garden" take aim at official versions of the removal of Native peoples from their lands and the stereotype of the alcoholic Aboriginal. Several stories relay traditional Native narratives in an interfusional fashion, relying on the syntax of the spoken word to rework biblical accounts of the Creation and to explore Christian rituals surrounding death from an Aboriginal perspective. In the title story white anthropologists come to the reserve to collect narratives that are stereotypically Native; Coyote deceives them into believing that they have heard an authentic tale that is, in fact, a parodic rendering of Genesis. "Magpies" depicts the conflict between Granny and her Catholic daughter, Wilma, over the former's impending death and burial. Wilma wants a church service and coffin, while Granny insists that her body be placed in a cottonwood tree. She persuades a local man to carry out this alternate plan after the funeral. The narrator, who is one of the magpies dancing on Granny's body in the tree, ensures that Wilma's efforts to rebury her mother are thwarted. The final tale in *One Good Story, That One*, "Borders," is narrated by a Blackfoot boy who accompanies his mother to the Canadian/American border on the way to see his older sister in Utah. When the mother refuses to identify herself as Canadian, describing herself to border guards as Blackfoot, a standoff ensues that is not resolved until the media arrive on the scene. By using the perspective of a boy to tell the story, King tempers his polemical message with humor and reminds readers of the vitality of Native communities today. King dramatized "The One about Coyote Going West," "Magpies," and "Borders" for the radio; he also adapted "Borders" for the CBC television series *Four Directions,* for which he served as story editor in 1993–1994.

King received a second nomination for the Governor General's Literary Award for his next novel, *Green Grass, Running Water* (1993). His most complexly layered text to date, with a circular narrative structure that frames multiple stories of contemporary political conflict and daily life on the reserve with Coyote's accounts of the world's creation, the work depicts the efforts of the Natives to hold onto reserve lands near Blossom, Alberta, that have been selected by the provincial government for the construction of a dam and cottages, to profit from the tourists who visit, and to preserve a sense of selfhood rooted in Native traditions and beliefs. The main characters are five Blackfoot men and women whose lives continually intersect. Lionel, a television salesman struggling to find focus in his life, and Charlie, a lawyer, compete for the affections of Alberta, a university professor who wants a child but refuses to marry. Lionel's uncle Eli, an English professor, comes back to Blossom to fight against the removal of his late mother's home from the site of the proposed dam. As the proprietor of the Dead Dog Café, Lionel's sister, Latisha, profits from the tourism industry by cashing in on Aboriginal stereotypes. She is recovering from an abusive marriage to a non-Native American, George, who returns to intrude on the community by trying to photograph a sacred tribal ceremony. Drawing on Aboriginal "Earth Diver" stories in which the main characters of Creation fall from the sky into water, each of the four sections of the novel recounts the appearance of a Native archetypal woman–First Woman, Changing Woman, Thought Woman, and Old Woman–who continues the process of Creation on her own terms. King also alludes to a wide range of British, American, and Canadian literary works, including Daniel Defoe's *Robinson Crusoe* (1719), Herman Melville's *Moby-Dick* (1851), and Timothy Findley's *Not Wanted on the Voyage* (1984), as well as key figures and events from Canadian and American history and politics such as George Armstrong Custer; Clifford Sifton, who served as Canadian federal minister of the interior and encouraged westward migration; and Archie Belaney, an Englishman who posed as an Indian named Grey Owl. Moreover, *Green Grass, Running Water* offers an extended commentary on the impact of movies and television on the local community: the easy migration of American mass culture to Canada and the reductive stereotypes of Aboriginal peoples that persist in Hollywood Westerns are shown to be especially destructive to the reserve population. Bill Bursum, a non-Native electronics-store owner who hopes to build a cottage near the proposed dam site and takes great delight in

watching Westerns, is a particular object of ridicule. His sense of control over the world is fundamentally challenged when his favorite John Wayne movie is altered by the four mythic female figures to make the Indians triumph over the cowboys.

The novel culminates with the destruction of the new dam. With Coyote's assistance, the four women send three cars–a Pinto, a Nissan, and a Karmann Gia (puns on the names of Columbus's ships, the *Niña,* the *Pinta,* and the *Santa María*–into the dam, causing it to crack; the cars are flushed down the dam, which resembles a giant toilet bowl. But Eli drowns in the resulting flood, creating a delicate balance between comedy and tragedy. The novel concludes in a circular fashion with Coyote sitting down to listen to the narrator relay yet another version of the Creation narrative; the pagination echoes this circularity, with the book finishing on page 360–the number of degrees in a circle.

During the filming of the 1993 movie version of *Medicine River,* for which he wrote the screenplay, King collaborated with the noted Aboriginal photographer Greg Staats on a series of twelve portraits of Native Canadian writers; the pictures were published, along with an essay by King, in a 1994 issue of *Books in Canada.* King has since produced several solo photography exhibits. The first, *The Medicine River Photographic Expedition,* begun in 1994, brings together portraits of a variety of Aboriginal writers and artists wearing "Lone Ranger"-style masks. The photographs, with King's commentary, have been shown at galleries in Minneapolis and San Francisco.

In 1995 King moved back to Canada as a full professor at the University of Guelph. That same year he became the writer and star of *The Dead Dog Café Comedy Hour,* an irreverent radio program with a cast of Native characters. Initially relegated by the CBC to regional programming, the show quickly became a hit and was broadcast nationally.

In 1998 King's exhibit *New Voices/New Visions* was shown at the Ansel Adams Center for Photography in San Francisco. It consists of a series of photographs in which his children pose at major Native American historical sites and also in front of shops that sell Native kitsch and perpetuate Aboriginal stereotypes.

Also in 1998 King returned to children's literature with *Coyote Sings to the Moon,* a gently humorous text inspired by bedtime stories he told his children. The moon, having been dismissed by Coyote, has gone into hiding, depriving the animals of their only source of light. Coyote is charged with enticing the moon to return; his voice is so terrible that the moon agrees to spend nights in the sky, far away from Coyote, and days at the bottom of the pond, where his voice will be muffled. The story provides a playful explanation of why coyotes howl at the moon.

King's darkest novel to date, *Truth and Bright Water* (1999), is set on a Native reserve that straddles the forty-ninth parallel. It is narrated by Tecumseh, an Aboriginal boy who is spending the summer working for a famous First Nations art restorer and trickster figure, Monroe Swimmer, who has returned to the reserve to reclaim the prairies for his ancestors. The narrator is named for the Shawnee war chief and pantribal leader who fought for an independent political confederacy based on Native ownership of lands in Canada and the United States in the late eighteenth and early nineteenth centuries; the original Tecumseh's desire to hold on to Native lands through tribal confederation parallels the struggles faced by King's narrator, who lives in a world in which borders and boundaries are defined by non-Natives but are undermined by Natives who regularly cross the river that divides Canada from the United States. Tecumseh's emerging sense of pride in his Aboriginal heritage is juxtaposed with the grim situation of his friend and relative Lum, who, beaten by his abusive father and haunted by the death of his mother, commits suicide by jumping off a half-built bridge that is to link Canada and the United States. Like *Green Grass, Running Water, Truth and Bright Water* relies heavily on puns, historical allusions (especially to the Cherokee "Trail of Tears"), and the parodic reworking of mass-culture icons such as Marilyn Monroe to criticize the power accorded to Eurocentric views of the world.

Dead Dog Café went off the air in 2000 to allow its cast to pursue other interests. They have reunited for special performances, including one for Victoria Day in Regina in May 2001. In 2000–2001 King mounted an exhibit of twenty prints at the Edmonton Art Gallery with the punning title *I Witness*.

Published under the pseudonym Hartley Good-Weather and intended to attract a wider audience than King's previous books, *DreadfulWater Shows Up* (2002) parodies the genre of the mystery novel generally and the work of Tony Hillerman in particular. Hillerman, a non-Native author, has written a best-selling series of mystery novels set in Arizona and New Mexico in which two Navajo tribal policemen solve crimes through a combination of insider cultural knowledge and hard work. Thumps DreadfulWater is a Cherokee former policeman who now works as a photographer in Chinook, a small town in the northwestern United States. He becomes involved in a murder investigation when he assists the police by taking photographs of the body of a computer programmer that has been found in a new luxury condominium and hotel development funded by the local Native band. When Stick Merchant, the son of his sometime lover and head of the

tribal council Claire Merchant, becomes the prime suspect, DreadfulWater decides that he must find Stick and solve the crime before the police take the teenager into custody. The actual criminal escapes at the end of the novel, leaving open the possibility of a sequel.

In November 2003 King became the first Native writer to deliver the prestigious Massey Lectures at McGill University. Published as *The Truth about Stories: A Native Narrative* (2003), King's five lectures combine humorous anecdotes, family narratives, and a wide range of references to Native and non-Native scholars and writers to examine how storytelling shapes people's lives. In the first lecture King replaces the Creation story presented in the Bible with "Woman Who Fell from the Sky." In subsequent lectures he discusses the representation and legislation of "Indian-ness" by Aboriginals and non-Aboriginals through photography, newspaper accounts, journal entries, paintings, sculpture, music, and laws such as Bill C-31, which redefined the status of Natives in Canada. He examines the differences between imagined and real Indians and the challenges that he and various relatives, friends, and historical figures such as Will Rogers have faced in coming to terms with their racial and national identities. As in his fiction, King avoids alienating his non-Native audience by using humor to temper his often confrontational and highly personal examination of the marginalization and persecution of Natives in Canada and the United States. In the afterword to the published version of the lectures, "Private Stories," King reverses white, Western assumptions about the superior value of the printed word by arguing that oral narratives are public while written stories are private. The black-and-white photograph on the cover, taken by King, of a collection of Indian memorabilia and kitsch marketed to non-Natives comments on the ways in which Aboriginals have been packaged for mass consumption.

In 2004 King published another children's book, *Coyote's New Suit,* in which Coyote's egotism and gullibility get him into trouble with the local animal and human population. After Raven dismisses Coyote's pride and joy, his beautiful fur coat, as just "okay," Coyote commits a series of burglaries so that he can try on the coats of others. Having accumulated a vast collection of animal suits and human garments, Coyote holds a garage sale. Chaos breaks out when the potential buyers recognize their stolen garments and accuse each other of committing the thefts. Raven sorts out the mess and ensures that everyone gets his or her suit back. Coyote expresses relief that the ordeal is over, but Raven starts another cycle of envy and greed by criticizing Coyote's coat again. Also in 2004 King published a photographic series titled "Indians on Vacation" in *Western American Literature.*

In 2006 King published *The Red Power Murders,* the second novel in his Thumps DreadfulWater series. Enlisted by the sheriff to help solve the murder of a retired FBI agent, DreadfulWater also tries to protect an old acquaintance, Noah Ridge, a Red Power activist who appears to be the next target. As he pursues the case, DreadfulWater revisits his own past involvement with the Red Power movement; his former romance with Dakota Miles, who is now Ridge's assistant; and the mystery of Lucy Kettle, who was second in command to Ridge until her disappearance years ago.

The Kettle case is based on the unsolved 1976 murder of Anna Mae Aquash, an American Indian Movement activist whose body, with a bullet through the skull, was found on the Pine Ridge Reservation ten days after her disappearance. Just as *Green Grass, Running Water* was published during the quincentenary celebrations of Columbus's discovery of the New World, *The Red Power Murders* was released on the thirtieth anniversary of Aquash's death.

King combines fast-paced action, gentle humor, and sharp irony in a narrative that both critiques the dangers of activist arrogance and looks at the lengths to which big business and the government have gone to silence Native activists.

Thomas King continues to attract new audiences by employing a diverse range of literary strategies to communicate his criticisms of dominant European cultural paradigms and the exploitation of Native peoples. He often depicts Aboriginals who have found innovative ways to reverse or subvert stereotypical notions of the Indian for their own gain. Though suspicious of nationalism when it is used to erase Native identities, King acknowledges the need for borders. His works trace the complexities of being Native from a range of viewpoints, employing humor, irony, and satire to present innovative and compelling representations of Aboriginal life in Canada and the United States.

Interviews:

Constance Rooke, "Interview with Tom King," *World Literature Written in English,* 30 (Autumn 1990): 62–76;

Beverley Daurio, "Coyote Lives: Thomas King," in *The Power to Bend Spoons: Interviews with Canadian Novelists,* edited by Daurio (Toronto: Mercury, 1998), pp. 90–97;

Jennifer Andrews, "Border Trickery and Dog Bones: A Conversation with Thomas King," *Studies in Canadian Literature,* 24, no. 2 (1999): 161–185;

Peter Gzowksi, "Peter Gzowksi Interviews Thomas King on *Green Grass, Running Water,*" *Canadian Literature,* 161–162 (1999): 65–76.

References:

Jennifer Andrews, "Reading Thomas King's *Green Grass, Running Water,*" *English Studies in Canada,* 28, no. 1 (2002): 91–116;

Andrews, Arnold Davidson, and Priscilla Walton, *Border Crossings: Thomas King's Cultural Inversions* (Toronto: University of Toronto Press, 2003);

Sharon M. Bailey, "The Arbitrary Nature of the Story: Poking Fun at Oral and Written Authority in Thomas King's *Green Grass, Running Water,*" *World Literature Today,* 73, no. 1 (1999): 43–52;

Barbara S. Bruce, "Figures of Collection and (Post) Colonial Processes in Major John Richardson's *Wacousta* and Thomas King's *Truth and Bright Water,*" in *Is Canada Postcolonial? Unsettling Canadian Literature,* edited by Laura Moss (Waterloo, Ont.: Wilfred Laurier, 2003), pp. 190–206;

Canadian Literature, special King issue, 161–162 (1999);

Maurice Collins, "King and Kodachrome: *Green Grass, Running Water*'s Models for Non-Native Participation," in *Telling the Stories: Essays on American Indian Literatures and Cultures,* edited by Elizabeth Hoffman Nelson (New York: Peter Lang, 2001): pp. 131–142;

Marie C. Davis, "Parable, Parody, or a 'Blip in the Canadian Literary Landscape': Tom King on *A Coyote Columbus Story,*" *Canadian Children's Literature,* 22, no. 4 (1996): 47–64;

Laura E. Donaldson, "Noah Meets Old Coyote; or Singing in the Rain: Intertextuality in Thomas King's *Green Grass, Running Water,*" *Studies in American Indian Literatures,* 7, no. 2 (1995): 27–43;

Marta Dvorak, "Thomas King's Christopher Cartier and Jacques Columbus," *Arachne,* 5, no. 1 (1998): 120–139;

Dvorak, "Thomas King's Fusion and Confusion: Or, What Happened to My Earth without Form?" *Commonwealth Essays and Studies,* 19, no. 1 (1996): 86–95;

Dvorak, "The World according to Thomas King," *Anglophonia,* 1 (1997): 67–76;

Teresa Gilbert, "Narrative Strategies in Thomas King's Short Stories," in *Telling Stories: Postcolonial Short Fiction in English,* edited by Jacqueline Bardolph (Amsterdam: Rodopi, 2001), pp. 67–76;

Ibis Gomez-Vega, "'Subverting the Mainstream' Paradigm through Magical Realism in Thomas King's *Green Grass, Running Water,*" *Journal of the Midwest Modern Language Association,* 33, no. 1 (2000): 1–19;

Renée Hulan and Linda Warley, in "Comic Relief: Pedagogical Issues Around Thomas King's *Medicine River,*" *Creating Community: A Roundtable on Canadian Aboriginal Literature,* edited by Renate Eigenbrod and Jo-Ann Episkenew (Penticton, B.C.: Theytus, 2002), pp. 125–146;

Linda Lamont-Stewart, "Androgyny as Resistance to Authoritarianism in Two Postmodern Canadian Novels," *Mosaic,* 30, no. 3 (1997): 115–130;

Patricia Linton, "'And Here's How It Happened': Trickster Discourse in Thomas King's *Green Grass, Running Water,*" *Modern Fiction Studies,* 45, no. 1 (1999): 212–234;

Mary M. Mackie, "Status, Mixedbloods, and Community in Thomas King's *Medicine River,*" *Journal of American Studies of Turkey,* 8 (1998): 65–71;

Thomas Matchie and Brent Larson, "Coyote Fixes the World: The Power of Myth in Thomas King's *Green Grass, Running Water,*" *North Dakota Quarterly,* 63, no. 2 (1996): 153–168;

Darrell Jesse Peters, "Beyond the Frame: Tom King's Narratives of Resistment," *Studies in American Indian Literatures,* 11, no. 2 (1999): 6–79;

Dieter Petzold, "Thomas King's *Green Grass, Running Water:* A Postmodern Postcolonial Puzzle; or, Coyote Conquers the Campus," in *Lineages of the Novel: Essays in Honour of Raimund Borgmeier,* edited by Bernhard Reitz and Eckart Voigts-Virchow (Trier: Wissenschaftlicher Verlag, 2000), pp. 243–254;

Robin Ridington, "Theorizing Coyote's Cannon: Sharing Stories with Thomas King," in *Theorizing the Americanist Tradition* edited by Lisa Philips Valentine and Regna Darnell (Toronto: University of Toronto Press, 1999), pp. 19–37;

Armand Garnet Ruffo, "From Myth to Metafiction, a Narratological Analysis of Thomas King's 'The One about Coyote Going West,'" *International Journal of Canadian Studies,* 12 (1995): 135–154;

Priscilla Walton, "'Tell Our Own Stories': Politics and the Fiction of Thomas King," *World Literature Written in English,* 30, no. 2 (1990): 77–84;

Gundula Wilke, "Re-Writing the Bible: Thomas King's *Green Grass, Running Water,*" in *Across the Lines: Intertextuality and Transcultural Communication in the New Literatures in English,* edited by Wolfgang Klooß (Amsterdam & Atlanta: Rodopi, 1998), pp. 83–90.

Joy Kogawa

(6 June 1935 –   )

Irene Sywenky
University of Alberta

BOOKS: *The Splintered Moon* (Fredericton: University of New Brunswick Press, 1968);

A Choice of Dreams (Toronto: McClelland & Stewart, 1974);

Jericho Road (Toronto: McClelland & Stewart, 1977);

Six Poems (Toronto: League of Canadian Poets, 1978);

Obasan (Toronto: Lester & Orpen Dennys, 1981; Boston: Godine, 1982); adapted by Kogawa for children as *Naomi's Road* (Toronto: Oxford University Press, 1986; enlarged edition, Markham, Ont.: Fitzhenry & Whiteside, 2005);

Woman in the Woods (Oakville, Ont.: Mosaic, 1985);

Itsuka (Toronto: Viking Canada, 1992; New York: Anchor, 1994); republished as *Emily Kato* (Toronto: Penguin Canada, 2005);

The Rain Ascends (Toronto: Knopf, 1995);

A Song of Lilith (Vancouver: Polestar, 2000);

A Garden of Anchors: Selected Poems (Oakville, Ont. & Niagara Falls, N.Y.: Mosaic, 2003).

PRODUCED SCRIPT: *The Pool: Reflections of the Japanese-Canadian Internment,* motion picture, Falcon Films, 1992.

OTHER: "Ancestors in Kurakawa," "Day of the Bride," "Hangnail," and "If Your Mirror Breaks," in *Poetry by Canadian Women,* edited by Rosemary Sullivan (Toronto: Oxford University Press, 1989), pp. 137–139;

"Is There a Just Cause?" in *Up and Doing: Canadian Women and Peace,* edited by Janice Williamson and Deborah Gorham (Toronto: Women's Press, 1989), pp. 157–162;

"From the Bottom of the Well, from the Distant Stars," in *Telling It: Women and Language across Cultures,* edited by The Telling It Book Collective (Vancouver: Press Gang Publishers, 1990), pp. 95–97;

"Obasan," in *Other Solitudes: Canadian Multicultural Fictions,* edited by Linda Hutcheon and Marion Richmond (Toronto: Oxford University Press, 1990), pp. 87–94;

"From *Obasan,*" in *Making a Difference: Canadian Multicultural Literature,* edited by Smaro Kamboureli (Don Mills, Ont.: Oxford University Press, 1996), pp. 120–140;

"Where There's a Wall," "Road Building by Pick Axe," "Minerals from Stone," and "Obasan," in *A New Anthology of Canadian Literature in English,* edited by Donna Bennett and Russell Brown (Don Mills, Ont.: Oxford University Press, 2002), pp. 732–742;

"When I Was a Little Girl," in *Literature: A Pocket Anthology, Canadian Edition,* edited by R. S. Gywnn and Wanda Campbell (Toronto: Pearson Longman, 2004), p. 737;

Gina Valle, ed., *Our Grandmothers, Ourselves: Reflections of Canadian Women,* foreword by Kogawa (Markham, Ont.: Fitzhenry & Whiteside, 2005).

SELECTED PERIODICAL PUBLICATIONS–UNCOLLECTED: "Pink Geranium," *Canadian Literature,* 99 (Winter 1983): 33;

"In the Forest" and "Grief Poem," *Canadian Literature,* 100 (Spring 1984): 171–172;

"Sunday Afternoon, September, 1983," *Quarry,* 40 (Spring 1991): 103–105;

"Itsuka," *Chatelaine,* 65 (December 1992): 85;

"For A.D.," *Canadian Literature,* 140 (Spring 1994): 12;

"For a Citizenship Swearing-in Ceremony," *Globe and Mail* (Toronto), 29 September 2001;

"Remember Nagasaki (Our Readers Write Peace)," *Peace Magazine,* 19 (July–September 2003): 5.

"There is a silence that cannot speak. There is a silence that will not speak. . . . The word is stone": the opening words of the novel *Obasan* (1981) define the spiritual quest for the articulation of memory in the work of Joy Kogawa, who became a voice of the three generations of Japanese Canadians who suffered internment and persecution during World War II. An award-winning author who became a member of the Order of Canada in 1986 and of the Order of

British Columbia in 2006, Kogawa is known for her novels, poetry, essays, children's stories, and social activism.

Joy Nozomi Nakayama was born on 6 June 1935 in Vancouver to issei parents. Her father, Gordon Goichi Nakayama, was an Anglican clergyman, and her mother, Lois Masui Yao Nakayama, was a kindergarten teacher. In 1942, the year following the attack on Pearl Harbor and Canada's declaration of war on Japan, some twenty-one thousand residents of Japanese ancestry living within one hundred miles of the Pacific Coast, most of whom were Canadian citizens, were moved to labor and detention camps in the interior of British Columbia. Except for personal belongings, all of their property was confiscated. The Nakayama family was sent to Slocan. After the end of the war in 1945, Japanese Canadians were given the choice of returning to Japan or going into internal exile east of British Columbia. As many of them identified themselves as Canadians, the latter option was the only acceptable one. The Nakayamas were relocated to Coaldale, Alberta.

In 1954 Joy Nakayama completed one year of study at the University of Alberta and took a teaching post at an elementary school in Coaldale. In 1955 she enrolled at the Anglican Women's Training College and Conservatory of Music in Toronto; the following year she transferred to a music school in Vancouver. She married David Kogawa in 1957. The couple had two children: Gordon, born in 1957, and Deidre, born in 1959. They lived in Vancouver; Grand Forks, British Columbia; Moose Jaw and Saskatoon, Saskatchewan; and Ottawa before divorcing in 1968.

In 1968 Kogawa published her first poetry collection, *The Splintered Moon*. The twenty-one poems offer a glimpse into a world of emotional intensity and spiritual longing underscored by Kogawa's characteristic minimalism. Kogawa's exploration of memory takes on a personal tone in her love lyric "In Memory," but her resort to the imagery of stone both as a metaphor of immutability and as a symbol of physicality and material "realness" of memory anticipate her use of the trope in *Obasan*. Similarly significant in view of her later work are her evocations of silence as a vehicle of memory, wisdom, and knowledge in "muted" sorrow with "no tears" in "Old Woman" or as a contained despair and emotional angst in "Snowflake." In "I Know Who I Am" the speaker's reflections on desire, loneliness, and emotional loss are counterbalanced by her need for freedom and her search for an identity that defies the limitations of the traditional male-female dichotomy. Kogawa's feminism is evident in her subversive evo-

cation of traditional fairy-tale imagery in "I Think I Am That Fabled Princess," in the subtexts of sexuality and sinfulness in the "red dress" image in "Pity My Dress," and in her openly revisionist rereading of the tale of the Nutcracker in the poem of that title. The theme of racial memory and history that is central to most of her work is addressed for the first time in "We Had Not Seen It," the only prose poem in the collection:

> We had not seen it. None of us had seen it. It was not that we were incapable of sight. But we were shielded from it. Some of us knew—most of us knew—that behind that shield it was there. Some of us chose to forget. A very few of us . . . tore at the shield, tore wildly. But none of us fully saw.

A reflection on the process of social awakening, the poem is the collective voice of a people whose memories of injustice have been silenced for decades.

In 1969 Kogawa traveled to Japan, remaining there for three months. Her second poetry collection, *A Choice of Dreams* (1974), resulted in part from that visit. It is more somber and reflective than her first volume, with meditations on the lessons of history in "For the Annual Service of Thanks That Kyoto Was Spared the Bomb" and "Hiroshima Exit." Many poems display themes that resurface in Kogawa's prose writing, and some sketches are incorporated in *Obasan*. For example, "Public Bath" anticipates the scene in *Obasan* in which the narrator reminisces about taking a bath with her grandmother: a trivial activity becomes meaningful as a ritual and as an experience of belonging to and sharing in the Japanese culture. The physicality of "warm soft body blending" with "neighbours strangers and friends" is transformed into a feeling of a spiritual communion and becomes a cultural rite of passage. Cultural memory is further explored in "Zen Graveyard," in which childhood experiences blend with mythology and mysticism. Retracing her father's "flight perpetual" and reflecting on her ancestors' graves in "Ancestors' Graves in Kurakawa" bring out an awareness of her beginnings, although "The hiddenness stretches beyond my reach." Similarly, her mother's "vaguely remembered girlhood" is associated with the muteness of aged items in a trunk with mothballs in "Trunk in the Attic." Kogawa revisits the racial discrimination she experienced in her childhood in "When I Was a Little Girl" and "What Do I Remember of the Evacuation." In "Chain Necklace" she explores the generation gap between herself and her mother in their responses to internment: her mother

wore her chains
Kept her cygnets in the
Ugly barnyard world
Told me constantly to be
Gentle and to wear
The heavy chains with joy
But I . . .
. . . pick and jab my noose
At every chance.

Kogawa's next poetry collection, *Jericho Road,* appeared in 1977. In "On the Jericho Road" the notion of silence generating meaning reappears:

Your tongue
was your weapon
I lay silent
on the Jericho Road

Silence is also
a two-edged sword

These words
are my donkey.

The creation of reality and identity through words is the theme of "As Though It Were the Earth" and "Therapist." Feeling trapped in a relationship and resenting her manipulated identity, the speaker of "As Those Who Are Too Old" struggles to break free from the structures of power and control:

he was inventing me
but I cannot say to him
she is not real
even as he held me
he was destroying me
and creating her
he was puzzled when
I walked away.

Finally, stone imagery is revived in "Bread to Stone." Kogawa's attention to detail and use of the small and the mundane to reveal the universal and the eternal shows her indebtedness to classical Japanese poetry.

Six Poems (1978) opens with "Offerings," which sets the tone of the collection:

We lift
the barricades
we take the edges
of our transience
we bury the ashes
of our wording
and sift
the silences.

Kogawa's minimalist world manifests a complex interweaving of the particular and universal, private and social. *Six Poems* displays a continuity with her previous collections through the exploration of the speech/silence dichotomy and the significance of collective memory.

Kogawa moved to Toronto in 1979. In 1981 she published *Obasan*. The novel, which includes many autobiographical details, is narrated by Naomi Nakane, a thirty-six-year-old sansei schoolteacher. Her 1972 trip to the funeral of her uncle, who helped to raise her, frames an internal journey through her memories, which are fragmented, elusive, and continuously reinterpreted by the narrator. To counterbalance the subjectivity of memory, the novel incorporates Naomi's activist aunt Emily Kato's diaries, correspondence, newspaper clippings, and copies of government documents. Naomi's narrative is more than a personal account of an individual caught in the workings of history: it is the voice of three generations lost to the indignities and displacements of a wartime period. Kogawa rejects postmodernist notions of memory as an unreliable narrative, a discursive labyrinth, or a game of construed subjectivities. In *Obasan* memory is holistic and healing and the only truth that is given to the narrator: "All our ordinary stories are changed in time, altered as much by the present as the present is shaped by the past. Potent and pervasive as a prairie dust storm, memories and dreams seep and mingle through cracks, settling on furniture and into upholstery." Furthermore, memory is closely related to identity as Naomi tries to relive the trauma of her displaced childhood. Kogawa observed in a 1990 interview with Magdalene Redekop that "there is a need for people to feel a sense of strength in belongingness." Naomi's "belongingness"—to a family, ethnic community, city, or country—was shaken at an early age. With her separation from her parents and relocation to an abandoned log hut, "shabby and sagging and overgrown with weeds," near Slocan in the interior of British Columbia; with her first exposure to denigrating newspaper comments on Japanese Canadians; and with the derogatory "Japs" from her students, the concept of "home," the epitome of "belongingness," was shattered. Naomi and her older brother, Stephen, have different responses to these childhood traumas. While Naomi represses her experiences, Stephen expresses his resistance through anger and violence. Usually gentle and kind, he alienates Naomi by sudden bouts of cruelty. Releasing his emotions at the sight of their dilapidated hut and seeking a momentary feeling of control, he leaves "the ground and grasses quivering with maimed and dismembered butterflies."

Naomi's earliest memories are of being one with her mother in womb-like comfort and belonging: "I am clinging to my mother's leg, a flesh shaft that grows from the ground, a tree trunk of which I am an off-

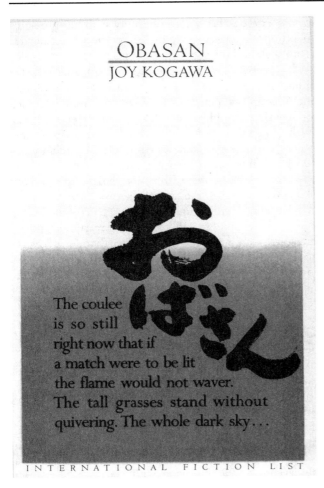

OBASAN
JOY KOGAWA

The coulee
is so still
right now that if
a match were to be lit
the flame would not waver.
The tall grasses stand without
quivering. The whole dark sky...

INTERNATIONAL   FICTION   LIST

Paperback cover for the first edition, 1981
(Bruccoli Clark Layman Archives)

enemy." A key moment in the process of coming to terms with her identity occurs when she reads Aunt Emily's diary, which is addressed to Emily's sister—Naomi's mother—in the hope that the latter will read it someday. To Naomi it feels like "breaking into a private house only to discover it's my own childhood house filled with corners and rooms I've never seen." Seeing familiar childhood scenes through Aunt Emily's eyes fills many gaps in her memories. Emily's unshakable Canadianness at the beginning of her epistolary diary evolves into a mix of bewilderment, disbelief, and anger at the segregation of Japanese Canadians. The idea of the redress movement gradually takes shape in her letters of protest to the government, which are based on the real-life letters of the Japanese Canadian activist Muriel Kitagawa.

The multiple silences in *Obasan* create a rich network of meanings and subtexts. On the most general level there is the decades-long silence of the Japanese Canadians—a silence that is powerfully broken by the book itself:

> We are the silences that speak from stone. We are the despised rendered voiceless, stripped of car, radio, camera and every means of communication, a trainload of eyes covered with mud and spittle. . . . We are sent to Siloam, the pool called "Sent." We are sent to sending, that we may bring sight. We are the scholarly and the illiterate, the envied and the ugly, the fierce and the docile. We are those pioneers who cleared the bush and the forest with our hands, the gardeners tending the soil with our tenderness, the fishermen who are flung from the sea to flounder in the dust of prairies. We are the Issei and the Nisei and the Sansei, the Japanese Canadians. We disappear into the future undemanding as dew.

shoot. . . . Her blood is whispering through my veins. The shaft of her leg is the shaft of my body and I am her thoughts." The actual separation from her mother, when her mother and grandmother left for Japan before the war, never to return, was preceded by the inner alienation Naomi felt after being sexually abused by their neighbor, Old Man Gower. Keeping the secret from her mother separated them long before her mother's physical departure; it not only made her "become other" from the maternal body but also marked her realization of the otherness of her own body, which no longer belonged to her but was used by another. This shift in her consciousness is symbolically reflected in her dreams: "My mother is on one side of the rift. I am on the other. We cannot reach each other. My legs are being sawn in half."

Naomi lives in a dichotomized world of two languages (Japanese and English), two countries, two nationalities, and being "both the enemy and not the

There are also the silence of the child Naomi, who does not comprehend the injustices she witnesses; the silence of Naomi's mother, who dies in the aftermath of the atomic bombing of Nagasaki; and the silence of Stephen, who outgrows his childhood anger and becomes alienated from everything Japanese. There is, finally, Naomi's aunt Obasan's silence—the most powerful silence in its meaningfulness: it is the silence of the generation and the community. During Naomi's stay with Obasan for her uncle's funeral their communication is minimal verbally but rich on other levels. Obasan speaks through her house, which is frozen in time and full of scraps and leftovers and historical junk; her memory houses every little detail. Naomi gradually wakes up to the need to face the past: "I would like to drop the lid of the trunk, go downstairs and back to bed. But we're trapped, Obasan and I, by our memories of the dead–all our dead–those who refuse to bury themselves. Like threads of old spiderwebs, still sticky and hovering, the past waits for us to submit, or depart." For Naomi, her two aunts are associated with two different strategies of resistance: "One lives in sound, the other in stone. Obasan's language remains deeply underground but Aunt Emily, BA, MA, is a word warrior."

Christian and Buddhist traditions are woven into the narrative both explicitly and implicitly. The first epigraph is taken from the Bible and structured by Kogawa as a poem:

To him that overcometh
will I give to eat
of the hidden manna
and will give him
a white stone
and in the stone
a new name written.

The stone imagery evokes connotations of silence, muteness, and stillness. The second epigraph flows smoothly into the narrative of the novel and reads as part of it: "Beneath the grass the speaking dreams and beneath the dreams is a sensate sea. The speech that frees comes forth from that amniotic deep." This epigraph highlights the difference between Christian and Buddhist treatments of life and death. Naomi accompanied her uncle on his annual trips to the coulee in the prairie on a full-moon night to pay respect to their dead and their history; although the younger Naomi did not comprehend the purpose and meaning of these trips, they gave her a powerful feeling of belonging: "My fingers tunnel through a tangle of roots till the grass stands up from my knuckles, making it seem that my fingers are the roots. I am part of this small forest." The image of the sea-like prairie– "Ripple after ripple of grass shadows, rhythmical as ocean waves"–is evoked in the allusion in the second epigraph to ancestral wisdom, knowledge, and spiritual power through "speaking dreams": if the silence is to be broken and speech is to be set free, it must come from the "amniotic deep" of the memory of the dead. In Japanese culture silence does not necessarily have a negative value but is associated with wisdom and revelation, allowing one to perceive, as Teruyo Ueki notes, the "very essence of a matter hidden behind silence." Kogawa utilizes both treatments of silence through Obasan's silence of memory, wisdom, and forgiveness, on the one hand, and, on the other hand, Aunt Emily's militant words and Naomi's narrative, both of which overcome the silence invoked in the two epigraphs.

Obasan incorporates a circular narrative structure, moving from Naomi's reminiscence of visiting the coulee with her uncle as an eighteen-year-old at the beginning of the first chapter to the older Naomi performing the same ritual in the last chapter after her uncle's death. The final trip to the coulee is an answer to the continuous uncomprehending "why?" of the younger Naomi. For Naomi it symbolizes coming back to the beginning, completing the circle and becoming one with the ancestral past: "my relatives, my ancestors, we have come to the forest tonight, to the place where the colors all meet. We have turned and returned to your arms as you turn to earth. My loved ones, rest in the world of stone."

The novel ends with a postscript that follows the final chapter. It is an excerpt from the memorandum sent by the Co-operative Committee on Japanese Canadians to the House and Senate of Canada in April 1946 that condemned the internment of Japanese Canadians as a violation of rights and liberties of Canadian citizens and demanded official recognition of this fact from the government. This document–the concluding "voice" in the novel–stands in direct contrast to the poetic and highly personal attempt at "speech" at the beginning of the narrative. The verbalization of the experiences of thousands of people in an official document reflects Naomi's personal evolution toward understanding the necessity of recognition of the past. *Obasan* won the *Books in Canada* First Novel Award in 1981 and the Canadian Authors Association Book of the Year Award, the Before Columbus Foundation American Book Award, and the American Library Association Notable Book Award in 1982. It also brought Kogawa international recognition.

In 1984 Kogawa visited Japan for the second time. The following year she published *Woman in the Woods,* which displays a more pronounced feminist voice than her previous poetry collections. The title of the book emphasizes the importance of nature as a sphere of freedom where a woman can abandon her socially imposed chains and return to her primordial roots as an uninhibited natural being. In "She Has Fled" Kogawa presents an image of a "wild woman" fleeing into a dream-like mythological landscape:

She (the wife
the nameless one)
has fled
to where the
name tree grows
its leaves
in the breezes
rustling.

In "Garden Poem" the speaker resents the proprietary chains of the male-female relationship:

> "Marigolds," he said
> rooting her firmly
> in his garden bed
> "are sacrificial plants
> for garden slugs."

In "Autumn" Kogawa experiments with the traditional Japanese tanka lyric form to capture the tranquility and beauty of a moment:

> A wrinkled leaf
> has fallen into
> the cup of tea.
>
> Instead of drinking
> we ponder the shape.

In a short series of six poems titled "Road Building by Pick Axe" Kogawa revisits the issei and nisei experience in British Columbia. Written in bold style that is close to journalism, the poems tell of particular people and refer to particular dates and places.

In 1992 Kogawa published *Itsuka,* a sequel to *Obasan.* The novel begins in 1983, the year Japanese Canadians began to petition through the Ad Hoc Committee for Japanese Canadian Redress, the National Association of Japanese Canadians, and the National Coalition for an official apology from the government and compensation for the wartime internments. The Liberal government of Prime Minister Pierre Trudeau treated the petition with indifference; Brian Mulroney, the opposition leader, promised to negotiate a settlement if his party won the upcoming election but failed to deliver on the promise after the Progressive Conservatives' 1984 victory. In 1988, after years of lobbying and petitioning, the Mulroney government was forced to offer a formal apology for "wrongful incarceration" and "disenfranchisement" of thousands of citizens of Japanese ancestry and a settlement of $21,000 each to the approximately twelve thousand surviving internees.

These facts provide the background for *Itsuka.* The title means "someday" in Japanese; Naomi's memories of her uncle invariably include his semi-meditative, semiprophetic references to "itsuka": "someday things will change, someday, the time for laughter will come." There is, however, a distinct difference between his use of *itsuka* and the connotation of the title of the second novel. Like Obasan's silence, the uncle's insistence on the coming of "someday" refers to reconciliation: the nisei–

Obasan's and the uncle's generation—forgave, and, although they did not forget, they let the past go. Naomi's *itsuka,* on the contrary, signals her awakening from the years of socially enforced amnesia and the beginning of her active contribution to the community. The death of Obasan is a significant moment in this process. Sitting with her dying aunt, Naomi feels herself part of the intergenerational connection: "we are there together, our hands speaking of the kitchen queendom and the past. Our language is gestures, the nodding and shaking of hands, the shrugging of shoulders." Naomi moves to Toronto and takes a trip to Japan and Hawaii, the latter of which has a Japanese diasporic community. Through Aunt Emily she becomes aware of the redress movement and gradually develops an activist political position.

Naomi is not beautiful and elegant like her mother, who is a symbol for her of the eternal feminine. She is also single and does not have children, signs of failure in a woman in both traditional and emancipated societies. Aunt Emily, an eternal rebel, proudly embraces her unmarried status and defies the "spinster" label: "if we laundered the term properly she'd put it on, but it's too covered with cultural accretions for comfort," Naomi says. Naomi, however, lacks the confidence to disregard social conventions; moreover, when the opportunity arises, she discovers she cannot maintain a relationship with a man. This inadequacy leads her to go deeper into her psyche to recover all the forgotten traumas: "Who knows what the psychogenesis of an illness may be? There are so many mysteries in the past—so many unknown and forbidden rooms." Her "whole body has been a foot binding all my life," she decides; it has been her worst enemy, holding her mind hostage.

On 22 September 1988 key members of the redress movement are invited to Parliament Hill for the official speech of apology and the signing of the settlement between the government and the Japanese Canadian community. The prime minister's speech is a "feast of words," and the ceremony is the beginning of a new life for Naomi and thousands like her: "I laugh. I am whole. I am as complete as when I was a very young child. . . . Reconciliation. Liberation. Belongingness. Home." After the ceremony, Naomi meditates on the hill, which overlooks the Ottawa river; the scene is reminiscent of her earlier ritual trips with her uncle to the coulee near Granton. Naomi's silent communion with her uncle and her ability to say that his hopes of "someday" have finally come true close the circle.

Kogawa received a Ryerson Polytechnical Institute Fellowship and an honorary LL.D. from the University of Lethbridge in 1991, an honorary

Litt.D. from the University of Guelph in 1992, an honorary LL.D. from Simon Fraser University in 1993, an Urban Alliance Race Relations Award in 1994, and a Grace MacInnis Visiting Scholar Award in 1995. In 1995 she published *The Rain Ascends,* a fictional account of sexual abuse by an Anglican priest in a small town in Alberta. The novel is narrated by Millicent, the only daughter of the Reverend Dr. Charles Barnabas Shelby, who is in his mid eighties. Millicent must deal with the fact that her father was guilty of sexually molesting an unspecified number of boys, including his own grandson—Millicent's son. She finds it impossible to reconcile the image of her father as she has known him all her life with the idea of him as a stranger with a terrible secret in the past:

> The wonder of your father has always existed—the warmth, the tenderness. He was a god. In the beginning he was the one who could do no wrong, the maker and the keeper of all laws. With the wave of his hand he formed the land. The clinging mist that surrounded the house could not extinguish the light, the bravely flickering light. Now, in his old age, it continues to glow through the mist. You move towards it. You trust it still.

The patriarchal structure of the Shelby family makes it even harder for Millicent to break down the myth of her father's god-like status. Meekness, obedience, and unconditional faith in her father, enforced by her mother, were the core of her upbringing. Her older brother, Charlie, the other male member of the family and another authority figure, invariably reminded her of her place: "You are asking too many questions. . . Stop asking questions." Millicent's sister-in-law Eleanor, who in her rebellious spirit and straightforward character is reminiscent of Aunt Emily in *Obasan* and *Itsuka,* forces Millicent to accept the necessity of facing the truth: "If there's just one thing that history teaches us . . . it's that bystanders and perpetrators are both on the same side."

Millicent is forced to reevaluate her life as a continuum of fictions: "We construct our lives out of the tales we tell ourselves, our myths and legends, the grids of understanding that chart the paths of good and evil, right and wrong." Reminiscing about her childhood, she realizes that the happy family scenes stored in her memory are fictional representations and that she has been living "in the house of lies." Millicent's path to finding peace lies in "slaying the fiction" and finding words to articulate the unspeakable truth. Kogawa shows, however, that there is not a distinct line of demarcation between good and evil: though a child molester, Shelby was well educated, charismatic, generous, and approach-

able and had a profoundly positive impact on the community. A surprising voice of support for Shelby comes from Eleanor's nephew, Martin, who was abused by Shelby. A homosexual, Martin knows what it is like to be scorned by society for one's sexuality: "You're jealous of our freedom. All through history it's been good people like you who stone people. You drown them. You burn them at the stake. You think you have the right to decide who the deviants are and then you sacrifice them. Now that's what I call abuse. It's abuse of power." Martin likens the persecution of those who engage in unorthodox sexual practices to the burning of witches. His refusal to consider himself a victim is thrown into question, however, when it is revealed that he tried twice to commit suicide. As Millicent ponders the events that made her reexamine her most sacred values, she realizes that speaking out for the victims of abuse was at the same time an act of love and absolution for her father.

Knox College of the University of Toronto bestowed an honorary doctorate of divinity on Kogawa in 1999. The previous year she had received a request from Kristine Bogyo, a classical-music performer, to write a narrative on the Lilith myth for a multimedia performance that would include narrated text, artwork, and music. Kogawa's first impulse had been to decline: community work was consuming most of her time, and she was not familiar with the Lilith material. But, she says in the "Author's Preface" to the published text of the work, when she received the artwork of Lilian Broca that was to be used in the project, she felt "deluged" with the "rich, powerful images." Broca also sent Kogawa an outline of her research on Lilith, and Kogawa was captivated by the beauty of the legend and the strong character of Lilith. The published version of the collaboration appeared in 2000 as *A Song of Lilith.*

While some feminist theorists view the legend of Lilith as having prebiblical roots and providing a clue to women's role in the evolution of social organization, Bible scholars point to the two different stories of creation in Genesis, which imply that another woman existed before Eve, as the basis of the myth. In Gen. 1:28 "God created human beings . . . male and female" and put both of them "in charge" of the animal world. Here the man and the woman are created independently of each other and equal. But in chapter 2 God creates Eve out of Adam's rib. According to feminists, the exclusion of the story from the canon and the later demonization of Lilith testify to the danger the myth presented to the patriarchal world.

In Kogawa's reinterpretation of the myth Lilith emerges as a powerful, independent, and intelligent woman who refuses to be subservient to Adam and prefers exclusion from society to male domination. Kogawa emphasizes that like Adam, Lilith was created "from dust . . . from earth's crust." The initial idyll ends when the man asserts his power over her:

> The lion finds its prey
> The hunter, the hunted;
> The bond of equality severed
> Is become the whip of domination.

Lilith despairs at first, but then she utters the ineffable name of God and is granted wings and freedom from Adam's domination. Characteristically for Kogawa, speech plays a crucial role in securing the character's freedom. Lilith's story is

> Not mediated through history
> Where she is locked in the turbulence
> Of man's memory.
> Her story is of her body, her blood
> Her wings and wanderings
> And her many new beginnings.

One of the important aspects of Lilith's freedom is that she, together with God, "creates / Names, re-names / Shapes and re-shapes." The word is an act, and she is an agent and a cocreator.

Adam is unhappy about losing his mate, and in the traditional Christian version of the myth God sends three angels to talk Lilith back into obedience. Kogawa, however, refers to the messengers as tempters and demons who try to call Lilith back to the security of enslavement and to the wifely role of "woman of silence." Lilith's rejection of both their threats and their lavish promises infuriates the demons, and they exile her into eternal "Otherness": she is

> bound and relegated to the region beyond memory
> To the land of legend
> Where at the whim of mythmaking man
> You are transformed into the needful
> Demon of the race.

The curse applies not to Lilith alone but to "every powerful woman" who will come in the future and represent Lilith in spirit. Kogawa is rewriting the traditional myth of the demonized Lilith as a product and a means of patriarchal ideology. Further, by bringing Eve into *A Song of Lilith* Kogawa departs from the traditional treatment of the two figures as archenemies and mutually exclusive symbolic opposites. Eve and Lilith become united through the solidarity of all women who "walk boldly / Out of the whirlwind of unspeakable memories / Into the mighty rivers / Of truth telling." These women regain the language of their own, "knit each tale of grief" through the voice of their memory and speak "Under the banner / Of our true and original name."

In 2001 Kogawa received a lifetime achievement award from the Association of Asian American Studies, an honorary Litt.D. from the University of British Columbia, and the National Association of Japanese Canadians National Award. In 2003 she received honorary LL.D.s from Queen's University and the University of Windsor. *Obasan* was chosen for One Book, One Community in Medicine Hat, Alberta, in 2004. The City of Vancouver designated 6 November 2004 Joy Kogawa Day; the following year *Obasan* was chosen for One Book, One Vancouver and 1 November was declared *Obasan* Cherry Tree Day in the city.

In the interview with Redekop, Kogawa said that "life is a matter of being chosen and choosing at the same time. The primary thing for me is a sense of being aligned to something that makes me feel at peace." In one of her earlier poems she reflects on her need to reevaluate the past without hatred and bitterness: "tell me how I may not live / or write of love." Although Joy Kogawa's contribution to Canadian literature is diverse, one of the more important aspects of her work is her concern with giving a hearing to marginalized voices and rethinking the processes of Canadian history, identity, truth, and memory.

Interviews:

Magdalene Redekop, *Other Solitudes: Canadian Multicultural Fictions,* edited by Linda Hutcheon and Marion Richmond (Toronto: Oxford University Press, 1990), pp. 94–101;

Janice Williamson, "In Writing I Keep Living, I Keep Breathing . . . ," in her *Sounding Differences: Conversations with Seventeen Canadian Women Writers* (Toronto: University of Toronto Press, 1993), pp. 148–159;

Karlyn Koh, "The Heart-of-the-Matter Questions," in *The Other Woman: Women of Colour in Contemporary Canadian Literature* (Toronto: Sister Vision Press, 1994), pp. 18–41.

References:

King-Kok Cheung, *Articulate Silences: Hisaye Yamamoto, Maxine Hong Kingston, Joy Kogawa* (Ithaca, N.Y.: Cornell University Press, 1993), pp. 126–167;

Cheung, "Attentive Silence in Joy Kogawa's *Obasan*," in *Listening to Silences: New Essays in Feminist Criti-*

cism, edited by Elaine Hedges and Shelley Fisher Fishkin (New York: Oxford University Press, 1994), pp. 113–129;

Cheng Lok Chua, "Witnessing the Japanese Canadian Experience in World War II: Processual Structure, Symbolism, and Irony in Joy Kogawa's *Obasan,*" in *Reading the Literatures of Asian America,* edited by Shirley Geok-lin Lim and Amy Ling (Philadelphia: Temple University Press, 1992), pp. 97–111;

Arnold Davidson, *Writing against the Silence: Joy Kogawa's* Obasan, Canadian Fiction Studies, no. 30 (Toronto: ECW Press, 1993);

Carol Fairbanks, "Joy Kogawa's *Obasan:* A Study in Political Efficacy," *Journal of American and Canadian Studies,* 5 (Spring 1990): 73–92;

Gayle K. Fujita, "'To attend the sound of stone': The Sensibility of Silence in *Obasan,*" *MELUS: The Journal of the Society for the Study of the Multi-Ethnic Literature of the United States,* 12 (Fall 1985): 33–42;

Donald C. Goellnicht, "Father Land and/or Mother Tongue: The Divided Female Subject in Kogawa's *Obasan* and Hong Kingston's *The Woman Warrior,*" in *Redefining Autobiography in Twentieth-Century Women's Fiction: An Essay Collection,* edited by Janice Morgan, Colette T. Hall, and Carol L. Snyder (New York: Garland, 1991), pp. 119–134;

Goellnicht, "Minority History as Metafiction: Joy Kogawa's *Obasan,*" *Tulsa Studies in Women's Literature,* 8 (Fall 1989): 287–306;

Erika Gottlieb, "The Riddle of Concentric Worlds in *Obasan,*" *Canadian Literature,* 109 (Summer 1986): 34–53;

Mason Harris, "Broken Generations in *Obasan:* Inner Conflict and the Destruction of Community," *Canadian Literature,* 127 (Winter 1990): 41–57;

Manina Jones, "The Avenues of Speech and Silence: Telling Difference in Joy Kogawa's *Obasan,*" in *Theory between the Disciplines: Authority/Vision/Politics,* edited by Martin Kreiswirth and Mark A. Cheetham (Ann Arbor: University of Michigan Press, 1990), pp. 213–229;

Jones, *"That Art of Difference": "Documentary-Collage" and English-Canadian Writing* (Toronto: University of Toronto Press, 1993), pp. 120–139;

Shirley Geok-lin Lim, "Asian American Daughters Rewriting Asian Maternal Texts," in *Asian Americans: Comparative and Global Perspectives,* edited by Shirley Hune, Hyung-chan Kim, Stephen S. Fugita, and Amy Ling (Pullman:

Washington State University Press, 1991), pp. 239–248;

Lim, "Japanese American Women's Life Stories: Maternality in Monica Sone's *Nisei Daughter* and Joy Kogawa's *Obasan,*" *Feminist Studies,* 16 (Summer 1990): 288–312;

A. Lynne Magnusson, "Language and Longing in Joy Kogawa's *Obasan,*" *Canadian Literature,* 116 (Spring 1988): 58–66;

P. Merivale, "Framed Voices: The Polyphonic Elegies of Hebert and Kogawa," *Canadian Literature,* 116 (Spring 1988): 68–82;

Robin Potter, "Moral–in Whose Sense? Joy Kogawa's *Obasan* and Julia Kristeva's *Powers of Horror,*" *Studies in Canadian Literature,* 15, no. 1 (1990): 117–139;

Marilyn Russell Rose, "Hawthorne's 'Custom House,' Said's Orientalism and Kogawa's *Obasan:* An Intertextual Reading of an Historical Fiction," *Dalhousie Review,* 67 (Summer–Fall 1987): 286–296;

Rose, "Politics into Art: Kogawa's *Obasan* and the Rhetoric of Fiction," *Mosaic: A Journal for the Interdisciplinary Study of Literature,* 21 (Spring 1988): 215–226;

B. A. St. Andrews, "Co-Wanderers Kogawa and Mukherjee: New Immigrant Writers," *World Literature Today: A Literary Quarterly of the University of Oklahoma,* 66 (Winter 1992): 56–58;

St. Andrews, "Reclaiming a Canadian Heritage: Kogawa's *Obasan,*" *International Fiction Review,* 13 (Winter 1986): 29–31;

Lynn Thiesmeyer, "Joy Kogawa's *Obasan:* Unsilencing the Silence of America's Concentration Camps," *Journal of the Faculty of Humanities, Japan Women's University,* 41 (1991): 63–80;

Margaret E. Turner, "Power, Language and Gender: Writing 'History' in *Beloved* and *Obasan,*" *Mosaic: A Journal for the Interdisciplinary Study of Literature,* 25 (Fall 1992): 81–97;

Eleanor Ty, "Struggling with the Powerful (M)Other: Identity and Sexuality in Kogawa's *Obasan* and Kincaid's *Lucy,*" *International Fiction Review,* 20, no. 2 (1993): 120–126;

Teruyo Ueki, "*Obasan:* Revelations in a Paradoxical Scheme," *MELUS: The Journal of the Society for the Study of the Multi-Ethnic Literature of the United States,* 18 (Winter 1993–1994): 5–20;

Gary Willis, "Speaking the Silence: Joy Kogawa's *Obasan,*" *Studies in Canadian Literature,* 12, no. 2 (1987): 239–249.

Dany Laferrière

(13 April 1953 –   )

Harry Vandervlist
University of Calgary

BOOKS: *Comment faire l'amour à un nègre sans se fatiguer: Roman* (Montreal: VLB, 1985); translated by David Homel as *How To Make Love to a Negro* (Toronto: Coach House, 1987);

Eroshima (Montreal: VLB, 1987); translated by Homel as *Eroshima: A Novel* (Toronto: Coach House, 1991);

L'odeur du café: Récit (Montreal: VLB, 1991); translated by Homel as *An Aroma of Coffee* (Toronto: Coach House, 1993);

Le goût des jeunes filles: Roman (Montreal: VLB, 1992); translated by Homel as *Dining with the Dictator* (Toronto: Coach House, 1994);

Cette grenade dans la main du jeune Nègre est-ell une arme ou un fruit? Roman (Montreal: VLB, 1993); translated by Homel as *Why Must a Black Writer Write about Sex?* (Toronto: Coach House, 1994);

Chronique de la dérive douce (Montreal: VLB, 1994); translated by Homel as *A Drifting Year* (Toronto: Douglas & McIntyre, 1997);

Pays sans chapeau: Roman (Outremont, Que.: Lanctôt, 1996); translated by Homel as *Down among the Dead Men* (Toronto: Douglas & McIntyre, 1997);

La chair du maître (Outremont, Que.: Lanctôt, 1997);

Le charme des après-midi sans fin: Récit (Outremont, Que.: Lanctôt, 1997);

Le cri des oiseaux fous: Roman (Outremont, Que.: Lanctôt, 2000);

J'écris comme je vis (Outremont, Que.: Lanctôt, 2000);

Je suis fatigué: Récits (Outremont, Que.: Lanctôt, 2001; revised and enlarged edition, Montreal: Typo, 2005);

Comment conquérir l'Amérique en une nuit: Scénario (Outremont, Que.: Lanctôt, 2004);

Les années 80 dans ma vieille Ford (Montreal: Mémoire d'encrier, 2005);

Je suis fou de Vava (Longueuil, Que.: Editions de la Bagnole, 2006);

Vers le Sud: Roman (Montreal: Boréal, 2006).

SELECTED PERIODICAL PUBLICATIONS– UNCOLLECTED: "Marie Chauvet," *Amour, Colère, Follie, Mot pour Mot,* 11 (July 1983): 7–10; "Le vert paradis des lectures enfantines," *Le Devoir* (Montreal), 9 November 1991, pp. 13–14.

PRODUCED SCRIPT: *Comment faire l'amour à un nègre sans se fatiguer,* motion picture, Angelika Films, 1989.

Outside of Quebec, the francophone writer Dany Laferrière is better known for the title of his first work, *Comment faire l'amour à un nègre sans se fatiguer* (1985, How to Make Love to a Negro without Getting Tired; translated as *How To Make Love to a Negro,* 1987) than for the eight novels and one linked short-story collection that followed. These works, written between 1985 and 2000, make up the tetralogy "Une autobiographie américaine" (An American Autobiography), a critical portrait of North America in the second half of the twentieth century. The heart of Laferrière's "America" is the Caribbean and Atlantic sections of the continent as seen mainly from Port-au-Prince, Montreal, Miami, and New York. To construct this extended exploration Laferrière works carefully with the multiple identities and perspectives available to him as black, Haitian, Quebecois, Canadian, francophone, North American, postcolonial, and male. Stylistically, Laferrière's writing has a sense of immediacy; his work has been called "journalistic," but the observations and impressions being "reported" are filtered through a carefully constructed persona closely associated with but not identical to Laferrière. The events of which each work is composed are drawn from Laferrière's autobiography but are selected and structured in highly organized sequences of short narrative and reflective segments. The resulting texts typically present themselves as simple and direct representations of lived experience; but like the pictures of the Haitian naive painters of whom Laferrière has declared himself fond, his writing is sim-

Dany Laferrière (Getty Images Entertainment)

ple only in appearance: it reflects artistic choices made in the context of his careful study of his predecessors and contemporaries. He aims for the hard-earned appearance of ease that he describes in the gestures of a dancer in *Cette grenade dans la main du jeune Nègre est-ell une arme ou un fruit?* (1993, Is That Grenade in the Young Negro's Hand a Weapon or a Fruit? translated as *Why Must a Black Writer Write about Sex?* 1994): "Ses mouvements semblent naturels, mais on sent derrière cette aisance un travail constant et des muscles d'acier même si très souples" ("Her movements seem natural, but behind this ease one senses long training and muscles at once supple and steel-hard").

Windsor Kléber Laferrière *fils* (Jr.) was born in Port-au-Prince on 13 April 1953 to Windsor Kléber Laferrière and Marie Nelson Laferrière. He has always been called "Dany," the nickname given to him by his maternal grandmother. According to Laferrière, the name change saved his life by disguising his connection to his father. Laferrière *père* (Sr.) had been a teacher, a popular journalist, the youngest mayor of Port-au-Prince, and minister of commerce and industry. A fiery public critic of the regime of François "Papa Doc" Duvalier, he was removed from the country when Dany Laferrière was four years old through ambassadorial appointments to Italy and Argentina. After his ambassadorship was revoked, he lived in exile in New York until his death in 1984. Dany Laferrière never saw his father after the latter's departure from Haiti, despite attempts to make contact in New York years later.

Laferrière's mother was the daughter of prosperous coffee wholesalers in the village of Petit-Goâve. After marrying Windsor Laferrière, she worked in the city-hall archives in Port-au-Prince; she managed to keep the job even after her husband was denounced and left the country. When Duvalier became president in 1957, she sent Laferrière to live in Petit-Goâve with his grandmother Amélie Jean-Marie Nelson, known as "Da." Laferrière received his primary education there, studying classic French authors such as Jean Racine, Molière, Voltaire, Jean-Jacques Rousseau, and Victor Hugo. The Haitian republic took pride in having thrown off foreign domination, and Laferrière was taught to regard these writers as masters of the French language rather than as representatives of a former colonial power. Laferrière's novels *L'odeur du café* (1991; translated as *An Aroma of Coffee,* 1993) and *Le charme des après-midi sans fin* (1997, The Charm of the Endless Afternoon) are set in Petit-Goâve under the Duvalier dictatorship.

Laferrière returned to Port-au-Prince in 1964 and completed his secondary studies at the Collège Canado-Haïtien, where the instructors were French-Canadian clerics. He returned to Petit-Goâve during summer vacations. In the novel *Le goût des jeunes filles* (1992; translated as *Dining with the Dictator,* 1994) and the story collection *La chair du maître* (1997, The Master's Flesh) Laferrière associates this period of his life with his sexual awakening and with his first experience of the city's complex and often violent racial, sexual, and class politics. This awareness, developed through his reading of works by authors such as D. H. Lawrence, informs his observations of Haitian and North American society.

As an adolescent Laferrière was an adventurous reader, partly by default. During the summers he was limited to the books available in Petit-Goâve's only library. Through the happenstance of a bequest, the collection consisted largely of modern poetry and criticism by writers such as Maurice Blanchot. Such books may not have been appropriate reading for a teenager, but Laferrière devoured them for lack of other material. Other early literary explorations included his discovery at nine or ten of André Maurois's *Climats* (1928, Climates; translated as *Whatever Gods May Be,* 1929), which his mother had hidden away along with a bottle of cherry liqueur. In *J'écris comme je vis* (2000, I Write as I Live) he recalls drinking in the writing and the alcohol together; the experience confirmed for him that reading was a sensual and bodily, as well as an intellectual, pleasure. He was also required to memorize literary selections at school, and passages from Denis Diderot's *Le neveu de Rameau* (1823; translated as *Rameau's Nephew,* 1878) and Albert Camus's *L'Etranger* (1942; translated as *The Stranger,* 1946) stayed with him for many years.

In 1972 *Le nouvelliste,* the major Haitian daily newspaper, began publishing Laferrière's short portraits of Haitian painters. In 1973 he began writing for *Le petit Samedi soir* and broadcasting on the radio station Haïti-Inter. He credits his beginnings as a newspaper writer for protecting him from seeing himself as an artist until he was already an experienced and published writer. "I began writing without realizing that I was doing it—the greatest stroke of luck I ever had," he told Carrol F. Coates in a 1988 interview. During this period he got to know the painters Rigaud Benoît, Jasmin Joseph, and Robert Saint-Brice; he also met the "Spiralist" writer Franketienne (pseudonym of Franck Etienne). By this time Jean-Claude "Baby Doc" Duvalier had succeeded his father, who had died in 1971. Laferrière was not an overtly political journalist, but refusal to engage in pro-regime propaganda was seen as an oppositional activity. When his journalist colleague and close friend Gasner Raymond was assassinated in 1976, Laferrière decided to leave Haiti. His novel *Le cri des oiseaux fous* (2000, The Crazed Bird's Cry) is a fictionalized portrayal of this period, focused on his last night in Haiti.

Laferrière arrived in Montreal in the summer of 1976. The novel *Chronique de la dérive douce* (1994, translated as *A Drifting Year,* 1997) is based on the early period of his life in Canada. For several years he lived in poverty, without the social status or family connections he had known in Haiti. But these hardships were combined with striking new freedoms. The socially liberal milieu of Quebec in the 1970s, where young cou-

ples could kiss in the streets, was a pleasant shock after the social conservatism of Port-au-Prince. Laferrière also reveled in having his own room, which offered a previously unknown degree of privacy and autonomy. He alternated between unemployment and various short-term jobs, including stints in a tannery and as a cleaner in office buildings.

Laferrière met his future wife, Margaret Berronet, in the late 1970s, when she was working as a nurse in New York. Their first child, Melissa, was born in New York in 1980. The initial version of Laferrière's first novel, *Comment faire l'amour à un nègre sans se fatiguer,* was composed while he was living in New York with his wife and infant daughter—circumstances quite different from those of the first-person narrator of the book. By the time the novel was published in 1985 the family had moved to Montreal. As a result, the author who enjoyed and endured succès de scandale of his novel was not a single young man like the fictional Vieux Os but a thirty-two-year-old married father.

Laferrière claims that all of his books begin as titles long before he puts a word on paper. In this case, the "scandalous" title has overshadowed the substance of the book. Laferrière told Coates that when he published *Comment faire l'amour à un nègre sans se fatiguer* he sought notoriety and hoped to avoid being pigeonholed as an immigrant writer. For these reasons he took Montreal as his subject rather than Haiti. "I wanted to talk about the city where I was living, but also about all of North America—and in a tone that was violent, tender, and provocative, all at once! I wanted to force them to talk about me without falling into that paternalistic attitude that they use when they're dealing with 'exotic' writers. The topic of interracial fucking hit them right in the solar plexus."

In fact, the novel is concerned as much with conversation as with sex. Two young unemployed black men, Bouba and the narrator, Vieux Os, are sharing an apartment during the infernal Montreal summer while Vieux Os writes the novel *Comment faire l'amour à un nègre sans se fatiguer.* He describes the work as his "last chance." Bouba passes the days listening to Miles Davis and reading the Qur'an. A series of white female students at nearby McGill University pass through the narrator's bed. Most of the novel, however, relates the conversations and philosophical speculations of the two main characters.

The success of *Comment faire l'amour à un nègre sans se fatiguer* brought Laferrière instant notoriety, at least within Quebec. He was interviewed by Denise Bombardier, recognized on the street, and hired as a weatherman by a new television station, Les Quatre Saisons; his distinctive approach to that assignment gained him wider popularity. He was frequently called on by Radio

Paperback cover for the first edition, 1992
(Bruccoli Clark Layman Archives)

Canada, the French-language arm of the Canadian Broadcasting Corporation as a commentator. In 1989 the novel was made into a motion picture of the same title.

The publisher of *Comment faire l'amour à un nègre sans se fatiguer,* Robert Lanctôt, deleted some scenes that he thought disrupted the progression of the work; those passages became Laferrière's second novel, *Eroshima* (1987, Hiroshima; translated as *Eroshima: A Novel,* 1991). The title indicates that the book takes the theme of interracial sexuality to an "explosive" level. Laferrière's previous novel had explored the power dynamic between white female and black male characters; in *Eroshima* the Asian female character has economic power, although both she and the black male narrator who refuses to leave her apartment bear racialized identities in which sexual stereotyping plays a large part. Laferrière replied in *J'écris comme je vis* to the charge that he was perpetuating the myth of the black man as a pre-eminently sexual being: "Au contraire, je suis en train de démonter le système en mettant à nu le jeu récip-

roque des phantasmes" (On the contrary, I'm dismantling the system by exposing the interplay of unreal images).

At the end of the 1980s Laferrière and his family moved to Miami; the city had become a point of connection to Haiti, and Laferrière's wife had relatives there. The couple's second child, Sarah, was fifteen days old when they left Montreal. At this point Laferrière had written, in effect, a single novel that the editing process had separated into two works. He was tired of writing and ready to try something else, but shortly after arriving in Miami he conceived of the long-term writing project that shaped his work for the next ten years. He quickly typed out a plan that included the overall title, "Une autobiographie américaine," and sketches of the ten books that were to make up this extended fictionalized autobiography, including the two novels already published.

The "America" of Laferrière's title takes in the entire North American continent and the Caribbean islands. By claiming all of America as his subject he intended to distance himself in style and subject matter from the Haitian writers by whom he felt most influenced: Jacques Roumain, the author of *Gouverneurs de la Rosée* (1944; translated as *Masters of the Dew*, 1947), and Jacques Stephen Alexis, the author of *Compère Général Soleil* (1955; translated as *General Sun, My Brother*, 1999). Haitian writers had not written about Haiti from the perspective that Laferrière intended to make his own: a perspective that would be agile, playful, and critical as it unveiled injustices and falsehoods. Though suffused with political awareness, Laferrière's approach would usually not involve overtly political arguments or anecdotes but would focus on capturing the emotional climates and sensual textures of daily life. Above all, Laferrière aimed to avoid nostalgia and folklore in evoking his Haitian origins.

With the new ten-volume plan in hand, Laferrière composed *L'odeur du café* in a monthlong burst of energy. Each of the short paragraphs in the novel appears under its own title, as if separate memory images were being consulted one after the other. The simple style and recursive structure of the work is calculated to suit the ten-year-old narrator, Vieux Os, who is living with his grandmother, "Da," in Petit-Goâve in 1963. The style also reflects Laferrière's fascination with Haitian naive painting. While the prose style is unadorned, there are complexities in the interplay between past and present in the person of the young narrator and his adult "present-day" self. The title of the final chapter, "The Book (Thirty Years Later)," explicitly raises this issue.

The following year Laferrière completed *Le goût des jeunes filles*. The novel does not follow *L'odeur du café* in autobiographical sequence but skips ahead to 1971 and Vieux Os's first months in Port-au-Prince. Aware that Vieux Os is unprepared for life in the crowded and dangerous city, his mother and aunts attempt to protect him by confining him to his room. A novel of initiation, *Le goût des jeunes filles* traces the narrator's discovery of young girls, whom he watches through the window: they are nearby, yet seemingly inaccessible to him. The major part of the novel consists of an imaginary movie, *Weekend à Port-au-Prince,* in which the narrator finally gains access to the room full of girls across the street. The movie takes place in April 1971, the month François Duvalier died; but it is being "screened" in the mind of the present-day narrator, who claims to be thirty-nine years old and soaking in his bathtub in Florida. In the late 1990s Laferrière wrote a screenplay based on the novel, but it has not been produced.

Published in 1993, *Cette grenade dans la main du jeune Nègre est-ell une arme ou un fruit?* begins by stating, "this is not a novel" but the narrative of a journalistic assignment accepted largely for financial reasons. Laferrière identifies himself as the narrator. While recognizing that he has been asked to write the article because black authors are "the flavour of the month," he refuses to adopt a predetermined "black" or "Caribbean" viewpoint. Nevertheless, he does arrive at a portrait of the United States and Canada as experienced by a celebrated black author. He claims his own place as the first black author among a lineage who have offered portraits of America, from Walt Whitman through Jack Kerouac. The book is divided into fifteen parts, which are further divided into short titled sections that consist of reflections or scenes presented entirely through dialogue. In an apparently plain journalistic style Laferrière offers insights into the America he has witnessed and comments on other chroniclers, including Woody Allen, Norman Mailer, Norman Rockwell, and Truman Capote.

Laferrière returns to his first year in Canada in his 1994 novel, *Chronique de la dérive douce,* which explores the contrasts that arise when high intellectual and artistic aspirations meet low socioeconomic status. The narrator says:

> To read the great Russian novels
> of the nineteenth century
> is the privilege
> of the unemployed man
> who has paid his rent.
> I began *War and Peace*
> this morning.

The book consists entirely of such poetic fragments, one for each day of the year (including the dedication and the epigraph from Whitman).

Laferrière's novel *Pays sans chapeau* (1996, World without a Hat; translated as *Down among the Dead Men,* 1997) alternates between scenes of a return visit to Haiti in 1995 and a parallel narrative of an attempted journey to the land of the dead. This dual sequence is signaled by the alternating titles "Pays Réel" (The Real World) and "Pays Revé" (World of Dreams). The narrator no longer bears the name Vieux Os but is called Laferrière.

The short stories in the 1997 collection, *La chair du maître,* employ many of Laferrière's characteristic strategies, including segmented narratives presented in short sections, to pursue the theme of sexual awakening and sexual politics as experienced in 1968 in Port-au-Prince. The publication of this book between *Pays sans chapeau* and *Le charme des après-midi sans fin* was calculated to offer a contrast to those "tender" novels, which are concerned with Laferrière's grandmother "Da." *La chair du maître* was his first book to be republished in France since *Cette grenade dans la main du jeune Nègre est-ell une arme ou un fruit?* This pattern has continued with Laferrière's subsequent publications and marks a new appreciation of his work in France and the rest of Europe.

In 2000 Laferrière published *Le cri des oiseaux fous,* the final novel in his ten-volume sequence. In a series of short segments, each assigned a specific time of day, the novel recounts Laferrière's final night in Port-au-Prince before his departure for Montreal in 1976 and offers a harrowing and angry depiction of the unwelcome choices into which the narrator is forced by the Duvalier dictatorship. The narrator seeks the freedom to live as if political concerns and guessing the next move of the dictator and his murderous personal police force *tonton macoutes* (Creole for "bogeymen"), were not the sole important matters.

Laferrière published two volumes of commentary in the form of extended interviews, *J'écris comme je vis* and *Je suis fatigué* (I Am Tired), in 2000 and 2001, respectively. *Je suis fatigué* closes with an apparent valediction to the writing life: "j'aimerais, si possible, qu'a partir de ce moment l'on me cesse de considerer comme un écrivain en activité" (I would like, if possible, that from this moment forward I no longer be considered a working writer). The editor's preface notes that it is difficult to imagine that Laferrière will cease writing.

In Quebec, Dany Laferrière has been a publicly recognized figure for many years. While he is less well known to anglophone readers, his audience in France has grown; since 2000 he has made several trips to read his work there. In 1991 he was awarded the Prix Carbet for *L'odeur du café,* and in 1993 *Le goût des jeunes filles* won the Prix Edgar-l'Espérance. In 2001 *Le cri des oiseaux fous* was awarded both the Prix Carbet and, in France, the Prix Littéraire Marguerite Yourcenar. When *Cette grenade dans la main du jeune Nègre est-ell une arme ou un fruit?* was republished in Paris in 2002, it was awarded the Prix RFO du Livre by Radio France d'Outremer (Radio France Overseas).

Interviews:

Ray Conlongue, "The Call of Soil and Blood," *Globe and Mail* (Toronto), 30 January 1993, p. C-1;

Francine Bordeleau, "Dany Laferrière sans arme et dangereux. Entrevue," *Lettres Québécoises,* 73 (Spring 1994): 9–10.

Bibliography:

Carrol F. Coates, "Dany Laferrière: A Bibliography," *Callaloo: A Journal of African-American and African Arts and Letters,* 22 (Fall 1999): 901–947.

References:

Pierre L'Hérault, "Le Je Incertain: Fragmentations et Dédoublements," *Voix et Images: Littérature Québécoise,* 23 (Spring 1998): 501–514;

Jean L. Prophète, "Dany Laferrière and the Autobiography of Disorderly Past Times," *Callaloo: A Journal of African-American and African Arts and Letters,* 22 (Fall 1999): 947–949.

Jeanette Lynes
(29 May 1956 –   )

Holly Luhning
University of Saskatchewan

BOOKS: *A Woman Alone on the Atikokan Highway* (Toronto: Wolsak & Wynn, 1999);

inglish prof with her head in a blender. turned on. high: a chapbook (Maxville, Ont.: Above/Ground Press, 2001);

The Aging Cheerleader's Alphabet (Toronto: Mansfield Press, 2003);

Left Fields (Toronto: Wolsak & Wynn, 2003).

OTHER: "Is Newfoundland inside That TV? Regionalism, Postmodernism, and Wayne Johnston's Human Amusements," in *A Sense of Place: Re-evaluating regionalism in Canadian and American Writing,* edited by Christian Riegel and Herb Wyile (Edmonton: University of Alberta Press / Kamloops, B.C.: Textual Studies in Canada, University College of the Cariboo, 1998), pp. 81–94;

"Hairnets and Giblets," in *Bad Jobs: My Last Shift at Albert Wong's Pagoda & Other Ugly Tales of the Workplace,* edited by Carellin Brooks (Vancouver: Arsenal Pulp Press, 1998), pp. 54–55;

"The Deep Side of Jade" and "Poem for the Unknown Trucker I Tailgated up the Atikokan Highway," in *Paradise Frost: The Thunder Bay Poetry Renaissance,* edited by Lynes, John Fell, and David Antilla (Thunder Bay, Ont.: Edgy Writers in Edgy Times, 1999);

"Can Lit" and "Six Smaller Landscapes," in *A Rich Garland: Poems for A. M. Klein,* edited by Seymour Mayne and Glenn Rotchin (Montreal: Vehicule, 1999), pp. 49, 62–63;

"Ten Years after High School," in *In Our Own Words: An Anthology of Poetry from a Generation Falsely Labeled Generation X,* edited by Marlowe Peerse Weever (Raleigh, N.C.: MW Enterprises, 1999);

Words out There: Women Poets in Atlantic Canada, edited by Lynes (Lockport, N.S.: Roseway, 1999);

"And You Thought This Was Only Love," "Real Life on Lake Superior," "Superior Homesickness," and "To Blur with Love," in *Great Lakes Logia,*

Jeanette Lynes (photograph by Bernice MacDonald; courtesy of the author)

edited by Joe Blades (Fredericton, N.B.: Broken Jaw Press, 2001);

"Cabin Fever" and "Markings," in *Landmarks: An Anthology of Atlantic Canadian Poetry,* edited by High MacDonald and Brent MacLaine (Charlottetown, P.E.I.: Acorn Press, 2001), pp. 84–86;

"The Fern Kidnappings," "What We Learned on the Highway Near St. John's," "Muskoxen," and "Brave," in *Coastlines: An Anthology of Contemporary*

Atlantic-Canadian Poetry, edited by Ross Leckie, Robin McGrath, Laurence Hutchman, and Ann Compton (Fredericton, N.B.: Goose Lane, 2002), pp. 139–143;

"My Sartorial Ruin," and "New Year's Resolutions," in *The Madwoman in the Academy,* edited by Debbie Keahey and Deborah Schnitzer (Calgary: University of Calgary Press, 2003).

SELECTED PERIODICAL PUBLICATIONS–UNCOLLECTED: "The Bright Particulars: Poems Selected and New," *Canadian Literature,* 122–123 (1989): 212;

"Strangely Strung Beads: Wayne Johnston's Story of Bobby O'Malley," *Studies in Canadian Literature,* 15, no. 2 (1990): 140–153;

"Mad Tea Parties–*Raw Material* by M. A. C. Farrant; *The Ghost of Bellow's Man* by Sasenarine Persaud," *Canadian Literature,* 144 (1995): 181;

"A Purple Sort of Girl: Sheree Fitch's Tales of Emergence," *Canadian Children's Literature* (1998): 28;

"Consumable Avonlea: The Commodification of the Green Gables Mythology," *Canadian Children's Literature* (1998–1999): 7;

"WTO in Seattle: Three Views," *Canadian Dimension,* 34, no. 6 (2000): 43.

Jeanette Lynes's poetry seamlessly weaves together humor, emotion, philosophy, and daily life. As writer and critic Gary Geddes notes, "Watch out for the face in the rearview mirror, the icy blip on the radar screen, or the voice emanating from the hair dryer, as it may well be Jeanette Lynes. . . . This is poetry that not only matters, but also entertains." Lynes herself has said that she engages "with the commonplace, everyday world." Primarily working in the lyric mode, Lynes has developed a sophisticated poetic voice that results in complex poems.

Jeanette Seim was born on 29 May 1956 in Hanover, Ontario, to Fred and Mabel Seim; she has an older brother, George. The parents were farmers in Grey County; to supplement the family's income Fred Seim also worked in a factory, and Mabel Seim worked for a time at a fish hatchery. After attending John Diefenbaker Secondary School and Grey Highlands Secondary School, Jeanette Seim entered York University in Toronto in 1975. She began by studying fine arts but switched her major to English in her junior year. She remained at York University for graduate study, obtaining her master's degree in 1980. In 1985 she married David Lynes, a sociologist. She completed her Ph.D. in English, with a specialization in Canadian literature, in 1987. From 1985 to 1991 she taught English at several colleges and universities in Canada and the United States, including the Augustana campus of the University of Alberta in Camrose; the University of British Columbia; Mount Allison University in Sackville, New Brunswick; Cottey College in Nevada, Missouri; and Northwest Missouri State University in Maryville. From 1991 to 1997 she taught at Lakehead University in Thunder Bay, Ontario, where she became associate professor of Canadian literature and creative writing. Lynes had written poetry as a college student but only started to write seriously during her time in Thunder Bay. In 1998 she became associate professor of English at St. Francis Xavier University in Antigonish, Nova Scotia; she is also associate editor of the university's literary journal, *The Antigonish Review.*

Lynes's first book, *A Woman Alone on the Atikokan Highway,* was published in 1999. Lynes has described the collection as "a book of memory and poetic memoir" and the poems as "unmediated, close to the bone, raw." It is divided into six sections. The poems in the first section, "Hay Seed," address the speaker's childhood and adolescence. "Getting Modern" recounts how the speaker "grew up / without plumbing without / automatic washer. There were rumours / you lived in a sty." In a time when "Even barns, in that boom / had hot water. You caught / the spirit of the times," the speaker and her mother set up a makeshift shower in the barn, tying a bucket of rainwater to a rope and rigging it over the roof beams. Mother and daughter take turns under the shower, which smells "of sheep / piss, pigeons, but it was worth / failing gym for / seeing your mother laughing / in the rain like that." "Lawrence's World" juxtaposes the rural Canadian existence of the 1960s with glossy American culture and the Vietnam War as the speaker remembers watching *The Lawrence Welk Show* with her family: they were attracted to the "American glamour" on the only station the television set received, while having "no idea / forests were filling / with agent orange while we watched / Lawrence's world." The speaker of "I Was a Teen-aged Shoe Mutilator" was taller than the boys in high school; she sawed off the heels of her new shoes, hoping that the small reduction in height "might inch me down / toward that sacred / mystery called a date."

The next two short sections involve the 4-H Club: "Taming Jello" focuses on the domestic skills the speaker learned in the club, while "Taming Monkeys" centers on livestock. In "Achievement Day," one of the poems in "Taming Jello," the speaker describes the 4-H Club examination/public carnival at which her recipe book was scrutinized as "the women of Grey county passed / the gingham tables, beheld how much / the word *dollop* / meant to you." "Taming Monkeys" includes "Livestock," in which the speaker admits that she joined 4-H to meet a boy; but she had to "tame a

Dust jacket for the first edition, 2003 (courtesy of the author)

wild steer before / Fair Day, parade him / beside the stern judges," and the steer stabbed her in the face with his horn. The speaker thus achieved the opposite of what she had set out to do: "Boys stayed / away from me, a disfigured girl who / failed 4-H." In the end she accepts the fact that "Things would / remain themselves: Gumby would never be Pokey; Fair Day would / never be fair." The prose poem "Hairnets and Giblets" describes the speaker's experience of working as "the giblet-girl" in a turkey-processing plant; when the "killing-guy," Mr. Ellis, asks her for a date via a note sent through her father, the speaker instructs her father to "tell Mr. Ellis no. Thank you." The poem ends with a turkey being served at a holiday dinner; the speaker imagines the words "'tell Mr. Ellis no' . . . streaming forth from the body cavity, everyone famished."

The poems in the fourth section, "Rides with Strangers," deal with travel, risk, and relationships. In "The Deep Side of Jade" the speaker is "rushing to my mother," who is dying. On the highway she overtakes "transports in torrents / nerves keened by / fear of logs / flying at me before I reach" the destination. In the

meantime, the mother has been told to have her room painted green and to think of "synonyms / for *calm*." The speaker paints her mother's room a deep jade, "and my mother / looked so pleased, I wondered how / long invention can / really keep someone / alive." "The Spandex Affair" chronicles the actions of Canadian men who travel to Cuba "bearing gifts of spandex for Cuban / women they'll pay." The speaker describes an uncomfortable gathering "with the Canadian men, me, & every bad / joke you tried to forget. / Some dinner party." In an effort to appear sensitive, the men give the women their denim jackets, which the speaker describes as a "consolation prize." At the end the speaker observes that the Cuban women look bored: "They don't / understand English and this, as far as I can see, / is their only / real consolation."

Section 5, "Coasts," treats themes of homesickness, distance, and attachment to place. In "Seattle" the speaker humorously describes becoming accustomed to the almost-constant rain: she refuses to use an umbrella, since "they're for / sissies"; goes to car washes and stands "inside them just for the / joy of it"; and orders "water as your main course" in restaurants. The poem ends with the speaker becoming "aquatic, the sky / your oyster." "The Cuban Professor" recounts the speaker's experience of being a guest lecturer at a Cuban university and explores cultural differences and social and political privilege. "On Trying to Leave the West Coast" addresses attachment to place: "this is not like other places, where / you simply say / *alas,* and drive away." The speaker is unable to bring the physical surroundings with her: "Rhododendrons / don't press well. . . . Mountains don't fold." But the most important loss is having to leave behind people such as the "jewelry-wagon girl at Capitol Hill" and "the drug-store cashier who / loves poetry."

In the final section, "Annuals and Perennials," Lynes touches on children, therapy, weddings, and dancing; images of gardens and flowers are woven throughout the poems. In "No Children" the childless speaker comments that "No yellow suns or stick people / live on my fridge—it's blank / finite, a / garden in winter." "The Wedding Spy" follows the speaker's hunt for weddings to observe in the Halifax Public Gardens. The book closes with an eight-part poem, "Edible Flowers: A Journey in Therapy," in which the speaker traces her experience with mental illness and her relationship with her therapist. The poem ends with the image of "the sad child still / in the orchard. . . . while she imagines / the perfect, milky dress, someone to / listen, a message."

A Woman Alone on the Atikokan Highway established Lynes's trademark comedic abilities. In a 2003 interview with Andrew Stubbs, Lynes said that her comedy contains elements of clowning and self-parody and that she views humor as an important tool in women's writing: "I like what Sandra Gilbert and Susan Gubar say about women's writing as a double-voiced discourse, a palimpsest—the idea that beneath the surface design of women's writing is a whole other level of meaning, and that in creating a double voice, women writers can seem to uphold and subvert the status quo (i.e. patriarchy) at one and the same time."

A Woman Alone on the Atikokan Highway was well received by critics. Helen Humphreys commented that "Lynes' poems . . . return the power of the ordinary and extraordinary moments of life with language that is vivid, humorous, intensely felt," and Don McKay wrote that "With nimble imagination and a humour that is tough and vulnerable as the heart of a country and western, Jeanette Lynes's poems speak in their own sharply tanged and quite unignorable voice." The *Ottawa Xpress* described Lynes as "a real discovery. There will not likely be another book of poetry this year as warm and suggestive of an entire life's experience."

Also in 1999 Lynes edited two anthologies: *Paradise Frost: The Thunder Bay Poetry Renaissance,* with John Fell and David Antilla, and *Words out There: Women Poets in Atlantic Canada.* The latter garnered positive critical attention: Governor General's Literary Award–winning poet Lorna Crozier described it as "a marvelous collection of voices that weave in and out of one another, speaking a woman's life, speaking a place, with authenticity, vitality and power. What a gift this book is to us!" Referring to the twenty-three poets whose works are included in the anthology, Brian Bartlett asserted that "Long into the future, we'll be grateful to Jeanette Lynes for bringing together into one book their voices, obsessions, opinions, aims, and influences. This anthology provides a fascination tour of contrasting poetics."

In 2001 Lynes received the Bliss Carman Poetry Award, and she won first-place prizes from *Grain* magazine in 2001 and 2002. From 1999 to 2001 she served as chairwoman of the National Status of Women Committee and was an executive member of the Canadian Association of University Teachers.

In 2001 Lynes published a chapbook, *inglish prof with her head in a blender. turned on. high,* which continues her humorous approach to poetry. As the title indicates, the work deals with teaching English literature to university students. In "it's only a shaggin' book" Lynes explores the gulf that separates first-year students who have no interest in literature from the professor for whom reading is an emotional experience:

lighten up, lady it's only
a shaggin' book, fer chrissake. If it's not this it's pomes
she cries then, too.

"pop quiz #17" displays inventiveness as well as hard-edged irony:

complete the following phrase:
MLA HAND_____

a)some
b)ful
c)shake
d)out
e)job
f)book
g)yman

In *inglish prof with her head in a blender. turned on. high* Lynes pays closer attention than in her previous work to the visual presentation of the poems on the page and to how language creates meaning. In "undelivered canlit lecture in 5 rapid movements" she refers to key Canadian poets who developed complex language-oriented poetics, such as bpNichol, Bill Bissett, Barry Mackinnon, and Eli Mandel, and she mimics some of their linguistic strategies: "the day bill bissett sitting in inglish 100 sed scroo it im border thn hell & im not goin' 2 / punctuate any more a poet / was born."

In 2003 Lynes was a visiting professor of Canadian studies at Princeton University. That year she published *The Aging Cheerleader's Alphabet*, which begins with an epilogue in which the aging cheerleader—who later in the book reveals that her name is the punning Maud-Lynn Hope—writes that she is "too young for an epilogue. But the team wants a memory book." Unable to let go of her identity as a cheerleader, she still haunts athletic stadiums. Section 2, "Jurassic Skin," opens with "Audition," in which Maud-Lynn tells the reader that she wanted to be a cheerleader since before she was born and that "I pulled myself up by my pom poms. Sartre said the world is what / you make it." In "Enigma in Red & White" she describes grocery shopping while wearing her old uniform with a fuzzy "F" on the front and doing a split to pick up something from a bottom shelf. She stays prepared, because "there's always a game somewhere." In "Face" the cheerleader recalls an Oil of Olay advertisement in which a student is attracted to his youthful-looking teacher; the students in the cheerleader's baton-twirling class do not find her attractive. "Invitation to Women's Studies Class" finds the aging cheerleader in another unpleasant situation: the students ask her how it felt to be a "bauble, / accessory to patriarchy?" and characterize her as an "air / head, sex toy, / no more than an exotic dancer," and "a contemporary of Barbie." Belying these stereotypes, in "Among the Books" she checks a volume of Sappho's poetry out of the library and tells the ancient Greek writer that "your poems are an ancient / lump of peat. In my palm. Smoldering." In "What the Neighbours Think" she celebrates the departure of her old neighbors, who thought she was "a freak show," and welcomes the arrival of a new one, a stand-up comic: "For once a spade's a spade, things are real— / the comic doesn't wear a mask, / she *is* a mask."

The title of the third section, "The Flames," is the name of the team for which Maud-Lynn used to cheer; it also foreshadows the fire that occurs near the end. The section opens with "Raze," in which she laments that the old stadium where she cheered is condemned and will be torn down to be replaced by a new coliseum with a dome, "a bloated egg. . . . How they'll miss / the sky, the fools." In "Original Chant" she shouts, "Heads up! Watch out! The Flames are gonna burn; / Go home—get lost—to ashes you will burn." Throughout this section Maud-Lynn looks back to the "great game of '71," the glory days of the now-aging quarterback, and her seemingly perpetual quest, which still continues, to lure him into her bedroom. In "Exhibit 8A: The Cheerleader as Relic" she portrays herself as a display

in the Museum of the Twentieth Century. Lynes uses extensive footnotes to "explain" pop-culture references such as King Kong and the Nancy Kerrigan-Tonya Harding figure-skating scandal of 1994. In "Soothsayer," which is structured like a play, Maud-Lynn warns that "Something terrible is going to happen"; then, the day before the stadium is to be demolished, she burns it down. The section closes with "Note Discovered by None Other Than Yourself," in which she explains that "After the fire, I became a recluse" and that "the fact you're reading this probably means / I'm dead"; but if she is not dead, "I expect Oprah's call / any day now." The book concludes with a prologue comprising a list of mysterious people whom readers should be careful not to mistake for Maud-Lynn and another list of thank-yous and messages to people such as sports fans, the college administration, and the aging quarterback. In *THIS Magazine* (2004) Sue McCluskey praised the "inventiveness of the conceit" of the aging cheerleader and noted that "Lynes pulls it off with . . . wit and elegance. Lynes throws pop culture and academia into the blender, mixing up Browning and Barbie, the Dionne Quints and T. S. Eliot, Nancy Drew and Caliban. The cycle of poems is almost symphonic in its thematic repetitions and variations." McCluskey also declared that "the poems deliver a subtle but firm ass-kicking to anyone who underestimates the accomplishments of women who, for whatever reason, choose not to break free from tradition."

In 2003 Lynes also published *Left Fields,* in which she returns to the themes of home and relationships and continues to mix pop culture, literary references, humor, and social commentary. The book is divided into three sections. The first, "Homeland, with Wreckage," opens with "Career Day at Diefenbaker High," which lists a variety of negative attributes of a particular student and concludes that the student has but one career option: to write poetry. Many of the poems in this section center on childhood, adolescence, school, friendships, and the relationship between daughter and parents. Lynes also writes on Canadian figures ranging from pop-country singer Shania Twain to pianist Glen Gould and includes a satirical piece on Canadian society, "Answering My American Friends."

Section 2 is titled "Can Anything Save a Daughter?" The poem "*The Guess Who* Play North Bay—One Night Only" is another example of Lynes's ability to juxtapose humor with social commentary. The speaker is surrounded by three women in a bar restroom who tell her that she "*must* party with them" while they listen to the aging rock band The Guess Who. When she reveals that she is in town to read poetry, the women urge her to read it right there, in the restroom. The speaker is "backed into / the Kotex machine" by the demanding women, whom she describes as "macho party-girls": "the cry for poetry *right here right now* / the way each day is lived like the last / gig you'll ever get."

The final section, "This Is Your Life," encompasses a wide range of topics: female mud wrestling, Tom Hanks, a professor's jealousy of her students' poetic typographical errors, Flanders Fields, Virginia Woolf, flowers, and the Paris Metro. In "Bog" the speaker has become a "Woman Mud Wrestler" to pay off her student loans; after a match, "the girls and I / like to go for a pint," and each time they say the "next gig, *really* our last." On their days off they "shower / and shower, try to awake, cleansed." In "Loosestrife" the speaker defends the maligned title plant; commenting that "Multiculturalism / doesn't extend to botany," she asks the reader to sympathize with loosestrife: "Have you ever been called floozy but / you're basically good? . . . Is your bad reputation / undeserved? Then you see what I mean."

Like Lynes's previous works, *Left Fields* is formally loose: it includes long lines, narratives, prose poems, short image-oriented poems, and strongly lyrical writing. Her stanzas are constructed to emphasize poetic effect: thus, in a given poem the reader may encounter a ten-line stanza followed by a one-line stanza followed by a five-line stanza. Lynes uses half lines, blank space, and enjambment to create suspense and

add complexity and ambiguity. Reviewing *Left Fields, The Toronto Star* (October 2003) said that "Lynes' outlook is offbeat and often funny. She is at her best when cultural worlds collide, for she has an appealing way of combining comedy and social observation."

Jeanette Lynes has received several arts grants and has read her poetry widely across Canada. In 2004 her sequence *The Beatrix Potter Poems* was short-listed for a Canadian Broadcasting Corporation Literary Award. She was writer-in-residence at the Saskatoon Public Library in 2005–2006. Her forthcoming work includes "Ghost Works: Improvisations in Letter and Poems," a chapbook co-authored with poet Alison Calder that is to be published by JackPine Press in the fall of 2007; and a novel, tentatively titled "The Girl Who Talked to Trees," to be published by Coteau Press in 2008. A fourth collection of poetry, as yet untitled, is scheduled to be published by Wolsak and Wynn in the fall of 2008. Lynes is also preparing a fifth poetry collection with the working title "It's Hard Being Queen: The Dusty Springfield Poems."

Interview:

Andrew Stubbs, "Female Poet as Clown and Outlaw: An Interview with Jeanette Lynes," *New Quarterly*, 87 (2003): 126–136.

Ann-Marie MacDonald

(29 October 1958 –   )

Craig Monk
University of Lethbridge

BOOKS: *Clue in the Fast Lane: A Mystery in Three Episodes,*
by MacDonald and Beverley Cooper (Toronto:
Playwrights Canada, 1985);

Goodnight Desdemona (Good Morning Juliet) (Toronto:
Coach House, 1990; New York: Grove, 1998);

The Arab's Mouth (Winnipeg: Blizzard, 1995); revised as
Belle Moral: A Natural History (Niagara-on-the-
Lake, Ont.: Academy of the Shaw Festival /
Toronto: Playwrights Canada, 2005);

Nigredo Hotel: An Opera for Baritone and Soprano, music by
Nic Gotham (Toronto: Playwrights Union of
Canada, 1996);

Fall on Your Knees (Toronto: Knopf Canada, 1996; New
York: Simon & Schuster, 1996; London: Cape,
1996);

The Attic, the Pearls, and 3 Fine Girls, by MacDonald, Jennifer Brewin, Leah Cherniak, Alisa Palmer, and
Martha Ross (Toronto: PUC Play Service, 1997);

The Way the Crow Flies (Toronto: Knopf Canada, 2003;
London: Fourth Estate, 2003; New York: Harper-
Collins, 2003).

PLAY PRODUCTIONS: *Nancy Prew: Clue in the Fast
Lane,* by MacDonald and Beverley Cooper,
Toronto, Nightwood Theatre, 1985;

This Is for You, Anna, by MacDonald, Suzanne Odette
Khuri, Patricia Nichols, Banuta Rubess, and Maureen White, Toronto, Nightwood Theatre, 1985;

Goodnight Desdemona (Good Morning Juliet), Toronto,
Annex Theatre, 1988;

The Arab's Mouth, Toronto, Factory Theatre, 1990;
revised as *Belle Moral: A Natural History,* Niagara-
on-the-Lake, Ontario, Court House Theatre, 15
July 2005;

Nigredo Hotel, music by Nic Gotham, Toronto, Tarragon
Theatre, 19 May 1992;

The Attic, the Pearls, and 3 Fine Girls, by MacDonald, Jennifer Brewin, Leah Cherniak, Alisa Palmer, and
Martha Ross, Toronto, 1995;

Anything That Moves, music by Allen Cole, Toronto,
2000; revised, Toronto, 2001.

Ann-Marie MacDonald (photograph by Cheryl Daniels;
from the dust jacket for Fall on Your Knees,
1996; Bruccoli Clark Layman Archives)

PRODUCED SCRIPT: "Whose Woods Are These,"
television, *Street Legal,* Canadian Broadcasting
Corporation, 25 November 1988.

SELECTED PERIODICAL PUBLICATION–
UNCOLLECTED: *This Is for You, Anna,* by Mac-
Donald, Suzanne Odette Khuri, Patricia Nichols,
Banuta Rubess, and Maureen White, *Canadian
Theatre Review,* 43 (Summer 1985): 127–166.

Ann-Marie MacDonald is an actor, novelist, and
playwright whose writings have found an audience
across Canada and around the world. Her training in

the theater informs much of her early work, and her preoccupation with questions of family, memory, and the treatment of marginalized figures has given readers a frank assessment of Canadian life that has resonated internationally.

MacDonald was born on a Royal Canadian Air Force Base in Baden-Baden, Germany, on 29 October 1958. Because of her father's military career, the family moved around a great deal; but, she told Rita Much in a 1990 interview, she has always recognized Cape Breton Island, Nova Scotia, where her older sisters were born and where her family has its roots, as "a kind of spiritual home." After attending high school in Ottawa, MacDonald spent a year at Carleton University before being accepted at the National Theatre School (N.T.S.). She likened her time at the school to "taking awful medicine that does you good. It was exactly what I needed to do, but thank God it's behind me." The N.T.S. underlined for MacDonald many of the failings in the traditional representation of women on the stage: "I always heard that if a girl could cry she had to be a good actress. Throughout theatre school I was forced to play a Chekhov character like a fucking gossamer thing, or a Shakespearean lady like a wimp. If you get a part with teeth in it it's usually negative: the character is a bitch or suicidal." Following her graduation from the program in 1980, she moved to Toronto and became involved as an actress with the fringe-theater movement. During this time she came out as a lesbian and decided to try writing for the stage. While theater school had emphasized specialization, "acting and writing were always dual passions for me ever since I was a little girl," she told Much. Her first effort was *Nancy Prew: Clue in the Fast Lane* (1985), a spoof of the Nancy Drew series written with Beverley Cooper in which detective Nancy Prew time travels from 1955 to 1985 to help a babysitter solve a mystery. It was first performed in 1985 at Nightwood Theatre's Rhubarb! Festival.

In an article that accompanied publication of the text in *Canadian Theatre Review* MacDonald describes her next play, *This Is for You, Anna* (1985), as her "first truly collaborative experience," as well as her first "feminist theatre experience." Calling themselves "The Anna Project," MacDonald, Suzanne Odette Khuri, Patricia Nichols, Banuta Rubess, and Maureen White dramatized the true story of Marianne Bachmeier, a German woman who was sentenced to six years in prison for murdering the man who had killed her daughter, Anna; the convicted sex offender had claimed in court that the seven-year-old had flirted with him. The sort of cooperative enterprise that gave rise to the play "makes a lot of sense" for women performers, MacDonald says in the *Canadian Theatre Review* article. "They don't have an old boys' network to rely on, so

the gals have got to get together to do their own stuff." But while collaboration brings together artists who hold similar interests, these partnerships inevitably require "constant striving for consensus in a process which is also a commitment to respect each artist's creative input."

While touring *This Is for You, Anna* in the United Kingdom, MacDonald had the idea for the play that became the breakthrough 1988 comedy *Goodnight Desdemona (Good Morning Juliet)* (published 1990). Work on the piece was completed quickly: four months passed, and three drafts were produced, before the first performance. Composed in prose and blank verse and placing William Shakespeare's words in fractured contexts, the play follows Constance Ledbelly, a lecturer in English at Queen's University, whose stalled doctoral research involves work on the untranslated "Gustav Manuscript" that is supposed to contain a lost source used in the writing of *Othello* and *Romeo and Juliet*. The fruits of her efforts are appropriated by her professor, Claude Night, and earn him a post at Oxford that the lowly lecturer covets. The "impossible event" in the play—made possible, according to the Chorus, "within the zone of the unconscious mind"—is that at the moment of abandoning her dissertation Constance is transported into the world of the plays she has studied so intensely. In Cyprus, where she is mistaken for an itinerant spinster, she shows Othello that Iago had Desdemona's handkerchief stolen and thereby saves the heroine from the Moor's jealous wrath. Long seen as the most delicate of the Bard's women, Desdemona proves herself an able warrior when her own quick temper allows Iago to convince her that Constance is cavorting with her husband. In the midst of the ensuing scuffle the scholar finds herself whisked off to Verona, where, mistaken this time for a man, she disrupts the feud between Romeo and Tybalt. This blurring of gender boundaries leads to a love triangle among Romeo, Constance, and Juliet, a complication that is resolved only with the sudden reappearance of Desdemona. The plays ends with a celebration of Constance's birthday. She has shown Shakespeare's characters that they need not be confined to the conventions of their tragic plots; they have shown her that she must not be too limiting in her readings of character.

While commenting pointedly both on academic life and on the theater, *Goodnight Desdemona (Good Morning Juliet)* transcends the narrowness of these milieus. Produced on a modest $20,000 budget at the Annex Theatre in Toronto, the play was revised in 1990 and taken on a successful five-city tour across Canada; since then it has been produced around the world. It received the Governor General's Literary Award for Drama, the

*Dust jacket for the first edition, 1996
(Bruccoli Clark Layman Archives)*

Canadian Authors' Association Award for Drama, and the Floyd S. Chambers Award for Outstanding Play.

During this period MacDonald was working extensively as an actress. She played guest roles in Canadian television series such as *Airwolf* and *Katts and Dog;* the part of Rowena Ross in the 1986 movie adaptation of Timothy Findley's novel *The Wars* (1977) led to her performance as Mary Joseph in Patricia Rozema's *I've Heard the Mermaids Singing* (1987), for which she received a Genie nomination. Filming her role as Julie in the 1987 musical *Island Love Song* gave her the first opportunity in nearly a decade to visit Cape Breton. In 1990 she won a Genie for Best Supporting Actress for her performance as a sympathetic teacher in *Where the Spirit Lives* (1989).

Also in 1990 MacDonald turned her attention back to the stage by writing *The Arab's Mouth.* Set in Scotland in 1899, the Gothic comedy deals with the aftermath of the death of family patriarch Ramsay MacIsaac. Pearl possesses her father's traits, while the maladjusted Victor is the image of his mother, Régine,

who supposedly died while giving birth to him. Ramsay's will disinherits Victor and bestows his fortune on Pearl on the condition that she remain childless, thereby severing a family line tainted with Roman Catholic blood. Seamus Reid, the family physician and Ramsay's best friend, proposes marriage to Pearl so that he can protect her and foster her scientific interests. The tense situation at Belle Moral, the family home, is complicated further by the creeping insanity that threatens to claim the MacIsaacs and the secret that could destroy the family: that Claire, Victor's slightly deformed twin, has been imprisoned in the attic since her birth. The reappearance of Régine, who chose exile over participation in the mistreatment of her daughter, brings this ghastly past to light. She drowns herself, and Victor, who has suffered a seizure, apparently returns from the dead. Dr. Reid is forced to certify Claire as the inheritor of the estate after Pearl finds herself mysteriously pregnant, and the play ends with his banishment from Belle Moral for his part in keeping Claire in the attic.

MacDonald drew on the psychoanalytic theories of Carl Gustav Jung in composing the libretto for Nic Gotham's chamber opera *Nigredo Hotel* (1992). After being involved in a minor car accident, Raymond, a successful brain surgeon, checks into a ramshackle hostelry run by the manic Sophie. There, in a "dark night of the soul," he confronts his past and is rewarded with a revelation.

MacDonald collaborated with Jennifer Brewin, Leah Cherniak, Alisa Palmer, and Martha Ross on the frantic comedy *The Attic, the Pearls, and 3 Fine Girls* (1995; published 1997). Called together by their dying father, the Fine sisters compare their disparate life experiences: Jo-Jo is an academic; Jelly is an artist; and Jayne is a businesswoman. An attic stuffed with trinkets prompts memories, and good and bad must be sorted out to reaffirm the bonds of family.

In the mid 1990s MacDonald wrote scripts for Canadian Broadcasting Corporation television programs, including *Liberty Street* and *Street Legal.* She began a play about the Piper family of New Waterford, Nova Scotia, but soon realized that it could not be confined to the stage; it became the blockbuster novel *Fall on Your Knees* (1996). At the turn of the twentieth century the marriage of James Piper and his child bride, Materia, is opposed on the grounds of culture and caste by her wealthy Lebanese parents, the Mahmouds, who have thrived in the dry-goods business in Sydney. The Pipers' daughter, Kathleen, shows remarkable musical ability from a young age. In an attempt to escape the demons that draw him to Kathleen, who reminds him of a prepubescent Materia, James conceives with his wife another daughter, Mercedes, and, soon after her birth, yet another, Frances. But only sending Kathleen to New York to study singing seems to promise her safety. The scheme goes horribly wrong when James intervenes in his daughter's life one last time. Kathleen dies in giving birth to twins Ambrose and Lily; Ambrose dies, and Lily is raised as a sister to Mercedes and Frances. Mercedes' development is stunted by the oppressive Catholicism she inherited from her mother and the burdensome domestic responsibilities that fall to her after Materia commits suicide. Discovering the secret of Lily's incestuous paternity in Kathleen's diary, Frances sends her on a pilgrimage to Harlem to find Rose, the woman her mother loved in defiance of race and gender expectations.

Perhaps the greatest achievement of *Fall on Your Knees* is the complexity of the characters. While the cherubic Mercedes appears obsessed and self-righteous, the malevolent James threatens at times to arouse the reader's pity. Knopf Canada made the novel the cornerstone of its new "New Faces of Fiction" series. In 1997 it won the Harlequin Literary Award for Fiction from the Canadian Authors' Association, the Dartmouth Book Award, and the Commonwealth Prize for Best First Fiction. The novel has been translated into more than a dozen languages; Lori Saint-Martin and Paul Gagné received the 2000 Governor General's Literary Award for Translation for the French version.

In the autumn of 1998 MacDonald became the host of the CBC television biography program *Life and Times*, narrating documentaries such as Erna Buffie's *The Pill* (1999) and Michel Jones's *Kim Campbell through the Looking Glass* (2000). She played Frances, the sexually repressed manager of a lesbian bookstore who battles the censorship of customs officials, in Anne Wheeler's "chick-chick flick" *Better than Chocolate* (1999).

In 2000 MacDonald wrote the libretto for *Anything That Moves,* a musical with a score by Allen Cole about a straight flower-shop owner and the woman who dates him only because she believes that he is gay. It received the 2002 Dora Mavor Moore Award for Best Musical. In 2001 MacDonald took for the first time the role of Constance Ledbelly in a Toronto production of the play that had brought her to prominence fifteen years before.

In February 2002 *Fall on Your Knees* was chosen as a selection for the "Book Club" segment on the *Oprah Winfrey Show;* MacDonald traveled to Chicago to tape the program, which was broadcast in April. "I promise you won't be able to stop reading it," Winfrey told her audience. "It just takes you everywhere." The attention renewed interest in the six-year-old book in Canada, where Vintage printed an additional 70,000 paperbacks to follow the quarter-million copies that had been sold since its initial release; in the United States, Charles Scribner's Sons printed 620,000 copies to supplement the 45,000 copies that had been sold there. "This book has been flying off the shelves," Winfrey observed to her audience. Also in 2002 MacDonald starred in Cassandra Nicolaou's short movie *The Girlfriend Interviews,* a mockumentary about a woman screening potential romantic prospects.

In July 2003 MacDonald married her longtime partner, Palmer, in a same-sex ceremony in Ontario. The couple had adopted a child the previous autumn.

In September 2003 MacDonald published *The Way the Crow Flies;* set during the Cold War, the novel draws on her experiences as an "air force kid." In 1962 Jack McCarthy returns with his wife, Mimi, and their children, Madeleine and Mike, to Royal Canadian Air Force Station Centralia in southern Ontario after an extended posting in West Germany. There he works with his old squadron leader on the top-secret "Project Paperclip," which involves smuggling an East German scientist into the United States through Canada. His reticence about his activities arouses Mimi's suspicions. Meanwhile, Madeleine and other girls at her school are preyed on by Mr. March, their third-grade teacher; Madeleine's inability to tell her father about the abuse duplicates his own secrecy. The growing tension in the McCarthy household is played out against the backdrop of the murder of Claire McCarroll, the daughter of an American unwittingly brought to Centralia to help with Project Paperclip. The blame falls on Ricky Froelich, the popular son of the McCarthys' next-door neighbor, concentration-camp survivor Henry Froelich. Henry suspects a war criminal he has spotted in a nearby city, a man known to Jack as Oscar Fried. But Henry is silenced by a powerful force Jack suspects to be connected with the United States government before he is able to clear his son. The last section of the novel picks up the story twenty-five years later. Madeleine has become a successful comedian; Mike has been killed in the Vietnam War; and Jack's enforced silence during Ricky Froelich's trial has left him disillusioned about military involvement in the space race. Madeleine pieces together the fragments of her past and discovers that Claire's murder brushed closer to her than she realized at the time. The solution to the murder mystery is overshadowed by Mimi's reaction to her daughter's confessed lesbianism.

Ann-Marie MacDonald's reputation as a strong Canadian voice has been affirmed internationally. As an individual, she has come to represent for many readers at home and abroad the tolerance and the respect for social justice that run throughout her work.

Interviews:

Rita Much, "Ann-Marie MacDonald Interview," in *Fair Play: 12 Women Speak,* edited by Much and Judith Much (Toronto: Simon & Pierre, 1990), pp. 127–143;

"The Mask of Comedy," *Books in Canada,* 19 (March 1990): 25–27;

"Ann-Marie MacDonald," *B&A: New Fiction,* 24 (Fall 1996): 37–39.

References:

Jennifer Andrews, "Rethinking the Relevance of Magic Realism for English-Canadian Literature: Reading Ann-Marie MacDonald's *Fall On Your Knees,*" *Studies in Canadian Literature,* 24 (Winter 1999): 1–19;

Marta Dvorak, "Goodnight William Shakespeare (Good Morning Ann-Marie MacDonald)," *Canadian Theatre Review,* 79–80 (Summer–Fall 1994): 128–133;

Michael Greenstein, "How They Write Us: Accepting and Excepting 'The Jew' in Canadian Fiction," *Shofar: An Interdisciplinary Journal of Jewish Studies,* 20, no. 2 (2002): 5–27;

Ellen Mackay, "The Spectre of Straight Shakespeare: New Ways of Looking at Old Texts in *Goodnight Desdemona* and *Mad Boy Chronicle,*" *Canadian Theatre Review,* 111 (Summer 2002): 10–14;

Marianne Novy, "Saving Desdemona and/or Ourselves: Plays By Ann-Marie MacDonald and Paula Vogel," in *Transforming Shakespeare: Contemporary Women's Re-Visions in Literature and Performance,* edited by Novy (New York: St. Martin's Press, 1999), pp. 67–85;

Laurin R. Porter, "Shakespeare's 'Sisters': Desdemona, Juliet, and Constance Ledbelly in *Goodnight Desdemona (Good Morning Juliet),*" *Modern Drama,* 38 (Fall 1995): 362–377;

Laura M. Robinson, "'Crossing Nature's Divide': Miscegenation and Lesbianism in Ann-Marie MacDonald's *Fall on Your Knees,*" in *Identity and Alterity in Canadian Literature,* edited by Dana Puiu (Cluj Napoca, Romania: Risoprint, 2003), pp. 213–225.

Daniel MacIvor

(23 July 1962 –   )

Marlene Moser
Brock University

BOOKS: *See Bob Run & Wild Abandon* (Toronto: Playwrights Canada Press, 1990);

House Humans (Toronto: Coach House Press, 1992; republished with new foreword, Toronto: Playwrights Canada Press, 1996);

2 Plays: Never Swim Alone & This Is a Play (Toronto: Playwrights Canada Press, 1993);

Here Lies Henry: A Play, by MacIvor and Daniel Brooks (Toronto: Playwrights Canada Press, 1996);

The Soldier Dreams (Winnipeg: Scirocco Drama, 1997);

Marion Bridge (Burnaby, B.C: Talonbooks, 1999; enlarged, 2006);

Monster, by MacIvor and Brooks (Winnipeg: Scirocco Drama, 1999);

In on It (Winnipeg: Scirocco Drama, 2001);

You Are Here (Winnipeg: Scirocco Drama, 2002);

I Still Love You: Five Plays (Toronto: Playwrights Canada Press, 2006)–comprises *Never Swim Alone, The Soldier Dreams, You Are Here, In on It,* and *A Beautiful View;*

How It Works (Winnipeg: Scirocco Drama, 2006);

Cul-de-Sac (Vancouver: Talonbooks, 2006).

PLAY PRODUCTIONS: *The Right One,* by MacIvor and Michele M. Jelley, Toronto, Buddies in Bad Times Theatre, 1987;

See Bob Run, Toronto, Poor Alex Theatre, 1987;

Wild Abandon, Toronto, Theatre Passe Muraille, 1988;

Theatre of Omaha's Production of the Sound of Music, Buddies in Bad Times Theatre, 1988;

Somewhere I Have Never Travelled, Toronto, Tarragon Theatre, 4 October 1988;

Yes I Am and Who Are You? Toronto, Buddies in Bad Times Theatre, 1989;

White Trash, Blue Eyes, Toronto, Buddies in Bad Times Theatre, 1990;

Sick, by MacIvor, Death Waits, Victoria Ward, and Rosalia Martini, Toronto, DNA Theatre, 1990;

2-2-Tango, Toronto, Buddies in Bad Times Theatre, 1991;

*Daniel MacIvor (photograph by Guntar Kravis;
<http://danielmacivor.com>)*

Never Swim Alone, Toronto, Theatre Centre, 26 February 1991;

Jump, Toronto, Theatre Passe Muraille, 7 February 1992;

House, Toronto, Factory Theatre, 23 May 1992;

This Is a Play, Toronto, Bathurst Street Theatre, June 1992;

The Lorca Play, by MacIvor and Brooks, Toronto, Theatre Centre, 15 October 1992;

Sleeproom, by MacIvor, Sally Clark, Robin Fulford, and John Mighton, Toronto, Theatre Passe Muraille, January 1993;

Excerpts from the Emo Journals, Toronto, Theatre Passe Muraille, 1994;

Sessions: A Document from the Psychoanalytic Tapes of Dr. Clifford Scott, by MacIvor, Brooks, and Clare Coulter, Toronto, Tarragon Theatre, 9 March 1995;

Here Lies Henry, by MacIvor and Brooks, Toronto, Buddies in Bad Times Theatre, June 1995;

The Soldier Dreams, Toronto, Canadian Stage, 26 March 1997;

Marion Bridge, Guysborough, N.S., Mulgrave Road Theatre, 1998;

Monster, by MacIvor and Brooks, Toronto, Canadian Stage, 21 April 1998;

In on It, Toronto, Vancouver East Cultural Centre, 24 January 2001; New York, P.S. 122, 7 October 2001;

A Beautiful View, Columbus, Ohio, Wexner Center for the Arts, 14 May 2001;

You Are Here, Toronto, Theatre Passe Muraille, 20 September 2001;

Cul-de-Sac, by MacIvor and Brooks, Montreal, Usine C, May 2002;

How It Works, Guysborough, N.S., Mulgrave Road Theatre, 2006.

PRODUCED SCRIPTS: *House,* motion picture, screenplay by MacIvor and Laurie Lind, Household Entertainment/Water Pictures, 1996;

Past Perfect, motion picture, imX Communications, 2002;

Marion Bridge, motion picture, Idlewild Films/Sienna Films, 2002;

Wilby Wonderful, motion picture, Palpable Productions/da da kamera, 2004;

Whole New Thing, motion picture, screenplay by MacIvor and Amnon Buchbinder, Acuity Productions/Palpable Productions/Whole Thing Productions, 2005.

OTHER: *2-2-Tango: A Two-Man-One-Man-Show,* in *Making, Out: Plays by Gay Men,* edited by Robert Wallace (Toronto: Coach House, 1992), pp. 193–217;

Theatre Omaha's Production of The Sound of Music, in *Rhubarb-o-rama: Plays and Playwrights from the Rhubarb! Festival,* edited by Franco Boni (Winnipeg: Blizzard Press, 1998), pp. 121–135.

SELECTED PERIODICAL PUBLICATIONS–UNCOLLECTED: "This Is an Article," *Theatrum,* no. 30 (September–October 1992): 15–17;

"Festival Antigonish," *Theatrum,* no. 31 (November 1992–January 1993): 36;

"Marion Bridge," *Malahat Review,* 130 (2000): 122–123.

In the foreword to *Here Lies Henry* (1996) Daniel MacIvor describes his play as "Experiential in that it is the whole experience of the piece (intellectual, emotional, visual, aural, etc.) which creates the 'narrative'– and this narrative varies for each person who experiences its elements." MacIvor often uses broadly theatrical metaphors that demand the audience's or reader's collaboration for their interpretation: for example, an oversized egg in a cage, watermelons rolling onstage, or a precise gridwork of lines of light that define a performance space. His works are metatheatrical but not abstract: the audience is of utmost importance to MacIvor and is acknowledged, surprised, challenged, and always entertained. In her introduction to *2 Plays: Never Swim Alone & This Is a Play* (1993) Carol Bolt notes that "In MacIvor's post-modern, meta-theatrical plays we're constantly reminded we're in the theatre. Together. It's a world full of poetry and ceremony and mystery. Where questions can be asked if not answered. It's a world where, when answers are riddles, we can still say, 'Ah, yes, of course.' And it's a world where we can make a difference."

MacIvor was born in Sydney, Cape Breton Island, Nova Scotia, on 23 July 1962, the youngest of five children of Buster MacIvor, a housepainter, and Lilian MacIvor, a waitress. His early life in industrial Sydney recurs in his later plays, especially *Marion Bridge* (1999), one of his most realistic works. After studying at Dalhousie University in Halifax from 1980 to 1982, he moved briefly to Newfoundland and then to Toronto. He studied theater at George Brown College from 1983 to 1985, receiving a diploma in performance. He contemplated moving to the United Kingdom to continue his studies but remained in Toronto.

In 1986 MacIvor founded the theater company da da kamera. Much of his early work found a venue at the Rhubarb! Festival at the Buddies in Bad Times Theatre in Toronto. Primarily trained as an actor, MacIvor performs in most of the plays he writes; he often directs and produces them, as well. He has had longstanding collaborations with other artists, especially actress Caroline Gillis, director Daniel Brooks, and producer Sherrie Johnson.

See Bob Run (produced 1987, published 1990) was written as a one-person play for Gillis. Bob, a girl who has been sexually abused by her father, takes a mental journey into her past as she hitchhikes along a highway. Her objective is to head east until she comes to "the water," a metaphor relating to both her father and rebirth: "the water knows everything . . . it knows everybody's biggest secrets . . . and it turns them into the sound of waves at night." Written in a realistic manner, the play reveals Bob's response to the cycle of abuse and makes clear her conflicted feelings about love and being loved.

Wild Abandon (published 1990), another one-person play, was first performed by MacIvor himself in 1988. The protagonist, Steve, sketches out his life in anecdotes, often speaking directly to the audience. The set is minimalist and symbolic, stripping theater to its barest constituents.

In *House* (1992), the title of which refers to the audience at a theater, Victor describes his experiences in therapy while demonstrating his awareness of the theatrical environment: "I know it's a theatre. I know it's a stage. I know it's a chair. I know it's a light." By snapping his fingers he brings up the lights and takes them back down. As Victor acknowledges his own "textuality," he moves seamlessly across the fourth wall and then slips back into the narrative of the play. *House* received the 1991 Chalmers New Canadian Play Award. It was published in 1992 with "Humans," a collection of prose fragments in which the everyday and the banal are seen anew; the fragments could be considered as written from the point of view of Victor.

MacIvor performed in *2-2-Tango: A Two-Man-One-Man-Show* (produced 1991, published 1992). Two almost identical men, Jim and James, negotiate their way through their relationship and playfully engage with the audience in highly structured words, movements, and gestures. MacIvor's *Jump,* produced in 1992, is pure choreography without dialogue.

Never Swim Alone (produced 1991, published 2006) has some of the same formal elements as *2-2-Tango*. It is also highly dependent on precise movement, staging, and the dialogue delivered by the three actors. The two male characters, Frank and Bill, are reminiscent of Jim and James in *2-2-Tango:* they dress alike, look alike, and speak in unison. A girl in a bathing suit acts as a referee for their competitive displays of masculinity, calling out rounds and awarding points. The three then return to a moment in their childhood: a competitive swim to an island during which the girl drowns. *This Is a Play* (produced 1992), published in the same volume, is a short exercise in metatheatricality in which MacIvor makes explicit the lives and thoughts of the actors in *Never Swim Alone*. *2-2-Tango* and *Never Swim Alone* were nominated for the 1991 Chalmers New Canadian Play Award.

The Lorca Play, produced in 1992, is an inquiry into the life and work of Federico García Lorca, especially his play *La casa de Bernarda Alba* (1944; translated as *The House of Bernarda Alba,* 1947). MacIvor directed and performed in the play, which won Doras (Dora

Paperback cover for the first edition, 1992
(Bruccoli Clark Layman Archives)

Mavor Moore Awards) in 1993 for Outstanding Direction and Outstanding Performance by a Female. *Sleep-room* was a collaborative project created with three other playwrights and a host of actors in 1993. The audience wandered through the play, rather than experiencing it in a linear fashion. Toronto's Theatre Passe Muraille became a kind of sleep institution; the actors instructed the audience in the experiments or interacted with them as patients. *Sessions: A Document from the Psychoanalytic Tapes of Dr. Clifford Scott,* produced at Tarragon Theatre in Toronto in 1995, was a collaborative undertaking with Brooks and Clare Coulter based on excerpts from nineteen hours of taped treatment sessions between a psychotherapist and a female patient. The script is highly mimetic, imitating the pauses, coughs, and smallest details of the tapes.

Here Lies Henry (produced 1995, published 1996) for which Brooks was given a writing credit, is a one-person play featuring MacIvor as Henry, a compulsive liar. Whereas *House* uses the pretext of a therapy group as a rationale for the exploration of Victor's psyche, here there is no pretense of realism: Henry, like theater

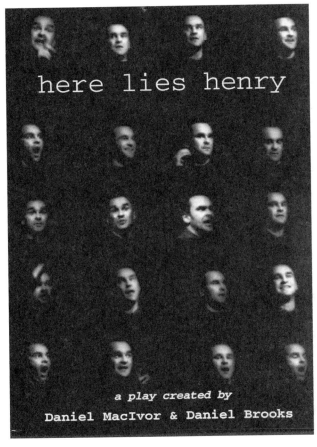

*Paperback cover for 2004 reprint
(Bruccoli Clark Layman Archives)*

itself, lies. Part confessional, part stand-up comedy act, the play, as Ann Wilson describes it, "is an exploration of lying in the context of performance." Lying is placed side by side with "dying" in both the theatrical sense of giving a bad performance and the real dying evoked by the title. The writing moves from the one-liners typical of MacIvor's work to a poetic stream of consciousness. Henry's shifting subjectivity is evoked by the use of a tiny microphone that affects the actor's voice on particular lines. As Brooks says of the main character, "He was dead, the audience was alive." Form and design play important roles in the realization of the play, especially in Brooks's use of light in performance. In directing the play, Brooks writes, he instructed MacIvor to resist the impulse to "perform" and "entertain" the audience and to strive instead to "fail." *Here Lies Henry* won the Chalmers New Canadian Play Award in 1997.

In *The Soldier Dreams* (1997) David is dying of AIDS. His family and friends gather around his deathbed while he plays out a past relationship with a lover. MacIvor uses monologue, dialogue, direct address to

the audience, and tape recordings to render the fluid demarcation between present and past and between life and death.

Marion Bridge (produced 1998, published 1999) is similar to MacIvor's earlier plays in the use of direct address to the audience in monologues delivered by the characters. Otherwise, however, it is quite traditional in form. Three sisters have gathered to spend time with their dying mother in Cape Breton; obstacles in their relationships are overcome, and the play has a happy, conciliatory ending that is free of irony. Forgiveness of self and others are prominent themes. The play is dedicated to MacIvor's sisters.

Monster (produced 1998, published 1999) is another one-person play by MacIvor and Brooks. MacIvor plays ten characters whose lives are in some way connected as the story of a man who kills and dismembers his father is told and retold. Robert Wallace suggests that "To make meaning of this play, the audience must restructure the sequence of events that MacIvor so deliberately disorganizes, in an act of restoration that is tantamount to piecing together Adam's fragmented body." Da da kamera won a Chalmers Award for Innovation in Theatre in 1998.

In on It (2001) returns to MacIvor's more-familiar stylistics and themes as a play about a man's death is presented with an overt awareness of the construction of the story and its own theatricality. Two characters, This One and That One, discuss the play and its development. As the play progresses, it becomes clear that This One and That One are lovers. Lighting, rather than set, divides the space into four areas of performance. *In on It* won a Village Voice Obie Award in New York in 2002.

In some ways a companion piece to *In on It,* a play for two male characters, *A Beautiful View* (produced 2001, published 2006) is the story of the relationship of two women over the course of several years. The play, which uses a sparse setting, reflects MacIvor's maturity: he still slyly implicates the audience but evokes a new poignancy.

You Are Here (produced 2001, published 2002) also plays with conventions of the theater; MacIvor describes it as "a one woman show with twelve characters." The audience follows Alison, played by Gillis in the premiere production, through her recollections of her life as lovers come and go and she reenacts moments of happiness, betrayal, and compromise. Lines are sometimes replayed until she responds "correctly." In his notes to the play MacIvor specifies that the actor who plays Alison needs to "claim a true presence in the room," overtly acknowledging any disruptions that may occur in the audience. The outcome is less cynical than in much of MacIvor's work in that Alison finds a kind of soul mate by the end of the play.

Cul-de-Sac (2002) is a one-person play in which MacIvor portrays fifteen characters who live in the same neighborhood and come together through the storytelling of one of them, Leonard. A major theme is the tentative and temporary nature of existence.

MacIvor returns to the Maritimes in *How It Works* (2006), a four-character play that probes family relationships and the nature of storytelling. Scenes of the past and present are interwoven as MacIvor deals less with overt theatricality and more with human issues than in his earlier plays.

In 2006 MacIvor published *I Still Love You: Five Plays,* which comprises *Never Swim Alone, The Soldier Dreams, You Are Here, In on It,* and *A Beautiful View.* The collection won the 2006 Governor General's Literary Award for Drama. In the preface to *A Beautiful View* MacIvor describes da da kamera as a company "where all artists are present in the process from the beginning of the idea, where each element of production is of equal and essential value, and where development continues years into the life of the production." In 2007, after remounting three of MacIvor's most popular solo works, the company dissolved.

MacIvor also directs, writes, and acts in movies. He performed all three functions for *Past Perfect,* which was screened at the Toronto Film Festival in 2002; it is an intimate story of a couple who meet on an airplane, fall in love, break up two years later, and reunite. He also wrote or co-authored the screenplays for *House* (1996) and *Marion Bridge* (2002), based on his plays, and wrote, directed, and appears in *Wilby Wonderful* (2004) and co-authored and appears in *Whole New Thing* (2005). MacIvor's attention has been increasingly directed to movies.

Daniel MacIvor's work pushes the boundaries of the theatrical form, inquiring in and around the poetics of space, of acting, and of representation, always engaging the audience in new questions. Ric Knowles, for example, describes how the actors in *Never Swim Alone*

and *2-2 Tango* "seem virtually to *perform* the subtext, and the interest of the audience lies in trying to work out—to construct—what the text, the context, and the specifics of any 'actual situation' might be." A complex theatrical inquiry is undertaken, often dependent on intimate collaborations between actor, director, writer, and designer. MacIvor's plays are most powerful when this exchange is most fluid. Although some of his plays, such as *Marion Bridge* and *The Soldier Dreams,* adhere to the conventions of realism, his most engaging works stretch the limits of the form, stripping theater to its utmost minimalism and inquiring into the nature of performance. As MacIvor said in an interview, "I want to find out where the nothing is in the everything." (The promotional tee shirts for da da kamera proclaimed, "Nothing is enough.") MacIvor's plays tour regularly throughout North America and Europe and have had a significant impact on the theater scene in Canada and internationally.

Interview:

Cordula Quint, "Reasons and/or Excuses for the Past, Present and Future: A Conversation with Daniel MacIvor," *Canadian Theatre Review,* 128 (Fall 2006): 126–130.

References:

Daniel Brooks, "Some Thoughts about Directing *Here Lies Henry*," *Canadian Theatre Review,* 92 (Fall 1997): 42–45;

Ric Knowles, *Theatre of Form and the Production of Meaning: Contemporary Canadian Dramaturgies* (Toronto: ECW Press, 1999), pp. 65, 68, 71–73, 124, 184, 198–199, 201–202, 209;

Robert Wallace, "Technologies of the Monstrous: Notes on the Daniels' *Monster* Trilogy," *Canadian Theatre Review,* 120 (Fall 2004): 12–17.

Ann Wilson, "Lying and Dying: Theatricality in *Here Lies Henry*," *Canadian Theatre Review,* 92 (Fall 1997): 39–41.

Dave Margoshes

(8 July 1941 –   )

Holly Luhning
University of Saskatchewan

BOOKS: *Small Regrets* (Saskatoon: Thistledown Press, 1986);

Walking at Brighton (Saskatoon: Thistledown Press, 1988);

Northwest Passage (Ottawa: Oberon Press, 1990);

Nine Lives (Saskatoon: Thistledown Press, 1991);

Saskatchewan, volume 8 of *Discover Canada* (Toronto: Grolier, 1992; revised, 1996);

Long Distance Calls (Regina: Coteau, 1996);

Fables of Creation (Windsor: Black Moss Press, 1998);

Tommy Douglas: Building the New Society (Montreal: XYZ, 1999);

We Who Seek: A Love Story (Windsor: Black Moss Press, 1999);

I'm Frankie Sterne (Edmonton: NeWest Press, 2000);

Purity of Absence (Vancouver: Beach Holme, 2001);

Drowning Man (Edmonton: NeWest Press, 2003);

Bix's Trumpet and Other Stories (Edmonton: NeWest Press, 2007).

OTHER: *Listening with the Ear of the Heart: Writers at St. Peter's,* edited by Margoshes and Shelley Sopher (Muenster, Sask.: St. Peter's Press, 2003).

SELECTED PERIODICAL PUBLICATIONS–UNCOLLECTED: "Pushing Plastic," *Saskatchewan Business,* 10, no. 8 (1989): 26;

"Swimming underwater: . . . Writing in Saskatchewan Is Still Working for Peanuts," *NeWest Review,* 16, no. 2 (1990): 12–16;

"Leave It to Lynda: The Political Stripe May Seem Familiar, but with a Fresh Approach, Lynda Haverstock Promises Government with a Difference," *Saskatchewan Business,* 12, no. 2 (1990): 7;

"Home Cooking," *Saskatchewan Business,* 12, no. 3 (1991): 14;

"There's Gold in the Garbage: Saskatchewan Boasts a Clean, If Not Dust-free Environment. But a Few Local Firms Would Like to Be Cleaning up in More Ways than One," *Saskatchewan Business,* 12, no. 4 (1991): 19;

Dave Margoshes (photograph by Bryan Schlosser; from the cover for Drowning Man, *2003; Bruccoli Clark Layman Archives)*

"Business al Dente," *Saskatchewan Business,* 12, no. 7 (1991): 12;

"The Duncan's Digital Dream," *Saskatchewan Business,* 12, no. 8 (1991): 11;

"Regina's Business Renaissance," *Saskatchewan Business,* 12, no. 8 (1991): 5;

"Arts Go Political: Arts Groups (in Saskatchewan) Co-operate in a Campaign to Raise Public Awareness of the Arts," *NeWest Review,* 17, no. 1 (1991): 6;

"Order of Magnitude: The Benedictine Monks of St. Peter's," *Western Living,* 30 (December 2000): 16–20;

"My Favourite Place: Memory and Solace Beside Saskatoon's Muscular River," *Globe & Mail* (Toronto), 17 November 2001, p. 1.

Dave Margoshes is a prolific author who, in his own words, approaches writing as "a juggler, a card shark, a tightrope walker." He is a poet, journalist, short-story writer, teacher, mentor, and novelist. Regarded in his adopted city of Regina, Saskatchewan, as an important prairie writer, Margoshes is also esteemed on the national Canadian literary scene.

Margoshes was born in New Brunswick, New Jersey, on 8 July 1941 to Harry and Berte Shally Margoshes; he has two sisters, Esther and Judy. His father, an uncle, and his grandfather were journalists. He attended public school in New York City and completed high school in Somerville, New Jersey. He studied for two years at Middlebury College in Vermont, where he attended the Breadloaf Writers' Conference with prominent writers such as Samuel R. Delany. He completed his B.A. in history at the University of Iowa in 1963. After graduation, he took a job as a copyboy at the *San Francisco Chronicle*. During the following years he worked as a reporter for newspapers in Chicago; New York City; Asbury Park, New Jersey; Iowa City, Iowa; Colorado Springs, Colorado; and Monterey, California. In 1967 he returned to the University of Iowa as a student in the renowned Writers Workshop, where he studied under writers such as Vance Bourjaily, Richard Yates, and Robert Coover. He earned his M.F.A. in 1969. In 1972 he moved to Calgary. He was a reporter for the *Calgary Herald* from 1972 to 1974, city editor at the *Calgary Albertan* in 1974–1975, and a reporter for the *Herald* again from 1977 to 1981; he also taught journalism at Mount Royal College in 1975–1976 and from 1981 to 1984 and at the Southern Alberta Institute of Technology in 1976–1977. He was a reporter for the *Vancouver Sun* from 1984 to 1986. In 1986 he moved to Regina and began writing full-time.

Margoshes's first book, a collection of short stories titled *Small Regrets,* was published in 1986. The stories are written in the realistic style that is his dominant narrative voice and address the issues of betrayal, moral indecision, and moral blindness to which he returned in subsequent work. The reviewer for the Toronto *Globe and Mail* said, "Margoshes has a fine ear for dialogue, and his characters communicate with razor-sharp exchanges reminiscent of those found in Raymond Carver's work."

In 1988 Margoshes published his first volume of poetry, *Walking at Brighton*. The poems deal with nature, relationships, geography, and time. In "Weather Report" he notes that

winter lasts too long to stand on ceremony,
life too short to look away
and love is fragile as snowflakes:
each one, science teaches, is different,
each a perfect creation
brittle as porcelain, splinters
thickening into ice under foot.

In 1990 Margoshes published another collection of poetry, *Northwest Passage*. The poems in this volume are informed by pop culture and news articles. Many are prefaced by an excerpt from a news item; for example, "Baby X" is preceded by "Baby Fae died Thursday night, but her doctor said today that the operation in which she received a baboon's heart had advanced science and one day would save the lives of many children." Mimicking the clipped style of newspaper headlines, the poem goes on to discuss "this baby / born / with a hole / in its heart." Unlike the news item, the poem does not comfort the reader with a potential silver lining but acknowledges the tragedy of the event.

In 1991 Margoshes returned to short fiction with *Nine Lives,* a collection of nine stories that explore unorthodox conventions, describe bizarre situations, and investigate the primal and fragile aspects of human emotion. "Striptease" draws attention to the commodification of a woman's body and self: Billie, "not a bad-looking woman, just a few years and pounds past her time," comes onstage at a strip club. After she removes her pasties, she "plucks off the nipple of her left breast, leaving a smooth, round surface." Billie continues to take off parts of her body and finally "removes her skull, and holds it out, a gift." Thus, by the end of the show the stripper no longer possesses even her own mind. In "The Cat Came Back," the title of which is borrowed from a children's song, a man named Carpenter returns to his apartment after having his cat neutered. He then begins to suffer an eerie string of misfortunes: his girlfriend berates his sexual abilities and leaves him; he loses his job; his telephone is cut off; he injures his foot; and he finds out, via his less-than-sympathetic sister, that their father has died. At the end, Miller, Carpenter's surly neighbor, discovers him "lying on the kitchen floor, doubled up, hands between his legs, moaning. The cat was standing in the doorway between the kitchen and the bedroom, a knife in his hand. '*The sonuvabitch*,' the cat said." The reviewer for *Saskatoon Star Phoenix* wrote that "Margoshes weaves a strange spell with these stories. You laugh a little, you wince a little, but you can't turn away." The *Vancouver Sun* commented that "Margoshes' imagination is fervid and eclectic."

In 1995–1996 Margoshes was writer-in-residence at the University of Winnipeg. In 1996 he received the Stephen Leacock Poetry Award. That same year he

Cover for the first paperback edition, 2003 (Bruccoli Clark Layman Archives)

published another short-story collection, *Long Distance Calls*. These character-driven stories differ greatly from the surreal tales of *Nine Lives*. In "Pennies on the Track" the narrator recalls his experiences as a boy: his father's love for him, his father's wayward behavior, and the ensuing tension between his father and mother. The story ends with the boy witnessing his mother's violent attack on his father, leaving the reader with the image of "him standing there, blood pouring down onto his collar, eyes closed as if, by shutting out the sight of it he could protect himself from her anger . . . his hands at his sides, the fingers jerking with concentration the way they had when they took the flames from me for themselves, waiting for the next blow."

In 1998 Margoshes published *Fables of Creation*. Many of the stories in this slim volume involve surreal elements. It opens with "Three Fables of Creation," which chronicles three aspects of the creation of the world. In "I. The History of Water," the narrator explains that "in the early days, before water, the Earth

was awash for a time in blood." In "II. Why the Sky is Blue," the reader is told that "Contrary to the story in the Bible, which often got things confused," in the beginning the sky was not blue; in fact, at first there was no sky. The final section, "III. When Wolves Were Lords," explains that "before the ascendancy of man, wolves were the undisputed lords of creation." Other fables include "The Woman in the Red Hat," in which a newlywed couple are the victims of a bizarre holdup, and "The Lie," about a man whose lies grow larger and more complicated until "the lie, as small as it had begun, consumed me, burning first blue, then red, then blinding white." *Fables of Creation* was short-listed for the 1998 Saskatchewan Book Award for Fiction.

In 1999 Margoshes branched out into nonfiction with *Tommy Douglas: Building the New Society*. He had been commissioned to write the work about former Saskatchewan prime minister Thomas Clement Douglas for XYZ Publishing's Quest Library series of biographies of notable deceased Canadians. Also that year he was writer-in-residence at the Writers Guild of Alberta Colony in Banff, Alberta. Finally, in 1999 he published the satirical novella *We Who Seek: A Love Story*. The inspiration for the work was the popularity of the drug Viagra; in the novella impotence is a metaphor for the anxieties and fears people feel when falling in love. Leo realizes that "he had a problem, too . . . it was this sex thing." He and his lover, Burr, "weren't making it the way they should have been." Leo engages in other sexual relationships and finally visits a confessional and confides his sins and his impotence to the priest. The next morning Burr informs him that she has decided to end their relationship. They argue, and their quarrel evolves into passionate sex. Leo develops a new attitude toward love, deciding that "the destination . . . is not as important as the motion itself."

Margoshes's first novel, *I'm Frankie Sterne* (2000), opens with an introduction by the title character: "My name is François Sterne. If you don't believe me, take a look at my driver's license. You can buy anything–hell, I can't even drive. Even passports, more expensive though. I don't have a need for one. Every place I'm likely to want to go, I've already been. I have a new life and an old one. I'm still figuring out the new, so it's the old one I'll tell you about." Also known as Francesco Sterne and Frankie Stein, Frankie is a mulatto who is raised by his Jewish father in Spanish Harlem. He is a member of a successful street-corner band during the early days of rock and roll in the 1950s and an itinerant folk musician in the 1960s; in the 1970s he moves to Canada and becomes a serious composer. Reviewer Dave Carpenter wrote, "Frankie Sterne does more one-night stands, dons and discards more outer layers than Gypsy Rose Lee. I can't think of a livelier way to revisit the sixties than to follow Frankie around the continent. This debut novel should travel nicely."

In 2001 Margoshes won the John V. Hicks Award for a collection in typescript form titled "Pornography and Other Stories"; it was published in 2007 as *Bix's Trumpet and Other Stories*. That same year he returned to poetry with *Purity of Absence*. The collection is divided into four sections. The first, "God's Tears," explores the darker portions of love; the poems in this section range from peacefully introspective to menacing. In "The Persistent Suitor" Yvonne is in a hospital bed "wrestling with Death, who slips / not *under* her bed as the demons / she feared as a child liked to do / but *into* it." The poem alludes to Emily Dickinson and the William Faulkner short story "A Rose for Emily" (1930) and ends on "just the fourth morning, days / before her hair turns white, before / her stomach turns itself inside / out, days before the first bouquet / of his roses arrives." Margoshes portrays death as a process, a threshold through which Yvonne passes.

In the title poem of section 2, "The Marriage Bed," the speaker describes crawling into bed late at night; he explains that "In sleep, you are always still / the girl I first came to all those years / ago, your porcelain skin tight / as the casing enfolding a rose / before it blossoms." The speaker is "that boy / who worshipped at the light radiating / from you, at your heat, the breath / stuttering through my ribs." The stanza concludes with the speaker's summation that "we are ghosts of ourselves, haunting / our present selves who cannot sleep." In "Saskatoons" the speaker describes in short, staccato lines seeing his wife come through the door with a peace offering of Saskatoon pie and feeling "my anger / crack open / the kernel / at its heart / fall / shards / of shell / littering / the floor." The poem ends with the spouses in each other's arms; but they hold "each other / carefully / mindful / of the teeth / below."

The third section, "The Satisfaction of Knowing," explores familial love and parent-child relationships. The poems allude to Elvis Presley, Adam and Eve, and old wives' tales. The section concludes with a poem about Robert Latimer, a Saskatchewan farmer who was convicted of second-degree murder and sentenced to life in prison for killing his twelve-year-old daughter in 1993 by piping exhaust fumes into the cab of his pickup truck; Tracy Latimer was severely disabled and in chronic pain with cerebral palsy. The case received nationwide media coverage and fueled heated debate over mercy killing. Margoshes's poem "Latimer's Statement to the Police" opens, "Let me be clear about one thing: / I killed my daughter," and works its way to a simple, yet emotional ending: "She didn't cry / and me neither. I stood in the

barnyard / in the snow, my boots open, no gloves, / my hands cold, looking / up at those damned stars."

The final section, "Radio Silence," addresses issues of history, aging, and reminiscence. Many of the poems in this section are longer than those in the earlier sections and picture the role of love against a backdrop of global scale. In "Dec. 6, Montreal" Margoshes writes about the present lives of the survivors of the 1989 "Montreal massacre," in which gunman Marc Lepine killed fourteen female engineering students at the Ecole Polytechnique. In "Ghosts and Poets at Batoche" Margoshes visits the site of the May 1885 battle that ended the Métis rebellion led by Louis Riel, where the "rifle pits have begun to fill / in like footsteps in snow / on the crest of hill overlooking / the river bend where they cabled down / the Northcote." The *Calgary Herald* noted that "Margoshes' poetry is singular among this year's many Canadian collections in that it points toward the eternal. When it's good, it's as good as it gets."

The protagonist of Margoshes's novel *Drowning Man* (2003) is Wilf Sweeny, a recovering alcoholic reporter "almost sixty-three years old, more than forty-five years in the racket." Sweeny returns to the small British Columbia town of his youth to try to make a comeback in his career. He notices a newspaper article about Nicholas Limousine, who was recently found dead in a local hotel room; the name is familiar to Sweeny, and he becomes involved in solving the mystery of Limousine's death. Along the way a young, beautiful woman named July joins Sweeny's investigation because she is attracted to him. As the plot unfolds, it becomes clear that Limousine and Sweeny are somehow linked. The novel is a realistic mystery story that challenges some of the conventions of the genre: Sweeny is not a conventionally attractive man, and he is initially uncomfortable with July's advances.

In 2003 Margoshes and the artist Shelley Sopher edited the anthology *Listening with the Ear of the Heart: Writers at St. Peter's*. St. Peter's Abbey near Muenster, Saskatchewan, hosts winter and summer writers' and artists' colonies that are well known throughout Canada; Sopher, the colony coordinator, and Margoshes, a member of the colony committee, solicited submissions from writers who had attended a St. Peter's colony. The book includes work from seventy-six writers, including Don McKay, Guy Vanderhaegue, Tim Lilburn, Lorna Crozier, and Jan Zwicky. In 2004 Margoshes won the City of Regina Writing Award for an untitled novel in progress.

Papers:

A collection of Dave Margoshes's papers is in the Dr. John Archer Library at the University of Regina.

Yann Martel

(25 June 1963 –   )

Jeanette Lynes
St. Francis Xavier University

See also the Martel entry in *DLB 326: Booker Prize Novels, 1969–2005.*

BOOKS: *The Facts behind the Helsinki Roccamatios* (Toronto: Knopf Canada, 1993; London: Faber & Faber, 1993);

Self: A Novel (Toronto: Knopf Canada, 1996; London: Faber & Faber, 1996);

Life of Pi: A Novel (Toronto: Knopf Canada, 2001; New York: Harcourt, 2001; Edinburgh: Canongate, 2002).

OTHER: "How I Wrote *Life of Pi,*" *Powells.com* <http://www.powells.com/fromtheauthor/martel.html> (accessed 22 February 2007).

Yann Martel has received international acclaim for work that celebrates the power of the imagination in the face of adversity, blending philosophical inquiry with metafiction and a Canadian preoccupation with survival. His second novel, *Life of Pi* (2001), received the 2002 Booker Prize, became an international best-seller, and in 2007 was being made into a feature motion picture.

The second of the two sons of Emile Martel, a Canadian diplomat, and Nicole Perron Martel, Martel was born on 25 June 1963 in Salamanca, Spain. He grew up, he told Sabine Sielke in a 2003 interview, in "Alaska, British Columbia, Costa Rica, France, Ontario and Mexico." He attended Ridgemont High School in Ottawa from 1976 to 1979 and Trinity College in Port Hope, Ontario, from 1979 to 1981. He studied at Trent University from 1981 to 1984 and at Concordia University in 1984–1985; in 1986 he returned to Trent University, where he received a bachelor of arts in philosophy in 1987.

Martel's first book, a collection of four stories titled *The Facts behind the Helsinki Roccamatios,* was published in 1993. In the title story—"more properly speaking . . . novella," he told Sielke—the unnamed narrator is a philosophy student at "Ellis University, in Roe-

town, just east of Toronto" who is forced to confront mortality when his nineteen-year-old friend, Paul Atsee, is diagnosed with AIDS. The story takes place over the nine-month period of Paul's decline and death. The friends decide that "between the two of us we had to do something constructive, something that would make something out of nothing, sense out of nonsense." The plan they devise is inspired by the parallel between the AIDS epidemic of the late twentieth century and the bubonic plague of the mid fourteenth century as depicted in Giovanni Boccaccio's *Decameron* (composed circa 1348–1353): "Such a simple idea: an isolated villa outside of Florence; the world dying of the Black Death; ten people gathered together hoping to survive; *telling each other stories to pass the time.*" The story the narrator and his dying friend will tell will "need a structure . . . some curb along which we blind could tap our white canes." The narrator conceives the structure "while picking weeds"—weeding, like storytelling, being an activity that imposes order on chaos: "we would use the history of the twentieth century." Paul and the narrator invent the Roccamatios, "a Finnish family of Italian extraction," and lay down the ground rule: "Each episode would be related in one sitting and would resemble one event from a consecutive year of the twentieth century." The friends agree to alternate years and keep the story "a secret between the two of us." Paul's hopeless condition and the rage it arouses in him are juxtaposed to the spiraling military conflict of World War I: after a long list of declarations of war in 1917, "For 1918 Paul wants to use further declarations of war." Thus, death is both highly particularized and universalized. Paul's final installment of the story, delivered to the narrator in a handwritten note, relates the death of Queen Elizabeth II and turns the story over to the narrator, underscoring the storyteller's mandate to keep history and memory alive. "The Facts behind the Helsinki Roccamatios" won the Journey Prize for the best short story in Canada in 1991; in 2004 it was adapted for the stage by Bruce M. Smith as a monologue in

Yann Martel (photograph by Danielle Schaub; from the dust jacket for the U.S. edition of Life of Pi, *2001; Bruccoli Clark Layman Archives)*

which the actor playing the narrator talks to an empty bed.

The second story in the collection, "The Time I Heard the Private Donald J. Rankin String Concerto with One Discordant Violin, by the American Composer John Morton," is narrated by a young Canadian who travels to Washington, D.C., to visit "an old high-school friend" who has joined the ranks of corporate America. Wandering the streets of the city, he discovers a dilapidated abandoned theater in which "The Maryland Vietnam War Veterans' Baroque Chamber Ensemble" is performing a concert. The ghostly Merridew Theatre resembles a battlefield, with "mould that covered the walls of the place and made them look like huge medieval maps tracing the spread of the Black Death." The concert provides the occasion for a sustained meditation on art; as the ensemble plays, the narrator's thoughts wander across a variety of topics that include "the brilliant use of semicolons" in Joseph Conrad's *Almayer's Folly: A Story of an Eastern River* (1895). By playing the Rankin Concerto "poorly," Morton, who is one of the musicians as well as the composer of the piece, becomes for the narrator the ideal artist, because his creative effort, devoid of "robotic flawlessness," is "truly human, a mix of perfect beauty and cathartic error." Confronted with the "blessed suffering" of great art, the narrator is transported to a state of sublime appreciation that is experienced as *"agony,"* and "The Merridew Theatre . . . was no longer a ruin: it was a magnificent temple." After the concert, the narrator follows Morton to the bank where he works as a janitor. With the vacuum cleaner roaring, Morton recounts how he became a composer while on tour in Vietnam, underscoring the theme of art arising from suffering. The janitor is now writing "The Laura Brooks Concerto" to commemorate the unsung worker exploited by capitalism—a different kind of soldier dying in a different kind of meaningless war. After his encounter with Morton, the narrator visits the Vietnam Veterans Memorial, touches the name Donald J. Rankin, and weeps "over this war that had nothing to do with me and that I know so little about." The work won the 1992 National Magazine Award for best short story.

Dust jacket for the first Canadian edition, 2001
(<http://www.canadacouncil.ca>)

The third story, "Manners of Dying," consists of nine letters written by a prison warden to the mother of an executed man; each letter recounts a different version of the hours before Kevin Barlow's hanging. These epistolary "takes" on Barlow's final hours reveal that it is never really possible to articulate the experience of someone's death. "Manners of Dying" was adapted by Jeremy Peter Allen for a 2004 motion picture of the same title.

The final story, "The Vita Aeterna Mirror Company: Mirrors to Last till Kingdom Come," about a young man visiting his grandmother, is the most formally innovative piece in the collection. The grandmother's story of her marriage to a doctor and her life in Quebec appear in a column running down the left side of the page; the grandson's mental responses to her story are printed on the right side, giving the story some of the visual effect of a poem. Often, the grandson's thoughts are unflattering comments such as "Man, she can go on," and sometimes the grandmother's remarks are replaced by *"blah-blah-blah-blah-/blah-blah-blah-blah,"* all of which reveals the grandson's

failure to value the past. But he learns that the past must be honored when he discovers a "mirror machine" among his grandmother's possessions. Pointing out that the mirror machine "runs on memories," the grandmother makes a mirror with her grandson. "The Vita Aeterna Mirror Company: Mirrors to Last till Kingdom Come" reveals how the colonial past is reflected in the present—the best sand for making mirrors comes from the Caribbean—and how mass production has replaced artisans. The grandson becomes "something of an expert" on old mirrors and, according to the final, parenthesized section of the story, which runs all the way across the page, he also becomes an artist whose task is to gaze through the mirror lens of history "and try to imagine all the words I so stupidly ignored."

Martel's first novel, *Self,* appeared in 1996. On his eighteenth birthday a young man turns into a woman; reflecting on the metamorphosis, she says, "My identity was tied to the English language. And I knew that I was a woman . . . English-speaking and a woman." The new woman is a student at Ellis University in Roetown, the institution depicted in "The Facts behind the Helsinki Roccamatios," and is also an aspiring writer. The "sexual history" the narrator craves is acquired during an intense relationship with an American woman, Ruth, in Greece and Turkey. When the narrator is raped by her neighbor, the text bifurcates into columns of rows of endless ellipses signifying silence. Seven years after becoming a woman, the narrator reverts to being a man. Though *Self* received the Hugh MacLennan Prize for Fiction, was nominated for the Governor General's Literary Award, and was a finalist for the Books in Canada First Novel Award, it did not sell well.

In 1997 Martel traveled to Matheran, near Mumbai (formerly Bombay), India, to write his next book. The novel he had envisioned did not come to fruition, but the idea for *Life of Pi* originated during the stay. A family of Indian zookeepers boards the Japanese ship *Tsimtsum* with some of their animals to immigrate to Canada; the ship sinks, leaving the narrator, young Piscine "Pi" Molitor Patel, adrift on a lifeboat for 227 days with a rat, a zebra, a hyena, an orangutan, and a Bengal tiger that, through a bureaucratic mix-up, has been named Richard Parker. The bulk of *Life of Pi*—the lengthy second of the three parts—deals with the daily challenges of survival at sea. The hyena eats the zebra and the orangutan; the tiger eats the hyena; and Pi feeds the rat to the tiger to keep from being eaten himself. Pi claims that he survived "because I forgot even the very notion of time." Time is depicted as a hellish, ecological aberration on the deadly island of meerkats, which Pi initially perceives as a place of refuge but discovers to be an omnivorous "ball of algae of leviathan proportions": "The entire forest was turning brown, an autumn that came in a few minutes." In part 3 the lifeboat washes up on the Mexican shore; Richard Parker runs off into the jungle; and Pi is thrust back into the world of rationalist temporality. Two men from the Japanese Ministry of Transport interview Pi, the lone survivor of the *Tsimtsum*. The exchange is presented as *"excerpts from the verbatim transcript."* The government officials do not believe Pi's story; they "would like to know what really happened . . . the 'straight facts.'" Pi responds, "Isn't telling about something–using words . . . already something of an invention? Isn't just looking upon this world already something of an invention?" He then tells them an alternative story in which the animals do not appear. The book concludes with Pi's story having been reduced to the pedestrian report submitted by the officials, who recommend that the *"case be closed."*

Florence Stratton reads the conflict between the bureaucrats and Pi as one between the positivist and poststructuralist dispositions. She also situates *Life of Pi* within a body of Canadian literature based on "the tropes of nationhood: that of orphanhood, for instance, or immigration," while June Dwyer locates the novel within the tradition of shipwreck narratives. Martel told Sielke that the work owes a debt to *Max e os felinos* (1981; translated as *Max and the Cats,* 1990), a novel by the Brazilian author Moacyr Scliar. The book has most engaged reviewers and critics as a philosophical novel. Specifically, there has been much discussion of what Stewart Cole calls the conflation of "belief in story with belief in God." Martel endorsed this interpretation in the interview with Sielke: "to say the book will make you believe in fiction, to me, isn't very far from saying

it'll make you believe in God. I think it's acceptable to say that God is a fiction, if you understand that this doesn't necessarily mean that this fiction doesn't exist. It just exists in a way that is only accessed through the imagination."

Yann Martel was the Samuel Fischer Professor of Literature in the Department of Comparative Literature at the University of Berlin in 2002 and the 2003–2004 writer-in-residence at the Saskatoon Public Library. He continues to live in Saskatoon, where he is a scholar-in-residence at the University of Saskatchewan. In early 2007 he was completing his third novel, which he described to Sielke as a "Holocaust fable . . . that takes place on a large shirt the size of a country."

Interviews:

Andrew Steinmetz, "Pi: Summing up Meaning from the Irrational: An Interview with Yann Martel," *Books in Canada,* 31, no. 6 (2002): 18;

Sabine Sielke, "'The Empathetic Imagination': An Interview with Yann Martel," *Canadian Literature,* 177 (Summer 2003): 12–32.

References:

Stewart Cole, "Believing in Tigers: Anthropomorphism and Incredulity in Yann Martel's *Life of Pi,*" *Studies in Canadian Literature,* 29 (Summer 2004): 22–37;

June Dwyer, "Yann Martel's *Life of Pi* and the Evolution of the Shipwreck Narrative," *Modern Fiction Studies,* 35 (Fall 1995): 9–21;

Florence Stratton, "'Hollow at the Core': Deconstructing Yann Martel's *Life of Pi,*" *Studies in Canadian Literature,* 29 (Summer 2004): 5–17.

Suzette Mayr

(1967 –)

Debra Dudek
Deakin University

BOOKS: *Zebra Talk* (Calgary: disOrientation Press, 1991);

Moon Honey (Edmonton: NeWest Press, 1995);

The Widows (Edmonton: NeWest Press, 1998);

Tale, by Mayr, Geoffrey Hunter, and Robin Arsenault (Calgary: Stride Gallery, 2001);

Venous Hum (Vancouver: Arsenal Pulp Press, 2004);

If, Adultery (Edmonton: Extra-Virgin Press, 2007).

OTHER: "Scalps," in *Boundless Alberta,* edited by Aritha van Herk (Edmonton: NeWest Press, 1993), pp. 163–168;

"Glass Anatomy," in *Eye Wuz Here: Short Stories by Women Writers under 30,* edited by Shannon Cooley (Vancouver: Douglas & McIntyre, 1996);

"Cross Oceans," "Visiting My Mother's Country: An Albino Pit Bull Lives Next Door," "Married Girlfriends (I)," "Married Girlfriends (II)," and "To Her Rainbow Tribe," in *Introductions: Poets Present Poets,* edited by Evan Jones (Markham, Ont.: Fitzhenry & Whiteside, 2001), pp. 45–49;

"Nipple Gospel," in *And Other Stories,* edited by George Bowering (Vancouver: Talonbooks, 2001), pp. 233–242;

"Toot Sweet Matricia," in *So Long Been Dreaming: Postcolonial Science Fiction and Fantasy,* edited by Nalo Hopkinson and Uppinder Mehan (Vancouver: Arsenal Pulp Press, 2004);

The Broadview Anthology of Short Fiction, edited by Mayr and Julia Gaunce (Peterborough: Broadview Press, 2004).

SELECTED PERIODICAL PUBLICATIONS–
UNCOLLECTED: "Eating My Mother's Country," *Open Letter,* 8 (Winter–Spring 1993): 64–66;

"Fine Stories Peopled by Crummy Characters," *Canadian Forum,* 78 (July 1999): 43;

"Am I Disturbing You?" and "Restlessness," *Canadian Forum,* 78 (December 1999): 42;

Suzette Mayr (photograph by Lisa Brawn; courtesy of the author)

"Absent Black Women in Dany Laferrière's *How to Make Love to a Negro,*" *Canadian Literature,* 188 (Spring 2006): 31–45.

Suzette Mayr is a poet, short-story writer, and novelist who is part of the Calgary Renaissance and is shaping both Canadian and African Canadian literature. George Elliott Clarke says in "Introduction

Paperback cover for the first edition, 1998
(Bruccoli Clark Layman Archives)

to Suzette Mayr" (2001) that she is the "upsetting upstart in Anglo-Canuck poetry, if you got ears to hear," and David Staines includes her among Canadians "who should become major poets of the future *and* the present. . . . She is a fascinating poet who deserves to be read carefully and seriously." Mayr refuses stereotypes, blurs rigid categories, and calls into question ideologies of race, gender, age, and sexuality. Alberta is central to her writing, although Mayr refuses to ally herself with what she called, in an unpublished December 2002 interview, the "conservative political forces in Alberta." Instead, she challenges the ways in which Canadian prairie literature is perceived in Canada and abroad:

> This whole notion of "Prairie literature" is one that needs some serious shaking up. I doubt that outside of post-secondary English departments people realize that Alberta literature is more than W. O. Mitchell and *Who Has Seen the Wind*. I want to shoot myself when I see Canadian Prairie Literature being represented by hay

bales, pioneers, and gophers, which I did at one "Canada Day" conference in Germany. It's W. O. Mitchell and gophers, *and* it's Fred Wah and Hiromi Goto. And it's me writing about Trudeau and how fucking sexy he was.

Mayr was born in 1967 in Calgary to Rose-Marie and Ulrich Mayr. She began her college career at the University of Calgary as a science major, because in high school she had found her English teachers boring but had excelled in biology. At the university, however, she did well in English and poorly in biology, and she realized that she wanted to become a writer when she took her first creative-writing course in 1988. While attending the university she worked as a waitress, an usher, a night-shift sandwich maker during the 1988 Olympics, and a receptionist for a publishing company. She graduated in 1990 with an honors degree in English.

Mayr's first book, a poetry chapbook titled *Zebra Talk* (1991), was originally written as part of her M.A. thesis. In both content and style it mediates between binaries such as black and white, homosexual and heterosexual, woman and man, mother and father, adult and child, and human and inhuman. It also examines the ways in which the body is often the site for both perpetuating and resisting such dualist thinking:

> When she dances she closes her eyes raises
> her arms from the elbows her knees sink together mermaid
> shape and her hair bounces back and forth back and forth back
> and forth like the tail of a pony. Mermaid shape. No legs.
> Nothing between them then don't you see you understand.

Mayr earned her M.A. in English, with a creative-writing focus, from the University of Alberta in 1992. From 1993 to 2002 she taught a variety of courses in second- and third-year English literature in the Liberal Studies Department at the Alberta College of Art and Design (ACAD) in Calgary, including Canadian multiculturalism, international literature, the novel and short story, poetry and drama, myth in literature, and women's literary perspectives.

Mayr's first novel, *Moon Honey* (1995), is a magic-realist work; Mayr explained in the 2002 interview that her use of magic realism is a way of making the metaphoric literal, which is important when she runs "into the dilemma of there not being a word or an operable concept for something I want to say. Metaphor is useful for filling in these gaps—a metaphor will always only be an approximation, but it'll still be closer than nothing." *Moon Honey* uses the genre of the love story to reveal how categories such as race, gender, and sexuality are not as stable as Western dualist thought might have one believe. The novel focuses primarily on the relationship between Carmen and Griffin, and all action connects in some way to these two characters. Carmen and Griffin are on the cusp of adulthood and are trying to have sex whenever and wherever they can avoid the watchful eye of Griffin's domineering, manipulative, passive-aggressive, racist mother, Fran. When Carmen is transformed into a black woman, the way in which she sees the world changes, and she begins to understand that identity is neither singular nor located only at the level of skin color. Mayr's interest in wordplay is apparent in both her poetry and her prose. Her playfulness extends into the ways that she shape-shifts not only words but also characters, both of which encourage readers to see identity as fluid, not static. Carmen leaves Griffin for Kevin, then returns to Griffin; Griffin loves Carmen but goes to Europe and falls in love

with Renata. Renata marries Griffin but runs away with Mika on the wedding day. Fran marries a man named God but has sex with the New Boss, then forsakes both of them when she turns into a magpie like her mother, Bedelia. The narrator says: "This is how metamorphoses work; angry old women transform into magpies, white girls turn brown, lose their lovers, but discover themselves in the television set. Metamorphosis always signals a happy alternative." The two epigraphs in the novel signal to the reader that metamorphosis and marriage are transformations of the body. The first epigraph is from Ovid's *Metamorphoses* (A.D. 8): *"My purpose is to tell of bodies which have been transformed into shapes of a different kind."* The second is from Beverly Clark's *Planning a Wedding to Remember: The Perfect Wedding Planner. Special Touches & Unique Ideas* (1985): *"Store the gown in a cedar chest or a lined wooden drawer. Air it out yearly and fold it in different places before restoring. Make sure it is stored in a dark, dry place."* In the unpublished 2002 interview Mayr said,

> Marriage is a transformation of how the body is seen and therefore how it functions within specific contexts. For a lot of women, it's a career and a way to become "normal"—you go from being unemployed and uncategorized and therefore an unknown and maybe dangerous quantity, to employed and useful and controlled. Marriage is all about putting women into a category in which they are easily managed—they "belong" to someone literally in the traditional marriage ceremony. For gays and lesbians who legally can't marry even if they want to, marriage shows how gay and lesbian unions are imaginary at best—they and their bodies will always be abnormal.

Moon Honey was short-listed for the Writers Guild of Alberta Best First Book and Best Novel Prizes.

In 1997 an excerpt from *Moon Honey* was published in Clarke's influential anthology, *Eyeing the North Star: Directions in African-Canadian Literature*. In *Introductions: Poets Present Poets* (2001) Clarke writes that he discovered Mayr's writing in 1995 and found it deft, imaginative, poetic, and political. He notes that she is part of the second generation of African Canadian writers and that "Along with poet Wayde Compton and poet-novelist David Odhiambo, she fronts a fresh generation of West Coast African-Canadian *avant-gardistes*."

Mayr's second novel, *The Widows* (1998), blends history and fiction in the story of three women who go over Niagara Falls in an egg-shaped structure, the Niagara Ball, and are haunted by the watery specter of Annie Edson Taylor, who in 1901 became the first person to go over the falls and live.

p. 88 – teacher scene – realistic?   p. 84 – orange group

RITUAL / CEREMONY

Paul. Lai Fen. Lloyd
Haroun. Kim. Daisy.
Ozzie

- Griffins – made from the sandstone quarries around the area, statues put up to commemorate the birth of the city. Mrs Blake (eg: knows one isn't pregnant, etc.) – wears down into blobs b/c sandstone lousy material for sculptures (part of vision for removal) – Griffins kidnap & eat children – Oscar / Freddy & fetus can't be griffins.
- Why do so many h. school kids die?
- Maureen & Lloyd – how does Charlotte / Hadley feel about them getting together? Lloyd was Hadley's bf. after all.
- Drama geeks – Kevon & Vincent & Ozzie
- Thor and Stefanya – high school sweethearts?
- Ghostly visitations @ La Barry before p. 182 & p. 204
- tape – scares off Mrs. Blake in her bid to over-protect her 38 year old daughter

- Shrub roses make no sense – plot wd have cutting flowers, not ornamental ones – perhaps teas do supernaturally well – red spots in the snow – because of the fertilizer

Hybrid Teas –
eg: "Prince Charles"   Angela
"Lady Di"   Carteresque

- Mrs. Blake – disappears @ graduation? Sub fills in for her – bf in dress – neck exposes bruises from Blake?

ch. 30 – 222.

Gargoyle Communications

ch. 20 – 173
ch. 21 – 177
ch. 22 – 182   Chapters for part II? maybe not.
ch. 23 – 186
ch. 24 – 190
ch. 25 – 210   ch. 26 – 211   ch. 27 – 212   ch. 28 – 215

ch. 1 – 18
ch. 2 – 32
ch. 3 – 38
ch. 4 – 43
ch. 5 – 53
ch. 29 – 220   ch. 17 – 160
ch. 18 – 164   ch. 19 – 165

ch. 6 – 65
ch. 7 – 67   Ch. 9 – 76   Ch. 10 – 93   Ch. 12 – 124
Ch. 8 – 74   Ch. 11 – 96   Ch. 13 – 132
Ch. 14 – 137
May – reunion in October   Ch. 15 – 145

Mrs. Beadle.

May June July August September October   Ch. 16 – 157

Page of notes by Mayr for a novel with the working title "Griffins on the Bridge" that was published in 2004 as Venous Hum *(courtesy of the author)*

Mayr said in the 2002 interview that she came across Taylor when she was

> writing a long poem about water and women who were involved with water somehow (e.g.: mermaids, selkies, Esther Williams). . . . Unfortunately, she wasn't Canadian, but the fact that she was 63 when she went over the Falls and the fact that she was the first person to do it and survive were just too hard to resist. I was appalled by the fact that hardly anyone outside of Niagara-on-the-Lake had ever heard of her. She completely confirmed my theory that there's a conspiracy to erase all old women, no matter how important they are.

Hannelore; her sister Clotilde; and Clotilde's lover, Frau Schnadelhuber, challenge the categorization of the aging female body as useless, sexless, and immobile. They grumble and curse, work and nurture, lose families and gain lovers, love both men and women and make love frequently. In a pivotal passage Mayr reveals how North American culture views old women—as she puts it in the unpublished 2002 interview—"one of the messy details that have been swept under the carpet":

> Now that she had nothing to do, Frau Schnadelhuber realized that her whole life had been a huge joke at her expense. Surviving two world wars, deaths and famine, the birth of her daughter, a husband from hell, and for what, for what? Simply to be told that because she had reached a certain age, she was taking up too much room, was no longer useful, no longer wanted. Her body was old, her hair grey and thinning, her skin soft and flabby where it used to be elastic and smooth, but she didn't feel old in her head until people told her she was old, hid things from her because they thought she was so old she was no longer connected with the world. . . .
>
> Frau Schnadelhuber didn't feel ugly and useless until people showed her she was ugly and useless. She felt like a spider. Every leg pulled off and a dying body left to throb in the middle of the web.
>
> Frau Schnadelhuber throbbed in the middle of the bed.

Frau Schnadelhuber's throbbing leads to robbery when Hannelore persuades her to return to her career as a thief, steal the egg prototype from the Royal Auditorium, and drive it across the prairies to Niagara Falls. Movement—across the Atlantic Ocean, across the prairies, and over Niagara Falls—symbolizes the way in which these three women refuse to sit still in terms either of literal physical motion or of emotional growth. The title indicates women whose husbands have died but also suggests the black widow spider, who devours the male after mating. Mayr is interested in exploring

the power of terms such as *widow* and *spinster* that, as she pointed out in the unpublished 2002 interview, do not have an equivalent for men: "The fact that so many kinds of women—gay, straight, old, young, rich, working-class—can be called 'spinsters' shows the problem with the whole concept of 'spinster.' It's just a good, name-calling way to put women who haven't taken the traditional marriage-route in their place—it really gets on my nerves. . . . Clotilde is the 'true' spinster in *The Widows,* but she's also very secure sexually, very competent, and very tough." *The Widows* was short-listed for the Commonwealth Prize for Best Book in the Canadian-Caribbean Region.

Mayr was honored in Clarke's poem "*Sur* Pélagie-la-charrette" (2001) for her depiction of figures who are rarely depicted in lead roles or who are simplified to the point of stereotype. The poem opens with the epigraph "*à la manière de Suzette Mayr*" and closes with the lines: "You've proven that *Poetry's* stern freedom / Depends on sluts, vampires, and assassins." Mayr said in the unpublished 2002 interview that Clarke's poem is "rude and great and addresses the messy, shitty taboo-lusts rooted in ugly history that still continue to this day . . . but which are disguised as euphemisms and in 'innocent' racist discourse." After teaching at the Institut für Anglistik/Amerikanistik at Ernst-Moritz-Arndt-Universität Greifswald in Germany in the summer of 2002—a position to which she was invited after the head of the department read *The Widows,* which had been translated into German in 2000—Mayr was the 2002–2003 Markin-Flanagan Writer-in-Residence at the University of Calgary.

Mayr's third novel, *Venous Hum,* was published in 2004. Lai Fun Kugelheim is a pregnant, lesbian, biracial, bispecies—human and vampire—mother who is having an affair with the husband of her best friend and neighbor and whose twenty-year high-school reunion is approaching. Mayr said in the unpublished 2002 interview,

> I am interested in vampires because they work as a metaphor for just about anything having to do with being an outsider. They violate the sexuality rules because they sexily suck anyone's blood, and being killed by a vampire is a glamorous, orgasmic way to die. What pisses me off about the vampire myth, though, is that all the major vampires seem to be tortured, rich, white, young-ish men—there is nothing tragic or horrific about being rich, white, and male, and I am going to write against this. Monsters in general work for me because sometimes I have felt "monstrous" and outside category—I grew up biracial and gay in Alberta with assholes telling me how "hard" it must be for me to be myself.

For most of the novel, and for the thirty years before the novel begins, Lai Fun's parents are vegetarians who have ceased their bloodsucking habits to set a good example for their child. The title comes from the scene in which Louvre, Lai Fun's mother, relapses into vampirism: "she could never resist a perfect vein, the sound of venous music, she even hears a light, unresolved venous hum around his throat that makes her cock her ears, and she darts her teeth forward to snap and tear off the waggling finger because she could never stand waggling fingers, ever since she was a girl."

Suzette Mayr is an assistant professor in the Department of English at the University of Calgary. She said in the unpublished 2002 interview that she is "overwhelmed by the passion and desolation and hopelessness that one sometimes feels as a female writer trying to do what she loves but still pay the bills. There's no money in it, people think it's a hobby, but if you don't do it it's like not breathing." Mayr writes against racism and sexism in provocative, challenging, passionate works that eschew simplicity and embrace complexity. She said in the unpublished 2002 inteview, "I do believe in the notion that nothing is simple—if it looks simple then some detail is being left out. This is the case with depictions of aging women, depictions of women in general, of race, of sexuality, of love, among many other things. I am interested in the details that make things difficult and complicated and messy and un-'universal.'"

Interview:

Nathaniel G. Moore, "TDR Interview: Suzette Mayr," *Danforth Review* (February 2005) <http://www.danforthreview.com/features/interviews/suzette_mayr.htm> [accessed 26 February 2007].

References:

George Elliott Clarke, "Introduction to Suzette Mayr," in *Introductions: Poets Present Poets,* edited by Evan Jones, introduction by David Staines (Markham, Ont.: Fitzhenry & Whiteside, 2001), pp. 43–44;

Clarke, "*Sur* Pélagie-la-charrette," in his *Blue* (Vancouver: Raincoast, 2001), pp. 60–61;

Harry Vandervlist, "Suzette Mayr's Big Problem," *ffwd: Calgary's News & Entertainment Weekly* (19 September 2002) <http://www.ffwdweekly.com/Issues/2002/0919/book1.htm> [accessed 22 February 2007].

Steve McCaffery

(24 January 1947 –   )

Rob Budde
University of Northern British Columbia

BOOKS: *Poems* (Toronto: grOnk, 1967);

Six Concrete Poems (Toronto: grOnk, 1969);

Ground Plans for a Speaking City (Toronto: Anonbeyond, 1969);

Cap(ture) (Toronto: grOnk, 1969);

Melons (Toronto: grOnk, 1970);

Transitions to the Beast: Post-Semiotic Poetry (Toronto: Ganglia Press, 1970);

Parallel Texts, by McCaffery and bpNichol (Toronto: Anonbeyond, 1971);

Maps: A Different Landscape (Toronto: grOnk, 1971);

Collbrations, by McCaffery and Nichol (Toronto: grOnk, 1971);

Carnival: Panel One: 1967–1970 (Toronto: Coach House, 1973);

Broken Mandala (Toronto: grOnk, 1974);

Dr. Sadhu's Muffins: A Book of Written Readings (Victoria: Press Porcépic, 1974);

'Ow's "Waif" (Toronto: Coach House, 1975);

Edge, by McCaffery and Steven Smith (Toronto: Anonbeyond, 1975);

Shifters (Toronto: grOnk, 1976);

Novel 7 (Toronto: Dreadnaught Press, 1976);

Horse d'Oeuvres, by McCaffery, Nichol, Paul Dutton, and Rafael Barreto-Rivera as The Four Horsemen (Toronto: General Publishing, 1976);

Carnival: Panel Two: 1971–1975 (Toronto: Coach House, 1977);

Crown's Creek, by McCaffery and Smith (Vancouver: Anonbeyond, 1978);

Every Way Oakly (Edmonton: Stephen Scobie, 1978);

Six Fillious, by McCaffery, Nichol, Robert Filliou, George Brecht, Dick Higgins, and Dieter Rot (Milwaukee: Membrane Press, 1978);

The Abstract Ruin: A Draft of Book I (Toronto: Coach House, 1978);

Epithalamium (Toronto: Underwhich Editions, 1979);

In England Now That Spring: polaroid poems, found texts, visions & collaborations records of a journey thru Scotland & England May 1978, by McCaffery and Nichol (Toronto: Aya Press, 1979);

Intimate Distortions: A Displacement of Sappho (Erin, Ont.: Press Porcépic, 1979);

Legend, by McCaffery, Bruce Andrews, Charles Bernstein, Ray Di Palma, and Ron Silliman (New York: Segue Foundation, 1980);

The Scenarios (Toronto: League of Canadian Poets, 1980);

Summary (Toronto: Curvd H&Z, 1981);

The Prose Tattoo: Collected Performance Scores, by McCaffery, Nichol, Dutton, and Barreto-Rivera as The Four Horsemen (Milwaukee: Membrane Press, 1983);

Knowledge Never Knew (Montreal: Véhicule Press, 1983);

Panopticon (Vancouver & Toronto: Blewointment Press, 1984);

North of Intention: Critical Writings 1973–86 (New York: Roof, 1986);

Evoba: The Investigations Meditations (Toronto: Coach House, 1987);

The Black Debt (London, Ont.: Nightwood Editions, 1989);

The Entries (London: Writers Forum, 1990);

Theory of Sediment (Vancouver: Talonbooks, 1991);

Modern Reading: Poems 1969–1990 (London: Writers Forum, 1991);

Rational Geomancy: The Kids of the Book-Machine. The Collected Research Reports of the Toronto Research Group 1972–83, by McCaffery and Nichol (Vancouver: Talonbooks, 1992);

The Cheat of Words (Toronto: ECW Press, 1996);

Poetry in the Pissoir (Calgary: House Press, 2000);

Prior to Meaning: The Protosemantic and Poetics (Evanston, Ill.: Northwestern University Press, 2001);

Seven Pages Missing: Selected Texts, 2 volumes (Toronto: Coach House, 2001, 2002);

Bouma Shapes (Gran Canaria, Spain: Zasterle Press, 2002).

RECORDINGS: *CaNADAda,* performed by McCaffery, bpNichol, Paul Dutton, and Rafael Barreto-Rivera as The Four Horsemen, 1972;

The 4 Horsemen at the Western Front, performed by McCaffery, Nichol, Dutton, and Barreto-Rivera, 1977;

Live in the West, performed by McCaffery, Nichol, Dutton, and Barreto-Rivera as The Four Horsemen, 1978;

Research on the Mouth, read by McCaffery, Underwhich Audiographics, 1979;

Wot We Wukkers Want / One Step to the Next, read by McCaffery, Underwhich Audiographics, 1979;

Manicured Noise, read by McCaffery and Richard Truhlar, Underwhich Audiographics, 1981;

Avoiding the Beautiful, read by McCaffery and Whitney Smith, Underwhich Audiographics, 1982;

Whispers, read by McCaffery, David Lee, and Bill Smith, blewointment Audio, 1984.

OTHER: *Sound Poetry: A Catalogue,* edited by McCaffery and bpNichol (Toronto: Underwhich Editions, 1978);

"for a poetry of blood," in *Text-Sound Texts,* edited by Richard Kostelanetz (New York: Morrow, 1980), p. 275;

"The Unreadable Text," in *Code of Signals: Recent Writing in Poetics,* edited by Michael Palmer (Berkeley, Cal.: North Atlantic, 1983), pp. 219–223;

"Intraview," in *The L=A=N=G=U=A=G=E Book,* edited by Bruce Andrews and Charles Bernstein (Carbondale: Southern Illinois University Press, 1984), p. 189;

"The Line of Prose," in *The Line in Postmodern Poetry,* edited by Robert Frank and Henry Sayre (Urbana: University of Illinois Press, 1988), pp. 198–199;

"Insufficiencies of Theory to Poetical Economy," in *The Ends of Theory,* edited by Jerry Herron, Dorothy Huson, Ross Pudaloff, and Robert Strozier (Detroit: Wayne State University Press, 1996), pp. 257–271;

"The Scandal of Sincerity: Towards a Levinasian Poetics," *Pretexts: Studies in Writing and Culture,* 6 (November 1997): 167–190;

"From Phonic to Sonic: The Emergence of the Audio-Poem," in *Sound States: Innovative Poetics and Acoustical Technologies,* edited by Adalaide Morris (Chapel Hill: University of North Carolina Press, 1997), pp. 149–168;

"Writing as a General Economy," in *Artifice and Indeterminacy: An Anthology of New Poetics,* edited by Christopher Beach (Tuscaloosa: University of Alabama Press, 1998), pp. 201–221;

Imagining Language, edited by McCaffery and Jed Rasula (Cambridge, Mass.: MIT Press, 1998);

"Parapoetics: A Soft Manifesto for the Nomad Cortex," <http://

www.poetics.yorku.ca article.php?sid=5&PHPSESS ID=1402644f90ec616ab1c8>.

SELECTED PERIODICAL PUBLICATIONS–UNCOLLECTED: "The Roots of Present Writing," by McCaffery, Daphne Marlatt, George Bowering, Fred Wah, Robert Creeley, Peter Culley, Victor Coleman, bpNichol, Joel Oppenheimer, and Robert Bertholf, and "Language Writing: From Productive to Libidinal Economy," by McCaffery, *Credences: A Journal of Twentieth-Century Poetry and Poetics,* 2 (Fall–Winter 1983): 211–228, 289–303;

"Jackson MacLow: Samasara in Lagado," *North Dakota Quarterly,* 55 (Fall 1987): 185–201;

"Zarathrustran 'Pataphysics,'" *Open Letter,* 9 (Winter 1997): 11–22;

"False Portrait of bpNichol as Charles Lamb," *Open Letter,* 10 (Fall 1998): 34–36;

"Blaser's Deleuzian Folds," *Discourse,* 20 (Fall 1998): 99–122;

Untitled, *Boundary 2,* 26 (Spring 1999): 29–30.

Steve McCaffery has inspired and represented experimental poetry in Canada for more than thirty years. Reading, writing, and researching in eccentric directions, he has produced a body of work that radically resists mainstream poetic theory. He has influenced nearly every innovative poetic movement in North America, including sound poetry and concrete poetry, as well as movie and video production, musical composition, and multimedia performance. Much of his work is described as "language poetry," "langpo," or "L=A=N=G=U=A=G=E" poetry, placing him in a community of writers that includes Charles Bernstein, Bruce Andrews, Lyn Hejinian, Barrett Watten, Ron Silliman, and Bob Perelman. Antilyrical, politicized, vocal, visual, self-reflexive, libidinal, and innovative in the extreme, his writing has created a whole new lexicon of poetic awareness. The short-listing of the first volume of his *Seven Pages Missing: Selected Texts* (2001, 2002) for the Governor General's Literary Award for Poetry in 2001 may signal the arrival of "language poetry" and the antilyrical into the mainstream canon of Canadian poetry.

McCaffery was born on 24 January 1947 in Sheffield, England, to Edwin and Kathleen McCaffery; his father was a glassblower and subsequently became a postman. He has no siblings. He went to Holy Rood Junior School and Broadview Technical Grammar School, both in Barnsley, Yorkshire, and received a joint B.A. Honors degree in philosophy and English from Hull University in 1968. While at Hull he published several visual poems in a small magazine, *Poet's Eye.* He married Margaret Shapland in 1968, and the two moved to Canada to enter the M.A. program at York University in Toronto. McCaffery completed his masters degree in 1969. His influences at this time included Gertrude Stein, Louis Zukofsky, John Cage, the Black Mountain poets, and the growing number of "language writers." These influences all fall into the category of "disjunctive" writing, which questions frames of reference and in which, according to Marjorie Perloff's *Radical Artifice* (1991), "Making strange . . . occurs at the level of phrasal and sentence structure rather than at the level of the image cluster." Also in 1969 he met the poet bpNichol (Barrie Phillip Nichol), and the two began a collaborative relationship that changed the way language functions in Canadian writing. McCaffery published a series of poetry chapbooks: *Six Concrete Poems* (1969), *Ground Plans for a Speaking City* (1969), *Cap(ture)* (1969), *Melons* (1970), *Transitions to the Beast: Post-Semiotic Poetry* (1970), and *Maps: A Different Landscape* (1971), and, with Nichol, *Parallel Texts* (1971) and *Collbrations* (1971). Much of his chapbook work consists of concrete poetry. In 1972 McCaffery and Nichol began calling themselves the Toronto Research Group (TRG) and embarked on a series of experiments in theoretical and critical writing that were published in the magazine *Open Letter,* edited by Frank Davey. The magazine also published their manifesto:

MANIFESTO

1) all theory is transient & after the fact of writing

2) writing never eliminates the need for action but action can sometimes eliminate the need for writing

3) where action eliminates the need for writing research can function to discover new uses for potentially outdated forms & techniques

4) where writing & action are necessary research can function to find new ways to unify them

5) all manifestos are simply statements of progressive awareness

6) all research is symbiotic & cannot exist separate from writing

7) no form or technique exists separate from what is said

first manifesto (may 1972) lost. second manifesto of the TORONTO RESEARCH GROUP january 5 1973.

The writings were published in book form in 1992 as *Rational Geomancy: The Kids of the Book-Machine: The Collected Research Reports of the Toronto Research Group 1972–83.*

McCaffery and Nichol also joined Paul Dutton and Rafael Barreto-Rivera to form The Four Horsemen, a sound-poetry ensemble that performed across Canada and around the world. These performances were captured in the audio recordings *CaNADAda* (1972), *Live in the West* (1978), and *Research on the Mouth* (1979) and the video *The 4 Horsemen at the Western Front* (1977). (The title *CaNADAda* is a combination of *nada,* Spanish for "nothing" and, in Hindu mythology, "the sound that never ends"; the name of the early-twentieth-century European poetic movement *Dada;* and *Canada.*) Transcripts of The Four Horsemen's performances were published as *Horse d'Oeuvres* in 1976 and *The Prose Tattoo: Collected Performance Scores* in 1983. Sound poetry, which can be traced to the Russian and Italian Futurists and the Dadaists, rejects technological enhancement and manipulation of voices, depends heavily on improvisation, emphasizes the unrepeatability of performance, and accesses prelinguistic and unconscious drives.

One of McCaffery's early "books" of poetry is technically not a book; it could, perhaps, more appropriately be considered an antibook. *Carnival: Panel One: 1967–1970* (1973) is a "cartographic" project made up of sixteen offset sheets of typewritten text, an "errata" sheet, and a postcard with the instructions: "In order to destroy this book please tear each page carefully along the perforation. The panel is assembled by laying out pages in a square of four." When arranged in this way, the sheets form a mural-like, multipanel visual poem; but to create the poem, the book has to be dismantled.

McCaffery's goal in his first full-length book, *Dr. Sadhu's Muffins: A Book of Written Readings* (1974), was to eliminate "all the *writing* from the writing" by randomly selecting fragments from literary and nonliterary texts. The title poem uses a "core structure of 13 phrases selected at random from the *Toronto Globe & Mail* and repeated and permuted according to a predetermined chance programme." Other source texts include the *Concise Oxford Dictionary,* works by William Shakespeare and John Donne, the *I Ching,* and *Life* and *Scientific American* magazines. Another piece, "Anamorphoses," is a series of attempts to "describe out of definition" and transform the thing "known into the thing seen." A third, "The Redwood Suite," which includes speed instructions such as "slow" and "moderately fast," was first performed at Carleton University in 1973.

'Ow's "Waif" (1975) is also made up of poems written formulaically from previously published texts; each poem is created from a "supply-text" by reading vertically or diagonally or making random word choices. The title poem is based on Henry Wadsworth Longfellow's poem "Waif." Other supply-texts include Sir Isaac Newton's *Opticks* (1730), Evelyn Waugh's biography of Edmund Campion (1935), Susanna Moodie's *Roughing It in the Bush, or, Life in Canada* (1852), a trigonometry textbook, Jacques Maritain's *Creative Intuition in*

Art and Poetry (1953), Edgar Allan Poe's "The Poetic Principle" (1850), and John Cage's *A Year from Monday* (1968). The supply-text for "Ten Portraits" is an interview with several prostitutes. One of McCaffery's messages is that exciting language effects can happen even without traditional human agency guiding the writing.

Carnival: Panel Two: 1971–1975 (1977) is made up of twenty-two sheets along with photocopied, rubber-stamped, stenciled, and handwritten texts. Both *Carnival* panels demand that the act of recomposition be accomplished "nonsequentially," a point McCaffery and Nichol emphasize in *Rational Geomancy*. The emphasis in these pieces on the reader's participation indicates McCaffery's interest in challenging the boundary between writer and reader. Both panels are available on-line at the Coach House Books website, <http://www.chbooks.com./archives/online_books/carnival/>.

In 1978 McCaffery published the chapbook *Every Way Oakly,* a series of "homolinguistic translations" of Stein's *Tender Buttons* (1912). McCaffery translates each of Stein's poems from English to English in a "free" rendering; sound, associations, and rhythms guide the process. Some of the original content and syntax remain, but new poetic possibilities emerge.

By collaborating with Nichol on *In England Now That Spring: polaroid poems, found texts, visions & collaborations records of a journey thru Scotland & England May 1978* (1979) McCaffery challenges the notion of the autonomous and definable authorial presence. Further challenging this notion are the reproductions of engravings underlying the poems. The book also includes "notebook" entries that comprise all of McCaffery's writings from a certain period of time. Long-distance collaboration with the American "language" poets Bernstein, Andrews, Silliman, and Ray Di Palma resulted in *Legend* (1980).

McCaffery and his wife were divorced in 1983. That same year McCaffery published *Knowledge Never Knew,* in which aphorisms run across the bottom of the page and an historical calendar runs across the top, with white space separating the two "bands." The historical calendar goes from 1 January to 19 April, but the years vary widely, and the historical reference often does not match the date. This kind of indeterminacy and paradox is typical of McCaffery's oeuvre.

Panopticon (1984) is McCaffery's only "novel," but it is hardly a sellout to a more accessible form: the book is a self-reflexive exposé of the nature of narrative. The plot, which is akin to a murder mystery, is confounded by embedded books and movies titled *The Mind of Pauline Brain, The Mark, Panopticon,* and *Summer Alibi.* The book is thus less about plot than about textual production itself. The title refers to the eighteenth-century British Utilitarian philosopher Jeremy Bentham's design for a model prison in which the guards could observe all of

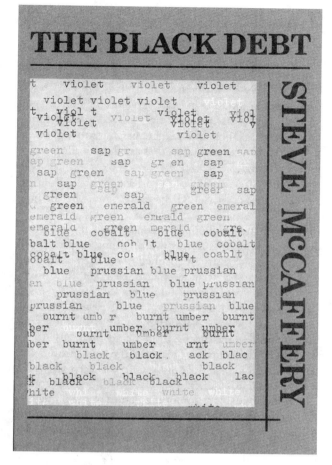

Paperback cover for the first edition, 1989
(Bruccoli Clark Layman Archives)

the inmates at all times; in McCaffery's text such an authoritative center of surveillance is obliterated. Uncertainty is materially manifested by the gluing together of two sets of pages so that the text inside is only partially readable. Filled with maze-like contradictions and obfuscations, the book reveals the structural effects that make up traditional narratives.

McCaffery's *North of Intention: Critical Writings 1973–86* (1986) was one of the few collections of essays about experimental writing in Canada and the United States at the time. Particularly influential was "Writing as a General Economy," in which McCaffery challenges traditional models of writing based on principles of capitalist exchange in favor of writing that interrupts and frustrates traditional modes of reading and revises conventional meaning-making processes.

In *Evoba: The Investigations Meditations* (1987) McCaffery uses drawings and cartoon-like sections to draw attention to the concrete aspects of printed text and the physical page. This aspect of his work is influenced by the Noigandres group in Brazil, especially Luiz Angelo Pinto and Decio Pigniatari, and by Ian Hamilton Finlay in England. *Evoba* is *above* spelled backward, as in proposition 160 of Ludwig Wittgenstein's *Philosophical Investigations* (1953), a work that is referred to extensively in the text. The title is emblematic of McCaffery's interest in "paragrammatic" techniques such as anagrams, palindromes, charades, and homolinguistic translation. Such language play subverts intention and produces meanings that are fluid, multiple, and indeterminate.

In 1989 McCaffery was a lecturer at the University of California at San Diego. That same year he published *The Black Debt,* which seems at first glance to be a new departure for him: it is constructed in a uniform and continuous manner as a long uninterrupted block of large type with strictly justified margins. The title is a Hegelian term for writing, and, once again, McCaffery addresses the act of writing in the book. *The Black Debt* consists of two sections: "Lag" and "An Effect of Cellophane." The sole formal difference between the two is the use of commas in the former and their absence in the latter. The transition between the two sections is a comment on syntax, grammar, and the ways in which text moves across junctures. "Lag," with its punctuated rhythm, is an exploration of the nature of the phrase: as the text proceeds, accumulated meaning scatters in the wake of the momentum of the individual phrases. McCaffery is responding here to the theorist Jean-François Lyotard's *Le Différend* (1983; translated as *The Differend: Phrases in Dispute* (1988). At the same time, the text critiques advertising through ironic use of commercial language and the evocation of billboards, ticker tape, and electronic mail. The narrative flow is interrupted as the reader moves from one phrase to the next, and even within phrases there are impediments: negations such as "sentence not sentence," numbers, and illogical definitions such as "three means a half-inch width." Each phrase is syntactically correct but semantically unstable. The phrases are language games of the most evasive kind in which words reinvent themselves and parts of speech are made strange. There is no clear image, no narrative motion, no autobiography, no exposition; for example,

ephemerides

by the hour, when all he asked was what will take its place, the sugar's case as evidence poured inward, pact not packed, Hollywood advancing messages on waves, the form the comets took in plunging, this official as a moment where culture went wrong, discovered to recognize both bodies are media, after Halloween one is drawn back to inference, the instrument which comes between its player and the music. . . .

McCaffery is, however, making statements about the world: as a cultural critic he is commenting on consumed language and information overload. *The Black Debt* was short-listed for the 1990 Before Columbus Award.

In *Theory of Sediment* (1991) McCaffery plays with the ideas of definition in "The Entries" and of lists in "The Printer to the Reader." Formal experiments include a poem, "Invariant," that submits to the rigors of a nine-character line, including spaces:

who is to
an act of
on some i
ink unity

in bussed
to return
pranks up
a what in

nest zero
chats fit
frivolity
colonized

Another poem, "Gnotes," runs parallel to a sentence by Michel Foucault that is printed vertically down the page letter by letter. The most critically discussed piece in the book is "Lastworda." This poem begins as continuous stream-of-consciousness prose but "retreats a few lines for each decade" as it traces the histories of the words; by the end of the poem the language has been transformed into Old English. *Lastworda* is Old English for "memorial" and is the last word of the poem:

naman thu sorgodest andwlita hal be wif eal areodode fram dam on geat cnihtum scufan mid motan in scynscada ænigne hetelic weard fela heahfæstne fleon lastworda.

Theory of Sediment was nominated for the Governor General's Literary Award for Poetry in 1992.

From 1993 to 1995 McCaffery was a lecturer in English at Queen's University in Kingston, Ontario. He received the Gertrude Stein Award for Innovative American Poetry for 1993–1994 and again for 1994–1995. In 1996 he published the collection *The Cheat of Words,* which, though it is nonlyrical and nonnarrative, seems more accessible than his other texts. Poems such as "Future Indicative" and "Writing a Sand Thinking" can almost be read as semilyrical pieces. "A Book: For Mallarmé" chants a catalogue of imaginary pages. In this book, as in much of his more recent work, McCaffery employs the "Lucretian clinamen," which Darren

Wershler-Henry described in a review in *Books in Canada* (March 1997) as "a minimal and at times almost imperceptible swerve away from an expected trajectory" (in the Epicurean metaphysics, as described by Lucretius in his first-century B.C. poem *De rerum natura* [On the Nature of Things], individual atoms sometimes spontaneously deviate from a straight downward path as they fall through the infinite void). In the poems this "swerve" constitutes subtle departures from normative syntax and habituated phrasings.

The most prominent poem in the book, "Teachable Texts," juxtaposes formal philosophical discourse with popular references such as "Donny Osmond is a linguist." In this clash of languages the popular becomes open to philosophical engagement, and high discourse is leveled, coexisting with Donald Duck. As in *Carnival* and many of his other books McCaffery includes instructions for reading his poems and self-reflexive references to the act of writing them: "The Self meets thought as thought / becomes a thinking other. // Truth / as a neighbourhood." "Instruction Manual" plays with the form of the definition: "Open the blade to read the word knife. // PROPERTY. // A loop-hole logic. // Films developed under water."

McCaffery married the poet Karen Mac Cormack in 1997. He earned his Ph.D. from the State University of New York at Buffalo in 1998. That same year he co-edited with Jed Rasula *Imagining Language,* an annotated anthology of two centuries of work on the written and spoken sign, and became an assistant professor of English at York University. There he founded and became director of the North American Center for Interdisciplinary Poetics (NACIP). He was promoted to associate professor in 2001.

Prior to Meaning: The Protosemantic and Poetics (2001) collects McCaffery's theoretical writings and research of the 1990s with chapters on Gilles Deleuze; Jacques Derrida; Alfred Jarry; the Marquis de Sade; Illya Prigogine and Isabelle Stengers, the founders of the science of nonequilibrium thermodynamics; Gottfried Wilhelm Leibniz; and Emmanuel Lévinas. He introduces the collection by stating that it is a study of "the ways in which language behaves rather than how it is designed to function." In a sophisticated and dense study McCaffery attempts to elucidate the ignored aspects of Ferdinand de Saussure's work on language function. McCaffery terms this counterlinguistic vision "protosemantic" and delineates three associated concepts: "the clinamen, the monad-fold, and the dissipative structure." McCaffery develops a language to describe the entropic—nonsystematic and noncommunicative—effects of material texts rather than the false security offered by the scientific models of linguistics and semantics. While seemingly opposed to traditional systems of

language study, McCaffery firmly locates himself in contemporary scientific thought, which recognizes the instability of natural systems: "if letters are to words what atoms are to bodies–heterogenous, deviant, collisional, and transmorphic–then we need earnestly to rethink what guarantees stability to verbal signs." Poets on whom McCaffery writes in *Prior to Meaning* include Mac Cormack, Robin Blaser, Charles Olson, and Jackson Mac Low.

The two volumes of McCaffery's *Seven Pages Missing* are essentially a history of poetic innovation in Canada. His collected work in these volumes ranges from 1968 to 2000 and covers the gamut of poetic styles from sound-poetry scores to concrete poems, long poems, and translations. McCaffery's work over those three decades charts the tensions that will remain in North American poetics for decades to come. No other Canadian author has consistently challenged latent or standardized poetic convention in so many ways. Volume two includes scores and concrete poems that have been carefully reproduced by Coach House Books. One of the scores is for "Dilemma of the Memo," commissioned for the "Exercise for the Ear" concert at New Langton Arts in San Francisco in 1991, curated by Dave Barrett. Performers at this event included Steve Adams on soprano saxophone, Ralph Cainey on contrabass clarinet, and Bill Fairbanks on bass, as well as Hejinian, Pauline Oliveros, and Nathaniel Mackey. The volume also includes a fragment of McCaffery's as-yet- unpublished work "The Abstract Ruin." A portion of the manuscript, *The Abstract Ruin: A Draft of Book I,* was published in 1978. "The Abstract Ruin" is the record of McCaffery's reading of Edward Gibbon's *The History of the Decline and Fall of the Roman Empire* (1776–1788) and Ezra Pound's *Cantos* simultaneously. In *Seven Pages Missing* McCaffery describes the choice of title:

> "Ruin" descends from the Latin "ruina," itself deriving from "ruere," to rush down. Ruination is a syntactic motion as through a porous agent. "Abstract" comes from the Latin "abstrahere," to draw away. The weave of thread, the path of syntagm, the author's composition ambivalence. None of this may hold.

Volume two also includes "Poetics: A Statement," in which McCaffery explains that "I have no steady poetics, no position or school that I defend, no fixist stance on art or anything else." In taking this "non-stance" McCaffery makes critical response to his work a difficult task.

McCaffery's *Bouma Shapes* was published in the Canary Islands in 2002. It is made up of shorter poems written between 1974 and 2002 and includes two series, "Ars Poetica" and "Pastoral," that reinvent archaic modes of thought through parody, irreverent play, and disjunction. The title of the book refers to the typographical development of words as separate units. McCaffery addresses the work of other poets, including Robert Creeley, Geoffrey Chaucer, Rainer Maria Rilke, Samuel Taylor Coleridge, and Paul Celan.

In 2004 McCaffery was appointed David Gray Professor of Poetry and Letters at the State University of New York at Buffalo, where he continues to direct NACIP. He has performed his poetry worldwide, and his work has been translated into French, Spanish, Chinese, and Hungarian. In 2007 he was editing an annotated collection of his letters to the poet Dick Higgins, which span more than three decades. The poet Stephen Cain is assisting him in this project, which is tentatively titled "The Zebras' Progress."

Critical attention to Steve McCaffery's work has come from Canada and the United States. In Canada his own work and critical writing on him frequently appear in journals such as *Open Letter* and *West Coast Line*. American critics such as Perloff and George Hartley have written extensively on McCaffery's books. Most critics associate him with the "language poets" at Buffalo and in San Francisco. While McCaffery and poets such as Bernstein share many aesthetic principles, much of McCaffery's sound poetry and many of his visual poems fall outside the loose rubric of "language writing."

Interviews:

Clint Burnham, "Unpunctuated Nature: Steve McCaffery," in *The Power to Bend Spoons: Interviews with Canadian Novelists,* edited by Beverley Daurio (Toronto: Mercury, 1998), pp. 105–114;

Peter Jaeger, "An Interview with Steve McCaffery on the TRG," *Open Letter,* 10 (Fall 1998): 77–96.

Bibliography:

bpNichol, "The Annotated, Anecdoted, Beginnings of a Critical Checklist of the Published Works of Steve McCaffery," *Open Letter,* 6 (Fall 1978): 67–92.

References:

Raphael Barret-Rivera, "Dr. Sadhu's Semi-Optics, or How to Write a Virtual-Novel by the Book: Steve McCaffery's *Panopticon,*" *Open Letter,* 6 (Fall 1978): 39–48;

Charles Bernstein, "Panoptical Artifice," *Open Letter,* 6 (Fall 1978): 9–16;

Bernstein, *A Poetics* (Cambridge, Mass.: Harvard University Press, 1992), pp. 9–89;

Christian Bök, "Nor the Fun Tension: Steve McCaffery and His Critical 'Paradoxy,'" *Open Letter,* 8, no. 3 (1992): 90–103;

Bök and Darren Wershler-Henry, "Walls That Are Cracked: A Paralogue on Panels 1 and 2 of Steve McCaffery's *Carnival,*" *Open Letter,* 10 (Summer 1999): 24–40;

Gerald Burns, "McCaffery's Moriarty: An Alchemy," *West Coast Line,* 26 (1992): 79–85;

Michael Coffey, "Grammatology & Economy," *Open Letter,* 6 (Fall 1978): 27–38;

Johanna Drucker, *Figuring the Word: Essays on Books, Writing and Visual Poetics* (New York: Granary, 1998);

George Hartley, *Textual Politics and the Language Poets* (Bloomington: Indiana University Press, 1989), pp. 66–72, 82–84;

Brian Henderson, "New Syntaxes in McCaffery and Nichol: Emptiness, Transformation, Serenity," *Essays on Canadian Writing,* 37 (1989): 1–29;

Peter Jaeger, *ABC of Reading TRG* (Burnaby: Talonbooks, 1999);

Alan R. Knight, "The Toronto Research Group Reports," *Line,* 5 (Spring 1985): 90–103;

Marjorie Perloff, "Inner Tension / In Attention: Steve McCaffery's Book Art," *Visible Language,* 25 (Spring 1991): 173–191;

Perloff, "'Modernism' at the Millennium," in her *21st-Century Modernism: The "New Poetics"* (Oxford: Blackwell, 2000), pp. 190–200;

Perloff, *Poetry on and off the Page: Essays for Emergent Occasions* (Evanston, Ill.: Northwestern University Press, 1998);

Perloff, *Radical Artifice* (Chicago: University of Chicago Press, 1991), pp. 93–133;

Perloff, "Signs Are Taken for Wonders: On Steve McCaffery's 'Lag,'" in *Contemporary Poetry Meets Modern Theory,* edited by Antony Easthope and John O. Thompson, Theory/Culture Series, volume 10 (Toronto: University of Toronto Press, 1991), pp. 108–114;

Perloff, "'Voice Whisht through Thither Flood': Steve McCaffery's *Panopticon* and *North of Intention,*" in her *Poetic License: Essays in Modernist and Postmodernist Lyric* (Evanston, Ill.: Northwestern University Press, 1990), pp. 285–296;

Steve Smith, "Language at the Limits: The Work of Steve McCaffery," *Poetry Canada Review,* 7 (Summer 1986): 64;

Barrett Watten, *Total Syntax* (Carbondale: Southern Illinois University Press, 1985), pp. 54–55.

Don McKay

(25 June 1942 –   )

Gary Draper
St. Jerome's University

BOOKS: *Moccasins on Concrete* (Montreal: Content, 1972);

Air Occupies Space (Windsor, Ont: Sesame Press, 1973);

Long Sault (London, Ont.: Applegarth Follies, 1975);

Lependu (Ilderton, Ont.: Nairn Coldstream, 1978);

Lightning Ball Bait (Toronto: Coach House Press, 1980);

Birding, or Desire (Toronto: McClelland & Stewart, 1983);

Sanding down This Rocking Chair on a Windy Night (Toronto: McClelland & Stewart, 1987);

Night Field (Toronto: McClelland & Stewart, 1991);

Apparatus (Toronto: McClelland & Stewart, 1997);

Fly Away Home: A Few Metamorphoses (Victoria: Published for the Hawthorne Society by Reference West, 1997);

Aria (Stratford, Ont.: Trout Lily Press, 2000);

The Book of Moonlight (Victoria: Outlaw Editions, 2000);

Another Gravity (Toronto: McClelland & Stewart, 2000);

Vis à Vis: Fieldnotes on Poetry & Wilderness (Wolfville, N.S.: Gaspereau Press, 2001);

Varves (Edmonton: Extra Virgin Press, 2003);

Camber: Selected Poems 1983–2000 (Toronto: McClelland & Stewart, 2004);

Deactivated West 100 (Kentville, N.S.: Gaspereau Press, 2005);

Strike/Slip (Toronto: McClelland & Stewart, 2006).

Collection: *Field Marks: The Poetry of Don McKay,* edited by Méira Cook (Waterloo, Ont.: Wilfrid Laurier University Press, 2006).

SELECTED PERIODICAL PUBLICATIONS–
UNCOLLECTED: "Dot, Line and Circle: A Structural Approach to Dylan Thomas's Imagery," *Anglo-Welsh Review,* 18, no. 41 (1969): 69–80;

"The Impulse to Epic in Goderich Ontario or The Huron County Pioneer Museum as a Form of Expression," *Brick,* 2 (January 1978): 28–32;

"At Work and Play in *The Ledger,*" *Open Letter,* fifth series, 8–9 (1984): 146–153;

"Crafty Dylan and the Altarwise Sonnets: 'I build a flying tower and I pull it down,'" *University of Toronto Quarterly,* 55 (Summer 1986): 375–394;

"What Shall We Do with a Drunken Poet? Dylan Thomas' Poetic Language," *Queen's Quarterly,* 93–94 (Winter 1986): 794–807;

"Local Wilderness," *Fiddlehead,* 169 (Autumn 1991): 5–6.

In the 1980s Don McKay emerged as one of the most influential poets and editors of his generation. His books of poetry have been short-listed for the Governor General's Literary Award four times and have won twice; two were short-listed for the prestigious Griffin Poetry Prize; and his only book of prose was nominated for the Governor General's Literary Award for Nonfiction. He is the senior editor of one of Canada's most important poetry publishers, Brick Books, and has served as the editor of Atlantic Canada's premier literary journal, *The Fiddlehead.* He has played significant roles in the literary life of Canada as both creator and mentor.

Donald Fleming McKay was born in Owen Sound, Ontario, on 25 June 1942 to John Brown McKay, a journalist, and Margaret Janet Fleming McKay, a social worker. Shortly after his birth the family moved to Cornwall, Ontario, where his father became editor of the *Cornwall Standard Freeholder.* McKay attended Bishop's University for two years; he then transferred to the University of Western Ontario, where he received his B.A. in 1965 and his M.A. in 1966. He taught English at the University of Saskatchewan from the mid to late 1960s. In 1971 he earned his Ph.D. from the University of Wales at Swansea with a dissertation titled "Mythological Elements in the Work of Dylan Thomas" and became an assistant professor of English at the University of Western Ontario.

In 1973 McKay published *Air Occupies Space,* a collection of twenty-five poems that had appeared in *Canadian Forum, Quarry,* and several short-lived literary

Don McKay (photograph by Jan Zwicky; courtesy of Kate Kennedy, Gaspereau Press)

journals. "Taking Your Baby to the Junior Hockey Game" evokes the casual rhythms of speech crossed with song; the diction is unpretentious and demotic, and the poem is concerned with the ordinary activities of ordinary people:

> Watch for it to happen out there on the ice:
> This music they fight for.
> You can feel her beside you as though poised in front of a net
> Circling.
> Circling.
> Christ, you'll say,
> Baby if you were a forty-three-year-old Montreal potato
>   merchant
> I'd be your five iron.

The poem is a series of metaphors for relationship. It also plays with the idea of metaphor itself, moving from the cryptic and dense "I would be your hawk / I would be silence / Forests" to the elaborate and funny:

> And baby, you'll say, if you conducted the Bach Society
>   Choir in town
> I'd be a dentist's wife
> Straining among sturdy contraltos after your unheard per-
>   fection
> Longing with them to devour your wrists, your boyish wit.

"Unmoving Day" includes the sort of vivid and surprising metaphors that have marked McKay's writing through much of his career: "Another hungry customer chats with the waitress / Biting into words like chunks of her inner thigh." The poem also provides hints of what became a major preoccupation for McKay: the epiphanic emergence and disappearance of a moment, place, or thing into and out of sudden importance or immanence.

> We enter this sudden pulse, this cleaving
> Catching its sprockets, churns
> And all slides safely back to landscape.

McKay's second book, *Long Sault* (1975), makes the transformation of the Long Sault into a part of the St. Lawrence Seaway a fable about the emasculation of wildness as the rapids give way to the placid and lifeless utility of the canal. In section 1, "So Long," the "once-famous Long Sault Rapids" have been put under human dominion and controlled. Things happen on schedule: "Boat leaving every 2 hours." Instead of straining or brimming behind the dam, the river "nuzzles the muddy shore as a vacuum cleaner / purrs across the carpet." But the closing lines of the third poem, "Bedrock," hint that the story is not over: "And only the Long Sault is laughing: Fuck your renaissance, get me a beer." Section 2, "Reading a Rapids," visits other rivers; in the opening poem, "Reading a Rapids on the Gens de Terre," the rapids have a voice that is seductive, enticing, arrogant, and erotic. The first poem in the third section portrays a campfire dance by the poet's daughter, Sally. The third poem, "Along about Then," is the first of McKay's longer narratives. In the final poem in this section, "The River is laughing to itself (continued)," the speakers make metaphors out of their experience: one says of the twisting creek they are following, "this heres a fallopian tube going nowheres"; another says, "nope this here's the ghost of the / pecker of the last guy tried to make the jump to the Capitachouane." But McKay's inclination always is to undercut the figurative by returning to the literal:

ah but there
I poise when
in
falls my papermate
ballpoint
pen.

In section 4, "The ghost with a hammer," the poem "Long Sault Blues" has the structure of a classic blues song: a call and response, with two couplets that are similar but not identical, followed by a third in which the tension is extended and then brought to a finish. The singer is the Long Sault's lover. In "The Long Sault Rapids in Kapuskasing" the rapids appears as a beer-drinking, saxophone-playing wisecracker: "Folks figured he was wise / he told me, because he never said a thing they could understand."

In 1975 McKay's friend and colleague at the University of Western Ontario, Stan Dragland, became the caretaker of a small chapbook-publishing venture, Nairn Publishing House in Ailsa Craig, Ontario, when the proprietors took what was meant to be a temporary leave. In 1976 Dragland and Jean McKay became co-editors of a literary magazine, Brick: A Journal of Reviews. Don McKay joined Nairn as editor and copublisher in 1977, and his Lependu (1978) was one of the first publications under the Nairn imprint. (The title page reads "Nairn Coldstream"; the McKays were living on Coldstream Road in Lobo Township, outside London, Ontario, at the time.) "Lependu"–the name means "the hanged man"–is Cornelius Burley, who was executed in London, Ontario, in 1830. Throughout the book the references to this figure slide between history and myth until the reader cannot be certain what is fact and what is fantasy. Language cannot be trusted, especially if it seems to be clear and simple. Lependu's essence is his very elusiveness:

You sense him inconspicuously coiled
on the unexpected stair, an old belt
perhaps a child's shed overalls he is waiting
to lurch–bottom falling out–back.

The world, as embodied by London, Ontario, responds to Lependu by clinging to the illusion of control. As his symbol of this illusion McKay uses the respectable corporate institution London Life Insurance. In the poem "London Life" he delineates the central oppositions on which the collection is structured: "The pastures of heaven are not more finely manicured / than the grass surrounding London Life," on the one hand, and a park where lunching secretaries sit "on / real grass which tickles their bare feet," on the other hand. The long final poem, "True confessions: a phrenology for the antlered man," is about language and history. It opens with ancient pictorial images: "Various figures were delineated on trees at the forks of the Thames, done with charcoal and vermillion, the most remarkable were the imitations of men with deer's heads–." This image is mediated not just by the poet's words but by those of the original recorder:

so says
Major Littlehales, who wrote them
doomed them in his diary as he passed through.

By the end of the collection Lependu has been transformed into a force of nature and life.

In 1980 McKay published Lightning Ball Bait, a collection of lyrics on a broad range of subjects that includes several poems from Air Occupies Space. The first section, "Nocturnal Animals," opens with "Fridge Nocturne," about the nighttime world of dreams and the unconscious, where words shift and elide, and silence has its own meaning. The title poem of the section evokes the theme of nature and language:

Two years ago the wolves took shape
in Lobo township, lifting the tombstone of its name
to lope across these snowy fields
                              between the woodlots
          spectral
                    legless as wind, their nostrils
wide with news of an automated pig barn
waiting for them like an all-night restaurant.

The second section, "Words for Snow," plays on the notion that the Inuit have an astonishing number of words for snow; the poems are about translation, both between languages and between language and the thing to which it refers. Seven brief lyrics trace the winter from "October Edge" to "March Snow" and probe the relation of language to the natural environment. "In blizzard," for example, takes the natural force of the title as a metaphor for the state of "prespeech." "Hoar Frost" suggests the sound of a cold engine cranking:

> My car
> also wishes it were dead, repeats
> were dead, were dead
> before it kicks and runs.

The first six of the eighteen lyrics in the final section, "After Supper," concern childhood, lost children, and the child's perception of the world. One poem, "Swallowings," comprises five short pieces, each on its own page, offering snapshots of swallows. In several cases, including the first piece, the layout of the text visually reflects the activity described:

> When we get close the barn goes
> schizophrenic, thoughts
> panicking from windows, swirling then
> banking, swirling
> more slowly, settling and
> returning to their
> nests.

The swallows in the fourth piece are onomatopoeic "snickersnacks." The word serves double duty, for the swallows are also "snacks" in the eyes of the hawk.

Though its output remained small, Nairn published several notable books, including Michael Ondaatje's *Elimination Dance* (1978) and Robert Kroetsch's *The Ledger* (1979). The name was changed to Brick/Nairn in 1979 and to Brick Books in 1981. McKay's commitment to publishing the work of both established and emerging poets is one of his most important contributions to the development of poetry in Canada.

The publication of *Birding, or Desire* (1983) by the major firm of McClelland and Stewart brought national attention to McKay's work. Almost two-thirds of the poems in *Lightning Ball Bait* reappear in the volume. Each of the four parts of the book corresponds to one of the seasons, beginning with autumn, although McKay does not identify them as such: not naming the seasons allows them to be free of the categorizations of the human mind and will. Part 1 deals with the encounter of imagination and language with nature, here in the form of birds; the bird is like, but is not subsumed under, its name. "Sparrows" in part 2 depicts bird sounds in anthropomorphized terms: the birds are "bickering," then they "jabber . . . clichés"; finally, their "group mind" begins to sing a scrambled version of "Je ne regrette rien," which ultimately blends with the poet's voice in a play on the word *feather:* "let the / space between our voices be my nom de plume." In parts 3 and 4 the bird sounds increasingly unite with music. The final poem in the volume, "September, Cyprus

Lake," set in an Ontario Provincial Park along the Bruce Trail, touches on the matter of naming—the human need to give voice to what is encountered and to impose, through language, significance on what is without obvious human "meaning":

> his name
> emerging into mind, fits strangely—
> —Goldfinch.

The fallen poplar leaves on the tent are "the shape of sharpened hearts" and are—McKay puts quotation marks around the word—"'insignia.'" But the poem follows the advice that it gives to the birds: "Sweet birds, / resist." Turning to "the causeless swell of Georgian Bay," the poem resists by refusing to impute meaning to the water:

> oracles in mumbo jumbo breaking
> boulder into pebble into
> syllables of sand
> which trickle through my fingers.

The poem ends with a simple observation of birds in motion:

> Redstarts: moving

Birding, or Desire won the Canadian Authors' Association Award for Poetry and was McKay's first to be short-listed for the Governor General's Literary Award for Poetry.

When *Sanding Down This Rocking Chair on a Windy Night* was published in 1987, McKay was living in Waterloo, Ontario; he was on sabbatical from the University of Western Ontario and had separated from his wife. The book is divided into seven parts. Most of the poems in the first section, which opens with "The Night Shift," are about translations or transformations. Section 2 consists of the extended prose poem from which the title of the volume is taken: in "Sanding Down This Rocking Chair on a Windy Night" the vaunted ash tree is transformed into a rocking chair, painted, then stripped back down to its essence. When, at the outset, the speaker says, "I'm erasing twenty years," the reader hears an echo of the impossible human longing to alter one's history. The twelve lyrics in section 3 explore the loss of love, the past, ghosts, sadness, dislocation, and disorientation. The poems in the fourth section, "Styles of Fall," describe ways of experiencing collective and individual falls from approximations of paradise or grace. One means of recovery is to see that the fall is not unique to human beings but is found in all forms of life. In "Buckling,"

Paperback cover for the first edition, 1987
(Bruccoli Clark Layman Archives)

Even the windhover makes mistakes—
some slight
miscalculation and he's prey
to ordinary cats.

Three poems make up the fifth section. The first, "Le Style," dazzles the reader with vivid and occasionally outrageous imagery; "Notes toward a Major Study of the Nose" allows McKay's gift for humor full rein; and "Sturnus Vulgaris" uses a starling as a kind of trickster figure. The sixth section, "Territoriality," shows how to become more like a bird by paying close attention; the final poem of this section, "Drinking Lake Superior," encourages readers to remake themselves, through reconnecting with nature, into the essence of what is human: "Blood bone flesh weather water." The concluding section, "Inhabiting the Map," identifies the place from which to begin the reconnecting. "For Laurel Creek," which opens the section, is a mock epic that

begins with the Miltonic apostrophe: "How Laurel Creek persists through the City of Waterloo . . . say / mongrel muse." Although it is a minor urban waterway that often runs underground, Laurel Creek is still a place where nature can be encountered. The speaker names all of the sad urban sites and then, addressing the creek with a respectful honorific, asks it to exert its power:

> o lost river
take revenge.
Waterbed King, reclaim your laureate, rising
up the drains like nightmare surging through the
Scotiabank Texas Bar-B-Q Bell Phonecentre . . .
> . . . lock us up
in some immersion course in wilderness, e.g.
Tom Thomson's *Stormy Sky.*

In 1991 McKay began teaching English and creative writing at the University of New Brunswick and editing *The Fiddlehead,* one of Canada's oldest and most influential literary journals. That same year he published *Night Field.* The first section, "The Wolf," opens with "Waking at the Mouth of the Willow River." An ode to the wordless connection with nature, it is about letting the thing be itself. "Black Spruce" takes the reader on a long hike along the White Gravel River near Lake Superior and ends in a quiet epiphany:

> All around us spruce
> distilling darkness out of sunlight,
> cradling it in their arms.

The title poem of section 2, "The Dumpe," borrows its epigraph from the *Oxford Companion to Music* to explain that a dumpe is "An old dance of which no one knows anything except that the word is generally used in a way that suggests a melancholy cast of expression." The opening sequence, "Bone Poems," looks at mind and body and then at bone in particular: "Bones attend to deep earth, while your heart is learning, year by year, to listen to your watch." The spirit is tethered to time and the body to earth, so that one is doubly bound; but there is music and dance, bone "carrying timbre of glaciers and French horns." Moreover, "it is through the bone self that the deaf hear symphonies." At the end of "Bone Poems" is a reminder of the readers' end:

> One day you will have to give yourselves
> to clutter and the ravages
> of air and be
> no good for nothing. . . .

The final section, "Metaxu," includes "Luke & Co.," an homage to a much-loved dog. Luke is an exemplar of living exactly in the place where one happens to be. The closing lines provide a perfect image of self-contained comfort:

> right here in this kitchen, Luke ate
> three-fifths of Hemingway's *For Whom*
> *The Bell Tolls,* fell asleep on his sofa
> wrapped in the perfect fur sleeping bag
>   of himself.

"Nostra," the long poem that closes the collection, spells out the meaning of the title of the section:

> No human being, Simone Weil declares,
> should be deprived of *metaxu*—creature comforts
> (home, country, culture) which allow
> the spirit to persist without the superhuman cost
> and benefit of sainthood.

The final lines of "Nostra," with their incantatory repetition and psalm-like structure of call and response, function as a kind of blessing of the earth and all its creatures. *Night Field* won the Governor General's Literary Award for Poetry.

In 1997 McKay left the University of New Brunswick and the editorship of *The Fiddlehead;* moved to Victoria, British Columbia, with his partner, Jan Zwicky; and published *Apparatus.* "Twinflower," the second poem in the first section of the book, "To Speak of Paths," is one of the most important for understanding McKay's sense of the relationship between humans and the rest of creation. The poem opens with the question "What do you call / the muscle we long with?" and answers, "A hole / which complements the heart." The poem goes on to evoke the biblical story of creation and Adam's naming of the animals: "Then God said, ok let's get this show / on the road, boy, get some names / stuck on these critters." At the end the speaker reads to a plant the description of it that appears in a field guide: "Listen now, / *Linnaea Borealis,* while I read of how / you have been loved." In succeeding poems McKay writes of other encounters and reflects on his own mortality. Section 2 includes "Snowlight," written "in memory of Jessica Naomi McKay Sharpe, 1980– 1994." The title of section 3, "Materiel," refers to the equipment used in war. The penultimate section, "Three Eclogues," evokes the tradition of English nature poetry: "Sunday Morning, Raisin River" praises one of McKay's favorite rivers; "On Foot to the Bypass Esso Postal Outlet" describes a journey to mail some poems; and in "Abandoned Tracks," Luke the dog has a nonfatal encounter with a passing train, after which,

> Back from the vet, stitched,
> still groggy from the drugs, he sensed the old throb
> troubling the air and struggled growling to his feet
> ready for round two.

The final section, "To Danceland," celebrates various kinds of apparatus. The alto saxophone and the drum are described in detailed, mechanical terms, in "Setting up the Drums" and "Acoustics of the Conical Tube." In "Ode to My Car" McKay devotes to the automobile the kind of attention he usually reserves for nature. In "Setting the Table" he takes on the ultimate challenge of ordinariness and familiarity with pieces on the knife, fork, and spoon. The final poem in the book is written for and about his mother, who is quoted in the epigraph: "No one is ever happier than when they're dancing." *Apparatus* was short-listed for the Governor General's Literary Award for Poetry.

In the latter half of the 1990s McKay was a major contributor to the poetry program of the Banff Centre for the Arts. During the same period he, Zwicky, and fellow poet Tim Lilburn presented a series of colloquia for writers and artists on wilderness, writing, and contemplation at St. Peter's College in Muenster, Saskatchewan.

McKay published *Another Gravity* in 2000. The poems of the opening section explore three of the basic concepts of flight: "Lift" and "Drag" echo many of the ideas that McKay explored in previous poems, while the concluding poem of the section, "Load," describes an encounter between the speaker and an exhausted white-throated sparrow and ends:

> I wanted
> very much to stroke it, and recalling
> several terrors of my brief
> and trivial existence, didn't.

The opening poem of the second section, "Before the Moon," examines the world that existed before the moon broke free of the Earth: "there was no second gravity and no / dark art of reflection. . . . there was no leaving home, and so / no dwelling in it either." Section 3 begins with "Nocturnal Migrants," the opening words of which are the title of the collection: "Another gravity" is the pull exerted by the moon. In a dream the speaker's feet take flight, leaving his body behind. In section 4 McKay recasts the myth of Icarus, who survives his fall and plans future airborne excursions: "Over and over he rehearses flight / and fall." At his moment of takeoff "he's up, / he's out of the story and into the song." In the penultimate poem of the section, "UFO," the speaker says that crows know something "about loss / made visible. Homing loves leaving / home." The section ends with "Plummet," the "unnumbered paths of air" are replaced by "the one shaft of your plunge." The final section opens with a revision of the opening poem of the volume, "Sometimes a Voice (2)." "Winter Solstice Moon: An Eclogue" is a meditation on the meaning of home. The moon and the ocean call to the speaker, and he responds; but in the end home is the cabin that enfolds the company of friends:

> Our cabin sat
> under its little party hat of lights, and to it,
> wanting its warmth, and supper, and to give our gifts,
> we went.

The volume closes with "On Leaving." It is about departure, including the departure into death: "There is a loneliness / which must be entered rather than resolved." The poet calls on the reader "To step off into darker darkness, / that no moon we call new." *Another Gravity* won the Governor General's Literary Award for

Poetry and was also a finalist for the 2001 Griffin Poetry Prize, which had become one of the country's most prestigious poetry awards despite having been launched only the preceding year.

In 2001 McKay published *Vis à Vis: Fieldnotes on Poetry & Wilderness,* a collection of essays. In the first piece, "Baler Twine: Thoughts on Ravens, Home and Nature Poetry," which was prompted by the appalling discovery of a dead raven, mutilated and strung up on a fence with baling twine, McKay reflects on four ideas that are central to his practice of poetry. "Materiel" is the "second-order appropriation" of something, which means not just its death but "the colonization of its death." By "wilderness" he means the quality of otherness possessed not just by wild places but by everything that is not oneself, including one's tools: "the capacity of all things to elude the mind's appropriations." "Poetic attention" is "a sort of readiness, a species of longing which is without the desire to possess." McKay begins "Remembering Apparatus: Poetry and the Visibility of Tools" by meditating on items set out for a yard sale; removed from their normal use, he observes, they become visible for the first time: "The wilderness is not just far away and dwindling, but implicit in the things we use every day." He moves on to a consideration of language as a tool; in metaphor, language is both magic and practical at the same moment:

> the excitement of metaphor stems from the injection of wilderness into language; it is quick, tricky, and . . . not easily domesticated to utility. The sadness of metaphor stems from an awareness of lost things as we waken to the teeming life outside the language we inhabit.

In the final piece, "Bushtits," McKay concludes that poetry "contemplates what language can't do: then it does something with language—in homage, or grief, or anger, or praise." Like the bushtits, who weave their homes out of scraps, the poet weaves with words. *Vis à Vis* was nominated for the Governor General's Literary Award for Nonfiction.

In 2004 Don McKay published *Camber: Selected Poems 1983–2000.* The range of dates would seem to exclude work published before *Birding, or Desire;* but because that book drew on all his previous publications, *Camber,* in fact, represents a summing up of his poetic oeuvre from the beginning. The poems are arranged chronologically, for the most part, and divided by original book titles. The only new poem in the collection is an untitled piece that opens the volume and begins:

Lifting off, letting go, seizing leave as though
departure were the first act ever, stepping
into air as sigh, as outbreath, hum,
commotion, whirr,
it's out of here, it's shucked us like
high school, like some stiff
chrysalis it lets fall from invisible
unfolding wings.

There are a few small changes in wording and in placement of the poems from their original appearance, but the collection offers the reader who is new to McKay's poetry the opportunity to experience his work in condensed form.

Interview:

Ken Babstock, "The Appropriate Gesture, or Regular Dumb-Ass Guy Looks at Bird," in *Where the Words Come From,* edited by Tim Bowling (Roberts Creek, B.C.: Nightwood Editions, 2002), pp. 44–61.

References:

Alanna F. Bondar, "Attending Guilt-Free Birdspeak and Treetalk: An Ecofeminist Reading of the 'Geopsyche' in the Poetry of Don McKay," *Canadian Poetry: Studies, Documents, Reviews,* 55 (Fall–Winter 2004): 65–85;

Bondar, "'That every feather is a pen, but living, // flying,' Desire: The Metapoetics of Don McKay's *Birding, or Desire,*" *Studies in Canadian Literature,* 19, no. 2 (1994): 14–29;

Kevin Bushell, "Don McKay and Metaphor: Stretching Language toward Wilderness," *Studies in Canadian Literature,* 21, no. 1 (1995): 37–55;

Adam Dickinson, "Lyric Ethics: Ecocriticism, Material Metaphoricity, and the Poetics of Don McKay and Jan Zwicky," *Canadian Poetry: Studies, Documents, Reviews,* 55 (Fall–Winter 2004): 34–52;

Stan Dragland, "Be-Wildering: The Poetry of Don McKay," *University of Toronto Quarterly,* 70 (Fall 2001): 881–888;

Susan Elmslie, "'Got to Meander If You Want to Get to Town': Excursion and Excursionist Figures in Don McKay," *Wascana Review,* 30 (Spring 1995): 77–92;

Sophia Forster, "Don McKay's Comic Anthropocentrism: Ecocriticism Meets 'Mr. Nature Poet,'" *Essays on Canadian Writing,* 77 (Fall 2002): 107–135;

Laurie Kruk, "To Scavenge and Invent: The Shamanic Journey in Don McKay's *Lependu,*" *Canadian Poetry: Studies, Documents, Reviews,* 24 (Spring–Summer 1989): 41–61.

Rohinton Mistry

(3 July 1952 –   )

Martin Genetsch
University of Trier

BOOKS: *Tales from Firozsha Baag* (Toronto: Penguin Canada, 1987); republished as *Swimming Lessons and Other Stories from Firozsha Baag* (Boston: Houghton Mifflin, 1989; London: Faber & Faber, 1992);

Such a Long Journey (Toronto: McClelland & Stewart, 1991; New York: Knopf, 1991; London: Faber & Faber, 1992);

A Fine Balance (Toronto: McClelland & Stewart, 1995; New York: Knopf, 1996; London: Faber & Faber, 1996);

Family Matters (Toronto: McClelland & Stewart, 2002; New York: Knopf, 2002; London: Faber & Faber, 2002).

PRODUCED SCRIPT: *Such a Long Journey,* motion picture, screenplay by Mistry and Sooni Taraporevala, Amy International Artists and The Film Works, 1998.

SELECTED PERIODICAL PUBLICATIONS—UNCOLLECTED: "Passages," *Books in Canada,* 17 (May 1988): 13–16;

"The More Important Things," *Canadian Fiction Magazine,* 65 (1989): 38–55;

"Edinburgh or Bust (Travelling in Scotland)," *Saturday Night Magazine,* 109 (May 1994): 39.

Most of Rohinton Mistry's fiction is set in the Parsi community of his native Bombay (today Mumbai), India. Concentrating on the individual's struggle to make life meaningful, his work is grounded in a liberal-humanist frame of reference and emphasizes solidarity, tolerance, and understanding. Mistry's works have won many prestigious awards and have been translated into many languages. He is a major voice on the contemporary Canadian literary scene.

Of Parsi descent, Mistry was born in Bombay on 3 July 1952 to Behram Mistry, who worked for an advertising agency, and Freny Mistry, née Jhaveri. He was the second of three brothers, the youngest of whom, Cyrus, also became a writer; he also has a

younger sister. He attended the Villa Theresa Primary School and St. Xavier High School. He watched the movies of Satyajit Ray and listened to the music of Ravi Shankar, but he also grew up with Enid Blyton's mystery and adventure novels and Captain W. E. Johns's Biggles books, enjoyed British theater and movies, and listened to American music. He learned to play the guitar at fourteen and later taught himself to play the harmonica, and he was a member of a folk-rock band that played the songs of Bob Dylan, Leonard Cohen, and Paul Simon and Art Garfunkel. Although Mistry is fluent in Hindi and Gujarati, he is most comfortable with English.

After completing a bachelor of science in economics and mathematics at St. Xavier's College of the University of Bombay in 1975, Mistry joined his fiancée, Freny Elavia, in Toronto, where she had been staying with relatives for a year. They had met at a music school in 1971 and had both attended Bombay University. Mistry became a Canadian citizen and married Elavia in 1975. Freny Mistry earned a B.A. in 1981 and a B.Ed. in 1982 from the University of Toronto and became a teacher at a high school in Brampton. The couple has no children.

Rohinton took a job as a clerk at the Canadian Imperial Bank of Commerce. After working for several years in the accounting department, he was made supervisor of customer services. After taking some classes at York University, in 1978 Mistry began studying literature and philosophy part-time at the University of Toronto. Around 1982 he began to write after working hours. He received his B.A. in 1983. That same year his story "One Sunday" won the $250 Hart House Literary Prize.

In 1984 Mistry's story "Auspicious Occasion" won another Hart House Literary Prize. Mavis Gallant, who at that time was writer-in-residence at the University of Toronto, was on the jury; she encouraged Mistry to continue writing and pointed him out to John Metcalf and Leon Rooke, who were putting together an anthology of new Canadian writing. A Canada Council

Rohinton Mistry (photograph by F. Mistry; from the dust jacket for the U.S. edition of Family Matters, *2002; Richland County Public Library)*

grant enabled him to give up his job at the bank in 1985 and commit himself to writing full-time. That same year he won the *Canadian Fiction Magazine* Annual Contributor's Award.

In 1986 Mistry accompanied his wife to Long Beach, California, where she had been offered a teaching position at a high school. In a 1989 interview with Geoff Hancock, Mistry said: "The killings and shootings we saw took place outside school property, but close enough to be frightening. One night, after a basketball game, a student was gunned down right outside that elaborate twenty-foot fence. Two other students on a long weekend were walking in the school neighbourhood and were shot from a passing car. That was the American experience for us." Comparing the United States and Canada, Mistry told Hancock: "I think I prefer Multiculturalism to the direct racism of the Melting Pot because I'd rather be alive and face the subtle discrimination. The overt racism of the Melting Pot often leads to a violent end."

The Mistrys returned to Canada in 1987; Rohinton Mistry's first book, *Tales from Firozsha Baag,* appeared that same year. In addition to "One Sunday" and "Auspicious Occasion," the volume includes the stories "The Ghost of Firozsha Baag," "Condolence Visit," "The

Collectors," "Of White Hairs and Cricket," "The Paying Guests," "Squatter," "Lend Me Your Light," "Exercisers," and "Swimming Lessons." The three that have attracted the most critical attention concern young Parsis who leave the Firozsha Baag apartment building in Bombay and immigrate to Canada or the United States. In "Squatter" Sarosh moves to Toronto, setting himself the goal of becoming a Canadian in ten years. On arrival he renames himself Sid, but he discovers that he is unable to use a toilet in the Western way: "Morning after morning, he had no choice but to climb up and simulate the squat of our Indian latrines. If he sat down, no amount of exertion could produce success." He considers the surgical implantation of the "Crappus Non Interruptus (CNI)," a device that enables one to empty one's bowels immediately by pressing a button. In the end he accomplishes the feat of sitting on a toilet without the help of the CNI; but he is able to do so only when he is on a flight to India and is, therefore, no longer on Canadian territory. He will remain a double entity, half Sarosh and half Sid, alienated from the old without being able to adapt to the new. In "Lend Me Your Light" the well-to-do Jamshed immigrates to the United States; the middle-class Kersi opts for Canada; and Kersi's brother Percy remains in India and commits himself to working for the underprivileged. Kersi reflects guiltily: "There you were, my brother, waging battles against corruption and evil, while I was watching sitcoms on my rented Granada TV." Kersi returns in the last story in the volume, "Swimming Lessons." He has now been living in Toronto for a year, but Bombay is constantly on his mind. While on the surface the story concerns Kersi's attempt to learn to swim, Gregory McElwain explains that "swimming is a metaphor for assimilating in the story, and his fear of the water and lack of effort in the lessons symbolize his inability to commit to Canada." Only when he explores his Indian past through art is Kersi able to come to terms with his country of adoption. *Tales from Firozsha Baag* was short-listed for the Governor General's Literary Award for Fiction in 1988.

The Parsis in Mistry's first novel, *Such a Long Journey* (1991), are concerned about the rise of the Shiv Sena, a radical right-wing party with considerable influence in the Bombay area. Shiv Sena's agitation for a national Hindu identity threatens the self-image of the Parsis, who were an elite in colonial times. Dinshawji, a friend of the protagonist, Gustad Noble, is confused by the changing of the names of Bombay streets from English to the local Marathi language. The Parsis live in the Khodadad Building; the wall surrounding the building is threatened by the municipality's road-widening scheme, as well as by "urinators and defecators" who use it as a public toilet. The loss of the wall will leave the Zoroastrian minority in an exposed position. According to Nilufer E. Bharucha, the "protecting/imprisoning wall" is symbolic of the siege mentality of the Parsi community in postcolonial times; David Williams notes that the wall preserves "the Parsi in his self-sameness and hierarchical privilege" and protects "him from the threat of difference, of Otherness itself." Gustad must also contend with the protracted illness of his daughter, Roshan; the waywardness of his youngest son, Darius; and the refusal of his eldest son, Sohrab, to attend a prestigious university. In addition, he becomes involved in a national scandal when he helps his old friend Jimmy Bilimoria, who once saved his life after he was injured in a traffic accident, hide a large sum of money; Dinshawji risks his job for Gustad by opening a bank account to launder Jimmy's illegal money. At the end of the novel the child-like, retarded Tehmul, who has been like a son to Gustad, is fatally injured; Gustad carries Tehmul in the same way Jimmy carried him after the accident. Gordon Ekelund finds that Mistry's first novel invites the reader to "discover shared values and a common humanity," while Barbara Leckie points out that "Mistry promotes a universal paradigm with respect to moral ideas." *Such a Long Journey* won the Governor General's Literary Award for Fiction in 1991

Cover for 2002 paperback reprint (Bruccoli Clark Layman Archives)

and the Trillium Award, the Commonwealth Writers Prize, and the Smith Books/*Books in Canada* Award for best first novel in 1992. It was a finalist for the 1991 Booker Prize in the United Kingdom and was made into a movie in 1998.

Part of Mistry's second novel, *A Fine Balance* (1995), is set at the time of India's independence from British rule in 1947; the bulk of it takes place during the 1975 to 1977 emergency declared by Prime Minister Indira Gandhi in an unnamed "city by the sea" that resembles Bombay. Two of the four protagonists, Maneck Kohlah and Dina Shroff, are Parsis; Ishvar Darji and his nephew, Omprakash (Om) Darji, are Hindus. Maneck comes from a rural background in the north of India; Dina was born into an upper-middle-class family in the city; the tailors Ishvar and Om belong to the Chamaar caste of untouchables. In a 1996 interview Mistry told Paul Wilson: "in the first two books, my setting was one

Cover for 2003 paperback reprint (<www.mcclelland.com>)

community, one narrow focus in a city, one apartment building, one neighbourhood, and even when we go outside it is still through the eyes of that one community. In *A Fine Balance* I wanted to deal with more of India, not just urban life." In the wake of independence Maneck's father, Farokh, is forced to give up his farm and is left with only a small shop; Ishvar and his brother Narayan are apprenticed to the Muslim tailor Ashraf Chacha; and the death of their father leaves Dina to face the domestic tyranny of her brother, Nusswan. In the 1970s Dina owns a textile factory that employs Ishvar and Om, and Maneck is Dina's lodger. During the emergency, Ashraf is killed in a police action; Maneck's friend Avinash, a student leader, is tortured to death because of his criticism of the prime minister's policy; and Om is castrated as a part of a mass-sterilization program. Narayan's death leaves Ishvar responsible for Om, Narayan's only surviving child. The employer-employee relationship between Dina, who has lost her father and her husband, and

the tailors, who have lost their entire family, is replaced by friendship; and Maneck, who has lost his father and his home, finds a new family with the three of them. Maneck, Dina, Ishvar, and Om make sense of their lives through storytelling. The proof-reader Vasantrao Valmik, a minor character whose last name echoes that of Valmiki, the poet to whom the Sanskrit epic *Ramayana* is ascribed, theorizes: "Perhaps the very act of telling created a natural design. Perhaps it was a knack that humans had, for cleaning up their untidy existences—a hidden survival weapon, like antibodies in the bloodstream." *A Fine Balance* won the 1995 Giller Prize, the 1995 Royal Society of Literature's Winifred Holtby Memorial Prize, the 1995 Canada-Australia Literary Prize, the 1996 *Los Angeles Times* Book Award for fiction, and the 1996 Commonwealth Writers Prize. It also received a prize from the Danish Literacy Council and was short-listed for the 1996 Booker Prize and the IMPAC Dublin Literary Award. Mistry received an honorary doctorate from the University of Ottawa in 1996. In autumn 2001 *A Fine Balance* became the first Canadian work—and only the second non-American book after Bernhard Schlink's *Der Vorleser* (1995; translated as *The Reader,* 1997)—to be chosen by the influential talk-show host Oprah Winfrey for her book club. A best-seller in Canada and the United States, the novel has been translated into many major languages, including German, Japanese, Swedish, Norwegian, and Danish.

Mistry's third novel, *Family Matters,* appeared in spring 2002. Yezad and Roxana and their sons, Murad and Jehangir, live in a tiny apartment. Yezad works in a sporting-goods store owned by the kindly Vikram Kapur, who, in spite of having suffered from Muslim aggression during the 1947 partition of the subcontinent into India and Pakistan, provides Husain, a traumatized Muslim victim of Hindu violence, with a job at the store. Vikram says to Husain: "You see how we two are sitting here, sharing? That's how people have lived in Bombay. That's why Bombay has survived floods, disease, plague, water shortage, bursting drains and sewers, all the population pressures." The lives of Yezad and Roxana are radically changed when they take in Roxana's father, Nariman Vakeel, a seventy-nine-year-old former professor of English literature who suffers from Parkinson's disease and a broken ankle, after he is cast out by his stepchildren, Coomy and Jal. To try to meet the additional expense that the care of Roxana's father entails, Yezad bets all of his money on the Indian Matka lottery but loses. He then attempts to extort money from Vikram Kapur by having friends pose as gangsters; but the plan fails when Vikram dies. The stress of his situation finally drives Yezad to identify completely with Zoroastrianism, from which he has hitherto been alienated, and become a religious bigot. *Family Matters* was short-listed for the 2002 Booker Prize.

Although he has published only four books, Rohinton Mistry is one of the most widely acclaimed Canadian writers. His analyses of Indian society and the Parsi community offer insights into history, politics, and life in general. As Singh points out, Mistry's books "take a full measure of the human experience—a domain no less worthy of a new Canadian writer than of a Dickens or a George Eliot."

Interviews:

Geoff Hancock, "An Interview with Rohinton Mistry," *Canadian Fiction Magazine,* 65 (1989): 143–150;

Dagmar Novak, "Interview with Rohinton Mistry," in *Other Solitudes: Canadian Multicultural Fictions,* edited by Linda Hutcheon and Marion Richmond (Toronto: Oxford University Press, 1990), pp. 255–262;

Paul Wilson, "Giving Free Rein: Paul Wilson Speaks with Rohinton Mistry," *Books in Canada,* 25 (March 1996): 2–4;

Robert McLay, "Rohinton Mistry Talks to Robert McLay," *Wasafiri,* 24 (Spring 1996): 16–18;

Stacey Gibson, "Such a Long Journey: From Bank Clerk to Writer, from Obscurity to the Oprah Winfrey Show, Rohinton Mistry's Path as a Writer Has Taken a Series of Unlikely Turns," *University of Toronto Magazine* (Summer 2002).

References:

Silvia Albertazzi, "Passages: The 'Indian Connection,' from Sara Jeannette Duncan to Rohinton Mistry," in *Imagination and the Creative Impulse in the New Literatures in English,* edited by M.-T. Bidella and G. V. Davis (Amsterdam & Atlanta: Rodopi, 1993), pp. 57–66;

Nilufer E. Bharucha, "'When Old Tracks are Lost': Rohinton Mistry's Fiction as Diasporic Discourse," *Journal of Canadian Literature,* 30 (1995): 57–64;

Dan Coleman, *Masculine Migrations: Reading the Postcolonial Male in "New Canadian" Narratives* (Toronto: University of Toronto Press, 1998), pp. 131–158;

Gordon Ekelund, "Left at the Station: The Portrayal of Women in Mistry's *Such a Long Journey,*" *Toronto Review of Contemporary Writing Abroad,* 14, no. 1 (1995): 6–14;

Ajay Heble, "'A Foreign Presence in the Stall': Towards a Poetics of Cultural Hybridity in Rohinton Mistry's Migration Stories," *Canadian Literature,* 137 (1993): 51–62;

Barbara Leckie, *Rohinton Mistry and His Works* (Toronto: ECW Press, 1995);

Amin Malak,, "The Shahrazadic Tradition: Rohinton Mistry's *Such a Long Journey* and the Art of Storytelling," *Journal of Commonwealth Literature,* 29 (1993): 108–118;

Hilary Mantel, "States of Emergency," *India: A Mosaic,* edited by Robert B. Silvers and Barbara Epstein (New York: New York Review of Books, 2000), 179–194;

Gregory McElwain, "Paddling away from the Past: Alienation and Assimilation in Rohinton Mistry's 'Swimming Lessons,'" *Kobe College Studies,* 41, no. 2 (1994): 15–26;

Peter Morey, "Post-Colonial DestiNations: Spatial Re(con)figurings in Khushwant Singh's *Train to Pakistan* and Rohinton Mistry's *A Fine Balance,*" in his *Fictions of India: Narrative and Power* (Edinburgh: Edinburgh University Press, 2000), pp. 161–190;

Laura Moss, "Can Rohinton Mistry's Realism Rescue the Novel?" in *Postcolonizing the Commonwealth: Studies in Literature and Culture,* edited by Rowland Smith (Waterloo, Ont.: Wilfrid Laurier University Press, 2000), pp. 157–165;

Arun Prabha Mukherjee, "Narrating India: Rohinton Mistry's *Such a Long Journey,*" in *Oppositional Aesthetics: Readings from a Hyphenated Space,* edited by Mukherjee (Toronto: TSAR, 1994), pp. 144–151;

Michael W. Pharand, "The Road to Salvation: Mythological and Theological Intertextuality in Rohinton Mistry's *Such a Long Journey,*" *Open Letter,* 8 (Winter 1994): 107–116;

Robert L. Ross, "Seeking and Maintaining Balance: Rohinton Mistry's Fiction," *World Literature Today,* 73 (1999): 239–244;

Amritjit Singh, "Rohinton Mistry," in *Writers of the Indian Diaspora: A Bio-Bibliographical Critical Sourcebook,* edited by Emmanuel S. Nelson (Westport, Conn.: Greenwood Press, 1993), pp. 207–217;

David Williams, "Cyberwriting and the Borders of Identity: 'What's in a Name' in Kroetsch's *The Puppeteer* and Mistry's *Such a Long Journey?*" *Canadian Literature,* 149 (1996): 55–71.

Daniel David Moses

(18 February 1952 –   )

Don Perkins
University of Alberta

BOOKS: *Delicate Bodies* (Vancouver: blewointment press, 1980);

Coyote City: A Play in Two Acts (Stratford, Ont.: Williams-Wallace, 1988);

The Dreaming Beauty: A Play (Toronto: Playwrights Union of Canada, 1990);

The White Line: Poems (Saskatoon: Fifth House, 1990);

Almighty Voice and His Wife: A Play in Two Acts (Stratford, Ont.: Williams-Wallace, 1992);

Kyotopolis: A Play in Two Acts (Toronto: Playwrights Union of Canada, 1993);

City of Shadows: A Play in One Act (Toronto: Playwrights Union of Canada, 1995);

The Indian Medicine Shows: Two One-Act Plays (Toronto: Exile Editions, 1995)—comprises *The Moon and Dead Indians* and *Angel of the Medicine Show;*

Brebeuf's Ghost: A Tale of Horror in Three Acts (Toronto: Playwrights Union of Canada, 1996);

Big Buck City: A Play in Two Acts (Toronto: Exile Editions, 1998);

The Witch of Niagara (Toronto: Playwrights Union of Canada, 1998);

Coyote City and City of Shadows: Necropolitei. Two Plays (Toronto: Imago Press, 2000);

Sixteen Jesuses (Toronto: Exile Editions, 2000);

Pursued by a Bear: Talks, Monologues, and Tales (Toronto: Exile Editions, 2005).

PLAY PRODUCTIONS: *Coyote City,* Toronto, Native Canadian Centre, 17 May 1988;

The Dreaming Beauty, Toronto, Innerstage, 18 October 1990;

Big Buck City, Toronto, Tarragon Theatre, 24 May 1991;

La belle fille de l'aurore, Saskatoon, La Troupe du Jour, 1991;

Almighty Voice and His Wife, Ottawa, Great Canadian Theatre Company, 18 September 1991;

Kyotopolis, Toronto, Graduate Centre for the Study of Drama, 17 March 1993;

The Moon and Dead Indians, Toronto, Cahoots Theatre Projects, 24 November 1993;

Daniel David Moses (photograph by John Reeves; from the cover for Sixteen Jesuses, *2000; Bruccoli Clark Layman Archives)*

City of Shadows, Windsor, University of Windsor Department of English and School of Dramatic Arts, 27 June 1995;

The Indian Medicine Show Plays (The Moon and Dead Indians and Angel of the Medicine Show), Toronto, Theatre Passe Muraille, 5 January 1996;

Brébeuf's Ghost, Windsor, University of Windsor Department of English and School of Dramatic Arts, 29 May 1996;

Red River, by Moses and Jim Millan, Toronto, Factory Studio Theatre, 21 September 1998;

The Witch of Niagara, Toronto, Centre for Indigenous Theatre, Robert Gill Theatre, 9 December 1998;

Songs of Love and Medicine (The Ballad of Burnt Ella and A Song for the Tall Grass), Kingston, Rotunda Theatre, Queen's University, 10 March 2005.

OTHER: "The King of the Raft," in *All My Relations,* edited by Thomas King (Toronto: McClelland & Stewart, 1990), pp. 171–174;

An Anthology of Canadian Native Literature in English, edited by Moses and Terry Goldie (Toronto: Oxford University Press, 1992; enlarged, 1998; enlarged again, 2005);

"Persistence of Songs," in *Unbury My Heart: An Exhibition of the Art of Shelley Niro. February 25–April 8, 2001* (Hamilton, Ont.: McMaster Museum of Art, 2001);

"Macintosh Moon," in *Lifeworlds–Artscapes, Contemporary Iroquois Art,* edited by Sylvia S. Kasprycki and Doris I. Stambrau (Frankfurt am Main: Galerie 37, Museum der Weltkulturen, 2003), p. 6;

"Smoke Blues," "Offhand Song," "Short Lines," "Early Pornography," and "A Song on the Wall," in *Without Reservation: Indigenous Erotica,* edited by Kateri Akiwenzie-Damm (Wiarton, Ont.: Kegedonce Press, 2003), pp. 72–74, 139–140.

SELECTED PERIODICAL PUBLICATIONS– UNCOLLECTED: "Gramma's Doing" and "The Trickster Theatre of Tomson Highway," *Canadian Fiction Magazine,* 60 (1987): 77–88;

"A Handful of Hallowe'ens," *Aboriginal Voices,* 4 (November–December 1997): 36–37;

"A Small Essay on the Largeness of Light," *Canadian Theatre Review,* 116 (Fall 2003): 57.

Daniel David Moses has been an independent writer in Toronto since 1979. He said in an unpublished September 2002 interview that he writes "for pleasure," but it is a "complex pleasure that mixes up the sensuality of words with the reverberations of ideas and the energy of morality." A poet, playwright, dramaturge, short-story writer, essayist, and educator, he has been an artist-, playwright-, and writer-in-residence at many theaters and universities across Canada. He has also served on the boards of the Association for Native Development in the Performing and Visual Arts, Native Earth Performing Arts, and the Playwrights Union of Canada (now known as the Playwrights Guild of Canada). In 1986 he and fellow writers Lenore Keeshig-Tobias and Tomson Highway founded the Committee to Re-Establish the Trickster; it has been instrumental in the literary rebirth of this paradoxical character, who serves as a teacher from whom Native people learn by example but whose examples include both mistakes and virtues.

Like many contemporary Native writers and artists, Moses feels a responsibility to help a damaged people heal by creating art that, as he told Wanda Campbell in 1994, allows them "to find a profound pleasure in their own existence," and Robert Appleford points out in a program note to *The Indian Medicine Show Plays* (1996) that even in his historical plays, Moses is "concerned less with elegies of past glory than with strategies of staying alive in the present." Moses points out, however, that given the variety that is covered by the term, "Native" is no more accurate a definition of him as a writer than "European" would be of a white one, and he has protested that it is not fair to him or to his work to see it as only, or essentially, "Indian." Moses explained to R. W. Gray in a 1999 interview that as an openly gay or "middle-gendered"–what in Native culture has been termed a "two-spirited"–writer, he occupies a "privileged" position that allows him freedom from the "expected."

A registered Delaware, Moses was born on 18 February 1952 in Ohsweken, Ontario, to David Nelson Moses, a farmer, and Blanche Ruth Jamieson Moses, a nurse's aide; he has a sister, Deborah Blanch Moses. He attributes his appreciation for the spoken word to the oral traditions in which he was raised on the Six Nations Reserve near Brantford, Ontario. As he explained to Gray, "So much of the writing of this century has been written for the page and I find it does not compel me at all." His interest in language that is written to be heard first led him to poetry but has found a fuller scope in drama, which allows him to speak in more than one voice. He told Hartmut Lutz in 1991 that he understood early that "language itself is the center to many things in the way society operates, and it would be useful to pay attention to it"; he explained to Gray that he strives to give his audiences language that will "actually stroke their ears and give them images to imagine." His drama is also rooted in his sense of the excitement that comes from being in a room with other people, all responding collectively to the experience of the words. He told Gray, "I think there's a dilemma in our current society where we're all off in our own cubbyholes . . . being fed the same material but we're not reacting together."

Moses gained a sense of the beauty of the English language from early exposure to the Anglican prayer book and hymns at the reserve mission. He suggested in the interview with Gray that "maybe with English we are working with a language that has had a lot of its power stripped away from it by being used as a tool for governance and imperialism" but insisted that it is still possible to have fun with the language. That fun often emerges as multilayered puns and metaphorically suggestive character names. It emerges also in Moses's reappropriation of the Trickster figure, in his ironic characters, and in highly ambiguous physical, cultural, and spiritual settings. The playfulness assures his prominence among a community of Native playwrights who, Appleford says in "The Desire to Crunch Bone: Daniel David Moses and the 'True Real Indian'" (1993), "hold funhouse mirrors up to our own desires for 'real Indians' in Canadian theatre."

Moses realized by his middle years in high school that he wanted to be a writer, and he tried to study every form of writing. He graduated from York University with an Honors B.F.A. in fine arts in 1975. He recalled in "'Adam' Means 'Red Man,'" an unpublished talk he gave to the Challenging Racism in the Arts forum in 1998 that is included in his *Pursued by a Bear: Talks, Monologues, and Tales* (2005), that he was the only student in his tutorial "who disagreed with the assumption that profit was an essential motive in human nature." The effect of materialism on individuals and families has remained a concern in his writing.

Moses went on to the University of British Columbia, where he won the creative-writing program's prize for playwriting in 1977 and produced a thesis project that included one-act plays and a body of poetry. He received his M.F.A. in 1977. His first published book, *Delicate Bodies* (1980), is a collection of poetry, but he revised most of his thesis poems for a later collection, *The White Line* (1990). The seasons are a key motif in *Delicate Bodies;* he told Gray that this motif reflects his concern for the cycles of life, of "everything changing but everything coming back and doing the same thing over again, even if it is infinitely different." That sense of the same things coming back time and again pervades his mythopoeic dramas reestablishing stories from the past, his history or "frontier" plays, and his contemporary or "city" plays.

Moses's first play, *Coyote City* (produced 1988, published 1990), incorporates the traditional Nez Perce tale of Coyote's journey to the World of the Dead to try to retrieve his wife as a thematic mirror to the contemporary story of Lena and Johnny. Johnny calls Lena and asks her to join him at the Silver Dollar Bar in Toronto, where he was killed in a brawl six months earlier. When her mother and sister fail to stop her, they follow her to the city in a failed effort to find and protect her. They are led on their journey by Thomas, a "reborn alcoholic" spirit guide. In the city Lena meets the "Dark Lady," Clarisse, who takes her to the Silver Dollar. When Lena fails to rescue Johnny from the shadow world, Clarisse sends her out as a prostitute to meet many "Johnnies." The play was nominated for the Governor General's Literary Award for Drama in 1991.

The first of Moses's mythopoeic plays, *The Dreaming Beauty* (1990)—in part a parody of the fairy tale "Sleeping Beauty"—is an allegory about the rebirth of Native cultures. A girl known only as Beauty must undergo a ritualized "death" to allow the spirit figures Corn Woman, Bean Woman, Squash Woman, and Grandmother Moon to restore her forgotten name and identity. The restoration will end a five-hundred-year-long decline into cultural dysfunction on the site of a lost "Old Village" on the shores of a shining great lake named Ontario. Though Toronto is never mentioned by name, the location is clear. The play won first prize in the One-Act Category in Theatre Canada's National Playwriting Competition.

The poems in Moses's 1990 collection, *The White Line,* explore the metaphorical potential of nature and seasonal cycles. While the poems in *Delicate Bodies* play the natural against the products of human hands, these poems integrate the two, reflecting Moses's growing sense that, as he told Campbell, "there isn't much difference between us and the rest of nature, even though we want to put ourselves on some high pedestal."

Moses's first frontier play, *Almighty Voice and His Wife* (performed 1991, published 1992), is a tragicomedy. He told Campbell: "I think humor is one of the best things I can achieve . . . because there are just some basic stupid realities about our existence that are humorous." Ric Knowles argues that the play serves as a "Native reclamation and re-appropriation" of a story that had been told by many white writers. The more realistic first act dramatizes the courtship of the young Cree warrior Almighty Voice and White Girl, Almighty Voice's arrest for stealing cattle, and his death at the hands of the police. Appleford describes the second act as "a grotesque vaudeville/minstrel show, with both White Girl (now the Interlocutor) and Almighty Voice (now Almighty Ghost) wearing whiteface and performing a bizarre mixture of racial slurs, melodramatic cliches, and never-ending puns." Through a mix of the tragic and the comic, the Trickster ghost and the Interlocutor expose the workings of history, art, and bureaucratic and anthropological language as they create and feed the public image of the "Indian." They also highlight the effect such images have on Native people and their cultures. In the final scene, Appleford says in "The Desire to Crunch Bone," "the ghost wipes the whiteface make-up from the Interlocutor's face, and gives her back her name." Appleford sees this gesture not as a "simple statement of identity" but as a reminder that the action of the play has been "an on-going battle for a soul." As such, he says, it exemplifies Moses's efforts to chronicle "the stories of a people whose survival is highly dependent upon how successfully they can resist and control the semiotic pressure to 'go Indian.'"

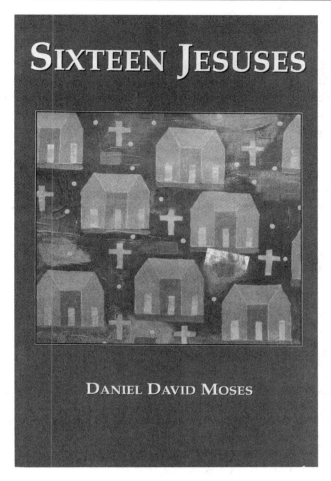

Paperback cover for the first edition, 2000
(Bruccoli Clark Layman Archives)

Moses's second city play, *Big Buck City* (produced 1991, published 1998), exposes the effects of the pursuit of wealth and urban status. On Christmas Eve, Barbara and Jack Buck long to escape their Indian identity and blend in as urbanized middle-class yuppies, but family entanglements keep pulling them back to their past. Complicating matters is a Trickster figure, Ricky Raccoon, who spends most of the play in a stolen Santa Claus suit as a disruptive "Christmas spirit." As the plumbing fails and the sewage backs up in the basement, a girl is born; but the mother, Lena from *Coyote City,* dies, and Ricky kidnaps the infant. The act is ambiguous: it may be seen as a crime or—given that the Bucks, her aunt and uncle, had selfishly wanted the child mainly to fill a void in their own lives—as a rescue.

The third city play, *Kyotopolis* (1993), is described in the text as "A darkly comic fantasia about the ways we communicate and the future of Native identity in the global village." The play explores the effect of writing on oral traditions through the contradictory media

accounts of Babe Fisher, the first Native in space. Babe, the child born to Lena and abducted from the Bucks at the end of *Big Buck City,* dies aboard the space shuttle *Crazy Horse* after it is blown by an exploding booster rocket into an increasingly erratic orbit from which the shuttle cannot recover and the crew cannot be rescued. Her family and official accounts tell conflicting stories of her life and her fate. Trying to collect and collate the evidence is Mary Oh, a reporter whose life becomes entangled with the lives and spectacular disappearances of her interviewees. The Trickster Ricky Raccoon, transfigured as Tommy Hawk, as a mysterious Lady in Black, and as Nicky, a cameraman, reappears to taunt the audience about its own confining vision of "Indian" identity. Playing with metaphors of cannibalism, Raccoon asks the audience, "We aren't Indian enough, are we? Or are we like too Indian for you to chew? Are you hungry enough to finally eat anything?"

City of Shadows (1995) revisits characters whose lives were lost or destroyed in the earlier city plays. In a shadowy limbo they retell the stories that brought them to the door of the Lodge of the Dead. Although they never say their names, they are recognizable to those who are familiar with the earlier plays.

As an undergraduate Moses had written a play about a homosexual relationship between Billy the Kid and Pat Garrett. In 1991, while taking part in a twenty-four-hour playwriting competition sponsored by Nakai Theatre Ensemble in Whitehorse, Yukon, he wrote a scene in which Billy, on the run, meets a widow and her son; the widow is crazy with fear of Indians. He expanded the scene into *The Moon and Dead Indians,* which won the DuMaurier One-Act Playwriting Competition in 1993. He added a comic companion piece, *Angel of the Medicine Show,* to balance out the bleakness of the first play, and in 1996 the two plays appeared as the next frontier play under the collective title *The Indian Medicine Show Plays. The Moon and Dead Indians* plays the myth of marauding Indians against the myth of the gunfighter—both of which were, by 1878 when the play is set, "vanished" species who, along with the frontier itself, may never truly have existed. Jon and Bill share deadly secrets: the murder of an effeminate Indian youth and their own homosexual attraction for each other. *Angel of the Medicine Show* is set two years after *The Moon and Dead Indians.* Jon, whose medicine show has been broken up and run out of town by angry residents, finds two other former members of the troupe: Angela and David, the "Indian entertainment," who was shot in the buttocks by the nervous Angela when he came up to her campsite. Trying to get a show back together, Jon drives the other two at gunpoint into a grotesque rehearsal. The badly injured David delivers promises of Indian secrets of health and relief from pain, before literally going up in smoke when his war bonnet catches fire. Angela, pregnant with Jon's baby, comes close to miscarrying. At the end she and Jon face an uncertain future.

Brebeuf's Ghost (1996), inspired by William Shakespeare's *Macbeth* (1606), focuses on the Ojibwa people living around Lake Nipissing in 1649. They are the innocent bystanders in a fur-trade war pitting the French and the Hurons against the English and the Iroquois. When a Jesuit missionary becomes possessed by a cannibal windigo spirit, the loyalties of Native Christian converts are tested as the Ojibwa seek to end the possession by traditional means. In 1996 Moses won the James Buller Award for Excellence in Aboriginal Theatre from the Centre for Indigenous Theatre for *The Indian Medicine Shows.*

In *The Witch of Niagara* (1998), a reestablishing of the story of the Maid of the Mist, an old man offers medicine to cure a village of a mysterious sickness that is killing the people. All he wants in return is to marry the sickly daughter of the chief. She refuses and flees, and her flight takes her over the falls into the caves of the God of Cloud and Thunder. She returns the following spring, "big with life" and with the knowledge that the old man is himself the witch who afflicted the village with the sickness. The Thunderer stops the old man's depredations in a battle with the giant snake who has been the old man's source of power.

Moses's next frontier play, *Red River* (1998), was co-authored with Jim Millan and carries echoes of Georg Büchner's tragedy *Woyzeck* (1879; translated as *Wozzeck,* 1927). During the Red River Rebellion in what is now Manitoba in 1869–1870, a Métis farmer, François David, has his marriage and his faith in the Church and civilized institutions undermined by the arrival and behavior of the army and the Orangemen (members of the Orange Order, a mainly Irish Protestant fraternal organization). These representatives of civilization treat the Métis and the Natives as disposable savages and the women as an outlet for their sexual appetites. David is powerless to protect his family, and he and his wife die tragically. But his earthy and occasionally comic mother, aided by David's best friend from the Native camp, escapes the settlement with her grandchild. As she flees, she stops to listen to migrating geese in flight—a natural sound associated with seasonal cycles of both return and change.

In 2000 Moses published a collection of poems, *Sixteen Jesuses.* "An Erratic Song"—the title is a pun on *erratic,* a rock pushed out of place by glacial activity, and on *erotic*—develops around an image of resurfacing after a long period of subterranean seclusion and begins with the question "What love is native to a stone?" The idea of reemergence echoes Moses's dramatic works, in which neglected or suppressed cultural practices or stories resurface as functional aspects of contemporary life. Parallels to the themes of his plays are also evident in poems such as "The Moon in Early Upper Canada." Playfulness with language is a constant throughout the collection, as in the opening line of "The Dogs of Free Speech": "I'd be glad to let sleeping dogs lie through their teeth in the sun." In "Cowboy Pictures" Moses comically wonders what is being said by black-and-white gay erotic photographs of well-oiled young men wearing nothing but cowboy hats and cheap feathers.

In 2001 Moses received the Harbourfront Festival Prize in recognition of his contributions to the literary and arts community by an artist in midcareer. In 2003 he and David McLaren were awarded a Chalmers Fellowship to write a play about the killing of Dudley George, an Ojibwa who was one of a group of protesters who peacefully occupied Ipperwash Park in 1995 to protest the destruction of their burial ground and the long delay in returning their tribal lands. Also in 2003

Moses was appointed a National Scholar to the Department of Theatre at Queen's University in Kingston, Ontario. His *Songs of Love and Medicine* (2005), comprising the one-act plays *The Ballad of Burnt Ella* and *A Song for the Tall Grass,* received its first workshop production at the university. As described in the promotional material from that production, *The Ballad of Burnt Ella* "reimagines a too familiar story by trying to answer the question—What if Cinderella had been a Mohawk girl with a prince of a guy in her heart and Country and Western music on her mind?"; *A Song of the Tall Grass* "expands an old Lakota ghost story, using a contemporary First Nation a cappella singing style that has roots in powwow, jazz and spirituals, to find healing for the wounds our wild hearts cause us."

In 2003–2004 and again in 2005–2006 Daniel David Moses was appointed poet-in-residence to the Prague-Toronto-Manitoulin Theatre Project, which seeks to create theater across languages and cultures. In 2005 he was short-listed for the prestigious Siminovitch Prize in Theatre. He was named playwright-in-residence at the National Arts Centre English Theatre Division for 2006–2007, where he worked on an adaptation of Thomas Heywood's play *The Fair Maid of the West* (1631). In 2006 he also received a commission from the Stratford (Ontario) Festival to adapt *Crazy Dave* (1999), by Ojibwa author Basil Johnston. A collection of essays, *Daniel David Moses: Written and Spoken Explorations of His Works,* is forthcoming from Guernica Editions.

Interviews:

Hartmut Lutz, "Daniel David Moses," in *Contemporary Challenges: Conversations with Canadian Native Authors,* edited by Lutz (Saskatoon: Fifth House, 1991), pp. 155–168;

Wanda Campbell, "The Rumour of Humanity: An Interview with Daniel David Moses," *Windsor Review,* 27 (Fall 1994): 55–63;

Terry Goldie, "Interview with Daniel David Moses and Drew Hayden Taylor," *Open Letter,* eighth series, 8 (Winter 1994): 41–51;

R. W. Gray, "'The nice thing about being two-spirited is it exists despite the patriarchy': An Interview with Daniel David Moses," *ARC: Canada's National Poetry Magazine,* 42 (Spring 1999): 29–39.

References:

Robert Appleford, "The Desire to Crunch Bone: Daniel David Moses and the 'True Real Indian,'" *Canadian Theatre Review,* 77 (Winter 1993): 21–26;

Ric Knowles, *The Theatre of Form and the Production of Meaning: Contemporary Canadian Dramaturgy* (Toronto: ECW Press, 1999), pp. 138–150.

M. NourbeSe Philip

(3 February 1947 –   )

Maureen Moynagh
St. Francis Xavier University

See also the Philip entry in *DLB 157: Twentieth-Century Caribbean and Black African Writers, Third Series.*

BOOKS: *Thorns* (Stratford, Ont.: Williams-Wallace, 1980);

Salmon Courage (Stratford, Ont.: Williams-Wallace, 1983);

Harriet's Daughter (London: Heinemann, 1988; Toronto: Women's Press, 1988; Portsmouth, N.H.: Heinemann, 1992);

She Tries Her Tongue, Her Silence Softly Breaks (Havana: Casa de las Americas, 1988; Charlottetown, P.E.I.: Ragweed, 1989; London: Women's Press, 1993);

Looking for Livingstone: An Odyssey of Silence (Stratford, Ont.: Mercury Press, 1991);

Frontiers: Essays and Writings On Racism and Culture (Stratford, Ont.: Mercury Press, 1992);

Showing Grit: Showboating North of the 44th Parallel (Toronto: Poui, 1993; revised and enlarged, 1993);

Caribana: African Roots and Continuities: Race, Space and the Poetics of Moving (Toronto: Poui, 1996);

A Genealogy of Resistance and Other Essays (Toronto: Mercury Press, 1997);

Coups and Calypsos (Toronto: Playwrights Union of Canada, 1999).

PLAY PRODUCTION: *Coups and Calypsos,* Toronto, Cahoots Theatre Project, 1999; London, 1999.

OTHER: "Managing the Unmanageable," in *Caribbean Women Writers: Essays from the First International Conference,* edited by Selwyn R. Cudjoe (Wellesley, Mass.: Calaloux, 1990), pp. 295–300;

"Commitment to Hardness," in *Erotique Noire: Black Erotica,* edited by Miriam DeCosta-Willis, Reginald Martin, and Roseann P. Bell (New York, London & Toronto: Doubleday, 1992), pp. 224–226;

"Trying Her Tongue," in *Dwelling in Possibility: Women Poets and Critics on Poetry,* edited by Yopie Prins and Maera Schreiber (Ithaca, N.Y.: Cornell University Press, 1997), pp. 116–123;

"Form and Improv," in *Epistrophe: Wall Paintings by Denyse Thomasos,* curated by Ingrid Jenkner and Gaëtane Verna (Lennoxville, Que.: Foreman Art Gallery of Bishop's University, 2006).

SELECTED PERIODICAL PUBLICATIONS–UNCOLLECTED:

POETRY

"Cashew #4," *Walrus Magazine,* 1 (July–August 2004): 57;

"Zong! #25 and #26," *Boundary 2,* 33 (Summer 2006): 8–9.

FICTION

"The Tall Rains," *Women's Review,* 12 (1986): 29–32;

"Just a Name," *Matrix,* 31 (1990): 17–18;

"Bad Words," *Wasafiri,* 11 (1990): 26–28;

"Stop Frame," *Prairie Schooner,* 67 (1993): 62–72;

"The Bearded Queen," *Ariel,* 28 (January 1997): 221–225.

In "The Absence of Language or How I Almost Became a Spy," the introductory essay in her book-length poem *She Tries Her Tongue, Her Silence Softly Breaks* (1988) that M. NourbeSe Philip characterizes as "something of a blueprint for my poetic and writing life," she addresses the image-making function of the artist in a colonial society in which language has been an instrument of imperial power. To create images that speak to and for subjugated peoples, she says, the artist must strive to rework the language, to fashion it anew, while remaining attentive to the silences that language inevitably produces. These intertwining themes of language, silence, and social justice inform both Philip's poetry and her activist writing.

In a 1993 interview with Janice Williamson, Philip observed: "As a writer, it has been very painful to survive here–where there was nothing that you could either resist or go along with as a tradition." While Philip's account of black writing in Canada is inaccurate—there is a tradition stretching back to the eighteenth- and nineteenth-century slave narratives of John Marrant and Boston King—her perception shaped her experience. Conversely, Philip acknowledged that "I could be more daring here in Canada. . . . Canada in a sense allowed me the space to produce something." One of the most important voices in contemporary African Canadian letters, Philip has published poetry, prose, dramas, and essays that address the experiences of women and girls in the African diaspora.

Marlene Irma Philip was born in Moriah, Tobago, on 3 February 1947 to Parkinson Philip-Yeates and Undine Bowles Philip. When she was eight, the family moved to Trinidad. Philip graduated from Bishop Antsey High School in 1965 with the Cipriani Memorial Scholarship in recognition of her first-place standing in a Caribbean-wide examination. She earned a B.S. in economics at the University of the West Indies in Mona, Jamaica, in 1968 and moved to Canada to pursue a master's degree in political science at the University of Western Ontario in London. She was married on 3 February 1969 and had a son, Bruce Omar, that same year. She completed her M.A. in 1970. She and her husband separated a year later, and she began to pursue a law degree at the University of Western Ontario. She also began to write. In "The Absence of Language or How I Almost Became a Spy" she contends that writing did not figure among the professions that scholarship-winning students were encouraged to pursue: "Only when we understand language and its role in a colonial society can we understand the role of writing and the writer in such a society; only then, perhaps, can we understand why writing was not and still, to a large degree, is not recognized as a career, profession, or way of being in the Caribbean and even among Caribbean people resident in Canada." She worked at a legal clinic, Parkdale Community Services, for eighteen months and then formed with Marva Jemmott the partnership Jemmott and Philip, the first law firm in Canada consisting of black women. She was divorced in 1974 and entered into a common-law marriage with Paul Chandless Chamberlain, an education administrator, in October 1975.

Philip's second child, Hardie Omar, was born in 1980. That same year she published her first poetry collection, *Thorns*. The title is taken from the final poem in the volume, "All that Remains of Kush Returns to the Desert," in which the speaker seeks a spiritual home in Africa: "gently I carry tiny thorns of Africa within." The poem "Oliver Twist" begins as a children's rhyme and develops into a powerful indictment of colonial education. On Empire Day schoolchildren gather in the heat to sing the praises of empire, even though "we had independence / an' massa day done." The majority of the poems are set in the Caribbean. "E. Pulcherrima" depicts a woman's transplantation from the Caribbean to Canada through the extended metaphor of a poinsettia that "bleeds" or reddens "normally / naturally in the tropic / days and nights of equal length" but must be forced to bloom in the Canadian winters. The poem implies that the northerly environment is hostile to the plant and to the writer from tropical climes.

Philip left her law partnership in 1982 and practiced law out of her home for the next two years. Her second book of poetry, *Salmon Courage,* was published in 1983, the year her daughter Hesper Zahra was born and that she became an interviewing lawyer for Ontario Legal Aid. *Salmon Courage* is marked by an increasing preoccupation with language and a growing self-consciousness about poetic form. While the poems in this volume, like those in *Thorns,* deal with a variety of themes, the title poem confers a loose thematic unity on the collection: several poems are preoccupied with the courage needed to swim against the current. In the autobiographical title poem a woman returns to the place of her birth, her "spawning ground," where she celebrates the life of her "salmon mother," who took the sharp hook of death

> in her mouth, broke free and beat
> her way upstream, uphill; spurned
> all but the challenge of gravity,
> answered the silver call of the moon,
> danced to the drag and pull of the
> tides, fate a silver thorn in her side.

The speaker contemplates her own insistence

> on swimming
> against the tide, upstream,
> leaping, jumping, flying floating,
> hurling myself at under, over,
> around all obstacles, backwards,

though she feels weighted by the "mill stone" of her father's dream of becoming a lawyer, "his milestone / to where he hadn't been."

In the mid 1980s Philip adopted the name Nourbese, which means "marvelous child" in the Edo language; she published for a time as Marlene Nourbese Philip and finally as M. NourbeSe Philip. Philip is not the only member of her family to have altered her name, and she suggests in the 1988 essay "A Genealogy of Resistance" (collected, 1997) that this proclivity stems from the disruption to ancestry and identity effected by the Middle Passage and the history of slavery: "As if we are all somehow uncomfortable in

She Tries Her Tongue

her silence softly breaks

Marlene Nourbese Philip

Paperback cover for the first edition, 1988
(<http://www.nourbese.com>)

these names; wearing them like strange and foreign clothes that generation after generation we keep changing and adjusting for a better fit. As if that first misnaming, after the Crossing, the *Maafa* [African Holocaust] has left us all fatally ill at ease."

Philip served as vice chairperson of the Workers' Compensation Appeals Tribunal from 1986 to 1988; also in 1988 she left the staff of Carswell Publishing. The relationship between naming and identity discussed in "A Genealogy of Resistance" is highlighted in Philip's novel for young adults, *Harriet's Daughter* (1988). The work is a teenage bildungsroman that addresses the challenges a girl faces as she seeks a role model to emulate and struggles against her socially conservative father and submissive mother. Margaret decides to change her name after reading about Harriet Tubman, who helped some three hundred slaves escape to freedom on the Underground Railroad, for a school project: "Harriet Tubman was brave and strong and she was black like me. I think it was the first time I thought of wanting to be called Harriet—I wanted to *be* Harriet."

The name also conjures a story her mother had told her about a family friend, Harriet Blewchamp, who had been in a Nazi concentration camp during World War II. Margaret tries to play Harriet Tubman by helping a friend, Zulma, escape from an abusive stepfather and return to her grandmother in Tobago. Margaret's own father plans to send her to his mother in Barbados for some "Good West Indian Discipline" because she is not appropriately feminine and submissive, but the forces of repressive masculinity are thwarted when Margaret enlists her mother, Zulma's mother, and Mrs. B., a kindly neighbor, in her scheme to send Zulma home. Margaret's mother intervenes to prevent Margaret from being sent to Barbados.

Philip had difficulty securing a publisher for *Harriet's Daughter*. She told Williamson in the 1993 interview that after two publishers informed her agent that "they weren't interested in work with Black kids," she decided to submit it to McClelland and Stewart herself. "They said that the readers' reports were all very good but that the manuscript wasn't marketable." Philip then turned to publishers outside of Canada. After Heinemann published the novel in England, The Women's Press in Toronto brought out a Canadian edition. In "Publish + Be Damned," collected in her *Frontiers: Essays and Writings On Racism and Culture* (1992), Philip says that the argument that there is no market for minority writers in Canada because the prospective audience is too small "assumes that if you are a Canadian writer of Native, Asian or African background, the only possible audience for your work is one comprised of individuals of the same ethnic background; this is erroneous, narrow-minded, and even racist." In 1989 *Harriet's Daughter* won the Canadian Children's Book Centre's Choice Award and was runner-up for the Canadian Library Association Prize and the Max and Greta Abel Award for Multicultural Literature. It has gone through multiple printings, has been brought out in English by three publishers, and has been translated into German. Until 2004 it was required reading on the English syllabus of the Caribbean-wide CXE (Caribbean Examinations).

In 1988 Philip won the Tradewinds Prize of Trinidad and Tobago in both the poetry and short-story categories. Most significantly, she was also awarded the Casa de las Américas Prize for *She Tries Her Tongue, Her Silence Softly Breaks*. This long poem was published by the prestigious cultural institute in Havana that same year and a year later by Ragweed Press in Canada. This work has garnered considerable critical interest for its sustained focus on questions of language and the legacies of colonialism, interrelated themes that are central to both of Philip's major poetic works, *She Tries Her Tongue, Her Silence Softly Breaks* and *Looking for Livingstone: An Odyssey of Silence* (1991).

Philip told Williamson in 1993 that the project she "was particularly engaged with in *She Tries Her Tongue* . . . was subverting in a very conscious way all the traditions of poetry. Poetry came to us in the Caribbean as another form of colonization and oppression." To subvert poetry within the frame of a long poem, Philip avails herself of techniques that, as she notes in *A Genealogy of Resistance and Other Essays* (1997), can be compared with L-A-N-G-U-A-G-E poetics. "Discourse on the Logic of Language," "Universal Grammar," and the title poem, "She Tries Her Tongue, Her Silence Softly Breaks," in particular, make use of syntactic disruptions, "found" texts, and jazz-like rhythms that de-emphasize semantics. Conventional distinctions between poetry and prose, science and art, and history and literature are suspended in the interest of her thematic and political concerns. Cristanne Miller argues that "Philip combines elements of postmodern formal experimentation with an engaged political stance—indeed, makes those aspects of her work inseparable." Formal experimentation is a means of challenging the ideological freight imbedded in language and of renewing language in order to formulate new "i-mages." Philip's eccentric spelling of *image*, as she points out in "The Absence of Writing or How I Almost Became a Spy," is meant to mark both her "deconstructive" impulse and her interest in African Caribbean popular forms, in this case the Rastafarian privileging of "I." For Philip "The power and threat of the artist, poet or writer lies in this ability to create new i-mages, i-mages that speak to the essential being of the people among whom and for whom the artist creates." With the aim of representing and transmitting African Caribbean cultural memory in a language that bears the weight of a colonial history, Philip creates a series of poems that both formally and thematically engage with history, the body, language, and race.

"Meditations on the Declension of Beauty by the Girl with the Flying Cheek-bones" makes compelling use of L-A-N-G-U-A-G-E poetry techniques to explore the role of language in producing markers of race, identity, and beauty:

> In whose
> In whose language
>   Am I
>   Am I not
>   Am I I am yours
>   Am I not I am yours
>   Am I   I am
> If not in yours
>   In whose
> In whose language
>   Am I
> If not in yours
>   Beautiful

The use of repetition with variation to suggest grammatical declension here becomes incantatory, an affirmation of identity and beauty achieved in language. The slippage between affirmation and denial—"Am I / Am I not"—and between the interrogative and the declarative—"Am I I am"—suggests the precariousness of this affirmation of the speaker's beauty, the precariousness of her very existence in a language that is alien. Language is made physical in the poem; it is made to embody, through its sketching of nose, hips, and cheekbones:

> Girl with the flying cheek-bones:
> She is
> I am
> Woman with the behind that drives men mad
> And if not in yours
> Where is the woman with a nose broad
> As her strength
> If not in yours
> In whose language

In "Managing the Unmanageable" (1990) Philip explains that "the body insisted on being present throughout *She Tries*" and adds, "When the African came to the New World she brought with her nothing but her body and all the memory and history which the body could contain. The text of her history and memory was inscribed upon and within the body which would become the repository of all the tools necessary for spiritual and cultural survival."

What Brenda Carr describes as the "entanglement of the historical subject's flesh-and-blood body with language" also informs "Discourse on the Logic of Language," the most frequently reprinted and anthologized of Philip's poems. Here Philip explores the difficulty of creating in a language that is at once foreign and not foreign to the speaker:

> English
> is my mother tongue.
> A mother tongue is not
> not a foreign lan lan lang
> language
> l/anguish
> anguish
> —a foreign anguish.

Philip uses the page as a framing device to present four different kinds of text simultaneously. This lyric meditation occupies the center column of the verso pages of the poem. Running sideways down the left side of the page is a prose passage describing a mother using her tongue to clean and nurture a newborn child: "WHEN IT WAS BORN, THE MOTHER HELD HER NEWBORN CHILD CLOSE: SHE BEGAN THEN

TO LICK IT ALL OVER." On the right side are "edicts," pronouncements by colonial authorities concerning the language use of slaves: *"Every owner of slaves shall, wherever possible, ensure that his slaves belong to as many ethnolinguistic groups as possible. If they cannot speak to each other, they cannot then foment rebellion and revolution."* The recto pages are reserved for contemplation of the physiological dimensions of language production, citing both the racialization and the gendering of language capacity:

A tapering, blunt-tipped, muscular, soft and fleshy organ describes
(a) the penis.
(b) the tongue.
(c) neither of the above.
(d) both of the above.

The lyric voice is caught between two mutually exclusive discourses. One bestows language—a "mother tongue"—on a girl child, and the other proscribes the use of a mother tongue: *"Every slave caught speaking his native language shall be severely punished."* The task of the speaker is to come to terms with this contradictory inheritance, to reconcile mother tongue and father tongue ("a father tongue is / a foreign language") in a way that simultaneously allows for creativity and mounts a challenge to the "anguish of English." "The linguistic rape and subsequent forced marriage between African and English tongues," Philip writes in the introductory essay, "has resulted in a language capable of great rhythms and musicality; one that is and is not English, and one which is among the most vital in the English-speaking world today." In wresting this vitality from a violent history, Philip emphasizes the transformative possibilities of language even as she reminds her readers of the material effects of language use.

One difficulty Philip confronted as a consequence of her efforts to "subvert the lyric voice" in *She Tries Her Tongue, Her Silence Softly Breaks* was that she limited the size of her audience. She observed to Williamson in 1993: "My poems have become impossible to read as a solo person. How do you read something in which three voices are happening at the same time? And I sometimes wonder if, in trying to subvert the colonial project, I haven't hoisted myself on my own petard." But in *A Genealogy of Resistance and Other Essays* she recounts replying to a student who asked her to read "Universal Grammar": "I will, if you read it with me." She realized that she "had so disrupted the lyric voice by interruptions, eruptions, digressions, and a variety of other techniques, that the text had now become a polyvocular text, requiring more than one voice to give voice to it." When several voices read poems such as

"Discourse on the Logic of Language" and "Universal Grammar," "each reading becomes a mini-performance, setting off resonances, disrupting and disturbing our inner texts and expectations," an experience Philip finds eminently preferable to a single voice:

> It seemed to me, long after the work was done, that the interruptions and the many-voiced quality of the work was a truer representation of the New World and its massive and traumatic interruptions of the aboriginal, African, Asian, and European texts. To attempt to "read" that experience, which continues today, in a logical and linear way was to do it a second violence.

The layering, dialogic effect achieved by multiple readers, who may even interrupt one another, is clearly a more fitting way to perform these poems. Engaging several readers also translates an apparently esoteric, page-bound experiment into a collective performance that can reach a broader audience, as the CBC Radio recording and broadcast of "Discourse on the Logic of Language" attests.

Philip served as a nonfiction jury member for the Canada Council in 1989 and as a lecturer on creative fiction at York University from 1989 to 1991. She was a resident at the Banff Centre of the Arts in July 1990. A 1990 Guggenheim Fellowship in poetry allowed her to complete *Looking for Livingstone,* which was published the following year. "It started out as the last poem in *She Tries Her Tongue,*" Philip explained to Williamson in 1993, "but grew so long it became a book in its own right." *Looking for Livingstone* is an allegorical work that combines prose narrative with lyric verse. The narrative follows the journey of The Traveller, an unnamed woman of African descent who undertakes to follow the British colonial explorer Dr. David Livingstone, vowing that, like him, "I will open a way to the interior or perish." While Livingstone was referring to the interior of the African continent when he uttered this phrase, The Traveller seems more intent on a psychic or spiritual journey, an exercise in cultural memory. As she explores the ramifications of silence through her sojourns with imaginary peoples whose names are anagrams for silence—the ECNELIS, the LENSECI, the CLEENIS, the SCENILE, the CESLIENS, and the NEECLIS—The Traveller is in part engaged in an exploration of what Philip described in an interview with Coomie D. Vevaina as the "echoes in the silence of another language that was obliterated." The reference is to the "obliteration" of African languages through the Middle Passage and their "echoes" in the Caribbean vernacular. Many words from African languages, such as *Twi* and *Wolof,* have been incorporated into the Creole English spoken in the West Indies, providing traces of the historical connection to Africa as well as evidence of the impact that colonialism has had on African languages in the New World. The severing of ties with Africa imposed on the slaves in the Middle Passage had multiple repercussions; Philip is striving to address some of them in this work, as she explained to Vevaina:

> What I was trying to do with *Looking for Livingstone* was to acknowledge the rupture, the wound. The wound is and will always be there mainly because I cannot ever successfully return to it. I do not know what group or groups we belonged to. I have often asked myself, particularly when working on *Looking for Livingstone,* "How can you make poetry out of nothing?" and "How does one work with silence?" You feel the reverberations of something that was there before, but I also acknowledge that I am a New World person as well.

Looking for Livingstone strives to represent this diasporic history without nostalgia, offering a vision of the interrelationship between silence and the word that ultimately refuses easy dichotomies. David Marriott suggests that "Philip's position on silence seems to be a dialectical one that, rather than simply reproduce the oral-scribal split of 'nation language' accounts of the Caribbean culture, depends rather on a deep understanding of the relation between voice, body, unconscious fantasy and psychic affect." *Looking for Livingstone* is thus an extension of the project Philip undertakes in *She Tries Her Tongue, Her Silence Softly Breaks,* since it considers the paths one might take through silence to a renewed relationship with the colonial languages of the Americas. Cristanne Miller notes that "in contrast to Livingstone, who practices discovery as conquest, in which the already known (Africa, female, silence) is erased or written over by the European word, the speaker practices discovery that requires the exploration, not the erasure, of multiple vocabularies and systems of silence, or what is to her unknown." The exploratory impulse of The Traveller—her willingness to undergo transformation—is, in the end, her strength. The commemorative work that is an implicit dimension of The Traveller's journey through different forms of silence and of her imagined encounter with Livingstone marks both the rupture to which Philip alludes and the creative resistance of writers like herself.

In June 1991 Philip spent several weeks at the MacDowell artists' colony in Peterborough, New Hampshire, working on a novel that she never completed. In 1992 she became a lecturer at the University of Toronto. Much of her writing in the 1990s has focused on racism in contemporary North American, especially Canadian, culture. *Frontiers,* published in 1992, collects essays that appeared from the mid 1980s through 1991. Among them are some of Philip's most important: "Museum Could Have Avoided Culture

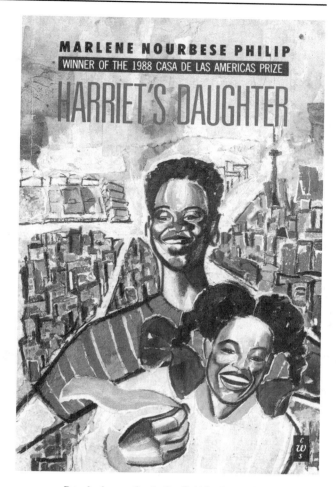

Paperback cover for the first British edition, 1988
(Bruccoli Clark Layman Archives)

Clash," about the Royal Ontario Museum exhibit *Into the Heart of Africa,* which the African Canadian community found to be insufficiently critical of colonialism and effectively racist; "Why Multiculturalism Can't End Racism," a critique of the official multiculturalism policy in Canada; and "The Disappearing Debate: Or, How the Discussion of Racism Has Been Taken over by the Censorship Issue," about the decision of The Women's Press not to publish work by white women that was deemed racist in its depiction of people of color. Philip's role as a public intellectual and analyst of the ways racism operates in Canadian cultural institutions is also evident in the pamphlet *Showing Grit: Showboating North of the 44th Parallel* (1993), an analysis of the assumptions about race in the Jerome Kern-Oscar Hammerstein II musical *Show Boat* (1927) and a critique of the Garth Drabinsky production that opened the publicly funded North York Centre for the Performing Arts in Toronto in 1993. The play that accompanies the second edition of this pamphlet (1993), *The Redemption of*

Al Bumen (a Morality Play): A Play in One Act, offers a witty rewriting of *Show Boat* that extends the argument Philip makes in *Showing Grit.*

Philip was a lecturer at the University of Toronto from 1992 to 1997; in 1993–1994 she was also a lecturer at the Ontario College of Art. She and Chamberlain were married on 7 June 1996. That same year Philip published *Caribana: African Roots and Continuities: Race, Space and the Poetics of Moving* (1996), a meditation on Carnival in Port of Spain, Notting Hill, and Toronto. The emphasis is on moving as metaphor for freedom and a form of resistance to slavery and racist efforts to police black movement in the New World after emancipation. The essay is richer for its use of the Caribbean vernacular and fictional devices such as the characters Maisie and Totoben, who are eager to "play marse" (parade in costume during Carnival). The 1997 collection *A Genealogy of Resistance and Other Essays* includes pieces Philip published in the 1990s on the legacies of colonialism. Like *The Redemption of Al Bumen (A Morality Play)* and *Caribana,* the essays blur the line between literature and nonfiction by combining argument and analysis with fiction, verse, diary entries, and drama. Philip dubs this style "word jazz."

Coups and Calypsos (1999), a two-act play that was produced in Toronto and London in 1999 and was a Dora Mavor Moore Award finalist, uses the 1990 coup attempt against the Trinidad government as the backdrop for an exploration of the tensions between those of African and Indian descent in Trinidad and Tobago. Rohan and Elvira, an estranged mixed-race couple (he is Indian Caribbean; she is African Caribbean), are thrust together again when it becomes impossible for Elvira to leave Tobago because of the hostage taking in Port of Spain. Rohan and Elvira revisit the problems in their relationship and attempt to come to terms with the racialized social dynamic that has driven them apart but ultimately retreat from any meaningful effort at reconciliation. The dialogue between Rohan and Elvira is periodically interrupted by a radio that alternately plays calypso music and provides highly unreliable updates on the coup situation, and by Rohan's elderly neighbor, Mrs. Samuels. The radio and Mrs. Samuels are devices for presenting the broader social scene and serve as a foil for the sophisticated professional couple, who by virtue of emigration are largely outside of the scene on which they are commenting and yet remain emotionally invested in these questions and in one another.

Each spring the Toronto-based arts company B Current presents new work by black women at the Rock.Paper.Sistahs Festival. Philip's poem cycle *Zong!*

was included in the 2006 festival at Harbourfront Theatre. The cycle addresses the massacre of African slaves aboard the slave ship *Zong* in 1781. In 2007 Philip had two books of poetry in manuscript: "Honey in the Window" and "Yesterdays of (K)not."

M. NourbeSe Philip's efforts to define an African-Caribbean-Canadian poetics that is attentive in its polyvocality, its performativity, and its thematic urgency to the lived history of the African diaspora are a hallmark of her work in all its guises. Her use of the vernacular and her taking up of a position that is deliberately situated between the inherited colonial language and poetic forms and an orality found in African Caribbean popular culture places her within a tradition of Caribbean writing that includes Edward Kamau Brathwaite, Derek Walcott, Edouard Glissant, and Grace Nichols. In the Canadian context her work is most frequently compared with that of Dionne Brand and Claire Harris, both of whom share Philip's concern with the vernacular, with gender, with the challenging of poetic boundaries, and with laying claim to a black Canadian imaginary while addressing an audience that encompasses but is hardly limited to the African diaspora. Philip's political activism and her writing about race and culture on the Canadian scene were recognized in 2001 by the "Rebels for a Cause" Award from the Elizabeth Fry Society and the 2001 YWCA Woman of Distinction Award in the Arts. A versatile writer whose work not only encompasses radical poetic experimentation and politically engaged essays but sometimes combines the two, Philip offers her readers a passionate engagement with language, colonialism, the body, and history that challenges orthodoxy and celebrates resistant artistry.

Interviews:

Barbara Carey, "Secrecy and Silence: M. Nourbese Philip's Search to Connect with Her Lost Cultural Heritage Fuels Her Writing," *Books in Canada,* 20, no. 6 (1991): 17–21;

Janice Williamson, "Blood on Our Hands: An Interview with M. Nourbese Philip," *Paragraph Magazine,* 14, no. 1 (1992): 18–19;

Jocelyne Doray and Julien Samuel, *The Raft of the Medusa: Five Voices on Colonies, Nations, and Histories* (Montreal: Black Rose, 1993);

Williamson, "Writing a Memory of Losing That Place," in her *Sounding Differences: Conversations with Seventeen Canadian Women Writers* (Toronto: University of Toronto, 1993), pp. 226–244;

Paul Naylor, "River City Interview with M. NourbeSe Philip," *River City: A Journal of Contemporary Culture,* 16 (Summer 1996): 22–34;

Coomie D. Vevaina, "Searching for Space: A Conversation with M. NourbeSe Philip," *Open Letter: A Canadian Journal of Writing and Theory,* ninth series, 9 (1997): 15–26;

Kristen Mahlis, "A Poet of Place: An Interview with M. NourbeSe Philip," *Callaloo,* 27, no. 3 (2004): 682–697;

Selina Horrell, "Bring the Private into the Public: An Interview with M. NourbeSe Philip," *Open Letter: A Canadian Journal of Writing and Theory,* twelfth series, 9 (2006): 27–32;

H. Nigel Thomas, "M. NourbeSe Philip," in his *Why We Write: Conversations with African Canadian Poets and Novelists* (Toronto: TSAR, 2006), pp. 198–208.

References:

Brenda Carr, "To 'Heal the Word Wounded': Agency and the Materiality of Language and Form in M. Nourbese Philip's *She Tries Her Tongue, Her Silence Softly Breaks,*" *Studies in Canadian Literature,* 19 (1994): 72–93;

George Elliott Clarke, "Harris, Philip, Brand: Three Authors in Search of Literate Criticism," *Journal of Canadian Studies,* 35 (Spring 2000): 161–189;

Elizabeth Deloughrey, "From Margin to the (Canadian) Frontier: 'The wombs of language' in M. Nourbese Philip's *She Tries Her Tongue, Her Silence Softly Breaks,*" *Journal of Canadian Studies,* 33 (Spring 1998): 121–145;

Barbara Godard, "Marlene Nourbese Philip's Hyphenated Tongue, or, Writing the Caribbean Demotic between Africa and Arctic," in *Major Minorities: English Literatures in Transit,* edited by Raoul Granqvist (Amsterdam & Atlanta: Rodopi, 1993), pp. 151–175;

Naomi Guttman, "Dream of the Mother Language: Myth and History in *She Tries Her Tongue, Her Silence Softly Breaks,*" *MELUS,* 21 (Fall 1996): 53–68;

David Marriott, "Figures of Silence and Orality in the Poetry of M. Nourbese Philip," in *Framing the Word: Gender and Genre in Caribbean Women's Writing,* edited by Joan Anim-Addo (London: Whiting & Birch, 1996), pp. 72–85;

Cristanne Miller, "M. Nourbese Philip and the Poetics/Politics of Silence," in *Semantics of Silences in Linguistics and Literature,* edited by Gudrun Grabher and Ulrike Jessner (Heidelberg: Universität C. Winter, 1996), pp. 139–160;

Miller, "Mixing It Up in M. Nourbese Philip's Poetic Recipes," in *Women Poets of the Americas: Toward a Pan-American Gathering,* edited by Jacqueline Vaught Brogan and Cordelia Chávez Candelaria (Notre Dame, Ind.: University of Notre Dame Press, 1999), pp. 233–253;

Leslie Sanders, "Marlene Nourbese Philip's 'Bad Words,'" *Tessera: Dialogue, Conversation, une écriture à deux,* 12 (Summer 1992): 81–89;

Elaine Savory, "The Poetry of Marlene Nourbese Philip and Pamela Mordecai," in *Framing the Word,* pp. 12–27.

Carol Shields

(2 June 1935 – 16 July 2003)

Christian Riegel
University of Regina

BOOKS: *Others* (Nepean, Ont.: Borealis Press, 1972);

Intersect (Nepean, Ont.: Borealis Press, 1974);

Small Ceremonies (Toronto: McGraw-Hill Ryerson, 1976; London: Fourth Estate, 1995; New York: Penguin, 1996);

Susanna Moodie: Voice and Vision (Nepean, Ont.: Borealis Press, 1977);

The Box Garden (Toronto: McGraw-Hill Ryerson, 1977; London: Fourth Estate, 1995; New York: Penguin, 1996);

Happenstance (Toronto: McGraw-Hill Ryerson, 1980);

A Fairly Conventional Woman (Toronto: Macmillan, 1982);

Various Miracles (Toronto: Stoddart, 1985; New York: Penguin, 1989; London: Fourth Estate, 1994);

Swann: A Mystery (Toronto: Stoddart, 1987); republished as *Swann: A Novel* (New York: Viking, 1989); republished as *Mary Swann* (London: Fourth Estate, 1990);

The Orange Fish (Toronto: Random House Canada, 1989; New York: Viking Adult, 1990);

Departures and Arrivals (Winnipeg: Blizzard, 1990);

A Celibate Season, by Shields and Blanche Howard (Regina: Coteau, 1991; New York: Penguin, 1999; London: Fourth Estate, 2000);

Coming to Canada: Poems, edited by Christopher Levenstein (Ottawa: Carleton University Press, 1992);

The Republic of Love (Toronto: Random House Canada, 1992; New York: Viking Adult, 1992; London: Fourth Estate, 1992);

The Stone Diaries (Toronto: Random House Canada, 1993; New York: Viking Adult, 1994; London: Fourth Estate, 1996);

Fashion, Power, Guilt, and the Charity of Families, by Shields and Catherine Shields (Winnipeg: Blizzard, 1995);

Larry's Party (Toronto: Random House Canada, 1997; New York: Viking Adult, 1997; London: Fourth Estate, 1997);

Anniversary, by Shields and David Williamson (Winnipeg: Blizzard, 1998);

Thirteen Hands (Winnipeg: Blizzard, 1998);

Dressing up for the Carnival (Toronto: Random House Canada, 2000; London: Fourth Estate, 2000; New York: Viking Adult, 2000);

Jane Austen (New York: Viking, 2001; London: Weidenfeld & Nicolson, 2001);

Unless (Toronto: Random House Canada, 2002; London: Fourth Estate, 2002);

Collected Stories of Carol Shields (Toronto: Random House Canada, 2004; London: Fourth Estate, 2004).

Collection: *Happenstance: Two Novels in One about a Marriage in Transition* (London: Fourth Estate, 1991; New York: Penguin, 1994)—comprises *Happenstance* and *A Fairly Conventional Woman.*

PLAY PRODUCTIONS: *Departures and Arrivals,* Winnipeg, The Black Hole Theatre, 1984;

Not Another Anniversary, Toronto, Solar Stage, 28 October 1986; revised by Shields and David Williamson as *Anniversary,* Winnipeg, Gas Station Theatre, 13 June 1996;

Thirteen Hands, Winnipeg, Prairie Theatre Exchange, 28 January 1993;

Fashion, Power, Guilt, and the Charity of Families, by Shields and Catherine Shields, Winnipeg, Prairie Theatre Exchange, 9 March 1995.

PRODUCED SCRIPT: *Sisters by Chance,* CBC Radio, 3 October 1999.

OTHER: "'Thinking back through Our Mothers': Tradition in Canadian Women's Writing," in *Re(Dis)covering Our Foremothers: Nineteenth-Century Canadian Women Writers,* edited by Lorraine McMullen (Ottawa: University of Ottawa Press, 1990), pp. 5–21;

"Travelwarp," in *Writing Away: The PEN Canada Travel Anthology,* edited by Constance Rooke (Toronto: McClelland & Stewart, 1994), pp. 276–280;

"Encounter," in *Without A Guide: Contemporary Women's Travel Adventures,* edited by Katherine Govier (St. Paul, Minn.: Hungry Mind, 1994), pp. 225–228;

Carol Shields (Getty Images Entertainment)

"Living at Home," in *Writing Home: A PEN Canada Anthology* (Toronto: McClelland & Stewart, 1997), pp. 286–289;

"The Orange Fish," in *Oxford Book of Stories by Canadian Women,* edited by Rosemary Sullivan (Don Mills, Ont.: Oxford University Press, 1999), pp. 234–239;

"Mrs. Turner Cutting the Grass," in *Great Stories from the Prairies,* edited by Birk Sproxton (Calgary: Red Deer Press, 2000), pp. 295–304;

Dropped Threads: What We Aren't Told, edited by Shields and Marjorie Anderson (Toronto: Vintage Canada, 2001);

Dropped Threads 2: More of What We Aren't Told, edited by Shields and Anderson (Toronto: Vintage Canada, 2003);

"Narrative Hunger and the Overflowing Cupboard," in *Carol Shields, Narrative Hunger, and the Possibilities of Fiction,* edited by Edward Eden and Dee Goertz (Toronto: University of Toronto Press, 2003), pp. 19–36;

"The Hardest Critics: A Collection from the *Washington Post* Book World," in *The Writing Life: Writers on How They Think and Work,* edited by Marie Arana (New York: Public Affairs Press, 2003), pp. 375–379;

"Collision," in *Short Fiction: An Anthology,* edited by Sullivan and Mark Levene (Don Mills, Ont.: Oxford University Press, 2003), pp. 546–557.

SELECTED PERIODICAL PUBLICATIONS–UNCOLLECTED: "Three Canadian Women: Fiction or Autobiography" and "'My Craft and Sullen Art': The Writers Speak," *Atlantis,* 4, no. 1 (1978): 49–54, 143–163;

"Leaving the Brick House behind Margaret Laurence and the Loop of Memory," *Recherches Anglaises et Nord-Americaines,* 24 (1991): 75–77;

"Jane Austen Images of the Body: No Fingers, No Toes," *Persuasions: Journal of the Jane Austen Society of North America,* 13 (December 1991): 132–137;

"Homing in on Winnipeg," *Canadian Living*, 17 (August 1992): 62;

"Fashion Power Guilt & the Charity of Families," *Quill & Quire*, 61 (November 1995): 36;

"Making Words / Finding Stories," *Journal of Business Administration and Policy Analysis*, 24–26 (1996): 36–52;

"Martians in Jane Austen?" *Persuasions: Journal of the Jane Austen Society of North America*, 18 (December 1996): 191–203;

"So That Every Child Is Certain of a Welcome," *Globe and Mail* (Toronto), 19 May 1997, p. A13;

"Coming to Canada," *Quill & Quire*, 63 (August 1997): 36;

"Giving Your Literary Papers Away," *Quill & Quire*, 64 (November 1998): 43;

"The Next Best Kiss," *Atlantic Monthly*, 283 (January 1999): 79–85;

"Opting for Invention over the Injury of Invasions," *New York Times*, 10 April 2000, pp. E1–E2;

"Faith, Flowers and Friends," *Canadian Living*, 25 (October 2000): 68;

"The question of fiction," *Event*, 31 (Spring 2002): 16;

"Mortality," *Brick*, no. 72 (Winter 2003): 14;

"Miracles en série," *Chatelaine*, 46 (March 2005): 22.

One of Canada's most celebrated authors, American-born Carol Shields was a best-selling novelist in her adopted country and around the world; she was also a noted poet and playwright. Shields was awarded many major literary prizes, including the Pulitzer Prize, the Orange Prize for Women's Fiction, the National Critics' Circle Prize, and the Prix Lire; she was also short-listed for the Booker Prize and nominated for the IMPAC Dublin Literary Award. She was made a Companion to the Order of Canada, a Fellow of the Royal Society of Canada, a member of the Order of Manitoba, and a Guggenheim fellow.

Carol Ann Warner was born on 2 June 1935 in Oak Park, Illinois, to Robert E. Warner, a manager of a candy company, and Inez Selgren Warner, a fourth-grade teacher. She had twin siblings, Barbara and Robert, who were two years her senior. In a 1989 interview with Eleanor Wachtel, Shields recalled reading the magazine *Better Homes and Gardens* when she was four: "For me, learning to read was the central mystical experience of my life." She began school at Nathaniel Hawthorne School, moving after three years to Ralph Waldo Emerson School. She graduated from Oak Park High School in 1953 and enrolled at Hanover College in Hanover, Indiana. She spent the 1955–1956 academic year at the University of Exeter in England as an exchange student. In 1957 she graduated from Hanover College and married Donald Hugh Shields, an engineer

from Saskatchewan. The newlyweds moved to Vancouver for three months, then to Toronto. Their first child, John, was born in 1958; Anne was born the next year. In 1960 the family moved to England while Donald Shields completed a Ph.D. at the University of Manchester. Their daughter Catherine was born in 1962. That same year Carol Shields sold several short stories to the Canadian Broadcasting Corporation and the British Broadcasting Corporation. While living in Manchester, Shields took several law courses. She told Wachtel, "Being in England turned me around a bit; I started waking up." She became more aware of the role of women in society and especially of how women were portrayed in fiction: "Around this time, I was conscious that women in the fiction I read were nothing like the women I knew. They weren't as intelligent. There was a real gap. And they weren't as kind."

In 1963 the family returned to Toronto; a third daughter, Margaret, was born that year. In 1964 Shields won the Canadian Broadcasting Corporation Young Writers Competition. In 1968 the Shieldses' final child, Sara, was born, and the family moved to Ottawa. Shields became a Canadian citizen in 1971.

Shields's first book was a collection of poems titled *Others*, which appeared in 1972. Several of the fifty-four poems had previously appeared in Canadian publications such as *The Candian Forum, Salt, The Far Point*, and *The West Coast Review*, or on the Canadian Broadcasting Corporation. "Margaret at Easter" is a portrait of Shields's daughter singing in the church choir: "From the choir she makes / angelic O's of song, / hosannas pumped from her seven-year-old lungs." In the majority of the poems the first-person plural is used to represent the speaker, as is shown by the titles "A Woman We Saw in an Antique Shop," "An Old Lady We Saw," "Our Artist Friends," and "What Our Toronto Friends Said," in which the speaker says, "Having an hour to kill we drove / around town, down streets with names / like Church, Jane, Martingrove, / past rows of houses set in frames." Christopher Levenstein notes in his introduction to Shields's *Coming to Canada* (1992) that "Shields avoids anything that could be construed as confessional; by remaining so obviously an observer she also deliberately conceals any overt personal reactions."

In 1973 Shields became an editorial assistant at the journal *Canadian Slavonic Papers* at Carleton University in Ottawa and began working on an M.A. in English at the University of Ottawa. Her second book, *Intersect* (1974), is a collection of forty-nine poems, some of which had previously appeared in literary magazines. In "Margaret, Aged Four" Shields examines her daughter's attempt to use language to explain the world around her. "Family at the Cottage" examines the experience of feeling slightly out of place in a new location but being grounded by belonging to a family unit:

> The children, dazed by novelty,
> pass supernatural
> through walls
>
> and at night
> we fall
> asleep in exotic lumbered corners
> almost touching but never quite.

"Pioneers: Southeast Ontario" is about the inexorable pace of development and how history quickly fades from consciousness. That the pioneers "existed" is evidenced by the artifacts they left behind: "Butter bowls / and hayrakes testify." But as time goes by, "they're melting to myth / every year harder to believe." "Volkswagen" deals with the automobile that was first produced in Nazi Germany: "At the auto show / the original Volkswagen / is on display." In a consumer culture "the black / era of its origin" is best forgotten; it is better to reflect on the qualities of the automobile as a beautiful and functional object:

> Think of its prim chrome lips
> instead, its likeable back,
> just humble enough for humans,
> the friendly hips
> enclosing those well meaning
> wheels, so anxious to get going.

Shields received her M.A. in 1975 with a thesis on the nineteenth-century Canadian author Susanna Moodie. She spent the next year in Brittany, returning to lecture part-time in the English department at the University of Ottawa.

Shields's first novel, *Small Ceremonies* (1976), is narrated by Judith Gill, who is writing a biography of Moodie. The novel takes place over the course of nine months, beginning in September; the family has just returned to Toronto from a year in Birmingham, where Judith's husband, Martin, was conducting research during his sabbatical. There they lived in the home of a family who were away in Greece. The year in England and the shadow of the family whose space they occupied hangs over Judith and her family as the novel progresses. A key theme of the work is Canadian identity, which was a major concern of cultural critics and commentators in the 1970s. In a letter the girl whose room Judith's son, Richard, occupied in England, writes: "my parents have told me that you are Canadians which I suppose is rather like being Americans." A secondary character, Roger, an expert on Canadian literature, espouses the view that the national theme of Canadian writing is "shelter. Shelter from the Storm of

life." This claim is an echo of conventional Canadian criticism in the 1970s. Another important theme is the nature of various types of writing. Judith comments that in a biography, "The characters are inert, having no details of person to make them fidget or scratch; they are toneless, simplified, stylized, myths distilled from letters; they are bloodless." She attempts to write a novel using a plot borrowed from an unpublished manuscript she found in the house in England; the plot is later borrowed by her friend, the well-known novelist Furlong Eberhart, who defends his action by saying, "But, my good Lord, writers can't stake out territories. It's open season. A free range. One uses what one can find. One takes an idea and brings to it his own individual touch. His own quality. Enhances it. Develops it."

In 1977 Shields published *Susanna Moodie: Voice and Vision,* a monograph that examines issues of personality, sexuality, and social structure in Moodie's writing. That same year she published the novel *The Box Garden,* in which the main character, Charleen Forrest, is Judith Gill's sister. Charleen, a poet, travels by train from Vancouver to Toronto with her boyfriend, Eugene, to attend her mother's surprise wedding to a lapsed priest she met during their cancer treatments at a clinic; while she is away, her son is kidnapped by her best friend, who was supposed to watch him but instead takes him on a lengthy road trip. On the train Charleen considers how she and Eugene are "the losers" in the marriage realm: "Both of us, Eugene and I, are secondary victims of separate modern diseases, mid-century maladies hatched by the heartless new social order: Eugene because his wife abandoned him for the Women's Movement and I, because I married a man who couldn't bear to leave his youth behind." Her husband's departure on a walking tour of Europe was a rejection of what he termed "Establishment values," which included his employment as a professor and the domestic role that his wife had taken on: "And then, overnight, it seemed I was part of the Establishment too. Wife. Kid. House. We were all part of it." The husband's departing note "was so terribly dumb. . . . It was just page after page of youth cult hash. Abstractions like freedom and selfhood." The husband is later revealed to be "Brother Adam," who writes letters filled with philosophical advice to Charleen. He has acquired a significant amount of knowledge about the propagation of grass, a pursuit that he elevates to a sacred search for knowledge. Charleen has gained some critical respect for her poetry but has found that the writing process itself is a significant aspect of her psychological well-being: "After Watson left us, after he walked out on Seth and me, poetry became the means by which I saved my life. I stopped assembling; I discovered that I could bury in my writing the greater part of my pain and humiliation. The usefulness of poetry was revealed to me."

In 1978 Shields took a position teaching creative writing at the University of British Columbia in Vancouver. Two years later, she began teaching English literature at the University of Manitoba in Winnipeg. Also in 1980 Shields published the novel *Happenstance,* about a week in the life of Jack Bowman. Middle-aged, Jack lives in Elm Park, a suburb of Chicago, with his wife, Brenda, and their two children; Brenda is spending the week in Philadelphia, where she is exhibiting her quilts at a crafts show. Jack is employed by the Great Lakes Research Institute and has been working for years on a book about North American Indians. When the novel opens, he and Bernie, a friend since their college days, are having their weekly meal at a local restaurant. Jack has misinterpreted the title of an announced book, *Indian Trading Practices Prior to Colonization,* by a former college lover, Harriet Post, to mean that she has written on the same topic as his, and he believes that his work has been wasted; it is later revealed that Harriet's book is about the Indian subcontinent. Jack notices that others, including his wife, do not see the past as he does: "He *had* taken it for granted, his vision of time, assuming that everyone perceived events as he did, through a multiple lens, a dense superimposed image composed of layers and layers of time." During the week covered by the novel Bernie's marriage dissolves; Jack's neighbor attempts suicide after a party; his son Rob realizes for the first time the complexity and harshness of life; and his secretary tells him that she loves him on her last day of work before retiring to Arizona.

In 1981 Shields became an assistant professor in the Department of English at the University of Manitoba. In 1982 she published *A Fairly Conventional Woman,* which relates the activities of Jack Bowman's wife, Brenda, during the same week that is depicted in *Happenstance.* Brenda has achieved success as a quilter, selling her pieces for significant prices and receiving acclaim in the magazine *Chicago Today* for the quality of her work. The novel opens with a typical domestic scene: "Every morning Brenda wakes up, slips into her belted robe, and glides–*glides*–down the wide oak stairs to make breakfast for her husband and children." Her quilting is far removed from this world of chores and mundane concerns: "When she was working on a quilt, she seldom looked out of the window, or anything else for that matter. . . . the patterns seemed to come from a simplified root of memory; sometimes they arrived as a pulsating rush when she was pulling weeds in the yard or shoveling snow off the front walk, but more often they appeared to her early in the morning before she opened her eyes, an entire design projected on the inte-

rior screen of her eyelids." The trip to Philadelphia, which will expose her to a national audience, is a much-anticipated event: "In recent days she has felt compelled to disguise her excitement, to affect calm. . . . She even managed a shrug of nonchalance when the printed program from the Philadelphia Exhibition arrived in the mail a week ago with her name listed on the back: Brenda Bowman, Quilter, Chicago Craft Guild." At home the face Brenda shows to the world is "Pleasant, pleasant, always pleasant." On the airplane, however, she tells a fellow passenger her destination "curtly, a sting of vinegar in her voice, not at all as she had pronounced it at home." Brenda shows that Jack was correct in his perception that she did not share his notion of history: "What he didn't seem to grasp (as Brenda did) was that history was no more than a chain of stories, stories that happened to everyone and that, in time, came to form the patterns of entire lives, her own included." In Brenda's view, history is far removed from the sterile academic accounts that occupy her husband. A fellow quilter tells her: "The thing is . . . I used to think stories only had the one ending. But then, this last year or so, I got to thinking that that's not right. The fact is, most stories have three or four endings, maybe even more." In Philadelphia she finds her roommate, a woman she has never met before, having sex in their hotel room; she gets drunk while being interviewed by a reporter for the local newspaper; and she has a drink in the room of a man she has encountered in an elevator. That encounter leads her to contemplate infidelity: "Now for the first time she felt she had stepped into faithlessness. So this was it! Not sex at all, but novelty, risk, possibility." Ultimately, Brenda does not become unfaithful: "'The trouble is I can't disconnect,' Brenda said. 'I don't mean just marriage vows. I mean my whole life.'"

In 1991 *Happenstance* and *A Fairly Conventional Woman* were republished together in paperback as *Happenstance: Two Novels in One about a Marriage in Transition.* Sarah Gamble notes in "Filling the Narrative Void: Narrative Dilemmas in *Small Ceremonies,* the *Happenstance* Novels, and *Swann,*" included in *Carol Shields, Narrative Hunger, and the Possibilities of Fiction* (2003): "Although originally published two years apart under different titles, the wife's and husband's stories are now printed together back-to-back, thus placing the dual ending squarely in the middle of the book. Once the story has been concluded, this structure draws the reader into the next and back, creating a never-ending Möbius strip of a narrative."

Shields's two-act comedy *Departures and Arrivals* premiered at The Black Hole Theatre at the University of Manitoba in 1984; it was published in 1990. Four actors portray a series of female characters in twenty-two vignettes set in an airport departure lounge.

In 1985 a documentary about Shields aired on the Alberta Access Network. That same year she published *Various Miracles,* a collection of twenty-one short stories prefaced by a passage from Emily Dickinson: "Tell the truth but tell it slant." In "Sailors Lost at Sea" Hélène is a child who has accidentally been locked in a church in a French village where she and her mother are spending several months away from their home in Winnipeg. Hélène thinks about her mother's relationship with her boyfriend, Roger, whose arrival in their household was, the mother asserted, "not how I planned things." In "Purple Blooms" the narrator contemplates her mother's attitude toward books: "What possible need does she have for books, she asks me. Life is all around her." In "Poaching" the narrator and her traveling companion, Dobey, discuss stories they have been told by other travelers. She wonders, "what had they offered?" Dobey responds that a story requires the listener or reader to be an active participant in its meaning: "Dobey says to be patient, that everything is fragmentary, that it's up to us to supply the missing links." In "Scenes" Frances explains her love of reading: "Learning to read was like falling into a mystery deeper than the mystery of airwaves or the halo around the head of the baby Jesus." Reading makes Frances feel "suffused with light." In "Others" Robert and Lila are honeymooning in France when they kindly cash a personal check for an English civil servant they have never met before. Every year for the next several decades they receive Christmas cards from the Englishman: "He signs them with a joint signature–Nigel and Jane–and adds a few words about the weather, the state of their health (both his and Jane's) and thanks them yet again for coming to their rescue in Normandy." Robert and Lila do not know Nigel and Jane's address and so can never respond. Over the years, as their children are born and raised; their careers falter; and they separate and are reunited; their lives are framed by the cards they receive annually.

Swann: A Mystery (1987) is a satire of the world of academic literary criticism. Mary Swann, a rural Canadian poet, is murdered. Little is known about her writing or her life. The novel is told from the perspectives of four characters and is divided into five sections. The first section is narrated by Sarah Moloney; the next three sections are narrated in the third person from the perspectives of each of the other main characters; and the final section is the script for a movie about the Mary Swann Symposium. Sarah, a young Chicago academic, stumbles on Swann's book of poems at a friend's cottage and turns the discovery into a major scholarly find: "In a sense I invented

Dust jacket for the first U.S. edition, 1989
(Bruccoli Clark Layman Archives)

Mary Swann and am responsible for her." The scholar is thus responsible for providing significance to a literary career that would otherwise go unnoticed. Morton Jimroy, an established Winnipeg scholar, is attempting to write a biography of Swann. He interviews Swann's daughter in California, but the information he gleans is superficial: he learns the size of the neighbors' farms and barns and that Swann only checked two books at a time out of the local library. He is reduced to writing in his notes that "It is highly probable that Swann read Jane Austen during this period" and concludes that she had "one of the dullest lives ever." Rose Hindmarch has established the Mary Swann Memorial Room in the Nadeau Local History Museum in Nadeau, Ontario, Swann's hometown. Since Swann left behind no material possessions, "Rose was forced to use her imagination when it came to furnishing the Mary Swann Memorial Room":

If you suggested to Rose that her room has been wrenched into being through duplicity, through countless small acts of deception, she will be sure to look injured and offer up a pained denial. These articles, after all, belong to the *time* and the *region* of which Mary Swann was a part, and therefore nothing is misrepresented, not the quilts, not the china, not even the picture of the cocker spaniel.

The narrator notes ironically: "The charm of falsehood is not that it distorts reality, but that it creates reality afresh." The final main character, Frederic Cruzzi, is a former newspaper editor in Kingston, Ontario. Swann arrived on Cruzzi's doorstep on a frozen afternoon with a paper bag filled with poems. Cruzzi decided to publish them; but his wife mistakenly put the remains of several whitefish in the bag, rendering many of the poems illegible. The couple reconstructed them, at times taking great liberties in their guesses as to what the smudgy scribbles could mean: "At one point, Hildë, supplying missing lines and even the greater part of a missing stanza, said she could feel what the inside of Mary Swann's head must look like." The result was Swann's only book, the posthumously published *Swann's Songs*. The last section of the novel is the script for a movie titled *Swann Symposium*. The novel won the Arthur Ellis Award for the Best Canadian Mystery and was short-listed for the Governor General's Literary Award for Fiction.

In 1988 Shields was writer-in-residence at the University of Winnipeg and at Douglas College in New Westminster, British Columbia; the following year she held a similar position at the University of Ottawa. A special issue of the feminist literary journal *A Room of One's Own* was devoted to her work in 1989. That same year she published a collection of twelve short stories, *The Orange Fish*. In "Chemistry" the narrator is one of a group of seven people who took a series of music lessons in the winter of 1972 in Montreal. She notes that one can only be certain about the basic elements of a remembered experience: "Unforgivable to forget, but at a certain distance the memory buckles." Though a special camaraderie—the "chemistry" of the title—developed among the participants, the narrator is unaware of any of them ever having made an effort to meet again: "We could take possession of each other once again, conjure our old undisturbed, unquestioning chemistry. The wonder is that it hasn't already happened. You would think we made a pact never to meet again." In "Hinterland" a middle-aged American couple, Roy and Meg Sloan, travel to Paris at the height of a terrorist threat and are mildly unsettled by being in a city under siege. The narrator comments on how the predictable shape of their lives has been thrown into question by their experiences in Paris: "Their robust North Ameri-

can belief that life consists of stages keeps them from sinking, though ahead of them, in a space the size of this small table, waits a series of intricate compromises: impotence, rusted garden furniture, disordered dreams, and the remembrance of specific events which have been worn smooth and treacherous as the stone steps of ancient buildings." In "Hazel" the recently widowed title character reflects on how her life has been a pale imitation of the novels she reads: "She had a sense of her own life turning over page by page, first a girl, then a young woman, then married with two young daughters, then a member of a bridge club and a quilting club, and now, too soon for symmetry, a widow. All of it fell into small childish paragraphs, the print over-large and blocky like a school reader." Hazel takes a sales job and rises quickly in the company. In the end she has moved away from the notion that life is like fiction; it is disordered, and things happen for no apparent reason: "Everything is an accident. Hazel would be willing to say if asked. Her whole life is an accident, and by accident she has blundered into the heart of it." "Collision" is a portrait of Martä Gjatä, a documentary moviemaker in an unnamed Eastern European country. The narrator points out that a biography cannot be written as an organized, well-ordered story; it must follow the constraints of the life that is its subject: "Biography is used to kinks and wherewithal, it expects to find people in odd pockets, it's used to surges of speechless passion that come out of nowhere and sink without a murmur. It doesn't care." *The Orange Fish* was named one of the top two books of short fiction of the year by *The Christian Science Monitor*.

In 1990 Shields received the Marian Engel Award, which recognizes the achievements of a female Canadian writer in midcareer. The following year Shields and the British Columbia writer Blanche Howard published the epistolary novel *A Celibate Season*, comprising a series of letters between Charles "Chas" and Jocelyn "Jock" Selby from September to June. Chas and Jock have been married for more than two decades and have two children. Jock has moved to Ottawa to take a temporary position as legal counsel for a government commission on women and poverty; Chas, a newly unemployed architect, has remained in Vancouver to take care of the children while he searches for a job. The new arrangement disrupts the rhythm of Chas's previously predictable life: "I feel this morning like a man reborn," he writes in one of his letters. Chas becomes a published poet, manages an unconventional household, and establishes his own architectural business. Jock returns at Christmas to find that Chas has undertaken an extensive addition to the house without consulting her. Later, she writes: "Of course I am sorry for the way I acted—bursting into tears when you walked into your very own home whose every corner you've mopped, scrubbed, painted, and loved, and whose interior reflects your soul just as faithfully as the clothing you wear and the shade of your lipstick–I can't go on. . . . To walk into a place you've longed for every day for four months and to find it has disappeared . . . you'd have cried too." Various characters with nowhere else to go end up in Chas and Jock's home: the cleaning lady and her daughter, the cleaning lady's neighbor and her daughter, his mother, and some of his friends from Ottawa. The home is no longer reserved as a space for the nuclear family. For Jock, moving to Ottawa is a liberating experience: it provides her with a sense of achievement as a professional woman, and she is exposed to feminist ideas about women's roles in society: "The Commission has been . . . the most tremendous experience of my life. I wouldn't give up these last months for the world, the people I've met, the things I've learned, the insights I've gained, the self-confidence. I suppose I *am* different." Over the course of *A Celibate Season* Chas and Jock find that despite their frequent letters, they have failed to communicate effectively, and their marriage seems on the brink of dissolution. Chas notes that when Jock left for Ottawa, "We didn't stop to discuss or even consider the problems that might accompany ten months of celibate life." Jock wonders: "We had a lot going for us before; surely we haven't changed enough to erase the happiness of twenty years?"

The Republic of Love appeared in 1992. Thirty-six-year-old Fay MacLeod, a mermaid researcher at the National Folklore Centre in Winnipeg, has inexplicably left her longtime lover. Tom Avery is a late-night-radio call-in-show host who has been through three failed marriages by his fortieth birthday. The two slowly come together and become lovers in a context of work, family, and friends. The narrator notes: "The problem with stories of romance is that lovers are always shown in isolation: two individuals made suddenly mythic by the size of their ardor, an ardor that is declared secretive or else incomprehensible to the rest of the wide buzzing world. . . . the lovers are magically released from a need for dentists, for tax advisers, for show salesmen, for anyone who stands outside their immediate sphere of passion." Fay thinks that in stories and movies lovers become separate from everyone and everything around them: "Their families, their friends, even their work and their separate histories pale beside their rapture, which lies outside of life, not within." The notion of the relationship between two people in love existing "within" life is central to *The Republic of Love*. Fay watches her parents' marriage suddenly disintegrate on the event of their fortieth anniversary when her father leaves because the relationship has been too

intense: "his long peaceful marriage had somehow overnourished him. He couldn't breathe. He felt watched, insulated, incapacitated." To Fay, the notion that there is more than one kind of love, or more than one dimension to love, is baffling: "Love is love. Her mother's only transgression, as far as she can see, is to have loved him deeply." Fay learns from witnessing this marital failure that life is not like the stories she reads: "Many people's lives don't wrap up nearly as neatly as they'd like to think. Fay's sure of that. Most people's lives are a mess." Such is the case with the path to love in Fay and Tom's case. Fay thinks, according to the narrator, that "love is not, anywhere, taken seriously. It's not respected. It's the one thing in the world everyone wants–she's convinced of that–but for some reason people are obliged to pretend that love is trifling and foolish." *The Republic of Love* won the 1992 U.K. Guardian Fiction Prize.

In 1992 Shields published *Coming to Canada,* a collection of poems that had appeared in magazines such as *Antigonish Review, Arc, Fiddlehead, Quarry, Canadian Forum,* and *Border Crossings.* The volume opens with a series of seventeen linked poems titled "Coming to Canada"; the middle section comprises twenty-two poems republished from *Others* and *Intersect;* thirty-three poems in a section titled "New Poems" end the collection. The largely autobiographical "Coming to Canada" sequence details experiences from her birth to her moving to Canada at age twenty-two. In the first poem, "Getting Born," she notes the facts surrounding her birth–"My time and place are fixed / at least–Chicago 1935"–and muses: "Odd that no one knows how / it feels to be born." "Learning to Talk" describes her growing awareness of language, and in "I / Myself" the three-year-old Shields becomes aware of herself as an individual. "Daddy" examines the mystery of her father's daily disappearance to go to work. "Visiting Aunt Violet" describes a visit to her aged aunt and the impertinent questions that Shields asked. In "When Grandma Died–1942" Shields writes of her first awareness of the physical reality of death:

When no one was looking I touched
her mouth–which had not
turned to dust
It was hard and cold
like pressing in the side
of a rubber ball.

The poems that close the volume include brief character sketches such as "Sunday Painter," in which an office worker is "expectant / but calm" as he approaches the task of painting as a means of escape from the vagaries of life; painting takes him "through the seasons, changes of government, / conditions of health and family history." "The Invention of Clocks," "At the Clock Museum," "Now," "Quartz," "Calendar Notes," "Spring," "Daylight Saving," "Fall," and "Season's Greetings" explore the theme of time. "In Daylight Savings" the speaker imagines possibilities for the one-hour time shift: "You could build a house there / in that hour and a garden, shining / windows flowers." Other poems return to the family themes of the "Coming to Canada" sequence, such as "Aunt Violet's Things" and "Relic," in which she recalls "Auntie Ruthie's fruited hat, / boat of truth / in a sea of right."

The Stone Diaries (1993) is the fictional autobiography of Daisy Goodwill; Daisy recounts the story of her life, and a second narrator provides commentary. The novel opens with her birth in a small town in Manitoba in 1905. Daisy's mother is preparing a meal in the kitchen while awaiting the return of her husband from the local quarry when she suddenly goes into labor. Various neighbors and passersby become witnesses to Daisy's birth: "Life is an endless recruiting of witnesses. . . . Our own memory is altogether too cherishing . . . Other accounts are required, other perspectives." Daisy's mother dies giving birth to her: "they cast their gaze one last time on the great white covered form of Mercy Stone Goodwill who lies before them, silent and still as a boat, a stranger in the world for all of her life, who has given her child the last of her breath." After Daisy dies, the second narrator remarks: "Only her body survives, and the problem of what do with it. It has not turned to dust." The thought of "her limbs and organs transformed to biblical dust or even funeral ashes" is "laughable." Daisy imagines herself in death: "Stone is finally how she sees herself, her living cells replaced by insentience of mineral deposition. It's easy enough to let it claim her." The novel ends with the benediction at Daisy's funeral that sums up her life as an ordinary woman whose story is not particularly notable: "Daisy Goodwill Flett, wife, mother, citizen of our century: May she rest in peace." Simone Vauthier points out: "Purporting to be the autobiography of Daisy Goodwill Flett, the narration, which oscillates between the first-person and the third, destabilizes the authority of the narrating voice(s). Devoting large chunks to people whose lives have sometimes only fleetingly touched Daisy's, the narrative decentres the (auto)biography." Wendy Roy notes in her article "Autobiography as Critical Practice in *The Stone Diaries*," included in *Carol Shields, Narrative Hunger, and the Possibilities of Fiction*, that "*The Stone Diaries* both imitates and undermines autobiography" and should be seen as "meta-autobiography, or a work of literature that comments on the genre," because "the first-person narrative is periodically replaced by other narrators and other narrative strategies . . . and the narrators muse repeat-

edly about the genre of autobiography." In "'She Enlarges on the Available Materials': A Postmodernism of Resistance in *The Stone Diaries*," included in the same volume, Lisa Johnson says that Shields "employs common postmodern aesthetic strategies." The novel achieved best-seller status and won the Governor General's Literary Award for Fiction, the McNally Robinson Award for Manitoba Book of the Year, the Canadian Booksellers' Association Prize, and the Pulitzer Prize and was short-listed for the Booker Prize.

Shields's two-act play *Thirteen Hands* was workshopped in 1990 by the Manitoba Association of Playwrights, had a staged public reading at the Tarragon Theatre in Toronto that same year, and was workshopped once more by the Canadian Stage Company in Toronto the following year. It was produced at the Prairie Theatre Exchange in Winnipeg with a run that began on 28 January 1993. It then toured across Canada, including a production at the National Arts Centre in Ottawa. It was published in 1998. *Thirteen Hands* is centered on the female players in a weekly bridge game between 1920 and 1993; over the course of the play the four founders of the bridge club age and die and are replaced by other women. Shields indicates in the "Playwright's Note" that she had a feminist purpose in writing the play: "For many years I've been interested in the lives of women, particularly those lives which have gone unrecorded. . . . one group seems consistently overlooked: a group who, for historical reasons mainly, were caught between movements, the so called 'blue rinse set,' the 'ladies of the club,' the bridge club 'biddies.' There were (are) thousands of these women, millions in fact. I am reluctant to believe that their lives are wasted or lost. Something important goes on around a bridge table, a place where many women have felt most brilliantly alive." *Thirteen Hands* was short-listed for the Dora Mavor Moore Award in 1997.

Shields spent a sabbatical year at the University of California, Berkeley, in 1994. In 1995 she received an honorary degree from the University of Ottawa and was promoted to full professor at the University of Manitoba. On 9 March of that year her play *Fashion, Power, Guilt, and the Charity of Families*, co-authored with her daughter Catherine, opened at the Prairie Theatre Exchange; it ran until 25 March and was published that same year. In her "Playwright's Note" Shields writes: "It seemed important to question the basic assumptions about the nuclear family by placing abstract commentary margin-to-margin with the ongoing life of a 'real' family, and bringing music and drama edge-to-edge in order to open that question as far as it would allow." Catherine Shields remarks in her own note that "I am fascinated by the power behind the drive we all share to find or create some kind of family (whatever form this may take: two people, or a commune). Yet the desire to escape the fury of family is just as strong. What's the deal here?" The production notes indicate that "The tone of the play varies from the surreal to the sharply realistic." The setting is the inside of a house; five actors play nine roles: a mother, a father, two children, and five minor characters. The play ends with a song: "Family on the fault line / One two three four, / Trouble always at the door. / Fam-i-lee-ee. / Carryin' on, / Carryin' on, / Carryiiin' oooooonnn."

In 1996 Shields was appointed chancellor of the University of Winnipeg, while retaining her status as a professor at the University of Manitoba. She was also awarded honorary degrees from the University of Winnipeg, Hanover College, Queen's University, and the University of British Columbia. On 13 June her play *Anniversary,* co-authored with her University of Manitoba colleague David Williamson, premiered at the Gas Station Theatre in Winnipeg; it was published in 1998. *Anniversary* is a revision in two acts of an unpublished one-act play, *Not Another Anniversary,* that was produced by Solar Stage in Toronto on 28 October 1986. Shields and Williamson remark in the "Playwrights' Note": "*Anniversary* is a fast-paced comedy built on a triple narrative irony. One couple in the play are married and pretending to be close to separation. Another couple, who are separated, are pretending to be married. The third and overriding irony is that the separated couple are still emotionally together, while the married couple have already emotionally separated. . . . We like to think this play will bring pleasure, laughter, recognition and perhaps even a little reflection."

In Shields's novel *Larry's Party* (1997) Larry Weller is a Winnipeg florist who visits the maze at Hampton Court while honeymooning in England with his wife, Dorrie. The experience signals to him a new way of living that takes into account the fluidity and uncertainty of existence: "And now, here in this garden maze, getting lost, and then found, seemed the whole point, that and the moment of willed abandonment, the unexpected rapture of being blindly led." Working his way into and finding his way out of the maze is a precursor to the shape that his life will take from this moment forward: "Departures and arrivals: he didn't know it then, but these two forces would form the twin bolts of his existence—as would the brief moments of clarity that rose up in between, offering stillness. A suspension of breath. His life held in his hands." In "Treading the Maze of *Larry's Party,*" included in *Carol Shields, Narrative Hunger, and the Possibilities of Fiction,* Dee Goertz remarks that "the maze functions not only as a symbol in the novel, but also as image, metaphor, and structural device." Goertz contends that "the maze as a symbol . . . underscores the main theme of

the novel—that the human quest for meaning and pattern in the universe is a quest for connectedness. To find meaning, people must push beyond symbols and reach out to each other." Larry becomes a successful maze designer in Chicago, then moves the business to Toronto. The novel ends twenty years after it began at Larry's forty-seventh-birthday party, at which he is reunited with his two former wives and his on-again, off-again girlfriend, Beth. There they all realize that he and his first wife, Dorrie, are still in love. Afterward, Beth writes to him: "Dear Larry, I always knew you loved her. And that she loved you. I knew! . . . It seemed to me that all that was required was the right frame or mood or circumstance. Or just taking the right corner at the right moment—like your beautiful mazes." *Larry's Party* won the Orange Prize, the National Book Critics Circle Award for Fiction, and France's Prix de Lire and was short-listed for the Giller Prize.

In 1998 Shields was appointed an officer of the Order of Canada, became a fellow of the Royal Society of Canada, and received honorary degrees from the University of Toronto, Concordia University, and the University of Western Ontario. She was diagnosed with breast cancer that year, and she retired from the University of Manitoba. In 1999 she was named professor emerita at the University of Manitoba and traveled to England on a Guggenheim Fellowship. That same year the first Carol Shields Winnipeg Book Award went to Gordon Sinclair Jr.'s *Cowboys and Indians.* In 2000 Shields and her husband moved to Victoria. By this time her cancer had spread to her liver. She was made professor emerita at the University of Winnipeg and received honorary degrees from Carleton University and Wilfred Laurier University.

In 2000 Shields published *Dressing up for the Carnival,* a collection of twenty-two stories. In the title piece, which opens the volume, Shields presents brief character sketches in which an individual is changed in some way by clothing or by an object. For thirty-year-old Roger the purchase of a mango instead of his usual apple shifts his perception of himself and his sense of how others see him; ten-year-old Mandy Eliot feels transformed when she is sent home to fetch her brother's forgotten football helmet: "Today, for a minute, she *is* her brother." "Keys" shows the significance of keys to several unconnected characters for whom the objects are important, such as the man who founded and operates the Museum of Keys in Buffalo and a sociologist at the fictional Agassiz University in Manitoba who studies keys and key use. In "Absence" a writer has to find a new vocabulary to express her ideas when a vowel key on her typewriter becomes stuck. In "A Scarf" a newly successful novelist buys herself a scarf that is mistaken for a gift by her old friend, a failed writer. In "Dying for Love" a series of women come close to killing themselves over lost love but conclude that life is worth living after all. In "Our Men and Women" the narrator finds that the lives of her colleagues are largely mundane and prone to the vagaries of existence: "There's no way people can protect themselves against surprise." In "Weather" a strike by meteorologists halts the weather; with no weather, there is no definition to the lives of the narrator and her husband. In "Flatties" the various types and uses of "flattie" bread are indicative of the varying beliefs and social histories of the inhabitants of an archipelago. In "Reportage" the discovery of a Roman arena in southwestern Manitoba transforms the economy from a primarily agrarian one to one based on tourism. In the final story, "Dressing Down," the narrator remembers his grandmother's reluctant acquiescence to his grandfather's philosophical need to spend a month every summer in a nudist colony he founded. Learning that "People with their limbs and creases and folds were more alike than I thought. . . . Take off your clothes and you are left with your dull suit of invisibility" had the effect of constraining the narrator, rather than freeing him as it freed his grandfather: "I was launched into the long business of shame, accumulating the mingled secrets of disgust and longing, that eventually formed a kind of rattling carapace that restricted natural movement and ease."

In 2001 Shields was named Winnipeg Citizen of the Year, given the Order of Manitoba, and received honorary degrees from Lakehead University, the University of Victoria, and the University of Calgary. That same year she co-edited with Marjorie Anderson a collection of essays by women writers, *Dropped Threads: What We Aren't Told,* which became a surprise best-seller. Anderson remarks in the introduction to *Dropped Threads 2: More of What We Aren't Told* (2003) that the first volume became "part of a country-wide discussion on what had been missing in women's conversations—those hidden nooks of pride, blessing, injury or shame that are revealed only when there's safety and a community of understanding. We were pleased to see that the anthology had been part of creating such a community."

Also in 2001 Shields published *Jane Austen,* a biography of the writer. Shields counters the notion that Austen was "impervious to the noises of the historical universe in which she was placed," arguing that "Her novels, each of them, can be seen as wide-ranging *glances* . . . across the material of the world she inhabited, and that material includes an implied commentary on the political, economic and social forces of her day."

She concludes: "Her legacy is not a piece of reportage from the society of a particular past, but a wise and compelling exploration of human nature. Her men and women speak their needs and define the barriers that separate them from peace and satisfaction. They are as alive today in their longings as they were two hundred years ago, when she first gave them breath." The biography won the Charles Taylor Prize for Literary Non-Fiction in 2002.

In 2002 Shields was raised to Companion of the Order of Canada, the highest level attainable; she also received the Queen Elizabeth Golden Jubilee Medal. *Unless,* her final novel, was published that year. The narrator, Reta Winters, is acclaimed as the translator of the work of the aged Holocaust survivor Danielle Westerman; wrote a best-selling short book she describes as "giftie," *Shakespeare and Flowers,* which is "sold in the kind of outlets that stock greeting cards and stuffed bears"; and has published a light novel, *Thyme's Up,* which achieved considerable commercial success and won a major literary prize and to which she is currently writing the sequel. She says, "My life as a writer and translator is my back story, as they say in the movie business; my front story is that I live in a house on a hill with Tom and our girls and our seven-year-old golden retriever, Pet."

Reta considers the role of writing in coping with life: "But more than anything else it is the rhythm of typing-and-thinking that soothes me, what is almost an athlete's delight in the piling of clause on clause. . . . On days when I don't know which foot to put in front of the other, I can type my way towards becoming a conscious being." The major drama of the novel revolves around the unexplained actions of Reta's eldest daughter, who has dropped out of college and organized society to beg on a Toronto street corner: "Norah sits cross-legged with a begging bowl in her lap and asks nothing of the world." She wears a sign around her neck that says, "goodness." Reta wonders, "How did this part of the narrative happen? We know it didn't ride out of the ordinary plot lines of a life story." She muses about the word on her daughter's sign: "Goodness but not greatness. . . . How long can she go on living her life knowing what she knows, that women are excluded from greatness?" The fractured family is ultimately able to bind itself back together.

Shields was awarded an honorary doctorate by the University of Manitoba in 2003. On 16 July 2003 she died of the cancer she had battled for more than five years. *Collected Stories of Carol Shields* (2004) includes all of the stories from her previous collections; "Segue," a chapter from an unpublished novel; and excerpts from *Swann* and *The Stone Diaries.*

Carol Shields was one of the most successful Canadian writers of her time. Georgiana M. M. Colville writes that "The brilliant wit, originality and structural intricacies she builds with frequently banal, dull characters in a wide variety of situations . . . explain her immense success in her adopted Canada, her native USA and frequently visited Britain. That specific English-speaking geographical triangle provides the background for most of her novels." Shields's works topped the best-seller lists in many countries, consistently met with critical acclaim, and spawned a great deal of literary criticism.

Interviews:

Eleanor Wachtel, "Interview with Carol Shields," *Room of One's Own: A Feminist Journal of Literature and Criticism,* 13, nos. 1–2 (1989): 5–45;

Marjorie Anderson, "Interview with Carol Shields," in *Carol Shields: The Arts of a Writing Life,* edited by Neil Besner (Winnipeg: Prairie Fire Press, 2003), pp. 57–72.

Bibliography:

Faye Hammill, "Carol Shields: An Annotated Bibliography," in *Carol Shields, Narrative Hunger, and the Possibilities of Fiction,* edited by Edward Eden and Dee Goertz (Toronto: University of Toronto Press, 2003), pp. 285–310.

Biography:

Susan L. Blake, "Carol Shields," in *American Writers: Supplement VII,* edited by Jay Parini (New York: Scribner, 2000), pp. 307–330.

References:

Neil Besner, ed., *Carol Shields: The Arts of a Writing Life* (Winnipeg: Prairie Fire Press, 2003);

Georgiana M. M. Colville, "Carol's Party and Larry's Shields: On Carol Shields' Novel *Larry's Party* (1997)," *Etudes Canadiennes/Canadian Studies,* 49 (2000): 85–96;

Edward Eden and Dee Goertz, eds., *Carol Shields, Narrative Hunger, and the Possibilities of Fiction* (Toronto: University of Toronto Press, 2003);

A *Room of One's Own: A Feminist Journal of Literature and Criticism,* special Shields issue, 13, nos. 1–2 (1989): 136–146;

Simone Vauthier, "Ruptures in Carol Shields's *The Stone Diaries,*" *Anglophonia: French Journal of English Studies,* 1 (January 1997): 177–192.

Papers:

Carol Shields Fonds, held by Library and Archives Canada, includes materials for the period 1954 to 1998.

Birk Sproxton
(12 August 1943 – 14 March 2007)

Christian Riegel
University of Regina

BOOKS: *Headframe:* (Winnipeg: Turnstone, 1985);

The Hockey Fan Came Riding (Red Deer: Red Deer College Press, 1990);

The Red-Headed Woman with the Black Black Heart (Winnipeg: Turnstone, 1997);

Phantom Lake: North of 54 (Edmonton: University of Alberta Press, 2005);

Headframe: 2 (Winnipeg: Turnstone, 2006).

OTHER: Bertram Brooker, *Sounds Assembling: The Poetry of Bertram Brooker,* edited by Sproxton (Winnipeg: Turnstone, 1980):

Trace: Prairie Writers on Writing, edited by Sproxton (Winnipeg: Turnstone, 1986)–includes "What the World Was Saying When I Made It," by Sproxton, pp. 221–226;

"*Figures on a Wharf:* Shaping Things to Come," in *Contemporary Manitoba Writers: New Critical Studies,* edited by Kenneth J. Hughes (Winnipeg: Turnstone, 1990), pp. 110–130;

"Blood and Guts" and "Bomb Threats," in *200% Cracked Wheat,* edited by Gary Hyland, Barbara Sapergia, and Geoffrey Ursell (Regina: Coteau, 1992), pp. 163–164;

"The Organized Woman Story," in *Due West: 30 Great Stories from Alberta, Saskatchewan and Manitoba,* edited by Tefs, Aritha van Herk, and Ursell (Regina: Coteau / Edmonton: NeWest Press / Winnipeg: Turnstone, 1996), pp. 187–191;

Great Stories from the Prairies, edited by Sproxton (Calgary: Red Deer Press, 2000);

"The Figure of the Unknown Soldier in *The Fire-Dwellers,*" in *Margaret Laurence: Critical Reflections,* edited by David Staines (Ottawa: University of Ottawa Press, 2001), pp. 99–127;

"The Novels That Named a City: The Fictional Pretexts of Flin Flon," in *Defining the Prairies: Region, Culture, and History,* edited by Robert Wardhaugh (Winnipeg: University of Manitoba Press, 2001), pp. 137–149;

Birk Sproxton (photograph by Mark Sproxton; courtesy of the author and the University of Alberta Press)

The Winnipeg Connection: Writing Lives at Mid-Century, edited by Sproxton (Winnipeg: Prairie Fire Press, 2006).

SELECTED PERIODICAL PUBLICATIONS–UNCOLLECTED: "Grove's Unpublished 'MAN' and its Relation to *The Master of the Mill,*" *Inscape,* 11 (Spring 1974): 35–54;

"E. J. Pratt as Psychologist, 1919–1920," *Canadian Notes and Queries,* 14 (November 1974): 7–9;

"Eugene O'Neill: Masks and Demons," *Sphinx: A Magazine of Literature and Society,* 3 (Winter 1975): 57–62;

"'Malcolm's Katie': Images and Songs," by Sproxton and Kenneth J. Hughes, *Canadian Literature,* 65 (Summer 1975): 55–64;

"Figures in the Night Wind: Riel and Dumont," by Sproxton and John Tobias, *Sphinx: A Magazine of Literature and Society,* 56 (Summer 1976): 42–46;

"Running" and "Sing While You Can," *CVII,* 7 (April 1983): 36;

"Two Poems: Phantom Lake and Return Visit," *Prairie Fire,* 5 (Winter 1984): 65–66;

"Untitled," *Capilano Review,* 35 (1985): 34;

"Making Mickey," *Prairie Fire,* 8 (Winter 1987): 81–87;

"A Kin to Strike," *Dinosaur Review,* 9 (Winter 1988): 49–52;

"'The Subjective Underground': The Stream of Consciousness," *Provincial Essays,* 7 (1989): 51–62;

"Tracing bpNichol," *Prairie Fire,* 12 (Autumn 1991): 93–96;

"Jon Whyte: 1941–1992," *Canadian Literature,* 135 (Winter 1992): 190;

"Reading Leonard Cohen: Reprise," *Canadian Poetry,* 33 (Fall–Winter 1993): 122–130;

"Kate Rice: Her Diary," *Prairie Fire,* 16 (Fall 1995): 149–159;

"Dennis Cooley and the Canadian Love Song," *Prairie Fire,* 19 (Spring 1998): 15–20;

"Imaginary Lines: Shield Notes," *Brick: A Literary Journal,* 60 (Fall 1998): 55–57;

"Smelter Smoke," *Grain,* 25 (Winter 1998): 97–105.

While Birk Sproxton's corpus is relatively small, he was a significant prairie writer. His poetry and fiction address the problems of writing about the local, and his aesthetic solutions involve complex textual maneuvering that defies easy generic categorization. Sproxton draws widely, from medieval and Renaissance models through contemporary postmodernist ones, to find how best to represent the world as he experiences it. Along with his creative work, Sproxton had an important role as an anthologizer of prairie writing.

The fifth of seven children—four boys and three girls—Birk Ernest Sproxton was born in Flin Flon, Manitoba, on 12 August 1943 to Keith Albert Sproxton, a miner, and Alice Maebelle Sproxton. His mother later worked as head matron in a retirement home. In September 1960 Sproxton entered United College in Winnipeg (since 1967 the University of Winnipeg), where he was captain of the varsity hockey team. He worked in the bush for Midwest Diamond Drilling in the summer of 1961, and in the summers of 1962 and 1963 he was a member of the track gang maintaining the railway for the Hudson Bay Mining and Smelting Com-

pany. After receiving his B.A. in English in May 1964, Sproxton enrolled in a special program in the Faculty of Education at the University of Manitoba. In September he took a position teaching English and physical education at Boissevain Collegiate in southern Manitoba. He returned to the University of Manitoba to continue his studies in education in the summer of 1965 and took a job marking tests for the High School Examination Board. In September he enrolled in a pre-M.A. year at the University of Manitoba; toward the end of the academic year he taught English at Sanford Collegiate outside Winnipeg. In June 1966 he married Lorraine Moffat, a former classmate at United College. In the fall he began work on his M.A. in English at the University of Manitoba, resulting in a thesis on Robert Frost; he received the degree in 1967. In June of that year the Sproxtons' first child, Richard Mark, was born. Soon thereafter, Sproxton became an instructor in the English department at the University of Regina. A second child, Denis James, was born in September 1970. In 1971 Sproxton returned to the University of Manitoba to begin work on a Ph.D. in English. In 1974 he published scholarly essays on the Canadian writers E. J. Pratt and Frederick Philip Grove. The Sproxtons' first daughter, Shannon, was born in 1974. A year later Sproxton became an English instructor at Red Deer College in Alberta.

Sproxton edited a special issue of *The Sphinx: A Magazine of Literature and Society* on Canadian Literature in 1977, and in 1980 he edited *Sounds Assembling: The Poetry of Bertram Brooker.* In this book Sproxton collected previously unpublished poems by Brooker, along with some of his essays and artwork. Sproxton earned his Ph.D. in 1983 with the dissertation "Subversive Sexuality in Four Middle Plays of Eugene O'Neill." On 22 November 1983 his wife gave birth to their fourth child, Andrea Caitlin. In 1985 he founded the Writers on Campus program, which continued until 1989 and featured important authors and scholars such as bpNichol (Barrie Phillip Nichol), Fred Wah, Aritha van Herk, Lorna Crozier, Smaro Kambourelli, and Robert Kroetsch. In the mid 1980s Sproxton was also involved with the *NeWest Review* and the Canadian Studies Advisory Committee of the Association for Canadian Community Colleges.

In 1985 Sproxton published *Headframe:.* Influenced by William Carlos Williams's multivolume poem about New Jersey, *Paterson* (1946–1958), Sproxton's work explores his hometown, Flin Flon. The title refers to the metal or wooden structure at the head of the shaft of an underground mine that supports the pulleys that hold the cables for the elevators, bucket, and so on. What comes after the curious colon in the title is what has been mined from the place. Like Williams, Sprox-

Paperback cover for the first edition, 1997
(Bruccoli Clark Layman Archives)

ton approaches the locality with which he is dealing with a language that is appropriate to that place; thus, he employs the vernacular and mining terminology. In "Wandering Men" the speaker says that he is "reading / the rock / reading / its / core." In a 2003 interview with Christian Riegel, Sproxton remarked on the similarities between mining and writing about a place: "I am interested in the nature of mining activity; the discovery of the unseen—at least initially—or to take a strike into the earth in the form of diamond drilling. . . . In diamond drilling the purpose is to take an extract from the earth, a core, and then read that core and imagine an ore body or a great body of riches."

One of the epigraphs to *Headframe:* is taken from Ken Dryden's *The Game: A Thoughtful and Provocative Look at a Life in Hockey* (1983): "Hundreds of tiny fragments of action, some leading nowhere, some leading somewhere, most going nowhere. Only one thing is clear. A fragmented game must be played in frag-

ments." Sproxton told Riegel: "I meant that as a clue to the nature of the book. The text is a collage, a series of fragments. That is how we understand the world anyway, it seems to me–in bits and pieces. So what I have given are fragments of narrative, fragments of document and, I guess, fragments of a larger story that all the smaller fragments make up." *Headframe:* consists of six titled sections—"The Open Pit," "Bitches Like Toe-Jam," "Finding," "Document Section," "A Likely Story: The Sub Text," and "Another Belly Button"—comprising short poems that offer fragmentary visions of Flin Flon but no overarching narrative. The epigraph provides another clue to Sproxton's aesthetic approach, for the text is rife with play. Sproxton told Riegel, "I am playing with these texts and then inviting the reader to play with them as well. . . . You can dip in and read the text for a bit and go quickly to another place and start again so that while the sequence may be important I think it's more important to the reader to find his or her way through the network and create a path."

Also like Williams, Sproxton incorporates into his work documents such as newspaper and magazine clippings and excerpts from history books and works of fiction. In the section "The Open Pit" the poem "Wandering Men," for example, opens with a quotation from a 1914 article in the *Canadian Mining Journal*:

GOLD–The first gold discoveries were made by Messrs. Mosher and Creighton in August 1913. Since that time a large part of the country around the north end of the lake has been staked. Many of these claims are of the usual *ho hum* type located during a gold rush. Even on claims where quartz veins have been found little work has been done.

The quotation is followed by a short poem that explains the lack of mining activity related in the article by referring to the problems posed by the natural world:

wind
carving
waves
lap
rock
on
shore
walking
thru the bush
poplar spruce birch
face-slapping willows
wet-snow puddles   spring
of soft muskeg

The first printing of *Headframe:* quickly sold out, and a second was ordered.

In 1986 Sproxton published the anthology *Trace: Prairie Writers on Writing*. Among the thirty-four writers represented are figures who were already important on the literary scene, such as Margaret Laurence, Henry Kreisel, Eli Mandel, Robert Kroetsch, and Rudy Wiebe, and newer talents such as Crozier, van Herk, Douglas Barbour, Dennis Cooley, Sandra Birdsell, Kristjana Gunnars, Monty Reid, and Wayne Tefs. In the preface Sproxton explains that "*Trace* began in the frustration that goes with not being able to find a book. I wanted a book that included statements on writing by major writers from the prairies, a book that I could use as a student and teacher of reading and writing. That book didn't exist." Since the volume appeared, many of the emerging writers Sproxton included have produced major bodies of work.

Marketed as a collection of short stories, Sproxton's *The Hockey Fan Came Riding* (1990) consists of fifty-nine titled pieces, none of which is more than four pages long and many of which comprise only one or two paragraphs. They are narrated by a man traveling to Europe with his sons, who are to play in a hockey tournament. This book continues the fragmentary approach that Sproxton employed in *Headframe:*; as in the earlier work, the reader is charged with piecing together the fragments and creating a whole. The sections include memories of the narrator's family and youth, reflections on hockey, ruminations on aging, and an examination of how the past affects the present. While the narrating "fan" is never identified as the author, his accounts of his past closely resemble Sproxton's life. In "The Hockey Fan Reflects on Beginnings" he says, "In Flin Flon he begins another beginning, a legendary place where the garden is called, yes, the Main Arena and the streets are paved with hockey pucks and gold. Or so the story goes and you never get away from the stories." In "Aurora Borealis" he says, "This story begins in snow. Light dusty flakes float down on the Laurentian Shield north of the 54th parallel." In "Hockey Is a Transition Game" the narrator muses on the role that storytelling plays in transmitting the past: "Stories are hand-me-down gifts you wear that don't wear out." In "The Hockey Fan on Site" a televised hockey game serves as a metaphor for the unifying nature of narrative and as a comment on how narrative only tells part of the story—the broadcast presents only what the cameras pick up: "Click back and forth, sew them together and there it is, a small story sutured up snug and tight." As with any story, "the camera always keeps secrets." All stories are, thus, subjective constructions: "Who runs those cameras anyway? Who hits the switch to make the suture? Who referees the switcher?" The narrator compares hockey to writing in part 5 of "A Stitch in Time":

On newly flooded ice, an accelerating skater leaves a string of oblique stitch marks

/
\
/
\
/
\
/

The strides open the ice, cut after cut. In typewriting you call it a slash. Emily speaks of telling the story slant, she knows how to sing the ice, sign the ayes, the eyes.

As the allusion to Emily Dickinson indicates, Sproxton's modus operandi in this book is to tell the story "slant"—that is, not in a linear fashion but from multiple perspectives. In the concluding piece, "Overtime," the narrator notes: "The letters of this story compose themselves in tidy lanes and skate across the page, they glide from gutter to margin and margin to gutter, run down the rivers of the page and turn with leaves in spring and fall." As the seasons change year in and year out, so does one's life: "They turn, you turn, I turn." One creates stories out of fragments in an attempt to understand oneself: "We ride these characters into a life sentence that turns through childhood to youth and middle age, a sentence that stretches until the buzzer sounds and he and she and you and I are body checked *belly up belly up* and found wanting."

Sproxton's novel *The Red-Headed Woman with the Black Black Heart* (1997) depicts the 1934 strike in Flin Flon against the Hudson Bay Mining and Smelting Company led by the title character, nineteen-year-old labor activist Mickey Marlowe. Sproxton employs conventions of the Old Comedy of Aristophanes, such as fantastic and farcical incidents, political satire, cheerful obscenity, and farcical names, such as Judge Knott, for some of the characters. The novel also includes historical and archival documents, newspaper articles, and photographs. A frame story, in which an unnamed researcher and writer tells how he put together the story, gives the reader an insight into how historical accounts are constructed and told. In the opening chapter the narrator appeals directly to the reader: "The judge had his problems, as you see. Slide that easy chair up to the desk, while I plug in the tea kettle." The narrator is, however, presented as unreliable; he tells the reader, "I am not always certain exactly what I hear and see. You know I am mostly deaf, surgeons carved a hole in my head large enough to land an airplane, so I need you to hear and see with me." Sproxton shows that history is a construction that is dependent on the historian's skill at discerning important features and details; thus, history is subjective rather than objective. When the narrator describes his discovery of Mickey Marlowe, the reader realizes that the words and deeds the narrator attributes to her, and even her very existence, are questionable:

> I hit upon this strategy by accident, I was playing around with my scissors as I am wont to do on days like this . . . and I cut a hole in the cardboard, a few quick turns and I had it. Then I set the cardboard on the page and it fell upon this woman with her arm upraised in the middle of a crowd. Just like that. I had not seen her there before, not in a dozen times. The hole in the cardboard helps you to focus. But the image is too small to make out her features.

In another passage the narrator presents a photograph of a group of people and invites the reader to imagine elements in the scene, such as "Bobo sticking out his tongue," because the "photo is too small" to show this detail. Creativity is needed to expand what is available in official history: "The historical records are incomplete and fragmented," and the role of the historian is to fill the spaces between the fragments: "I have collected newspapers, letters, magazine articles–all kinds of archival documents to fill in the gaps. To give Mickey a proper setting for her red red hair, you must imagine the geography of her peculiar world." At one point the narrator asserts the value of photographs in providing an objective version of events: "I had found a story, one photo led into another. . . . The photos told a story. . . . I listened to the photos." Later, however, he admits: "I see that photos are not easily lined up in sequence. Despite the strict order imposed by the rings of my binder, they have begun to slide and wiggle under their plastic covers. When I look at them again I see huge puzzling silences." One answer is to supplement one mode of historical chronicle with another: "To stabilize things I add clippings from the newspapers." In another place the narrator admits, "I'm making it up as we go, stringing a line."

In the 1920s and 1930s the Manitoba government invested heavily in the northern part of the province. The fictitious Premier Bramble's vision for the north is that of "A future so bright you daren't look it straight on . . . a future rising like a fireball out of the brooding rocks and swamps and lakes of the Manitoba Shield." Judge Knott "gave Bramble credit for opening up this town, and ensuring a flow of $27 million into the plant construction–no small matter that, in 1928." But that the money was used purely for the gain of the company is clear when the judge asks, "How could a man take pride in the muddy slophole they call streets?" Mickey notes in one of her speeches that neither the company

nor the government is interested in promoting a healthy environment for the residents of Flin Flon: "at home your kids are puking their guts out and running every fifteen minutes because of the stinking water they are trying to feed us and then charge us for. . . . You get a little cut, you wash, you get infected from the filthy water, guts wrenched, little cuts puffed up and oozing with pus and slime. Like the water, dogs in there, the shit pipe right there by the drinking water pipe."

A quotation from the *Winnipeg Tribune* explains the motivation for the strike: "The first demand was that the corporation recognize the United Mine Workers of Canada. The officials flatly refused to do this." In the eyes of the mine management and the government, the workers are communists and foreigners. When Judge Knott arrives in Flin Flon to hear the case against Mickey, who has been arrested as an agitator, he thinks: "Aliens, most of them, egged on by Moscow. . . . Moscow calls the tune." The daughter of the city councilman Smallbearing points out that he identifies only those who are not of Anglo-Saxon descent as foreign: "Father . . . you don't sound like me, and I am Canadian through and through." He thinks, "She intimates that there's no difference between my English accent and the accent of that European girl."

The government attempts to break the strike and the union through heavy-handed and violent methods. Mickey Marlowe remembers the response to a strike in southern Saskatchewan: "She thought of Estevan, the RCMP rifles. . . . One two three men (dead) in the street. Here, in this town in the spruce deep bush, they knew it could happen again." The strike is broken, and Mickey is convicted; the length of her sentence is not mentioned.

At the end of the novel the narrator walks through Union Station in Winnipeg: "I have just now entered the north end where she must have walked." As he sits under the lobby rotunda, he hears "the sounds of the past, the times between Mickey's time and now." Contemplating the fragmentary nature of historical knowledge, he recalls a 1967 documentary radio program produced by the pianist Glenn Gould titled "The Idea of North" that was "a collage of voices": "Gould fragmented the voices into bits of sound and inflection: his voices do not speak together in conversation, but rather play against each other, in counterpoint." The narrator has employed a similar method to tell his story. The result is that Gould's listener, like the reader of *The Red-Headed Woman with the Black Black Heart,* is given "the pleasure of making the story. He leaves it to you to fill in the gaps."

In the summer of 1999 Sproxton edited a special issue of the journal *Prairie Fire* titled "Winnipeg in Fiction: 125 Years of English-Language Writing" that included a long-forgotten poem by Laurence. In 2000 he edited *Great Stories from the Prairies,* in which canonical writers such as Grove, Laurence, Sinclair Ross, Ken Mitchell, and Jack Ludwig appear along with newer voices such as Gunnars, van Herk, Greg Hollingshead, David Bergen, and Joan Crate. The anthology filled an important gap in textbooks for undergraduate courses in Canadian literature.

In April 2005 Sproxton lectured at the Postcolonial Spring School at Berlin's Freie Universität. That same year he published *Phantom Lake: North of 54,* a nonfictional examination of his life and his relationship to the area around Flin Flon that he calls "a personal essay and a biography of place." He notes in the "Comments on Sources" section at the end that "This book grows out of travels in summer (and winter) to Flin Flon and Phantom Lake over the past forty years." In the first chapter, "Imaginary Lines," as Sproxton approaches Flin Flon and Phantom Lake he considers the effects of decades of mining on the landscape; his daughter does not share his fascination with the place, choosing instead to read a popular novel. Sproxton is reminded of Barbara Moon's *The Canadian Shield* (1970): "A woman named Moon writes at length in a book called *The Canadian Shield* about a land often described as a moonscape, a world of desolation and barrenness. At the same time, her name, Moon, calls forth associations of dreams and gentle beauty and love." At the end of the chapter he muses about the craft of writing: "I scrabble to become a writer, searching for ways to tie together words and world, world and words. To string them together, I incise dark grey letters on the white pages and send them winging to you–imaginary lines." In chapter 12, "Phantom Lake, December 1996," he travels to Flin Flon to attend his mother's funeral. As in the other chapters, he reflects on the past as the present unfolds. A winter trip thirty years earlier is compared to the current one. The road has been straightened and leveled: "The highway ran its old course at the time. The distance between Cranberry Portage and Flin Flon meant curve after curve, dip after hill, then curve after more curves. . . . The trip was many kilometers longer then." As a teenager he worked at Hillside Cemetery, where his mother is being buried: "On that December day, I did not swagger through the cemetery with a rake over my shoulder, as I did that first year. This time I felt my way among the stones, heading for the telltale clods of earth. With my siblings I looked for the one who bore us." Sproxton received the $25,000 Grant MacEwan Author's Award, Canada's second largest monetary prize, for *Phantom Lake.* The book won the Manitoba Historical Society Margaret McWilliams Award for Local History.

Dust jacket for the first edition, 2005 (courtesy of the author and the University of Alberta Press)

In 2006 Sproxton edited *The Winnipeg Connection: Writing Lives at Mid-Century,* a collection of thirty-four essays that attempt to answer the question he asks in the introduction: "What makes Winnipeg a writing centre?" The essays, by contemporary Winnipeg writers such as Dennis Cooley, Dave Williamson, and Margaret Sweatman, deal with writers who emerged in Winnipeg in the 1940s and 1950s, including Jack Ludwig, Margaret Laurence, and Sinclair Ross.

Also in 2006 Sproxton published a second collection of poems, *Headframe: 2.* The volume is divided into nine sections; "The Screen Door Chronicles," "Benchmark," "Notes for a Father," "Hillside," "Beaver Lake Notes," "Scratch an Epitaph," "Riverhurst Entries," "Run to the Sea," and "The Screen Door Revisions." With the exception of "Benchmark," each section comprises a thematically and formally linked sequence of poems; the poems in "Benchmark" are linked by key themes—rocks, mining, family, and the speaker's sense of a developing sense of self—but are not formally connected as those of the other sections are. The first section, "The Screen Door Chronicles," presents nine with similar titles, beginning with "Chronicle #1" and ending with "Chronicle #9," that are concerned with an action or contemplation that occurs "in the moment between / the swing the slam" of a screen door. The idea and form of the final poem in the sequence are borrowed from Williams and indicate the mode of the first section:

> so much depends
> upon
>
> a red screen
> door
>
> framed with pine
> slats
>
> outside the white
> cabin

The third section, "Notes for a Father," comprises a series of elegiac poems about the life and death of the speaker's father. The following section, "Hillside," consists of nine numbered poems about the speaker's work as a young man at Hillside Cemetery in Flin Flon. The titled poems in the fifth section, "Beaver Lake Notes," are concerned with the contemplation of an aspect of the lake. The next section, "Scratch and Epitaph," is a single long poem that deals with the life and death of the speaker's mother, Maebelle. The ten numbered poems in the seventh section, "Riverhurst Entries," relate the fleeting bits of family history that the speaker gleans from his visits to the cemetery where his grandparents and great-grandparents are buried and to the nearby town. The title of the penultimate section, "Run to the Sea," is taken from a section of Williams's *Paterson*. The closing section, "The Screen Door Revisions," brings the main themes of the volume together. The four concluding poems deal with family history and loss ("Family Reunion 1980," "Family Reunion 2005," and "The Screen Door Revisions") and with the processes involved in transforming images and ideas into language ("Begin, again"). Sproxton died of massive heart failure on 14 March 2007.

Master of the fragmentary narrative, Birk Sproxton was a significant prairie writer who worked within a postmodernist aesthetic. He summarized his approach in the interview with Riegel: "I think play is central to the writer and I guess for the reader as well. When you come to the game, then you butt up against notions of convention. Part of what I do . . . is to play with the conventions of reading and writing. The nature of the game is to play with the conventions or the 'rules' that we work with."

Interviews:

Martin Kuester, "Retracing Prairie Voices: A Conversation with Birk Sproxton," *Prairie Fire*, 8 (Summer 1997): 4–10;

Christian Riegel, "Interview with Birk Sproxton," *Antigonish Review*, 132 (Winter 2003): 81–92.

Judith Thompson

(20 September 1954 –   )

Len Falkenstein
University of New Brunswick

BOOKS: *The Crackwalker* (Toronto: Playwrights Canada, 1981);

White Biting Dog (Toronto: Playwrights Canada, 1984);

The Other Side of the Dark: Four Plays (Toronto: Coach House, 1989)–comprises *The Crackwalker, Pink, Tornado,* and *I Am Yours*;

Lion in the Streets (Toronto: Coach House, 1992);

Sled, introduction by Ann Wilson (Toronto: Playwrights Canada, 1997);

I Am Yours (London & Boston: Faber & Faber, 1998);

Perfect Pie (Toronto: Playwrights Canada, 2000);

Habitat (Toronto: Playwrights Canada, 2002);

Capture Me (Toronto: Playwrights Canada, 2006);

Enoch Arden in the Hope Shelter, music by Richard Strauss (Toronto: Playwrights Canada, 2006).

Collection: *Late 20th Century Plays, 1980–2000,* introduction by Ric Knowles, afterword by Helen Gilbert (Toronto: Playwrights Canada, 2003)–comprises *The Crackwalker, White Biting Dog, Pink, I Am Yours, Lion in the Streets, Sled,* and *Perfect Pie.*

PLAY PRODUCTIONS: *The Crackwalker,* Toronto, Theatre Passe Muraille, 12 November 1980; revised, Montreal, Centaur Theatre, 4 February 1982;

White Biting Dog, Toronto, Tarragon Theatre, January 1984;

I Am Yours, Toronto, Tarragon Theatre, 17 November 1987;

Lion in the Streets, Toronto, du Maurier Theatre, June 1990; revised, Toronto, Tarragon Theatre, 6 November 1990;

Sled, Toronto, Tarragon Theatre, February 1997;

Perfect Pie, Toronto, Tarragon Theatre, 11 January 2000;

Serge Boucher, *Motel Hélène,* translated by Morwyn Brebner, adapted by Thompson, Toronto, Tarragon Theatre, June 2000;

Habitat, Toronto, Bluma Appel Theatre, 20 September 2001; Manchester, U.K., Royal Exchange Theatre, 12 November 2002;

Capture Me, Toronto, Tarragon Theatre, 2004;

Judith Thompson (from Lion in the Streets, *1992; Bruccoli Clark Layman Archives)*

Henrik Ibsen, *Hedda Gabler,* adapted by Thompson, Toronto, Buddies in Bad Times Theatre, Spring 2005;

My Pyramids; or, How I Got Fired from the Dairy Queen and Ended up at Abu Ghraib by Private Lynndie England, Edinburgh, Traverse Mainspace, August 2005.

PRODUCED SCRIPTS: *Quickening,* radio, *Vanishing Point,* Canadian Broadcasting Corporation, 24 November 1984;

Kissing Way, radio, *Vanishing Point,* Canadian Broadcasting Corporation, 20 January 1986;

Turning to Stone, television, Canadian Broadcasting Corporation, 25 February 1986;

"Tornado," radio, *Sextet,* Canadian Broadcasting Corporation, 29 November 1987;

A Big White Light, radio, Canadian Broadcasting Corporation, 17 December 1989;

White Sand, radio, Canadian Broadcasting Corporation, 1991;

Life with Billy, television, Canadian Broadcasting Corporation, 1994;

The Gliding, radio, Canadian Broadcasting Corporation, 1998;

Lost and Delirious, motion picture, adapted from Susan Swan's novel *The Wives of Bath,* Lions Gate Films, 2001;

Perfect Pie, motion picture, Astral Films, 2002;

Pony, motion picture, adapted by Thompson from her play *White Biting Dog,* 3 Legged Dog Films, 2002;

Pink, motion picture, 3 Legged Dog Films, 2003.

OTHER: "One Twelfth," in *Language and Her Eye: Views on Writing and Gender by Canadian Women Writing in English,* edited by Libby Scheier, Sarah Sheard, and Eleanor Wachtel (Toronto: Coach House, 1990), pp. 263–267;

White Sand, in *Airborne: Radio Plays by Women,* edited by Ann Jansen (Winnipeg: Blizzard, 1991);

"Why Should a Playwright Direct Her Own Plays?" in *Women on the Canadian Stage: The Legacy of Hrotsvit,* edited by Rita Much (Winnipeg: Blizzard, 1992), pp. 104–108;

"No Soy Culpable," in *Writing Away: The PEN Canada Travel Anthology,* edited by Constance Rooke (Toronto: McClelland & Stewart, 1994), pp. 307–316;

"Mouthful of Pearls," in *The Monkey King and Other Stories,* edited by Griffin Ondaatje (Toronto: HarperCollins, 1995), pp. 209–217;

Stop Talking Like That, in *Airplay: An Anthology of CBC Radio Drama,* edited by Dave Carley (Toronto: Scirocco Drama, 1996);

"'I Will Tear You To Pieces': The Classroom as Theatre," in *How Theatre Educates: Convergences & Counterpoints,* edited by Kathleen Gallagher and David Booth (Toronto: University of Toronto Press, 2003), pp. 25–35;

She Speaks: Monologues for Women, edited by Thompson (Toronto: Playwrights Canada, 2004).

SELECTED PERIODICAL PUBLICATIONS– UNCOLLECTED:
DRAMA

Off the 401, Canadian Theatre Review, 89 (Winter 1996): 65–69;

Tornado, Canadian Theatre Review, 89 (Winter 1996): 46–64.

NONFICTION

"Second Thoughts (What I'd Be If I Were Not a Playwright)," *Brick,* 51 (Winter 1995): 26–29;

"Epilepsy and the Snake: Fear in the Creative Process," *Canadian Theatre Review,* 89 (Winter 1996): 4–7;

"It's My Birthday Forever Now: Urjo Karenda and Me," *Canadian Theatre Review,* 113 (Winter 2003): 11–14.

Since arriving on the Canadian theater scene with *The Crackwalker* (produced 1980, published 1981), Judith Thompson has become one of the major names in contemporary Canadian drama; according to Jerry Wasserman, she is "considered by many the most exciting playwright in English Canadian theatre." Thompson's plays have a fierce intensity born of her emotionally relentless and theatrically challenging explorations of the guarded corners of psyche and society. A Freudian and feminist who draws inspiration from fairy tales, her Catholic upbringing, social injustice, and the states of possession she has experienced both as an actor and as an epileptic, Thompson is fascinated by the subterranean undercurrents of darkness and violence beneath the placid and civilized surfaces of the world around her. Her plays combine vivid language and imagery, startling reversals, shocking violence, and a theatricality that frequently walks a fine line between realism and the landscape of dream. They explore themes of abuse, fear, desire, and longing in ways that leave audiences and critics enraptured or hostile but rarely indifferent.

Thompson was born in Montreal on 20 September 1954 and grew up in Kingston, Ontario. Her father, William Robert Thompson, was a professor of psychology specializing in behavioral genetics at Queen's University and for many years was chairman of the psychology department. Her mother, Mary Therese Forde Thompson, was the daughter of Francis Michael (Frank) Forde, a former prime minister of Australia and ambassador to Canada; she was a part-time English instructor at Queen's but was, Thompson told Sandra Tomc in 1989, "mainly a mother—and a writer, and she worked as a director when she was younger and an actress." When Thompson was eleven, her mother directed her in a play. Thompson told Tomc that her mother's college friends "became very rich people and married very rich people, so we'd stay in their houses. And then I also at the same time went to a tough Catholic elementary school in Kingston. . . . There were a couple of other daughters of professionals in the class, but mainly it was Kingston underprivileged."

Catholicism has been a significant influence on Thompson's life and work. She told Cynthia Zimmerman in 1990 that she finds the "immense kind of poetry" and stark depictions of the battle between good and evil that are central to Catholicism highly compelling. But, she said in "Look to the Lady: Re-examining Women's Theatre," a 1995 panel discussion chaired by Soraya Peerbaye: "Growing up a girl, and a Catholic girl at that, means I grew up bound. I grew up with a psyche bound like the feet of women in ancient China, mangled and bloody. . . . And a mask had been created for me . . . a ridiculous fey mask of a girl, and I stepped into it as soon as I could talk and inhabited it thoroughly." She suggested in the same discussion that a "resistance fighter" or "stranger" within her was working to subvert "the paper doll . . . character of Judith" she had created for herself. The result, she claimed, was the epilepsy that first surfaced in a grand mal seizure when she was nine: "I almost died. I think, I'm sure now, that I almost died basically of being a girl."

Thompson graduated from Queen's University in 1976 and enrolled in the three-year acting program at the National Theatre School (NTS) in Montreal. In one of her classes she created a character named Theresa who was based on a mentally handicapped woman she had met while working one summer at Adult Protective Services in Kingston. After graduating from NTS, she spent a year working as an actor; then, realizing that she preferred writing, she built *The Crackwalker* around her Theresa character. Set in the lower-class slums of Kingston, *The Crackwalker* centers on two destitute couples: the mentally handicapped, part-Native Theresa and her simpleminded, emotionally damaged, and doting boyfriend, Alan; and tough, resourceful Sandy and her thuggish and abusive husband, Joe, who is idolized by Alan. The fifth character is the "Crackwalker," a drunken Native man who wanders the streets screaming obscenities, a bogeyman figure who represents insanity, death, and what Zimmerman quotes Thompson as calling "the abyss." Unable to hold a job, Alan strangles his and Theresa's mentally damaged infant in an explosion of rage and frustration (this action was also based on an incident that happened during Thompson's time with Protective Services). At the end of the play Alan has joined the Native man, and a numbed Theresa has returned to life on the streets; the only character for whom there is some cause for hope is Sandy, who has achieved some measure of insight into her situation as a result of the tragedy.

The Crackwalker premiered at the Theatre Passe Muraille in Toronto on 12 November 1980. It was largely ignored and not favorably reviewed at that time, but a 1982 Montreal Centaur Theatre revival was widely praised. The play presented middle-class audiences with a world that had rarely been seen on the Canadian stage. In a 1990 interview with Judith Rudakoff and Rita Much, however, Thompson rejected the notion that *The Crackwalker* depicts "the underbelly of society" and attacked the complacency that allows an audience to say "Oh that play is not about me, it's about the underbelly." According to Zimmerman, for Thompson "the play is neither exaggerated, nor unreal, nor restricted in its applicability" but depicts characters who could just as easily be middle-class. George Toles argues, however, that the heightened language and emotions, the symbolic figure of the Crackwalker, and the incorporation of extended confessional monologues make the play much less naturalistic in style than it appears at first glance to be.

Thompson was an instructor in playwriting at the University of Toronto in 1983–1984. She married University of Toronto English professor Gregor Campbell on 28 October 1983. She spent a year and a half studying the theories of Sigmund Freud at the University of Toronto prior to writing *White Biting Dog* (1984), which she described in her interview with Tomc as her "toughest" and "least accessible" play. Cape is saved from throwing himself off Toronto's Bloor Street viaduct when a talking white dog gives him the mission of saving his father, Glidden. Glidden is dying of a mysterious disease that he has contracted through his obsession with peat moss and gardening. The dog's owner, a young woman named Pony, arrives and tells Cape that the only way to save Glidden is to reunite him with his estranged wife, Cape's mother, Lomia. Lomia, however, has a much younger lover, Pascal, and rejects the notion of reconciling with Glidden. Cape seduces Pony, who has fallen in love with him, to ensure her compliance with his plot, then drives Pascal away. Having succeeded in bringing his parents back together, he rejects Pony. Glidden dies anyway, however, and Pony hangs herself in an attempt to save Cape, whose evil she believes she has absorbed. The play ends on an ambivalent note as Cape and Lomia wonder whether Pony's act will make any difference in their lives.

White Biting Dog premiered at Tarragon Theatre in Toronto in January 1984. Audience and critical response varied from outright bafflement to rave reviews; the published text received the Governor General's Literary Award for Drama. Critical interpretations of the work are also divergent. Craig Stewart Walker reads the play as a "dream vision" that "resembles a modern version of the medieval genre of 'psychomachia'" and suggests that it might also be seen as an exploration of Freud's theory of the Oedipus complex, as depicted in the relationships among Glidden, Lomia, and Cape, or as a contemporary rewriting of William Shakespeare's *Hamlet* (circa 1600–1601) with Cape as

Prince Hamlet, Glidden as King Hamlet, Lomia as Gertrude, Pony as Ophelia, and Pascal as Claudius. Focusing on Pony's act of martyrdom for the flawed Cape, Zimmerman and Toles see the play as a parable or fairy tale about salvation and sacrifice that suggests that individuals and societies that have fallen prey to selfishness and cynicism can be healed through the selfless gestures of others. Walker contends that the "unity" of the play lies in "its exploration of the psychic warfare and subliminal connections among the desires and taboos of the subconscious."

Between 1984 and 1987 Thompson gave birth to the first two of her and Campbell's five children. She was playwright-in-residence at Smith College in 1986. She also wrote several radio and television scripts for the Canadian Broadcasting Corporation (CBC). She comments in her introduction to the published text of her radio play *White Sand* (1991): "I like this idea of voices in the dark, whispering; schizophrenics hear voices in the dark, it affects them deeply. The voice and you—I just love that, no distractions. It's a pure experience." Her 1984 radio drama *Quickening* depicts the unraveling of a marriage, while her 1986 radio play *Kissing Way* dramatizes a date that ends in the revelation of dark, suppressed impulses: misogyny that leads to homicidal desires by the man, Philip, and self-loathing that expresses itself as a death wish on the part of the woman, Barbara. Also airing in 1986 was Thompson's first television drama, *Turning to Stone,* about a young woman who experiences a profound moment of self-revelation when she is arrested for drug smuggling.

Thompson's next work to be staged was *Pink,* a fifteen-minute monologue written for the 1986 Toronto Arts Against Apartheid Benefit; it is included in Thompson's collection *The Other Side of the Dark* (1989). Set in apartheid-era South Africa, the monologue is addressed by a ten-year-old white girl to the corpse of her black nanny, who has been killed in a protest march. Her sense of loss and abandonment results in a stream of racist vitriol, showing that subterranean hatreds are often far more powerful than bonds of love.

In Thompson's 1987 radio play *Tornado* Mandy, a social worker, plots to save her failing marriage by tricking her pregnant client, Rose—an epileptic welfare mother and incest survivor—into giving Mandy her newborn. In a typical Thompson reversal, the play depicts the emptiness of Mandy's life and the comparative richness of Rose's, owing to her loving relationships with her other children and to her epilepsy, which is shown as a window into the primal unconscious. At the end of the play Mandy, too, becomes epileptic.

Thompson's *I Am Yours* opened at the Tarragon Theatre on 17 November 1987; it was published in 1989. Thompson told Tome that in this play "I wanted to do a study of an amoral woman, Dee—I guess you could describe her as sociopathic—whose mother hated her and was jealous of her so she had no feeling for motherhood herself. She's terrified of anything taking over her. . . . So when that's translated into the body she fears pregnancy." Dee is a middle-class woman who eventually drives her patient and selfless husband, Mack, away. Her less respectable sister, Mercy, who takes refuge with Dee, is a neurotic who has sought intimacy with a series of men over the course of her life. Just as Dee was rejected by their mother, Mercy was rejected by their father, who gave Dee a locket engraved with the German words *Ich bin dein* (I am yours) when they were children. Dee seduces Toilane, the former-convict superintendent of her apartment building, even though she finds him repulsive both for his ugliness and his lower-class origins, and becomes pregnant. Horrified, she plans to give the baby up for adoption; but at the instigation of his mother, Pegs, Toilane demands the baby for his own. Dee counters by charging Toilane with rape, but Toilane and Pegs begin a campaign of stalking and intimidation to pressure Dee into giving them the child. At the end of the play they are present when Dee goes into labor; when she wakes up in the hospital, the baby is gone. Walker argues that *I Am Yours* reveals impulses toward love and sex to be a form of suppressed "animal"—a word that recurs repeatedly in the play and in Thompson's comments on it. Walker also claims that the play is largely a rewriting of the fairy tale "Rumpelstiltskin." *I Am Yours* was positively received by critics and audiences. It was published, along with *The Crackwalker, Pink,* and *Tornado,* in *The Other Side of the Dark,* which won the Governor General's Literary Award for Drama in 1989. In 1989–1990 Thompson was resident instructor and director at the University of New Brunswick in Fredericton.

Thompson further exposes and probes the "animal within" in her most acclaimed, darkest, and most emotionally intense and disturbing play to date, *Lion in the Streets,* which premiered at the du Maurier Theatre in June 1990; a revised version opened at the Tarragon Theatre on 6 November 1990 under Thompson's direction. It was published in 1992. In this case the animal—the "lion" of the title—is the impulse toward violence. The play comprises what Thompson called in her interview with Zimmerman "a series of soul murders or physical murders." *Lion in the Streets* grew out of a radio script, *A Big White Light,* which was broadcast on the CBC on 17 December 1989. Thompson retains the "daisy-chain" structure of the radio play, in which the episodes are linked by the reappearance in each scene of one character from the previous scene. *Lion in the Streets* is also unified by the setting, an urban neighborhood, and by the character Isobel, a nine-year-old Portuguese

Paperback cover for the first edition, 1992
(Bruccoli Clark Layman Archives)

girl who serves as a commentator on the events. The audience discovers that Isobel is a ghost; she was murdered seventeen years earlier in the same neighborhood by a young man. Over the course of the play, scenes of abuse and trauma gradually escalate in severity: children bully others on a playground; a woman is humiliated by her husband at a dinner party; a middle-class woman reprimands a lower-class day-care worker for giving the children in her charge too much sugar; a respected reporter researching a story on cerebral palsy kicks a disabled woman to death in an outburst of loathing; and a man browbeats his wife into admitting that she provoked and enjoyed the rape she suffered years earlier. Isobel attempts to alert the other characters to the danger of the "lions" that stalk them. In the last scene she comes face to face with the man who murdered her. She considers taking violent revenge on him; instead, she forgives him, achieving a divine apotheosis in which she is taken up to heaven as she

implores the audience to "take your life." Thompson told Eleanor Wachtel in 1991 that the goal of the play is to point out that "there IS evil and good warring in the culture at all times. And I do think it's in every human being." She went on to argue that the solution is "to change your sense of who you are in the world. See that you are an active and effective person in the world. See that you can actually make a difference. Isobel says, 'Take back your life.' 'I will no longer be a victim. I won't be sent to war. I will take back my life.'" She told Rudakoff and Much: "My real hope is to hold a mirror up to all of us, because I think that awakening, slipping out of our comas, is what it's all about. Otherwise, we do not live—it's the unexamined life. The coma lifting, then, becomes political. Art is political, should be political, but only in this really essential way. . . . It's not at all about a particular platform."

Despite Thompson's rejection of polemics, several of the plays she has written since *Lion in the Streets* are overtly political. *White Sand,* for example, deals with the white supremacist slaying of a Caribbean immigrant woman. Having the murder committed not by the skinhead Carl but by his adoring girlfriend, Kim, allows Thompson to explore the common roots and effects of racism and patriarchy. In 1992 Thompson became an associate professor in the School of English and Theatre Studies at the University of Guelph, where she teaches courses in playwriting and writing for radio, television, and movies. *Life with Billy,* broadcast on CBC television in 1994, dramatizes a true-life "battered-wife syndrome" murder. *Off the 401* (1996) is a short play in which a middle-class woman reacts with horror on discovering a pedophile abusing a child at a highway rest stop but takes no action to stop him. The radio play *Stop Talking Like That* (1996) delves into the death wish that prompts the anorexia of a Canadian teenager vacationing in Australia.

Sled premiered at the Tarragon Theatre in 1997 and was published the same year. The drama has been read as a commentary both on the pathology of violence in general and on a specific manifestation of violence endemic to contemporary Canada. The action shifts between two symbolic poles of Canadian culture: the northern wilderness and multicultural Toronto. At a northern lodge Kevin, a hunter, murders Annie, a lounge singer, in reprisal for a humiliation Kevin suffered at the hands of Annie's husband, Jack. Kevin and Jack drift back to Toronto, where Kevin breaks into the home of his long-lost sister, Evangeline, forces her into an incestuous relationship, and bullies her into becoming a stripper. Jack and Evangeline meet and begin a relationship. Jack learns that Kevin is his wife's killer, and the two men fight; Evangeline kills Jack to save Kevin. After Kevin kills Joe, their Italian immigrant neighbor who is a repository of the history of the neighborhood, Evangeline takes him north to the site of Annie's murder. There the ghosts of the dead confront him as he dies of hypothermia. Walker suggests that "*Sled* uses the Canadian political context to explore the disintegration of social goodwill into the kinds of xenophobic hostility and violent self-protectiveness that destroy the possibilities of peaceful civilization." Reading the play more generally as a study of the pathology of violence and drawing a parallel between the high body count in it and in classical tragedy, Ann Wilson writes in the introduction to the published text of the work that "Thompson is not content to suggest that violence is a simple matter of 'evil'; rather violence occurs within a social context, and so is an exercise of power which is related to issues of power and gender." This conclusion suggests a kinship between *Sled* and *Lion in the Streets,* but *Sled* diverges from the earlier play, Wilson contends, by implying "that violence doesn't

shatter a community but is incorporated into its identity" and by the presence of the ghosts, who call for acts of healing and community building that address not just present but also historical wrongs. *Sled* did not fare well with audiences, and many reviewers criticized what they saw as a bewildering profusion of imagery and allusion and a convoluted and often unbelievable plot. Nevertheless, in 1998 it was nominated for ten Jessie Richardson Theatre Awards and received a Canadian Author's Association Award.

Perfect Pie, which Thompson directed in its 2000 Tarragon Theatre premiere, was received more favorably. Developed from a monologue Thompson had written in 1993, *Perfect Pie* is set in a rural Ontario town. Patsy, a housewife, is making a rhubarb pie when she is visited by her long-estranged friend, Marie, who has become a well-known performer under the name Francesca. Their conversation is interspersed with flashback scenes in which two other actors play the young Patsy and Marie. Patsy befriended the exotic and mysterious outsider Marie, whose torment at the hands of the local boys climaxed in her being gang-raped after a school dance. After this incident, the two made a suicide pact and went to lie on the train tracks before an oncoming locomotive. What happened then is unclear. Patsy asserts that Marie saved her life, a version of events that Marie seems to have trouble believing. Marie leaves shortly thereafter. It is strongly hinted that Marie's visit is a figment of Patsy's imagination—that Patsy actually abandoned her friend to die on the tracks and has fantasized the reunion to assuage her guilt. Another motive for Patsy's fantasy is her lifelong obsession with the mysterious and charismatic Marie, who represents all the dark and destructive yet seductive forces that Patsy suppresses in her respectable but dull daily life.

Habitat, coproduced by Toronto's Canadian Stage Company and Manchester's Royal Exchange Theatre, opened at the Bluma Appel Theatre in Toronto on 20 September 2001. The play questions whether the renowned tolerance of Canadian society is real or illusory. Businessman Lewis Chance establishes a group home for troubled teens in a house he buys in the quiet, prosperous enclave of Mapleview Lanes in the Toronto suburb of Etobicoke. The wealthy residents of the community are horrified and, led by the matriarch Margaret Deacon and her initially reluctant liberal lawyer daughter, Janet, try to force the group home out. Just when it seems that Chance might have won over the residents of the neighborhood, allegations about his past surface. He confirms and embellishes the rumors in a speech to the city council in which he admits to being a homosexual; to having a relationship with one of his young charges, the gay petty crook Sparkle; and to misappropriating group-home funds to aid his impoverished family. The city orders the group home closed, and Sparkle and the disaffected suburban teen Raine burn it to the ground. The only prospect of hope at the end of the play is the newly politicized, activist, and humanitarian outlook of the formerly apathetic Raine. Dysfunctional mother-child relationships, a repeated motif in Thompson's works, are central to *Habitat:* Raine's indifference to her dying mother, Margaret's distant relationship with Janet, Janet's confession that she does not particularly like her own children, and Chance's flawed—and, in his relationship with Sparkle, potentially exploitative—"mothering" of the children at the group home lead to unhappy consequences. For many reviewers, however, the welter of issues in the play, ranging from class and sexuality to race in the form of Raine's Jewishness, drowned out Thompson's commentary on the connection between flawed parenting and societal dysfunction. *Habitat* has come to be regarded an overly ambitious failure.

In 2000 Thompson received an honorary degree from Thorneloe University. Her adaptation of Canadian novelist Susan Swan's *The Wives of Bath* (1993) for the motion picture *Lost and Delirious* (2001) was an official selection of the Sundance Film Festival in 2001, was named by critic Roger Ebert as one of the ten best movies of the year, won a 2001 Stockholm Film Festival Audience Award, and was nominated as Best Screenplay at the Genie Awards in March 2002. She also wrote the screenplay for the 2002 movie version of her own *Perfect Pie;* it was selected for the Toronto Film Festival, the Kingston Film Festival, Vancouver Film Festival, and Milan Film Festival and was nominated Best Screenplay at the Genie Awards in March 2003. Thompson was promoted to full professor at the University of Guelph in 2004, and in 2006 she was invested as an Officer of the Order of Canada.

Although the height of Judith Thompson's career may have been 1990–1991, when five productions of her plays were staged within weeks of each other at major theaters in Ontario and Quebec, she is still one of the top two or three Canadian playwrights of her generation in terms of critical recognition and popularity and one of only a few who has an international reputation. Her plays have won many awards and enjoyed successful productions both at home and abroad, have garnered considerable critical and scholarly attention, and feature prominently in anthologies of Canadian plays and on the syllabi of Canadian drama courses, and she has inspired a younger generation of playwrights. Appreciation of her works is, however, by no means universal. In the introduction to *White Sand* Thompson describes herself as a writer "not into subtlety"; the remark, which few would dispute, is reinforced by a dis-

closure she proffered in the 1995 panel discussion "Look to the Lady: Re-examining Women's Theatre": "When I have young babies I like to let my breast milk leak through my blouse in public at nice restaurants. I will not wear those breast pads! And the looks of disgust on people's faces are the same looks on the people that walk out of my plays." Clearly, Thompson's provocative, confrontational style of theater, which she described to Tomc as a desire to "penetrate" the audience, is not for everyone. Thompson has been criticized for her excesses, for the unrelenting bleakness of her plays, for her reliance on monologues in lieu of dramatic action, for her unconventional melding of disparate styles, and for the promises of redemption that some critics think are too neatly and unconvincingly grafted onto the endings of plays that otherwise offer little reason for optimism. Such criticisms have for the most part been outweighed, however, by praise for Thompson's ability to conjure startling flights of imagery from the most banal and unexpected starting points, for her skill in capturing dialogue that is true to the Canadian vernacular yet filled with an insight and intensity that lifts it into the realm of the poetic, for her challenging experimentation with dramatic form, and the social and political vision that invests her observations on culture and society with such visceral impact—in short, for her ability to create the type of theater to which she told Rudakoff and Much she most aspires: a theater of "pure experience."

Interviews:

Sandra Tomc, "Revisions of Probability: An Interview with Judith Thompson," *Canadian Theatre Review,* 59 (Summer 1989): 18–23;

Judith Rudakoff and Rita Much, "Judith Thompson: Interview," in *Fair Play: 12 Women Speak* (Toronto: Simon & Pierre, 1990), pp. 87–104;

Cynthia Zimmerman, "A Conversation with Judith Thompson," *Canadian Drama,* 16 (1990): 184–194;

Eleanor Wachtel, "An Interview with Judith Thompson," *Brick,* 41 (Summer 1991): 37–41;

"Revisions: Offending Your Audience," *Theatrum,* 29 (June–August 1992): 33–34;

Ric Knowles, "Computers Keep Your Office Tidier: Interview with Judith Thompson," *Canadian Theatre Review,* 81 (Winter 1994): 29–31;

Soraya Peerbaye, "Look to the Lady: Re-examining Women's Theatre," *Canadian Theatre Review,* 84 (Fall 1995): 22–25;

Jennifer Fletcher, "The Last Things in *Sled:* An Interview with Judith Thompson," *Canadian Theatre Review,* 89 (Winter 1996): 39–41.

Bibliography:

Ahnes Hong, "Judith Thompson: A Bibliography," *Canadian Theatre Review,* 89 (Winter 1996): 42–44.

References:

Julie Adam, "The Implicated Audience: Judith Thompson's Anti-Naturalism in *The Crackwalker, White Biting Dog, I Am Yours* and *Lion in the Streets,*" in *Women on the Canadian Stage: The Legacy of Hrotsvit,* edited by Rita Much (Winnipeg: Blizzard, 1992), pp. 21–29;

Dianne Bessai, "Women Dramatists: Sharon Pollock and Judith Thompson," in *Post-Colonial English Drama,* edited by Bruce King (New York: St. Martin's Press, 1992), pp. 97–117;

Canadian Theatre Review, special Thompson issue, 89 (Winter 1996);

Sherrill Grace, "Going North on Judith Thompson's *Sled,*" *Essays in Theatre,* 16 (May 1998): 153–164;

Jennifer Harvie, "(Im)Possibility: Fantasy and Judith Thompson's Drama," in *On-Stage and Off-Stage: English Canadian Drama in Discourse,* edited by Albert-Reiner Glaap and Rolf Althorp (St. John's, Nfld.: Breakwater, 1996), pp. 240–256;

Ric Knowles, "The Plays of Judith Thompson: The Achievement of Grace," *Brick,* 41 (Summer 1991): 33–36;

Knowles, ed., *Judith Thompson,* Critical Perspectives on Canadian Theatre in English, volume 3 (Toronto: Playwrights Canada, 2005);

Robert Nunn, "Spatial Metaphor in the Plays of Judith Thompson," *Theatre History in Canada,* 10 (Spring 1989): 3–29;

George Toles, "'Cause You're the Only One I Want': The Anatomy of Love in the Plays of Judith Thompson," *Canadian Literature,* 118 (Autumn 1988): 116–135;

Craig Stewart Walker, "Judith Thompson: Social Psychomachia," in his *The Buried Astrolabe: Canadian Dramatic Imagination and Western Tradition* (Montreal: McGill-Queen's University Press, 2001), pp. 355–411;

Jerry Wasserman, "Judith Thompson," in *Modern Canadian Plays,* volume 2, fourth edition (Vancouver: Talonbooks, 2001), pp. 257–259;

Cynthia Zimmerman, "Judith Thompson: Voices in the Dark," in her *Playwriting Women: Female Voices in English Canada* (Toronto: Simon & Pierre, 1994), pp. 176–209.

Papers:

Judith Thompson's papers are at the University of Guelph.

Maxine Tynes

(30 June 1949 –)

Laura M. Robinson
Royal Military College

BOOKS: *Borrowed Beauty* (Porters Lake, N.S.: Pottersfield Press, 1987);
Woman Talking Woman (Porters Lake, N.S.: Pottersfield Press, 1990);
Save the World for Me (Porters Lake, N.S.: Pottersfield Press, 1991);
The Door of My Heart (Porters Lake, N.S.: Pottersfield Press, 1993).

PRODUCED SCRIPT: *In Service,* motion picture, screenplay by Tynes and Lulu Keating, Red Snapper Films, 1993.

RECORDING: *Borrowed Beauty,* read by Tynes, Deep Nine Recording Studio, Pottersfield Press, 1994.

OTHER: "Poet, Weaver, Woman, Dreamer," in *Nearly an Island: A Nova Scotian Anthology,* edited by Alice Hale and Sheila Brooks (St. John's, N.S.: Breakwater, 1979), p. 176;
"Womanskin" and "The Profile of Africa," in *Other Voices: Writings by Blacks in Canada,* edited by Lorris Elliott (Toronto: Williams-Wallace, 1985), pp. 162–163;
Beetles and Blue Jeans: Poems, edited, with contributions, by Tynes (Scarborough, Ont.: Nelson Canada, 1993).

SELECTED PERIODICAL PUBLICATIONS–UNCOLLECTED: "Raising the Flag on the Disabled Community," *Ability Network,* 2 (April–May 1994): 3-5;
"Canada Loses to U.S. on Accessibility Score," *Daily News* (Halifax, N.S.), 8 September 1994, p. D3;
"Smokers Playing Russian Roulette with Us All," *Daily News* (Halifax, N.S.), 6 October 1994, p. D2;
"WTN Doesn't Reflect Canada's Ethnic Diversity," *Daily News* (Halifax, N.S.), 12 January 1995, p. D2;
"Disabled Traveller Finds Friendlier Skies," *Daily News* (Halifax, N.S.), 2 February 1995, p. D2;

Maxine Tynes (from the cover for Woman Talking Woman, *1990; Bruccoli Clark Layman Archives)*

"Conversation Creates Invisible Woman in 1995," *Daily News* (Halifax, N.S.), 9 February 1995, p. D2;
"Justice System Wracked by Miscues, Mishaps and Biases," *Daily News* (Halifax, N.S.), 16 March 1995, p. D2;

"Economic Ministers Never Admit the Human Deficit,"
    Daily News (Halifax, N.S.), 23 March 1995, p. D2;

"Personal Heroes the Antidote to Rash of Fallen Icons,"
    Daily News (Halifax, N.S.), 6 April 1995, p. D2;

"Words Impotent in Face of Oklahoma City Bombing,"
    Daily News (Halifax, N.S.), 27 April 1995, p. D2;

"Spanking Now May Lessen Pain for Society Later,"
    Daily News (Halifax, N.S.), 4 May 1995, p. D2;

"G-7 Summit Sends Metro into Flag-Waving Tizzy,"
    Daily News (Halifax, N.S.), 22 June 1995, p. D2;

"Bernardo: Viewers Want Information, Not Titillation," *Daily News* (Halifax, N.S.), 7 September 1995, p. D2;

"'Don't Trust Anyone' Is the Rallying Cry for Life in the '90s," *Daily News* (Halifax, N.S.), 21 September 1995, p. D2;

"Smelly Bus Drama Illustrates the Politics of Scent,"
    Daily News (Halifax, N.S.), 5 October 1995, p. D2;

"It's Halloween Already? Let's Slow the Seasons Down," *Daily News* (Halifax, N.S.), 19 October 1995, p. D2;

"Majority Must Break Silence on Quebec Referendum," *Daily News* (Halifax, N.S.), 26 October 1995, p. D2;

"Referendum Means Nothing Will Ever Be the Same," *Daily News* (Halifax, N.S.), 2 November 1995, p. D2;

"Province Taking an Axe to the Tree of Education," *Daily News* (Halifax, N.S.), 16 November 1995, p. D2;

"Day of the Child Leaves Bad Taste: Our Society Seems to Hold a Burgeoning Desire to Consume Our Young People," *Daily News* (Halifax, N.S.), 30 November 1995, p. D2;

"Zero Tolerance Too Often Adds up to Less than Zero," *Daily News* (Halifax, N.S.), 21 December 1995, p. D2;

"Press Biased in Favor of Murder, Mayhem," *Daily News* (Halifax, N.S.), 25 January 1996, p. D2;

"A Miss Manners–Style Guide to Movie Etiquette," *Daily News* (Halifax, N.S.), 8 February 1996, p. D2;

"Stiff Sentences for Watts Beaters Send Message," *Daily News* (Halifax, N.S.), 7 March 1996, p. D2.

Black Nova Scotian poet Maxine Tynes insists in her lyric poetry on the literal need to raise one's voice. Calling Tynes a "vibrant, pop poet," George Elliott Clarke remarks that she speaks "for and of herself in the full-breathed way of Baptist 'Exhorters.'" At readings Tynes conveys a majestic appearance with her colorful attire, her many noisy bracelets, and her distinctive cane. Her deep, resonant voice, carefully projecting and modulating her words, captivates her audiences. She makes her identity as a black disabled woman central to her poetry, and she is also an uncompromising activist for African Canadians, the disabled, women, peace, and the environment.

Descended from black Loyalists, Tynes was born in Dartmouth, Nova Scotia, on 30 June 1949. She was the seventh of twelve children of Joe Tynes, a dockworker, and Ada Maxwell Tynes. In 1955 she contracted polio, which left her with a lifelong need to use a cane. Tynes's parents were not well educated, but they encouraged their children's learning. Her father brought home visiting sea captains from all over the world, exposing the family to a variety of languages, foods, and cultures. The home was filled with magazines, and Tynes developed a love of reading and writing that was encouraged by her parents.

Because the family lived in a white, working-class area, Tynes was the only black girl in her class at Dartmouth High School. Her career as a poet began at seventeen when her poem "Pro Patria" was read on television by Edmund Morris, the host of a current-affairs program. Tynes attended Dalhousie University from 1970 to 1976, earning a B.A. in English and a bachelor of education degree. As a student she published poetry in *The Dalhousie Review* and won the Dennis Memorial Prize for Poetry, an award sponsored by the English department. After graduation, she became a teacher of Canadian literature at Cole Harbour District High School. In 1979 her poem "Poet, Weaver, Woman, Dreamer" appeared in the textbook *Nearly an Island: A Nova Scotian Anthology.* In 1983 she recited her poetry on a local radio station. In 1985 her poems "Womanskin" and "The Profile of Africa" were included in the anthology *Other Voices: Writings by Blacks in Canada.* In 1986 she was the first African Canadian invited to join the board of governors of Dalhousie University. As a board member she has taken controversial positions and frequently sided with the underdog: in 1992, for example, she was one of five members who voted against a 10 percent tuition hike; the other four were the student representatives.

In the late 1980s a spate of racial violence erupted in Halifax and Dartmouth. In response, Cole Harbour District High School hosted a human-rights conference and instituted a black-literature course taught by Tynes. In 1992 Sylvia Hamilton reported that "after these many years," the course was "still the only one of its kind taught in Nova Scotia schools. Students take the class as an extra English course and may not receive credit for it. Nevertheless, the class is full."

Tynes's short story "In Service," about black women who work for upper-class whites, appeared in the textbook *The Maritimes: Tradition, Challenge & Change* in 1987. That same year Tynes published her first book,

Borrowed Beauty. It opens with a prose piece, "Mirrors," in which she declares that "My poems, my poetry are great shouts of the joy that I feel and share" and says of her identity as a black female: "I wear it joyfully. I wear it big. I wear it womanly. And I wear it Black. Black. Black." In the poem "Family Portrait" Tynes celebrates her family, her past, and her heritage. The title poem praises the often undervalued beauty of African women. While many of these poems are about Nova Scotia, "Avec Mes Soeurs / Con Mis Hermanes / With My Sisters" pledges solidarity with the women of Nicaragua in their struggle for peace. The first press run of one thousand copies of *Borrowed Beauty* sold out in nine months, and the collection garnered Tynes the Milton Acorn People's Poetry Award in 1988.

Tynes's poetry was included in the anthology *Celebrating Canadian Women: Prose and Poetry by and about Women* (1989), edited by Greta Hofmann Nemiroff. In 1990 the Maxine Tynes Reading Room was established at the Alderney Gate Public Library in Dartmouth, and Tynes published her second book, *Woman Talking Woman.* The volume is divided into four sections. The first, "Woman Talking Woman," explores women's identities and roles in lighthearted and ironic poems such as "Enamoured of the Black and White Cow," as well as in serious pieces such as "For the Montreal Fourteen," which commemorates the women killed by gunman Marc Lepine at Montreal's Ecole Polytechnique on 6 December 1989. The second section, "Black Song Nova Scotia," focuses on racism. Several of the poems deal with Africville, the black community razed by the city of Halifax between 1964 and 1967. While Tynes's family did not live in Africville, her speaker identifies with the community in such poems as "Africville Spirit" and "Africville." In "Africville Is My Name" Tynes lists the names of the former Africville residents in the manner of a war memorial. Section 3 is a series of poems about the portrait of Tynes that is reproduced on the cover of the book. The fourth section consists of three prose pieces about working-class Black Nova Scotia. Reviewer Anita Hurwitz wrote in *Poetry Canada Review* (1993): "Tynes cries against injustice, not with venom, but with productive anger." Also in 1990 the Canadian Research Institute for the Advancement of Women presented Tynes with the Muriel Duckworth Award for her work in the field of social justice leading to the advancement of women in Canada.

Tynes's collection of poetry for children, *Save the World for Me,* was published in 1991. "I Have Three Legs, You Have Two" explains the perspective of a disabled person. Many of her children's poems offer a direct and unabashed didacticism, such as "War is Not Healthy for Children or Other Living Things," "The 'No' Word," and "What Can I Do for the World

WOMAN TALKING WOMAN

Maxine Tynes

*Paperback cover for the first edition, 1990
(Bruccoli Clark Layman Archives)*

Today?" The poems are playful and accessible and similar in tone to her "adult" poems. The collection also includes the story "In Service." Also in 1991 Tynes was elected to the Board of the Writers Federation of Nova Scotia. In 1992 Mount Saint Vincent University presented Tynes with an honorary doctorate.

Tynes's next volume of poetry, *The Door of My Heart,* came out in 1993. While the poems are still concerned with large political issues such as racism, sexism, and ableism, they have a more personal voice. The section "Rolling Thunder Titans" describes the experiences of a disabled woman, revealing the pain of the condition but rejoicing in life nonetheless. In "Handprints on the Wall" a woman stumbles through her apartment, clinging for support to walls that "never want for human touch." Other poems deal with her students at Cole Harbour High School and the black American writer Zora Neale Hurston. Also in 1993 Tynes edited an anthology for children, *Beetles and Blue Jeans,* that includes poems by bpNichol, Rita Joe, Jean

Little, and Tynes herself. *In Service,* a short movie based on her story with a screenplay by Rynes and the director, Lulu Keating, was also released that year.

In 1994 Tynes moved from Cole Harbour District High School to Auburn Drive High School in Dartmouth. From 1994 to 1996 she wrote a weekly column for the Halifax *Daily News.* The columns deal with topics ranging from the Quebec Referendum, the 1995 G-7 meeting in Halifax, and black South African politician Winnie Mandela's fall from grace to the changing seasons, proper etiquette at the movies, travel, and gardening. A typical Tynes column, however, is a rant against an outrage. She expounds on racism and accessibility issues, but her most frequent focus is on crime. In "the violent 90s," she wrote in her column for 21 September 1995, the mantra is "don't trust anyone." On 27 April 1995 she combined her outrage with her poetic voice in reacting to the 19 April bombing of the Murrah Federal Building in Oklahoma City:

> Violence is no longer an unexpected event in contemporary society. Instead, it has become a regular punctuation point in our lives. We hear the statistics of overnight brawls and wanton street violence and vandalism. We swallow the facts of molestation and abuse as easily as throating oysters from the halfshell. We digest headlines and sound bites of murder and of abduction, of the desecration of human lives and human dignity. And now this.

Many columns criticize the justice system for not being harder on criminals. On 4 May 1995 she claimed that spanking children would go a long way toward decreasing the crime rate. While her ideas about crime suggest a conservative outlook, Tynes's position was generally perceived as liberal; her colleague John McLeod, business editor of *The Daily News,* publicly cautioned her against "propagating lefty myths" after a column in which she referred to long unemployment lines.

In 1994 Tynes made an audio recording of *Borrowed Beauty.* In an article announcing its release she told *Daily News* reporter Andy Pedersen: "I'm not one to sit quietly in a corner. I don't laugh modestly and cover my mouth with my hand. I take huge lusty bites out of life—I smack my lips over the feast of my passions. And I don't know why I shouldn't follow with that same passion when I'm practicing my art." Also in 1994 she was a finalist for the Dartmouth Book Award for *The Door of My Heart* and was included in the Dartmouth Heritage Museum exhibit "Dartmouth's Memorable Women 1750–1994."

Tynes has given many public readings as part of her activist agenda: as tournament poet laureate for the 1992 Peter Gzowski Invitational golf tournament to raise money for the Dartmouth Literacy Network, an event at which a copy of one of her poems was framed and auctioned off; at a 1994 Women's Day benefit for the Spryfield Anti-Poverty Network; at a benefit for the now-defunct Red Herring Co-operative Book Store in June 1994; at Word on the Street, a literary street festival held in Halifax in 1995; at Showcase Halifax 1995, a celebration of Nova Scotian artists; and at a variety show in 1999 to raise money for the Avalon Sexual Assault Centre after the acquittal of former Nova Scotia premier Gerald Regan on sexual assault charges. In the late 1990s, for undisclosed reasons, Tynes abruptly severed her relationship with her publisher, Lesley Choyce of Pottersfield Press.

In the only sustained academic treatment of Maxine Tynes's work in the context of her female maritime-provinces colleagues, *Writing the Everyday: Women's Textual Communities in Atlantic Canada* (2004), Danielle Fuller explains that Tynes's poetry conveys a sense of orality because it is primarily written for performance. By recognizing the "legacy of black Nova Scotian women" through "'lady talk', oral stories, and laughter," Fuller says, Tynes's poetry "establishes a continuity between oral expression and print literature." According to Marjorie Stone, Tynes's poetic and artistic influences range from Alden Nowlan, Leonard Cohen, Dylan Thomas, Margaret Laurence, Margaret Atwood, and Alice Munro to a black female tradition of artists and writers that includes Hurston, Portia White, Edith Clayton, Diana Ross, Sojourner Truth, Alice Walker, and Audre Lorde. With the exceptions of Fuller and Stone, Tynes's work has generally been neglected by the academic community and is absent even from anthologies of Canadian writing that focus on black authors such as Ayanna Black's *Fiery Spirits: A Collection of Short Fiction and Poetry by Canadian Writers of African Descent* (2000) and Donna Bailey Nurse's *Revival: An Anthology of Black Canadian Writing* (2006). In his 1997 critical work, *Black Like Who? Writing Black Canada,* Rinaldo Walcott overlooks not only Tynes but also the critically acclaimed black Nova Scotian writer Clarke. Fuller suggests that these oversights can be explained by the marginalized identities, in terms of race, region, and sex, that Tynes occupies as a black Nova Scotian woman. Furthermore, Fuller argues in "'Raising the Heart': The Politics of the Popular and the Poetics of Performance in the Work of Maxine Tynes" (1999), academics have difficulty engaging with work that focuses on orality and simplicity of tone. Tynes's poetry is, however, undeniably popular. In 2007 Shauntay Grant published a poem in the Halifax *Daily News* that celebrates black heritage; the final lines indicate the impact that Tynes has had on her culture: "I am . . . / english: harlem renaissance poets, spoken word, George Elliott Clarke, Maxine Tynes . . . beautiful."

Interview:

Jeanette Lynes, "Medicine, Magic, Weaponry, Love: Maxine Tynes' Poetry," in *Words out There: Women Poets in Atlantic Canada,* edited by Lynes (Lockeport, N.S.: Roseway, 1999), pp. 117–128.

References:

George Elliott Clarke, "Tynes Gaining on Muses," *Halifax Chronicle Herald,* 19 November 1993, p. D3;

Danielle Fuller, "'Raising the Heart': The Politics of the Popular and the Poetics of Performance in the Work of Maxine Tynes," *Essays in Canadian Writing,* 67 (Spring 1999): 76–112;

Fuller, *Writing the Everyday: Women's Textual Communities in Atlantic Canada* (Montreal & Kingston, Ont.: McGill-Queen's University Press, 2004);

Shauntay Grant, "Scream to Be Heard," *Daily News* (Halifax, N.S.), 1 February 2007, p. H5;

Sylvia Hamilton, "A Way to Light a Candle: The Real Significance of Black History Month," *Daily News* (Halifax, N.S.), 2 February 1992, p. 3;

John McLeod, "Sniping, Lefty Myths, Shudder, Winning Yap," *Daily News* (Halifax, N.S.), 24 March 1995, p. 24;

Andy Pedersen, "A Passionate Woman: Dartmouth Writer Maxine Tynes Releases Recorded Poetry," *Daily News* (Halifax, N.S.), 22 December 1994, p. 31;

Leslie Smith, "A Chronicler of Current Events," *Nova Scotian,* 10 October 1987, pp. 12–13;

Marjorie Stone, "The Poet as Whole-Body Camera: Maxine Tynes and the Pluralities of Otherness," *Dalhousie Review,* 77 (Summer 1997): 227–257.

"Tynes Proud to Be People's Poet," *Mail-Star* (Halifax, N.S.), 7 June 1988, p. 16.

Jane Urquhart

(21 June 1949 –)

Holly Luhning
University of Saskatchewan

BOOKS: *False Shuffles* (Victoria: Press Porcépic, 1982);
I Am Walking in the Garden of His Imaginary Palace: Eleven Poems for Le Nôtre (Toronto: Aya Press, 1982);
The Little Flowers of Madame de Montespan (Erin, Ont.: Porcupine's Quill, 1984);
The Whirlpool: A Novel (Toronto: McClelland & Stewart, 1986; New York: Simon & Schuster, 1989);
Storm Glass (Erin, Ont.: Porcupine's Quill, 1987);
Changing Heaven (Toronto: McClelland & Stewart, 1990; Boston: David R. Godine, 1993);
Away: A Novel (Toronto: McClelland & Stewart, 1993; New York: Viking, 1994; London: Bloomsbury, 1994);
The Underpainter (Toronto: McClelland & Stewart, 1997; New York: Viking 1997; London: Bloomsbury, 1997);
The Stone Carvers (Toronto: McClelland & Stewart, 2001; New York: Viking, 2002; London: Bloomsbury, 2002);
A Map of Glass (Toronto: McClelland & Stewart, 2005; London: Bloomsbury, 2005; San Francisco: Mac-Adam/Cage, 2006).

OTHER: "Returning to the Village," in *Writing Away: The PEN Canada Travel Anthology,* edited by Constance Rooke (Toronto: McClelland & Stewart, 1994), pp. 281–194;
"The Frozen Lake," in *Writing Home: A PEN Canada Anthology,* edited by Rooke (Toronto: McClelland & Stewart, 1997), pp. 349–356.

SELECTED PERIODICAL PUBLICATIONS–UNCOLLECTED: "Night Walk (Jane Urquhart Remembers Ken Adachi)," *Brick,* 35 (1989): 37–38;
"The Way Angel Spreads Her Wings," *Canadian Literature,* 130 (1991): 132–134;
"An Innocent Bystander," *Canadian Literature,* 130 (1991): 132–134;
"Familiar Roads Home (Second Thoughts on Rereading *The Lost Salt Gift of Blood* by Alistair

Jane Urquhart (photograph by Tony Urquhart; from the cover for Away: A Novel, *1993; Bruccoli Clark Layman Archives)*

MacLeod)," *Globe and Mail* (Toronto), 4 May 1991, pp. E1, E4;
"Away," *Canadian Forum,* 72 (1993): 24–28;
"Imaginary Landscape," *Canadian Geographic,* 116, no. 2 (1996): 84;
"Five Wheelchairs," *Canadian Fiction Magazine Annual* (1997): 120–140;
"The Last Words We Spoke: 'Drive Carefully,' I Said. At 3 A.m., He Still Wasn't Home. By Morning, I Was a 24-Year-Old Widow," *National Post,* 5 April 2003, p. SP1;
"Author's Generosity of Spirit Enriched Lives of Her Readers (Carol Shields: 1935–2003)," *Globe and Mail* (Toronto), 18 July 2003, p. A1.

Jane Urquhart is one of Canada's leading novelists. Her preoccupations with history, familial pasts, myth, and desire have produced texts popular both with critics and with the reading public. Like Robertson Davies and Margaret Atwood, Urquhart looks beneath the calm surfaces of towns and countrysides and finds bizarre occurrences, passionate attachments, and supernatural encounters. In a 1998 interview with Jeffrey Canton, Urquhart said that telling stories is "an important part of the human psyche. Wanting to shape the events of our lives, to give them order. Transforming our daily lives into the stuff of myth."

Jane Carter was born in Little Long Lac in a remote region north of Lake Superior, on 21 June 1949 to W. A. "Nick" Carter, a mining engineer and gold prospector, and Marianne Quinn Carter, a nurse. She has two older brothers. The mine where her father worked closed in the mid 1950s, and the family moved to Toronto. Urquhart told Canton, "an already established Northern Mythology moved with us in the form of anecdotes about the people and events of the community": her father related stories about characters such as brothel owner "Coffee Annie" and men named "Pipefitter Slim" and "Broken Leg Bill." Her mother's large Irish family, the Quinns, were farmers in southeastern Ontario, and Urquhart told Canton that "that side of the family also spent a lot of time keeping the oral tradition alive." From them she heard stories about strong grandmothers, town drunks, "various babies that died of awful childhood diseases, brides that died on the bed in their wedding gowns, magic lantern shows."

After seeing *My Fair Lady* and *The Music Man* during a visit to New York when she was eight, Carter became "obsessed" with musicals and dreamed of becoming an actress. When she was ten, she began to study acting at the New Play Society in Toronto. She performed in a youth choir, took piano lessons, and spent a summer at the Banff School of Fine Arts. At eleven she wrote to the composer Richard Rodgers that she wanted to run away from home and become a Broadway star and asked him to meet her at the airport in a month. Rodgers wrote back that he would meet her—after she turned eighteen. She told Canton that as an adolescent, "I realized that I could use my imagination in other ways. I began writing poetry and became serious about reading, especially the modernist poets. I was attracted to work I didn't quite understand. I thought if you read something often enough and carefully enough, a wonderful mystery will be explained to you. I was probably right."

In 1968 Carter enrolled at the University of Guelph, where she met art student Paul Keele; they were married on 1 January 1969. Jane Keele received her B.A. in English in 1971. The couple moved to Halifax; while Paul studied at the Nova Scotia College of Art and Design, Jane worked as a civilian information officer for the Royal Canadian Navy. In 1973 they moved to a farm on Lake Ontario east of Toronto. Paul Keele was killed in an automobile accident later that year. Jane Keele returned to the University of Guelph to study art history and received a B.A. in that subject in 1975. On 5 May 1976 she married Tony Urquhart, a painter and sculptor fifteen years her senior and a divorced father of four. Their daughter, Emily, was born in 1977.

Around this time Jane Urquhart's poems began appearing in literary journals, and in 1982 she published her first book of poetry, *False Shuffles*. She told Geoff Hancock in 1986 that this collection "connects to my interest in the past. The narrating daughter is the speaker and the oral tradition plays, and has played an enormous role in that both the grandmother and the mother have passed the interpretation of events down to the daughter." Later in 1982 she published *I Am Walking in the Garden of His Imaginary Palace: Eleven Poems for Le Nôtre,* about the seventeenth-century French garden and landscape designer André Le Nôtre, illustrated with drawings by her husband. It was followed in 1984 by *The Little Flowers of Madame de Montespan,* a series of poems on the gardens of Louis XIV. Anne Compton notes that the "Niagara Landscape is a nightmare to the orderly mind, to the mind of that arch-architect of gardens, Louis XIV." According to Compton, Urquhart's poetry "emphasizes visual memory, which, for her, is both perceptual and fantastical since it combines memory, fantasy, and actuality."

In 1984 Urquhart submitted a manuscript to the Seal First Novel Contest; it was one of the five finalists. Ellen Seligman, McClelland and Stewart's fiction editor, read the manuscript, gave Urquhart suggestions on how she might develop it, and McClelland and Stewart published *The Whirlpool* in 1986. The novel is set during the summer of 1889. Maud Grady has taken over the undertaking business of her late husband, Charles, and has become obsessed, as he was, with trying to identify the nameless bodies fished from the Niagara River near the falls. The beautiful Fleda is involved in a dismal marriage to David, a military historian. David is disturbed by Fleda's obsession with Robert Browning's poetry; Fleda risks spiritual death if she succumbs to David's perverse eroticism and fascination with mock necrophilia.

Urquhart's collection of short stories, *Storm Glass,* was published by the small literary house Porcupine's Quill in 1987. Although the readership for *Storm Glass* was small, the book was critically well received and caught the attention of the Boston publisher David R. Godine; he published Urquhart's next novel, *Changing Heaven* (1990), in the United States in 1993. The French

translation of *The Whirlpool* won the French Prix du Meilleur Livre Etrange in 1992.

While working on *Changing Heaven,* Urquhart spent some time on the Yorkshire moors near Haworth, the home of Emily Brontë: "I need more than a superficial connection with the landscape I'm going to discuss in a novel. I need to actually live in the place for awhile. When I lived near Haworth, I would take long walks on the moors—not because I thought that I was a reincarnation of Emily Brontë and could experience everything she did by being out there—but so as to be able to pick up details of the world surrounding me." Ann Frear, an awkward Canadian teenager with braces, reads Brontë's novel *Wuthering Heights* (1847) and becomes obsessed with the Romantic character Heathcliff: "'Oh Heathcliff, Heathcliff,' she whispers in the dark of her own pink bedroom, any winter night the wind chooses to howl through the city in which she lives." As an adult she veils her obsession by becoming a Brontë scholar and goes to live near Haworth. Other characters in the novel are the ghosts of Brontë and Ari-

anna, a balloonist who died while parachuting over the moor at the turn of the twentieth century. According to Urquhart, "Emily and Arianna do not manifest themselves as howling, shrieking phantoms dragging their chains behind them. They are not out to drive anyone mad with fear." On the whole, they are lighthearted ghosts, but they do talk about serious issues. Emily tells Arianna: "My dog Keeper and I set out on our daily walk and, suddenly, the landscape had altered. There it was, the landscape of my novel! I could never see it any other way again. It was mine, mine!" *Changing Heaven* was critically well received; Janice Kulyk Keefer called it "one of the strangest, most powerful texts in the English language," and *Saturday Night* (November 1993) described it as "a beautifully written book" that "throbs with the storm and wind of passion." J. Russel Perkin notes that "Jane Urquhart and her protagonist have a relationship with *Wuthering Heights* that goes beyond mere critical esteem, becoming something immoderate and obsessive."

Urquhart's next novel, *Away* (1993), begins as Esther O'Malley prepares to die; her last act is to "give shape to one hundred and forty years" by remembering the family story told to her by her grandmother Eileen. Esther's retelling of the story of her grandmother and Eileen's mother, Mary, comprises the bulk of the novel. In the early nineteenth century Mary falls in love with a sailor she finds shipwrecked on the shore of Rathlin Island. Before he dies in her arms, he whispers the name "Moira"; from then on, Mary believes that Moira is her new name and new identity. She marries the schoolmaster Brian O'Malley but cryptically tells him, "I will be your wife but I will not be your wife." After they immigrate to Canada, she leaves Brian and their children, renames herself Moira, and goes to live on the shore of Moira Lake in Ontario. Her frozen body is returned to her family seven years later by her Ojibway friend, Exodus Crow. Mary's daughter Eileen becomes infatuated with Aidan Lanighan, a political activist seemingly aligned with the Irish nationalist Fenians but secretly a spy for D'Arcy McGee, one of the fathers of Confederation in Canada. When they go to hear McGee speak in Parliament, Eileen insists on concealing a pistol that Aidan takes as "a precaution"; she gives the pistol to Aidan's cohort Patrick, who assassinates McGee. Aidan blames Eileen for the killing and accuses her of being under the influence of a dream or a supernatural power. For Eileen, the romantic and political spell is broken, but Aidan leaves his mark on the rest of her life; years later, she tells Esther, "I can't, you see, get the face of a certain young man out of my mind." Esther, an artist, is tempted by an "otherworldly" romance when a fisherman, whose physical description echoes those of Mary's sailor and Aidan, takes shelter from a storm in her house on Loughbreeze Beach: "It was his swimming to her land, the storm, his journey over beach stones that mattered." But she has learned from the experiences of Eileen and Mary and has chosen a life of stability. Thus, she lies on her deathbed, alone and childless, telling the family story to an empty house. The story will die with Esther, the last descendant of the O'Malley line.

Away remained on the Toronto *Globe and Mail* bestseller list for 132 weeks, a record for a Canadian book; won the Trillium Award; and was short-listed for the International IMPAC Dublin Literary Award. Herb Wylie says that the novel "combines the verisimilitude and plausibility typical of the historical novel with the spectral and magical, constructing a fairly detailed historical context while retaining the sense of exoticism, mystery, and otherness typical of the romance." Cynthia Sugars argues that *Away* is, on the one hand, "postcolonial in its recuperative drive to celebrate the foundations of Canada's national history; on the other, its romance of Canadian 'beginnings' is contentious." Patricia Smart describes the novel as an Irish Canadian "story of extremes: of material poverty and imaginative, mystical richness, of stark beauty of the rocky coast of northern Ireland and the overwhelming power of the Canadian forest, and of the political passion of the Irish settlers who clung to the Fenian dream of nation after centuries of British oppression." Timothy Findlay described the novel as "a great romantic tale—rich in imagery and with language worthy of Emily Brontë and Thomas Hardy. Like these writers, she is unafraid of words and spends them fearlessly. The uses to which she puts her command of language are beautiful and breathtaking."

Urquhart received the Marian Engel Award for an outstanding body of prose by a Canadian woman writer in 1994 and was named a Chevalier of France's Order of Arts and Letters in 1996. In her fourth novel, *The Underpainter* (1997), seventy-five-year-old American minimalist painter Austin Fraser, a cold and emotionally distant man, recounts the story of his life. He tells of two people he betrayed: Sara, his model, mistress, and companion during his annual sketching trips to the Canadian wilderness north of Lake Superior; and George, his friend from his youth. George loved Vivian, who suddenly left him; Fraser shattered George's fragile world when he thoughtlessly brought Vivian to see George after her long absence. Austin's paintings, called "erasures," symbolize his withdrawal from human relationships: he carefully creates a picture, then applies layers of paint to blur, obscure, and eliminate the image. *The Underpainter* won the 1997 Governor General's Literary Award for Fiction.

The protagonist of *The Stone Carvers* (2001) is Klara, a thirty-eight-year-old self-described spinster who lives in the village of Shoneval, Ontario. The village was established in 1867 by Father Archangel Gstir, who came from Bavaria. Gstir dreamed of building a stone church inspired by the castle of the mad King Ludwig of Bavaria, with a large bell "which would ring out to an established village and whose song would carry over beautifully cultivated fields." Gstir's quest drew together the community, including Klara's grandfather, a woodcarver, who tried to pass on his skills to Klara's brother, Tilman. Tilman was prone to wandering away from home; to keep him from roaming, his mother chained him to his cot. Klara unchained him, and Tilman ran away again and did not return. Klara learns her grandfather's craft and also the tailoring skills of her mother. In her younger years "romance had disturbed and illuminated her life, had cast its lights and its shadow over her for one intense, confusing season," but her lover, Eamon O'Sullivan, was killed in World War I. One day Tilman returns, maimed from fighting in France. Tilman's return and her memories of Eamon inspire Klara to become involved with the project to construct a Canadian war memorial at the site of the April 1917 battle at Vimy Ridge in France. Klara persuades Tilman to become involved also, and the two work on the memorial designed by the Toronto sculptor Walter Seymour Allward. Klara and Tilman make a pilgrimage to the memorial after its completion in 1936; the sculpture sheds "light and strength and consolation" and eases Klara's and Tilman's suffering. *The Stone Carvers* was short-listed for the Giller Prize for 2001.

Jane Urquhart has an honorary degree from the University of Waterloo and was writer-in-residence at the University of Ottawa in 1997, Memorial University of Newfoundland in 1992, and the University of Toronto in 1997. She has been hailed as one of the most compelling and accomplished voices in contemporary Canadian fiction. Urquhart lives with her husband in a small town in southeastern Ontario.

Interviews:

Geoff Hancock, "An Interview with Jane Urquhart," *Canadian Fiction Magazine,* 55 (1986): 23–40;

Beverly Slopen, "Jane Urquhart: Writing for Art's Sake," *Publishers Weekly,* 244 (24 November 1997): 48–49;

Jeffrey Canton, "Ghosts in the Landscape: Jane Urquhart," in *The Power to Bend Spoons: Interviews with Canadian Novelists,* edited by Beverley Daurio (Toronto: Mercury, 1998), pp. 194–199.

References:

Libby Birch, "The Irish Female Presence in Jane Urquhart's Fiction," *Canadian Woman Studies/Les Cahiers de la Femme,* 17 (Summer–Fall 1997): 115–119;

Georgianna M. M. Colville, "The Quest for a Literary and Mythical Past in Three Novels by Jane Urquhart," *Etudes Canadiennes/Canadian Studies: Revue Interdisciplinaire des Etudes Canadiennes en France,* 44 (1998): 61–76;

Anne Compton, "Romancing the Landscape: Jane Urquhart's Fiction," in *Literature of Region and Nation: Proceedings of the 6th International Literature of Region and Nation Conference, 2–7 August 1996* (Saint John, N.B.: Social Sciences and Humanities Research Council of Canada & University of New Brunswick in Saint John, 1998), pp. 431–443;

Katherine K. Gottschalk, "Isabel Hugan and Jane Urquhart: Feminine in This?" in *Canadian Women Writing Fiction,* edited by Mickey Pearlman (Jackson: University Press of Mississippi, 1993), pp. 99–115;

Laura Hancu, "Escaping the Frame: Circumscribing the Narrative in *The Whirlpool*," *Studies in Canadian Literature/Etudes den Litterature Canadienne,* 20, no. 1 (1995): 45–64;

J. Russel Perkin, "Inhabiting Wuthering Heights: Jane Urquhart's Rewriting of Emily Brontë," *Victorian Review: The Journal of the Victorian Studies Association of Western Canada and the Victorian Studies Association of Ontario,* 21, no. 2 (1995): 115–128;

Patricia Smart, "Weighing the Claims of Memory: The Poetry and Politics of the Irish-Canadian Experience in Jane Urquhart's *Away*," *International Journal of Canadian Studies/Revue Internationale d'Etudes Canadiennes,* 10 (1994): 63–70;

Patsy Stoneman, "From Classic Text to Intertext: *Wuthering Heights* in a Post-Kristevan World," *Versus: Quaderni di Studi Semiotici,* 77–78 (May–December 1997): 75–96;

Cynthia Sugars, "Haunted by (a Lack of) Postcolonial Ghosts: Settler Nationalism in Jane Urquhart's *Away*," *Essays on Canadian Writing,* 79 (2003): 1–32;

Sugars, "Settler Fantasies, Postcolonial Guilt: The Compromised Postcolonialism of Jane Urquhart's *Away*," *Australian-Canadian Studies: A Journal for the Humanities & Social Sciences,* 19, no. 2 (2001): 101–118;

Herb Wylie, "The Opposite of History is Forgetfulness: Myth History, and the new Dominion in Jane Urquhart's *Away*," *Studies in Canadian Literature/Etudes en Littérature Canadienne,* 24, no. 1 (1999): 20–45.

Papers:

Jane Urquhart's diary is in the Doris Lewis Rare Book Room of the Dana Porter Library at the University of Waterloo.

Guy Vanderhaeghe
(5 April 1951 –)

Alison Calder
University of Manitoba

BOOKS: *Man Descending* (Toronto: Macmillan, 1982; New York: Houghton Mifflin, 1985; London: Bodley Head, 1986);

The Trouble with Heroes (Ottawa: Borealis, 1983);

My Present Age (Toronto: Macmillan, 1984; New York: Ticknor & Fields, 1985; London: Bodley Head, 1986);

Homesick (Toronto: McClelland & Stewart, 1989; Boston: Ticknor & Fields, 1990);

Things as They Are? (Toronto: McClelland & Stewart, 1992);

I Had a Job I Liked. Once (Saskatoon: Fifth House, 1992);

Dancock's Dance (Winnipeg: Blizzard, 1996);

The Englishman's Boy (Toronto: McClelland & Stewart, 1996; London: Doubleday, 1997; New York: Picador USA, 1997);

The Last Crossing (Toronto: McClelland & Stewart, 2002; New York: Atlantic Monthly Press, 2004).

PLAY PRODUCTIONS: *I Had a Job I Liked. Once,* Saskatoon, Persephone Theatre, 18 April 1991;

Dancock's Dance, Saskatoon, Persephone Theatre, 1 April 1995.

PRODUCED SCRIPT: *Cages,* motion picture, Beacon Films, 1985.

OTHER: "Poetic Desire and Authentic Rendering: Linked Collections," in *Writing Saskatchewan: 20 Critical Essays,* edited by Kenneth G. Probert (Regina: Canadian Plains Research Centre, 1989), pp. 170–172;

Mordecai Richler, *St. Urbain's Horseman,* afterword by Vanderhaeghe (Toronto: McClelland & Stewart, 1989);

"The Jimi Hendrix Experience," in *Turn of the Story: Canadian Short Fiction on the Eve of the Millenium,* edited by Joan Thomas and Heidi Harms (Toronto: Anansi, 1991), pp. 57–68; repub-

Guy Vanderhaeghe (photograph by Margaret Vanderhaeghe; from the dust jacket for the U.S. edition of The Last Crossing, *2004; Richland County Public Library)*

lished in *Ghost Writing: Haunted Tales by Contemporary Writers,* edited by Roger Weingarten (Montpelier, Vt.: Invisible Cities, 2000), pp. 245–256;

Margaret Laurence, *The Tomorrow-Tamers,* afterword by Vanderhaeghe (Toronto: McClelland & Stewart, 1993);

The Journey Prize Anthology: The Best of Canada's New Writers, edited by Vanderhaeghe (Toronto: McClelland & Stewart, 1993);

"'Brand Name' vs. 'No-Name': A Half-Century of the Representation of Western Canadian Cities in Fiction," in *The Urban Prairie,* edited by Dan Ring (Saskatoon: Fifth House, 1993), pp. 111–129.

SELECTED PERIODICAL PUBLICATIONS– UNCOLLECTED:

POETRY

"There Is No Accounting for Taste," *Queen's Quarterly*, 88 (1981): 523–524;

"The Doctrine of Water," *Dalhousie Review*, 61 (1981–1982): 686–687;

"Death Should Be an Elephant," *Malahat Review*, 63 (1982): 68.

FICTION

"Happy Jack," *Grain*, 2, no. 1 (1974): 5–13;

"And No Man Could Bind Him," *Chelsea Journal*, 6 (1980): 22–28;

"He Scores! He Shoots!," *Matrix*, 13 (1981): 3–15;

"Snell," *Quarry*, 30, no. 1 (1981): 48–52;

"The King Is Dead," *Wascana Review*, 32, no. 1 (1997): 45–56.

NONFICTION

"A Magician of the Austere," *Globe and Mail* (Toronto), 21 June 1997, p. D16.

While Guy Vanderhaeghe has long been known to those interested in Canadian literature as a fine storyteller, he did not gain popular attention in Canada until he published *The Englishman's Boy* in 1996. The success of this Western novel thrust Vanderhaeghe into the national spotlight and garnered him a reputation as a tough-talking, straight-shooting writer. Such a reputation, while upheld by his 2002 novel, *The Last Crossing*, threatens to eclipse his earlier accomplishments: three short-story collections, one of which won the Governor General's Literary Award; two previous novels published in Canada and abroad; and two plays, both of which have been produced. His works have been translated into Dutch, Swedish, Norwegian, Danish, and French and have been reviewed in such publications as *The New Yorker*, *TLS: The Times Literary Supplement*, *The Guardian* (London), *The Sunday Times* (London), and *The Irish Times* (Dublin). Though his literary career might have progressed faster if he had moved to a major publishing center, Vanderhaeghe remains committed to Saskatchewan, the setting for many of his works. In a 1984 interview with Doris Hillis he said that Saskatchewan is a good place for a writer to live "because it's isolated from the extraliterary activity associated with the literary world. There are not the same pressures here as [on] a writer living in Toronto. But, at the same time, the writer in Saskatchewan is less inclined to be thought of as a national writer, and has fewer markets available. Yet I think the benefits of living in Saskatchewan outweigh the disadvantages." He also told Hillis that "I believe you can live almost anywhere as a writer and not be isolated because you can always get your hands on books. The intellectual communion that I have does not necessarily have to be personal. It can go on through books. And I can get a book from anywhere in the world in Saskatoon."

Guy Clarence Vanderhaeghe was born on 5 April 1951 in Esterhazy, a mining town 120 miles northeast of Regina, the only child of Clarence Earl and Alma Beth Allen Vanderhaeghe. His father was a mill worker in a potash mine; his mother was a secretary. When he was six years old, he offered to write a Western and sell it to his grandfather for five cents. The family moved to a farm when he was thirteen.

At seventeen Vanderhaeghe enrolled at the University of Saskatchewan in Saskatoon, where he majored in history. He earned a B.A. with great distinction in 1971. In September 1972 he married Margaret Nagel, a fellow history major. He completed additional history courses, earning an honors degree and meeting the admission requirements for the M.A. program. In 1973 he worked as a researcher for the university's Institute for Northern Studies; the following year he took a job as an archivist at the university library. His first published story appeared in *Grain* magazine that year. In 1975 he received his M.A. in British imperial history. He maintained his archivist position while also working as a freelance writer and editor and continuing to place stories in literary journals. He received his bachelor of education with great distinction from the University of Regina in 1978 and taught English and history for a year in the small town of Herbert, Saskatchewan. By this time his stories were being published in leading literary journals such as *The Malahat Review*, *The Journal of Canadian Fiction*, and *Canadian Fiction Magazine*.

In 1979 Vanderhaeghe returned to Saskatoon to work as a researcher for Access Consulting, a firm of health-care consultants; he held the position for one year before turning to writing full-time. His wife, meanwhile, was establishing a reputation as a painter; her work has been shown in galleries from Saskatoon, Edmonton, and Toronto to the Netherlands and Hong Kong.

In 1982 Vanderhaeghe published his first collection of short stories, *Man Descending*. Many of the pieces are narrated by characters who watch events unfold without being the main participants in them or who lack the power to change them. Charlie, the child narrator of "The Watcher," observes the hostile dance between his tough grandmother and the psychobabbling and sadistic man his mother brings home. Caragan, the psychically damaged narrator of "Going to Russia," seeks to expiate his guilt for fathering a mentally retarded child. Dieter Bethge in "Dancing Bear" and Tom Ogle in "A Taste for Perfection" are held captive by failing bodies and by the institutions designed to aid them. Though the stories are marked by moments of epiphany, such as in Billy Simpson's sudden understanding in "Cages" of the literal and figurative cages that confine him and his father, transcendence is only momentary: the best the characters can hope to do is recognize the limits on their lives. Joe's despairing realization at the end of "The Expatriates' Party" that he had "been lost for thirty years, an expatriate wandering" can be applied to almost any of these alienated characters. The last two stories, however, which introduce Vanderhaeghe's recurring character Ed, offer some hope for transformation. In "Man Descending" Ed is an unemployed, embittered slacker whose marriage dissolves because he is drifting through life; in "Sam, Soren, and Ed," however, he is writing a novel and holding down a job. *Man Descending* won the Governor General's Literary Award for Fiction, beating out Alice Munro's collection *Who Do You Think You Are?* Vanderhaeghe was named writer-in-residence at the Saskatoon Public Library in 1982. Published in Britain in 1986, the collection won the 1987 Geoffrey Faber Memorial Prize. The title story was adapted for television in 1992.

Man Descending was followed in 1983 by *The Trouble with Heroes,* although several of the stories in this collection predate the publication *Man Descending:* "Lazarus," for example, first appeared in 1976. The stories range in setting from biblical times to the present and introduce protagonists at various stages of their lives. The collection has a strong masculine bent: female characters, when present at all, are tangential to the self-exploration undertaken by the male protagonists. "Café Society" contrasts the historical awareness of Gabriel Dumont, who led the Métis forces in the Northwest Rebellion of 1885, with the self-absorbed and effete fin de siècle society of Paris. In the title story a war veteran muses on the lies necessary to maintain the illusion of heroism. Several stories are concerned with power and weakness and the cruelties associated with that dynamic: "The King Is Dead," for example, juxtaposes a boy's response to the assassination of President John F. Kennedy with his brutal killing of a dog. Vanderhaeghe told Hillis, "I believe there is an element of *original sin* in all of us which makes us self-centred. In some people it is blatantly gross and cruel; in others less so, and certainly less apparent. *But it is a fact of human nature.* It is clearly evident in children." The hapless, rootless protagonists of the final two stories, "The Prodigal" and "Parker's Dog," resemble Ed in "Man Descending"; the endings of these stories, however, provide a glimmer of hope.

Ed himself returns in *My Present Age* (1984), Vanderhaeghe's first novel. Although he had seemed to be getting his life together in "Sam, Soren, and Ed," here he is even worse off than he was in "Man Descend-

ing": a deeply damaged human being, unemployed, paranoid, cynical, and supercilious, with delusions of genius, he is obsessed with his pregnant wife, Victoria, who is divorcing him. He gradually drives everyone away except Rubacek, a former convict who is a student in the creative-writing class Ed teaches at night. When Ed suffers what he believes to be a heart attack brought on by a rage-infused dance to torment his downstairs neighbor, Rubacek moves into Ed's apartment to care for him. Though there are glimmerings of romantic potential with an acquaintance, Martha, Ed's self-destructive behavior, culminating in a drunken and inappropriate toast at Martha's brother's wedding, cuts off that possibility. Vanderhaeghe parallels Ed's descent from a young man with some promise to an alienated loner with a scene from the Western novel Ed is writing: his hero, Sam Waters, walks into a saloon and meets a drunken barfly who eventually gives his name as Huck Finn. The epigraph to *My Present Age* is a quotation from the nineteenth-century Danish philosopher Søren Kierkegaard that sums up the modern age as one of listlessness and lack of ambition. This characterization makes Ed a representative Everyman. Predating Douglas Coupland's novel *Generation X* by seven years, *My Present Age* presents some of the same themes: alienation, angst, dissatisfaction with life, and the feeling that one's generation has been cheated out of one's inheritance by the very people who should have preserved it. Many of the other characters criticize Ed for his lack of ambition and refusal to conform to the doctrine of success as manifested by career and wealth, but conformity to social norms is not the solution to Ed's anomie; ultimately, even Victoria, who remained idealistic throughout her miserable marriage to Ed, is revealed to be breaking down. *My Present Age* is an intensely literary novel, repeatedly engaging with the construction of narratives and the relation of art to life. Ed deals with the world through books: a book he wrote led to his nervous breakdown five years previously, and he is engaged in a custody battle with Victoria over a set of works by Honoré de Balzac.

In Vanderhaeghe's second novel, *Homesick* (1989), Vera Miller moves back to her family home in the fictional town of Connaught, Saskatchewan, with her twelve-year-old son, Daniel. Vera and her father, Alec Monkman, have not spoken in nineteen years: Vera has never forgiven her father for taking her out of high school and making her keep house for him and her younger brother, Earl, after their mother's death; Alec has never forgiven Vera for abandoning him by leaving home at sixteen to join the army. The novel is told from Vera's, Daniel's, and Alec's perspectives, allowing the narrators to comment on each other's behavior and to reveal to the reader thoughts they would never speak

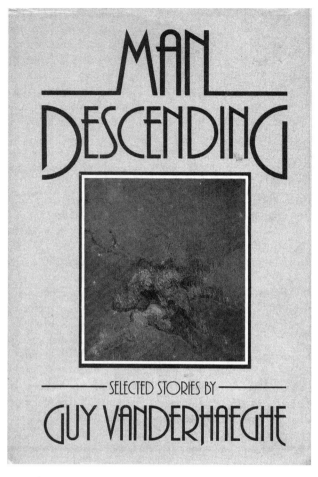

Dust jacket for the first edition, 1982
(Bruccoli Clark Layman Archives)

aloud. Eventually, Vera finds it impossible to remain in Alec's home, and she and Daniel move to another house. She believes that Alec is keeping Earl's whereabouts from her to punish her for leaving, but Alec reveals the secret to Daniel: some years after Vera's departure, Earl had to be committed to a mental hospital, where he died of an infection and was buried. When Alec has a stroke, Vera tells Daniel that it is their duty to stay with him in the hospital: "it has to be done and there's no one else to do it but us, the family. This is part of being a family." In the final paragraph, Vera embraces her dying father in an attempt to warm him. *Homesick* was the cowinner of the City of Toronto Book Award in 1990.

Vanderhaeghe's short story "Home Place," originally published in *The London Review of Books* in 1987 and republished in *Grain* magazine in 1990, won the Western Magazine Award for Fiction in 1991. It depicts the power struggle between land-proud Gil and his weak son Ronald and is included in his third collection,

Things as They Are? (1992). The opening piece, "King Walsh," is narrated by King's brother, who observes the relationship between King and King's son as King ages. "The Master of Disaster" opens: "Norman Hiller and Kurt Meinecke, both dreamers, and me caught sticky between them, the jam in the sandwich." The narrator, Bernie Berman, is an accessory to Hiller's plan to turn Meinecke into a boxer. Spending the summer with his grandmother, the eleven-year-old narrator of "Loneliness Has Its Claims" is befriended by "Uncle Cecil," a neighbor who initially seems to be attracted to the grandmother but switches his attentions to the boy; while the narrator seemingly remains unaware of the sexual nature of Cecil's interest, he is far from an innocent and manipulates Cecil into buying him a gun. "The Teacher" details a boy's battles with a wicked teacher, and "Fraud" presents a con man who is ultimately ensnared by his intended victim.

Also in 1991 Vanderhaeghe's first play, *I Had a Job I Liked. Once,* premiered at Persephone Theatre in

Saskatoon; it was published in 1992. In the police station of a prairie mining town Les Grant, a young man accused of attempting to rape the daughter of a prominent citizen, is being interrogated by Finestad, an aging Royal Canadian Mounted Police sergeant who clings to the belief that strict adherence to the law will produce a just outcome. Grant finally confesses that he stripped the girl and left her stranded to repay her for the humiliations he suffered at her hands and at the hands of the town's other "upstanding" citizens. Finestad is devastated: no law can fully accommodate the specifics of this case. Grant will go to prison, confirming the prejudices of the town's upper crust, who deplore the working class; his confinement echoes his earlier "imprisonment" in the snack bar where he had to work while the rich youngsters played at the swimming pool. *I Had a Job I Liked. Once* won the Canadian Authors Association Award for Drama.

Vanderhaeghe's second play, *Dancock's Dance*, premiered at the Persephone Theatre in 1995 and was published the following year. In 1919 Lieutenant John Dancock, a patient at the Saskatchewan Hospital for the Insane, struggles with a shadowy soldier figure who is the embodiment of his guilt-ridden shell shock. Adhering to a strict military rule in the madness of war, Dancock shot the soldier for refusing to leave his trench and attack the enemy; he now considers the man he killed to have been blameless. The soldier points to Dancock's role in his death and asks why Dancock is still alive. Dancock's obedience to the rules is paralleled by the hospital superintendent's adherence to senseless policies that deny the inmates meaningful work and interactions in favor of administration-approved rituals. Dancock's only solace is his relationship with Dorothea, a fellow patient who is afraid that she will spontaneously combust. When the influenza epidemic strikes the hospital, the staff deserts; Dancock is able to persuade the superintendent to relax the rules and allow the patients to look after themselves and each other. The play ends with Dancock and Dorothea dancing together.

Vanderhaeghe's 1996 novel, *The Englishman's Boy,* is set in 1923. Hollywood studio head Damon Ira Chance, whose hero is D. W. Griffith, director of the pro–Ku Klux Klan epic *The Birth of a Nation* (1919), regards movies as a way of weaning immigrants away from their traditions and converting them into "real" Americans. Chance hires aspiring young Canadian screenwriter Harry Vincent to write the script for a movie about the 1873 Cypress Hills Massacre in Saskatchewan. From Shorty McAdoo, an old cowboy, Harry learns the true story of the massacre, in which a band of Assiniboine Indians were killed and an Assiniboine girl was raped and murdered by a gang of American "wolfers"–trappers who poisoned buffalo carcasses and harvested the furs from the wolves and coyotes who died from eating the tainted meat. When he turns in his screenplay, Chance demands that he rewrite it to have the girl kill herself: "Change the girl, Harry," he insists, "the enemy is never human." In addition to winning the Governor General's Literary Award for Fiction, *The Englishman's Boy* won Saskatchewan Book Awards for best book of fiction and for book of the year, was a finalist for the Giller Prize, and was shortlisted for the International IMPAC Dublin Literary Award. Vanderhaeghe received an honorary Litt.D. degree from the University of Saskatchewan in 1997.

In interviews Vanderhaeghe has said that he discarded from *The Englishman's Boy* a subplot about a Victorian painter's search for his brother. He used this story for his next novel, *The Last Crossing* (2002), in which the painter Charles Gaunt travels from England to the American West to try to find his brother Simon, a missionary who disappeared while trying to convert the Indians to Christianity. Other characters are also searching: Lucy Stoveall, a young woman abandoned by her abusive husband, is pursuing the murderers of her sister; Custis Straw, an aging Civil War veteran, is following Lucy in the hope of persuading her to love him; saloon keeper Aloysius Dooley seeks to protect his friend Custis; and Jerry Potts, a Métis guide alienated from both the Native and the white communities, is in search of a place where he can belong. Their quests intersect on the American plains in an uneasy convoy led by Charles's other brother, Addington, a military officer driven mad by syphilis. Charles has been sent in pursuit of Simon to protect his family's honor, which rests on notions of propriety, masculinity, and class privilege; when he returns to England, he discovers that the ancestral home is in ruins and that he has been serving decadent and degraded ideals. Lucy does not find the killer of her sister, and her pursuit of vengeance nearly destroys Custis. The American novelist Annie Proulx, reviewing *The Last Crossing* for *The Globe and Mail* (Toronto), praised the "brilliant writing" in the novel and called Vanderhaeghe "one of North America's best writers." The novel won the Saskatoon Book Award and was named Book of the Year at the 2002 Saskatchewan Book Awards, but its exclusion from the Giller Prize and Governor General's Literary Award shortlists caused a national controversy.

While applauding Guy Vanderhaeghe's talent, some critics have found his works bleak and pessimistic. The increasing complexity of his narratives, however, recommend them to popular and academic readers alike, and the number of scholarly articles on his works is growing. With *The Englishman's Boy* and *The Last Crossing* he has emerged as one of Canada's major writers. He has taught at workshops such as the Booming Ground Creative Writing Program, and he serves frequently as a visiting professor in the Department of English at the University of Saskatchewan's St. Thomas More College.

Interviews:

Doris Hillis, "An Interview with Guy Vanderhaeghe," *Wascana Review of Contemporary Poetry and Short Fiction,* 19, no. 1 (1984): 17–28;

Alan Twigg, "Guy Vanderhaeghe," in his *Strong Voices: Conversations with 50 Canadian Authors* (Vancouver: Harbour, 1988), pp. 270–274.

Bibliography:

Tony Horava, "Guy Vanderhaeghe: A Bibliography," *Essays on Canadian Writing,* 58 (1996): 241–264.

Biographies:

David Staines, "Vanderhaeghe, Guy," in *The Concise Oxford Companion to Canadian Literature,* edited by William Toye (Don Mills, Ont.: Oxford University Press, 2001), pp. 489–490;

Dennis Cooley, "Vanderhaeghe, Guy" in *Encyclopedia of Literature in Canada,* edited by W. H. New (Toronto: University of Toronto Press, 2002), pp. 1161–1163.

References:

Alison Calder, "Unsettling the West: Nation and Genre in Guy Vanderhaeghe's *The Englishman's Boy,*" *Studies in Canadian Literature,* 25 (2001): 96–107;

Tom Gerry, "Violence and Narrative Metalepsis in Guy Vanderhaeghe's Fiction," *Studies in Canadian Literature,* 12 (1987): 199–211;

Reinhold Kramer, "Nationalism, the West, and *The Englishman's Boy,*" *Essays on Canadian Writing,* 67 (1999): 1–22;

Patricia Linton, "Narrative Geography in Guy Vanderhaeghe's *The Englishman's Boy,*" *American Review of Canadian Studies,* 31 (Winter 2001): 611–621;

Herb Wylie, "Dances with Wolfers: Choreographing History in *The Englishman's Boy,*" *Essays on Canadian Writing,* 67 (1999): 23–52.

Papers:

Correspondence, manuscripts, screenplays, promotional materials, interviews, and critical materials about Guy Vanderhaeghe are at the University of Calgary Library.

Aritha van Herk

(26 May 1954 –   )

Kathryn Sloan
University of Calgary

BOOKS: *Judith* (Toronto: McClelland & Stewart, 1978; Boston: Little, Brown, 1978; London: Deutsch, 1978);

The Tent Peg (Toronto: McClelland & Stewart, 1981; New York: Seaview Press, 1982; London: Virago, 1989);

No Fixed Address: An Amorous Journey (Toronto: McClelland & Stewart, 1986; Oslo: Cappelen, 1987; London: Virago, 1988);

Places Far from Ellesmere: A Geografictione: Explorations on Site (Red Deer, Alta.: Red Deer College Press, 1990);

In Visible Ink: Crypto-Frictions (Edmonton: NeWest Press, 1991);

A Frozen Tongue: Selected Criticism and Ficto-Criticism (Mundelstrup, Denmark: Dangeroo Press, 1992);

Restlessness (Red Deer, Alta.: Red Deer College Press, 1998);

Mavericks: An Incorrigible History of Alberta (Toronto: Penguin Canada, 2001);

Audacious and Adamant: The Story of Maverick Alberta (Toronto: Key Porter, 2007).

Edition: *No Fixed Address: An Amorous Journey,* introduction by Karin E. Beeler (Red Deer, Alta.: Red Deer College Press, 1998).

OTHER: "Biocritical Introduction," in *The Robert Kroetsch Papers: First Accession. An Inventory of the Archive at the University of Calgary Libraries,* compiled by Jean F. Tener, Sandra Mortensen, and Marlys Chevrefils, edited by Jean F. Tener and Apollonia Steele (Calgary: University of Calgary Press, 1986), pp. ix–xxxix;

"Women in Anita Desai's *In Custody*," in *Canada-India Opportunities,* edited by Ashis Gupta (Calgary: University of Calgary, International Centre, 1988), pp. 170–174;

"A Re/position on Death," in *The Second Macmillan Anthology,* edited by John Metcalf and Leon Rooke (Toronto: Macmillan Canada, 1989), pp. 258–261;

Aritha van Herk (Trudie Lee Photography, Calgary, Alberta; courtesy of the author)

"*Bear* in the Head," in *Bear,* by Marian Engel (Toronto: McClelland & Stewart, 1990), pp. 143–147;

"Post-Modernism: Homesick for Homesickness," in *The Commonwealth Novel since 1960,* edited by Bruce King (London: Macmillan Academic and Professional, 1991), pp. 216–230;

"The Fictioneer as Ficto-Critic: Footnotes on the Edge of Nowhere," in *Literary Genres/Les Genres litteraires,* edited by I. S. MacLaren and C. Potvin (Edmonton: University of Alberta, Research Institute for Comparative Literature, 1991), pp. 63–72;

"Canada," in *Bloomsbury Guide to Women's Literature,* edited by Claire Buck (London: Bloomsbury, 1992), pp. 141–150;

"Allowances," in *200% Cracked Wheat,* edited by Gary Hyland, Barbara Sapergia, and Geoffrey Ursell (Regina: Coteau, 1992), pp. 16–18;

"The Erased and Eroding Languages of Alberta," in *The Road Home: New Stories from Alberta Writers,* edited by Fred Stenson (Edmonton: Reidmore Books, 1992), pp. 134–143;

"The Pea," in *Hearts Wild,* edited by Wayne Tefs (Winnipeg: Turnstone, 1993), pp. 175–197;

"At Land," in *Boundless Alberta,* edited by van Herk (Edmonton: NeWest Press, 1993), pp. 308–326;

"Instructions from Our Mothers: A Loving Matricide," in *Shades of Empire in Colonial and Post-Colonial Literatures,* edited by C. C. Barfoot and Theo D'Haen (Amsterdam & Atlanta: Rodopi, 1993), pp. 199–210;

"Edging off the Cliff," in *Woman as Artist: Papers in Honour of Marsha Hanen,* edited by Christine Mason Sutherland and Beverly Matson Rasporich (Calgary: University of Calgary Press, 1993), pp. 211–221;

"Why I Write" and "Especially Jericho," in *Into the Nineties: Post-Colonial Women's Writing,* edited by Rutherford, Lars Jensen, and Shirley Chew (Aarhus: Dangeroo Press, 1994), pp. 403–415;

"Death in Vienna," in *Writing Away: The PEN Travel Anthology,* edited by Constance Rooke (Toronto: McClelland & Stewart, 1994), pp. 326–334;

"Dissolving Boundaries: Writing Past the Line, or a Meditation on Hopscotch," in *Nationalism versus Internationalism: (Inter)National Dimensions of Literatures in English,* edited by Wolfgang Zach and Ken Goodwin (Tübingen: Stauffenburg, 1996), pp. 289–292;

"Pioneers and Settlers," in *New National and Post-Colonial Literature,* edited by King (Oxford: Clarendon Press, 1996), pp. 81–101;

"Anna Rutherford's Excursions," in *A Talent(ed) Digger,* edited by Hena Maes-Jelinek, Gordon Collier, and Geoffrey V. Davis (Amsterdam & Atlanta: Rodopi, 1996), pp. 1–5;

"Prairie Writing, 1983 to 1996," in *The Oxford Companion to Canadian Literature,* edited by Eugene Benson and William Toye (Toronto: Oxford University Press, 1997), pp. 963–965;

"Driving toward Death," in *Great Dames,* edited by Elspeth Cameron and Janice Dickin (Toronto: University of Toronto Press, 1997), pp. 55–71;

"Creating Willem Barentsz; Piloting North," in *Echoing Silence: Essays on Arctic Narrative,* edited by John Moss (Ottawa: University of Ottawa Press, 1997), pp. 79–92;

"Undressing in the Dark: A Literary Transparency on Regions and Regionalisms, with a Gesture toward the Inevitability of Maps," in *People and Places: Changing Relations in Canada,* edited by F. J.

Toppen and J. van Weesep, Canada Cahiers, no. 9 (Nijmegen: Stichting Studiegenootschap Canada, 1998), pp. 61–72;

"The Ethnic Gasp/The Disenchanted Eye Unstoried," in *Literary Pluralities,* edited by Christl Verduyn (Peterborough, Ont.: Broadview Press, 1998), pp. 75–80;

"The Fetid Breath of Class; or, How to Pass the Translation Test," in *Translating Cultures,* edited by Isabel Carrera Suárez, Aurora García Fernández, and M. S. Suárez Lafuente (Hebden Bridge, U.K.: Dangaroo Press / Oviedo, Spain: KRK, 1999), pp. 57–66;

"Margaret Laurence: The Shape of the Writer's Shadow," in *Margaret Laurence: Critical Reflections,* edited by David Staines (Ottawa: University of Ottawa Press, 2001), pp. 135–143;

"Canada," in *Good Fiction Guide,* edited by Jane Rogers (Oxford: Oxford University Press, 2001), pp. 19–22;

"The Surfless Ocean: A Prose-Poetry Meditation on the Arctic Ocean, and How It Resists Writerly Interventions," in *Rediscovering Canada: Image, Place and Text,* edited by Gudrun Björk Gudsteins, Nordic Association for Canadian Studies Text Series, vol. 16 (Reykjavik: Nordic Association for Canadian Studies / Nordiques d'Etudes Canadiennes and Institute for Foreign Languages, University of Iceland, 2001), pp. 1–10;

"Late Hands," in *Early Voices,* edited by T. L. Waters and James King (Edmonton: Juvenalia Press, 2001), pp. 36–46;

"Cross-Dressed Writing in Canada," in *Caught between Cultures: Women, Writing and Subjectivities,* edited by Elizabeth Russell (Amsterdam & New York: Rodopi, 2002), pp. 2–14;

"Body Shock," in *Landscapes of the Heart: Narratives of Nature and Self,* edited by Michael Aleksiuk and Thomas Nelson (Edmonton: NeWest Press, 2002), pp. 153–166;

"Publishing and Perishing with No Parachute," in *How Canadians Communicate,* edited by David Taras, Frits Pannekoek, and Maria Bakardjieva (Calgary: University of Calgary Press, 2003), pp. 121–141;

"Bail Skippers and Bacchants," in *The Wild Rose Anthology of Alberta Prose,* edited by George Melnyk and Tamara Palmer Seiler (Calgary: University of Calgary Press, 2003), pp. 299–309;

"A Guide to Academic Sainthood," in *The Madwoman in the Academy,* edited by Deborah Keahey and Deborah Schnitzer (Calgary: University of Calgary Press, 2003), pp. 155–163;

"Looking for the Writer behind the Door," in *Coming of Age,* edited by E. Lisbeth Donaldson (Calgary: Detselig, 2004), pp. 9–14;

Robert Kroetsch, *The Studhorse Man,* introduction by van Herk (Edmonton: University of Alberta Press, 2004);

"Ladies and Escorts," in *Writing Addiction: Towards a Poetics of Desire and Its Others,* edited by Bela Szabados and Kenneth G. Probert (Regina: Canadian Plains Research Center, University of Regina, 2004), pp. 11–22;

"Shooting a Saskatoon (Whatever Happened to the Marlboro Man?)" in *Challenging Frontiers: The Canadian West,* edited by Lorry Felske and Beverly Rasporich (Calgary: University of Calgary Press, 2004), pp. 14–25;

Nellie McClung, *Clearing in the West,* introduction by van Herk (Toronto: Thomas Allen, 2005);

"Inventing a Family Tree: Is it Possible to be a Dutch-Canadian?" in *Building Liberty: Canada and World Peace, 1945–2005,* edited by van Herk and Conny Steenman-Marcusse (Groningen, Netherlands: Barkhuis, 2005), pp. 33–51;

"The City Small and Smaller," in *The Small Cities Book on the Cultural Future of Small Cities,* edited by W. F. Garrett-Petts (Vancouver: New Star, 2005), pp. 135–143;

"Albertans: Our Citizenship and Identity," in *Alberta: A State of Mind,* edited by Sydney Sharpe, Roger Gibbins, James H. Marsh, and Heather Bala Edwards (Toronto: Key Porter, 2005), pp. 269–275;

"Encountering Himself: Peter Fidler Takes Advice," in *First Nations of North America: Politics and Representation,* edited by Hans Bak (Amsterdam: VU University Press, 2005), pp. 356–373;

"'There's no reason for letting my mind lose its colour': Sheila Watson's Modernism," in *Re:Generations: Canadian Women Poets in Conversation,* edited by Di Brandt and Barbara Godard (Windsor: Black Moss Press, 2005), pp. 184–191;

"Washtub Westerns," in *Unsettled Pasts: Reconceiving the West through Women's History,* edited by Sarah Carter, Lesley Erickson, Patricia Roome, and Char Smith (Calgary: University of Calgary Press, 2005), pp. 251–266;

"Epilogue, or 'Prove Yourself a Fidler': Instructions on Surveying and Surviving," in *Narratives of Exploration and Discovery,* edited by Wolfgang Klooss (Trier: Wissenschaftlicher Verlag, 2005), pp. 233–237;

"Riposte to *Caprice:* Being an address to the purported author of *Caprice,* itself delicious and capricious enough but also a model and emulation of that

genre . . . ," in *71+ for GB: An Anthology for George Bowering on the Occasion of His 70th Birthday,* edited by Jean Baird, David W. McFadden, and George Stanley (Toronto: Coach House, 2005), pp. 14–16;

"Work and Its Dubious Delights," in *Dropped Threads 3: Beyond the Small Circle,* edited by Marjorie Anderson (Toronto: Vintage Canada, 2006), pp. 197–207.

SELECTED PERIODICAL PUBLICATIONS–UNCOLLECTED:

FICTION

"The Road Out," *Miss Chatelaine,* 14 (February 1977): 58–59, 76–79;

"A Minor Loss," *Gasoline Rainbow* (March 1977), pp. 41–43;

"Stationed," *NeWest Review* (May 1978);

"Who Travels Too," *Room of One's Own,* 7 (Spring 1982): 81–89;

"Waiting for the Rodeo," *Canadian Fiction Magazine,* 50–51 (1985): 196–205;

"Bail-Skippers and Bacchants," *Canadian Fiction Magazine,* 53 (March 1986): 89–97;

"Eating Elephant," *SPAN: South Pacific Association Newsletter,* 22 (April 1986);

"Another Incursion between Tomes," *Last Issue,* 15 (Autumn 1986): 23;

"A Latin for Thieves," *Dandelion,* 14, no. 2 (1987): 103–109;

"Planning a Future," *Canadian Forum,* 68 (March 1990): 22–26;

"Djakarta's Forgetting," *Tessera,* 14 (Summer 1993): 76–82;

"Dal away Dutch," *Rungh,* 3, no. 1 (1995): 10;

"Temporarily Innocent, or a Dextrous Textation for Rumplestilzchens Everywhere," *Text,* 8 (June 1997): 10–13;

"Leeuwenhoek's Eyebrows, Circa 1687," *Mattoid,* 52–53 (1998): 27–30;

"A Fondness for the Bay," *Alberta Views,* 1 (Spring 1998): 42–49;

"Bicycle Blues," *TransLit,* 4 (1999): 37–39;

"Numbering Tulip Streaks," *Dandelion,* 25, no. 2 (1999): 30–48;

"Corpus Delicti," *West Coast Line,* 29 (Fall 1999): 53–64;

"Occasions for Decay," *Tessera,* 27 (Winter 1999): 16–21;

"Leading the Parade," *American Review of Canadian Studies,* 33 (Winter 2003–2004), pp. 493–502;

"Traffic," *filling station,* no. 30 (2004): 36–40;

"Zola and the Laundrymaids," *filling station,* no. 34 (2006): 51–53.

NONFICTION

"Surveys," *Interface* (April 1981);

"Desire in Fiction: De-siring Realism," *Dandelion*, 8 (Fall 1981);

"Mapping as Metaphor in Canadian Fiction," *Zeitscrift der Gesellschaft fur Kanada-Studien*, 2 (1982): 75–86;

"Seeing the Dinner Party," *Monday Magazine* (Victoria) (11–18 February 1983);

"The Art of Blackmail: Secrets and Seeing," *Canadian Literature*, 100 (Spring 1984): 329–332;

"Stranded Bestride in Canada," *World Literature Written in English*, 24 (Summer 1984): 10–16;

"Picaro and Priestess: Repentant Rogues," *Humanities Association of Canada Newsletter*, 13 (Fall 1984): 14–18;

"Women Writers and the Prairie: Spies in an Indifferent Landscape," *Kunapipi*, 6, no. 2 (1984): 315–325;

"Marian Engel's Pleasured Texts," *Calgary Herald*, 23 February 1985, p. A9;

"An (other) Third World: Girls in Children's Literature," *Komparatistische Heft*, 12 (1985): 33–37;

"Progressions toward Sainthood: There Is Nothing to Do but Die," *Border Crossings*, 5 (May 1986): 46–50;

"Calgary, this Growing Graveyard," *NeWest Review*, 13 (December 1987): 5–11;

"no parrot/no crow/no parrot," *Prairie Fire*, 8 (Winter 1987–1988): 12–20;

"Audiencing Calgary," *Books in Canada* (March 1988);

"An Armchair (Reader's) Companion to Club Cars and Ladies Crossing Canada by Train or Will the Real Picara Please Leave Town (Please Haul Ass)," *Malahat Review*, 83 (Summer 1988): 115–126;

"The Incredible Woman: Margaret Atwood," *Elle* (December 1988): 49–50;

"We Are Robbing Artists," *Gazette* (Montreal), 30 December 1989, p. F7;

"Extrapolations from *Miracles*," *Room of One's Own*, 13, nos. 1–2 (1989): 99–108;

"Symposium on the New Decade," *Canadian Forum*, 68 (January 1990): 10–11;

"Crowb(e)ars and Kangaroos: The Post-Colonial Ga(s)p," *World Literature Written in English*, 30 (Autumn 1990): 42–54;

"First the Chores and Then the Dishes," *Psychological Perspectives*, 23 (1990): 38–48;

"Laying the Body on the Line," *Border Crossings*, 9 (October 1990): 86–88;

"Rituals for a Pagan Midwinter," *Western Living*, 20 (December 1990): 33–34;

"Stealing Inside after Dark," *Journal of Educational Thought*, 24 (December 1990): 34–45;

"Henry Kreisel: Leading Writer, Teacher Dies," *Calgary Herald*, 25 April 1991, p. D2;

"Critical Contamination, or Going Boudoir: A Diallage," by van Herk and Charlene Diehl-Jones, *Room of One's Own*, 14, no. 4 (1991): 7–22;

"Ghost Narratives: A Haunting," *Open Letter*, seventh series, no. 9 (Winter 1991): 61–70;

"And Silence Is Also a Nakedness," *West Coast Line*, 6 (Winter 1991–1992): 175–84;

"First Fictions," *University of Toronto Quarterly*, 62 (Fall 1992): 1–21;

"Oral Thuggery," *Open Letter*, eighth series, 5–6 (Winter–Spring 1993): 134–141;

"Of Dykes and Boers and Drowning," *West Coast Line*, 10 (Spring 1993): 40–45;

"Fiction," *University of Toronto Quarterly*, 63 (Fall 1993): 26–48;

"Spectral Tattoo: Reconstructive Fictions," *SPAN: South Pacific Association for Commonwealth Literature and Language Studies*, 36 (October 1993), pp. 15–24;

"Talking Back," *Border Crossings*, 13 (April 1994): 10–13;

"The Reader's Cul de Sac: Writing on Writing on Writing," *Paragraph*, 16 (Summer 1994): 14–22;

"Smoke and Mirrors," *Journal of Canadian Studies*, 29 (Autumn 1994): 158–162;

"Boxing the Critics: Sucker Punches, Shooting Niagara and Other Boys' Games of Criticism," *Canadian Forum*, 74 (December 1994): 32–35;

"First Fictions," *University of Toronto Quarterly*, 64 (Winter 1994): 1–25;

"Gazing at Coffins: A Meditation on Erectile Death, for Robert Kroetsch," *Open Letter*, ninth series, 5–6 (Spring–Summer 1996): 147–157;

"The Map's Temptation; or the Search for a Secret Book," *Journal of Commonwealth Literature*, 31, no. 1 (1996): 128–136;

"Windswept Seduction," *Canadian Geographic*, 117 (January–February 1997): 92;

"Warm Heart, Weak Pulse," *Canadian Forum*, 76 (January–February 1998): 16–20;

"De-binarizing the Erotic Kroetsch," *New Quarterly*, 18 (Spring 1998): 126–137;

"The Woman on the Side," *Prairie Fire*, 19 (Spring 1998): 128–130;

"Poetics Statements," *Open Letter*, tenth series, 3 (Summer 1998): 131–132;

"Grave Thoughts," *Canadian Geographic*, 118 (September–October 1998): 54;

"Scant Articulations of Time," *University of Toronto Quarterly*, 68 (Fall 1999): 925–938;

"The Privacies of Silence, Part One," *freeLance*, XX19 (December 1999–January 2000): 8–10;

"The Privacies of Silence, Part Two," *freeLance*, XX19 (February 2000): 8–10;

"Occupational Heretics for Writing Women," *Contemporary Verse 2*, 23 (Summer 2000): 59–66;

"The Man Who Loved the Smell of His Own Farts," *Prairie Fire*, 22 (Spring 2001): 152–159;

"Type/Caste: A Poetics of Class," *Moving Worlds*, 1 (2001): 105–114;

"Living with Snow," *Calgary Herald*, 18 January 2002, p. SS3;

"Invisibled Laundry," *Signs*, 27 (Spring 2002): 893–900;

"How the West Was Divided," *Canadian Geographic* (January–February 2005): 40–47; republished as "Was Dividing the West a Bad Idea?" *Reader's Digest* (July 2005): 116–123;

"Seduction: Catherine Gildiner's New Novel Is a Psychological Thriller," *Calgary Herald*, 12 February 2005, pp. G1–G2;

"Curious Oliver," *Calgary Herald*, 2 April 2005, pp. G1–G2;

"Tapping into a Season of Murder," *Calgary Herald*, 16 April 2005, p. G3;

"The Chocolate Soldiers," *Calgary Herald*, 7 May 2005, p. G3;

"Alberta Rides into Town," *Ottawa Citizen*, 20 May 2005, p. B2;

"We Were Always a Territory Too Big for Its Beans," *Calgary Herald*, 22 May 2005, p. A12;

"Absolute Irving," *Calgary Herald*, 23 July 2005, pp. G1–G2;

"Elusive Fortune," *Calgary Herald*, 27 August 2005, pp. G1–G2;

"Map of Glass," *Calgary Herald*, 3 September 2005, p. G3;

"In the Jaws of Writing," *Calgary Herald*, 24 September 2005, pp. F1–F2;

"Booker Front-Runner," *Calgary Herald*, 8 October 2005, p. F7;

"A Practical Sibyl," *Calgary Herald*, 15 October 2005, pp. F1–F2;

"Dave of Our Lives," *Calgary Herald*, 10 December 2005, pp. F1–F2;

"Double Take," *Calgary Herald*, 31 December 2005, pp. F1–F2;

"Who You Callin' Cultured?" *Alberta Views* (December 2005–January 2006): 28–32;

"Of Fig Leaves and Voluptuous Cities," *Calgary Herald*, 4 March 2006, pp. F1–F2;

"Time Travel," *Calgary Herald*, 11 March 2006, pp. F1–F2;

"Melbourne Blog," *Calgary Herald*, 18 March 2006, p. F3;

"40 Ways the U of C is Changing the World," *U Magazine* (Spring 2006): 15;

"Vancouver Chronicles," *Calgary Herald*, 22 April 2006, pp. F1–F2;

"Confidence Man," *Calgary Herald*, 20 May 2006, pp. F1–F2;

"The View from Without," *Avenue Magazine* (June 2006): 60–64;

"Unsentimental Tourist," *Calgary Herald*, 16 July 2006, pp. E1–E2;

"Fiction by Numbers," *Calgary Herald*, 13 August 2006, pp. C1–C2;

Maritime Gothic," *Calgary Herald*, 24 September 2006, pp. C1–C2.

In April 1978 twenty-three-year-old graduate student Aritha van Herk earned a place in Canadian literary history and garnered international attention by winning the $50,000 inaugural Seal First Novel Award for her M.A. thesis. The work, about a woman who abandons city life to become a pig farmer, was published the following October as *Judith;* later translated into nine languages, it received critical recognition across North America and Europe and in Australia. Equally comfortable with fiction and with literary and cultural criticism, van Herk is recognized as the creator of the genres of "fictocriticism" and "geograficcione."

van Herk (she insists that the *v* be lowercase, even at the beginning of a sentence) was born on 26 May 1954 in Wetaskiwin, Alberta, a small town between Red Deer and Edmonton, to Dutch-immigrant farm laborers William and Maretje van Herk. At the time of van Herk's birth her parents and three siblings were living on a rented property that had neither electricity nor running water. She was the first of the five van Herk children to be born in Canada. Her first language was Dutch, but she lost her fluency in it as her family turned to English.

In 1956 van Herk's parents bought a farm near the Battle River, about eighty-seven miles southeast of Edmonton. As a child van Herk read early and obsessively and always kept a notebook and pencil within reach. In a 1984 interview with Ingwer Nommensen she said: "After a certain point, I really retreated into fiction, into stories instead of into real life. And real life to me was a big fiction and stories were real."

van Herk attended primary and secondary school in the hamlet of Edberg. Her first publication was a poem in the *Alberta Poetry Yearbook* for 1966. She earned her high-school diploma at seventeen by skipping a grade. In 1972 she entered the University of Alberta in Edmonton. She received the James Patrick Folinsbee Prize in English during her two final years as an undergraduate. On 14 September 1974 she married geologist and cartographer Robert Sharp. She received her B.A. in English literature with honors in 1976 and began working on her M.A. in English, with a specialty in creative writing, under the supervision of the writer Rudy Wiebe; she received Province of Alberta Graduate

*Dust jacket for the first edition, 1978 (Bruccoli
Clark Layman Archives)*

Scholarship Awards for both of her years in graduate school.

Robert Kroetsch's fiction showed van Herk how elements of the fantastic and the mythic could be integrated into the realism that typified Western narratives. She also found inspiration in the work of Marian Engel, who was writer-in-residence at the university during van Herk's final year. Engel's novel *Bear,* which won the 1976 Governor General's Literary Award for Fiction, also showed van Herk how mythic or extraordinary components could intertwine with realism. van Herk stated in the *Calgary Herald* (23 February 1985) on the occasion of Engel's death, "if there is one novel I wish I had written, it's *Bear.*"

While she struggled in 1976–1977 to extend a seventeen-page short story, "Pigs," into the book-length master's thesis that became *Judith,* van Herk wrote several other stories; three of them were published while she was still in graduate school. "The Road Out" won the 1977 *Miss Chatelaine* Short Fiction Contest and appeared in the February issue of the magazine. This story is one of the earliest examples of van Herk's inser-

tion of biblical themes into realistic Canadian settings, an approach she most notably revisits in her second novel, *The Tent Peg* (1981). In "The Road Out" Tabitha resists the expectation of her family and rural community that she marry a young man from a neighboring farm. Her name is the same as that of the woman who was raised from the dead by the disciple Peter (Acts 9:36–40) because she was particularly good and charitable, and in a final hallucinatory scene she is raised from her bed by a figure who seems to be St. Peter. van Herk leaves it for the reader to decide whether Tabitha will take to the untraveled road that passes in front of her mother's house or be trapped in the "dead end" that the marriage represents. "A Minor Loss" appeared in *Gasoline Rainbow* in March 1977. A woman collapses in a department store after a visit to the dentist; she is helped by a man she does not know and later returns to the site of her collapse to meet her husband. "'Yes,' Lina thought, 'we're all led into it, marriage and toothache, husbands and dentists.'" "A Woman of Moderate Temperament," about a woman seeking to escape from her conventional suburban married life by taking a night class, was included in Wiebe's anthology *Getting Here* (1977). In 1977 van Herk became book-review editor for *Branching Out,* a feminist literary magazine; later she moved to fiction editor.

van Herk wrote most of her master's thesis, then titled "When Pigs Fly," on a portable typewriter while working as a camp cook for a geological expedition in the Yukon during the summer of 1977. She also collected impressions that later coalesced in *The Tent Peg.* After returning to the university for her final year, she approached Alberta Culture, a department of the provincial government, about entering the manuscript in its novel contest; she was told that she could not do so if she also submitted it for the newly inaugurated Seal First Novel Award. van Herk chose to try for the $50,000 Seal prize rather than the $2,500 offered by Alberta Culture. Between the announcement of the Seal prize in April and the publication of *Judith* in October, what eventually became van Herk's most-anthologized short story, "Transitions," appeared in the August 1978 issue of *Miss Chatelaine.* The narrator, Marikje, describes her childhood fascination with her beautiful older sister, Hannike. Marikje rejects Hannike when she ignores her own longing for freedom from the burdens of caring for home and children and follows the expected route into marriage and motherhood. Refusing to follow in her sister's path, Marikje remains single and childless in the face of her family's disapproval.

The first line of *Judith* confronts the reader with the hard reality of farm life: "Pig shit and wet greasy straw were piled high in the wheelbarrow." Judith Pierce grows up on a farm and then moves to the city, where she works as a secretary and becomes involved in an oppressive and unsatisfying affair with an older man. Feeling that she is slowly suffocating in the urban environment, she buys a pig farm and ten sows. There she contends with the hostility of the local farmers toward her infiltration of their masculine domain. The narrative flashes back and forth between her childhood on her father's farm, her life in the city, and her present situation without resorting to italics, white space, or any of the other devices that usually indicate such shifts. The pigs become important characters in their own right as Judith tends to their needs, helps them to give birth, and castrates the male piglets. Viga Boland wrote in her review in *Canadian Author and Bookman* (May 1979): "Enhancing and heightening the portrayal of Judith, these sows are engaged in an almost spiritual union with her"; Judith "loves and loathes them as she does herself, she places all her hopes in them, and at the same time despairs of them." Boland found a playful tone in van Herk's direct references to the legend of the sorceress Circe's transformation of Odysseus's men into swine, a reversal of traditional power roles in which men are depicted as a necessary, sometimes enjoyable, evil that is peripheral to the serious business of life as a woman. William French in *The Globe and Mail* (Toronto) for 7 October 1978, on the other hand, lambasted *Judith* as a lightweight romance and the author as a rampant feminist interested in literary and literal male castration. References in the novel to the virtuous widow in the Apocrypha's Book of Judith, who helped defeat the invading Babylonians by seducing and decapitating their general, Holofernes, added to the gender-based controversy over the novel.

Having affixed a license plate reading "NOVEL1" to the white Porsche she purchased with some of her Seal Award winnings, van Herk returned to work at *Branching Out*. In November 1978 she received the Province of Alberta Achievement Award for Literature.

In a *Calgary Herald* interview with Kevin Peterson in January 1979 van Herk commented on the lack of meaningful funding for writers in Alberta. She pointed out that a $500 grant she had received as a graduate student, which she had returned after winning the Seal Award, had provided little real benefit over the "six years that I spent learning the craft of writing." At the end of 1980 *Branching Out* ceased publication because of lack of funding. Angry with the failure of the Alberta government to continue supporting the magazine and generally unhappy with the lack of government interest in the local literary scene, van Herk took a position as sessional instructor in English at the University of British Columbia.

In Vancouver, van Herk began to publish scholarly articles in addition to fiction. At this time she created a new kind of writing, fictocriticism, which uses fiction to respond to and interpret other literary works. Her first piece of fictocriticism, "Desire in Fiction: Desiring Realism," originally given as a paper at the 1980 Annual NeWest Forum on the Arts in Edmonton, appeared in the Fall 1981 issue of *Dandelion*.

In 1981 van Herk published *The Tent Peg*. In the essay "*Judith* and *The Tent Peg*: A Retrospective," included in her collection *A Frozen Tongue: Selected Criticism and Ficto-Criticism* (1992), van Herk writes: "Think of this. A nation of almost four million square miles and most of its twenty-six million people cling to the band-aid of its southern fringe." In *The Tent Peg* she hoped to map at least a tiny slice of the Canadian north. Set in a geological exploration camp in the Yukon mountains during a summer expedition, *The Tent Peg* employs thirteen first-person narrators in a diary format; van Herk admits in "*Judith* and *The Tent Peg*: A Retrospective" that she took the form from William Faulkner's *As I Lay Dying* (1930). Twelve of the voices are male, most of them named for historic explorers and cartographers; the single female perspective belongs to J.L., the camp cook, who briefly disguises herself as a man to obtain the job. J.L.'s name is taken from Jael, the woman in Judg. 4:16–:22 who gave refuge to the Canaanite general Sisera after his army was defeated by the Israelites; while Sisera slept in her tent, Jael killed him by hammering a tent peg through his temple. She hoped thereby to end the war that was destroying her country and her people. J.L. acts as a mystical go-between for the men and what van Herk understands as a feminine landscape; she rescues the crew boss, Mackenzie, from spiraling into isolation and despair after the departure of his wife and family, and by the end of the summer she has helped all of the men except the misogynist Jerome to a new level of self-knowledge. The crew discovers gold in the northern mountains; van Herk depicts J.L. as a kind of gold, and the parallels between the landscape and the woman are made increasingly clear as the novel progresses. J.L. speaks to grizzly bears, dances on fire, and heals with her touch; she appears to be able to call down landslides and to comprehend the language of the earth she traverses. She is the elusive magical element in the lives of the quintessentially Canadian explorers, surveyors, and geologists, men of reason who are inexplicably drawn to the north. J.L. offers an enigmatic focus for each of the men, even as she explodes male-generated myths concerning women. van Herk has said in many interviews that *The Tent Peg* is a reversal of *Judith*: Circe transformed men into swine to reflect their true nature; J.L. is a witch-like woman who helps men to escape that nature.

Reviewing *The Tent Peg* in the March 1981 issue of *MacLean's,* Cathleen Hoskins complained that van Herk had returned to an attack on men that had grown stale and dismissed her as a writer with only one story to tell. Other critics, however, noted that *The Tent Peg* was a much tighter, riskier, and more experimental novel than *Judith* and praised the complexity of the narrative.

In February 1982 van Herk presented a paper at the annual Canadian Studies Congress in Grainau, Germany, and in September she delivered another at the Gothenburg University Congress of Commonwealth Language and Literature in Sweden. That same year she received a grant from Canada Council for the Arts. She served as the guest chairperson in Canadian studies at the University of Kiel in Germany from April until August 1983. In September she became an assistant professor of English at the University of Calgary; she was promoted to associate professor in July 1985.

In her short story "Waiting for the Rodeo" (1985) van Herk created the character Tip, who is an almost twin of Arachne Mantea, the protagonist of her next novel. She returned to Tip in two later stories, "Mining Darkness" (1989) and "Corpus Delecti" (1991).

van Herk considers her third novel, *No Fixed Address: An Amorous Journey* (1986), as forming a loose trilogy with *Judith* and *The Tent Peg:* all three works depict women as active and empowered rather than as background dressing or as victims. Arachne Mantea is an itinerant underwear saleswoman who refuses to wear such garments herself; she travels the roads of western Canada with no destination in mind, pausing briefly for an occasional fling but always with an eye on the horizon. The novel disrupts the reader's expectation of a linear narrative, and at the end Arachne drives off the page, "headed into nowhere." The final chapter, "Notebook on a Missing Person," addresses the reader directly: "you" inquire into the whereabouts of a certain Arachne Mantea, only to be told that she is headed down a road with no end. "You" trace her route, discovering a variety of discarded panties along the way. The last line of the novel states: "There is no end to the panties; there will be no end to this road." *No Fixed Address* received widespread critical acclaim and won the 1986 Howard O'Hagan Prize for best novel of the year. In 1986 van Herk also won a "45 Below" Award, given to the ten best Canadian fiction writers under the age of forty-five. *No Fixed Address* was nominated for the Governor General's Literary Award for Fiction in 1987.

During this period van Herk published several short stories, including "Bail-Skippers and Bacchants" (1986), "Eating Elephant" (1986), and "A Latin for Thieves" (1987). In 1988 she was nominated for the Women of Distinction Award in the area of Arts and Culture and received a writing grant from the Alberta Foundation for the Literary Arts and a Department of External Affairs grant for a reading tour of the United Kingdom. The following year she received yet another Department of External Affairs grant and embarked on a reading tour of Australia. In all, during the 1980s van Herk published nine short stories and nearly twenty essays, articles, and pieces of fictocriticism and gave 140 readings. She also wrote reviews, edited magazines and anthologies, and presented papers at conferences.

Job security freed van Herk from the need to produce popular as well as literary work, and she tested the generic elasticity of the novel in *Places Far from Ellesmere: A Geografictione: Explorations on Site* (1990). It was her first book not published by McClelland and Stewart, the firm responsible for the Seal prize; instead, van Herk turned to Red Deer College Press, an Alberta publisher. *Places Far from Ellesmere* resembles the fictocritical essays van Herk had been writing during the latter half of the 1980s. Incorporating elements of fiction, prose poetry, biography, memoir, travel journal, history, and criticism, it is a narrative about imagining and creating narratives.

The "geografictione"—text that explores place and uses geography as character—is divided into four sections: "Edberg," "Edmonton," "Calgary," and "Ellesmere." In the first three sections the narrator, whose name is van Herk, travels to the places named, revisiting and relearning each as a specific geography that changes with each new "reading." The narrator is shaped by each location, and she reshapes the locations through her reading and writing. Geography is thus shown to be a text that molds individual identity even as individual identity molds geography as a text, and the concepts of reality and fiction are turned back on themselves to reveal the constructed nature of each. In the final section van Herk travels to Ellesmere Island to circumnavigate Lake Hazen, the world's largest lake lying entirely north of the Arctic Circle. During this expedition she rereads Leo Tolstoy's epic novel *Anna Karenina* (1875–1877; translated, 1886). Tolstoy's heroine has appeared briefly in the three preceding sections; thus, the narrator and the reader have already established a relationship with her before the journey to Ellesmere. This relationship takes on greater depth as the narrator engages with Tolstoy's text in an environment that allows Anna to tell her own story, which until now has been subverted by Tolstoy's male perspective. Every reading, van Herk posits, creates a fiction that is specific to the time and place of that reading. *Places Far from Ellesmere* is a difficult work in which it is frequently impossible to distinguish fact from fiction and in which there is no plot other than the uncovering of Anna's alternative position outside of Tolstoy's novel. It caused little stir in the world of popular fiction but generated a great deal of interest in literary and scholarly circles and was nominated for the 1991 Howard O'Hagan Prize in literature.

van Herk was elected honorary president of the Library Association of Alberta for 1990–1991 and was made a full professor at the University of Calgary in 1991. In 1992 she was again nominated for the Arts and Culture Women of Distinction Award and presented a paper at the meeting of the Association of Commonwealth Literature and Language Studies in Kingston, Jamaica.

Two nonfiction collections, *In Visible Ink: Cryptofrictions* and *A Frozen Tongue: Selected Criticism and Ficto-Criticism,* appeared in 1991 and 1992, respectively. Many of the pieces in *In Visible Ink* had previously been published, but in her acknowledgments van Herk states, "I confess to much dissatisfied revision and re-inscription." The thirteen pieces include meditations on the silence of the Arctic, reflections on Carol Shields's *Various Miracles* (1985), responses to the work of Kroetsch, and explanations of van Herk's own creative language. *A Frozen Tongue* opens with an autobiographical section that includes photographs of the young van Herk; the rest of the volume comprises fictocritical essays and a few more-traditional academic analyses of works by such authors as Engel, Kroetsch, and Margaret Laurence. van Herk also examines the forces that shape her own writing and outlines some of the structural and artistic choices she made in her first three novels.

van Herk wrote 214 entries on Canadian writers and books for *The Bloomsbury Guide to Women's Literature* (1992). She served a short residency at the Djerassi Resident Artists Program in Woodside, California, in 1993; received another Department of Foreign Affairs Grant in 1995; and was elected a fellow of the Royal Society of Canada in 1997. Also in 1997 she gave an invited paper at the Centers d'Etudes Canadiennes de l'Universite Libre de Bruxelles in Brussels. During the 1990s she was a visiting professor at universities in Germany, Spain, and Denmark.

Restlessness, van Herk's fourth novel, was published in 1998. Dorcas is an international courier who longs to escape from her life of empty motion into a final, absolute stillness. She arranges for professional assassin Derek Atman, a quiet, polished, gentle man from Winnipeg, to kill her at the Palliser Hotel in Calgary. Dorcas and Atman spend the evening together as Dorcas readies herself for the denouement; Atman will not take her life until she tells him to do so. As they walk around the city, stop to eat, and explore Dorcas's restless past and present despair, Dorcas holds all the power; Atman, the hit man, becomes the submissive reflection of her desire for stability. A sort of Scheher-azade in reverse, he endeavors to draw from Dorcas stories about her life in an effort to prevent her death; but he only succeeds in uncovering her inability to remain in any one place. As much as she loves Calgary or Vienna, Dorcas's restlessness drives her on to the next city and the next country. "My insatiable restlessness will turn me into a hotel, coming and going personified," she says at the end of the novel. The actual murder is not described but is left to the reader's imagination.

In a joint interview with van Herk for the Autumn 2001 issue of *Canadian Literature* Kroetsch called *Restlessness* "mind-boggling and unnerving to read," describing the novel as "fluid" and Dorcas as a character who "subverts submissiveness." Reviewing the book in the Summer 2001 issue of *Herizons,* Maria Stanborough noted that "*Restlessness* is not an easy novel"; it is, she contended, "less a story than an intellectual journey." While the reviews were generally favorable, the novel failed to stir the interest of the reading public.

Asked by Penguin Books Canada to write a history of Alberta as part of a series of provincial histories by novelists, van Herk accepted with a certain amount of trepidation but soon completed an 1,800-page manuscript. She and her editor cut it down, and the result was the 434-page *Mavericks: An Incorrigible History of Alberta* (2001). The fourteen chapters of the book are arranged more or less chronologically, opening with a description of Alberta's geological history and moving on to early exploration, the fur trade, immigration, First Nations peoples, politics, and culture. van Herk does not shy away from revealing the historical intolerance and sheer contrariness of her home province, and she discusses the source of tensions between central and western Canada. She never pretends to be uninvolved or unbiased but attempts to illuminate an Alberta that is invisible to outsiders through an interpretive, engaging, and idiosyncratic point of view. van Herk calls *Mavericks* "creative nonfiction": it is a story rather than a strict history and makes scanty use of footnotes, but it supplies a lively and accessible survey of a geography and a culture and detailed commentaries on the forces that have fashioned the present Alberta. Ranchers, surveyors, Mounties, and reprobates all find a place in van Herk's text, and individual as well as collective stories are offered. The work brought van Herk back into the public eye, and critics generally concluded that her venture into the field of historical nonfiction was successful. On 23 March 2007 Calgary's Glenbow Museum opened a new permanent gallery to showcase Alberta history and culture; it is named "Mavericks," after van Herk's book, and includes texts contributed by her. She produced an exhibition book titled *Audacious and*

Adamant: The Story of Maverick Alberta (2007) to accompany the opening of the gallery.

Aritha van Herk continues to teach at the University of Calgary and to write. Her reputation as a creative writer is rivaled only by her stature as an academic and a critic. Always feminist and Western Canadian, van Herk has produced a body of innovative and articulate literature that inspires readers, writers, and students alike.

Interviews:

Kevin Petersen, "Writers and Words," *Calgary Herald*, 6 January 1979, p. F15;

Ingwer Nommensen, "Das Thema der Verwandlung in Dem Romanwerk Aritha van Herk," M.A. thesis, University of Kiel, 1984;

Karin E. Beeler, "Shifting Form: An Interview with Aritha van Herk," *Canadian Literature*, 157 (Summer 1998): 80–96;

J'nan Morse Sellery, "Robert Kroetsch and Aritha van Herk on Writing and Reading Gender and Genres: An Interview," *Canadian Literature*, no. 170–171 (Autumn 2001): 21–55;

Dawne McCance, "Crossings: An Interview with Aritha van Herk," *Mosaic*, 36 (March 2003): 1–20.

References:

Susanne Becker, "Ironic Transformations: The Feminine Gothic in Aritha van Herk's *No Fixed Address*," in *Double Talking: Essays on Verbal and Visual Ironies in Contemporary Canadian Art and Literature*, edited by Linda Hutcheon (Toronto: ECW Press, 1992), pp. 115–133;

Karin E. Beeler, "Re-creating Cassandra and Anna Karenina: Unheard Voices in Christa Wolf's *Cassandra* and Aritha van Herk's *Places Far from Ellesmere*," *Critique*, 336 (Summer 1995): 227–327;

Isabel Carrera, "Caprice and *No Fixed Address:* Playing with Gender and Genre," *Kunapipi*, 16, no. 1 (1994): 432–439;

Marlene Goldman, "Earth-quaking the Kingdom of the Male Virgin: A Deleuzian Analysis of Aritha van Herk's *No Fixed Address* and *Places Far from Ellesmere*," *Canadian Literature*, 137 (Summer 1993): 21–38;

Linda Hutcheon, *The Canadian Postmodern: A Study of Contemporary English-Canadian Fiction* (Toronto: Oxford University Press, 1988), pp. 122–132;

H. Lutz and J. Hindersmann, "'Meat and Bones Don't Matter': Mythology in *The Tent Peg*," *Ariel: A Review of International English Literature*, 20 (April 1989): 41–67;

Matthew Manera, "The Act of Being Read: Fictional Process in *Places Far from Ellesmere*," *Canadian Literature*, 146 (Autumn 1995): 87–94;

Asta Mott, "Aritha van Herk's *Places Far from Ellesmere:* The Wild and Adventurous North?" *Canadian Literature*, 157 (Summer 1998): 99–111;

Christl Verduyn, ed., *Aritha van Herk: Essays on Her Works* (Toronto: Guernica, 2001).

Papers:

An Aritha van Herk collection, including manuscripts, letters, photographs, and media clippings, is at the Mackimmie Library of the University of Calgary.

M. G. Vassanji

(30 May 1950 –)

John Clement Ball
University of New Brunswick

BOOKS: *The Gunny Sack* (Oxford & Portsmouth, N.H.: Heinemann, 1989);

No New Land (Toronto: McClelland & Stewart, 1991);

Uhuru Street (Oxford & Portsmouth, N.H.: Heinemann, 1991; Toronto: McClelland & Stewart, 1992);

The Book of Secrets (Toronto: McClelland & Stewart, 1994; London: Picador, 1995; New York: Picador, 1996);

Amriika (Toronto: McClelland & Stewart, 1999);

The In-Between World of Vikram Lall (Toronto: Doubleday, 2003);

When She Was Queen (Toronto: Doubleday, 2005).

PRODUCED SCRIPT: "The Ghost of Bagamoyo," radio, *Morningside,* Canadian Broadcasting Corporation, 26 December 1992.

OTHER: *A Meeting of Streams: South Asian Canadian Literature,* edited by Vassanji (Toronto: TSAR, 1985);

"The Postcolonial Writer: Myth Maker and Folk Historian," in *A Meeting of Streams: South Asian Canadian Literature,* edited by Vassanji (Toronto: TSAR, 1985), pp. 63–68;

"A Tin of Cookies," in *The Whistling Thorn: South Asian Canadian Fiction,* edited by Suwanda Sugunasiri (Oakville, Ont.: Mosaic, 1994), pp. 49–54;

"Life at the Margins: In the Thick of Multiplicity," in *Between the Lines: South Asians and Postcoloniality,* edited by Deepika Bahri and Mary Vasudeva (Philadelphia: Temple University Press, 1996), pp. 111–120;

"Canada and Me: Finding Ourselves," in *Passages: Welcome Home to Canada,* foreword by Michael Ignatieff, preface by Rudyard Griffiths (Toronto: Doubleday Canada, 2002), pp. 15–33.

SELECTED PERIODICAL PUBLICATIONS–
UNCOLLECTED: "Waiting for the Goddess," *Toronto South Asian Review,* 1, no. 2 (1982): 78–83;

M. G. Vassanji (photograph by Denise Grant; from the cover for The Book of Secrets, *1994; Bruccoli Clark Layman Archives)*

"Canadian Punjabi Literature–An Introduction," by Vassanji and Surjeet Kalsey, *Toronto South Asian Review,* 2 (Spring 1983): 47–54;

"Is There a South Asian Canadian Literature?" *Toronto South Asian Review,* 6 (Spring 1988): 1–8; republished as "South Asian Literature in Canada," *Canadian Review of Comparative Literature/Revue canadienne de littérature comparée,* 16 (1989): 801–808;

"Editorial: Growing Out," *Toronto South Asian Review,* 11 (Spring 1993): 1–8;

"Community as a Fictional Character," *Studies in Humanities and Social Sciences,* 1 (November 1994): 13–18;

"The Little Warrior," *Toronto Life,* 32 (August 1998): 78–81;

"The Sky to Stop Us," *Toronto Life,* 34 (August 2000): 98–102.

"Wanderlust," M. G. Vassanji writes in "Canada and Me: Finding Ourselves" (2002), "is part of my heritage, as is the quest for home. With every departure comes a sense of loss, of something left behind; and if you are a novelist, you find yourself out on that quest for comprehensibility, for the beginning of history and the sources of memory." Since the publication of his first novel in 1989, this self-described "East African Canadian of Indian origin" has been scrupulously attentive to the complex dynamics of identity and belonging among people who lead unsettled, nomadic lives. In his stories of the Ismaili Muslim community and of the Africans, Britons, Indians, Canadians, and Americans with whom it has come in contact, this Toronto-based author has illuminated some previously shadowy corners of the tumultuous twentieth century. In the process he has given a voice to a people that had been virtually unrepresented in English-language literature and put a distinctive stamp on the century's dominant themes of war, colonialism, dislocation, race relations, and the individual's formation by, and liberation from, community norms.

Moyez Gulamhussein Vassanji was born on 30 May 1950 in Nairobi, Kenya, the third of four children of Gulamhussein Vassanji and Daulatkhanu Vassanji (née Manji Jiwani); a cousin also lived with the family. His paternal great-grandfather had immigrated to Kenya from the Indian state of Gujarat in the 1880s; his mother, who was born in Zanzibar and grew up in Mombasa, was also of Indian descent. The man Vassanji describes in "Canada and Me" as "my somewhat vagabond of a father" was a salesman in a department store catering to Europeans. He died when Vassanji was five; within a year the family moved to Dar es Salaam, Tanzania, where Vassanji's mother opened a clothing shop. Apart from a few months of nursery school in Nairobi, Vassanji acquired his early education in Dar es Salaam; he has written about this city more than about any other and continues to think of it as his home.

Despite the family's modest means, Vassanji was sent to private Aga Khan schools run by Ismailis. Growing up in a multilinguistic society, he learned English, Cutchi, Gujarati, Swahili, and some Hindi. In 1969 he successfully sat the Cambridge A-level examinations in physics, chemistry, applied mathematics, and pure mathematics. During the first three months of 1970 he performed his national service, which involved light military training and work on a banana plantation near Lake Victoria. He was accepted into a postsecondary civil-engineering program in Nairobi; but his first choice had been electrical engineering, and he withdrew in the summer of 1970, three months into the program. In the autumn he entered the Massachusetts Institute of Technology on a government scholarship. There he studied science and engineering, eventually specializing in physics; he also took a writing course. He graduated in 1974 and entered the doctoral program in theoretical nuclear physics at the University of Pennsylvania. He was attracted to campus radicalism and supported the anti–Vietnam War movement, though as a foreign national he was careful not to make himself officially unwelcome. During his final year in Philadelphia he began studying Indian history and philosophy, as well as Sanskrit, which he learned to translate into English.

After earning his doctorate in 1978, Vassanji had the choice of postdoctoral fellowships at the University of California in Berkeley and with Atomic Energy of Canada in Chalk River, Ontario. He recalled in a 1992 profile by Stephen Smith that "Berkeley was vacillating about whether they had the money or not, and Chalk River was definite, so I took it. It was just that, to be honest." A similar pragmatism motivated his wedding to Nurjehan Aziz on his arrival in Chalk River. They had been acquainted in Dar es Salaam but had gotten to know each other and become engaged in Boston; they planned to marry at home the following year, but, Vassanji remembers in "Canada and Me," "to qualify for my luxurious (as it seemed then) furnished apartment" in nearby Deep River, "company rules demanded that I be married." He and Aziz, who was helping him move, asked a Lutheran minister to marry them the day after they arrived. Aziz returned to Boston, but the couple met every few weekends in Montreal. They had "the real, traditional wedding some eight months later" in Mombasa, Vassanji says in "Canada and Me."

During his first two years in Canada, Vassanji wrote a story that has since been lost. He also wrote a novel drawing on his experiences in the United States; it remained unpublished, but he later reworked the material for his novel *Amriika* (1999). Aziz joined him in the spring of 1980. Later that year they moved to Toronto, where Vassanji had been hired as a full-time research associate in the University of Toronto physics department. Also in 1980 Vassanji began writing his multigenerational novel *The Gunny Sack* (1989).

In 1982 Vassanji and Aziz founded a literary journal, *The Toronto South Asian Review,* that was published three times a year. After some early difficulties, Vassanji wrote in an editorial in the last issue of 1993, the journal became an "institution": "We never tried to use well-known names to put a rubber stamp of quality on us, but rather became the rubber stamp." In 1983 Vassanji participated in a conference on South Asian Canadian literature at the University of Toronto's Hart House. He and Aziz took on a leadership role in subsequent discussions about publishing the proceedings; the result was the first book produced by TSAR Publications. *A Meeting of Streams: South Asian Canadian Literature* appeared in 1985, the same year that Vassanji and Aziz's son, Anil Karim, was born.

In the introduction to the volume Vassanji characterizes the late twentieth century as an age dominated by exiles, refugees, immigrants, and other displaced people. While there have always been travelers, "At no time in history has there been such a massive movement across geographical, political, and cultural barriers." As a result, there is a "specific need for a new literature or literary consciousness to define itself" on behalf of particular migrant groups so their culture and history—everything that "differentiates" them and enables them to "survive"—can be preserved. In an essay in the volume, "The Postcolonial Writer: Myth Maker and Folk Historian," Vassanji sees various writers of the Indian diaspora as jointly producing "the literary record of a collective experience. As such they are like no other records. A future historian of that culture will have no recourse but to walk those imaginative landscapes." The writer's role in an era of decolonization, transition, and dispersal is, therefore, to act

as a preserver of the collective tradition, a folk historian and myth maker. He gives himself a history; he recreates the past, which exists only in memory and is otherwise obliterated, so fast has his world transformed. He emerges from the oral, preliterate, and unrecorded, to the literate. In many instances this reclamation of the past is the first serious act of writing. Having reclaimed it, having given himself a history, he liberates himself to write about the present. To borrow an image from physics, he creates a field of space—of words, images and landscapes.

Vassanji goes on to state that "the writer as myth maker creates Adam and stipulates a year zero, the events leading from which give meaning and coherence to his life and his time." The works of fiction he has written since then exemplify these principles. As his narrator says in the novel *No New Land* (1991), "We are but creatures of our origins, and however stalwartly we march forward, paving new roads, seeking new worlds, the ghosts from our pasts stand not far behind and are not easily shaken off."

In 1989 Vassanji published *The Gunny Sack,* an episodic epic covering a hundred years of the history of the Indian community in East Africa. The narrator, Salim, sits in his North American hotel room and writes the story of his complex origins and inheritances, prompted by objects he pulls from a gunnysack that belonged to his recently deceased great-aunt. The sack, which he calls "Shehrbanoo," is a kind of inanimate Scheherazade from which a proliferation of stories burgeons forth; the narrative that results is, however, chronological and orderly. Salim's great-grandfather, Dhanji Govindji, emigrated from India to Zanzibar, where he sired Salim's grandfather, Huseini, with an African slave girl. As he details the lives of ordinary people caught up in European wars, anticolonial rebellions, cross-border migrations, and the disenfranchisement of Indians in newly independent nations, Salim locates himself and his forebears in the contexts of family, community, nation, and diaspora. Salim's name echoes those of V. S. Naipaul's Salim in *A Bend in the River* (1979), who also observes Indian-African relations in an African country, and Salman Rushdie's Saleem in *Midnight's Children* (1981), who also tells a multigenerational, personal, unofficial national history. His unsuccessful relationship with the militant student Amina conveys the challenge of bridging the divide between black and Indian Africans, even as the novel emphasizes hybrid cultural identities and subtly critiques notions of ethnic, religious, or racial purity. The narration is complicated by the introduction of correspondence between Salim and his brother, Sona, who is in the United States researching a scholarly history of East Africa's Indian community. The novel thus introduces epistemological and moral questions about the truths told by narrative history—a theme that has preoccupied many postcolonial and Canadian writers. Replete with dramatic incidents and populated by dozens of characters, *The Gunny Sack* won the African regional Commonwealth Writers' Prize for Best First Book and established Vassanji as the unofficial literary spokesperson for his community. Peter Nazareth considers the work "the first Tanzan/Asian Novel," and Paul Williams Roberts in the *Toronto Star* (12 May 1990) called it "the African answer to Salman Rushdie's *Midnight's Children.*"

Although Vassanji had visited Kenya periodically throughout the 1970s and 1980s, he stayed away from Tanzania because he had broken a contract with the government when he left Nairobi for M.I.T. His trip to Dar es Salaam in 1989 in connection with the publication of *The Gunny Sack* was, in his view, a return from exile, and he has traveled to Tanzania regularly since then. Also in 1989 his story "In the Quiet of a Sunday Afternoon," which appeared in the *Toronto South Asian Review* and was later included in the collection *Uhuru Street* (1991), was short-listed for the Journey Prize for

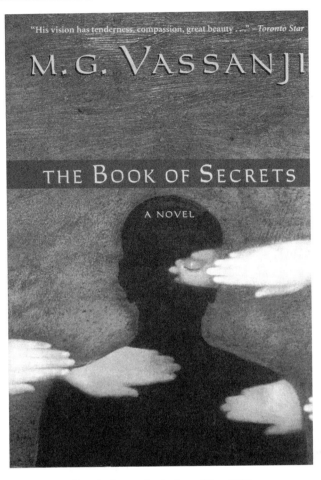

Paperback cover for the first edition, 1994
(Bruccoli Clark Layman Archives)

best short story published in a Canadian literary periodical. That same year he was appointed a visiting writer in the University of Iowa's International Writing Program.

In 1991 Vassanji followed his first success with a shorter novel, *No New Land,* about a group of Tanzanian expatriates dwelling in a Toronto high-rise apartment building. The main protagonist, middle-aged Nurdin Lalani, has trouble adapting to life in Toronto. After accidentally eating a forbidden pork sausage, he equates the corrupting atmosphere of Canada with bestial behavior and godlessness and laments, "you become, morally, like *them.* The Canadians." He sees the CN Tower, which blinks incessantly through his window, as the new land's only god. Nurdin himself becomes morally suspect after being unjustly accused of rape by a white woman. The failure of his attempts to join the Canadian mainstream—he has trouble finding a job—creates a sense of unbridgeable racial differences and leads him to assess Canada's multicultural policy as

"multivulturalism." The stories of Nurdin's family's easier adaptations, together with the narratives of his friends the immigration lawyer Jamal, the philosopher Nanji, the artist Esmail, and the spiritual guru "Missionary," give this novel something of the community focus of *The Gunny Sack,* and scenes set in Dar es Salaam flesh out the contrasts and correspondences between "here" and "there." *No New Land* remains Vassanji's only book set in Canada, and its scale seems to reflect his view of the limited fictional possibilities his adopted homeland affords. The year the novel was published, he remarked in an interview with Chelva Kanaganayakam that a novel such as Rushdie's *The Satanic Verses* (1988) could not be written in Canada, because "there is not enough depth here, I think, to warrant that. There is no intensity of experience in this country."

Klay Dyer quotes the Canadian writer Neil Bissoondath's argument that in *No New Land* Vassanji "fails to present his background material with sufficient subtlety, so that community submerges character (i.e. the individual)." Vassanji responds in his essay "Community as a Fictional Character" (1994) that Nurdin "does not exist without the community. In a sense, then, Nurdin Lalani is the community." He concludes the essay:

My literary project, although this is not how I think when I write, has been to trace the origins of a community, its development in a British colony, and finally its dispersal in the postcolonial era. In this way I look at the present century from the perspective of a simple community as it evolves and arrives at a metropolitan consciousness and loses a large part of its traditional identity. One could say that such a community is acted upon by history, and thus enters a historical consciousness. In all of this, however, the individual within the community is of central concern. And in a final reversal, even as my novels make the community historical–paralleling what the modern world has done to it– by fictionalizing the community, they have mythologised it.

Like similarly titled early collections by Naipaul (*Miguel Street,* 1959) and Mordecai Richler (*The Street,* 1969), Vassanji's 1991 book, *Uhuru Street,* makes a street the organizing site for a social portrait of an ethnic-minority group in a cosmopolitan city. Alternating between comic and melancholy tones and between child and adult and first- and third-person perspectives, the work comprises sixteen linked short stories about the shopkeepers, servants, schoolboys, and refugees who populate a Dar es Salaam neighborhood during the transition from colonialism to independence. Vassanji writes in the foreword that Uhuru, which means "independence," was a new name given to an old street to mark "a great event in the country." He highlights the street's and Dar es Salaam's worldly orientation by pointing out that Africa's east coast "over the centuries was visited by Arab, Indian, and European: traveller and merchant, slave trader, missionary and coloniser"; now, Uhuru Street "seeks access to the world." The stories "English Lessons," "Leaving," "The London-Returned," and "All Worlds Are Possible Now" trace a psychological change from colonial anglophilia, institutionalized in the educational system, to a sense of new opportunities for international travel and career building, particularly for the young. The ironically titled "What Good Times We Had" departs from the prevailing gentle and affirmative irony of the book to portray an interracial murder.

Vassanji made the first of several trips to India, a country his parents had never seen, in January 1993. "Going to India," he said in an interview with John Clement Ball shortly after the visit, "was like going to a place with all your nerves exposed, because I knew everything I would see would bring out a response from me." Having "romanticized India as a student" but later

"put India behind me," he realized in middle age "that if you claim yourself to be of Indian ancestry, then you are in some ways responsible for what goes on there." Much was going on when he arrived: his visit coincided with the communal riots that followed the bombing of the Ayodhya mosque in December 1992. In an interview with Shane Rhodes in 1997, by which time he had made at least two more trips to India, he recalled how "shocked" he was at the violence he witnessed, as well as by "the sanguinity of the middle class" toward it. At the same time, he recognized that going to India had enhanced his writing and his understanding of himself and his people: "India was a whole new world that had come alive, a world that had been closed off, that now opened to complicate my life even further."

Vassanji and Aziz's second son, Kabir Amin, was born in 1993. The following year year Vassanji published *The Book of Secrets.* His most celebrated novel, it is part love story, part war story, part mystery, part national history, and part journey of self-discovery. *The Book of Secrets* begins in 1988 with the finding of a slim, brittle book that turns out to be the 1913 diary of a British colonial administrator, Alfred Corbin. The narrator, Pius Fernandes, a retired history teacher who immigrated to Dar es Salaam from Goa, India, as a young man, uses the diary as a basis for the depiction of the life and times of Corbin and those who came into possession of his book after he lost it. Fernandes re-creates the colonial world of the kindly neophyte administrator Corbin and the fragile Indian community under his rule in the inland village of Kikono, Kenya. Particularly notable is his portrait of the "Great Riddle" that was World War I, with its enormous effect on peoples bordering German and British African territories who suddenly found their lives transformed and their families often divided by confusing new allegiances and territorial restrictions. Most of the major characters change nations, and often continents, of residence at least once; the novel compassionately explores the ways their multiple affiliations complicate their identities, their relationships, and their sense of where "home" is located. As in *The Gunny Sack,* Vassanji creates a large cast of ordinary people swept up in the events of a turbulent century. And through the divisions and breakdowns that occur in various families and small communities he figures the larger societal rifts caused by colonial rule, wars and their aftermaths, and postindependence politics.

Through the central story of the shopkeeper Pipa and his son Aku, whose true father is the central unrevealed secret of the diary, Fernandes connects Corbin's involvement in Dar es Salaam's Indian community and his own. The framing narrative that shows how he traces these links, together with the controversial history of the changing ownership of the diary, enables Vassanji to introduce questions common to many contemporary postmodern novels and of particular importance to displaced and migratory communities: how should history's multiple and ultimately subjective truths be gathered, sifted, and told? To whom do the artifacts and stories of history really belong? What is the historian's moral responsibility to the real-life players in the pageant of the past? At the end Pius, who has revealed the serendipitous investigations that led to his own act of history writing, declares his book to be "as incomplete as the old one [the diary] was, incomplete as any book must be. A book of half lies, partial truths, conjecture, interpretation, and perhaps even some mistakes." Indian and Swahili terms such as *mukhi, mzungu,* and *dhoti* are sprinkled throughout the novel, and Vassanji includes a glossary at the end of the book.

The Book of Secrets was the inaugural winner of the prestigious Giller Prize for Canadian fiction; it also won the Bressani Italian Canadian Award. Also in 1994 Vassanji received the Harbourfront Literary Award and was included in the *Maclean's* annual honor roll of twelve distinguished Canadians. That same year *The Toronto South Asian Review* became *The Toronto Review of Contemporary Writing Abroad.*

Vassanji spent five years working on his next novel, *Amriika.* In the late 1960s Ramji comes from "a small people" and "an innocent world," Dar es Salaam, to Boston as a diffident and impressionable college student. Despite his innate conservatism and passivity he joins an anti–Vietnam War march on Washington, lives in an ashram, and has an affair with the wife of his American host. He does not feel guilty about betraying his host, but he agonizes over whether his antiwar activities make him seem "ungrateful" for the nation's hospitality. Vassanji thus shows that the moral confusions of the late 1960s, which were hard enough for native-born Americans to sort out, were especially difficult for an immigrant. Ramji becomes implicated in a bombing incident and, fearing deportation, lies to the college president. As he moves over the next twenty-five years from Boston to Chicago to a Santa Monica beach, the complexion of the political agitators among whom he falls changes from white Americans to East-African Indian Americans. In the 1990s a letter campaign against Muslims provokes communal tensions and retaliations, and Ramji becomes embroiled in the crisis in a way that is almost a repetition of his earlier experience.

The Toronto Review of Contemporary Writing Abroad ceased publication in 2003. That same year Vassanji published *The In-Between World of Vikram Lall,* which opens with the title character introducing himself as "having been numbered one of Africa's most corrupt men, a cheat of monstrous and reptilian cunning. . . . I head my country's List of Shame." But he claims that he is an "ordinary" and "moderate" man who gained this dubious distinction simply by muddling his way through a half-century of "exceptional" times. From a hideout in southern Ontario he reconstructs his experiences at several key points. As an eight-year-old in provincial Kenya in 1953, Vikram's best friends are Njoroge, a Kikuyu, and two British children, Bill and Annie. The Lall family celebrates the British queen's coronation at the same time as Mau Mau rebels are slaughtering white families to protest colonial rule. In that "year of our loves and friendships" Vikram takes the Mau Mau oath to cement his bond with Njoroge but loves a girl–Annie–who will soon become a victim of Mau Mau terrorism. Later, as a student in Dar es Salaam, the Hindu Vikram forms a relationship with an Ismaili girl, only to have it destroyed by her community's antagonism to him. Still later, Vikram is caught in the middle of the taboo courtship of his sister Deepa and Njoroge; it, too, ends tragically. Finally, his career in the Kenyan civil service requires him to become a middleman in furtive financial deals that, despite his initial resistance, produce dividends for him: "If you don't take it, someone else will," his boss tells him. Soon he is asking favors of the aging Jomo Kenyatta, former Mau Mau leader and now president of the young nation. "Total corruption," Vikram remarks in retrospect, "occurs in inches and proceeds through veils of ambiguity." As Vikram reaches the end of his memoir he decides to return to post-Kenyatta Kenya in a quixotic pursuit of "truth and reconciliation."

Vassanji's most political novel, *The In-Between World of Vikram Lall* earned the writer his second Giller Prize. The jury called the work "an astonishing tapestry of irresistible vignettes, brilliantly exploring the painful lessons of history–national, culture and personal– amidst the fragility of human relationships."

Vassanji's second short-story collection, *When She Was Queen,* appeared in 2005. More varied and experimental in tone and style and more contemporary and international in focus than those in *Uhuru Street,* the dozen stories are set in Canada, the United States, Tanzania, Kenya, and India. Mysteries that link people across time and space, which often drive the narratives of Vassanji's novels, are evident on the smaller scale, as well. In the title story a middle-aged Toronto resident uses the fact that his father gambled away his mother to a friend back in Kenya to solve the question of his parentage. "The Girl on the Bicycle" begins with a woman spitting on a corpse in a Toronto funeral home; the reason for her action is gradually traced back to her wedding night in Dar es Salaam decades earlier. In the epistolary tale "Dear Khatija" childhood friends separated by the partition of the Indian subcontinent into India and Pakistan in 1947 reunite fifty years later as grandmothers in San Francisco; their letters and those of their family members subtly imply that if not for historical and cultural boundaries, their girlhood intimacy could have taken their lives down a radically different course. The stories explore the seemingly infinite dimensions of human bonding and disconnection—emotional, sexual, geographical, cultural, religious, and national—that affect even the most apparently settled and successful diasporic lives.

M. G. Vassanji has read from his works at literary festivals across Canada and around the world and regularly lectures and participates in panels on literary and publishing topics. He has served as a visiting writer or fellow at institutions in the United States, India, and Tanzania. A documentary, *The In-between World of M. G. Vassanji,* directed by Robin Benger, was broadcast on Canadian television in 2006. Vassanji told Kanaganayakam in an updated 1995 version of their interview, "ultimately I see myself as everything that's gone into me—Africa, India, Britain, America, Canada, Hinduism, Islam." In his essay "Life at the Margins: In the Thick of Multiplicity" (1996) he laments, "The condition of the world today brings home to us—those of us who had forgotten—the pervasiveness of smaller ethnic, communal, or sectarian identities and the tenacity with which they survive. We have seen pluralism-based national identities—built on the idea that human equality and fraternity should ultimately override ethnic or other communal differences—disintegrate and these smaller components reasserting themselves, shaking off the old idealism." Vassanji's fiction counteracts such factionalism by compassionately evoking the identities of those whose multiple affiliations exemplify the syncretism of the increasingly mobile and global societies of the twenty-first century.

Interviews:

Chelva Kanaganayakam, "Broadening the Substrata: An Interview with M. G. Vassanji," *World Literature Written in English,* 31, no. 2 (1991): 19–35; updated as "M. G. Vassanji," in his *Configurations of Exile: South Asian Writers and Their World* (Toronto: TSAR, 1995), pp. 127–137;

John Clement Ball, "Interview with M. G. Vassanji," *Paragraph: Canadian Fiction Review,* 15, nos. 3–4 (1993–1994): 3–8; republished as "Taboos: M. G. Vassanji," in *The Power to Bend Spoons: Interviews with Canadian Novelists,* edited by Beverley Daurio (Toronto: Mercury, 1998), pp. 200–209;

Shane Rhodes, "M. G. Vassanji: An Interview," *Studies in Canadian Literature/Études en littérature canadienne,* 22, no. 2 (1997): 105–117.

References:

John Clement Ball, "Locating M. G. Vassanji's *The Book of Secrets:* Postmodern, Postcolonial, or Otherwise?" in *Floating the Borders: New Contexts in Canadian Criticism,* edited by Nurjehan Aziz (Toronto: TSAR, 1999): 89–105;

Frank Davey, "Return to History: Ethnicity and Historiography in Some Recent English-Canadian Fiction," *British Journal of Canadian Studies,* 12, no. 1 (1997): 24–31;

Klay Dyer, "A Book of Secrets: M. G. Vassanji," *Canadian Forum,* 74 (June 1995): 17–21;

Rosemary Marangoly George, *The Politics of Home: Postcolonial Relocations and Twentieth-Century Fiction* (Cambridge: Cambridge University Press, 1996), pp. 176–197;

Amin Malak, "Ambivalent Affiliations and the Postcolonial Condition: The Fiction of M. G. Vassanji," *World Literature Today,* 67 (Spring 1993): 277–282;

Peter Nazareth, "The First Tanzan/Asian Novel," *Research in African Literatures,* 21 (Winter 1990): 129–133;

Shane Rhodes, "Frontier Fiction: Reading Books in M. G. Vassanji's *The Book of Secrets,*" *ARIEL,* 29, no. 1 (1998): 179–193;

Charles Ponnuthurai Sarvan, "M. G. Vassanji's *The Gunny Sack:* A Reflection on History and the Novel," *Modern Fiction Studies,* 37, no. 3 (1991): 511–518;

Stephen Smith, "Stories Not Yet Told: M. G. Vassanji Wants to Capture the Past before It 'Disappears into the Sunlight,'" *Books in Canada,* 21 (Summer 1992): 26–29.

Guillermo Verdecchia

(7 December 1962 –   )

Don Perkins
University of Alberta

BOOKS: *The Noam Chomsky Lectures,* by Verdecchia and Daniel Brooks (Toronto: Coach House, 1991);

Final Decisions/War (Toronto: Playwrights Union of Canada, 1991);

Fronteras Americanas (Toronto: Coach House, 1993);

A Line in the Sand, by Verdecchia and Marcus Youssef (Vancouver: Talonbooks, 1997);

Citizen Suárez (Vancouver: Talonbooks, 1998);

Insomnia, by Verdecchia and Brooks (Vancouver: Talonbooks, 1999);

The Adventures of Ali and Ali and the Axes of Evil: A Divertimento for Warlords, by Verdecchia, Youssef, and Camyar Chai (Vancouver: Talonbooks, 2005);

Another Country: bloom (Vancouver: Talonbooks, 2007).

PLAY PRODUCTIONS: *i.d.,* by Verdecchia and members of the Canadian Stage Hour Company, Toronto, The Free Downstairs, 11 May 1989;

The Noam Chomsky Lectures, by Verdecchia and Daniel Brooks, Toronto, Buddies in Bad Times Theatre, 14 February 1990;

Final Decisions (War), Calgary, Alberta Theatre Projects, 13 February 1991;

Get off the Stage, by Verdecchia and Jim Warren, Toronto, Tarragon Theatre, 20 April 1991;

Fronteras Americanas, Toronto, Tarragon Theatre, 21 January 1993;

A Line in the Sand, by Verdecchia and Marcus Youssef, Vancouver, New Play Centre, 29 March 1995; revised, Toronto, Tarragon Theatre, April 1996;

True Lies, by Verdecchia and Youssef, Vancouver, Rumble Theatre, 9 September 1995;

The Terrible but Incomplete Journals of John D., Vancouver, Rumble Theatre, 6 October 1996;

Insomnia, by Verdecchia and Brooks, Toronto, Theatre Centre, 20 May 1997;

The Adventures of Ali and Ali and the Axes of Evil, by Verdecchia, Youssef, and Camyar Chai, Vancouver, Vancouver East Cultural Centre, 11 February 2004;

bloom, Toronto, Theatre Centre, 1 March 2006.

PRODUCED SCRIPT: *Crucero/Crossroads,* adapted by Verdecchia from his *Fronteras Americanas,* Snake Cinema, 1994.

SELECTED PERIODICAL PUBLICATIONS–UNCOLLECTED: *The Terrible but Incomplete Journals of John D., Canadian Theatre Review,* 92 (Fall 1997): 50–67;

"Spanglish," *In 2 Print* (Summer 2000): 10.

Argentinian-born Guillermo Verdecchia is a playwright, actor, director, and short-story writer. He is best known for metatheatrical works that explore the ways in which politics and culture are filtered and distorted through media representations and that examine the effects of such representations. His many honors include the Governor General's Literary Award for Drama and four Chalmers Awards. As a playwright, Verdecchia avoids condescending to his audiences. He explained to Jennifer Harvie in a 1997 interview: "People *do* want to concern themselves with things. People *do* want to contend with things. People *do* want to think. They want to use their critical abilities." Popular forms of theater, he said, tell the audience to "just sit back and be stupid for a while."

Guillermo Luis Verdecchia was born in Buenos Aires on 7 December 1962 to Raphael Verdecchia, an engineer, and Elvira Pedreira Verdecchia, a clerical worker. When he was two, the family immigrated to Canada and settled in Kitchener, Ontario. In his essay "Spanglish" (2000) he recalls: "Even as I was putting together my first phrases and simple sentences in Spanish, my parents were teaching me English words, in preparation for our imminent emigration to Canada." At first he refused to speak the new language, but finally, "surrounded, outnumbered, and overwhelmed, I gave in and learned words and phrases, rhymes and songs." Eventually, he found himself embarrassed trying to carry on conversations in Spanish, while, para-

Guillermo Verdecchia (courtesy of the author)

doxically, he longed to hear the language spoken. The experience left him feeling "like a liar" in any claim either to Canadian or Argentinean identity.

As a result of exposure to high-school and community theater, Verdecchia realized by the eleventh grade that he wanted to make drama his career. He left school to study acting at the Ryerson Theatre School, then performed for some years in collective and collaborative pieces in the alternative theater, mainly in Toronto. In this creative atmosphere he often contributed to the texts of the plays; but he did not begin to consider himself a playwright until around 1989, when he and Daniel Brooks were creating *The Noam Chomsky Lectures* (produced 1990, published 1991). He explained in an unpublished 19 November 2002 interview:

> Writing was a development of my initial engagement with the theatre as an actor. I soon discovered that I had a lot I wanted to explore and address, and that the traditional "passive" role of the actor wasn't going to allow me to undertake that exploration.
>
> What I've tried to do is make art. Sometimes I do that as an actor, sometimes as a writer/director, sometimes as a dramaturgical collaborator. Sometimes as a short story writer. The stories, well . . . they are stories that don't fit onstage. Different impulses require different forms.

In 1990 Verdecchia won his first Chalmers Award for his collaboration on *i.d.*, a play for young audiences created and toured by the Canadian Stage

Hour Company that premiered on 11 May 1989. The piece followed so closely on the events of a matter that was before the courts at the time that the audience was repeatedly reminded that the characters bore no similarity to any actual person. After two police officers shoot and kill a young black man, television interviewers repeat the officers' version of the incident rather than the testimony of a woman who was in the car with the victim. The young man's friends and mother eventually wins their fight for an independent investigation of the shooting instead of an internal police inquiry. The play has never been published.

Verdecchia's first nomination for the Governor General's Literary Award was for: *The Noam Chomsky Lectures*. Verdecchia and Brooks note in the published version that each performance was a "workshop" of a "work in progress" and that the text is "little more than the transcript of one performance which took place on March 31, 1991 at Theatre Passe Muraille in Toronto." The published version includes footnotes with information on sources, as well as extensive options for alternative approaches to performance of the work. Verdecchia explained to Harvie that the play asks what happens when the media and the corporate interests they serve become barriers to collective knowledge and when public "information" sources become a form of "denial mechanism . . . a mechanism of systematic repression." He and Brooks attempted, he said, "to put us back in the problem, literally put the playwrights in the problem, put the actors in the problem, and by extension, obviously, the audience." The piece also asks, according to Joyce Nelson's introduction to the published text, how it is possible for the public to "know together"—to form a public consciousness or conscience—in the face of such countermanding forces. If theater is a kind of "Memory Machine," as it has been termed in critical discourse, then *The Noam Chomsky Lectures,* as Nelson explains, takes the audience "through the Memory Hole" to "help us retrieve not only lost strands of our own contemporary history, but also the concept of public conscience."

The Noam Chomsky Lectures has been described by Nigel Hunt as "anti-theatre" and by Lisa Coulthard as "a course in 'intellectual self-defense'" and in "semiological guerrilla warfare." Coulthard emphasizes that the piece functions in several ways as political theater: "as a play about politics, a play about the politics of theatre (that is a play about the politics of working in the theatre) and a play about the politics of theatrical representation, reception and form"; she says that it "encourages readers to resist manipulation and control from the mass media" and translates "Chomsky's notions of the manufacture of consent and thought control into theatrical forms and concerns." The play turns its own genres and conventions back on themselves as problems, as when it says that it is not to be taken as a satire while openly satirizing topical issues and telling theatrical insider jokes. A gaudily decorated "Artstick" is used to silence the actors whenever they cross the reputed line between art and polemic or demagoguery; Coulthard explains that the stick serves as "a physical manifestation of aesthetic judgement and represents the critics' ability to silence a production because it does not meet their aesthetic standards."

In the play the performers introduce, through captions, slides, flowcharts, and "brief, and by no means exhaustive" histories of Latin America and the Middle East, a wide range of facts on corporate concentration, political interconnections, and missed connections. They examine three historical examples that "challenge the notion that Canada is, in fact, a nation of peacekeepers." Attention then shifts to Noam Chomsky and Edward S. Herman's *Manufacturing Consent: The Political Economy of the Mass Media* (1988), and the performers create theatrical demonstrations of how the media shape the news to establish a particular political agenda. The play goes on to demonstrate other ways in which information gets distorted and to examine the effect of such distortions. These scenes include moments when Brooks and Verdecchia openly and sometimes comically "abuse" their ownership of the medium of the play to promote their own concerns and interests in the face of critical condemnation and belittlement. A Verdecchia "Digression" that polemically

proclaims theater as a place to get at "who we are" brings a ringing slam from the Artstick, and a list of politically desirable dos and don'ts occasions a blast on the "Whistle of Indignation." Following the narration of a story borrowed from Eduardo Galeano, inserted to provide an element supposedly lacking in the play, *The Noam Chomsky Lectures* ends with readings from Chomsky's works and a slide with a quotation that condemns Canadian comfort at being accomplices to mass murder.

In early 1991 Verdecchia collaborated with Jim Warren to produce a short piece, *Get off the Stage,* for the Tarragon Spring Arts Fair. The work centers on two four-hundred-year-old actors, the Lords Geoffrey and Jeffrey, transplanted from England to the colonies and, according to Verdecchia in the unpublished 2002 interview, "naturally, hating every minute of it." Also in 1991 Verdecchia moved to Vancouver, where he formed creative links with Marcus Youssef, Camyar Chai, Norman Armour, and Dennis Foon.

Verdecchia's first work as a solo playwright, *Final Decisions,* premiered on 13 February 1991 at the Alberta Theatre Projects playRites '91 Festival; it had previously received public readings under the working title *War.* The play dramatizes how disturbingly "normal" and middle-class the agents of evil can be and the effects on the agents of order when their work cheapens human lives, their own included. In an article in the *Calgary Herald* (19 January 1991) before the premiere of *Final Decisions* Martin Morrow asked Verdecchia, "A Canadian play about torture? Surely that doesn't happen here?" He answered: "Torture is instituted in over 100 countries in the world. . . . We don't have to stretch our imaginations too far to see it here in Canada." He referred to recent incidents "of people who have died while in police detention, who have had burn marks, grill marks, on their bodies." What is more important in the play, he went on, is the "direct relationship between First-World wealth and Third-World oppression."

Bea and Tony seem to be a typical young, upwardly mobile, urban, middle-class Canadian couple. Bea works for an advertising agency; the nature of Tony's work is at first unspecified, but later the audience learns that he is the head of human-resource management for the Political Section with responsibility for "transfers." Bea designs a humorous ad campaign featuring B-movie images of torture. Monica, an employee who questions the ad, is driven from the company. Monica's objections stem not from aesthetics but from experience and fear: she is hiding her sister, Maria, who is a member of what Tony's supervisor, Mark, defines as an "extremist political organization." When the police catch up with them, Monica claims to be Maria and is taken to jail, where Tony is one of her inquisitors.

When the stress of his work causes problems in their marriage, Tony tells Bea that he is just a civil servant who keeps track of people and information. Yet, when she jokes that she "has ways of making him talk"—the theme of her ad—and tries to tickle him, he pulls away violently. Trying to rescue her sister, Maria informs the disbelieving Bea of the true nature of Tony's work and the tools of his trade: electric cattle prods and a blowtorch. Monica is beaten to death by Mark, who considers it an accident and part of the job of keeping the "scum" in their place. When Tony vanishes after threatening to quit his job and talk about it, Bea assumes that Maria and her friends have kidnapped him; it is clear to the audience that the government has taken him away to keep him silent. Maria tries to educate Bea as to the nature of the state in which she lives: "People like you can work up a real fury about problems on the other side of the globe but do you give a shit about what happens in your own back yard?" Maria learns that Tony is about to be "transferred" and explains to Bea this term means that he will be executed. Bea kills Mark and flees with testimonies of those who have been tortured. Opening-night reviews of *Final Decisions* mention audience members leaving early, one in an obvious rage. Morrow's review in the *Herald* (14 February 1991) saluted the festival organizers for offering such a brutal "provocation" but also criticized them for giving the play a much shorter run than other pieces. *Final Decisions* was published in 2007 under the title *Another Country.*

The quasi-autobiographical play *Fronteras Americanas* (1993) is Verdecchia's most celebrated and most analyzed work. He explained to Harvie that the play is an attempt to "look at the whole problem of representation of Latinos in North American popular culture." Rather than simply dramatize racism, however, he examines his own susceptibility to and complicity in it: "What's more interesting and more important, I think, is to say 'This is racist, and outrageous, and wrong. And this is how I contribute to the problem. This is how I participate in it. This is how I am complicit in this.'" The effect of such an "auto-critique" is to allow the audience to "enter into the spirit of self-examination and self-criticism." The sole actor—originally, Verdecchia himself—performs before a backdrop of slides of distorted depictions of historical and current events. The combination produces a tension that is described by Anne Wilson: "Verdecchia . . . plays a double-sided game by repudiating the cultural stereotypes which the technologies of capital produce and selectively using images produced by the technologies of late capital to forge a sense of identity." In one scene Verdecchia auditions for the role of a Latino criminal selling stolen guns; he mentions other Latino roles for which he has

auditioned, all of them stereotypes. In another scene he is a tourist on a trip "home": when a man is gunned down outside his hotel in Santiago, Chile, he takes photographs from the window of the police standing around smoking and talking to each other, "and I realize that I have willed this to happen." In addition to dramatizing himself as an Argentinean Canadian, Verdecchia plays a second character, Facundo Morales Segundo. Facundo has tried to blend into the dominant Anglicized culture—to become "Saxonized," in the terminology of the play—by calling himself Wideload McKennah, a comically improbable name he appropriated from a character in a television show. Wideload's attempt to Saxonize his name mirrors the autobiographical scene "Roll Call," in which the young Verdecchia's teacher contorts her mouth "into shapes hitherto unknown to the human race as she attempts to pronounce my name." He tells the teacher, "You can call me Willy," thereby gaining momentary relief from the feeling of belonging to a different species from the rest of the class. The cure for this internal division that he sees as a "border wound" comes to Verdecchia when he realizes that living on the border is not a problem but a kind of "third space"; the border is not a margin but a center of new possibilities: "I am learning to live on the border. I have called off the Border Patrol. I am a hyphenated person but I am not falling apart, I am putting together. I am building a house on the border." The play earned Verdecchia another Chalmers Award and the 1993 Governor General's Literary Award for Drama. He later adapted the piece as a movie, *Crucero/Crossroads* (1994), which garnered many awards at national and international film festivals.

A Line in the Sand (produced 1995, published 1997), co-authored by Verdecchia and the Arab Canadian playwright Youssef, is set shortly before the 1991 Persian Gulf War and incorporates elements of the 1993 murder of Shidane Arone, a sixteen-year-old Somali, by members of the Canadian army on a peacekeeping mission. In act 1, Mercer, a young private in the Royal Canadian Regiment, sees Sadiq, a young Palestinian, as an Arab and, therefore, as the enemy; Sadiq sees Mercer as an "American" and a "Military Man." When Mercer says that he is Canadian, Sadiq responds with a hint of irony, "Oh, Canadian. Yes! The peacekeepers." He then offers a list of "facts" about Canada that he learned in school from a textbook supplied by the Canadian government: Canadians are peacekeeping, French-speaking inhabitants of a snowbound country. He then sells Mercer pornography, a business through which he hopes to earn enough to join his rich slumlord uncle in the United States. Sadiq's knowledge of America comes from Cable News Network, which, he believes, portrays "all sides" of the country; Mercer disabuses him of this notion. But while Mercer can see

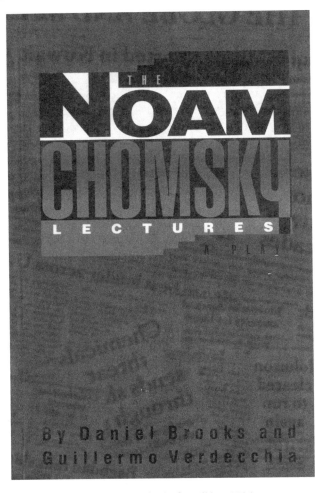

Paperback cover for the first edition, 1991
(Bruccoli Clark Layman Archives)

how Sadiq's image of America is distorted by the media, he cannot recognize that his own image of Arabs has been equally distorted by similar sources. When Sadiq suggests that the Iraqi soldiers are just like Mercer—lonely, a long way from home, and not volunteers but conscripts—Mercer replies with the military line: "No way, Sadiq. They're crack troops, elite. The Republican Guard, they beat the fucking Iranians, for Christ's sake. And you know how crazy they are." Sadiq is forced to take sides: "No, I do not. . . . You think we want to die? Because we are Muslim. We don't have wives? Families? Children?" He gives Mercer a brief history lesson, showing how the violence and instability of the Middle East are the result of interference by outsiders, but Mercer is indifferent.

In the original script, as performed in Vancouver in 1995, the second act consisted of a conversation between "Marcus Youssef" and a character named Norman. In response to Norman's ironic questioning and

misunderstandings based on stereotypes, Marcus explains the evolution of his sense of himself as an Arab living in Canada. When Norman observes that the play is about the Gulf War, Marcus replies that the war is only the setting, not the topic: "I felt that the Gulf War was a really concrete example of how cultural stereotypes and propaganda can convince us to accept the wholesale slaughter of other human beings." In the version presented in Toronto in 1997 and published the same year, the second act features an actor reading a transcript of a speech Prime Minister Brian Mulroney made to the House of Commons justifying military action against Iraq, which a second actor repeatedly interrupts with statistics and information about military spending, media representation of Arabs, and weapons research.

Act 3 opens with a colonel interrogating Mercer about the death of Sadiq, who was killed after being tortured by two other members of the unit. Mercer claims that a pistol that the others had left a table went off accidentally as he and Sadiq struggled over it. The colonel asks about Mercer's background, since one of the torturers is a member of a White Power organization. Mercer does not think of himself as a racist, though his comments in act 1 clearly show that he thinks in programmed racialized terms about "the enemy." To the colonel, an unfortunate aspect of Sadiq's death is its timing: a day or two later, after the shooting had started, he would be just another dead Arab; but the "peacetime" killing has become a matter of national interest. Mercer has sixteen photographs of the event that the soldier took turns in taking; one photograph shows him holding a pistol in Sadiq's mouth. Other possible motives for the killing emerge: the need to hide a homosexual relationship, a desire to punish Sadiq for the soldiers' guilt or boredom, a macho "hero" game based on distorted models of masculinity, or even a distorted act of mercy to save the boy from further pain. *A Line in the Sand* won the 1996 Chalmers Award for its Toronto production.

Verdecchia collaborated with Youssef, Chai, and Armour on *True Lies,* which premiered on 9 September at the 1995 Vancouver Fringe Festival. Promotional releases for this as-yet-unpublished play explain that it "places the intimacies of three men's lives at the epicentre of a media culture predicated on the hard-sell of half-truths and obscured facts." The three protagonists—a movie and television director, an actor preparing for an audition, and a former photographer—work, or worked, in various image-creating industries. In her review of the play in *FFWD Weekly* (8 January 1998) Nikki Sheppy quoted Armour, artistic director of Rumble Theatre, who explained that the play "draws on ideas about visuality by cultural critics John Berger and Brian Fawcett"; Verdecchia also acknowledges borrowing from Paul Auster, Tony Barr, Roland Barthes, and Susan Sontag. Sheppy noted that the plot centers on a crisis that links the three as participants in "a search for authenticity in a field that relies upon the power of appearance" and referred to a scene in which the actor rehearses the same few lines over and over, looking for a version that will convey "something meaningful," before slipping into an interior monologue about "the kind of fraud his life has become." The photographer has ceased taking pictures because he realizes that photographs he had taken of a former lover are a record of what had existed at a particular moment but now convey a lie. This type of "decay or ambiguity of truth," Sheppy wrote, is the thematic core of the play and the source of the title.

Following these collaborations, Verdecchia wrote *The Terrible but Incomplete Journals of John D.,* which was first produced on 6 October 1996 as a "live radio

drama" in Rumble Theatre's Wireless Graffiti series. Billed by Rumble Theatre as "a melancholy, funny, and musical look at the multifarious strains of a deception," the piece has minimal requirements: one actor, a cellist, and a sound-effects technician. The title character is a "curmudgeonly . . . quasi-Everyman" who describes himself as "an average, regular, straight, white, fin de siècle kind of guy." The day before he leaves for a trip to Mexico to do research for a book he is writing, John D. receives a postcard from M., a woman with whom he has been having a love affair, with the 1932 Henri Cartier-Bresson photograph of a man in midleap, "Behind the Gare St.-Lazare"; on the reverse is the message "It's over. M." He thinks:

I thought love would take care of itself.

That it was just there, perfect, immovable, inviolable.

That it didn't need to be tended or defended.

I thought we would live happily ever after.

Where does it go? Where does all the love go?

In Mexico City he records his observations of the desperate citizens scrambling to make a living any way they can. He wonders, "Maybe I'm nothing more than a machine in the shape of a man condemned to take notes," while chiding himself for "thinking about sex all the time." He decides that "The only true law is decay" and that "Mexico City is a funhouse mirror distorting, enlarging all my anxieties." His anxieties increase with his return to Canada, where infomercials for exercise machines are the most erotic thing on television, and Reform Party logic explains that since children do not work and generate wealth, they cannot be poor: "So with this clever piece of free market sophistry, she explains away all those children who go to school hungry; all those children who lack adequate supervision, stimulation. They're not really poor, not really hungry, not really abused, not really suffering. . . . And we believe this shit. . . . How did we come to this? Was nobody paying attention?" Connecting the political and economic deterioration he observes with his personal relationships, especially with M., he wonders, "Why did I cheat?" He notes that the fast-food restaurants all around him supply a basic human need for a place that says "Come on in, nothing here will surprise you." Someday, he thinks, "there will be nothing unique or local left in the world." His attack on globalization ends with a disgruntled and fearful "This isn't funny anymore." Yet, when he is asked to join a collective at a local radio station, he declines, because "collectives make me break out in shingles" and because Jean-Paul Sartre was right that "Hell is other people." Eventually, this change-resistant yuppie faces up to his regrets and shares a moment of understanding and laughter with M. when they encounter each other in a grocery store.

Verdecchia's next play, *Insomnia* (produced 1997, published 1999), is another collaboration with Brooks. In one long act and a procession of scenes that may represent waking reality, paranoid fantasies, waking dreams, or insomniac delusions, it focuses on the nightmare life of John F., a doubt-plagued artist. John F. is married to Gwen, played in the original production by Verdecchia's partner, the actress Tamsin Kelsey. They are visited by his brother, William, originally played by Verdecchia, and his wife, Kate. Tensions abound over a range of domestic and personal issues: marital decay, sibling jealousies, and real or imagined infidelities. The published version, which includes the typical caveat that it represents only the stage of development at the time of publication and that the play remains a work in progress, opens with the repeated word "Doubt. Doubt." John F. and the audience remain in that state throughout the play. John F.'s unspecified "opus" seems to be perpetually in progress. William, a wealthy employee of the Disney Corporation, says in response to the perceived disapproval of his brother, "I'm comfortable in my corruption." Conversations about the corrupted content of news sources—magazines sold to sell her advertising, doctored photographs that paint pretty pictures to encourage consumption, and so forth—emerge from John F.'s preoccupation with the question "How do you know?" The play ends with three disturbing scenes. In the first, John F. delivers an increasingly distracted monologue in which he attempts to list twenty-seven "protocols for living in the Republic of Doubt." He cannot sleep until he gets answers, and his intensity has created the widening rift between him and those around him. The second scene opens with protocol 27, "the possibility of redemption," but spirals down into a nightmare in which Gwen, who seems to have been hypnotized appears to have served their baby daughter, Lilly, as an ingredient in a special dish for their guests. The final scene is, perhaps, the most disturbing: it is one of almost Disney-like "normality," possibly a "doctored" scene in which everything is fine with John F. and Gwen's marriage, the baby, and John F.'s relationship with his brother. It is a seductive dream from which the audience would prefer not to wake up. *Insomnia* received a Chalmers nomination.

In 1998 Verdecchia returned to Toronto and published *Citizen Suárez,* a collection of short stories; five had been published over the previous three years, and the other five had not been published previously. The narrators vary from first- to third-person, from adults to children, and from insiders to outsiders of various societies. Reviewing the book in *Canadian Forum* (November 1998), Nicole Markotic noted: "The stories range from the overtly political to the explicitly literary to the complicated social relations that develop from characters' desires to maintain personal histories and to belong completely." Verdecchia served as artistic director of Cahoots Theatre Projects in Toronto from 1999 to 2004. In the latter year he joined Chai and Youssef to write *The Adventures of Ali and Ali and the Axes of Evil: A Divertimento for Warlords,* which was selected for the 2004 Magnetic North Theatre Festival, "Canada's National Festival of Contemporary Theatre in English," and published in 2005. The title characters, played by Chai and Youssef in the original production, are refugees from the fictional Middle Eastern country of Agraba. Ali and Ali perform a cabaret of off-color humor, songs, skits, videos, puppet theater, and parodies of the standard fare of Canadian theater. Stick puppets representing members of the American administration meet in the Oval Office to review the occupation of Iraq. A linked pair of skits repeats the familiar plot and sentimentality of the type of politically correct multicultural, multiethnic family drama that has become familiar to Canadian audiences. In her review in *Canadian Theatre Review* (Fall 2004), "Theatre as a Weapon against Mass Delusion," Rosalind Kerr noted that the objective of the play is to challenge "'the good people of Real Life Canada' in the audience to examine their own position vis-à-vis terrorism." Kerr termed the parodies "Howlingly funny for audiences too familiar with the overt nationalist propaganda directed against immigrants" and said that they "slowly retell the heavily mediatized version of 9/11 and its aftermath in the form of a sentimentalized Hollywood movie. . . . We cannot escape the fact that we know this trivialized version of events only too well because we've seen it on 'CBCNN.'"

Verdecchia's 2006 play, *bloom,* draws on T. S. Eliot's *The Waste Land* (1922), Samuel Beckett, Dante, William Shakespeare's *Hamlet* (circa 1600–1601), and Geoffrey Chaucer. On the fringes of a ruined world Gerontion, an ancient war veteran, has shut himself up in a damaged house filled with books he can no longer read. A war orphan, known only as the Boy, appears; he digs up memories and stirs up ghosts that threaten the peace that Gerontion has carved out. Surviving together, they argue and play and annoy and forgive each other, unearthing a past that the Boy needs to remember and Gerontion would like to forget. In a 2006 interview with Jon Kaplan, Verdecchia suggested that the play is more "interior and personal" than his earlier works, "But I can't escape from infusing it with the historical moment we're living in, just as Eliot did in 'The Waste Land.' The central figure in *bloom* is in a state of mental war, living with the consequences of his actions." The play was published in 2007.

In 2006 Verdecchia completed his master's thesis, "Staging Memory, Constructing Canadian Latinidad," for the University of Guelph. The thesis examines the work of the Latin Canadian playwrights Carmen Aguirre, Rosa Loborde, and Beatriz Pizano.

In his work Guillermo Verdecchia seeks to counteract a popular culture of easily digested, watered-down "news" as entertainment and of entertainment that provides easy, stereotyped "understanding" of complex issues. He and his collaborators insist that such "knowledge" is inadequate and immoral as they engage their audience's intelligence and confront the audience with questions that call its own knowledge into doubt. Verdecchia also raises questions about how artists themselves become complicit in such distortions.

Interviews:

Jennifer Harvie, "The Nth Degree: An Interview with Guillermo Verdecchia," *Canadian Theatre Review,* 92 (Fall 1997): 46–49;

Jon Kaplan, "Old Poem, New Bloom: Guillermo Verdecchia Takes Inspiration from T. S. Eliot's The Waste Land," *NOW,* 25 (23 February–1 March 2006).

References:

Lisa Coulthard, "'The Line's Getting Mighty Blurry': Politics, Polemics and Performance in *The Noam Chomsky Lectures,*" *Studies in Canadian Literature/ Etudes literraires Canadiens,* 20 (1995): 45–56;

Mayte Gomez, "Healing the Border Wound: *Fronteras Americanas* and the Future of Canadian Multi-culturalism," *Theatre Research in Canada/Recherches theatrales au Canada,* 16, no. 1 (1995): 26–39;

Nigel Hunt, "The Chomsky Boys," *Brick,* 45 (Winter 1993): 38–43;

Martin Morrow, "Guillermo Verdecchia," *Calgary Herald,* 19 January 1991, p. C5;

Anne Wilson, "Border Crossing: The Technologies of Identity in *Fronteras Americanas,*" *Australasian Drama Studies,* 29 (October 1996): 7–15.

Jon Whyte

(15 March 1941 – 6 January 1992)

Harry Vandervlist
University of Calgary

BOOKS: *Three,* by Whyte, Charles Noble, and J. O. Thompson, introduction by Eli Mandel (Banff: Summerthought, 1973);

Open Spaces (Banff: Peter Whyte Gallery, 1977);

The Rockies, High Where the Wind Is Lonely, photographs by Shin Sugino (Toronto: Gage, 1978);

Gallimaufry (Edmonton: Longspoon Press, 1981);

Homage, Henry Kelsey: A Poem in Five Parts, Illuminated with Eight Ink Drawings by Dennis Burton (Winnipeg: Turnstone, 1981);

Lake Louise: A Diamond in the Wilderness (Banff: Altitude, 1982);

Rocky Mountain Madness: A Bittersweet Romance, photographs by Edward Cavell (Banff: Altitude, 1982);

The Fells of Brightness: Some Fittes and Starts (Edmonton: Longspoon Press, 1983);

Tommy and Lawrence: The Ways and Trails of Lake O'Hara (Banff: Lake O'Hara Trails Club, 1983);

The Fells of Brightness, Second Volume: Wenkchemna (Edmonton: Longspoon Press, 1985);

Carl Rungius, Painter of the Western Wilderness, by Whyte and E. J. Hart (Calgary: Glenbow-Alberta Institute / Vancouver: Douglas & McIntyre, 1985);

Indians in the Rockies (Banff: Altitude, 1985);

Mountain Glory: The Art of Peter and Catharine Whyte (Banff: Whyte Museum of the Canadian Rockies, 1988);

Transitions (Springbank, Alta.: Springbank Press, 1990);

Mountain Chronicles: A Collection of Columns on the Canadian Rockies from the Banff Crag and Canyon, 1975–1991, edited by Brian Patton (Banff: Altitude, 1992);

Mind over Mountains: Selected and Collected Poems, edited by Harry Vandervlist (Red Deer, Alta.: Red Deer Press, 2000).

PRODUCED SCRIPTS: *Jimmy Simpson: Mountain Man,* motion picture, Filmwest Associates, 1973;

"The Fells of Brightness: Some Fittes and Starts," radio, *Alberta Anthology,* Canadian Broadcasting Corporation, 25 May 1984;

Jon Whyte (photograph by Craig Richards; from the cover for The Fells of Brightness: Some Fittes and Starts, *1983; Bruccoli Clark Layman Archives)*

"Swansong," radio, *State of the Arts,* Canadian Broadcasting Corporation, 1986;

"Magnificent Obsession," radio, *State of the Arts,* Canadian Broadcasting Corporation, 1987;

Minisniwapta, radio, Canadian Broadcasting Corporation, 1988.

OTHER: "Peter Pond, His True Confession," in *Stories from Western Canada,* edited by Rudy Wiebe (Toronto: Macmillan, 1972), pp. 35–40;

Pete 'n' Catharine: Their Story, Drawn from Diaries, Letters, and Notes, edited by Whyte (Banff: Peter and Catharine Whyte Foundation, 1980);

Catherine Robb Whyte–Peter Whyte: A Commemorative Port-folio, edited by Whyte (Banff: Peter and Catharine Whyte Foundation, 1980);

Exceptional Pass: The Quests, the Expeditions, the Explorations, contribution by Whyte (Banff: Peter Whyte Gallery, 1982);

John Davenall Turner, *Sunfield Painter: The Reminiscences of John Davenall Turner,* edited by Whyte (Edmonton: University of Alberta Press, 1982);

"Cosmos: Order and Turning," in *Trace: Prairie Writers on Writing,* edited by Birk Sproxton (Winnipeg: Turnstone, 1986), pp. 269–274.

SELECTED PERIODICAL PUBLICATIONS–
UNCOLLECTED: "The Agony of Mrs. Stone," *Matrix,* 3 (Summer 1977): between pp. 14 and 15;

"Now the light fades . . .," *Paper Bag Poems,* 1 (Spring 1980): 6;

"Koans for a September Monday Afternoon," *Paper Bag Poems,* 2 (Spring 1981): 11;

"Slow walk in the forest of . . .," "For F. R. Scott," and "Geosophy," *Contemporary Verse Two,* 27 (April 1983): 38–39;

"Canadian Rockies Legacy," by Whyte and E. J. Hart, *Equinox,* 20 (1985): 66–77;

"Mountain Painters," *Horizon Canada,* 1 (1985): 80–85;

"Eli Mandel, Comedian Cosmologist," *Essays on Canadian Writing,* 45–46 (Winter–Spring 1991–1992): 45–46, 80–88.

The epithet "poet of place" aptly describes Banff poet, local historian, and museum curator Jon Whyte, who remained passionately rooted in this mountain town during his lifetime. Whyte's strong local focus was balanced by an inclusive poetics that ensured that few literary or intellectual passions were foreign to his approach to his subjects. "My poems declare their epic intent," he writes in his 1986 essay "Cosmos: Order and Turning." He defined epic as "something akin to 'the narrative that defines the universe at the time.'" Whyte both celebrated and poked fun at the grandiose mythic connotations of his chosen genre, by using the term "bigness" to capture the range of tone and subject matter his own writing aimed to accommodate: "Bigness is part of it–a grand theme, lots of language to roll around in, so we can shake ourselves like a dog standing up after a roll in a manure heap and say, gosh that felt good. Ain't no room for simple language in an epic. If you like your language full, robust, redolent, vibrating, full of echoes in the vault of myth and mind, you'll like the type of epic I like." Three volumes of *The Fells of Brightness* (1983, 1985), Whyte's planned five-volume epic poem on the Canadian Rockies, were completed before his death in 1992; only the first two volumes

appeared in print, while part 3, "Minisniwapta," was broadcast as a performance for several voices on Canadian Broadcasting Corporation (CBC) radio. This unfinished Rockies epic forms the heart of Whyte's poetic work. He also produced an energetic outpouring of local history, arts journalism, book editing, and cultural and environmental advocacy. The common element in this diverse activity is Whyte's view of the Rocky Mountains not as an unpeopled and "sublime" landscape but as a theater where local, human, and planetary history are interwoven. As a screen for human consciousness the mountains both confer and reflect complex types of order and dissolution. Whyte links these threads of culture, environment, and local history with his own reinterpretation of the epic genre. By doing so he contributed to a reinvention of the artistic vision of postcentennial Canada in the 1970s and of the Canadian long poem in the 1980s.

Whyte was born in Banff on 15 March 1941 to Dave and Barbara Carpenter Whyte White, a teacher from New York State. Whyte took the spelling of his surname from his mother, who played the larger part in his upbringing. His aunt and uncle, the painters Peter Whyte and Catharine Robb Whyte, were at least as influential as his parents in forming Whyte's future interests. Peter and Catharine Whyte had been painting in and around Banff since the Great Depression and were acquainted with a wide range of local and visiting artists, including Belmore Browne, Carl Rungius, and Group of Seven members J. E. H. MacDonald, Lawren Harris, Arthur Lismer, and A. Y. Jackson. In a 1 March 1984 interview with Carol L. Foreman for the CBC radio program *Anthology* Whyte recalled listening, as a nine-year-old, to his aunt as she recorded interviews with long-time Banff-area residents such as the outfitter Jimmy Simpson. Whyte retained a lifelong interest in "local legends" such as Simpson and Ike Mills, whose trail-riding stable was across the street from his home.

In 1956 Whyte moved with his mother to Medicine Hat, Alberta, where he completed high school. As an adolescent he read E. J. Pratt's *Newfoundland Verse* (1923), *The Titanic* (1935), and *Towards the Last Spike* (1952). Impressed by these Canadian poetic epics, Whyte took up the story of the Frank Slide in Alberta's Crowsnest Pass in a youthful effort. If Pratt could write "a poem as long as the CPR," Whyte says in the introduction to the first volume of *The Fells of Brightness,* "I would write a poem as big as a mountain." In September 1959 he enrolled at the University of Alberta in Edmonton. Initially he majored in psychology, then switched to a bachelor of education program, and in 1963 settled into the B.A. program in English, which he completed in 1964. He remained at the university until 1967, working as a sessional lecturer and teaching creative writing while completing his master's thesis, "*Pearl: A Study in Individuation.*" He worked at CKUA, the college radio station, the beginning of a life-long involvement with radio, and immersed himself in jazz and folk-music clubs, the Focus Gallery, and the Citadel Theatre. The university was home to the little magazine *White Pelican,* in which Whyte published his early work. People who taught or inspired Whyte at the time included Wilfred and Sheila Watson, Henry Kreisel, Eli Mandel, Dianne Besai, and Mel Hurtig, who was then a publisher and bookseller.

After completing his master's degree in English, Whyte spent the winter of 1967–1968 at Stanford University working on an M.A. in communications. In June 1968 he returned to Banff, where he became manager of the Book and Art Den bookstore. In October 1968 he began a weekly column in Banff's *Summit News.* In 1969 he added the feature "Whyte's Weather," a series of daily haiku on the town's changeable climate. The newspaper ceased publication in 1970. That year Whyte joined the board of the Peter Whyte Foundation (now the Whyte Museum of Canadian Rockies) and began a long involvement with the Bow Valley Naturalists.

Whyte was already drafting the poems that make up *Homage, Henry Kelsey: A Poem in Five Parts, Illuminated with Eight Ink Drawings by Dennis Burton* (1981) and *The Fells of Brightness.* On 23 July 1971 the poet Robert Kroetsch wrote to Whyte, praising the originality of an early segment of *Homage, Henry Kelsey* that he had read. Whyte published the short story "Peter Pond, His True Confession" in an anthology edited by Rudy Wiebe in 1972. By 1973 Whyte had begun contributing regular brief arts reports on CBC radio. In 1973 a selection of Whyte's poetry appeared in *Three,* a volume that also featured poems by Charles Noble and J. O. Thompson. The book was published by Summerthought Press, which Whyte had helped to establish with Peter Steiner, the owner of the Book and Art Den. Along with several of Whyte's lyric poems displaying a fascination for sound and wordplay, the volume includes his narrative poem "Paley," about the young mathematician Edward Paley, who was killed in an avalanche near Skoki, west of Banff. Eli Mandel's introduction points out that Whyte's "mountain tale" would "inevitably invite comparisons with Earle Birney's *David* [1942]." In fact, Birney had commented on "Paley" in a letter to Whyte dated 7 February 1969: "you are a poet undoubtedly, and able to get many different effects . . . you have a strangeness, a voice of your own." The volume also includes "The Dreambearer," which was revised and republished in *Homage, Henry Kelsey.* In this version of just under one hundred lines Whyte sketches a creation tale in which a sort of precursor to the human order of

thought is being born for the first time in a landscape so far "undreamt":

the great bear's mind
comes together warming out of the reaches
to find order amid the first dream
of all dreams and imaginings born of darkness

As consciousness and landscape encounter one another, a mutual shaping takes place in which the land is dreamed into a new kind of order.

Whyte's Stanford thesis documentary, *Jimmy Simpson, Mountain Man,* premiered in 1973 and was broadcast three times on CBC television; he received his M.A. in 1974. In October 1974 Whyte began writing "Where Man and Mountain Meet," a weekly column for *The Banff Crag and Canyon* newspaper. The eclectic column addressed artistic, political, and environmental issues and remained a feature of the newspaper until 1991. (In 1987, recognizing feminist arguments about the importance of everyday language, Whyte changed the title to "Where Peaks and People Meet.") Selections are reprinted in *Mountain Chronicles,* edited by Brian Patton.

On 2 October 1976 Kroetsch, who had read an early draft of *The Fells of Brightness,* wrote to Whyte that he admired the ambition and design of the poem. Whyte's evocation of *The Anathemata* (1952), by Welsh poet David Jones, as one model for his own work struck Kroetsch as ambitious but appropriate.

In 1977 *Matrix* magazine published a portfolio that included "The Agony of Mrs. Stone," Whyte's narrative poem based on a 1921 mountain rescue that took place south of Banff. Margaret Stone, an American, became stranded on a ledge on Mount Eon after her husband, Winthrop, fell to his death. The poem might easily have been made into a heroic tale of the rescuers, Bill Peyto and Swiss guide Rudolf Aemmer, who had to rely on packhorses to reach the then-isolated area. Instead, Whyte focuses on his female protagonist. He concerns himself with Margaret Stone's endurance, alone and without food or water during the seven days it took for rescuers to realize that the pair were missing and to make the forty-five-mile journey. His other main theme is the elusiveness of his subject's concrete reality: "Margaret Stone is the questions she has become." The poem traces the impossibility of entirely recapturing the events, well documented though they may be. The last sections of the poem narrate Whyte's failed effort to make contact with Mrs. Stone more than fifty years after her ordeal. The portfolio included photographs of the Stones and of the cairn erected on the spot where Winthrop Stone died.

Also in 1977 Whyte's *Open Spaces* appeared. In this volume of concrete poetry he cultivates formal innovation and the adventurous use of typography and page design. That same year he traveled with his aunt on an extended Trans-Siberian and Far East tour that is reflected in the poems "Yokohama Episode" and "The Irkutsk Tournament" in his *Gallimaufry* (1981).

What became a series of exhibitions and publications based on a fantasy landscape began in 1978 with *Beyond Exceptional Pass,* a concept originated by Whyte and Karen McDiarmid. This collaboration among artists in several media aimed to document a region shrouded in mist and mystery, accessible only by Exceptional Pass, that the explorer Sir Ronald Hamilton is held to have first penetrated in 1934. The exhibit and resulting publication include maps, drawings, photographs, and expedition journals by artists and writers including Barbara Spohr, Stephen Hutchings, Patricia Askren, and Edward Cavell. The concept was employed again in the 1982 volume *Exceptional Pass: The Quests, the Exhibitions, the Explorations,* to which Whyte contributed, and in 1991 in *Return to Exceptional Pass.*

Whyte became curator of the Heritage Collection at the Whyte Museum of Canadian Rockies in 1980, following the death of his aunt Catharine. He held the post for twelve years. In 1981 he became involved in the formation of the Writers Guild of Alberta and published *Gallimaufry* and *Homage, Henry Kelsey.*

The term *gallimaufry* refers literally to a dish made up of odds and ends. The figurative meanings, as given in the *Oxford English Dictionary,* include "A heterogeneous mixture, a confused jumble, a ridiculous medley" and extend to a derogatory term for "A man of many accomplishments; a composite character." This mildly self-mocking title suggests the miscellaneous nature of the book, which includes concrete poems, short lyrics, and longer narratives in verse. The poem "Sta Sit" is practically a found poem, listing words derived from the Indo-Germanic root *sta* (place). Several children's lyrics appear, along with poems that respond to Whyte's readings, such as "Monad," "Gestalt," "Bicameral" (a poem for two speakers), and "The Ambidextrous Universe." The longest piece is "Sources," a section from *The Fells of Brightness.* In the introduction to *Gallimaufry* Whyte describes *The Fells of Brightness* as "an anatomy of personal reminscence, history, myth, geology, and all else I encounter."

Critical reaction was divided between admiration for the promise displayed in many of the poems and exasperation at an overexuberant indulgence in wordplay and intellectual associations. In *Books In Canada* (July 1982) Kroetsch said that "Sources" was "proof positive" that *The Fells of Brightness* "is on its way to greatness." The rest of the volume, wrote Kroetsch, pre-

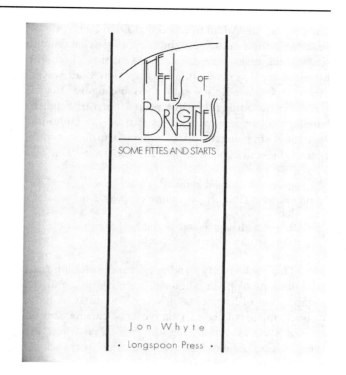

Title page for the first edition, 1983 (Bruccoli Clark Layman Archives)

sents Whyte in the guise of the "poet as magpie" and "rejoicer in the extravagance of our given world."

Begun in 1968, the book-length poem *Homage, Henry Kelsey* underwent several major revisions. Whyte had read the 1690 journals of the Hudson's Bay Company explorer Henry Kelsey in *The Kelsey Papers* (1929), edited by Arthur G. Doughty and Chester Martin. Kelsey provided the first descriptions in the English language of the area west of Hudson's Bay and of animals such as grizzly bears and bison. Though Whyte describes Kelsey's verse notes as "doggerel," he sees the potential for a poetic epic that would "reset" Kelsey's words as a jeweler resets a stone. In addition to *White Pelican* and *Three,* during the long gestation period of the poem several sections had appeared in the little magazine *Elfinplot* in 1971 and in *Freelance,* the Saskatchewan Writers Guild magazine, in 1979. The book includes original prints by the artist Dennis Burton.

Whyte makes use of both Kelsey's field notes, recorded in a commonplace book during the summer of 1689, and Kelsey's poem about his explorations, which he reprints at the end of *Homage.* The figure of Kelsey offers Whyte the opportunity to elaborate a tale of origin for Western Canadian landscape as represented in the English language. Kelsey could not serve as a Western Canadian "Adam," however, since the land was already inhabited by several First Nations. For this reason Whyte describes him in "Cosmos: Order and

Turning" as an "Adam in a peopled Eden" who "disappears into the landscape," thus realizing what Whyte sees as an essentially Canadian yearning. Like the Echimamish River, which is held to "flow both ways," the poem makes Kelsey into a double figure. In one sense, he becomes a kind of primal bard of English-language Canada. In another sense, he embodies "primacy"—the direct and seemingly wordless experience of the land evoked in part 1 of the poem "List":

> Language falls behind in the river's newness
> rumoured to run red as murderous blood in summer's
>   flood,
> of flesh-smooth land as soft as youth,
> as old as archaic stone the glacier bared to sun.

The book creates striking effects through unusual combinations of plain language, page layouts, and the juxtaposition of fragments of Kelsey's writings. A more abstract, intellectually speculative bent can be seen in sections such as part 5, "Arbor," which envisions the interpretation of landscape and perception or consciousness:

> Sphere of the eye
> Sphere of the world
> together a lens each focussing
> the other

In 1982 Whyte published two well-received books of local history, *Lake Louise: A Diamond in the Wilderness* and *Rocky Mountain Madness: A Bittersweet Romance*. He also edited *Sunfield Painter: The Reminiscences of John Davenall Turner*. In 1983 the Writers Guild of Alberta awarded *Homage, Henry Kelsey* its inaugural Stephan Stephansson Award for poetry. That year Whyte traveled to Greece and Africa. The unpublished manuscript "Black Markets," a substantial collection of poems based on this trip, remains among Whyte's papers.

In 1983 *The Fells of Brightness: Some Fittes and Starts* appeared. The design of the book involves columns of text, both parallel and angled across the page, along with drawn concrete poems—or "technopagneia," as Whyte dubbed them. Mixed typefaces and black-and-white landscape images also appear. In his preface Whyte lays out the plan for the next four volumes of the work. The second, "Wenkchemna," will focus on the ten peaks of the Wenkchemna range; the third, not yet titled, will be "fluvial in form"; the fourth is to be autobiographical; and the fifth volume, "Summits," will conclude the series with "a sort of *Paradiso*." Whyte casts *Homage, Henry Kelsey* as a prologue to this projected five-part epic, "for it incorporates history, myth, landscape, a literary past, and is a foray into 'anatomical epic,' lying like the prairies before the mountains."

The autobiographical elements in *The Fells of Brightness* serve as a case study in the formation of perception and memory in the interplay with environment. Meditations on this theme are interspersed with "yarns" about local figures such as Peyto, Simpson, and Whyte's grandfather. The verbal registers of the writing span the distance between the plain diction in passages of oral recollection and highly abstract conjunctions of words laid out in two or three parallel strips vertically or horizontally across the page. Whyte's approach to language in the poem binds together earthy, often factual passages on the roots of daily life in the Bow Valley with airy speculative sections that evoke the sweep of time embodied in the surrounding mountains. The strata of rock formations visible on all sides are seen as concrete analogues for the strata of meaning and association embedded in language.

The Fells of Brightness, Second Volume: Wenkchemna was published in 1985. The name of the mountain range in the title comes from the Stoney word for "ten": the area around Moraine Lake, near Lake Louise, had been called "The Valley of the Ten Peaks," and the names first given to these summits, the Stoney numerals 1 through 10, provide the titles for chapters 4 through 13 of Whyte's book. The opening sections, "Rockfall," "Tower of Babel," and "Mount Babel," pursue the theme of creation through dissolution and scattering, as in the Tower of Babel myth and in the formation of mountain landscapes through subsidence. The parallels between language and geology reverberate throughout the volume, most explicitly in "Sagowa." Here Whyte conflates myths of dragons that writhe beneath the earth and the scientific narrative of the violent formation of tectonic-plate formation. Etymological "formations" mirroring formations of rock are deployed on several pages in columns and alluvial fans of words. In other poems the narrative history of mountain exploration and first ascents, drawn from sources that include early issues of the *Alpine Journal*, provide found narratives that Whyte reworks in a fashion that recalls his adaptation of Kelsey's poems and journals. In the concluding poem, "Wenkchemna," Whyte simultaneously narrates two hikes over Wenkchemna Pass. S. E. S. Allen wrote in 1896–1897 of his journey through the pass, and passages from his account are printed in parallel with Whyte's narrative of his hike through the pass with Pamela Knott, the Special Events Coordinator for the Whyte Museum, in September 1983.

Whyte's publications on the visual art of the Rockies continued with *Carl Rungius, Painter of the Western Wilderness* (1985), co-authored with E. J. Hart. His local history *Indians in the Rockies* appeared the same year. Travels to New Zealand occupied part of the winter of

1985–1986. Whyte's work began to be featured regularly on CBC radio with the short story "Swansong," broadcast on *State of the Arts* in 1986. In 1987 another short story, "Magnificent Obsession," was aired, and the CBC in Calgary recorded "Minisniwapta," part 3 of *The Fells of Brightness,* as a poem for four voices.

"Minisniwapta" traces the genesis of a mountain river from its birth as a few drops of glacial meltwater. To echo the shape of the river in an extended work of concrete poetry, Whyte wrote the poem in landscape format on a continuous series of joined sheets of accordion-folded paper. The poem was not published, and the manuscript remains among his papers.

When a literary dinner party was held in Calgary on 28 October 1987, Whyte was present along with such figures as W. O. Mitchell, Aritha van Herk, Sid Marty, Andrew Wreggit, Claire Harris, and Fred Stenson. He became vice president of the Writers Guild of Alberta in 1989 and president in 1990. He traveled to Italy in the fall of 1991. He died of cancer on 6 January 1992 and is buried in the Banff Cemetery.

In the late 1990s the growing influence of ecologically based criticism and increased interest in the topic "writing the land" created fresh interest in Jon Whyte's contributions to the renewed poetic and artistic representation of the Rocky Mountains. Whyte's attention to the pioneering contributions of women in all areas of Rocky Mountain culture and his lifelong emphasis on the primordial presence of aboriginal peoples on the land he wrote about anticipated literary-critical debates pursued with increasing vigor in the years after his death. Red Deer Press published a representative collection of his work in 2000. Part of *The Fells of Brightness* was adapted by Winnipeg composer Diana McIntosh for chamber orchestra and voice in *Wenkchemna,* which premiered at the Banff Centre for the Arts in November 2001. The Writers Guild of Alberta continues to recognize Whyte with its annual Jon Whyte Memorial Essay Prize.

References:

Tim Heath, "Landscape Delitescent": Cultural Nationalism in Jon Whyte's *Homage, Henry Kelsey," Canadian Poetry,* 41 (Fall–Winter 1997): 53–84;

Eli Mandel, "The Post Structural Scene in Contemporary Canadian Poetry: A Note," *Poetry Canada Review,* 5 (Summer 1984): 10;

Birk Sproxton, "Jon Whyte 1941–1992," *Canadian Literature,* 135 (Winter 1992): 1992.

Papers:

Jon Whyte's papers are at the Whyte Museum of the Canadian Rockies in Banff, Alberta.

Jan Zwicky

(10 May 1955 –   )

Nancy E. Batty
Red Deer College

BOOKS: *Where Have We Been* (Iderton, Ont.: Brick Books, 1982);

Wittgenstein Elegies (Coldstream, Ont.: Brick Books, 1986);

The New Room (Toronto: Coach House, 1989);

Lyric Philosophy (Toronto: University of Toronto Press, 1992);

Songs for Relinquishing the Earth (London, Ont.: Brick Books, 1998);

Twenty-One Small Songs (Mission, B.C.: Barbarian Press, 2000);

Wisdom & Metaphor (Kentville, N.S.: Gaspereau, 2003);

Robinson's Crossing (London, Ont.: Brick Books, 2004);

Thirty-Seven Small Songs & Thirteen Silences (Kentville, N.S.: Gaspereau, 2005).

OTHER: *Why I Sing the Blues: Lyrics and Poems,* edited by Zwicky and Brad Cran (Vancouver: Smoking Lung Press, 2001);

"'Dream Logic' and the Politics of Interpretation," in *Thinking and Singing: Poetry and the Practice of Philosophy,* edited by Tim Lilburn (Toronto: Cormorant, 2002);

Harold Coward and Andrew J. Weaver, eds., *Hard Choices: Climate Change in Canada,* introduction by Zwicky (Waterloo, Ont.: WLU Press, 2004).

SELECTED PERIODICAL PUBLICATIONS–
UNCOLLECTED: "Wittgenstein and the Logic of Inference," *Dialogue: Canadian Philosophical Review,* 21 (December 1982): 671–692;

"Unsong," *Malahat Review* (Winter 1995): 68;

"What am I doing when I'm writing poetry?" *Grain,* 23 (1996): 111;

"Relay 1: PKP to Pablo Neruda," by Zwicky and Don McKay, *Malahat Review* (Winter 1996): 59;

"Relay 2: PKP to Rilke," by Zwicky and McKay, *Malahat Review* (Winter 1996): 60;

"Relay 3: PKP to Wallace Stevens," by Zwicky and McKay, *Malahat Review* (Winter 1996): 61;

"Solitude: A Philosophical Encounter," *Dialogue: Canadian Philosophical Review,* 36 (Fall 1997): 866;

Jan Zwicky (photograph by Danielle Schaub; courtesy of Kate Kennedy, Gaspereau Press, by permission of the author)

"Being, Polyphony, Lyric: An Open Letter to Robert Bringhurst," *Canadian Literature,* no. 156 (Spring 1998): 181–184;

"Freud's Metapsychology and the Culture of Philosophy," *Canadian Journal of Philosophy,* 25 (1999): 211;

"Partir de chez soi," "Cordes a vide," and "La geologie de la Norvege," *Ellipse,* no. 63 (Spring 2000): 65, 69, 73;

"Oracularity," *Metaphilosophy*, 34 (2003): 488–509;

"Song," *Arc*, no. 50 (Summer 2003): 91;

"The Ethics of the Negative Review," *Malahat Review*, 144 (Fall 2003): 55–63;

"Study: Disciplines," *Prism International*, 41 (Winter 2003): 45.

Jan Zwicky won the Governor General's Literary Award for Poetry in 1999 and was a double Governor General's Award nominee in 2004. Her work, which has been compared to that of Margaret Avison, Jay Macpherson, and P. K. Page, is heavily influenced by her philosophical training and her interest in music. Her poetry does not shrink from presenting her readers with intellectually challenging material; as a result, she has a reputation as a difficult, and perhaps even elitist, poet. Some of her work is highly allusive and abstruse; but her language, even in her most philosophical moments, is evocatively sensuous and remains grounded in poetic conventions of rhythm and sound and in an enduring poetic concern to reflect the natural world and communicate its ineffable beauty in language. In its citation, the nominating committee for the Governor General's Literary Award said that Zwicky's *Songs for Relinquishing the Earth* (1998) is governed by "A compelling and versatile intelligence, along with exquisitely modulated rhythms of feeling." Zwicky insists on poetry as a mode of thought; in the words of the nominating committee, "Grounding her elegant metaphysical and aesthetic insights in the physicality of the natural world and our own sensual natures, Zwicky shows that poetry is the best manifestation of philosophy."

Jan Keeley Zwicky was born in Calgary, Alberta, on 10 May 1955 to Robert William Zwicky, an engineer, and Jean Nellie Keeley Zwicky, a music teacher. Although her family lived briefly in Texas and Oklahoma, she spent much of her early life attending school in Calgary, with summers on her grandparents' farm on the north bank of the Paddle River near Mayerthorpe, Alberta. In collections such as *The New Room* (1989), *Songs for Relinquishing the Earth*, and *Robinson's Crossing* (2004) Zwicky draws poetic inspiration from her childhood, particularly times spent on the family homestead. A third-generation Canadian, Zwicky traces her maternal ancestry to Ireland and France. Both of her parents were strong social activists within the Unitarian Church tradition. Her mother and great-aunt have been civil-rights activists in such organizations as the New Democratic Party, the Voice of Women, and the Co-operative Commonwealth Federation. Zwicky's younger sister, Lynn, is an editor at Duvall House.

After graduating from high school in Calgary, Zwicky completed her bachelor of arts in philosophy at University of Calgary in 1976; she earned a master of arts in 1977 and a Ph.D. in 1981, both in philosophy, at the University of Toronto. Her dissertation was on the work of Sigmund Freud, but the title, "A Theory of Ineffability," points to her early interest in the Austrian philosopher Ludwig Wittgenstein. Zwicky recalls reading Wittgenstein's *Tractatus Logico-Philosophicus* (1922) in a single, life-altering sitting in 1976, and Wittgenstein's theories about how language approaches, apprehends, and communicates (or fails to communicate) are the subject of some of her poetry. While devoting most of her time to studying philosophy, Zwicky also wrote poetry and was encouraged to continue doing so by Christopher Wiseman at Calgary and Dennis Lee at Toronto. Zwicky took up a one-year postdoctoral fellowship at University of Waterloo and then taught for a year at Princeton University. In 1982 she published her first book of poetry, *Where Have We Been*. During the editing of the book she met and worked with Don McKay, cofounder of Brick Books.

Where Have We Been is more direct, conventional, and accessible than some of Zwicky's later, more allusive and philosophically informed poetry. Unified by poems that sensuously detail a tumultuous romantic relationship, the collection explores familiar poetic ground: the intense and fickle nature of sexual love. Although the poems at times slip into cliché or overly sentimental expression, they also exhibit trademarks of Zwicky's later work: a meticulous attention to diction, rhythm, and line length, and a characteristic, aphoristic final couplet that revises or intensifies the poetic thought. The influence of John Donne and other metaphysical poets on these poems, in terms of both form and content, is apparent in their preoccupation with the intense and sometimes contrary emotions of lovers and their battles against love's enemies: time and infidelity.

For example, in "It Is What We Are Always Asking" Zwicky raises the age-old question: what does one risk when one gives oneself to another? Her answer uses chiasmus and alliteration: "For in this abdication, self lost is / self found, our grace restored. To offer / all is to have all returned." Similarly, the cliché of pain caused by a lover's absence is redeemed in "Summer Nights" through paradox, as the lover imagines this absence not as empty and hollow but as alive and growing, even fetal. Poems such as "Emendation" hint at Zwicky's early preoccupation with ineffability:

. . . Transluscent, your skin, you know
in those milk-white rooms. Betrayals.
For all this, love, words have always been inadequate.

Yet stranded in this leafless season, even memories now

only of leaflessness, what do we have
but words?
The mind is stilled; to stretch the understanding
past the slow grey crack of trees that shows us the horizon,
impossible. There are only words with which
to promise, only images to remind.

These lines prepare the reader for the philosophical turn that Zwicky's poetry takes in subsequent work.

While there are only hints of Zwicky's philosophical training in her first book of poetry, her second, *Wittgenstein Elegies* (1986), announces clearly her intention to use poetry as a vehicle for the exploration of philosophy and philosophers. This poem in five parts was inspired by the foreword to *Philosophical Remarks* (1975), in which Wittgenstein contrasts analytical philosophy with what he considers to be true philosophical inquiry: a "spirit" that "remains where it is and what it tries to grasp is always the same." The sections of the poem express four voices: those of the public and private personae of Wittgenstein; that of Georg Trakl, a modernist poet who received financial support from Wittgenstein and whose experiences in World War I drove him to commit suicide; and that of the speaker. The use of the term *elegies* in the title is significant not only to this volume of poetry but to all of Zwicky's work. Zwicky said in a 2002 interview with Anne Simpson that "lyric art is essentially celebratory/elegiac. There are some . . . lyric poems that are purely celebratory—that manage to relive that fused moment of joy without contextualizing it in any way—but as soon as you get context, you've got loss. Hence, the preponderance of the elegiac tone."

The poems in *Wittgenstein Elegies* stage a dialectical interplay between the exigencies of the flesh and the strivings of the spirit, all the while acknowledging that it is only through the material instrument of language that—humans can even hope to bridge this unbridgeable gap. In these poems, Zwicky directly confronts the dilemma of the elusive nature of experience and the poet's (and philosopher's) impossible duty to represent it to others without knowing whether he or she has succeeded:

We communicate
With others without knowing
If it is the same for them.

What goes unrepresented and perhaps remains unrepresentable, except in the visual arts, is the provenance of poetry and philosophy. But purely analytical thought is incapable of communicating these gestures. It is only through paradox and silence that the poet and philosopher can approach the ineffable, as Zwicky says in "Rosro, County Galway":

Perhaps what is inexpressible is this:

The huge faint height beyond the shadowed heart
Against which we must measure lives,
the possibility of truth.

Against which, only,
Death might mean,
the emptied voice

at last begin to speak.

While knowledge of Wittgenstein's work is not needed to appreciate many of the poems in *Wittgenstein Elegies,* Zwicky was concerned enough about the potential difficulties lay readers might encounter that she provided a foreword and explanatory notes for each of its sections. Some familiarity with Wittgenstein's life enriches the reading particularly of the first two sections. But Zwicky's notes, rather than providing the biographical context, often merely provide references to other works. Some reviewers of the book were frustrated by such indirection. In a review in *Essays on Canadian Writing* (1989) John Harris argued that "The poem's apparatus is maddeningly vague," that "Some of the notes seem designed more to intimidate than inform," that "Zwicky's poetry is not that good," and that "Zwicky-Wittgenstein's" style is addicted "to the use of sentence fragments, which, after a while, become tiresome to the ear."

While completing *Wittgenstein Elegies* for publication, Zwicky began her close relationship with Brick Books editor and Governor General's Literary Award-winning poet McKay. Since 1986 Zwicky and McKay have engaged in a continuing and often public discussion of poetry and ecology with poets Lee, Robert Bringhurst, and Tim Lilburn. After McKay left his teaching position at University of Western Ontario to take up a position at University of New Brunswick in Fredericton, Zwicky and McKay moved throughout Canada, taking up short-term teaching and writer-in-residence appointments until Zwicky's appointment to a teaching position at the University of Victoria in 1996. Poems in *The New Room* collection reflect Zwicky's reaction to the death of her father from cancer in 1987, and in them Zwicky returns to more conventional poetic topics and a personal lyric voice. Taken together, these poems can best be characterized as restless, exploring notions of home and homelessness, searching for rootedness. The poems travel among landscapes and domestic spaces from Canada's west coast to the east, with landfalls in Alberta, rural Ontario, and Ireland. The book is divided thematically, rather than geographically, into four parts: the first section comprises sixteen short lyrics; the second consists of one long poem set on the

Keeley homestead near Mayerthorpe; the third comprises eight lyric poems, including the title piece; and the final sequence is "Seven Elegies: Robert William Zwicky (1927–1987)."

The New Room offers candid glimpses of Zwicky's early life, particularly her relationship with her parents and grandparents. These relationships are portrayed as difficult, complex, and haunting. The last poem of the first section, "Last Steps," prepares the reader for the longer poem that follows. "Leaving Home" begins as a meditation on moving houses as an adult: Zwicky establishes the motif of an avocado plant that endures repeated household moves but is subtly diminished each time it is uprooted. The plant's struggle is a metaphor for the speaker's sense of tenacity and diminishment when, as a child, she endures abandonment and the tough discipline of a bitter, unloving grandmother at the family homestead:

> And then the things I never quite learned:
> how not to reply, or to reply with silence . . .
> How to turn my back,
> stuff hands in pockets, amble off.
> The rules.

The traumas of childhood continue to haunt some of Zwicky's later poetry, most notably in "Lilacs," published in *Songs for Relinquishing the Earth.*

In much of Zwicky's poetry, objects in nature provide the objective correlatives to intense, ineffable emotion. In "Your Body," the final poem in *The New Room,* Zwicky compares the moment of steeling herself to enter the hospital room to view her father's cancer-ravaged body to the reaction of a couple who hit an owl with their car on a snowy night:

> I can imagine them
> not saying anything, sitting,
> snow swirling in the headlights, wondering
> how much blood, how broken, what if
> it's still alive, what if it looks
> at us.

Even the description of her father's body draws on the concrete imagery of nature: "your arms like snapped lilacs, bruises / pooling at your elbows, ankles, knees." The elegies for her father are some of the most powerful pieces in this volume. Here the speaker feels most keenly and most pertinently the inadequacy of language to express irrevocable loss. The speaker must either attempt to convey these emotions indirectly through the images of nature, as in the dual-voiced, haunting "Mourning Song," or she must attempt to define them through negation,

*Paperback cover for the first edition, 1986
(Bruccoli Clark Layman Archives)*

as in "Spring Light," in which she enumerates the many things that death is not.

In a review in the *Journal of Canadian Poetry* (1991) Peter McCormick praised *The New Room* for "The sharply observed details with the quick unexpected comparisons and juxtapositions, the musicality of the lines with their unobtrusive but closely calculated rhythms and stresses and rests, and the thematic suggestiveness of memory, memorializing, and commemoration." Elizabeth Thompson in *Canadian Literature* (1991) described "Zwicky's landscape" as "grounded in specific detail; places and things are real," while acknowledging that it is a landscape in which "the knowable segments of the world become mysterious." In *The New Room* Zwicky demonstrates that philosophically informed poetry, when it engages directly with the senses and with concrete images from nature, need not be inaccessible. Insisting on the relevance of ecology to her poetry, Zwicky told Simpson that "Lyric and philosophy converge where thought is governed by a twinned eros, when it seeks clarity and coherence simultaneously. All ecologies are coherent to some degree or another, and the world as a whole is an ecology. In the desire to understand clearly the nature of what-is, lyric, philosophy and ecology converge."

Zwicky's next work, *Lyric Philosophy* (1992), addresses more directly and more rigorously the interrelationship of poetry and philosophy. She described the impetus for the book to Simpson as "an attempt to write the poetics for *Wittgenstein Elegies*." *Lyric Philosophy* is unusual in several ways: its format of nineteen by twenty-seven centimeters; its length of 566 pages, including notes and index; and its content, which consists of the work of other poets and philosophers and even of musicians and visual artists on the recto pages and Zwicky's own, usually short, texts on the versos. In her foreword to this three-part olio, Zwicky describes the relation of the two sides of the book as "somewhere between counterpoint and harmony, somewhere between a double helix and the allemande of the earth and moon." Less a book of poetry than a book about thinking lyrically (it bears University of Toronto's Studies in Philosophy imprimatur), it nonetheless contains poems by authors such as Lilburn, McKay, Bringhurst, Trakl, William Blake, Philip Larkin, Pablo Neruda, Roo Borson, and Elizabeth Bishop. Some of Zwicky's commentary borders on the poetic. Opposite an excerpt from philosopher John Locke, Zwicky writes: "But it is an economy of movement, not merely a stinginess with words, that is close to [lyric's] heart: lyric is lithe. . . . Lyric is an attempt to comprehend the whole in a single gesture." In a review in the *Journal of Aesthetics and Art Criticism* (Summer 1994) philosopher Alex Neill argued that the book "is more like poetry than it is like philosophy; but part of the book's success lies in the ways it blurs that boundary."

Aside from her indebtedness to Wittgenstein, Freud, and analytical philosophers of the rationalist western tradition, Zwicky also reveals in her texts a strong interest in Eastern philosophies such as Taoism:

> [Lyric] is orphic. The note whose pitch and timbre quickens the entire resonant structure into which it issues. (Lyric assumes the resonant structure of the universe.) . . .
> Lyric occurs in emptiness: a particular gesture locates itself exactly in a particular emptiness.
> It speaks the radiant embodiment that makes the possibility of absence immediately present to it.
> It is vision rooted in the preciousness, the losability, of the world. . . .
> Lyric art is the fullest expression of the hunger for wordlessness.

Through an eclectic juxtaposition of many traditions, styles, and genres, Zwicky attempts to present a poetics of philosophy and a philosophy of poetics that is neither prescriptive nor entirely rational. Although at times Zwicky's comments reflect specific literary theories, such as formalism, the dialectical presentation of the material belies such didacticism. Each page offers a proposition, an hypothesis, that, in the next page, may be questioned or elaborated. Above all, *Lyric Philosophy* is an ongoing argument—not just an argument with the tradition of analytic philosophy but also an internal struggle, within the poet herself, to articulate why and how poetry means and continues to be meaningful and how one might use lyric to distill thought: "Lyric philosophy: thought in love with clarity, informed by the intuition of coherence; by a desire to respond to the preciousness of the world." Once again straying from the conventional path of the contemporary poet, Zwicky challenges readers of *Lyric Philosophy* to think deeply about the way that words reflect the world. She invites them to read interactively, to "substitute at any point a work, or passage . . . more illustrative . . . or challenging, than the one I have chosen." In a review in *Literature and Philosophy* (1994) Donald Phillip Verene lauded Zwicky's attempt to "have a lyric-philosophical form of thinking." Phyllis Webb, in *Malahat Review* (Spring 1993), also praised *Lyric Philosophy*, describing it as "beautiful and heavily seductive." The book is now out of print.

Zwicky's next published book of poetry was the Governor General's Literary Award–winning *Songs for Relinquishing the Earth* (1998). While the philosophically oriented *Wittgenstein Elegies* provided the contrapuntal score to the more sensually grounded books that come before and after it, *Songs for Relinquishing the Earth* emerges from the poetics established in *Lyric Philosophy*. Her most mature and successful collection of poetry to date, *Songs for Relinquishing the Earth* was reprinted multiple times. The collection began as a hand-bound, limited edition that Zwicky prepared herself, in 1996, for friends; her intention was "to connect the acts of publication and publicity with the initial act of composition, to have a book whose public gestures were in keeping with the intimacy of the art." Word of the handcrafted collection soon spread, however, prompting Brick Books, for whom Zwicky has been an editor since 1986, to publish a facsimile copy.

The poems in this collection engage subjects that have always been important to Zwicky—the fragility and ineffability of experience; the significance of nature, music, and ecology to human lives; and the insight that philosophy and philosophers' lives can provide, as in the long poem "The Geology of Norway," written from the point of view of Wittgenstein. There is, however, a new synthesis here of philosophical and lyrical thought, as though the poet has discovered a way of infusing her practice with those principles of philosophy with which she has so long grappled. "April" is poetry as proposition:

How the light is sad.
How it will not leave us alone.
How we are tugged up staircases
by the way it angles across landings

There is also a new litheness and elasticity in the form of Zwicky's poetry as she moves with agility from the prose line to the aphoristic couplet in such poems as "Kant and Bruckner: Twelve Variations." The emotional range in this group of poems is striking: from the serious, reflective tone of poems like "Poppies," "Recovery," and "Shade" that readers have come to expect of Zwicky's work, to the whimsical, humorous tone that she adopts in the first lines of the opening poem, "Open Strings":

E, laser of the ear, ear's
vinegar, bagpipes
in a tux, the sky's blue, pointed;
A, youngest of the four, cocksure
and vulnerable, the white kid
on the basketball team.

A relaxed humor informs many of the poems, striking the reader when least expected—as in "Variations," where Zwicky creates a motif from the minor detail that the composer Anton Bruckner was once detected wearing mismatched socks. In the preface to these "Variations," Zwicky describes their structure, and, in doing so, may also be describing the structure of many of the poems in this collection, indeed, the structure of the collection itself: "Not infrequently, especially in the works of Haydn and Beethoven, the sublime and the ridiculous are deliberately juxtaposed—the meditative tension is relieved by a scherzo. This goofing-off usually occurs about two-thirds or three-quarters of the way through."

In "Lilacs" Zwicky contrasts a magical, happy memory from her childhood with her sister's more pragmatic vision, reluctantly giving in to the latter:

if I say there were moments when the sun came out
like her hair in the shadows of the leaves, heavy, like
	cream, cut
blunt as a spoon, her small teeth
as she laughed up at me, the bee
humming in my palm as she stroked it, and though I
think hope may be a better guide to the past than despair

I now doubt it, too.

Like many of the poems in this volume, "Lilacs" filters joy and sorrow through the mind of someone wise enough to know that life is also lived in the interstices of these emotions.

In the long poem "Cashion Bridge" Zwicky gestures toward the profundity of the liminal; in this case, the ineffable sensation that can be located on the threshold of experience:

that held breath
between the future and the past that's neither, but is still
the only place we'll ever be arriving
to, the only place it's possible
we are.

Marnie Parsons says of this poem that "what is enacted here is a sensual and cerebral visitation of the pause. The cadences of lines, the variation of phrases, the compounding of words . . . take us into the energies of that moment." Rob McLennan commented in *Books in Canada* (1999) that "Zwicky's is a thinking lyric, with a coherent and complex philosophical musicality." Anne Simpson, in *The Antigonish Review,* says that "This is radiant language; these words are made of light. Sometimes they sear the heart."

In *Songs for Relinquishing the Earth* Zwicky translates philosophical principle into poetic practice: the poems in this book enact the poet's "lyric philosophy," not abstractly, but through the concrete and sensual. In "Being, Polyphony, Lyric: An Open Letter to Robert Bringhurst" (1998) Zwicky says that "a lyric mind is one for which the world lives as a complex, intricately structured, mortal & resonant whole: elapsing through time, that world makes from time the space of what is."

Zwicky's next two publications—*Wisdom & Metaphor* (2003) and *Robinson's Crossing*—earned her a double Governor General's Literary Award nomination in 2004 in the nonfiction and poetry categories, respectively. Like *Lyric Philosophy* and *Wittgenstein Elegies,* these two books reveal complementary aspects of Zwicky's identity as philosopher/poet/musician and therefore stand in contrapuntal relationship to each other.

Wisdom & Metaphor echoes the format and design of *Lyric Philosophy.* The poet's thoughts, or "aphorisms," occupy the verso text, set in apposition to the thoughts of other philosophers and poets, as well as geometrical and gestalt figures. Zwicky justifies her use of this form by noting that it responds to the "demand that form follow sense and . . . to the need to mediate between the lyric and the scholarly." She concludes the foreword with the hope that "the book is able to defend the necessity of both love and wisdom to the continued life of philosophy." As critic Michael Greenstein notes,

"Connecting the linked pages is akin to combining the tenor and vehicle of a metaphor."

While the concepts of "lyric" and "domesticity" that occupied Zwicky in *Lyric Philosophy* are still in evidence in *Wisdom & Metaphor*, here Zwicky focuses on the proposition that "those who think metaphorically are enabled to think truly because the shape of their thinking echoes the shape of the world" (foreword). She undertakes the task of demonstrating this proposition through a diverse range of thinkers: Lilburn, Wittgenstein, Heraclitus, Max Wertheimer, Charles Simic, Simone Weil, Robert Hass, and so forth. In dialogue with these philosophers and poets Zwicky illustrates and defends in "Left" the value of metaphor to an ethical approach to "being" in the world:

> Being is the interconnectedness, the resonant ecology, of things.
> The meaning of what-is is the live, metaphorical relation between things and the resonant structure of the world.

As in *Lyric Philosophy,* Zwicky deliberately confounds the boundary between poetry and philosophy. She also continues to explore the notion of "domesticity" that she first introduced in that volume. She says in the foreword to *Wisdom & Metaphor:*

> My use of "domesticity". . . sets aside connotative associations with clean aprons and contentment to focus on the attempt to lead a life that is neither swept up in the objectifying project of tool-use (which includes the use of language) nor in the impossible goal of sustained lyric comprehension. Domesticity . . . is not so much a static mid-point between these two contrary moments in human desire as it is an active acknowledgement that the tension between them cannot be resolved. It is an attempt to come home to ourselves in the presence of that tension.

A proximate reading of *Wisdom & Metaphor* and *Robinson's Crossing* suggests that it is precisely through metaphor that the journey "home to ourselves" is undertaken and communicated.

The poems in *Robinson's Crossing* are presented in three sections, or movements, but the book is unified by its focus on "domesticity" through an exploration of personal and family history. The poems return to places in the poet-speaker's past, notably Fredericton and the homestead on the Paddle River near Mayerthorpe, Alberta. Memory is metaphorically invoked in the opening poem, "Prairie," by "the big hasp on the underside [of the farmhouse kitchen table] that locked the two main leaves." Later in the poem, the speaker experiences "some rusty weight in my chest stick / then give, a slow opening to the sky." As if recognizing the potential of such excavation of personal history to descend into

mere sentiment and cliché, however, in "Nostalgia" the speaker questions her sudden irrational attachment to an object from her past—her grandmother's clock—discovered after her grandmother has been consigned to a nursing home. The speaker realizes, finally, that her nostalgia is for something that never was.

In keeping with the larger theme of exploring the past, several of the poems in this volume are titled "History" but are distinguished from each other by italicized subtitles that refer to particular classical musical compositions. Some of these poems link memory and history mnemonically to the aural senses. This linkage is most evident in the poem that closes the volume, "Glen Gould: Bach's 'Italian' Concerto, BWV 971":

> North of Superior, November,
> bad weather behind, more
> coming in from the west, the car windows furred
> with salt, the genius of his fingers
> bright, incongruous, cresting a ridge
> and without warning the sky
> has been swept clear . . .
> . . . .
> I'd stepped into my real life, the one
> that's always here, right here,
> but outside history. . . .

Memory is also inscribed in, as well as erased from, particular childhood landscapes that haunt the speaker. In three long poems in the middle of the volume—"Robinson's Crossing," "Track," and the prose poem "Black Spruce"—Zwicky returns to the homestead in Mayerthorpe and creates a palimpsest of the alterations wrought on the landscape by human and natural actors. Mere traces of that history can be located in snatches of family legend, arrowheads found in a plowed field, a grandmother's failing memory, and overgrown wagon tracks. In these and many other poems in the volume the speaker is haunted by a past that both occupies and eludes her.

Both *Wisdom & Metaphor* and *Robinson's Crossing* met with considerable critical success, each receiving a Governor General's Literary Award nomination. Allison Sivak, in a review for *Canadian Book Review Annual* (2003), called *Wisdom & Metaphor* "an outstanding example of small-press printing, a true collaboration between the author and the press, and a fascinating philosophical work that will continue to provide insight as it is reread." *Wisdom & Metaphor* was reviewed widely in poetry journals, and it was also the focus of a long discussion among Simpson, Brian Bartlett, and Ross Leckie in the Winter 2004 issue of *Fiddlehead*. In his review of *Robinson's Crossing* in the *Saskatoon Star-Phoenix* (26 February 2005) Bill Robertson said that "Rather than layer her poems with philosophical concept and conjecture, or jam them with tricks of language and catalogues of synonyms for desire, Zwicky goes for the clean line, the open image." George Murray in the *Globe and Mail* (Toronto) for 11 December 2004, while conceding that *Robinson's Crossing* is "not as strong as . . . Songs for Relinquishing the Earth,* argued that "when she finds the right subject and dips deep for words, . . . this is as good as anything by Anne Carson or Sharon Olds."

Zwicky's next major publication, *Thirty-Seven Small Songs & Thirteen Silences* (2005), is composed entirely of lyric poems. Twenty-one of the thirty-seven "songs" were previously published in a limited-edition (146 copies) Barbarian Press volume, *Twenty-One Small Songs* (2000). The titles of both volumes are self-explanatory. The latter book comprises thirty-seven "Small Songs" addressed to various ideas and objects with which the poet feels a deep connection, while the "Thirteen Silences" consist of "Seven Studies," poems focused primarily on nature, and "Six Variations on Silence," a series of six short imagistic poems. None of these poems takes up more than a single page; the closing "Variations" are two or three lines long. A sampling of the "song" titles gives some indication of their precision and focus: "Small Song: Anger," "Small Song: Bath," "Small Song: Blue," "Small song in praise of ears." Best described as lyrical meditations on or apostrophes to (mostly) concrete objects, the poems in the first two parts of this volume illustrate one of Zwicky's most important poetic principles: close observation of the "thing" itself. In the simply titled "Small Song," for example, the poet-speaker evokes concretely the abstract meaning of the end of summer with the precise image of an abandoned object: "The window will fill up with stars. My straw hat / will hang upon the wall."

In the section "Six Variations on Silence" Zwicky turns to a modified haiku form to capture, in a more condensed and imagistic form than that found in the "Songs" and "Studies," those moments of insight that rely on association and gesture, rather than analytic thought. Once again, nature provides the inspiration for most of these poems:

> Deep in the ravine, pollen settles
> to the eddy's swirl. You could watch all day
> and never see it move

In these poems Zwicky practices the art of observing and "knowing" that she advocates in *Wisdom & Metaphor:* "Being is the interconnectedness, the resonant ecology, of things."

Jan Zwicky continues to combine her interests in philosophy, poetry, music, and ecology. She currently teaches part-time at the University of Victoria, most recently designing and teaching a general introduction to the humanities, while continuing to write poetry with an ecological and ethical focus, informed by the wordless rhythms of music. Poetry, as she made clear in her Governor General's Literary Award acceptance speech in 1999, is also serious, life-altering, and ethical work: "Lyric art is intimate–when it is good it is always, whatever its medium, a struggle to achieve an integrity of spirit, body, and mind. When we engage with it, we are forced to reflect on the degree of our own integrity, and in so doing, we may be led to see that we must change our lives."

Interview:

Anne Simpson, "There Is No Place That Does Not See You," in *Where the Words Come From: Canadian Poets in Conversation,* edited by Tim Bowling (Roberts Creek, B.C.: Nightwood, 2002).

References:

Brian Bartlett, Ross Leckie, and Anne Simpson, "In Conversation: Brian Bartlett, Ross Leckie, and Anne Simpson Discuss Jan Zwicky's *Wisdom & Metaphor,*" *Fiddlehead,* 222 (Winter 2004): 83–104;

Marnie Parsons, "Poetry," *University of Toronto Quarterly,* 68, no. 1 (1999): 275–306;

Peter Sanger, "Almost blind with light. . . .: Jan Zwicky," *Antigonish Review,* 136 (2004): 7–14;

Simpson, "Three Women Poets," *Antigonish Review,* 120 (Winter 2000): 153–155.

Appendices:
Literary Awards in Canada
The Canada Council

Appendix 1: Literary Awards in Canada

Christian Riegel
University of Regina

Canadian writers are recognized by national and provincial-level awards. This appendix outlines the main awards and lists the winners.

The longest-standing awards are the Governor General's Literary Awards, which have been presented since 1936 and are considered the pinnacle of recognition in the nation in all but two categories. The Giller Prize for Fiction, inaugurated in 1994, rapidly became the highest-profile award in that area. A comparable award, the Griffin Trust Prize for Excellence in Poetry, was created in 2001. The Writers' Trust of Canada Awards are administered by a nonprofit organization devoted to the welfare of Canadian authors. The Canadian Booksellers Association and the Canadian Authors Association maintain awards programs in the major categories of writing. The Amazon.ca/Books in Canada First Novel Award recognizes work by a new novelist. The Chalmers Awards were major prizes for playwrights until they were discontinued in 2002.

British Columbia, Alberta, Saskatchewan, and Manitoba provide comprehensive and well-promoted literary awards that are primarily organized by provincial arts boards and writers' organizations. A comparable set of awards is presented by the Nova Scotia Writers' Federation to recognize both Nova Scotian writing and writing from the larger Atlantic Canada region; they are the only regional writing awards in the country. The other Atlantic provinces—New Brunswick and Newfoundland and Labrador—maintain modest awards programs, as do the two largest provinces, Ontario and Quebec.

National-Level Awards

Governor General's Literary Awards

The first Governor General's Literary Awards were organized by the Canadian Authors Association (CAA) in 1936 and were presented by Governor General Sir John Buchan, first Baron Tweedsmuir, the author of the novel *The Thirty-Nine Steps* (1915). The Canada Council for the Arts, established in 1957, began sponsoring the awards in 1959, though the CAA continued to administer them until 1971. The awards were initially given for fiction and nonfiction written in English; over the years the categories of poetry, drama, translation, and children's literature—illustration and text—were added. Parallel French-language awards were added in 1959. There was no monetary prize until $250 was awarded in 1951; the amount has now grown to $15,000. The publisher of each winning book receives $3,000 to support promotional activities. Each nonwinning finalist—currently there are five, but the number has varied over the years—receives $1,000, bringing the total value of the awards to more than $300,000.

2006

ENGLISH

Fiction: Peter Behrens, *The Law of Dreams*

Poetry: John Pass, *Stumbling in the Bloom*

Drama: Daniel MacIvor, *I Still Love You*

Nonfiction: Ross King, *The Judgement of Paris: The Revolutionary Decade That Gave the World Impressionism*

Children's Literature–Illustration: Leo Yerxa, *Ancient Thunder*

Children's Literature–Text: William Gilkerson, *Pirate's Passage*

Translation (French to English): Hugh Hazelton, *Vetiver*, by Joël Des Rosiers

FRENCH

Fiction: Andrée Laberge, *La rivière du loup*

Poetry: Hélène Dorion, *Ravir: les lieux*

Drama: Evèlyne de la Chenelière, *Désordre public*

Nonfiction: Pierre Ouellet, *A force de voir: histoire de regards*

Children's Literature–Illustration: Rogé (Roger Girard), *Le gros monstre qui amait trop lire*

Children's Literature–Text: Dany Laferrière, *Je suis fou de Vava*

Translation (English to French): Sophie Voillot, *Un jardin de papier,* by Thomas Wharton

2005

ENGLISH

Fiction: David Gilmour, *A Perfect Night to Go to China*

Poetry: Anne Compton, *Processional*

Drama: John Mighton, *Half Life*

Nonfiction: John Vaillant, *The Golden Spruce: A True Story of Myth, Madness and Greed*

Children's Literature–Illustration: Rob Gonsalves, *Imagine a Day*

Children's Literature–Text: Pamela Porter, *The Crazy Man*

Translation (French to English): Fred A. Reed, *Truth or Death: The Quest for Immortality in the Western Narrative Tradition,* by Thierry Hentsch

FRENCH

Fiction: Aki Shimazaki, *Hotaru*

Poetry: Jean-Marc Desgent, *Vingtièmes siècles*

Drama: Geneviève Billette, *Le Pays des genoux*

Nonfiction: Michel Bock, *Quand la nation débordait les frontières: les minorités françaises dans la pensée de Lionel Groulx*

Children's Literature–Illustration: Isabelle Arsenault, *Le cœur de monsieur Gauguin*

Children's Literature–Text: Camille Bouchard, *Le Ricanement des hyènes*

Translation (English to French): Rachel Martinez, *Glenn Gould: une vie,* by Kevin Bazzana

2004

ENGLISH

Fiction: Miriam Toews, *A Complicated Kindness*

Poetry: Roo Borson, *Short Journey Upriver toward Ōishida*

Drama: Morris Panych, *Girl in the Goldfish Bowl*

Nonfiction: Lt.-Gen. Roméo Dallaire, *Shake Hands with the Devil: The Failure of Humanity in Rwanda*

Children's Literature–Illustration: Stéphane Jorisch, *Jabberwocky*

Children's Literature–Text: Kenneth Oppel, *Airborn*

Translation (French to English): Judith Elaine Cowan, *Mirabel,* by Pierre Nepveu

FRENCH

Fiction: Pascale Quiviger, *Le cercle parfait*

Poetry: André Brochu, *Les jours à vif*

Drama: Emma Haché, *L'intimité*

Nonfiction: Jean-Jacques Simard, *La Réduction: L'autochtone inventé et les Améindiens d'aujourd'hui*

Children's Literature–Illustration: Janice Nadeau, *Nul poisson où aller*

Children's Literature–Text: Nicole Leroux, *L'Hiver de Léo Polatouche*

Translation (English to French): Ivan Steenhout, *Les Indes accidentelles,* by Robert Finley

2003

ENGLISH

Fiction: Douglas Glover, *Elle*

Poetry: Tim Lilburn, *Kill-site*

Drama: Vern Thiessen, *Einstein's Gift*

Nonfiction: Margaret MacMillan, *Paris 1919: Six Months That Changed the World*

Children's Literature–Illustration: Allen Sapp, *The Song within My Heart*

Children's Literature–Text: Glen Huser, *Stitches*

Translation (French to English): Jane Brierley, *Memoirs of a Less Travelled Road: A Historian's Life,* by Marcel Trudel

FRENCH

Fiction: Elise Turcotte, *La maison étrangère*

Poetry: Pierre Nepveu, *Lignes aériennes*

Drama: Jean-Rock Gaudreault, *Deux pas ver les étoiles*

Nonfiction: Thierry Hentsch, *Raconter et mourir: aux sources narratives de l'imaginaire occidental*

Children's Literature–Illustration: Virginie Egger, *Recette d'éléphant à la sauce vieux pneu*

Children's Literature–Text: Danielle Simard, *J'ai vendu ma soeur*

Translation (English to French): Agnès Guitard, *Un Amour de Salomé,* by Linda Leith

2002

ENGLISH

Fiction: Gloria Sawai, *A Song for Nettie Johnson*

Poetry: Roy Miki, *Surrender*

Drama: Kevin Kerr, *Unite (1918)*

Nonfiction: Andrew Nikiforuk, *Saboteurs: Wiebo Ludwig's War against Big Oil*

Children's Literature–Illustration: Wallace Edwards, *Alphabeasts*

Children's Literature–Text: Martha Brooks, *True Confessions of a Heartless Girl*

Translation (French to English): Nigel Spencer, *Thunder and Light,* by Marie Claire Blais

FRENCH

Fiction: Monique LaRue, *La Gloire de Cassiodore*

Poetry: Robert Dickson, *Humains paysages en temps de paix relative*

Drama: Daniel Danis, *Le Langue-à-Langue des chiens de roche*

Nonfiction: Judith Lavoie, *Mark Twain et la parole noire*

Children's Literature–Illustration: Luc Melanson, *Le grand voyage de Monsieur*

Children's Literature–Text: Hélène Vachon, *L'oiseau de passage*

Translation (English to French): Paul Pierre-Noyart, *Histoire universelle de la chasteté et du célibat*, by Elizabeth Abbott

2001

ENGLISH

Fiction: Richard B. Wright, *Clara Callan*

Poetry: George Elliott Clarke, *Execution Poems*

Drama: Kent Stetson, *The Harps of God*

Nonfiction: Thomas Homer-Dixon, *The Ingenuity Gap*

Children's Literature–Illustration: Mireille Levert, *An Island in the Soup*

Children's Literature–Text: Arthur Slade, *Dust*

Translation (French to English): Fred A. Reed and David Homel, *Fairy Ring,* by Martine Desjardins

FRENCH

Fiction: Andrée A. Michaud, *Le ravissement*

Poetry: Paul Chanel Malenfant, *Des ombres portées*

Drama: Normand Chaurette, *Le Petit Köchel*

Nonfiction: Renée Dupuis, *Quel Canada pour les Autochtones? La fin de l'exclusion*

Children's Literature–Illustration: Bruce Roberts, *Fidèles éléphants*

Children's Literature–Text: Christiane Duchesne, *Jomusch et le troll des cuisines*

Translation (English to French): Michel Saint-Germain, *No Logo: La Tyrannie des marques,* by Naomi Klein

2000

ENGLISH

Fiction: Michael Ondaatje, *Anil's Ghost*

Poetry: Don McKay, *Another Gravity*

Drama: Timothy Findley, *Elizabeth Rex*

Nonfiction: Nega Mezlekia, *Notes from the Hyena's Belly*

Children's Literature–Illustration: Marie-Louise Gay, *Yuck, a Love Story*

Children's Literature–Text: Deborah Ellis, *Looking for X*

Translation (French to English): Robert Majzels, *Just Fine,* by France Daigel

FRENCH

Fiction: Jean Marc Dalpé, *Un vent se lève qui éparpille*

Poetry: Normand de Bellefeuille, *La Marche de l'aveugle sans son chien*

Drama: Wajdi Mouawad, *Littoral*

Nonfiction: Gérard Bouchard, *Genèse des nations et cultures du Nouveau Monde*

Children's Literature–Illustration: Anne Villeneuve, *L'Écharpe rouge*

Children's Literature–Text: Charlotte Gingras, *Un été de Jade*

Translation (English to French): Lori Saint-Martin and Paul Gagné, *Un parfum de cèdre,* by Ann-Marie MacDonald

1999

ENGLISH

Fiction: Matt Cohen, *Elizabeth and After*

Poetry: Jan Zwicky, *Songs for Relinquishing the Earth*

Drama: Michael Healey, *The Drawer Boy*

Nonfiction: Marq de Villiers, *Water*

Children's Literature–Illustration: Gary Clement, *The Great Poochini*

Children's Literature–Text: Rachna Gilmore, *A Screaming Kind of Day*

Translation (French to English): Patricia Claxton, *Gabrielle Roy: A Life,* by François Ricard

FRENCH

Fiction: Lise Tremblay, *La danse juive*

Poetry: Herménégilde Chiasson, *Conversations*

Drama: Jean Marc Dalpé, *Il n'y a que l'amour*

Nonfiction: Pierre Perrault, *Le Mal du Nord*

Children's Literature–Illustration: Stephane Jorish, *Charlotte et l'île du destin*

Children's Literature–Text: Charlotte Gingras, *La Liberté? Connais pas . . .*

Translation (English to French): Jacques Brault, *Transfiguration,* by E. D. Blodgett

1998

ENGLISH

Fiction: Diane Schoemperlen, *Forms of Devotion*

Poetry: Stephanie Bolster, *White Stone: The Alice Poems*

Drama: Djanet Sears, *Harlem Duet*

Nonfiction: David Adams Richards, *Lines on the Water: A Fisherman's Life on the Miramichi*

Children's Literature–Illustration: Kady MacDonald Denton, *A Child's Treasury of Nursery Rhymes*

Children's Literature–Text: Janet Lunn, *The Hollow Tree*

Translation (French to English): Sheila Fischman, *Bambi and Me,* by Michel Tremblay

FRENCH

Fiction: Christiane Frenette, *La Terre ferme*

Poetry: Suzanne Jacob, *La Part de feu précédé de Le Deuil de la rancune*

Drama: François Archambault, *15 secondes*

Nonfiction: Pierre Nepveu, *Intérieurs du Nouveau Monde: Essais sur les littératures du Québec et des Amériques*

Children's Literature–Illustration: Pierre Pratt, *Monsieur Ilétaitunefois*

Children's Literature–Text: Angèle Delaunois, *Variations sur un même "t'aime"*

Translation (English to French): Charlotte Melançon, *Les Sources du moi–La Formation de l'identité moderne,* by Charles Taylor

1997

ENGLISH

Fiction: Jane Urquhart, *The Underpainter*

Poetry: Dionne Brand, *Land to Light On*

Drama: Ian Ross, *fareWel*

Nonfiction: Rachel Manley, *Drumblair–Memories of a Jamaican Childhood*

Children's Literature–Illustration: Barbara Reid, *The Party*

Children's Literature–Text: Kit Pearson, *Awake and Dreaming*

Translation (French to English): Howard Scott, *The Euguelion,* by Louky Bersianik

FRENCH

Fiction: Aude (Claudette Charbonneau-Tissot), *Cet imperceptible mouvement*

Poetry: Pierre Nepveu, *Romans-fleuves*

Drama: Yvan Bienvenue, *Dits et Inédits*

Nonfiction: Roland Viau, *Enfants du néant et mangeurs d'âmes–Gueure, culture et société en Iroquoisie ancienne*

Children's Literature–Illustration: Stéphane Poulin, *Poil serpent, dent d'araignée*

Children's Literature–Text: Michel Noël, *Pien*

Translation (English to French): Marie José Thériault, *Arracher les montagnes,* by Neil Bissoondath

1996

ENGLISH

Fiction: Guy Vanderhaeghe, *The Englishman's Boy*

Poetry: E. D. Blodgett, *Apostrophes: Woman at a Piano*

Drama: Colleen Wagner, *The Monument*

Nonfiction: John Ralston Saul, *The Unconscious Civilization*

Children's Literature–Illustration: Eric Beddows, *The Rooster's Gift*

Children's Literature–Text: Paul Yee, *Ghost Train*

Translation (French to English): Linda Gaboriau, *Stone and Ashes,* by Daniel Danis

FRENCH

Fiction: Mari-Claire Blais, *Soifs*

Poetry: Serge Patrice Thibodeau, *Le Quatuor de l'errance suivi de La Traversée du désert*

Drama: Normand Chaurette, *Le Passage de l'Indiana*

Nonfiction: Michel Freitag, *Le Naufrage de l'université-Et autres essais d'épistémologies politique*

Children's Literature–Illustration: No prize awarded

Children's Literature–Text: Gilles Tibo, *Noémie–Le Secret de Madame Lumbago*

Translation (English to French): Christiane Teasdale, *Systèmes de survie: Dialogue sure les fondaments moraux du commerce et de la politique,* by Jane Jacobs

1995

ENGLISH

Fiction: Greg Hollingshead, *The Roaring Girl*

Poetry: Anne Szumigalski, *Voice*

Drama: Jason Sherman, *Three in the Black, Two in the Head*

Nonfiction: Rosemary Sullivan, *Shadow Maker: The Life of Gwendolyn MacEwen*

Children's Literature–Illustration: Ludmila Zeman, *The Last Quest of Gilgamesh*

Children's Literature–Text: Tim Wynne-Jones, *The Maestro*

Translation (French to English): David Homel, *Why Must a Black Writer Write about Sex?* by Dany Laferrière

FRENCH

Fiction: Nicole Houde, *Les Oiseaux de Saint-John Perse*

Poetry: Emile Martel, *Pour orchestre et poète seul*

Drama: Carole Fréchette, *Les Quatre Morts de Marie*

Nonfiction: Yvan Lamonde, *Louis-Antoine Dessaulles: Un seigneur libéral et anticlérical*

Children's Literature–Illustration: Annouchka Gravel Galouchko, *Sho et les dragon d'eau*

Children's Literature–Text: Sonia Sarfati, *Comme une peau de chagrin*

Translation (English to French): Hervé Juste, *Entre l'ordre et la liberté,* by Gérald Bernier and Daniel Salée

1994

ENGLISH

Fiction: Rudy Wiebe, *A Discovery of Strangers*

Poetry: Robert Hilles, *Cantos from a Small Room*

Drama: Morris Panych, *The Ends of the Earth*

Nonfiction: John A. Livingston, *Rogue Primate*

Children's Literature–Illustration: Murray Kimber, *Josepha: A Prairie Boy's Story*

Children's Literature–Text: Julie Johnston, *Adam and Eve and Pinch-Me*

Translation (French to English): Donald Winkler, *The Lyric Generation: The Life and Times of the Baby Boomers,* by François Ricard

FRENCH

Fiction: Robert Lalonde, *Le Petit aigle à tête blanche*

Poetry: Fulvio Caccia, *Aknos*

Drama: Michel Ouellette, *French Town*

Nonfiction: Chantal Saint-Jarre, *Du sida*

Children's Literature–Illustration: Pierre Pratt, *Mon chien est un éléphant*

Children's Literature–Text: Suzanne Martel, *Une bell journée pour mourir*

Translation (English to French): Julie Des Chênes, *Le mythe du sauvage,* by Olive Patricia Dickason

1993

ENGLISH

Fiction: Carol Shields, *The Stone Diaries*

Poetry: Don Coles, *Forests of the Medieval World*

Drama: Guilermo Verdecchia, *Fronteras Americanas*

Nonfiction: Karen Connelly, *Touch the Dragon*

Children's Literature–Illustration: Mireille Levert, *Sleep Tight, Mrs. Ming*

Children's Literature–Text: Tim Wynne-Jones, *Some of the Kinder Planets*

Translation (French to English): D. G. Jones, *Categorics: 1, 2 & 3,* by Normand de Bellefeuille

FRENCH

Fiction: Nancy Huston, *Cantique des plaines*

Poetry: Denise Desautels, *Le Saut de l'ange*

Drama: Daniel Danis, *Celle-là*

Nonfiction: François Paré, *Les littératures de l'exiguïté*

Children's Literature–Illustration: Stéphane Jorisch, *Le Monde selon Jean de . . .*

Children's Literature–Text: Michèle Marineau, *La Route de Chlifa*

Translation (English to French): Marie José Thériault, *L'Oeuvre du Gallois,* by Robert Walshe

1992

ENGLISH

Fiction: Michael Ondaatje, *The English Patient*

Poetry: Lorna Crozier, *Inventing the Hawk*

Drama: John Mighton, *Possible Worlds and A Short History of the Night*

Nonfiction: Maggie Siggins, *Revenge of the Land: A Century of Greed, Tragedy and Murder*

Children's Literature–Illustration: Ron Lightburn, *Waiting for the Whales*

Children's Literature–Text: Julie Johnston, *Hero of Lesser Causes*

Translation (French to English): Fred A. Reed, *Imagining the Middle East,* by Thierry Hentsch

FRENCH

Fiction: Anne Hébert, *L'enfant chargé de songes*

Poetry: Gilles Cyr, *Andromède attendra*

Drama: Louis-Dominique Lavigne, *Les petits orteils*

Nonfiction: Pierre Turgeon, *La Radissonie: Le pays de la baie James*

Children's Literature–Illustration: Gilles Tibo, *Simon et la ville de carton*

Children's Literature–Text: Christiane Duchesne, *Victor*

Translation (English to French): Jean Papineau, *La mémoire postmoderne: Essai sur l'art canadienne contemporain,* by Mark A. Cheetham and Linda Hutcheon

1991

ENGLISH

Fiction: Rohinton Mistry, *Such a Long Journey*

Poetry: Don McKay, *Night Field*

Drama: Joan MacLeod, *Amigo's Blue Guitar*

Nonfiction: Robert Hunter and Robert Calihoo, *Occupied Canada: A Young White Man Discovers His Unsuspected Past*

Children's Literature–Illustration: Joanne Fitzgerald, *Doctor Kiss Says Yes*

Children's Literature–Text: Sarah Ellis, *Pick-Up Sticks*

Translation (French to English): Albert W. Halsall, *A Dictionary of Literary Devices: Gradus, A–Z,* by Bernard Marie Dupriez

FRENCH

Fiction: André Brochu, *La Croix du Nord*

Poetry: Madeleine Gagnon, *Chant pour un Québec lointan*

Drama: Gilbert Dupuis, *Mon oncle Marcel qui vague près du métro Berri*

Nonfiction: Bernand Arcand, *Le Jaguar et le Tamanoir*

Children's Literature–Illustration: Sheldon Cohen, *Un champion*

Children's Literature–Text: François Gravel, *Deux heures et demie avant Jasmine*

Translation (English to French): Jean-Paul Sainte-Marie and Brigitte Chabert Hackiyan, *Les Enfants d'Aataentsic: L'histoire du peuple huron*, by Bruce G. Trigger

1990

ENGLISH

Fiction: Nino Ricci, *Lives of the Saints*

Poetry: Margaret Avison, *No Time*

Drama: Ann-Marie MacDonald, *Goodnight Desdemona (Good Morning Juliet)*

Nonfiction: Stephen Clarkson and Christina McCall, *Trudeau and Our Times*

Children's Literature–Illustration: Paul Morin, *The Orphan Boy*

Children's Literature–Text: Michael Bedard, *Redwork*

Translation (French to English): Jane Brierly, *Yellow-Wolf and Other Tales of the Saint Lawrence*, by Philippe Aubert de Gaspé

FRENCH

Fiction: Gérald Tougas, *La Mauvaise foi*

Poetry: Jean-Paul Daoust, *Les Cendres bleues*

Drama: Jovette Marchessault, *Le Voyage magnifique d'Emily Carr*

Nonfiction: Jean-François Lisée, *Dans l'oeil de l'aigle*

Children's Literature–Illustration: Pierre Pratt, *Les Fantaisies de l'oncle Henri*

Children's Literature–Text: Christiane Duchesne, *La Vraie histoire du chien de Clara Vic*

Translation (English to French): Charlotte Melançon and Robert Melançon, *Le Second Rouleau*, by A. M. Klein

1989

ENGLISH

Fiction: Paul Quarrington, *Whale Music*

Poetry: Heather Spears, *The Word for Sand*

Drama: Judith Thompson, *The Other Side of the Dark*

Nonfiction: Robert Calder, *Willie: The Life of W. Somerset Maugham*

Children's Literature–Illustration: Robin Muller, *The Magic Paintbrush*

Children's Literature–Text: Diana Wieler, *Bad Boy*

Translation (French to English): Wayne Grady, *On the Eighth Day*, by Antonine Maillet

FRENCH

Fiction: Louis Hamelin, *La Rage*

Poetry: Pierre Desruisseaux, *Monème*

Drama: Michel Garneau, *Mademoiselle Rouge*

Nonfiction: Lise Noël, *L'Intolérance: Une problématique générale*

Children's Literature–Illustration: Stéphane Poulin, *Benjamin et la saga des oreillers*

Children's Literature–Text: Charles Montpetit, *Temps mort*

Translation (English to French): Jean Antonin Billard, *Les Ages de l'amour*, by Dorothy Livesay

1988

ENGLISH

Fiction: David Adams Richards, *Nights below Station Street*

Poetry: Erin Mouré, *Furious*

Drama: George F. Walker, *Nothing Sacred*

Nonfiction: Anne Collins, *In the Sleep Room*

Children's Literature–Illustration: Kim LaFave, *Amos's Sweater*

Children's Literature–Text: Welwyn Wilton Katz, *The Third Magic*

Translation (French to English): Philip Stratford, *Second Chance*

FRENCH

Fiction: Jacques Folch-Ribas, *Le Silence ou le Parfait Bonheur*

Poetry: Marcel Labine, *Papiers d'épidémie*

Drama: Jean Marc Dalpé, *Le Chien*

Nonfiction: Patricia Smart: *Ecrire dans la maison du père*

Children's Literature–Illustration: Philippe Béha, *Les Jeux de Pic-Mots*

Children's Literature–Text: Michèle Marineau, *Cassopée ou L'Eté Polonais*

Translation (English to French): Didier Holtzwarth, *Nucléus*, by Robert Bothwell

1987

ENGLISH

Fiction: M. T. Kelly, *A Dream Like Mine*

Poetry: Gwendolyn MacEwen, *Afterworlds*

Drama: John Krizanc, *Prague*

Nonfiction: Michael Ignatieff, *The Russian Album*

Children's Literature–Illustration: Marie-Louise Gay, *Rainy Day Magic*

Children's Literature–Text: Morgan Nyberg, *Galahad Schwartz and the Cockroach Army*

Translation (English to French): Patricia Claxton, *Enchantment and Sorrow: The Autobiography of Gabrielle Roy*

FRENCH

    Fiction: Gilles Archambault, *L'Obsédante obèse et autres agressions*

    Poetry: Fernand Ouellette, *Les Heures*

    Drama: Jeanne-Mance Delisle, *Un oiseau vivant dans la gueule*

    Nonfiction: Jean Larose, *La Petite Noirceur*

    Children's Literature–Illustration: Darcia Labross, *Venir au monde*

    Children's Literature–Text: David Schinkel and Yves Beauchesne, *Le Don*

    Translation (English to French): Ivan Steenhout and Christiane Teasdale, *L'homme qui se croyait aimé; ou, La vie secrète d'un premier ministre*, by Heather Robertson

1986

ENGLISH

    Fiction: Alice Munro, *The Progress of Love*

    Poetry: Al Purdy, *The Collected Poems of Al Purdy*

    Drama: Sharon Pollock, *Doc*

    Nonfiction: Northrop Frye, *Northrop Frye on Shakespeare*

FRENCH

    Fiction: Yvon Rivard, *Les silences du corbeau*

    Poetry: Cécile Cloutier, *L'écouté*

    Drama: Anne Legault, *La visite des sauvages*

    Nonfiction: Régine Robin, *Le réalisme socialiste: une esthétique impossible*

1985

ENGLISH

    Fiction: Margaret Atwood, *The Handmaid's Tale*

    Poetry: Fred Wah, *Waiting for Saskatchewan*

    Drama: George F. Walker, *Criminals in Love*

    Nonfiction: Ramsay Cook, *The Regenerators: Social Criticism in Late Victorian English Canada*

FRENCH

    Fiction: Fernand Ouellette, *Lucie ou un midi en novembre*

    Poetry: André Roy, *Action Writing*

    Drama: Maryse Pelletier, *Duo pour voix obstinées*

    Nonfiction: François Ricard, *La littérature contre elle-même*

1984

ENGLISH

    Fiction: Joseph Skvorecky, *The Engineer of Human Souls*

    Poetry: Paulette Jiles, *Celestial Navigation*

    Drama: Judith Thompson, *White Biting Dog*

    Nonfiction: Sandra Gwyn, *The Private Capital: Ambition and Love in the Age of MacDonald and Laurier*

FRENCH

    Fiction: Jacques Brault, *Agonie*

    Poetry: Nicole Brossard, *Double Impression*

    Drama: René-Daniel Dubois, *Ne blâmez jamais les Bédouins*

    Nonfiction: Jacques Hamelin and Nicole Gagnon, *Le XXe siècle: Histoire du catholicisme québecois*

1983

ENGLISH

    Fiction: Leon Rooke, *Shakespeare's Dog*

    Poetry: David Donnell, *Settlements*

    Drama: Anne Chislett, *Quiet in the Land*

    Nonfiction: Jeffrey Williams, *Byng of Vimy: General and Governor General*

FRENCH:

    Fiction: Suzanne Jacob, *Laura Laur*

    Poetry: Suzanne Paradis, *Un goût de sel*

    Drama: René Gingras, *Syncope*

    Nonfiction: Maurice Cusson, *Le contrôle socials du crime*

1982

ENGLISH

    Fiction: Guy Vanderhaeghe, *Man Descending*

    Poetry: Phyllis Webb, *The Vision Tree: Selected Poems*

    Drama: John Gray, *Billy Bishop Goes to War, a Play by John Gray with Eric Peterson*

    Nonfiction: Christopher Moore, *Louisbourg Portraits: Life in an Eighteenth-Century Garrison Town*

FRENCH

    Fiction: Roger Fournier, *Le cercle des arènes*

    Poetry: Michel Savard, *Forages*

    Drama: Réjean Ducharme, *Ha ha! . . .*

    Nonfiction: Maurice Lagueux, *Le marxisme des années soixante: une saison dans l'histoire de la pensée critique*

1981

ENGLISH

    Fiction: Mavis Gallant, *Home Truths: Selected Canadian Stories*

    Poetry: F. R. Scott, *The Selected Poems of F. R. Scott*

    Drama: Sharon Pollock, *Blood Relations*

    Nonfiction: George Calef, *Caribou and the Barren-Lands*

FRENCH

    Fiction: Denys Chabot, *La province lunaire*

Poetry: Michel Beaulieu, *Visages*

Drama: Marie Laberge, *C'était avant la guerre de l'Anse à Gilles*

Nonfiction: Madeleine Ouellette-Michalska, *L'échapée des discours de l'oeil*

1980

ENGLISH

Fiction: George Bowering, *Burning Water*

Poetry or Drama: Stephen Scobie, *McAlmon's Chinese Opera*

Nonfiction: Jeffrey Simpson, *Discipline of Power: The Conservative Interlude and the Liberal Restoration*

FRENCH

Fiction: Pierre Turgeon, *La première personne*

Poetry or Drama: Michel van Schenkel, *De l'oeil et de l'écoute*

Nonfiction: Maurice Champagne-Gilbert, *La famille et l'homme à délivrer du pouvoir*

1979

ENGLISH

Fiction: Jack Hodgins, *The Resurrection of Joseph Bourne*

Poetry or Drama: Michael Ondaatje, *There's a Trick with a Knife I'm Learning to Do*

Nonfiction: Maria Tippett, *Emily Carr: A Biography*

FRENCH

Fiction: Marie-Claire Blais, *Le sourd dans la ville*

Poetry or Drama: Robert Melançon, *Peinture aveugle*

Nonfiction: Dominique Clift and Sheila McLeod Arnopolous, *Le Fait Anglais au Québec*

1978

ENGLISH

Fiction: Alice Munro, *Who Do You Think You Are?*

Poetry or Drama: Patrick Lane, *Poems New and Selected*

Nonfiction: Roger Caron, *Go Boy*

FRENCH

Fiction: Jacques Poulin, *Les grandes marées*

Poetry or Drama: Gilbert Langevin, *Mon refuge est un volcan*

Nonfiction: François-Marc Gagnon, *Paul-Emile Borduas: Biographie critique et analyse de l'oeuvre*

1977

ENGLISH

Fiction: Timothy Findley, *The Wars*

Poetry or Drama: D. G. Jones, *Under the Thunder the Flowers Light Up the Earth*

Nonfiction: Frank Scott, *Essays on the Constitution*

FRENCH

Fiction: Gabrielle Roy, *Ces enfants de ma vie*

Poetry or Drama: Michel Garneau, *Les célébrations et Adidou Adidouce* (declined)

Nonfiction: Denis Monière, *Le Développement des idéologies au Québec des origines à nos jours*

1976

ENGLISH

Fiction: Marian Engel, *Bear*

Poetry or Drama: Joe Rosenblatt, *Top Soil*

Nonfiction: Carl Berger, *The Writing of Canadian History*

FRENCH

Fiction: André Major, *Les rescapés*

Poetry or Drama: Alphonse Piché, *Poèmes 1946–1968*

Nonfiction: Fernand Ouellet, *Les Bas Canada 1791–1840, changement structuraux et crise*

1975

ENGLISH

Fiction: Brian Moore, *The Great Victorian Collection*

Poetry or Drama: Milton Acorn, *The Island Means Minago*

Nonfiction: Marion MacRae and Anthony Adamson, *Hallowed Walls*

FRENCH

Fiction: Anne Hébert, *Les enfants du sabbat*

Poetry or Drama: Pierre Perrault, *Chouennes*

Nonfiction: Louis-Edmond Hamelin, *Nordicité canadienne*

1974

ENGLISH

Fiction: Margaret Laurence, *The Diviners*

Poetry or Drama: Ralph Gustafson, *Fire on Stone*

Nonfiction: Charles Ritchie, *The Siren Years*

FRENCH

Fiction: Victor-Levy Beaulieu, *Don Quichotte de la démanche*

Poetry or Drama: Nicole Brossard, *Mécanique jongleuse suivi de Masculin grammaticale*

Nonfiction: Louise Dechêne, *Habitants et marchands de Montréal au XVIIe siécle*

1973

ENGLISH

Fiction: Rudy Wiebe, *The Temptations of Big Bear*

Poetry or Drama: Miriam Mandel, *Lions at Her Face*

Nonfiction: Michael Bell, *Painters in a New Land*

FRENCH

Fiction: Réjean Ducharme, *L'hiver de force*

Poetry or Drama: Roland Giguère, *La main au feu* (declined)

Nonfiction: Albert Faucher, *Québec en Amérique au XIXe siècle*

1972

ENGLISH

Fiction: Robertson Davies, *The Manticore*

Poetry or Drama: Dennis Lee, *Civil Elegies and Other Poems;* John Newlove, *Lies*

FRENCH

Fiction: Antonine Maillet, *Don l'Original*

Poetry or Drama: Gilles Hénault, *Signaux pour les voyants*

Nonfiction: Jean Hamelin and Yves Roby, *Histoire économique du Québec 1851–1896*

1971

ENGLISH

Fiction: Mordecai Richler, *St. Urbain's Horseman*

Poetry or Drama: John Glassco, *Selected Poems*

Nonfiction: Pierre Berton, *The Last Spike*

FRENCH

Fiction: Gérard Bessette, *Le cycle*

Poetry or Drama: Paul-Martin Lapointe, *Le réel absolu*

Nonfiction: Gérald Fortin, *La fin d'un règne*

1970

ENGLISH

Fiction: Dave Godfrey, *The New Ancestors*

Poetry or Drama: bpNichol, *Still Water, The True Eventual Story of Billy the Kid, Beach Head, The cosmic chef: an evening of concrete*

Prose and Poetry: Michael Ondaatje, *The Collected Works of Billy the Kid*

FRENCH

Fiction: Monique Bosco, *La femme de Loth*

Poetry or Drama: Jacques Brault, *Quand nous serons heureux*

Nonfiction: Fernand Ouellette, *Les actes retrouvés* (declined)

1969

ENGLISH

Fiction: Robert Kroetsch, *The Studhorse Man*

Poetry or Drama: Gwendlyn MacEwen, *The Shadow-Maker;* George Bowering, *Rocky Mountain Foot* and *The Gangs of the Kosmos*

FRENCH

Fiction: Louise Maheux-Forcier, *Une forêt pour Zoé*

Poetry or Drama: Jean-Guy Pilon, *Comme eau retenue*

Nonfiction: Michel Brunet, *Les canadiens après la conquête*

1968

ENGLISH

Fiction: Alice Munro, *Dance of the Happy Shades*

Poetry or Drama: Leonard Cohen, *Selected Poems 1956–68* (declined)

Fiction and Essays: Mordecai Richler, *Cocksure* and *Hunting Tigers under Glass*

FRENCH

Fiction: Hubert Aquin, *Trou de mémoire* (declined); Marie-Claire Blais, *Manuscrits de Pauline Archange*

Nonfiction: Fernand Dumont, *Le lieu de l'homme*

1967

ENGLISH

Poetry or Drama: Eli Mandel, *An Idiot Joy;* Alden Nowlan, *Bread, Wine and Salt*

Nonfiction: Norah Story, *The Oxford Companion to Canadian History and Literature*

FRENCH

Fiction: Jacques Godbout, *Salut Galarneau*

Poetry or Drama: François Loranger, *Encore en cinq minutes*

Nonfiction: Robert-Lionel Séguin, *La civilisation traditionelle de l'"Habitant" aux 17 et 18 siècles*

1966

ENGLISH

Fiction: Margaret Laurence, *A Jest of God*

Poetry or Drama: Margaret Atwood, *The Circle Game*

Nonfiction: George Woodcock, *The Crystal Spirit: A Study of George Orwell*

FRENCH

Fiction: Claire Martin, *La joue droite*

Poetry or Drama: Réjean Ducharme, *L'avalée des avalés*

Nonfiction: Marcel Trudel, *Le comptoir, 1604–1627*

1965

ENGLISH

Poetry or Drama: Alfred Purdy, *The Cariboo Horses*

Nonfiction: James Eayrs, *In Defence of Canada*

FRENCH

Fiction: Gérard Bessette, *L'incubation*

Poetry or Drama: Gilles Vigneault, *Quand les bateaux s'en vont*

Nonfiction: André S. Vachon, *Le temps et l'espace dans l'oeuvre de Paul Claudel*

1964

ENGLISH

Fiction: Douglas LePan, *The Deserter*

Poetry or Drama: Raymond Souster, *The Colour of the Times*

Nonfiction: Phyllis Grosskurth, *John Addington Symonds*

FRENCH

Fiction: Jean-Paul Pinsonneault, *Les terres sèches*

Poetry or Drama: Pierre Perrault, *Au coeur de la rose*

Nonfiction: Réjean Robidoux, *Roger Martin du Gard et la Religion*

1963

ENGLISH

Fiction: Hugh Garner, *Hugh Garner's Best Short Stories*

Nonfiction: J. M. S. Careless, *Brown of the Globe*

FRENCH

Poetry or Drama: Gatien Lapointe, *Ode au Saint-Laurent*

Nonfiction: Gustave Lanctot, *Histoire du Canada*

1962

ENGLISH

Fiction: Kildare Dobbs, *Running to Paradise*

Poetry or Drama: James Reaney, *Twelve Letters to a Small Town* and *The Killdeer and Other Plays*

Nonfiction: Marshall McLuhan, *The Gutenberg Galaxy*

FRENCH

Fiction: Jacques Ferron: *Contes du pays incertain*

Poetry: Jacques Languirand, *Les insolites et les violons de l'automne*

Nonfiction: Gilles Marcotte, *Une littérature se fait*

1961

ENGLISH

Fiction: Malcolm Lowry, *Hear Us O Lord From Heaven Thy Dwelling Place*

Poetry or Drama: Robert Finch, *Acis in Oxford*

Nonfiction: T. A. Goudge, *The Ascent of Life*

FRENCH

Fiction: Yves Thériault, *Ashini*

Nonfiction: Jean Le Moyne, *Convergences*

1960

ENGLISH

Fiction: Brian Moore, *The Luck of Ginger Coffey*

Poetry or Drama: Margaret Avison, *Winter Sun*

Nonfiction: Frank H. Underhill, *In Search of Canadian Liberalism*

FRENCH

Poetry or Drama: Anne Hébert, *Poèmes*

Nonfiction: Paul Toupin, *Souvenirs pour demain*

1959

ENGLISH

Fiction: Hugh MacLennan, *The Watch That Ends the Night*

Poetry or Drama: Irving Layton, *Red Carpet for the Sun*

FRENCH

Fiction: André Giroux, *Malgré tout, la joie*

Nonfiction: Félix-Antoine Savard, *Le barachois*

1958

Fiction: Colin McDougall, *Execution*

Poetry or Drama: James Reaney, *A Suit of Nettles*

Nonfiction: Pierre Berton, *Klondike;* Joyce Hemlow, *The History of Fanny Burney*

Juvenile: Edith L. Sharp, *Nkwala*

1957

Fiction: Gabrielle Roy, *Street of Riches* (translation)

Poetry or Drama: Jay Macpherson, *The Boatman*

Nonfiction: Bruce Hutchison, *Canada: Tomorrow's Giant;* Thomas H. Raddall, *The Path of Destiny*

Juvenile: Kerry Wood, *The Green Chief*

1956

Fiction: Adele Wiseman, *The Sacrifice*

Poetry or Drama: Robert A. D. Ford, *A Window on the North*

Nonfiction: Pierre Berton, *The Mysterious North;* Joseph Lister Rutledge, *Century of Conflict*

Juvenile: Farley Mowat, *Lost in the Barrens*

1955

Fiction: Lionel Shapiro, *The Sixth of June*

Poetry or Drama: Wilfred Watson, *Friday's Child*

Nonfiction: N. J. Berrill, *Man's Emerging Mind;* Donald G. Creighton, *John A. MacDonald, the Old Chieftain*

Juvenile: Kerry Wood, *The Map-Maker*

1954

Fiction: Igor Gouzenko, *The Fall of a Titan*

Poetry or Drama: P. K. Page, *The Metal and the Flower*

Nonfiction: Hugh MacLennan, *Thirty and Three;* A. R. M. Lower, *This Most Famous Stream;*

Juvenile: Marjorie Wilkins Campbell, *The Nor'westers*

1953

Fiction: David Walker, *Digby*

Poetry or Drama: Douglas LePan, *The Net and the Sword*

Nonfiction: N. J. Berrill, *Sex and the Nature of Things;* J. M. S. Careless, *Canada: A Story of Challenge*

Juvenile: John F. Hayes, *Rebels Ride at Night*

1952

Fiction: David Walker, *The Pillar*

Poetry or Drama: E. J. Pratt, *Towards the Last Spike*

Nonfiction: Bruce Hutchison, *The Incredible Canadian;* Donald G. Creighton, *John A. Mac-Donald, the Young Politician*

Juvenile: Marie McPhedran, *Cargoes on the Great Lakes*

1951

Fiction: Morley Callaghan, *The Loved and the Lost*

Poetry or Drama: Charles Bruce, *The Mulgrave Road*

Nonfiction: Josephine Phelan, *The Ardent Exile;* Frank MacKinnon, *The Government of Prince Edward Island*

Juvenile: John F. Hayes, *A Land Divided*

1950

Fiction: Germaine Guèvremont, *The Outlander* (translation)

Poetry or Drama: James Wreford Watson, *Of Time and the Lover*

Nonfiction: Marjorie Wilkins Campbell, *The Saskatchewan;* W. L. Morton, *The Progressive Party of Canada*

Juvenile: Donald Dickie, *The Great Adventure*

1949

Fiction: Philip Child, *Mr. Ames against Time*

Poetry or Drama: James Reaney, *The Red Heart*

Nonfiction: Hugh MacLennan, *Cross-Country;* R. MacGregor Dawson, *Democratic Government in Canada*

Juvenile: R. S. Lambert, *Franklin of the Arctic*

1948

Fiction: Hugh MacLennan, *The Precipice*

Poetry or Drama: A. M. Klein, *The Rocking Chair and Other Poems*

Nonfiction: Thomas H. Raddall, *Halifax, Warden of the North;* C. P. Stacey, *The Canadian Army, 1939–1945*

1947

Fiction: Gabrielle Roy, *The Tin Flute* (translation)

Poetry or Drama: Dorothy Livesay, *Poems for People*

Nonfiction: William Sclater, *Haida;* R. MacGregor Dawson, *The Government of Canada*

1946

Fiction: Winifred Bambrick, *Continental Revue*

Poetry or Drama: Robert Finch, *Poems*

Nonfiction: Frederick Philip Grove, *In Search of Myself;* A. R. M. Lower, *Colony to Nation*

1945

Fiction: Hugh MacLennan, *Two Solitudes*

Poetry or Drama: Earle Birney, *Now Is Time*

Nonfiction: Evelyn M. Richardson, *We Keep a Light;* Ross Munro, *Gauntlet to Overlord*

1944

Fiction: Gwethalyn Graham, *Earth and High Heaven*

Poetry or Drama: Dorothy Livesay, *Day and Night*

Nonfiction: Dorothy Duncan, *Partner in Three Worlds;* Edgar McInnis, *The War: Fourth Year*

1943

Fiction: Thomas H. Raddall, *The Pied Piper of Dipper Creek*

Poetry or Drama: A. J. M. Smith, *News of the Phoenix*

Nonfiction: John D. Robins, *The Incomplete Anglers;* E. K. Brown, *On Canadian Poetry*

1942

Fiction: G. Herbert Sallans, *Little Man*

Poetry or Drama: Earle Birney, *David and Other Poems*

Nonfiction: Bruce Hutchison, *The Unknown Country;* Edgar McInnis, *The Unguarded Frontier*

1941

Fiction: Alan Sullivan, *Three Came to Ville Marie*

Poetry or Drama: Anne Marriott, *Calling Adventurers*

Nonfiction: Emily Carr, *Klee Wyck*

1940

Fiction: Ringuet (pseudonym), *Thirty Acres* (translation)

Poetry or Drama: E. J. Pratt, *Brébeuf and His Brethren*

Nonfiction: J. F. C. Wright, *Slava Bohu*

1939

Fiction: Franklin D. McDowell, *The Champlain Road*

Poetry or Drama: Arthur S. Bourinot, *Under the Sun*

Nonfiction: Laura G. Salverson, *Confessions of an Immigrant's Daughter*

1938

Fiction: Gwethalyn Graham, *Swiss Sonata*

Poetry or Drama: Kenneth Leslie, *By Stubborn Stars*

Nonfiction: John Murray Gibbon, *Canadian Mosaic*

1937

Fiction: Laura G. Salverson, *The Dark Weaver*

Poetry or Drama: E. J. Pratt, *The Fable of the Goats*

Nonfiction: Stephen Leacock, *My Discovery of the West*

1936

Fiction: Bertram Brooker, *Think of the Earth*

Nonfiction: T. B. Roberston, *T.B.R.–Newspaper Pieces*

Scotiabank Giller Prize

The Giller Prize was founded in 1994 by Jack Giller in honor of his wife, Doris, a literary journalist who had died of cancer the previous year. The Giller Prize became the richest award in English-language writing, offering $25,000 in prize money and significant publicity, including a prime-time televised awards ceremony. In 2005, with the corporate sponsorship of Scotiabank, the award was renamed the Scotiabank Giller Prize, and the prize money was increased to $40,000. The Scotia-bank Giller Prize is awarded to the author of the best Canadian novel or short-story collection published in English. Each finalist, of whom there are typically five or six, receives $2,500.

2006   Vincent Lam, *Bloodletting and Miraculous Cures*

2005   David Bergen, *The Time in Between*

2004   Alice Munro, *Runaway*

2003   M. G. Vassanji, *The In-Between World of Vikram Lall*

2002   Austin Clarke, *The Polished Hoe*

2001   Richard B. Wright, *Clara Callan*

2000   David Adams Richards, *Mercy among the Children;* Michael Ondaatje, *Anil's Ghost*

1999   Bonnie Burnard, *A Good House*

1998   Alice Munro, *The Love of a Good Woman*

1997   Mordecai Richler, *Barney's Version*

1996   Margaret Atwood, *Alias Grace*

1995   Rohinton Mistry, *A Fine Balance*

1994   M. G. Vassanji, *The Book of Secrets*

The Griffin Trust Prize for Excellence In Poetry

The Griffin Trust Prize for Poetry was founded in 2000 by businessman Scott Griffin with the guidance of writers such as Michael Ondaatje and Margaret Atwood. Two prizes are given for collections of poetry published in English during the preceding year; one goes to a living Canadian poet, the other to a living poet from any country, which may include Canada. Prize money was initially $40,000 and was raised in 2005 to $50,000.

2006   Sylvia Legris, *Nerve Squall;* Kamau Brathwaite, *Born to Slow Horses*

2005   Roo Borson, *Short Journey Upriver toward Ōishida;* Charles Simic, *Selected Poems: 1963–2003*

2004   Anne Simpson, *Loop;* August Kleinzahler, *The Strange Hours Travelers Keep*

2003   Margaret Avison, *Concrete and Wild Carrot;* Paul Muldoon, *Moy sand and gravel*

2002   Christian Bök, *Eunoia;* Alice Notley, *Disobedience*

2001   Anne Carson, *Men in the Off Hours;* Paul Celan, *Glottal Stop: 101 Poems,* translated by Nikolai Popov and Heather McHugh

Writers' Trust of Canada Awards:

Rogers Writers' Trust Fiction Prize

Established in 1997, this prize recognizes Canadian writers of the year's best novel or short-story collection. The winner receives $15,000; finalists, of whom there are typically five, receive $2,000.

2006   Kenneth J. Harvey, *Inside*

2005   Joseph Boyden, *Three Day Road*
2004   Alice Munro, *Runaway*
2003   Kevin Patterson, *Country of Cold*
2002   Paulette Jiles, *Enemy Women*
2001   Margaret Sweatman, *When Alice Lay down with Peter*
2000   Helen Humphreys, *Afterimage*
1999   Peter Oliva, *The City of Yes*
1998   Greg Hollingshead, *The Healer*
1997   Austin Clarke, *The Origins of Waves*

Marian Engel Award

This $15,000 award was established by the Writers' Trust to honor the memory of one of Canada's most respected writers. Marian Engel won the Governor General's Literary Award for Fiction in 1976 for her novel *Bear* and was the first chairperson of the Writers' Union of Canada in 1973–1974. The award is presented to a female Canadian writer for a body of work and in anticipation of her future contribution to Canadian literature.

2006   Caroline Adderson
2005   Gayla Reid
2004   Dianne Warren
2003   Elisabeth Harvor
2002   Terry Griggs
2001   Elizabeth Hay
2000   Anita Rau Badami
1999   Janice Kulyk Keefer
1998   Sharon Butala
1997   Katherine Govier
1996   Barbara Gowdy
1995   Bonnie Burnard
1994   Jane Urquhart
1993   Sandra Birdsell
1992   Joan Barfoot
1991   Joan Clark
1990   Carol Shields
1989   Merna Summers
1988   Edna Alford
1987   Audrey Thomas
1986   Alice Munro

Writers' Trust of Canada/McClelland & Stewart Journey Prize

This $10,000 prize is awarded annually to a writer at the beginning of his or her career for a short story or excerpt from a fiction work in progress published in a Canadian literary venue. The publisher of the work receives $2,000. The award is made possible by James A. Michener's donation of his Canadian royal-

ties from his novel *Journey*, published by McClelland and Stewart in 1988.

2006   Heather Birrell, "BriannaSusannaAlana"
2005   Matt Shaw, "Matchbook for a Mother's Hair"
2004   Devin Krukoff, "The Last Spark"
2003   Jessica Grant, "My Husband's Jump"
2002   Jocelyn Brown, "Miss Canada"
2001   Kevin Armstrong, "The Cane Field"
2000   Timothy Taylor, "Doves of Townsend"
1999   Alissa York, "The Back of the Bear's Mouth"
1998   John Brooke, "The Finer Points of Apples"
1997   Gabriella Goliger, "Maladies of the Inner Ear"; Anne Simpson, "Dreaming Snow"
1996   Elyse Gasco, "Can You Wave Bye Bye, Baby?"
1995   Kathryn Woodward, "Of Marranos and Gilded Angels"
1994   Melissa Hardy, "Long Man the River"
1993   Gayla Reid, "Sister Doyle's Men"
1992   Rozena Maart, "No Rosa, No District Six"
1991   Yann Martel, "The Facts behind the Helsinki Roccamatios"
1990   Cynthia Flood, "My Father Took a Cake to France"
1989   Holley Rubinsky, "Rapid Transits"

Timothy Findley Award

This $15,000 award recognizes a body of work, comprising no fewer than three works of literary merit, predominantly fiction, by a male Canadian writer.

2006   Douglas Glover
2005   Rohinton Mistry
2004   David Adams Richards
2003   Guy Vanderhaeghe
2002   Bill Gaston

Drainie-Taylor Biography Prize

This $10,000 prize honors the year's best biography, autobiography, or memoir. It is named for John Drainie, the most prominent of Canada's first generation of actors, and Nathan A. (Nat) Taylor, founder of the Cineplex movie-theater chain. The two men are linked through the writer and actress Claire Drainie Taylor, who was married to Drainie from 1942 until his death in 1966 and then to Taylor, who died in 2004.

2005   Nelofer Pazira, *A Bed of Red Flowers: In Search of My Afghanistan*
2004   Peter C. Newman, *Here Be Dragons: Telling Tales of People, Passion and Power*

2003 Geoffrey Stevens, *The Player: The Life & Times of Dalton Camp*

2002 Warren Cariou, *Lake of the Prairies: A Story of Belonging*

2001 Ken McGoogan, *Fatal Passage*

2000 Trevor Herriot, *River in a Dry Land: A Prairie Passage*

1999 François Ricard, author, and Patricia Claxton, translator, *Gabrielle Roy: A Life*

Vicky Metcalf Award for Children's Literature

This $15,000 prize, created in 1963 by the Toronto librarian for whom it is named, is given to the author of a body of work in children's literature that demonstrates the highest literary standards.

2006 Kenneth Oppel
2005 Marie-Louise Gay
2004 Deborah Ellis
2003 Roslyn Schwartz
2002 Julie Johnston
2001 Linda Granfield
2000 Sheree Fitch
1999 Joan Clark
1998 Kit Pearson
1997 Tim Wynne-Jones
1996 Margaret Buffie
1995 Sarah Ellis
1994 Welwyn Wilton Katz
1993 Phoebe Gilman
1992 Kevin Major
1991 Brian Doyle
1990 Bernice Thurman Hunter
1989 Stephane Poulin
1988 Barbara Smucker
1987 Robert Munsch
1986 Dennis Lee
1985 Edith Fowke
1984 Bill Freeman
1983 Claire Mackay
1982 Janet Lunn
1981 Monica Hughes
1980 John Craig
1979 Cliff Faulknor
1978 Lyn Cook
1977 James Houston
1976 Suzanne Martel
1975 Lyn Harrington
1974 Jean Little
1973 Christie Harris
1972 William E. Toye
1971 Kay Hill
1970 Farley Mowat
1969 Audrey McKim
1968 Lorrie McLaughlin
1967 John Patrick Gillese
1966 Fred Swayze
1965 Roderick Haig-Brown
1964 John F. Hayes
1963 Kerry Wood

Nereus Writers' Trust Nonfiction Prize

This $15,000 prize is for a work of nonfiction that shows the highest literary merit. Finalists, of whom there are typically five, receive $2,000.

2006 Dragan Todorovic, *The Book of Revenge*

2005 John Vaillant, *The Golden Spruce: A True Story of Myth, Madness and Greed*

2004 Elaine Dewar, *The Second Tree: Of Clones, Chimeras, and Quests for Immortality*

2003 Brian Fawcett, *Virtual Clearcut; or, The Way Things Are in My Hometown*

2002 Jake MacDonald, *Houseboat Chronicles: Notes from a Life in Shield Country*

2001 Clark Blaise, *Time Lord*

2000 Erna Paris, *Long Shadows: Truth, Lies and History*

1999 Modris Eksteins, *Walking Since Daybreak: A Story of Eastern Europe, World War II and the Heart of Our Century*

1998 Rudy Wiebe and Yvonne Johnson, *Stolen Life: The Journey of a Cree Woman*

1997 Ernest Hillen, *Small Mercies: A Boy after War*

Writers' Trust of Canada's Matt Cohen Prize—In Celebration of a Writing Life

Established in 2001 by the Writers' Trust of Canada and a group of anonymous donors, this $20,000 award recognizes a lifetime of distinguished work by a Canadian writer of poetry or prose in French or English.

2006 Marie-Claire Blais
2005 Janet Lunn
2004 Howard Engel
2003 Audrey Thomas
2002 Fred Bodsworth
2001 Norman Levine
2000 Mavis Gallant

Writers' Trust of Canada W. O. Mitchell Prize

This $15,000 prize is given to a writer who has produced an outstanding body of work, has been a "caring mentor" for other writers, and has published a work of fiction or had a new play produced during the three-year period specified for each competition.

2003 Nicole Brossard
2002 Leon Rooke
2001 Audrey Thomas
2000 Marie-Claire Blais
1999 Austin Clarke
1998 Barry Callaghan

Canadian Booksellers Association Libris Awards
No monetary award is given in any category.

Author of the Year

This award is given to the Canadian author of an outstanding literary work from the previous year that is a contribution to Canadian culture and that combines readability with strong sales.

2006 Stephen Lewis
2005 Alice Munro
2004 Romeo Dallaire
2003 Carol Shields
2002 Richard B. Wright
2001 David Adams Richards
2000 Alistair MacLeod
1999 Alice Munro
1998 Mordecai Richler
1997 Margaret Atwood
1996 Timothy Findley
1995 Alice Munro
1994 Carol Shields
1993 Michael Ondaatje
1992 Eric Wilson
1991 Robert Munsch
1990 David Suzuki

Fiction Book of the Year

This award is for a Canadian work of fiction published in the previous year that created wide media attention, brought people into bookstores, and had strong sales.

2006 Joseph Boyden, *Three Day Road*
2005 Miriam Toews, *A Complicated Kindness*
2004 Ann-Marie MacDonald, *The Way the Crow Flies*
2003 Guy Vanderhaeghe, *The Last Crossing*
2002 Richard B. Wright, *Clara Callan*
2001 David Adams Richards, *Mercy among the Children*
2000 Alistair MacLeod, *No Great Mischief*
1999 Alice Munro, *The Love of a Good Woman*
1998 Ann-Marie MacDonald, *Fall On Your Knees*

Nonfiction Book of the Year

This award is for a Canadian work of nonfiction published in the previous year that created wide media attention, brought people into bookstores, and had strong sales.

2006 Stephen Lewis, *Race against Time*
2005 Ronald Wright, *A Short History of Progress*
2004 Romeo Dallaire, *Shake Hands with the Devil*
2003 Margaret MacMillan, *Paris 1919: Six Months That Changed the World*
2002 Will and Ian Ferguson, *How to Be a Canadian*
2001 Don Gilmor and Pierre Turgeon, *Canada: A People's History*
2000 Charlotte Gray, *Sisters in the Wilderness*
1999 Katherine Barber, *The Canadian Oxford Dictionary*
1998 John C. Crosbie, *No Holds Barred*

Children's Author of the Year

This award is given to the Canadian author of a work for children published during the previous year that combines readability with strong sales.

2006 Kenneth Oppel

Children's Illustrator of the Year

This award goes to a Canadian illustrator who demonstrated artistic merit and creativity while complementing and enhancing the story line of a literary work for children in the previous year, attracted customer attention, and contributed to the overall sales of the work.

2006 Michael Martchenko

The Chalmers Awards for Creation and Excellence in the Arts

Discontinued in 2002, the Chalmers Awards for Creation and Excellence in the Arts honored Canadians for contributions to the arts. Winners received $5,000 to $25,000.

Floyd S. Chalmers Play Awards

2001 Florence Gibson, *Belle;* Chris Earle, *Radio: 30;* Michael Redhill, *Building Jerusalem;* George F. Walker, *Heaven*
2000 Linda Griffiths, *Alien Creatures: A Visitation from Gwendolyn MacEwan;* Michel Tremblay, *Encore une fois, si vous permettez;* Ronnie Burkett, *Street of Blood;* Michael Healey, *The Drawer Boy*
1999 Michel Marc Bouchard, *The Orphan Muses;* Leah Cherniak, Oliver Dennis, Maggie Huculak,

Robert Morgan, Martha Ross, and Michael Simpson, *The Betrayal;* Jason Sherman, *Patience;* George F. Walker, *The End of Civilization*

1998 George F. Walker, *Problem Child;* Djanet Sears, *Harlem Duet;* Carole Fréchette, *The Four Lives of Marie;* David Rubinoff, *Stuck*

1997 Don Druick, *Where Is Kabuki?;* Ted Dykstra and Richard Greenblatt, *2 Pianos, 4 Hands;* Daniel MacIvor and Daniel Brooks, *Here Lies Henry;* Guillermo Verdecchia and Marcus Youssef, *A Line In the Sand*

1996 Timothy Findley, *The Stillborn Lover;* Brad Fraser, *Poor Super Man;* Andrew Moodie, *Riot;* John Murrell, *The Faraway Nearby*

1995 Robert Lepage, *Needles and Opium;* Geoff Kavanagh, *Ditch*

1994 Michael Hollingsworth, *The Life and Times of MacKenzie King;* Hillar Liitoja, *The Last Supper;* Alisa Palmer, *A Play about the Mothers of Plaza de Mayo;* Guillermo Verdecchia, *Fronteras Americanas;* Ken Garnhum, *Pants on Fire;* Diane Cave and Nadia Ross, *The Alistair Trilogy*

1993 Normand Chaurette (author) and Linda Gaboriau (translator), *The Queens;* Joan MacLeod, *The Hope Slide;* Jason Sherman, *The League of Nathans;* George F. Walker, *Escape from Happiness*

1992 Michel Marc Bouchard (author) and Linda Gaboriau (translator), *Lilies;* Daniel Brooks and Guillermo Verdecchia, *The Noam Chomsky Lectures;* Daniel MacIvor, *House;* John Mighton, *A Short History of Night*

1991 Marie Brassard and Robert Lepage, *Le Polygraphe;* Brad Fraser, *Unidentified Human Remains and the True Nature of Love;* Judith Thompson, *Lion in the Streets;* Michel Tremblay, *La Maison suspendue*

1990 Sally Clark, *Moo;* Tomson Highway, *Dry Lips Oughta Move to Kapuskasing;* John Krizanc, *The Half of It;* George F. Walker, *Love and Anger*

1989 Paul Ledoux and David Young, *Fire;* Ann-Marie MacDonald, *Goodnight Desdemona (Good Morning Juliet);* Michel Tremblay, *Le Vrai Monde?;* George F. Walker, *Nothing Sacred*

1988 Tom Wood, *B Movie: The Play;* Robert Fothergill, *Detaining Mr. Trotsky;* Judith Thompson, *I Am Yours;* Ralph Burdman, *Tête-à-Tête*

1987 John Murrell, *Farther West;* Linda Griffiths, *Jessica;* Don Hannah, *The Wedding Script;* Tomson Highway, *The Rez Sisters*

1986 Michel Tremblay, *Albertine, in Five Times;* Michael Hollingsworth, *History of the Village of Small Huts: New France;* Michael Mercer, *Goodnight Disgrace;* Allan Stratton, *Papers*

1985 George F. Walker, *Criminals in Love;* David French, *Salt Water Moon;* John Krizanc, *Prague;* Sharon Pollock, *Doc*

1984 Sherman Snukal, *Talking Dirty;* Claude Meunier, Jean-Pierre Plante, Francine Ruel, Louis Sala, Michel Côté, Marcel Gauthier and Marc Messier, *Brew;* Betty Lambert, *Jennie's Story;* Margaret Hollingsworth, *Ever Loving*

1983 Anne Chislett, *Quiet in the Land;* John and Joe Lazarus, *Dreaming and Dueling;* Tom Walmsley, *White Boys*

1982 Allan Stratton, *Rexy!;* Charles Tidler, *Straight Ahead / Blind Dancers;* George Walker, *Theatre of the Film Noir*

1981 Erika Ritter, *Automatic Pilot;* Neil Munro, *F.C.U.;* George Luscombe, Mac Reynolds, and Larry Cox, *Mac Paps;* John Craig and George Luscombe, *Ain't Lookin'*

1980 David Fennario, *Balconville;* David French, *Jitters;* John Gray, *Billy Bishop;* Antonine Maillet, *La Sagouine;* John Murrell, *Waiting for the Parade*

1979 Roland Lepage, *Le temps d'une vie*

1978 Rick Salutin, *Les Canadiens*

1977 W. O. Mitchell, *Back to Beulah;* Larry Fineberg, *Eve*

1976 John Herbert, *Fortune and Men's Eyes*

1975 James Reaney, *Saint Nicholas Hotel*

1974 David French, *Of the Fields, Lately*

1973 David Freeman, *Creeps*

Chalmers Canadian Play Awards: Theatre for Young Audiences

2001 Sean Reycraft, *Pop Song;* Richard Lacroix, André Laliberté, and Richard Morin, *The Star Keeper/Le Porteur*

2000 Gail Nyoka, *Mella Mella;* Leslie Arden, *The Happy Prince*

1999 David S. Craig and Robert Morgan, *Dib and Dob and the Journey Home;* Robert Morgan, *The General*

1998 Ronnie Burkett, *Old Friends;* Robert Priest, *Minibugs and Microchips*

1997 David S. Craig, *Napalm the Magnificent: Dancing with the Dark;* Ron Reed, *Book of the Dragon*

1996 Anne Chislett, *Flippin' In;* Rex Deverell, *Belonging*

1995 Joan MacLeod, *Little Sister;* Dennis Foon, *The Short Tree and The Bird That Could Not Sing*

1994 Maristella Roca, *Pinocchio;* Kathleen McDonnell, *Loon Boy;* Edward Roy, *A Secret Life*

1993 Michael Miller, *Birds of a Feather;* Shirley Barrie, *Carrying the Calf;* Paula Wing, *Naomi's Road*

1992   Drew Hayden Taylor, *Toronto at Dreamer's Rock;* Maristella Roca, *The Servant of Two Masters;* Colin Thomas, *Flesh and Blood*

1991   Martha Brooks, *Andrew's Tree;* Colin Thomas, *Two Weeks Twice a Year*

1990   The Great Unwashed Fish Collective, *i.d.;* Jim Betts, *The Groundworld Adventure;* Shirley Barrie, *Straight Stitching*

1989   Carol Bolt, *Ice Time;* Marvin Ishmael, *Forever Free*

1988   Beverley Cooper and Banuta Rubess, *Thin Ice;* Frank Etherington, *The Snake Lady;* Robert Morgan, *Not as Hard as It Seems*

1987   Dennis Foon, *Skin;* Robert Morgan and David Craig, *Morgan's Journey*

1986   Suzanne Lebeau, *Little Victories/Les Petits Pouvoirs;* Duncan McGregor, *Running the Gauntlet;* John Lazarus, *Not So Dumb;* Paul Shilton and Jim Biros, *The Fabulous Farming Show*

1985   Colin Thomas, *One Thousand Cranes;* Robert Bellefeuille and Isabel Cauchy, *Les Nez*

1984   Jim Betts, *Mystery of the Oak Island Treasure;* Anne Dansereau, *Une histoire à dormir debout;* Joel Greenberg, *The Nuclear Power Show*

1983   Marcel Sabourin, *Pleurer pour rire*

Canadian Authors' Association Awards Program

CAA Award for Fiction

The author of the winning novel receives $2,500.

2006   Joseph Boyden, *Three Day Road*
2005   Jeffrey Moore, *The Memory Artists*
2004   Douglas Coupland, *Hey Nostradamus*
2003   Rohinton Mistry, *Family Matters*
2002   Will Ferguson, *Generica*
2001   Elizabeth Hay, *A Student of Weather*
2000   Alistair MacLeod, *No Great Mischief*
1999   Wayne Johnston, *The Colony of Unrequited Dreams*
1998   Rita Donovan, *Landed*
1997   Ann-Marie MacDonald, *Fall on Your Knees*
1996   L. R. Wright, *Mother Love*
1995   Bernice Morgan, *Waiting for Time*
1994   Margaret Atwood, *The Robber Bride*
1993   Neil Bissoondath, *The Innocence of Age*
1992   Alberto Manguel, *News from a Foreign Country Came*
1991   David Adams Richards, *Evening Snow Will Bring Such Peace*
1990   James Houston, *Running West*
1989   Joan Clark, *The Victory of Geraldine Gull*
1988   Brian Moore, *The Colour of Blood*
1987   No award given
1986   Robertson Davies, *What's Bred in the Bone*
1985   Timothy Findley, *Not Wanted on the Voyage*
1984   Heather Robertson, *Willie: A Romance*

1983   W. P. Kinsella, *Shoeless Joe*
1982   Joy Kogawa, *Obasan*
1981   Hugh Maclennan, *Voices in Time*
1980   No award given
1979   Marian Engel, *The Glassy Sea*
1978   Jane Rule, *The Young in One Another's Arms*
1977   Carol Shields, *Small Ceremonies*
1976   No award given
1975   Fred Stenson, *Lonesome Hero*

CAA Award for Poetry

This $1,000 prize is for a volume of poetry by one poet.

2006   Barry Dempster, *The Burning Alphabet*
2005   Peter Trower, *Haunted Hills and Hanging Valleys*
2004   Chris Banks, *Bonfires*
2003   Margaret Avison, *Concrete and Wild Carrot*
2002   Tim Bowling, *Darkness and Silence*
2001   Carmine Starnino, *Credo*
2000   Helen Humphreys, *Anthem*
1999   Janice Kulyk Keefer, *Marrying the Sea*
1998   Anne Szumigalski, *On Glassy Wings*
1997   E. D. Blodgett, *Apostrophies: Woman at a Piano*
1996   Di Brandt, *Jerusalem, Beloved*
1995   Tim Lilburn, *Moosehead Sandhills*
1994   George Bowering, *Selected Poems*
1993   Lorna Crozier, *Inventing the Hawk*
1992   Anne Michaels, *Miner's Pond*
1991   Richard Lemm, *Prelude to the Bacchanal*
1990   Don Bailey, *Homeless Heart*
1989   Bruce Rice, *Daniel*
1988   Pat Lane, *Selected Poems*
1987   Al Purdy, *The Collected Poems, 1956–1986*
1986   P. K. Page, *The Glass Air*
1985   Leonard Cohen, *Book of Mercy*
1984   Don McKay, *Birding, or Desire*
1983   George Amabile, *The presence of fire*
1982   Gary Geddes, *The Acid Test*
1981   Leona Gom, *Land of the Peace*
1980   Michael Ondaatje, *There's a Trick with a Knife That I'm Learning To Do*
1979   Andrew Suknaski, *The Ghosts You Call Poor*
1978   Alden Nowlan, *Smoked Glass*
1977   Sid Stephen, *Beothuck Poems*
1976   Jim Green, *North Book*
1975   Tom Wayman, *For and against the moon: blues, yells, and chuckles*

CAA Award for Plays

A prize of $1,000 and a silver medal are given for first publication or performance of a full-length play.

2006   John Mighton, *Half Life*

2005 Mieko Ouchi, *The Red Priest (Eight Ways to Say Goodbye)*

2004 Florence Gibson, *Home Is My Road*

2003 Daniel Goldfarb, *Adam Baum and the Jew Movie*

2002 Kent Stetson, *The Harps of God*

2001 Award suspended

2000 Award suspended

1999 David Young, *Inexpressible Island*

1998 Judith Thompson, *Sled*

1997 Jane Sherman, *The League of Nathans*

1996 Vittorio Rossi, *The Last Adam*

1995 Elise Moore, *Live with It*

1994 Timothy Findley, *The Stillborn Lover*

1993 Guy Vanderhaeghe, *I Had a Job I Liked. Once*

1992 Drew Taylor, *Bootlegger Blues*

1991 Ann-Marie MacDonald, *Goodnight Desdemona (Good Morning Juliet)*

1990 Kelly Rebar, *Bordertown Café*

1989 George F. Walker, *Nothing Sacred*

1988 John Gray, *Rock and Roll*

1987 John Murrell, *Farther West*

1986 David French, *Salt-Water Moon*

1985 Ken Mitchell, *Gone the Burning Sun*

1984 W. D. Valgardson, *Granite Point*

1983 W. O. Mitchell, *Back to Beulah*

1982 Allan Stratton, *Rexy!*

1981 Ted Galay, *After Bob's Funeral and Sweet and Sour Pickles*

1980 Sheldon Rosen, *Ned and Jack*

1979 No award given

1978 Rex Deverell, *Boiler Room Suite*

1977 No award given

1976 John Hirsh, *The Dybbuk*

CAA Jubilee Award for Short Stories

Discontinued after 2005, this award for a collection of short stories by a single author recognized Canadian writers who were not eligible for the CAA Award for Fiction.

2005 Frances Itani, *Poached Egg on Toast*

2004 Stuart McLean, *Vinyl Café Diaries*

2003 Lisa Moore, *Open*

2002 Melissa Hardy, *Uncharted Heart*

2001 Lynn Coady, *Play the Monster Blind*

2000 Uma Parameswaran, *What Was Always Hers*

1999 Dennis Bock, *Olympia*

1998 Joanne Gerber, *In the Misleading Absence of Light*

1997 Alice Munro, *Selected Stories*

CAA Lela Common Award for Canadian History

This $2,500 award is for excellence in the writing of a work of Canadian history, excluding biography.

2006 J. L. Granatstein, *The Last Good War*

2005 Charlotte Gray, *The Museum Called Canada*

2004 Ishmael Alunik, *Eddie D. Kolausok and David Morrison—Across Time and Tundra: The Inuvialuit of the Western Arctic*

2003 Derek Hayes, *Historical Atlas of Canada*

2002 Ken McGoogan, *Fatal Passage: The Untold Story of John Rae, the Arctic Adventurer Who Discovered the Fate of Franklin*

2001 Will Ferguson, *Canadian History for Dummies*

2000 D'Arcy Jenish, *Indian Fall: The Last Great Days of the Plains Cree and Blackfoot Conspiracy*

1999 Rod McQueen, *The Eatons*

1998 Dorothy Harley Eber, *Images of Justice*

1997 Phil Jenkins, *An Acre of Time*

CAA Birks Family Foundation Award for Biography

Discontinued after 2003, this award presented $2,500 and a silver medal for a biographical or autobiographical work about a Canadian written by a Canadian.

2003 Janet Lunn, *Maud's House of Dreams*

2002 Julian Sher, *Until You are Dead: Steven Truscott's Long Ride into History*

2001 Anna Porter, *The Storyteller*

2000 Roy MacGregor, *A Life in the Bush: Lessons from My Father*

1999 Leslie Yeo, *A Thousand and One First Nights*

1998 Charlotte Gray, *Mrs. King: The Life and Times of Isabelle MacKenzie King*

CAA Vicky Metcalf Body of Work Award

This $10,000 award was created in 1963 by Toronto librarian Metcalf for a body of work—fiction, nonfiction, poetry, or picture books. It was suspended in 2002.

2001 Linda Granfield

2000 Sheree Fitch

1999 Joan Clark

1998 Kit Pearson

1997 Tim Wynne-Jones

1996 Margaret Buffie

1995 Sarah Ellis

1994 Welwyn Wilton Katz

1993 Phoebe Gilman

1992 Kevin Major

1991 Brian Doyle

1990 Bernice Thurman Hunter

1989 Stéphane Poulin

1988	Barbara Smucker
1987	Robert Munsch
1986	Dennis Lee
1985	Edith Fowke
1984	Bill Freeman
1983	Claire Mackay
1982	Janet Lunn
1981	Monica Hughes
1980	John Craig
1979	Cliff Faulknor
1978	Lyn Cook
1977	James Houston
1976	Suzanne Martel
1975	Lyn Harrington
1974	Jean Little
1973	Christie Harris
1972	William E. Toye
1971	Kay Hill
1970	Farley Mowat
1969	Audrey McKim
1968	Lorrie McLaughlin
1967	John Patrick Gillese
1966	Fred Savage
1965	Roderick Haig-Brown
1964	John F. Hayes
1963	Kerry Wood

CAA Vicky Metcalf Short Story Award

This $3,000 award was created in 1963 by Toronto librarian Metcalf for a short story published in an English-language periodical or anthology; a $1,000 prize goes to the editor responsible for publishing the prize-winning story if it appeared in a Canadian periodical or anthology.

2005	Frances Itani, "Poached Egg on Toast"
2004	Stuart McLean, "Vinyl Café Diaries"
2003	Lisa Moore, "Open"
2002	Melissa Hardy, "Uncharted Heart"
2001	Lynn Coady, "Play the Monster Blind"
2000	Uma Parameswaran, "What Was Always Hers"
1999	Anne Carter, "Leaving the Iron Lung"
1998	W. D. Valgardson, "Chicken Lady"; Shelly Tanaka, editor
1997	Not awarded
1996	Bernice Friesen, "The Seasons Are Horses"; Susan Musgrave, editor
1995	Not awarded
1994	Tim Wynne-Jones, "The Hope Bakery"; Shelly Tanaka, editor
1993	R. P. MacIntyre, "The Rink"; Peter Carver, editor
1992	Edna King, "Adventure on Thunder Island"; Linda Sheppard, editor

1991	Not awarded
1990	Patricia Armstrong, "Choose Your Grandmother"; Wendy McArthur and Geoffrey Ursell, editors
1989	Martha Brooks, "A Boy and His Dog"; Nancy Marcotte, editor
1988	Claire MacKay, "Marvin and Me and the Files"; Brian Cross, editor
1987	Isabel Reimer, "The Viking Dagger"
1986	Diana J. Wieler, "The Boy Who Walked Backwards"
1985	Martyn Godfrey, "Here She Is, Ms. Teeny-Wonderful"
1984	P. Colleen Archer, "The Dog Who Wanted to Die"
1983	Monica Hughes, "The Iron-Barred Door"
1982	Barbara Greenwood, "A Major Resolution"
1981	James Houston, "Long Claws"
1980	Estelle Salata, "Blind Date"
1979	Marina McDougall, "The Kingdom of Riddles"

CAA Book Television Emerging Writer Award

This award, which grants $500 and a silver medal, replaces the CAA Air Canada Award.

2006	Souvankham Thammavongsa

CAA Air Canada Award

Until funding ceased after 2001, the $500 award and a silver medal went to the Canadian or landed immigrant under thirty who showed the most promise in any field of literary creation.

2001	Madeleine Thien
2000	Treen Kortje
1999	Rob McLennan
1998	Lynn Coady
1997	Richard van Camp
1996	Gregory Scofield
1995	Kenneth Oppel
1994	Lesley-Anne Bourne
1993	Yann Martel
1992	Leslie Smith Dow
1991	Vivienne Laxdal
1990	Evelyn Lau
1989	Steven Heighton
1988	Wayne Johnston
1987	Nancy Painter
1986	Karen Connelly
1985	Andrea Lang
1984	Mary di Michele
1983	Kevin Longfield

1982   Gail Hamilton
1981   Gordon Korman
1980   Larry Krotz
1979   Russel Martin

CAA Allan Sangster Award

Given to a member of the CAA for extraordinary service to the association, this award, which carries no monetary prize, was established in memory of a Canadian Broadcasting Corporation producer of classical music.

2006   Karleen Bradford
2005   Russ Harvey
2004   Bernice Lever
2003   Deborah Ranchuk
2002   Harvey Grossman
2001   Ishbel Moore
2000   Beth Greenwood
1999   Bert Reynolds
1998   Anna Marie Kowalski
1997   Eleanor McEachern
1996   Larry Muller
1995   Doug Waugh
1994   Jeffrey Holmes
1993   Kevin Longfield
1992   Gillian Foss
1991   Don Wetmore
1990   Cora Taylor
1989   Murphy Shewchuk
1988   Anne Fairly
1987   Anne Osborne
1986   Betty Dyck
1985   James Fritch
1984   Betty Millway
1983   Rosemary Bauchman
1982   Fred Kerner
1981   C. H. Little
1980   Mary Dawe
1979   Max Goldin
1978   Will R. Bird
1977   Isabel Reimer
1976   Carol Wilson
1975   Dorothy Powell
1974   H. R. Percy
1973   Joe Holliday
1972   Vinia Hoogstraten
1971   John Patrick Gillese
1970   Don and Terry Thomson
1969   Lyn Harrington
1968   W. G. Hardy

Amazon.ca/Books in Canada First Novel Award

This $5,000 award is for the best first novel in English published the previous year by a citizen or resident of Canada.

2005   Joseph Boyden, *Three Day Road*
2004   Colin McAdam, *Some Great Thing*
2003   Michel Basilières, *Black Bird*
2002   Mary Lawson, *Crow Lake*
2001   Michael Redhill, *Martin Sloane*
2000   Eva Stachniak, *Necessary Lies*
1999   David McFarlane, *Summer Gone;* Ian Wilson, *Before the Flood*
1998   André Alexis, *Childhood*
1997   Margaret Gibson, *Opium Dreams*
1996   Anne Michaels, *Fugitive Pieces;* Keath Fraser, *Popular Anatomy*
1995   Shyam Selvadurai, *Funny Boy*
1994   Deborah Joy Corey, *Losing Eddie*
1993   John Steffler, *The Afterlife of George Cartwright*
1992   Rohinton Mistry, *Such a Long Journey*
1991   Nino Ricci, *Lives of the Saints*
1990   Sandra Birdsell, *The Missing Child*
1989   Rick Salutin, *A Man of Little Faith*
1988   Marion Quednau, *The Butterfly Chair*
1987   Karen Lawrence, *The Life of Helen Alone*
1986   Wayne Johnston, *The Story of Bobby O'Malley*
1985   Geoffrey Ursell, *Perdue; or, How the West Was Won*
1984   Heather Robertson, *Willie: A Romance*
1983   W. P. Kinsella, *Shoeless Joe*
1982   Joy Kogawa, *Obasan*
1981   W. D. Valgardson, *Gentle Sinners*
1980   Clark Blaise, *Lunar Attractions*
1979   Joan Barfoot, *Abra*
1978   Oonah McFee, *Sandbars*
1977   Michael Ondaatje, *Coming through Slaughter;* Ian McLachlan, *Seventh Hexagram*

Major Provincial Awards

Alberta

Alberta Book Awards

Administered by the Writers Guild of Alberta, each of these awards carries a cash prize of $1,000.

Georges Bugnet Award for Fiction (Novel)

2005   Marie Jakober, *Sons of Liberty*
2004   Paul Anderson, *Hunger's Brides*
2003   Tim Bowling, *The Paperboy's Winter*
2002   Thomas Trofimuk, *The 52nd Poem: A Novel*
2001   Thomas Wharton, *Salamander*
2000   Fred Stenson, *The Trade*
1999   Catherine Simmons Niven, *A Fine Daughter;* Peter Oliva, *The City of Yes*
1998   Greg Hollingshead, *The Healer*
1997   Margie Taylor, *Some of Skippy's Blues*

1996   Kristjana Gunnars, *The Garden Rose*
1995   Marion Douglas, *Bending at the Bow*
1994   Richard Wagamese, *The Keeper 'n Me*
1993   Roberta Rees, *Beneath the Faceless Mountain*
1992   Robert Hilles, *Raising Voices*
1991   Greg Hollingshead, *Spin Dry*
1990   Thomas King, *Medicine River*
1989   Jacqueline Dumas, *Madeleine and the Angel*
1988   Helen Forrester, *Yes, Mama*
1987   Mary Walters Riskin, *The Woman Upstairs*
1986   Aritha van Herk, *No Fixed Address*
1985   Marie Jakober, *Sandinisita: A Novel of Nicaragua*
1984   Pauline Gedge, *The Twelfth Transforming*
1983   Sam Selvon, *Moses Migrating*
1982   W. P. Kinsella, *Shoeless Joe*

Stephan G. Stephansson Award for Poetry

2005   sheri-d wilson, *Re:Zoom*
2004   Walter Hildebrandt, *Where the Land Gets Broken*
2003   Robert Hilles, *Wrapped within Again: Poems New and Selected*
2002   Weyman Chan, *Before a Blue Sky Moon*
2001   Marilyn Dumont, *green girl dreams mountains*
2000   Shane Rhodes, *The Wireless Room*
1999   Shawna Lemay, *All the God-Sized Fruit*
1998   Monty Reid, *Flat Side*
1997   Tim Bowling, *Dying Scarlet*
1996   Kristjana Gunnars, *Exiles among You*
1995   Charles Noble, *Wormwood Vermouth, Warphistory*
1994   Bert Almon, *Earth Prime*
1993   Richard Stevenson, *From the Mouths of Angels*
1992   Roberta Rees, *Eyes Like Pigeons*
1991   Fred Wah, *So Far*
1990   Monty Reid, *These Lawns*
1989   Andrew Wreggett, *Making Movies*
1988   Christopher Wiseman, *Postcards Home*
1987   E. D. Blodgett, *Musical Offerings*
1986   Claire Harris, *Travelling to Find a Remedy*
1985   Monty Reid, *The Alternate Guide*
1984   Douglas Barbour, *Visible Visions*
1983   E. D. Blodgett, *Arche/Elegies*
1982   Jon Whyte, *Homage, Henry Kelsey*

Wilfred Eggleston Award for Nonfiction

2005   Ted Bishop, *Riding with Rilke: Reflections on Motorcycles and Books*
2004   Mark Lisac, *Alberta Politics Uncovered: Taking Back Our Province*
2003   Lorie Miseck, *A Promise of Salt*
2002   A. K. Hellum, *A Painter's Year in the Forests of Bhutan*
2001   Chic Scott, *Pushing the Limits: The Story of Canadian Mountaineering*

2000   No award given
1999   Alla Tumanov, *Where We Buried the Sun*
1998   Rudy Wiebe and Yvonne Johnson, *Stolen Life*
1997   Judy Schultz, *Mamie's Children*
1996   David Bercuson, *Significant Incident*
1995   Hugh Dempsey, *The Golden Age of the Canadian Cowboy*
1994   Stacy Schiff, *Saint-Exupéry*
1993   Myrna Kostash, *Bloodlines*
1992   F. L. Morton, *Morgentaler v. Borowski*
1991   Kenneth McGoogan, *Canada's Undeclared War*
1990   Donald B. Smith, *Land of Shadows*
1989   Stephen Hume, *Ghost Camps*
1988   Peter Jonker, *The Song and the Silence*
1987   Myrna Kostash, *No Kidding*
1986   Daniel Dancocks, *Legacy of Valour*
1985   Douglas Curran, *In Advance of the Landing*
1984   Edward Brado, *Cattle Kingdom*
1983   E. J. Hart, *The Selling of Canada*
1982   John Davenall Turner, *Sunfield Painter*

Henry Kreisel Award for Best First Book

2005   Laura J. Cutler, *This Side of Bonkers*
2004   Thomas Wharton, *The Logogryph*
2003   Jacqueline Baker, *A Hard Witching*
2002   Sarah Murphy, *Die, Tinkerbell, Die*
2001   Gloria Sawai, *A Song for Nettie Johnson*
2000   Todd Babiak, *Choke Hold*
1999   Catherine Simmons Niven, *A Fine Daughter*
1998   Rajinderpal Pal, *Pappaji wrote poetry in a language I cannot read*
1997   Curtis Gillespie, *The Progress of an Object in Motion*
1996   Lisa Christensen, *A Hiker's Guide to Art of the Canadian Rockies*
1995   Thomas Wharton, *Icefields*
1994   Stacy Schiff, *Saint Exupery*
1993   Peter Oliva, *Drowning in Darkness*

Howard O'Hagan Award for Short Fiction

2005   Laura J. Cutler, *This Side of Bonkers*
2004   Thomas Wharton, *The Logogryph*
2003   Jacqueline Baker, *A Hard Witching*
2002   Sarah Murphy, *Die Tinkerbell Die*
2001   Gloria Sawai, *A Song for Nettie Johnson*
2000   Caterina Edwards, *Island of the Nightingales*; Candace Jane Dorsey, *Vanilla and Other Stories*
1999   Barbara Scott, *The Quick*
1998   Sally Ito, *Floating Shore*
1997   Cecilia Frey, *Salamander Moon*
1996   Fred Wah, *Diamond Grill*

1995 Greg Hollingshead, *The Roaring Girl*

1994 Rosemary Nixon, *Cock's Egg*

1993 Martin Sherman, *Elephant Hook and Other Stories*

1992 Greg Hollingshead, *White Buick*

1991 J. Jill Robinson, *Saltwater Trees*

1990 Cecilia Frey, *The Love Song of Romeo Paquette*

1989 W. O. Mitchell, *According to Jake and the Kid*

1988 Merna Summers, *North of the Battle*

1987 Cecilia Frey, *The Nefertiti Look*

1986 Diane Schoemperlen, *Frogs and Other Stories*

1985 No award given

1984 Mark Anthony Jarman, *Dancing Nightly in the Tavern*

1983 W. P. Kinsella, *Moccasin Telegraph*

1982 Merna Summers, *Calling Home*

R. Ross Annet Award for Children's Literature

2005 Colleen Hefferman, *A Kind of Courage*

2004 Joan Marie Galat, *Dot to Dot in the Sky: Stories of the Moon*

2003 Glen Huser, *Stitches*

2002 Katherine Holubitsky, *Last Summer in Agatha*

2001 Tololwa Mollel, *My Rows and Piles of Coins;* Anita Horrocks, *Topher*

2000 Clem Martini, *Illegal Entry*

2000 No award given

1999 Barbara Demers, *Willa's New World*

1998 Anita Horrocks, *What They Don't Know*

1997 Hazel Hutchins, *The Prince of Tarn*

1996 Don Trembath, *Tuesday Café*

1995 Tololwa M. Mollel, *Big Boy*

1994 Beth Goobie, *Mission Impossible*

1993 David Bly, *The McIntyre Liar*

1992 Monica Hughes, *The Crystal Drop*

1991 Hazel Hutchins, *A Cat of Artimus Pride*

1990 Jan Hudson, *Dawn Rider*

1989 Don Meredith, *Dog Runner*

1988 William Pasnak, *Under the Eagle's Claw*

1987 Marilyn Halvorson, *Nobody Said It Would Be Easy*

1986 Monica Hughes, *Blaine's Way*

1985 Cora Taylor, *Julie*

1984 William Pasnak, *In the City of the King*

1983 Monica Hughes, *Space Trap*

1982 Monica Hughes, *Hunter in the Dark*

Gwen Pharis Ringwood Award for Drama

2005 Sharon Pollock, *Sharon Pollock: Collected Works, Volume One*

2004 Karen Hines, *The Pochsy Plays*

2003 Marty Chan, *The Forbidden Phoenix*

2002 Stephen Massicotte, *Mary's Wedding*

2001 Chris Craddock, *naked at school*

2000 Clem Martini, *A Three Martini Lunch*

1999 Clem Martini, *Illegal Entry*

1998 Brad Fraser, *Martin Yesterday;* Greg Nelson, *Spirit Wrestler*

1997 Ron Chambers, *Three Really Nasty Plays*

1996 Brad Fraser, *Love and Human Remains*

1995 Brad Fraser, *Poor Super Man*

1994 Pamela Boyd, *Odd Fish*

1993 Greg Nelson, *Castrato*

1992 John Murrell, *Democracy*

1991 Clem Martini, *Nobody of Consequence*

1990 Brad Fraser, *Unidentified Human Remains and the True Nature of Human Love*

1989 Robert Clinton, *The Mail Order Bride*

1988 No award given

1987 Michael D. C. McKinlay, *"Walt Roy" New Works I*

1986 Sharon Pollock, *Doc*

1985 Raymond Storey, *Angel of Death*

British Columbia

British Columbia Book Prizes

These prizes, which carry a monetary award of $2,000, comprise the Roderick Haig-Brown Regional Prize, the Ethel Wilson Fiction Prize, the Dorothy Livesay Poetry Prize, the Sheila A. Egoff Children's Prize, the Christie Harris Illustrated Children's Literature Prize, the Hubert Evans Nonfiction Prize, and the Lieutenant Governor's Award for Literary Excellence.

Roderick Haig-Brown Regional Prize

This prize is awarded to the authors of the book that contributes most to the enjoyment and understanding of British Columbia.

2006 John Vaillant, *The Golden Spruce: A True Story of Myth, Madness and Greed*

2005 Alexandra Morton, Betty C. Keller, Rosella M. Leslie, Otto Langer, and Don Staniford, *A Stain upon the Sea: West Coast Salmon Farming*

2004 Donald Luxton, *Building the West: The Early Architects of British Columbia*

2003 Ernest Perrault, *Tong: The Story of Tong Louie, Vancouver's Quiet Titan*

2002 Keith Thor Carlson, Colin Duffield, Albert (Sonny) McHalsie, Jan Perrier, Leeanna Lynn Rhodes, David M. Schaepe, and David Smith, *A Stó:lo–Coast Salish Historical Atlas*

2001 Dan Francis, *The Encyclopedia of British Columbia*

2000 Margaret Horsfield, *Cougar Annie's Garden*

1999   Mark Hume and Harvey Thommassen, *River of the Angry Moon: Seasons on the Bella Coola*

1998   Richard Bocking, *Mighty River*

1997   Alan Haig-Brown, *The Fraser River*

1996   Ken Drushka, *A Biography of H. R. MacMillan*

1995   Howard White, *Raincoast Chronicles: Eleven-Up*

1994   Alex Rose, ed., *Nisga'a: People of the Nass River*

1993   Harry Robinson and Wendy Wickwire, *Nature Power: In the Spirit of an Okanagan Storyteller*

1992   Herb Hammond, *Seeing the Forest among the Trees: The Case for Holistic Forest Use*

1991   Paul Tennant, *Aboriginal Peoples and Politics: The Indian Land Question in B.C., 1849–1989*

1990   Various artists, *Carmanah: Artistic Visions of an Ancient Rainforest*

1989   Celia Haig-Brown, *Resistance and Renewal*

1988   W. A. Hagelund, *Whalers No More*

1987   Ruth Kirk, *Wisdom of the Elders*

1986   Donald Graham, *Keepers of the Light*

1985   Hilary Stewart, *Cedar*

Ethel Wilson Fiction Prize

2006   Charlotte Gill, *Ladykiller*

2005   Pauline Holstock, *Beyond Measure*

2004   Caroline Adderson, *Sitting Practice*

2003   Carol Shields, *Unless*

2002   Madeleine Thien, *Simple Recipes*

2001   Eden Robinson, *Monkey Beach*

2000   Michael Turner, *The Pornographer's Poem*

1999   Jack Odgins, *Broken Ground*

1998   Marilyn Bowering, *Visible Worlds*

1997   Gail Anderson-Dargatz, *The Cure for Death by Lightning*

1996   Audrey Thomas, *Coming down from Wa*

1995   Gayla Reid, *To Be There with You*

1994   Caroline Adderson, *Bad Imaginings*

1993   W. D. Valgardson, *The Girl with the Botticelli Face*

1992   Don Dickinson, *Blue Husbands*

1991   Audrey Thomas, *Wild Blue Yonder*

1990   Keith Maillard, *Motet*

1989   Bill Schermbrucker, *Mimosa*

1988   George McWhirter, *Cage*

1987   Leona Gom, *Housebroken*

1986   Keath Fraser, *Foreign Affairs*

1985   Audrey Thomas, *Intertidal Life*

Dorothy Livesay Poetry Prize

2006   Meredith Quartermain, *Vancouver Walking*

2005   Jan Zwicky, *Robinson's Crossing*

2004   Philip Kevin Paul, *Taking the Names down from the Hill*

2003   Bill Bissett, *peter among th towring boxes*

2002   Karen Solie, *Short Haul Engine*

2001   Don McKay, *Another Gravity*

2000   Lorna Crozier, *What the Living Won't Let Go*

1999   David Zieroth, *How I Joined Humanity at Last*

1998   Patricia Young, *What I Remember from My Time on Earth*

1997   Margo Button, *The Unhinging of Wings*

1996   Patrick Lane, *Too Spare, Too Fierce*

1995   Linda Rogers, *Hard Candy*

1994   Gregory Scofield, *The Gathering: Stones for the Medicine Wheel*

1993   Bill Bissett, *inkorrect thots*

1992   Barry McKinnon, *Pulp Log*

1991   Jeff Derksen, *Down Time*

1990   Victoria Walker, *Suitcase*

1989   Charles Lillard, *Circling North*

1988   Patricia Young, *All I Ever Needed Was a Beautiful Room*

1987   Diana Hartog, *Candy From Strangers*

1986   Joe Rosenblatt, *Poetry Hotel*

Sheila A. Egoff Children's Prize

This prize is awarded to authors of novels, including chapter books, aimed at juveniles and young adults, as well as nonfiction books for children, including biographies, that have not been highly illustrated.

2006   Barbara Nickel, *Hannah Waters and the Daughter of Johann Sebastian Bach*

2005   Susan Juby, *Miss Smithers*

2004   Dennis Foon, *Skud*

2003   James Heneghan, *Flood*

2002   Polly Horvath, *Everything on a Waffle*

2001   James Heneghan, *The Grave*

2000   Vivien Bowers, *WOW Canada! Exploring the Land from Coast To Coast to Coast*

1999   Sandra Lightburn (text) and Ron Lightburn (illustrations), *Driftwood Cove*

1998   James Heneghan, *Wish Me Luck*

1997   Sarah Ellis, *Back of Beyond*

1996   Nan Gregory (text) and Ron Lightburn (illustrations), *How Smudge Came*

1995   Lillian Boraks-Nemetz, *Old Brown Suitcase*

1994   Julie Lawson, *White Jade Tiger*

1993   Shirley Sterling, *My Name Is Seepeetza*

1992   Alexandra Morton, *Siwiti: A Whale's Story*

1991   Nancy Hundal, *I Heard My Mother Call My Name*

1990   Paul Yee, *Tales from Gold Mountain*

1989   Mary Ellen Collura, *Sunny*

1988   Nicola Morgan, *Pride of Lions*

1987   Sarah Ellis, *The Baby Project*

1986   Joe Rosenblatt, *Poetry Hotel*

Christie Harris Illustrated Children's Literature Prize

This prize is awarded to the author and illustrator of picture books, picture storybooks, and illustrated non-fiction books.

2006 Tanya Lloyd Kyi, *The Blue Jean Book: The Story behind the Seams*
2005 Marilynn Reynolds and Renné Benoit, *Goodbye to Griffith Street*
2004 Linda Bailey and Bill Slavin, *Stanley's Party*
2003 Annette LeBox and Karen Reczuch, *Salmon Creek*

Hubert Evans Nonfiction Prize

This prize is awarded to the author of the best original nonfiction literary work, including philosophy, belles lettres, biography, or history.

2006 Stan Persky, *The Short Version: An ABC Book*
2005 Charles Montgomery, *The Last Heathen*
2004 Maria Tippett, *Bill Reid: The Making of an Indian*
2003 Sandra Shields and David Campion, *Where Fire Speaks: A Visit with the Himba*
2002 Susan Crean, *The Laughing One: A Journey to Emily Carr*
2001 Terry Glavin, *The Last Great Sea*
2000 Rita Moir, *Buffalo Jump: A Woman's Travels*
1999 Peter Newman, *Titans: How the New Canadian Establishment Seized Power*
1998 Suzanne Fournier and Ernie Crey, *Stolen from Our Embrace*
1997 Catherine Lang, *O-Bon in Chimunesu*
1996 Claudia Cornwall, *Letter from Vienna*
1995 Lisa Hobbs Birnie, *Uncommon Will: The Death & Life of Sue Rodriguez*
1994 Sharon Brown, *Some Become Flowers: Living with Dying at Home*
1993 Lynne Bowen, *Muddling Through*
1992 Rosemary Neering, *Down the Road: Journeys through Small-Town British Columbia*
1991 Scott Watson, *Jack Shadbolt*
1990 Philip Marchand, *Marshall McLuhan*
1989 Robin Ridington, *Trail to Heaven*
1988 P. K. Page, *Brazilian Journal*
1987 Doris Shadbolt, *Bill Reid*
1986 Bruce Hutchison, *The Unfinished Country*
1985 David R. Williams, *Duff: A Life in the Law*

Lieutenant Governor's Award for Literary Excellence

This award was established in 2003 by the Honorable Iona Campagnolo to recognize British Columbia writ-ers who have contributed to the development of literary excellence in the province.

2006 Jack Hodgins
2005 Robert Bringhurst
2004 P. K. Page

City of Vancouver Book Award

This $2,000 prize is presented to authors of books in any genre that demonstrate excellence and contribute to the appreciation and understanding of Vancouver's history, its unique character, or the achievements of its residents.

2006 Jean Barman, *Stanley Park's Secret;* James Delgado, *Waterfront*
2005 Lance Berelowitz, *Dream City: Vancouver and the Global Imagination*
2004 Daniel Francis, *L.D.: Mayor Louis Taylor and the Rise of Vancouver*
2003 Lincoln Clarkes, *Heroines;* Reid Shier, ed., *Stan Douglas: Every Building on 100 Block West Hastings*
2002 Keith Thor Carlson, Colin Duffield, Albert (Sonny) McHalsie, Jan Perrier, Leeanna Lynn Rhodes, David M. Schaepe, and David Smith, *A Sto:lo–Coast Salish Historical Atlas*
2001 Madeleine Thien, *Simple Recipes*
2000 Lilia D'Acres and Donald Luxton, *Lions Gate*
1999 Bud Osborn, *Keys to Kingdoms*
1998 Chuck Davis, *The Greater Vancouver Book: An Urban Encyclopaedia*
1997 Rhodri Windsor Liscombe, *The New Spirit: Modern Architecture in Vancouver, 1938–1963*
1996 Wayson Choy, *The Jade Peony*
1995 Elspeth Cameron, *Earle Birney: A Life*
1994 Denise Chong, *The Concubine's Children*
1993 Bruce Macdonald, *Vancouver: A Visual History*
1992 Gerald Straley, *Trees of Vancouver: A Guide to the Common & Unusual Trees of the City*
1991 Michael Kluckner, *Vanishing Vancouver*
1990 Sky Lee, *Disappearing Moon Cafe*
1989 Paul Yee, *Saltwater City: An Illustrated History of the Chinese in Vancouver*

Manitoba

Manitoba Book Awards

McNally Robinson Book of the Year Award

This $3,000 award is presented to the Manitoba writer of the best-written English-language book for adults.

2005 David Bergen, *The Time in Between*

2004   Miriam Toews, *A Complicated Kindness*

2003   Armin Wiebe, *Tatsea*

2002   Jake MacDonald, *Houseboat Chronicles: Notes from a Life in Shield Country*

2001   Margaret Sweatman, *When Alice Lay Down with Peter*

2000   Miriam Toews, *Swing Low: A Life*

1999   Gordon Sinclair Jr., *Cowboys and Indians*

1998   Miriam Toews, *A Boy of Good Breeding*

1997   Catherine Hunter, *Latent Heat*

1996   David Bergen, *A Year of Lesser*

1995   Victoria Jason, *Kabloona in the Yellow Kayak*

1994   Patrick Friesen, *Blasphemer's Wheel*

1993   Carol Shields, *The Stone Diaries*

1992   Sandra Birdsell, *The Chrome Suite*

1991   Margaret Sweatman, *Fox*

1990   Di Brandt, *Agnes in the Sky*

1989   Kristjana Gunnars, *The Prowler*

1988   Jan Horner, *Recent Mistakes*

McNally Robinson Book for Young People Award

In 1997 this $2,500 award was split into two categories: Older and Younger. It is presented to the Manitoba author of the best-written book for young people.

McNally Robinson Book for Young People Award– Older

2005   Diane Juttner Perreault, *Breath of the Dragon*

2004   Margaret Buffie, *The Finder*

2003   Duncan Thornton, *The Star-Glass*

2002   Linda Holeman, *Search of the Moon King's Daughter*

2001   Eva Wiseman, *My Canary Yellow Star*

2000   Linda Holeman, *Raspberry House Blues*

1999   Martha Brooks, *Being with Henry*

1998   Diana Wieler, *Drive*

1997   Diana Wieler, *RanVan: Magic Nation*

McNally Robinson Book for Young People Award– Younger

2005   Colleen Sydor, *Camilla Chameleon*

2004   Award deferred until 2005

2003   Connie Colker Steiner, *Shoes for Amélie*

2002   Award deferred until 2003

2001   Sheldon Oberman, *The Wisdom Bird*

2000   Award deferred until 2001

1999   Colleen Sydor, *Smarty Pants*

1998   Award deferred until 1999

1997   Sheldon Oberman, *By the Hanukkah Light*

McNally Robinson Book for Young People Award

1996   Margaret Shaw-MacKinnon, *Tiktala*

1995   Margaret Buffie, *The Dark Garden*

Margaret Laurence Award for Fiction

This $3,500 award is presented to the Manitoba writer of the best book of adult fiction written in English.

2005   David Bergen, *The Time in Between*

2004   Miriam Toews, *A Complicated Kindness*

2003   Armin Wiebe, *Tatsea*

2002   Don Bailey, *A Stranger to Myself*

2001   Margaret Sweatman, *When Alice Lay Down with Peter*

2000   Wayne Tefs, *Moon Lake*

Carol Shields Winnipeg Book Award

This juried annual award carries a monetary prize of $5,000.

2005   David Arnason and Mhari Mackintosh, eds., *The Imagined City: A Literary History of Winnipeg*

2004   Chandra Mayor, *Cherry*

2003   Barbara Huck, ed., *Crossroads of the Continent: A History of the Forks of the Red and Assiniboine Rivers*

2002   David Bergen, *The Case of Lena S.: A Novel*

2001   Margaret Sweatman, *When Alice Lay down with Peter*

2000   Caelum Vatnsdal, *Kino delirium: The Films of Guy Maddin*

1999   Gordon Sinclair Jr., *Cowboys and Indians*

Eileen McTavish Sykes Award for Best First Book

This $1,500 award is given annually to the Manitoba author of the best-written first book.

2005   Michael Van Rooy, *An Ordinary Decent Criminal*

2004   Lori Cayer, *Stealing Mercury*

2003   Rick Ranson, *Working North: DEW Line to Drill Ship*

2002   Chandra Mayor, *August Witch: Poems*

2001   Joil Alpern, *No One Awaiting Me*

2000   Heather Frayne, *Last Night's Dream*

1999   Ingeborg Boyens, *Unnatural Harvest*

Prix littéraire Rue-Deschambault

The $3,500 prize, sponsored by the Ministry of Culture, Heritage and Citizenship of Manitoba, is presented to the Manitoba writer of the best book in French.

2004   Charles Leblanc, *L'appétit du compteur: Poèmes accumulés*

2002   J. R. Léveillé, *Le soleil du lac qui se couche*

2000   Jean-Pierre Dubé, *Ma cousine Germaine*

1998   Marie Jack, *Tant que le fleuve coule*

1996   Jean-Pierre Dubé, *La Grotte*

1993   Roger Léveillé, *Causer l'amour*

1991   Simone Chaput, *Un piano dans le noir*

1989   Simone Chaput, *La Vigne Amère*

John Hirsch Award for Most Promising Manitoba Writer

This $2,500 award was established by the Manitoba Foundation for the Arts with a bequest from Hirsch, who cofounded the Manitoba Theatre Centre and was its first artistic director from 1958 to 1966.

2005   Lori Cayer

2004   Caelum Vatnsdal

2003   Chandra Mayor

2002   Marvin Francis

2001   Suzanne Matczuk

2000   Alissa York

1999   Melissa Steele

1998   Deborah Keahey

1997   Todd Bruce

1996   Miriam Toews

1995   Ian Ross

1994   Elise Moore

1993   David Bergen

1992   Patrick O'Connell

Alexander Kennedy Isbister Award for Nonfiction

This $3,500 award is presented to the Manitoba writer of the best book of adult nonfiction in English.

2005   Peter Kulchyski, *Like the Sound of a Drum: Aboriginal Cultural Politics in Denendeh and Nunavut*

2004   Raymond M. Hébert, *Manitoba's French-Language Crisis: A Cautionary Tale*

2003   Mark Morton, *The Lover's Tongue: A Merry Romp through the Language of Love and Sex*

2002   Jake MacDonald, *Houseboat Chronicles: Notes from a Life in Shield Country*

2001   Joil Alpern, *No One Awaiting Me*

2000   Miriam Toews, *Swing Low: A Life*

New Brunswick

New Brunswick Excellence Awards

Before 1997, these awards were made on a biennial basis to specified disciplines; since then they have been open to all disciplines and are given annually. Each award carries a monetary prize of $5,000, and a maximum of four per year may be awarded. Only literary awards are listed here.

Alden Nowlen Award for Excellence in English Language Literary Arts

2003   M. Travis Lane

2001   Douglas Lochhead

2000   Elizabeth Harvor

1999   Nancy Bauer

1998   Robert Gibb

1995   Fred Cogswell

1993   David Adams Richards

1991   Clara Kathleen (Kay) Smith

1984   Alfred G. Bailey

Pascal Poirier Award for Excellence in French Language Literary Arts

2003   Herménégilde Chiasson

2002   Antonine Maillet

2000   Claude LeBouthillier

1998   Raymond Guy Leblanc

1995   Père Anselme Chiasson

1993   Gérald Leblanc

1991   France Daigle

1984   Ronald Déspres

Newfoundland and Labrador

Writers' Alliance of Newfoundland and Labrador Provincial Book Awards

The $1,500 Newfoundland and Labrador Book Awards are administered by the Writers' Alliance of Newfoundland and Labrador under the patronage of the lieutenant governor. Prizes are awarded for nonfiction and poetry in one year and for fiction and children's/young adult literature the following year.

Bennington Gate Fiction Award

2004   Susan Rendell, *In the Chambers of the Sea*

2002   Ed Kavanagh, *The Confessons of Nipper Mooney*

2000   Carmelita McGrath, *Stranger Things Have Happened*

Newtel Fiction Award

1998   Patrick Kavanagh, *Gaff Topsails*

Rogers Cable Nonfiction Award

2005 Stan Dragland, *Apocrypha*
2003 Ed Smith, *From the Ashes of My Dreams*

Newfoundland Herald Nonfiction Award

2001 Mary Pratt, *A Personal Calligraphy*
1991 Patrick O'Flaherty, *Old Newfoundland: A History to 1843*

Nonfiction Award

1999 Berni Stapleton, *They Let Down Baskets*
1997 Dorothy Inglis, *Bread and Roses*

E. J. Pratt Poetry Award

2005 Mary Dalton, *Merrybegot*

Craig L. Dobbin Poetry Award

2003 John Steffler, *Helix: New and Selected Poems*

Poetry Award

2001 Al Pittman, *Thirty-for-Sixty*

Darmonkow Associates Poetry Award

1999 John Steffler, *That Night We Were Ravenous*

Poetry Award

1997 Michael Crummey, *Arguments with Gravity*

Bruneau Family Children's Literature Award

2004 Janet McNaughton, *An Earthly Knight*
2002 Janet McNaughton, *The Secret under My Skin*

NewTel Children's/Young Adult Award

2000 Janet McNaughton, *Make or Break Spring*

Hibernia Children's/Young Adult Award

1998 Joan Clark, *The Dream Carvers*

Nova Scotia

Writer's Federation of Nova Scotia Literary Prizes

Atlantic Poetry Prize

Full-length books of adult poetry written by Atlantic Canadians and published as a whole for the first time in the current calendar year are eligible for this $1,000 award.

2006 Anne Compton, *Processional*
2005 David Helwig, *The Year One*
2004 Brian Bartlett, *Wanting the Day*
2003 Anne Compton, *Opening the Island*
2002 M. Travis Lane, *Keeping Afloat*
2001 Anne Simpson, *Light Falls through You*
2000 Ken Babstock, *Mean*
1999 John Steffler, *That Night We Were Ravenous*
1998 Carmelita McGrath, *To the New World*

Evelyn Richardson Memorial Literary Award

The province's highest award for a book of nonfiction by a Nova Scotian is named for the writer whose *We Keep a Light* won the Governor General's Literary Award for Nonfiction in 1945. It carries a $1,000 monetary prize.

2006 Linda Johns, *Birds of a Feather: Tales of a Wild Bird Haven*
2005 Marq de Villiers and Sheila Hirtle, *A Dune Adrift*
2004 Harry Thurston, *Island of the Blessed: The Secrets of Egypt's Everlasting Oasis*
2003 Stephen Kimber, *Sailors, Slackers and Blind Pigs: Halifax at War*
2002 Kent Thompson, *Getting out of Town by Book and Bike*
2001 Joan Baxter, *A Serious Pair of Shoes: An African Journal*
2000 Robin Metcalfe, *Studio Rally*
1999 Silver Donald Cameron, *The Living Beach*
1998 Harry Bruce, *An Illustrated History of Nova Scotia*
1997 Harry Thurston, *The Nature of Shorebirds: Nomads of the Wetlands*
1996 Simone Poirier-Bures, *That Shining Place*
1995 Elizabeth Pacey, *Landmarks: Historic Buildings of Nova Scotia*
1994 Peter Brock, *Variations on a Planet*
1993 Sally Ross and Alphonse Deveau, *The Acadians of Nova Scotia: Past and Present*
1992 Robert Pope, *Illness and Healing: Images of Cancer*
1991 Harry Thurston, *Tidal Life: A Natural History of the Bay of Fundy*
1990 Judith Fingard, *Dark Side of Life in Victorian Halifax*
1989 Dean Jobb, *Shades of Justice: Seven Nova Scotia Murder Cases*
1988 Harold Horwood, *Dancing on the Shore: A Celebration of Life at Annapolis Basin*
1987 Tony Foster, *Meeting of Generals*
1986 P. B. Waite, *The Man from Halifax: Sir John Thompson, Prime Minister*

1985   Lilias M. Toward, *Mabel Bell: Alexander's Silent Partner*

1984   Brian C. Cuthbertson, *The Loyalist Governor: Biography of Sir John Wentworth*

1983   J. Murray Beck, *Joseph Howe,* volume one: *Conservative Reformer, 1804–1848*

1982   Bruce Armstrong, *Sable Island*

1981   Kay Hill, *Joe Howe: The Man Who Was Nova Scotia*

1980   Joan and L. J. Payzant, *Like a Weaver's Shuttle: A History of the Halifax-Dartmouth Ferries*

1979   Alden Nowlan, *Double Exposure*

1978   Harry Bruce, *Lifeline: The Story of the Atlantic Ferries and Coastal Boats*

Thomas Head Raddall Atlantic Fiction Award

This $10,000 award was established by the Writers' Federation of Nova Scotia and the Writers' Development Trust in 1990 to honor the author of *His Majesty's Yankees* (1942), *The Governor's Lady* (1960), *The Nymph and the Lamp* (1950), and *Halifax, Warden of the North* (1948) and to recognize the best Atlantic Canadian adult fiction. Raddall willed an endowment to the federation that augments the initial prize in perpetuity.

2006   Donna Morrissey, *Sylvanus Now*

2005   Edward Riche, *The Nine Planets*

2004   Kenneth J. Harvey, *The Town That Forgot How to Breathe*

2003   Donna Morrissey, *Downhill Chance*

2002   Michael Crummey, *River Thieves*

2001   Carol Bruneau, *Purple for Sky*

2000   Alistair MacLeod, *No Great Mischief*

1999   Wayne Johnston, *The Colony of Unrequited Dreams*

1998   Shree Ghatage, *Awake When All the World Is Asleep*

1997   Alfred Silver, *Acadia*

1996   M. T. Dohaney, *A Marriage of Masks*

1995   Bernice Morgan, *Waiting for Time*

1994   David Adams Richards, *For Those Who Hunt the Wounded Down*

1993   John Steffler, *The Afterlife of George Cartwright*

1992   Herb Curtis, *The Last Tasmanian*

1991   Wayne Johnston, *The Divine Ryans*

Ann Connor Brimer Award for Children's Literature

This $1,000 prize is awarded for a book that makes an outstanding contribution to children's literature in Atlantic Canada.

2006   Kevin Major, *Aunt Olga's Christmas Postcards*

2005   Alice Walsh, *Pomiuk, Prince of the North*

2004   Don Aker, *The First Stone*

2003   Lesley Choyce, *Shoulder the Sky*

2002   Francis Wolfe, *Where I Live*

2001   Janet McNaughton, *The Secret under My Skin*

2000   David Weale, *The True Meaning of Crumbfest*

1999   Janet McNaughton, *Make or Break Spring*

1998   Kevin Major, *The House of Wooden Santas*

1997   Janet McNaughton, *To Dance at the Palais Royale*

1996   Don Aker, *Of Things Not Seen*

1995   Sheree Fitch, *Mabel Murple*

1994   Lesley Choyce, *Good Idea Gone Bad*

1993   Budge Wilson, *Oliver's War*

1992   Kevin Major, *Eating between the Lines*

1991   Joyce Barkhouse, *Pit Pony*

Ontario

Trillium Book Award

The Ontario government established this $20,000 award in 1987 to recognize excellence, support marketing, and foster increased public awareness of the quality and diversity of Ontario writers and writing. It is the province's leading award for literature.

2005   English prose: Camilla Gibb, *Sweetness in the Belly;* English poetry: Kevin Connolly, *drift;* French prose: Jean Mohsen Fahmy, *L'Agonie des dieux;* French poetry: Eric Charlebois, *Centrifuge*

2004   English prose: Wayson Choy, *All That Matters;* English poetry: Maureen Scott Harris, *Drowning Lessons;* French prose: Antonio D'Alfonso, *Un vendredi du mois d'aout;* French poetry: no prize was given this year, as there were fewer than five submissions; the prize money is being used to create a scholarship for emerging French-language poets.

2003   English prose: Thomas King, *The Truth about Stories;* English poetry: Adam Sol, *Crowd of Sounds;* French prose: Serge Denis, *Social-démocratie et mouvements ouvriers;* François Paré, *La distance habitée;* French poetry: Angèle Bassolé-Ouédraogo, *Avec tes mots*

2002   English: Austin Clarke, *The Polished Hoe;* Nino Ricci, *Testament;* French: Michel Ouellette, *Le testament du couturier;* Eric Charlebois, *Faux-fuyants*

2001   English: Richard B. Wright, *Clara Callan;* French: Michèle Matteau, *Cognac et Porto*

2000   English: Don Coles, *Kurgan;* French: Didier Leclair, *Toronto, je t'aime*

1999   English: Alistair MacLeod, *No Great Mischief;* French: Andrée Christensen and Jacques Flamand, *Lithochronos ou le premier vol de la pierre*

1998   English: André Alexis, *Childhood;* Alice Munro, *The Love of a Good Woman;* French: Daniel Poliquin, *L'homme de paille;* Stefan Psenak, *Du chaos et de l'ordre des choses*

1997 English: Dionne Brand, *Land to Light On;* French: Roger Levac, *Petite Crapaude!*
1996 English: Anne Michaels, *Fugitive Pieces;* French: Nancy Vickers, *Le Pied de Sappho;* Alain Bernard Marchand, *Tintin au pays de la ferveur*
1995 English: Margaret Atwood, *Morning in the Burned House;* Wayson Choy, *The Jade Peony;* French: Maurice Henrie, *Le Balcon dans le ciel*
1994 English: Donald Harman Akenson, *Conor: A Biography of Conor Cruise O'Brien,* volume one: *Narrative;* French: Andrée Lacelle, *Tant de vie s'égare*
1993 Jane Urquhart, *Away;* Margaret Atwood, *The Robber Bride*
1992 Michael Ondaatje, *The English Patient*
1991 Margaret Atwood, *Wilderness Tips*
1990 Alice Munro, *Friend of My Youth*
1989 Modris Eksteins, *Rites of Spring*
1988 Timothy Findley, *Stones*
1987 Michael Ondaatje, *In the Skin of a Lion*

City of Toronto Book Award

This award carries a monetary prize totaling $15,000: $1,000 is given to each of the four to seven finalists, with the remainder going to the winner or winners. Established by the Toronto City Council in 1974, the award honors authors of books of literary or artistic merit that are evocative of Toronto.

2006 Dionne Brand, *What We All Long For*
2005 David Bezmozgis, *Natasha and Other Stories*
2004 Kevin Bazzana, *Wondrous Strange: The Life and Art of Glenn Gould;* Kate Taylor, *Mme. Proust and the Kosher Kitchen*
2003 Joe Fiorito, *The Song beneath the Ice*
2002 Sarah Dearing, *Courage My Love*
2001 A. B. McKillop, *The Spinster and the Prophet: Florence Deeks, H. G. Wells and the Mystery of the Purloined Past*
2000 Camilla Gibb, *Mouthing the Words*
1999 Richard Outram, *Benedict Abroad*
1998 Helen Humphreys, *Leaving Earth*
1997 Anne Michaels, *Fugitive Pieces*
1996 Rosemary Sullivan, *Shadow Maker: The Life of Gwendolyn MacEwen*
1995 Ezra Schabas, *Sir Ernest MacMillan: The Importance of Being Canadian*
1994 Timothy Findley, *Headhunter*
1993 Carole Corbeil, *Voice-Over;* David Donnell, *China Blues*
1992 Katherine Govier, *Hearts of Flame*
1991 Cary Fagan and Robert MacDonald, eds., *Streets of Attitude: Toronto Stories*
1990 Hilary Russell, *Double Take: The Story of the Elgin and Winter Garden Theatres;* Guy Vanderhaeghe, *Homesick*
1989 Margaret Atwood, *Cat's Eye*

1988 Michael Ondaatje, *In the Skin of the Lion*
1987 William Dendy and William Kilbourn, *Toronto Observed: Its Architecture, Patrons and History*
1986 Morley Callaghan, *Our Lady of the Snows;* Robertson Davies, *What's Bred in the Bone*
1985 Warabe Aska, *Who Goes to the Park;* J. M. S. Careless, *Toronto to 1918;* Josef Skvorecky, *The Engineer of Human Souls*
1984 Edith G. Firth, *Toronto in Art;* Gerald Killan, *David Boyle: From Artisan to Archaeologist;* Eric Wright, *The Night the Gods Smiled*
1983 Michael Bliss, *The Discovery of Insulin;* Lucy Booth Martyn, *The Face of Early Toronto: An Archival Record 1803–1936*
1982 Claude Bissell, *The Young Vincent Massey;* Marian Engel, *Lunatic Villas*
1981 Timothy Colton, *Big Daddy: Frederick G. Gardiner and the Building of Metropolitan Toronto;* Mary Larratt Smith, *Young Mr. Smith in Upper Canada;* Helen Weinzweig, *Basic Black with Pearls*
1980 Raymond Souster, *Hanging In;* Stephen A. Speisman, *The Jews of Toronto: A History to 1937*
1979 Michael Bliss, *A Canadian Millionaire;* William Dendy, *Lost Toronto;* John Morgan Gray, *Fun Tomorrow*
1978 Christopher Armstrong and H. V. Nelles, *The Revenge of the Methodist Bicycle Company;* Timothy Findley, *The Wars*
1977 Margaret Atwood, *Lady Oracle;* Margaret Gibson, *The Butterfly Ward*
1976 Robert F. Harney and Harold Troper, *Immigrants: A Portrait of the Urban Experience 1890–1930;* Hugh Hood, *The Swing in the Garden*
1975 Claude Bissell, *Halfway up Parnassus;* The Labour History Collective, *Women at Work;* Loren Lind, *The Learning Machine*
1974 William Kurelek, *O Toronto;* Desmond Morton, *Mayor Howland;* Richard B. Wright, *In the Middle of a Life*

Quebec

Prix Athanase-David

The $30,000 prize is awarded to a writer for his or her complete oeuvre. The literary genres recognized for the prize are fairy tales, short stories, poetry, narrative stories, novels, dramas, cartoons, essays, literary criticism, journalism, and all forms of writing for children.

2006 Mavis Gallant
2005 Pierre Nepveu
2004 Naïm Kattan
2003 Pierre van Schendel
2002 Madeleine Gagnon
2001 Victor-Lévy Beaulieu
2000 Pierre Morency

1999	Roland Giguère
1997	Gilles Marcotte
1996	Monique Bosco
1995	Jacques Poulin
1994	Réjean Ducharme
1993	Gilles Hénault
1992	André Major
1991	Nicole Brossard
1990	Andrée Maillet
1989	Jean Ethier-Blais
1988	Michel Tremblay
1987	Fernand Ouellette
1986	Jacques Brault
1985	Jacques Godbout
1984	Jean-Guy Pilon
1983	Gaston Miron
1982	Marie-Claire Blais
1981	Gilles Archambault
1980	Gérard Bessette
1979	Yves Thériault
1978	Anne Hébert
1977	Jacques Ferron
1976	Pierre Vadeboncoeur
1975	Fernand Dumont
1974	Rina Lasnier
1973	Hubert Aquin, Marcel Dubé
1972	Paul-Marie Lapointe
1971	Gabrielle Roy
1970	Alain Grandbois
1969	Félix-Antoine Savard

Prix Gilles-Corbeil

The triennial $100,000 prize is awarded to a citizen of Canada or the United States for poetry, fiction, dramas, or literary essays written in French; works translated into French or written collaboratively are not admissible. The prize is awarded for the whole writing career of an author and not for an individual work.

2005	Marie-Claire Blais
2002	Fernand Ouellette
1999	Paul-Marie Lapointe
1996	Jacques Brault
1993	Anne Hébert
1990	Réjean Ducharme

Saskatchewan

Saskatchewan Book of the Year Award

This $3,000 award is presented to the Saskatchewan author or pair of authors of the best-written book or books of the year.

2006	Michael Trussler, *Encounters*

2005	Steven Ross Smith, *FLUTTERTONGUE 3: Disarray*
2004	Candace Savage, *Prairie: A Natural History*
2003	Donald Ward, *Nobody Goes to Earth Any More*
2002	Guy Vanderhaeghe, *The Last Crossing*
2001	Sandra Birdsell, *The Russländer*
2000	Trevor Herriot, *River in a Dry Land;* Patricia Monture-Angus, *Journeying Forward*
1999	Tim Lilburn, *To the River*
1998	Susan Andrews Grace, *Ferry Woman's History of the World*
1997	Sandra Birdsell, *The Two-Headed Calf*
1996	Guy Vanderhaeghe, *The Englishman's Boy*
1995	Anne Szumigalski, *Z: A Meditation on Oppression, Desire and Freedom*
1994	Bonnie Burnard, *Casino & Other Stories*
1993	Dianne Warren, *Bad Luck Dog*

Saskatchewan Book Award for Fiction

This $2,000 award is presented to the Saskatchewan author of the best-written novel or collection of short fiction.

2006	Martha Blum, *The Apothecary*
2005	Sandra Birdsell, *Children of the Day*
2004	Larry Gasper, *Princes in Waiting*
2003	J. Jill Robinson, *Residual Desire*
2002	Guy Vanderhaeghe, *The Last Crossing*
2001	Sandra Birdsell, *The Russländer*
2000	Leona Theis, *Sightlines*
1999	Brenda Baker, *The Maleness of God*
1998	Larry Warwaruk, *The Ukrainian Wedding*
1997	Joanne Gerber, *In the Misleading Absence of Light*
1996	Guy Vanderhaeghe, *The Englishman's Boy*
1995	Byrna Barclay, *Crosswinds*

Saskatchewan Book Award for Nonfiction

This $2,000 award is presented to a Saskatchewan author or pair of authors for the best-written book or books of nonfiction.

2006	Marie Elyse St. George, *Once in A Blue Moon: An Artist's Life*
2005	Sharon Butala, *Lilac Moon*
2004	Candace Savage, *Prairie, A Natural History*
2003	Bill Waiser, *All Hell Can't Stop Us*
2002	Frances Greenslade, *A Pilgrim in Ireland*
2001	Tom Molloy, *The World Is Our Witness*
2000	Warren Goulding, *Just Another Indian*
1999	Tim Lilburn, *Living in the World As If It Were Home*
1998	Yvonne Johnson and Rudy Wiebe, *Stolen Life: The Journey of a Cree Woman*
1997	Anne Szumigalski, *Sermons on Stones*

1996   David Carpenter, *Courting Saskatchewan;* J. R. Miller, *Shingwauk's Vision*

1995   Sharon Butala, *The Perfection of the Morning*

Anne Szumigalski Poetry Award

This $2,000 award is presented to a Saskatchewan author of the best-written book of poetry.

2006   Daniel Scott Tysdal, *Predicting the Next Big Advertising Breakthrough Using a Potentially Dangerous Method*

2005   Allan Safarik, *When Light Falls from the Sun*

2004   Gerald Hill, *Getting to Know You*

2003   Elizabeth Brewster, *Jacob's Dream*

2002   Sheri Benning, *Earth after Rain*

2001   Ken Howe, *Household Hints for the End of Time*

2000   Elizabeth Philips, *A Blue with Blood In It*

1999   Hilary Clark, *More Light*

1998   Steven Michael Berzensky, *Variations on the Birth of Jacob*

1997   Anne Szumigalski, *On Glassy Wings*

1996   Tonya Gunvaldsen Klaassen, *Clay Birds*

1995   Elizabeth Philips, *Beyond My Keeping*

Saskatchewan Book Award for Children's Literature

This $2,000 award is presented to a Saskatchewan author or pair of authors for the best-written book or books of children's or young-adult literature.

2006   Arthur Slade, *Megiddo's Shadow*

2005   Beth Goobie, *Fixed*

2004   Beth Goobie, *Flux*

2003   Judith Silverthorne, *Dinosaur Hideout*

2002   Candace Savage, *Wizards*

2001   Arthur Slace, *Dust*

2000   Beth Goobie, *Before Wings*

1999   David Richards, *The Lady at Batoche*

1998   Betty Dorion, *Bay Girl*

1997   Sandra Birdsell, *The Town That Floated Away*

1996   Judith Silverthorne, *The Secret of Sentinel Rock*

1995   Lois Simmie, *Mister Got to Go*

Saskatchewan First Book Award

This $2,000 award is presented to a Saskatchewan author or pair of authors of the best-written first book or books.

2006   Annette Lapointe, *Stolen*

2005   Eric Greenway, *The Darkness beneath All Things*

2004   Bonnie Dunlop, *The Beauty Box*

2003   Michael Hetherton, *Grasslands*

2002   Sheri Benning, *Earth after Rain*

2001   Katherine Lawrence, *Ring Finger, Left Hand*

2000   Tom Molloy, *The World Is Our Witness*

1999   Martha Blum, *The Walnut Tree*

1998   Harriet Richards, *The Lavender Child*

1997   Joanne Gerber, *In the Misleading Absence of Light*

1996   Dave Little, *Catching the Wind in a Net*

1995   Kate Sutherland, *Summer Reading*

1994   Terry Jordan, *It's a Hard Cow*

Regina Book Award

This $2,000 award is presented to a Regina author or pair of authors of the best-written book or books; it is a multigenre category.

2006   Michael Trussler, *Encounters*

2005   Maggie Siggins, *Bitter Embrace: White Society's Assault on the Woodland Cree*

2004   Byrna Barclay, *The Room with Five Walls*

2003   Bruce Rice, *The Illustrated Statue of Liberty*

2002   Edward Willett, *Spirit Singer*

2001   Sandra Birdsell, *The Russländer*

2000   Trevor Herriot, *River in a Dry Land;* Maggie Siggins, *In Her Own Time*

1999   Paul Wilson, *The Long Landscape*

1998   Britt Holmstrom, *The Man Next Door*

1997   Ven Begamudre, *Laterna Magika;* Sandra Birdsell, *The Two-Headed Calf;* Joanne Gerber, *In the Misleading Absence of Light*

1996   Connie Gault, *Inspection of a Small Village*

1995   Dianne Warren, *Club Chernobyl*

1994   Maggie Siggins, *Riel: A Life of Revolution*

1993   Dianne Warren, *Bad Luck Dog*

Saskatoon Book Award

This $2,000 award is presented to the Saskatoon author or pair of authors of the best-written book or books in any genre.

2006   Annette Lapointe, *Stolen*

2005   Don Kerr, *The Garden of Art: Vic Cicansky, Sculptor*

2004   Robert Calder, *Beware the British Serpent*

2003   J. Jill Robinson, *Residual Desire*

2002   Guy Vanderhaeghe, *The Last Crossing*

2001   Glen Sorestad, *Leaving Holds Me Here*

2000   Leona Theis, *Sightlines*

1999   Martha Blum, *The Walnut Tree*

1998   R. P. MacIntyre, *The Crying Jesus*

Saskatchewan Book Award for Scholarly Writing

This $2,000 award is presented to a Saskatchewan author, pair of authors, or contributing editor for the best contribution to scholarship. The book must recognize or draw on specific theoretical work within a community of scholars, participate in the creation and transmission of knowledge, and be accessible to non-academics.

2006 Jim Warren and Kathleen Carlisle, *On the Side of the People: A History of Labour in Saskatchewan*
2005 University of Regina, Canadian Plains Research Centre, *The Encyclopedia of Saskatchewan*
2004 Robert Calder, *Beware the British Serpent*
2003 Ross Green and Kearney Healy, *Tough on Kids*
2002 Greg Marchildon and Sid Robinson, *Canoeing the Churchill*
2001 Peter Phillips and George Khachatourians, *The Biotechnology Revolution in Global Agriculture*
2000 James Youngblood Henderson, Marjorie L. Benson, and Isobel Findlay, *Aboriginal Tenure in the Constitution of Canada*
1999 William A. Stahl, *God and the Chip*

Prix du Livre Français

The biennial $2,000 prize is awarded to the Saskatchewan author(s) or editor(s) of the best book published in French.

2006 Martine Noël-Maw, *Amélia et les Papillons*

Saskatchewan Book Award for Publishing

This award is presented to the Saskatchewan publisher of the best book, based on literary or artistic value, quality of editing, design, and production.

1996 Fifth House Publishers, *Buffalo Nation,* by Valerius Geist

Saskatchewan Book Award for Publishing in Education

1996 Thistledown Press, *Takes,* by R. P. MacIntyre

Spirit of Saskatchewan Award

1994 Sharon Butala, *The Perfection of the Morning*

Saskatchewan Award

1993 Dianne Warren, *Bad Luck Dog*

Appendix 2: The Canada Council

Christian Riegel
University of Regina

A wide-ranging examination of the state of Canadian culture by the Royal Commission on the National Development in the Arts, Letters and Sciences, was conducted from 1949 to 1951. The commission's report is known as the Massey Report after its chairman, Vincent Massey, chancellor of the University of Toronto. One of the central problems identified by the Massey Report was that there appeared to be no identifiable national literature. The report asked: "Is it true, then, that we are a people without a literature?" It cited E. A. McCourt, professor of English at the University of Saskatchewan: "The palpable truth is that today in Canada there exists no body of creative writing which reflects adequately, or with more than limited insight, the nature of the Canadian people and the historic forces which have made them what they are." The report concluded that "Canadian letters have no . . . great names."

The lack of "great names" was in large part owing to the paucity of publishing opportunities for writers in Canada. In *The Beginnings of the Book Trade in Canada* (1985) George L. Parker states that in 1900 Canadian bookselling and publishing was dominated by foreign books and magazines: "Most . . . magazines, such as *Macmillan's* or *Frank Leslie's,* were imported from Britain and the United States. Most . . . books were international best-sellers or standard classics that were made in Britain or the United States, although occasionally one found a Canadian author and a Canadian-made book. . . . Canadian books . . . were a far cry from handsome, well-bound British books."

In the late 1940s publishing was still dominated by foreign books rather than by works by Canadian authors. The Massey Report presents data that in 1948, 1,830 books of fiction were published in Britain, 1,102 in the United States, and 14 in Canada. Parker notes that Toronto publishers "were accustomed to having their publishing programs determined in New York and London. The fact is that Canadian publishers rarely obtained world rights for the authors they published, a situation possibly connected to the relatively unimportant place of Canadian authors in the international book world."

The Massey Report concluded with the recommendation "That a body be created to be known as the Canada Council for the Encouragement of the Arts, Letters, Humanities and Social Sciences to stimulate and to help voluntary organizations within these fields, to foster Canada's cultural relations abroad, to perform the functions of a national commission for UNESCO, and to devise and administer a system of scholarships as recommended."

The Canada Council was created by an act of Parliament in 1957 "to foster and promote the study and enjoyment of, and the production of works in, the arts." Robert Lecker notes that "the introduction of the federal agency served to formalize the conception of Canadian literature and to circumscribe the conditions of its production" and "it remains clear that it was the Council and its funding policies . . . that contributed most to the creation of the publishing industry."

While it operates at arm's length from the Canadian government, the Canada Council receives an annual grant from the government; it is used, in conjunction with income from an endowment that was established when the council was formed, to fund more than one hundred programs in its six sections: Dance, Music and Opera, Theatre, Writing and Publishing, Visual Arts, and Media Arts. Several writing-specific programs are administered by the council, including grants to publishers and authors and the Governor General's Literary Awards. In 1978 funding and programming in the humanities and social sciences was taken over by the newly formed Social Sciences and Humanities Council of Canada. In 2004–2005 more than $132 million was distributed to artists and writers through the Canada Council's programs.

The grants that have had the most effect on the development of Canadian writing during the years of the Canada Council's existence are the Grants for Professional Writers, which provide support to writers to complete their books, and the Block Grants for Publishers, which support the development and maintenance of publishing programs that are devoted to Canadian authors and content. Other programs that promote writing and related activities include the Aboriginal Emerging Writers Residencies, Travel Grants for Professional Writers; Grants to Aboriginal Writers, Storytellers and Publishers; Emerging Publisher Grants; International Translation Grants; and Grants to Literary and Arts Magazines, Literary Readings, Literary Festivals, Author Residencies, and Author Tours.

In 2004 *Newsweek* magazine noted that in the previous fifty years Canadian authors had garnered a level of international literary success that was previously nearly impossible to attain: "Mordecai Richler had to leave Canada and go to Britain to make a name for himself. Today that's not necessary: Canada's literary scene is flourishing." Much of the successful development of Canadian writing at home and abroad is due to the federal and provincial governments actively supporting authors and book publishing.

The Canada Council supports writing and publishing at the national level; several provincial governments have followed the model of the council by establishing parallel programs to support the develop-

ment of writing, as well as other areas of the arts, in their provinces. These councils are the Alberta Foundation for the Arts, the British Columbia Arts Council, the Manitoba Arts Council, the New Brunswick Arts Board, the Newfoundland and Labrador Arts Council, the Nova Scotia Arts and Culture Council, the Ontario Arts Council, the Prince Edward Island Arts Council, the Conseil des arts et lettres du Quebec, and the Saskatchewan Arts Board.

References:

Robert Lecker, "The Canada Council's Block Grant Program and the Construction of Canadian Literature," *English Studies in Canada,* 25, nos. 3–4 (1999): 439–470;

George L. Parker, *The Beginnings of the Book Trade in Canada* (Toronto: University of Toronto Press, 1985);

Liat Radcliffe, "Canada: The Literary Life: Authors Revel in Global Acclaim and Public Funding," *Newsweek* (26 July 2004): 49;

Royal Commission on National Development in the Arts, Letters and Sciences, 1949–1951 (Ottawa: Department of External Affairs, Information Division, 1951).

Checklist of Further Readings

Armstrong, Jeannette, ed. *Looking at the Words of Our People: First Nations Analysis of Literature*. Penticton, B.C.: Theytus, 1993.

Atwood, Margaret, and Robert Weaver, eds. *The New Oxford Book of Canadian Short Stories in English*. Toronto & New York: Oxford University Press, 1995.

Beaudoin, Rejean, and Andre Lamontagne. "A Firm Balance: Questions d'equilibre et rapport de froce dans les representations des litteratures anglophone et francophone du Canada," *Canadian Literature,* 175 (Winter 2002): 96–114.

Bentley, D. M. R. "Literary Sites and Cultural Properties in Canadian Poetry," *Studies in Canadian Literature,* 23, no. 1 (1998): 90–127.

Berry, Reginald, and James Acheson, eds. *Regionalism and National Identity*. Christchurch, N.Z.: Association for Canadian Studies in Australia and New Zealand, 1985.

Blodgett, E. D. *Five-Part Invention: A History of Literary History in Canada*. Toronto: University of Toronto Press, 2003.

Borovilos, John. *Images: Canada through Literature*. Scarborough, Ont.: Prentice Hall, 1996.

Brydon, Diana. "Reading Postcoloniality, Reading Canada," *Essays on Canadian Writing,* 56 (Fall 1995): 1–19.

Buss, Helen M. *Mapping Our Selves*. Montreal: McGill-Queen's University Press, 1993.

Careless, J. M. S. *Frontier and Metropolis: Regions, Cities and Identities in Canada before 1914*. Toronto: University of Toronto Press, 1989.

Carriere, Marie J. *Writing in the Feminine in French and English Canada: A Question of Ethics*. Toronto: University of Toronto Press, 2002.

Carter, Adam. "Namelessness, Irony, and National Character in Contemporary Canadian Criticism and the Critical Tradition," *Studies in Canadian Literature,* 27, no. 1 (2003): 5–25.

Chalykoff, Lisa. "Overcoming the Two Solitudes of Canadian Literary Regionalism," *Studies in Canadian Literature,* 23, no. 1 (1998): 160–177.

Clarke, George Elliot. *Odysseys Home: Mapping African-Canadian Literature*. Toronto: University of Toronto Press, 2002.

Clarke, ed. *Eyeing the North Star: Directions in African-Canadian Literature*. Toronto: McClelland & Stewart, 1997.

Coleman, Daniel. *Masculine Migrations: Reading the Postcolonial Male in "New Canadian" Narratives*. Toronto: University of Toronto Press, 1998.

Compton, Wade, ed. *Bluesprint: Black British Columbian Literature and Orature*. Vancouver: Arsenal Pulp Press, 2002.

Cook, Ramsay. "Imagining a North American Garden: Some Parallels and Differences in Canadian and American Culture," *Canadian Literature,* 103 (Winter 1984): 10–23.

Corse, Sarah M. *Nationalism and Literature: The Politics of Culture in Canada and the United States*. Cambridge: Cambridge University Press, 1997.

Creelman, David. *Setting in the East: Maritime Realist Fiction*. Montreal: McGill-Queen's University Press, 2003.

Danas-Beautell, Eva. *Contemporary Theories and Canadian Fiction*. Queenston, Ont.: Edwin Mellen Press, 2000.

Davey, Frank. *Canadian Literary Power*. Edmonton: NeWest Press, 1994.

Davey. *From There to Here: A Guide to English-Canadian Literature since 1960*. Erin, Ont.: Porcepic, 1974.

Davey. *Post-National Arguments*. Toronto: University of Toronto Press, 1993.

Davey. "Surviving the Paraphrase: Thematic Criticism and Its Alternatives," *Canadian Literature*, 70 (Autumn 1976): 5–13.

Davidson, Arnold E. *Coyote Country: Fictions of the Canadian West*. Durham, N.C.: Duke University Press, 1994.

Davidson, ed. *Studies in Canadian Literature: Introductory and Critical Essays*. New York: Modern Language Association of America, 1990.

Davies, Gwendolyn. *Studies in Maritime Literary History*. Fredericton, N.B.: Acadiensis Press, 1991.

DeCook, Travis. "The History of the Book, Literary History, and Identity Politics in Canada," *Studies in Canadian Literature*, 27, no. 2 (2002): 71–87.

Dickinson, Peter. *Here Is Queer: Nationalisms, Sexualities and the Literatures of Canada*. Toronto: University of Toronto Press, 1999.

Downie, Marie Alice, and Barbara Robertson, eds. *The New Wind Has Wings*. Toronto: Oxford University Press, 1984.

Dragland, Stan. *The Bees of the Invisible: Essays in Contemporary English Canadian Writing*. Toronto: Coach House, 1991.

Emberley, Julia. *Thresholds of Difference: Feminist Critique, Native Women's Writings, Postcolonial Theory*. Toronto: University of Toronto Press, 2001.

Fisher, Susan. "'Our Next Neighbour across the Way': Japan and Canadian Writers," *Canadian Literature*, 174 (Autumn 2002): 29–42.

Freiwald, Bina Toledo. "Nation and Self-Narration: A View from Quebec/Quebec," *Canadian Literature*, 172 (Spring 2002): 17–40.

Frye, Northrop. *The Bush Garden: Essays on the Canadian Imagination*. Toronto: Anansi, 1971.

Glickman, Susan. *The Picturesque and the Sublime: A Poetics of the Canadian Landscape*. Montreal: McGill-Queen's University Press, 1998.

Goldie, Terry. *Fear and Temptation: The Image of the Indigene in Canadian, Australian, and New Zealand Literatures*. Montreal: McGill-Queen's University Press, 1989.

Good, Graham. "Northrop Frye and Liberal Humanism," *Canadian Literature*, 148 (Spring 1996): 75–95.

Gudsteins, Gudrun Bjork, ed. *Rediscovering Canada: Image, Place and Text*. Reykjavik: Nordic Association for Canadian Studies, University of Iceland Press, 2001.

Hammill, Faye. *Literary Culture and Female Authorship in Canada 1760–2000*. Amsterdam & New York: Rodopi, 2003.

Hart, Jonathan Locke. *Northrop Frye: The Theoretical Imagination*. New York: Routledge, 1994.

Henighan, Stephen. *When Words Deny the World: The Reshaping of Canadian Writing*. Erin, Ont.: Porcupine's Quill, 2002.

Hough, Michael. *Out of Place: Restoring Identity to the Regional Landscape*. New Haven & London: Yale University Press, 1990.

Hoy, Helen. *How Should I Read These: Native Women Writers in Canada*. Toronto: University of Toronto Press, 2001.

Huggan, Graham, and Winfried Siemerling. "U.S./Canadian Writers' Perspectives on the Multiculturalism Debate: A Round-Table Discussion at Harvard University," *Canadian Literature*, 164 (Spring 2000): 82–111.

Hunter, Lynette. *Outsider Notes: Feminist Approaches to Nation State Ideology, Writers/Readers and Publishing*. Burnaby, B.C.: Talonbooks, 1996.

Hutcheon, Linda. *The Canadian Postmodern: A Study of Contemporary English-Canadian Fiction.* Don Mills, Ont.: Oxford University Press, 1988.

Juneja, Om P. and Chandra Mohan, ed. *Ambivalence: Studies in Canadian Literature.* New Delhi: Allied, 1990.

Kamboureli, Smaro. *Scandalous Bodies: Diasporic Literature in English Canada.* Don Mills, Ont.: Oxford University Press, 2000.

Keefer, Janice Kulyk. *Under Eastern Eyes: A Critical Reading of Maritime Fiction.* Toronto: University of Toronto Press, 1987.

Kelly, Peggy. "Anthologies and the Canonization Process: A Case Study of the English-Canadian Literary Field, 1920–1950," *Studies in Canadian Literature,* 25, no. 1 (2000): 73–94.

Kertzer, Jonathan. *Worrying the Nation.* Toronto: University of Toronto Press, 1998.

King, Thomas, ed. *All My Relations: An Anthology of Contemporary Native Canadian Fiction.* Toronto: McClelland & Stewart, 1990.

Kroetsch, Robert. *The Lovely Treachery of Words: Essays Selected and New.* Don Mills, Ont.: Oxford University Press, 1989.

Kroetsch and Reingard M. Nischik, eds. *Gaining Ground: European Critics on Canadian Literature.* Edmonton: NeWest Press, 1985.

Lecker, Robert. *Canadian Canons: Essays in Cultural Value.* Toronto: University of Toronto Press, 1991.

Lecker. *Making it Real: The Canonization of English-Canadian Literature.* Concord, Ont.: Anansi, 1995.

Lecker. "Would You Publish This Book? Material Production, Canadian Criticism, and *The Theatre of Form*," *Studies in Canadian Literature,* 25, no. 1 (2000): 15–36.

Lundgren, Jodi. "'Being a Half-Breed': Discourses of Race and Cultural Syncreticity in the Works of Three Métis Women Writers," *Canadian Literature,* 144 (Spring 1995): 62–81.

Lutz, Hartmut. "Canadian Native Literature and the Sixties: A Historical and Bibliographical Survey," *Canadian Literature,* 152–153 (Spring–Summer 1997): 167–191.

Lynch, Gerald. *The One and the Many: English-Canadian Short Story Cycles.* Toronto: University of Toronto Press, 2001.

Mailhot, Laurent. *La litterature quebecoise.* Montreal: Typo, 1997.

Marchand, Philip. *Ripostes: Reflections on Canadian Literature.* Erin, Ont.: Porcupine's Quill, 1998.

Maugiere, Benedicte, ed. *Cultural Identities in Canadian Literature/Identites culturelles dans la litteratures canadienne.* New York: Peter Lang, 1998.

Melnyk, George. *The Literary History of Alberta,* 2 volumes. Edmonton: University of Alberta Press, 1998, 1999.

Morton, Desmond, and Morton Weinfeld. *Who Speaks for Canada? Words That Shape a Country.* Toronto: McClelland & Stewart, 1998.

Moss, John. *Paradox of Meaning: Cultural Poetics and Critical Fictions.* Winnipeg: Turnstone, 1999.

New, W. H. *Dreams of Speech and Violence: The Art of the Short Story in Canada and New Zealand.* Toronto: University of Toronto Press, 1987.

New. *A History of Canadian Literature,* second edition. Montreal: McGill-Queen's University Press, 2003.

New. *Land Sliding: Imagining Space, Presence, and Power in Canadian Writing.* Toronto: University of Toronto Press, 1997.

Pacey, Desmond. *Creative Writing in Canada.* Toronto: Ryerson, 1952.

Padolsky, Enoch. "Ethnicity and Race: Canadian Minority Writing at a Crossroads," *Journal of Canadian Studies,* 31 (Fall 1996): 129–147.

Petrone, Penny. *Native Literature in Canada: From the Oral Tradition to the Present.* Toronto: Oxford University Press, 1990.

Riegel, Christian, and Herb Wyile, eds. *A Sense of Place: Re-evaluating Regionalism in Canadian and American Writing.* Edmonton: University of Alberta Press, 1998.

Ruffo, Armand Garnet, ed. *(Ad)dressing Our Words: Aboriginal Perspectives on Aboriginal Literatures.* Penticton, B.C.: Theytus, 2001.

Saint-Martin, Fernande. "Fonctions de l'art dans la cuture quebecoise," *Canadian Literature,* 152–153 (Spring–Summer 1997): 145–159.

Schechels, Theodore F. *The Island Motif in the Fiction of L. M. Montgomery, Margaret Laurence, Margaret Atwood and Other Canadian Women Novelists.* New York: Peter Lang, 2003.

Scherf, Kathleen. "A Legacy of Canadian Cultural Tradition and the Small Press: The Case of Talon Books," *Studies in Canadian Literature,* 25, no. 1 (2000): 131–149.

Scobie, Stephen. *Signature Event Cantext.* Edmonton: NeWest Press, 1989.

Thomas, Clara. *All My Sisters: Essays on the Work of Canadian Women Writers.* Ottawa: Tecumseh, 1994.

Thompson, Barbara. *Talking about Ourselves: The Literary Productions of Native Women of Canada.* Ottawa: Canadian Research Institute for the Advancement of Women, 1985.

Trikha, Manorama, ed. *Canadian Literature: Recent Essays.* Delhi: Pencraft International, 1994.

Turner, Margaret E. *Imagining Culture: New World Narrative and the Writing of Canada.* Montreal: McGill-Queen's University Press, 1995.

Vautier, Marie. *New World Myth: Postmodernism and Postcolonialism in Canadian Fiction.* Montreal: McGill-Queen's University Press, 1998.

Veraina, Coomi S., and Barbara Godard. *Intersexions: Issues of Race and Gender in Canadian Women's Writing.* New Dehli: Creative Books, 1996.

Wardhaugh, Robert, ed. *Toward Defining the Prairies: Region, Culture, and History.* Winnipeg: University of Manitoba Press, 2001.

Williamson, Janice. *Sounding Differences: Conversations with Seventeen Canadian Women Writers.* Toronto: University of Toronto Press, 1993.

Wyile, Herb. *Speculative Fictions: Contemporary Canadian Novelists and the Writing of History.* Montreal: McGill-Queen's University Press, 2002.

Contributors

Cumulative Index

Dictionary of Literary Biography, Volumes 1-334
Dictionary of Literary Biography Yearbook, 1980-2002
Dictionary of Literary Biography Documentary Series, Volumes 1-19
Concise Dictionary of American Literary Biography, Volumes 1-7
Concise Dictionary of British Literary Biography, Volumes 1-8
Concise Dictionary of World Literary Biography, Volumes 1-4

Cumulative Index

DLB before number: *Dictionary of Literary Biography*, Volumes 1-334
Y before number: *Dictionary of Literary Biography Yearbook*, 1980-2002
DS before number: *Dictionary of Literary Biography Documentary Series*, Volumes 1-19
CDALB before number: *Concise Dictionary of American Literary Biography*, Volumes 1-7
CDBLB before number: *Concise Dictionary of British Literary Biography*, Volumes 1-8
CDWLB before number: *Concise Dictionary of World Literary Biography*, Volumes 1-4

373

O

ISBN-13: 978-0-7876-8152-4
ISBN-10: 0-7876-8152-0